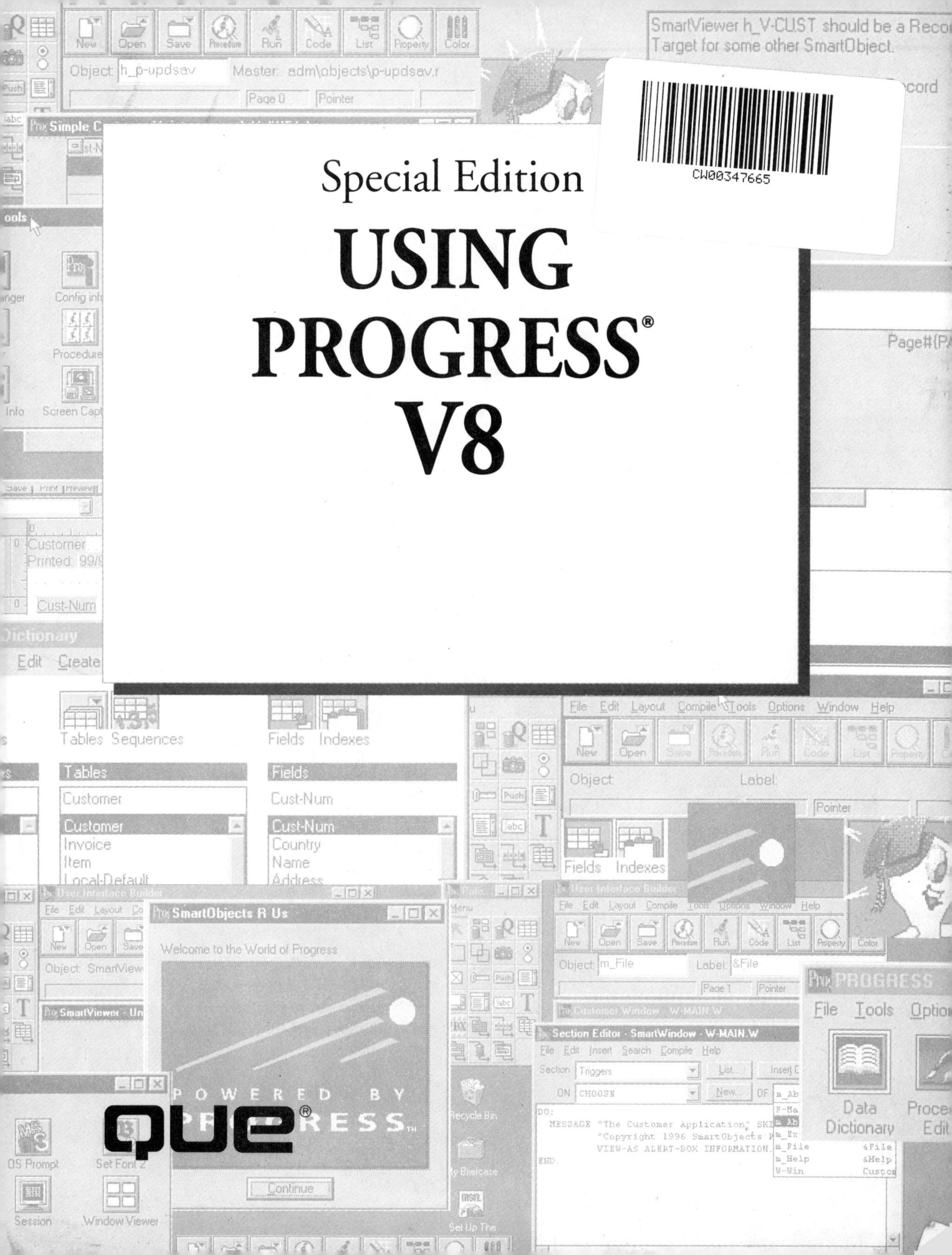
Special Edition
USING
PROGRESS®
V8
QUE®
CW00347665

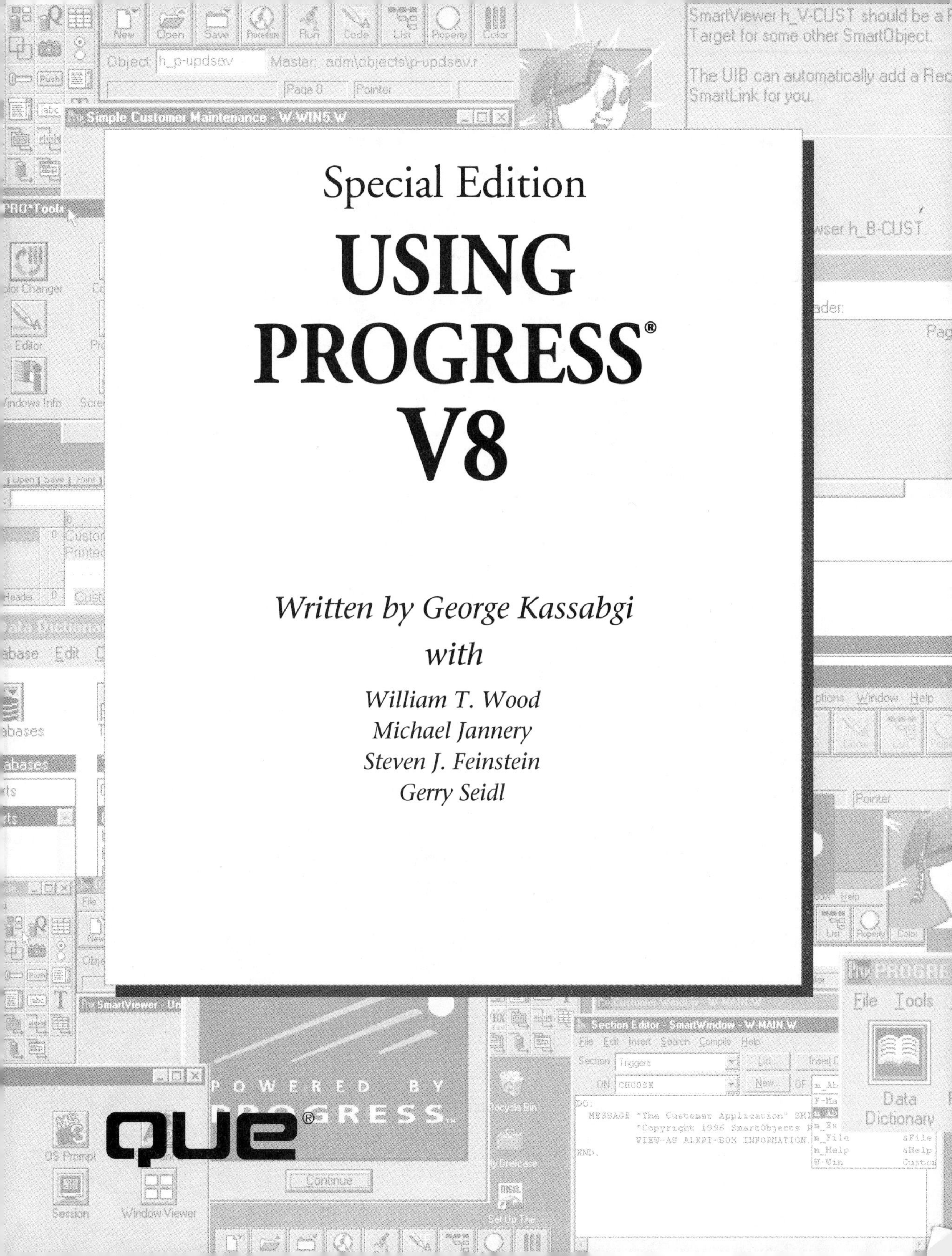

Special Edition

USING PROGRESS® V8

Written by George Kassabgi

with

William T. Wood
Michael Jannery
Steven J. Feinstein
Gerry Seidl

que®

Special Edition Using PROGRESS V8

Library of Congress Catalog No.: 95-71739

ISBN: 0-7897-0493-5

98 97 96 6 5 4 3 2 1

Interpretation of the printing code: the rightmost double-digit number is the year of the book's printing; the rightmost single-digit number, the number of the book's printing. For example, a printing code of 96-1 shows that the first printing of the book occurred in 1996.

Screen reproductions in this book were created using Collage Plus from Inner Media, Inc., Hollis, NH.

Composed in *Stone Serif* and *MCPdigital* by Que Corporation

Credits

President and Publisher
Roland Elgey

Associate Publisher
Joseph B. Wikert

Editorial Services Director
Elizabeth Keaffaber

Managing Editor
Sandy Doell

Director of Marketing
Lynn E. Zingraf

Senior Series Editor
Chris Nelson

Title Manager
Bryan Gambrel

Acquisitions Editor
Fred Slone

Product Director
Stephen L. Miller

Production Editor
Jeff Riley

Editors
Danielle Bird
Susan Christophersen
Noelle Gasco
Chuck Hutchinson
Gill Kent
Susan Moore
Nanci Sears Perry
Linda Seifert
Nancy E. Sixsmith

Technical Editors
Rick Ralston
John T. Suzanne
Tex Texin

Assistant Product Marketing Manager
Kim Margolius

Technical Specialist
Nadeem Muhammed

Acquisitions Coordinator
Angela C. Kozlowski

Operations Coordinator
Patricia J. Brooks

Editorial Assistant
Michelle Newcomb

Assistant to the Publisher
Jane Brownlow

Book Designer
Ruth Harvey

Cover Designer
Dan Armstrong

Production Team
Steve Adams
Claudia Bell
Brian Buschkill
Jason Carr
Anne Dickerson
Chad Dressler
Joan Evan
Trey Frank
Jason Hand
John Hulse
Bob LaRoche
Glenn Larsen
Stephanie Layton
Michelle Lee
Bobbi Satterfield
Mike Thomas
Kelly Warner

"Even if you are on the right track, you will get run over if you just sit there!"

The author's work is dedicated to the memory of Jonathan B. Kast (1959-1995).

A good friend, colleague, and avid Progress consultant. He is sorely missed.

About the Authors

Originally from Milan, Italy, **George Kassabgi** is a principal consultant with Progress Software's Consulting Group. He manages consulting activity in Canada and the eastern United States. Fluent in both Italian and French, George travels extensively throughout Europe for consulting and technical presentations.

He has orchestrated large Progress development projects with such clients as ROCHE (Switzerland), WalMart (Amarillo, Texas), Cargill (Minneapolis, Minn.), Johnson & Johnson (New Brunswick, N.J.), and Tupperware (Orlando, Fla.).

He is responsible for Progress Consulting's "Shell" methodology and Frame Level Objects under Progress Version 7, which were developed into Version 8 SmartObjects. George lives in Massachusetts with his wife Maria and their Alaskan Malamute "Cassimere."

William T. Wood is one of the principal developers of the Progress Application Development Environment (ADE) and he is a coauthor of the Progress User Interface Builder. Bill is a graduate of the Massachusetts Institute of Technology, where his postgraduate work explored issues in human-computer interaction. He has worked as a consultant for several years, building decision-support systems focusing on resource allocation.

Bill joined George Kassabgi on PROGRESS' Silver Medal team at the 1993 World Championship in 4GL Programming (Stockholm, Sweden). The team also competed in the 1994 Data Based Advisor Competition in Raleigh, N.C. and finished with the highest-placed MS-Windows application in the competition's history. They also scored first in database reports (using the Progress Report Builder, of course).

Michael Jannery, who has a B.A. in Computer Science from Dartmouth, is Director of International Products at Progress Software. He is responsible for determining international requirements for the product line, as well as the planning and implementation of specific features.

He has been responsible for the introduction of PROGRESS Version 6 and Version 7 Double-Byte Enabled products, supporting Chinese, Japanese, and Korean, as well as an overall architecture in Version 7 for providing advanced codepage and collation support in client-server configurations. In this position, he travels to roughly 30 countries throughout the world each year.

Steven J. Feinstein, a native Bostonian (without the accent), has been an employee with Progress Software since 1986 and Version 3.2D. He has held positions in Technical Support, Training, Quality Assurance, and most recently in the Sales organization as a Corporate Systems Engineer. He has a B.S. in Computer Science from the School of Engineering at Tulane University in New Orleans.

Steven also founded the New England Software Quality Assurance Forum. This regional group of QA professionals meets on a monthly basis to promote software quality. Steven answers e-mail addressed to sjf@progress.com.

Gerry Seidl is a Software Engineer with Progress Software Corporation and is currently working on the UIB and other ADE tools. His major contributions are in the areas of support for SmartObjects, PRO*Tools, XFTRs, Cue Cards, Wizards, and GUI expertise.

Gerry also worked for PSC's Technical Support team, where he assisted countless customers with PROGRESS programming questions. Gerry lives in Massachusetts with his wife Monica and son Andrew.

Acknowledgments

The following people were of immense help in getting this work and the work of PROGRESS V8 completed.

To my wife Maria for her patience and understanding. To coauthors' wives Sue Wood, Linda Jannery, and Monica Seidl for putting up with late nights of typing.

To Rich Wolverton for giving me time to write and being "sanguine" about it.

Thanks to Sue Wood for her valuable word-smithing review of the first drafts. Thanks to Tex Texin for his work in proofing Michael Jannery's Internationalization chapters.

To Jay Lee, Anthony Tomasino, and Stephen Cross in Progress Consulting for putting their creativity and vision into our SmartObjects. To John Sadd for turning a consulting methodology into a polished product. To Lisa Weil and Tom Bright for putting their hearts into the V8 product and its market introduction. To Bill Coakley, Rod Gaither, and John Cave for believing in our early ideas about Frame Level Objects and components (and to Dave Chappell for adding `KEEP-FRAME-Z-ORDER` to V7.3), without which our early prototypes would not have been feasible.

Thanks to David Lee for his contributions to the VBX material in the book.

Special thanks to Libby Wilson for her strong editorial work of the introduction and the first three chapters.

Indeed the saying is true: "One can see very far when standing on tall shoulders."

We'd Like to Hear from You!

As part of our continuing effort to produce books of the highest possible quality, Que would like to hear your comments. To stay competitive, we *really* want you, as a computer book reader and user, to let us know what you like or dislike most about this book or other Que products.

You can mail comments, ideas, or suggestions for improving future editions to the address below, or send us a fax at (317) 581-4663. For the online inclined, Macmillan Computer Publishing has a forum on CompuServe (type **GO QUEBOOKS** at any prompt) through which our staff and authors are available for questions and comments. The address of our Internet site is **http://www.mcp.com** (World Wide Web).

In addition to exploring our forum, please feel free to contact me personally to discuss your opinions of this book: I'm at 76103,1334 on CompuServe, and I'm smiller@que.mcp.com on the Internet.

Thanks in advance—your comments will help us to continue publishing the best books available on computer topics in today's market.

Stephen L. Miller
Product Development Specialist
Que Corporation
201 W. 103rd Street
Indianapolis, Indiana 46290
USA

Contents at a Glance

Appendixes

Contents

G Contents of CD 681

Index 699

Introduction

Welcome to the exciting world of PROGRESS. *Special Edition Using PROGRESS V8* launches you into the powerful world of enterprise client/server development.

Progress Software has provided solutions for fourth-generation languages and databases in the DOS/UNIX environment for over a decade. Numerous awards from *VAR Business* magazine represent its strength in the vertical market applications development arena. Indeed, thousands of PROGRESS developers are building and selling PROGRESS-written applications globally.

Special Edition Using PROGRESS V8 exposes the tools, language, and techniques of this powerful development environment. It leads you through the development of a graphical application focusing on objects, reusability, and structure. You will learn from the pros how to maximize your productivity and you will also gain insights on the inner workings of this programming model. It's easy to watch and listen to the pros as they build objects and screens with the CD's "Voice of Experience" screen cams.

Ideally, this book serves you in two ways:

- As a tutorial with a step-by-step development of a sample application.
- As an in-depth study of the PROGRESS environment and its inner workings.

To understand as much as possible about PROGRESS SmartObject technology and the PROGRESS Application Development Model, look no further.

The sample application was carefully designed to illustrate a broad set of development techniques. The Application Development Environment (ADE) and Application Development Model (ADM) tutorials cover each tool and SmartObject so that you get the "big picture" quickly.

The enclosed CD contains all the sample programs and objects. Several extra programs and usable objects collected from the vast Progress development world are also included on the CD.

The "Voice of Experience" recordings allow you to watch and listen as the authors actually create programs and objects.

The book is a training class, a tutorial with tool developers, and a consultant visit all rolled into one. With this book, you will quickly become a skilled application developer using PROGRESS graphical enterprise tools.

The Expanding Realm of Graphical Client/Server Development

Since the inception of the Apple Macintosh and, more recently, with the enormous popularity of Microsoft Windows, the graphical user interface (GUI) has revolutionized the appearance of software applications. Graphical user interfaces bring their own new paradigm to a development effort. It is essential that the development environment not only *supports* the GUI, it must allow the developer to *take advantage* of it.

The concept of "event-driven" programming is built into the graphical user interface. As we shall see, PROGRESS allows programmers of different skill levels to work with this event-driven model. A novice PROGRESS programmer can use tools such as the User Interface Builder (UIB) to handle the various user interface events. An experienced PROGRESS developer can use the powerful PROGRESS 4GL language to handle more complex scenarios.

By definition, in a client/server connection, the machine serving the data is called the "server" and the machine asking for the data is the "client." In this book, our client is the computer providing the user interface.

The realm of GUI applications is expanding at a rapid pace. PROGRESS has the unique power to deploy an application in *both* a GUI environment (examples: Windows 95, UNIX Motif) and a TTY environment (example: UNIX terminal). Hence the application takes advantage of the emergence of GUI while at the same time realizing, quite correctly, that many of the "back office" functions still utilize a TTY interface.

> **Note**
>
> PROGRESS can be used to develop applications that run on many different platforms and user interface types. The screen shots in this text relate to the Windows 95 version of the tools unless otherwise specified.

Client/server is, simply stated, a means of separating the data and the user interface. The benefit of this is a distribution of the CPU effort between the database functions (server) and interface functions (client). Since the user interface under this model is typically on a different machine than the data, we have today many client/server applications which access data stored on a so-called "legacy" machine and a user interface on newer Windows-based systems.

The legacy hardware houses existing legacy applications and their data. Although we often are rewriting modules into client/server, many times certain modules and/or the "back-office" functions of an application remain the same. The legacy hardware is often a very cost-effective way to "serve" data to a separate client machine.

The latter notion shows itself in countless client/server applications accessing legacy data from large UNIX systems and minis such as IBM's AS400. Such hardware is very capable of serving data with the performance and high-volume attributes of so-called "mission critical" systems.

Generally speaking, the maturity and price/performance characteristics of today's graphical desktop workstations has aided the proliferation of client/server applications. This is a classic case of one emerging technology supporting the other. We shall see in greater detail how the PROGRESS environment serves the needs of this expanding realm of GUI client/server and how it provides a complete solution.

The PROGRESS Environment

The advent of client/server has brought about an emergence of client-level tools that have no data storage functionality to speak of. These client tools create front-end graphical user interfaces connected to some external data server. Such tools have had reasonable success in the recent years. While PROGRESS can create a client-level GUI capable of communicating with external databases, it also embodies a powerful native database engine and external database "DataServer" that allows a more direct access path to data.

In terms of data access, we come across two general options around which we must architect our systems:

- An "open" data-access path that incorporates generally accepted and adhered to protocols such as (ODBC)
- A direct-access path that is customized for the client machine's access to a specific database

PROGRESS supports both approaches, allowing the ensuing client applications access to both ODBC-connected databases *and* access to PROGRESS DataServer databases such as Oracle, Sybase, AS400, and DB2.

The emphasis in the ODBC data access is clearly on standardization and open interface; the emphasis on direct-access connectivity is on performance and volume. In the PROGRESS environment we have the flexibility to use either or both options.

If the PROGRESS database server is chosen, you have a large array of hardware platforms to choose from. Most UNIX machines are readily supported and are the choice of most large-volume, transaction-oriented sites. The PROGRESS database is explored in greater detail later in this section.

Tools and Flexibility

The PROGRESS environment is one of balance between powerful development tools and a comprehensive language.

In terms of the development of the application client (for example, the application user interface and its associated processes), we have two general options to choose from:

- A "tool-centric" approach utilizing a code generation tool which creates a deployable application
- A language and compiler that are used to create source code and the resulting "executables"

Neither option is necessarily better or worse. These are general options that an environment leans towards.

Many of the tools we see today embody the tool-centric approach with reasonable success. As a programmer, you're limited to the fullness (or lack thereof) of the tool(s) provided unless one drops down to a 3GL such as Visual-C. The tool approach is highly effective for rapid development concentrated at what we refer to as the "desktop" level applications. Such desktop applications are often limited in scope, covering the lower range of transaction volume/performance, and do quite well for departmental level systems. With the emergence of external interface constructs such as Visual Basic Extensions (VBX) and Object Linking & Embedding (OLE) in the Windows environment, more doors—or shall we say more windows?—are opened. Even though a particular tool may not embody a certain interface control or mechanism, the job can be done with an OLE or VBX purchased or developed externally.

Indeed, the tool-centric approach to the client side of the development effort has had its successes. Flexibility is an essential element in developing large, transaction-oriented, enterprise-wide applications. We will explore the PROGRESS 4GL language and its ability to leverage the PROGRESS toolset and the work of developers on a team.

Again, we see that the PROGRESS environment is one of balance between powerful development tools and a comprehensive language.

One of the most significant testaments to PROGRESS' balance of tools and language lies in the fact that all of the tools (with the exception of the Report Builder, which was acquired) are written in the PROGRESS 4GL language itself. It can be said that if the language is strong enough to support the engineering intricacies of development tools, it should perform nicely in the development of the average business application.

The complete solution comes not simply because tools, databases, and language are strong but because of the balance which they strike together in the development efforts.

Who Should Read This Book?

The authors intend this book to be of value to several types of readers:

- Programmers and analysts interested in the PROGRESS suite of development tools for future projects
- Programmers and analysts new to the PROGRESS environment and in the process of developing an application
- Existing PROGRESS V7 or V6 developers making the migration to the new V8 release
- Project managers wishing to find out more about the overall development environment
- Students interested in client/server application development, object-oriented principles, component-based development, or graphical user interface development

This book is clearly focused on V8 and its significance in developing within the PROGRESS environment. The objective is to understand as much as possible about PROGRESS V8 SmartObject technology and the PROGRESS Application Development Model (V8 ADM).

How This Book Is Organized

Since each chapter builds upon information found in preceeding chapters, it is suggested that you read the chapters in sequence.

Part I: Introduction to PROGRESS

Part I introduces you to the PROGRESS environment: its components and tools. Explore the language and its powerful functions. Learn about record locking and transactions. Find out how VBXs can expand your interface's potential.

Chapter 1, "Introducing PROGRESS," introduces the development environment, including the Application Development Environment (ADE), the Application Development Model (ADM), and the database engine. You'll also find tips on where to find source code for V8 tools and tips on quick setup parameters that make your work easier.

Chapter 2, "Getting Started with ADE Tools," gives a guided tour through the development tools. These include the User Interface Builder, Data Dictionary, Compiler, and Librarian.

Chapter 3, "Using ADE End-User Tools," takes you through the tools used by end-users and re-sellers. Tools covered include Report Builder, PROGRESS Results, and the Data Administration tool.

Chapter 4, "Introducing PROGRESS Language," teaches you the essential elements and constructs of this powerful fourth-generation language (4GL). Learn how one PROGRESS 4GL statement is equivalent to hundreds of lines of COBOL or 3GL code.

Chapter 5, "Further Exploration: Locking, Transactions, and VBXs," explores PROGRESS record locking and transaction management. Learn how VBXs can be integrated into your PROGRESS programs.

Part II: Application Development Model

In Part II, you will explore the ADM in great detail, starting with component-based development and continuing with the essential elements of PROGRESS SmartObjects.

Chapter 6, "Utilizing Component-Based Development," discusses the significance of the programmer's evolution through a new paradigm. The impact of component-based development is explored through the eyes of the ADM.

Chapter 7, "SmartObject Links and Messages," gives an in-depth tour through the model and its associated toolset. Each type of SmartObject is explored. The encapsulated SmartObject method for passing messages (also called *message linking)* is described.

Chapter 8, "SmartObject Internals," describes the inner workings of the PROGRESS SmartObjects and their SmartLinks. Learn how these powerful objects are put together and how they communicate.

Part III: Creating a Sample Application

In Part III, you will develop a modest application. The various objects involved in the application are created and linked together. In addition to the development effort, you consider the deployment steps and client/server performance issues.

Chapter 9, "A Sample GUI Application," takes you through the development of each object associated with the sample application. This is a powerful tutorial for learning about V8 SmartObjects and the V8 User Interface Builder.

Chapter 10, "Connecting the Components," illustrates message linking (discussed in Chapter 7) and shows the object links connecting the sample application objects.

Chapter 11, "Adding Menu Bar and Report Components," demonstrates how to create reports for the application using the Report Builder tool. Deployment issues are explored along with review of a client/server performance check list.

Part IV: Application Design

Part IV teaches you the techniques which are successful in designing graphical user interfaces and relational databases. For user interfaces, the "paper modeling" technique is an extremely powerful tool for effectively gathering feedback from end users early. For database design, we review basic themes and general applied principles in this broad topic.

Chapter 12, "Introduction to User Interface Design," explores the simple—yet powerful—techniques involved in the iterative process of paper user-interface modeling. Usability testing is an important part of the design process which will be covered in this chapter.

Chapter 13, "Understanding Database Design," reviews key principles behind database design. We review entity-relationship (ER) diagrams, Database Normalization, and optimal selection of key fields.

Part V: Internationalization

Part V shows you how to globalize your Progress applications. Introduce your applications in the global market by understanding international software decisions and the tools associated with translation.

Chapter 14, "Designing Your Global Applications," details how to ensure that your application will satisfy your international customer base. Supporting other languages and national requirements is much easier and more cost effective if you design internationalization into your application from the beginning. This chapter reviews the major issues involved in designing an application for the global marketplace.

Chapter 15, "Developing Your Global Application," describes the capabilities of PROGRESS to address the issues covered in the preceding chapter. It covers PROGRESS startup parameters and 4GL functions that can be used to develop culturally flexible applications. It also covers double-byte enablement in PROGRESS—the capability to develop and support applications for Japan, China, Taiwan, and Korea markets.

Chapter 16, "Preparing for Translation," reviews the translation process, and introduces you to two tools available with Version 8 to translate a PROGRESS-based application: Translation Manager and Visual Translator. In this chapter, you will begin to translate the sample application developed earlier in Part III.

Chapter 17, "Translating Your Application," continues the process of translating the sample application using Visual Translator. It concludes by building a multilingual application without changing a single line of the application source code.

Chapter 18, "Deploying Your Application Globally," concludes the international discussion by reviewing the challenges of deploying an application abroad. There are international challenges that have been introduced with the advent of client/server computing, and this chapter reviews those challenges as well as the powerful solutions PROGRESS provides.

Part VI: Tips from the Pros

Part VI goes in depth into the User Interface Builder (UIB), active templates and other high-powered, sometimes-lesser-known features. In "UIB Exposed," you will get tricks and techniques from the programmers who created the User Interface Builder tool.

Chapter 19, "Using Active Templates," explores the concepts behind active templates and their role in defining new SmartObjects. You learn how to create a template easily with all the features used by the pros.

Chapter 20, "Extending the Development Tools," shows you the hidden techniques and entries into the UIB. Learn advanced "smarts" and smart message debugging.

Chapter 21, "Making the Most of the Application Component Environment," is like a conference with a consultant, an ADE developer, a database engineer, and a database tuner. This chapter brings you tricks and techniques not available anywhere else. Read highlights of hundreds and thousands of hours of V8 application effort.

Chapter 22, "PROGRESS Programming Tips," explains how to write code that is as reusable as possible. You'll learn to write code to change your user interface dynamically. Avoid the common mistakes made by many PROGRESS programmers while improving the portability of your application across deployment platforms.

Appendixes

The appendix section is intended as reference material. Additional information on SmartObjects, the PROGRESS language, internationalization, and the User Interface Builder is contained within the appendixes.

Appendix A, "Attribute Reference Guide," is a reference for all widget attributes and methods.

Appendix B, "SmartObject Method Reference," provides a quick reference of all SmartObject methods.

Appendix C, "Important Information for PROGRESS Software Users," provides a worldwide list of contacts and phone numbers. Get in touch with the global Progress community.

Appendix D, "Internationalization," provides additional information on internationalization issues.

Appendix E, "Custom Object Options," provides options for the development of new UIB objects.

Appendix F, "Structure of .w Files," explains the structure of UIB-generated .w files.

Appendix G, "Contents of CD," provides a directory of the CD-ROM contents.

Conventions Used in This Book

PROGRESS V8 allows for the selection of commands from its pull-down menus like all Windows applications. Also, like most Windows applications, the use of toolbars allows the user to quickly access a particular function. Letters that activate menu items are underlined, as in File, New.

Text that you're supposed to type is **boldface**. Control sequences that are used for certain functions are joined by a "+" sign, as in Shift+F10.

Throughout *Special Edition Using PROGRESS V8*, you'll see the following special elements.

Caution

This paragraph format warns the reader of dangerous procedures (for example, activities that result in files being deleted).

Note

This paragraph gives additional information about the topic in focus. It's designed to draw attention to special details about a particular subject.

Voice-of-Experience Movies

This special element alerts you to the fact there are Voice-of-Experience files on the CD-ROM and tells you where to find the files in Appendix G, "Contents of CD."

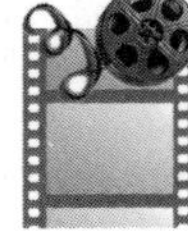

Tip

This paragraph format suggests easier or alternative ways to use PROGRESS.

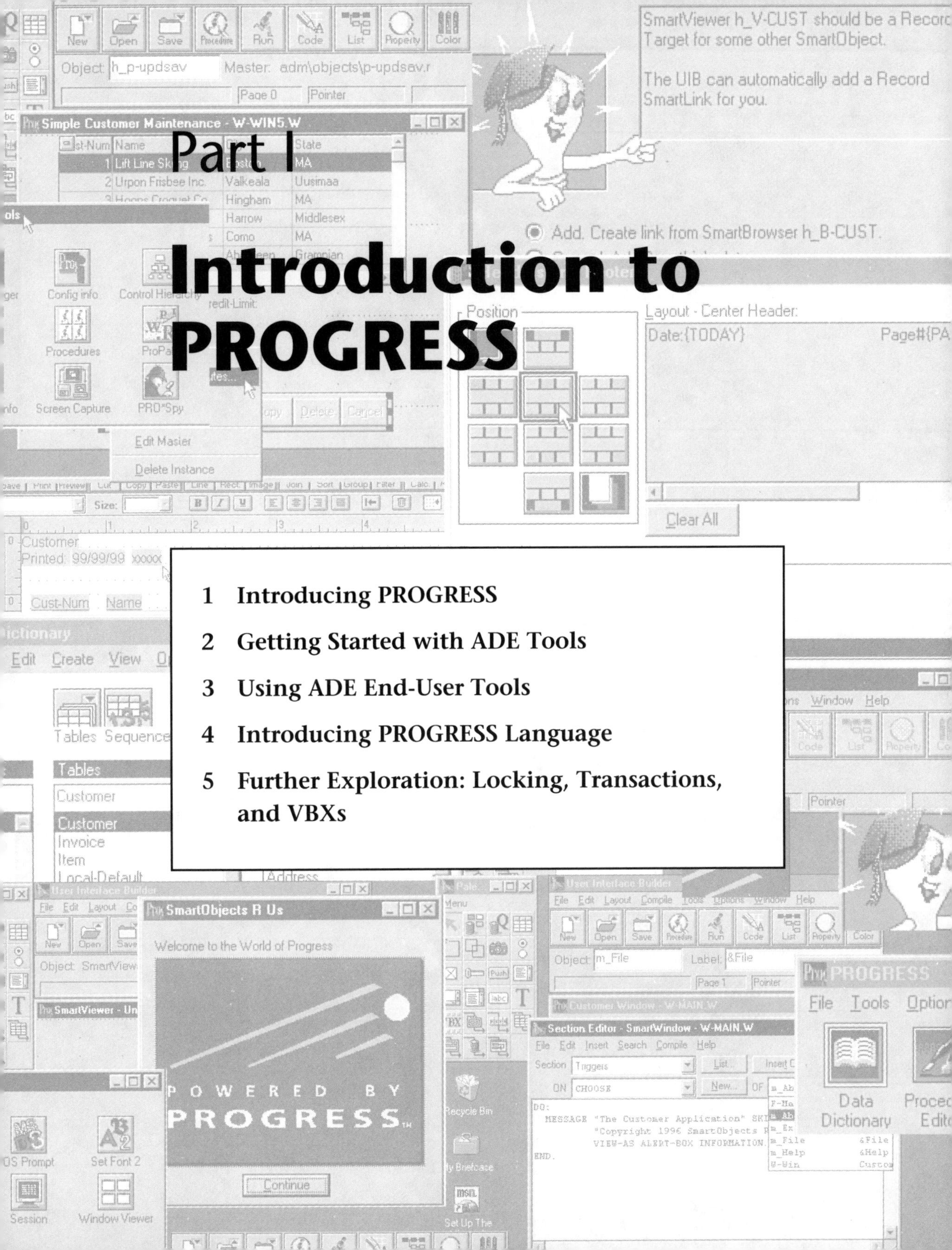

Part I

Introduction to PROGRESS

New
Open
Save
Procedure
Run
Code
List
Property
Color
Object: h_p-updsav
Master: adm\objects\p-updsav.r
Page 0
Pointer
SmartViewer h_V-CUST should be a
Target for some other SmartObject.
The UIB can automatically add a Rec
SmartLink for you.
Add. Create link from SmartBrowser h_B-CUST.
Simple Customer Maintenance - W-WIN5.W
Name
City
State
Lift Line Skiing
Boston
MA
Urpon Frisbee Inc.
Valkeala
Uusimaa
Hingham
MA
Harrow
Middlesex
Como
MA
Aberdeen
Grampian
Config info
Control Hierarchy
Editor
Procedures
ProPath
Screen Capture
PRO*Spy
Edit Master
Delete Instance
Headers and Footers
Position
Layout - Center Header:
Date:{TODAY}
Clear All
Function List:
{TODAY} Today's date
{TIME} Time report started
{NOW} Current time
{COUNT} Records listed so far
{PAGE} Current page number
Size:
Customer
Printed: 99/99/99
Cust-Num
Name
City
State
Edit
Create
View
Options
Tools
Help
Tables
Sequences
Fields
Indexes
Tables
Fields
Customer
Cust-Num
Customer
Invoice
Item
Cust-Num
Country
Name
User Interface Builder
File
Edit
Layout
Compile
Tools
Options
Window
Help
New
Open
Object
Label:
Pointer
Fields
Indexes
SmartObjects R Us
Welcome to the World of Progress
POWERED BY
PROGRESS
Continue
OS Prompt
Set Font 2
Session
Window Viewer
Recycle Bin
Set Up The
Object: m_File
Label: &File
Page 1
Pointer
Section Editor - SmartWindow - W-MAIN.W
File
Edit
Insert
Search
Compile
Help
Section
Triggers
List...
ON
CHOOSE
New...
DO:
MESSAGE "The Customer Application"
"Copyright 1996 SmartObjects
VIEW-AS ALERT-BOX INFORMATION.
END.
File
Tools
Data
Dictionary

CHAPTER 1

Introducing PROGRESS

This chapter introduces you to the PROGRESS V8 development environment. It addresses the scope of the PROGRESS toolset and serves as a foundation for understanding future chapters.

After reading this chapter, you should be able to do the following:

- Identify the major components of PROGRESS V8
- Know how the PROGRESS database and DataServers integrate into the environment
- Know the location for source code for PROGRESS tools
- Install PROGRESS V8 with proper Windows parameters

Introduction to the PROGRESS Development Environment

Before we look at the specific parts of PROGRESS and its functions, let's start with an overview of application development in general. This is important due to the way PROGRESS tools, language, and database are interconnected.

You can look at an application as being comprised of three major areas: data area, executable area, and deployment area, shown in figure 1.1.

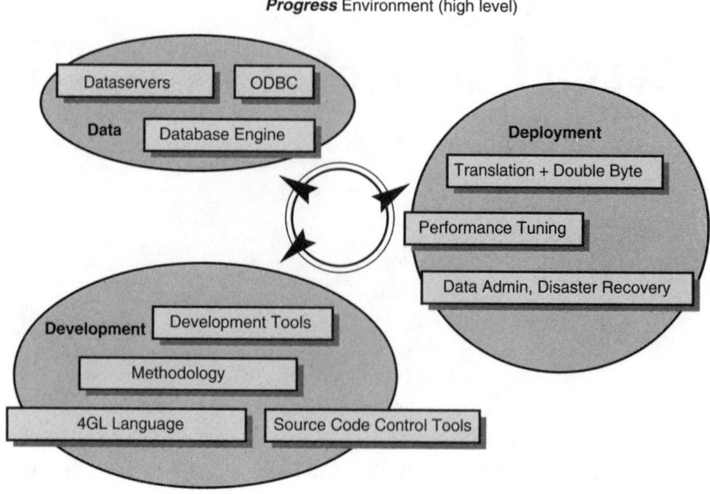

Fig. 1.1

The environment: Three areas of the PROGRESS environment.

The Data Area

Almost all applications require the manipulation of stored data. A PROGRESS application can access data from a PROGRESS database, any database supported by a PROGRESS DataServer, or any combination of these. A PROGRESS application can also access an ODBC-compliant data source through the PROGRESS ODBC drivers. The data area is, to a large extent, transparent to the developer and end user. Programmers don't need to use database-specific code to access a database. The same PROGRESS code can retrieve, manipulate, and store data in any supported database. The supported databases include Sybase, ORACLE, AS400, and VAX-RDB.

The reality of today's business is that it uses many data sources that you must integrate into your application. The data area of an application must be flexible.

The Development Area

The development area (for example, application code) is the primary focus of this book. At the core of a PROGRESS executable is a powerful fourth-generation language that serves as the foundation for the toolset and the code it generates. More than a scripting language, the PROGRESS 4GL stands on its own as a robust, complete programming language.

There are four major types of files within the PROGRESS developer's environment, which are identified by their default file extensions:

- 4GL code or .p, as in main.p
- User Interface Builder code, a window or .w
- Include files, .i
- Compiled program .r. (in a deployed environment, only the compiled .r files exist)

We cover all of the preceding files types in detail throughout the book. The fact that PROGRESS tools such as the User Interface Builder (UIB) generate PROGRESS 4GL code is essential for large-scale development *flexibility*. This allows the developer to modify the generated 4GL code or, better yet, to extend the tools to suit the requirements.

The Deployment Area

You must deploy an application before it is of any use to anyone. In enterprise-wide systems, deploying an application is an increasingly more complex task because of the number of different hardware platforms, networking protocols, and databases. You usually have an easier time deploying desktop or departmental systems (applications used either by a single person or a department/group) because there are fewer variables to consider. The real challenge comes in trying to scale up a desktop application to support a large group of users or an entire organization or company. This is often referred to as an "enterprise wide" system.

There are numerous issues to consider when deploying an application. These issues include hardware configuration, performance tuning, user interface translation, and disaster recovery. This book contains extensive information about deployment, concentrating especially on translating an application from one spoken language to another.

To become a fluent PROGRESS programmer, you must understand how the PROGRESS environment addresses the data, development, and deployment areas of an application. Because the language and toolset are so highly integrated, you can effectively ignore many issues around data and deployment and still develop effective enterprise applications. The better you understand how PROGRESS addresses each area, however, the better your application design can make use of the flexibility that PROGRESS offers.

Using a Programming Methodology

A programming methodology is critical when a development team works together to create a single application. The methodology prescribes a way to accomplish development tasks with consistency and efficiency. The PROGRESS toolset supports the development methodology presented in that the tools guide you through the steps in the development process. In most cases, the tools generate 4GL code as an end product. Although, many times, the programmer need not study the generated code, it is helpful to understand the relationship between tools and language.

Figure 1.2 shows the development area. It is comprised of development tools, development methodology, and 4GL language. Source Code Control (SCC) tools are included because they are essential for organizing application programs. PROGRESS Software bundles an SCC tool with V8, called Roundtable. Although the use and configuration of Roundtable are beyond the scope of this book, it is important to highlight its position within the development environment.

Fig. 1.2

The development environment.

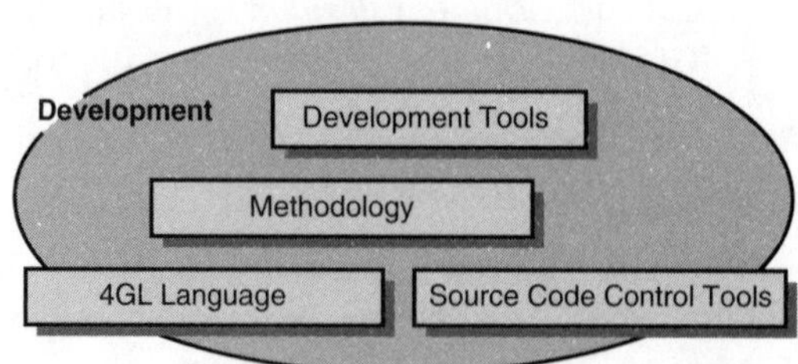

The best way to begin learning PROGRESS is to acclimate yourself to the environment by using the tools. After you gain some familiarity with the toolset, you should study methodology, and then learn the 4GL. This book is structured to support this learning path.

What's New in PROGRESS V8

This section is primarily for the benefit of PROGRESS V7 and V6 developers. It details the changes from PROGRESS V7.3 and makes reference to discussions of a topic elsewhere in this book.

This should allow seasoned PROGRESS developers to make quick use of the improvements of the V8 release.

After reading this section, you should be able to do the following:

- Understand the new features of V8
- Get a glimpse of possible V9 directions

The PROGRESS V8 Enhancements

The following features and concepts are new with V8:

- *Application Development Model (ADM).* Extensively covered throughout this book, the ADM is a Progress-endorsed and supported model for developing 4GL GUI client/server applications. The focus is on structured and organized code following the object-oriented model and exhibiting high reusability. The ADM consists of 4GL standards, SmartObjects, UIB support, documentation, and training courses. The ADM enters you, the developer, into the PROGRESS component-based development world.
- *Progress SmartObjects.* Progress SmartObjects support the new ADM by combining object-oriented technology with the PROGRESS 4GL. The V8 UIB revolves around its support for the V8 SmartObjects: SmartViewer, SmartContainer, TabFolder, SmartPanel, SmartBrowse, and SmartQuery. The V8 SmartObjects bring about organized, consistent, and reusable component-based development on the small or large scale.

- *UIB Enhancements* include the following:

  Open ADE. The Open ADE strives for a meta-tool—an interfaceable tool that the development team can enhance or extend in its work.

  PRO*Tools. A UIB palette with many mini-tools with time-saving development utilities such as font dialog, persistent procedure list, widget hierarchy, PROPATH editor, and many more. PRO*Tools is easily extended by the developer wishing to expand the toolset.

  Support for VBX controls!

  Windows 95 enhancements.

- *GUI enhancements* include the following:

  Updatable Browser! A browser control that allows data update.

  Frames owning (parenting) Frames. This feature allows a SmartObject (built on top of a Frame) to contain other SmartObjects within itself.

  Windows parenting Windows. This feature greatly enhances the potential for multiwindow applications, and allows for the Multi-Document Interface (MDI) look popular with Windows 3.x applications.

- *4GL language enhancements* include the following:

  `ASSIGN "WHEN"` option allowing conditional assignment in one statement.

  Upgrade Query/Buffer lock status allowing the upgrade of a lock without having to reread the record!

  `RECORD-CHANGED` function. Indicates a modification to the record buffer.

  `ROW-ID` datatype and function. The `ROW-ID` is fully portable and takes the place of `RECID` which does not ensure portability.

The following are database and dataserver enhancements:

- *PROGRESS Database Engine enhancements* include the following:

  Field Lists. Handles the transfer of specified fields for records minimizing network traffic. Imagine a 60K record coming across your client/server network for 100,000 records in order to locate a Social Security number. With field lists, only the SSN field would be transferred (for all 100,000 records). If the SSN field is approximately 12 percent of the record, this represents a network traffic reduction of 82 percent.

  Query Optimization/Record Selection. Server-based record selection for client/server. Server is able to select which records are to be sent across to the client, minimizing network traffic.

  Server-based DATE&TIME stamp. Avoids the troubles of data and time stamping at the client level. Because each client can have a different time, date/time stamping cannot be 100 percent effective. With server-based data/time stamp, this problem is resolved.

  SQL Engine II. Self-tuning SQL engine supporting outer joins. Better support for ANSI SQL.

Support for `ROW-ID` (see language enhancements).

- *Oracle 7 DataServer enhancements* include the following:

  ROW-ID support (see language enhancements).

  Select Pass through. Selection criteria is passed to the Oracle server for increased efficiency.

  Join by the Server. Join criteria are passed to the Oracle server.

  Look-Ahead Cursor and Prefetch. Capability to perform server-based record prefetch and record look-ahead.

- *Sybase System 10 enhancements* include the following:

  `ROW-ID` support (see language enhancements).

  Look-Ahead Cursor and Prefetch (see Oracle 7 DataServer).

  Join by Server (see Oracle 7 DataServer).

  Select Pass Through (see Oracle 7 DataServer).

- *DB2 DataServer Product* is new to the list of DataServers. Using an OS/2 Router to access existing DB2 data.

- *Enhancements to the RESULTS Report Builder tool* include the following:

  3D look and feel.

  Data Governor. Allowing developer to test run a report against a limited number of records.

  `ROW-ID` support (see language enhancements).

  Enhanced calculated fields.

  Enhanced table joins.

  Enhanced TTY conversion.

  Double Byte Enabled (see internationalization chapters).

  Product Translation to 12 languages!

  Field List Support (see database enhancements).

- *ReportBuilder enhancements* include the following:

  Deployment Engine. A reporting server for UNIX platforms allowing RB reports to be executed at the server level.

  Outer joins.

  Connection to multiple databases.

  Culturally Expected Behavior (not sure what Progress meant by this but it sounds good!).

  Product Translation to 12 languages!

- *Translation Manager V2 enhancements* include the following:

  Capability to view the actual interfaces on-screen while translating strings. This feature improves Visual Translator's ability to detect when translations result in screen real-estate challenges.

  Product Translation to 12 languages!

- *Support for team development enhancements* include the following:

  Source Code Change Management tool bundled with PROGRESS V8 product. Starbase's Roundtable product (a PROGRESS-built SCC package).

  Progress Software certifies SCM (Source Code Management) products (Starbase's Roundtable product and Intersolv's PVCS product) for integration with Progress ADE.

- *Internationalization enhancements* include the following:

  Additional translations of PROMSG file.

  Additional translations of PROGRESS error and system messages.

  Translations to error and system message include: Arabic, Persian, Japanese, Chines, Korean, Croatian, and Bahasa Indonesian.

- *New documentation sets* include the following:

  Getting Started tutorial.

  Programming Guide for SmartObjects.

  Online help enhancements.

  Translating PROGRESS applications.

  DB2 DataServer.

- *New training courses* include "Using the PROGRESS Application Component Environment (ACE)," which covers the Application Development Model and SmartObjects.

- *New programs* include the following:

  Source Code Management (SCM) Partners Program. A vehicle for working closely with SCM vendors to certify their products with the PROGRESS ADE.

  Early Access Program. Getting clients involved with the new release as soon as possible.

All this is new for version 8!

Moving Beyond V8

It is of no use to speculate the features of the next release. It is clear, however, that the object-oriented constructs of a "PRO-Class" will be introduced. With the PRO-Class, new object types at a lower level than SmartObjects will be created by developers.

The V8 SmartObjects will serve as containers and component structures for PRO-Class objects.

For example, a SmartObject such as the SmartPanel (toolbar) could easily contain a PRO-Class instance of a specialized button or graphic.

Imagine the power of SmartObject and low-level object orientation together. Although SmartObjects encapsulate and organize business application functions providing component-based solutions, a lower level of object orientation is sometimes desired.

In figure 1.3, you see the overall base of SmartObjects as providing true component-based development solutions to the PROGRESS developer. The SmartObjects are pure, 100 percent PROGRESS 4GL and are the foundation on which applications are built.

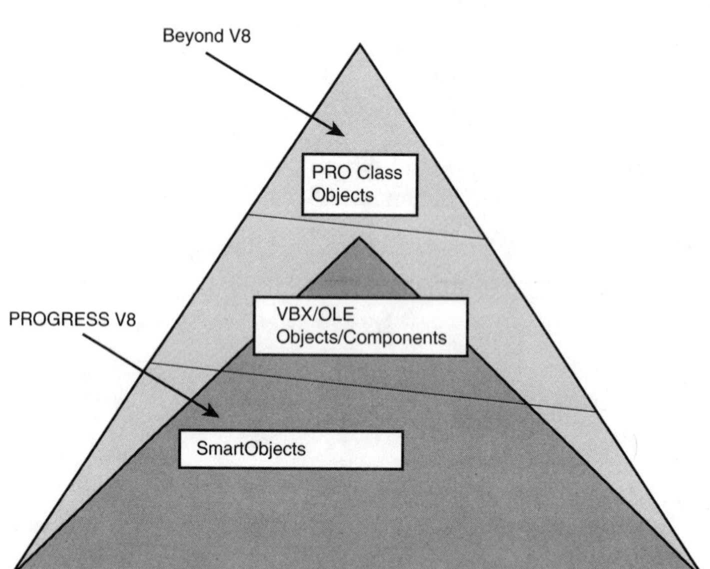

Fig. 1.3

PROGRESS object orientation, V8 and beyond.

VBX and OLE support would lie on top of the SmartObjects in the triangular structure shown in figure 1.3. Such components have a place *within* SmartObjects to increase the flexibility and available interface options.

Finally, the PRO-Classes lie at the top of the structure providing the low-level object orientation using PROGRESS 4GL code. Instances of PRO-Classes and their corresponding PRO-Objects will certainly make a presence in themselves. Their existence within SmartObjects will add additional flexibility even beyond VBX and OLE integration.

Whatever does lie ahead beyond V8, this certainly seems to be the path to efficiency, productivity, and quality.

Installation and Setup for PROGRESS V8

It is not the purpose of the text to describe the installation process for PROGRESS V8. We advise you to follow the steps outlined by the PROGRESS Installation procedure. It is assumed that you have PROGRESS installed and are using a Windows client because most developers will be residing on Windows 3.x or Windows 95.

This section is primarily to explain options and parameters that will make your job easier. First, we examine the command line for the PROGRESS icon in your Program Manager.

> **Note**
>
> To see the command line for a selected icon, press Alt+Enter after the icon has been selected.

The command line for the typical PROGRESS Desktop icon is as follows:

```
c:\dlc\bin\_prowin.exe -p _desk.p
```

Look at some of the most important parts of the command line:

- Start program file (`-p`). The `-p` parameter specifies the startup program. Using `_desk.p` causes the desktop to start. The desktop is written in the PROGRESS 4GL and is called `_desk.p`. If the `-p` parameter is omitted, you will start in the Procedure Editor, from which you may reach any tool by using the Tools option from the menu.
- Temporary files directory (`-T`). The `T` must be capitalized. Temporary files are created by the database engine and by tools such as the UIB during development. Temporary files should be placed in their own directory. This will facilitate possible cleanup of the temporary files. To place your temporary files in a directory called \temp, use the parameter `-T \temp` in the command line.

> **Note**
>
> If you have sufficient memory, you can create a RAM drive using the MS-DOS `RAM-Drive` command to house your temporary files. Be sure to create a RAM drive of no less then 1.5 megabytes. This is recommended only for development sessions, not deployment startup.

- Database connect at startup (`-db`). To connect to a database at startup, you may include the `-db` parameter. To connect to the sports database, use `-db sports -1` in the command line. This assumes that a copy of the sports database is in your working directory (see Chapter 3, "Using ADE End-User Tools"). The `-1` indicates 1 user, or single user. An omission of the `-1` parameter causes a strange network-related error that confuses most novices. PROGRESS looks for a server on the network (if one exists) if the `-1` is left out.

Parameters are combined into a single command line, such as:

```
\dlc\bin\_prowin.exe -p _desk.p -T \temp -db sports -1
```

Note the working directory for the Desktop icon. It should be set to the directory that your working files are in. It is a good idea to create a working directory such as c:\appdir and set this in the working directory slot. Do not use \dlc as your working directory; PROGRESS files are stored there.

All working files and programs will be placed in your working directory (as opposed to your root directory or some other place). If you have used the `-T` parameter (as shown in the previous command line), then PROGRESS' temporary files will be directed to the temporary directory while your working files (programs, data, and so on) will be placed in your working directory.

Now that you have established a working directory, it is a good idea to place a sample database in that directory for use in the ADE Tour chapter and beyond. The PROGRESS sports database is a good sample database. To copy the sports database into the working directory c:\appdir, copy the sports.* files from PROGRESS' DLC\BIN directory with File Manager or issue the DOS command: The sports database is included with the PROGRESS product.

Assuming that you installed PROGRESS in the root directory; issue the following MS-DOS command to copy the sports database.

```
copy \dlc\bin\sports.* \appdir
```

You now have a copy of the sports database in your working directory. Now that you have your PROGRESS environment setup, I'll go over the different components of PROGRESS itself.

The Application Development Environment (ADE) Components

This section introduces the tools that comprise the ADE. The PROGRESS Application Development Environment (ADE) is a conceptual group of tools that you use to create the executable portion of your application. In Chapters 2 and 3, you get plenty of detailed descriptions and hands-on work with the ADE.

Figure 1.4 points to the development tools. This area will be the first you will focus on in this book.

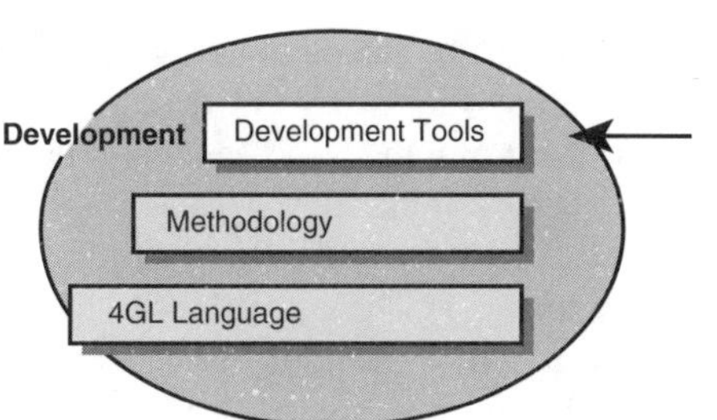

Fig. 1.4

The Tools section of the development area.

The first thing you see when you start PROGRESS is the PROGRESS desktop toolbar (see fig. 1.5). The toolbar displays an icon for each tool in the ADE.

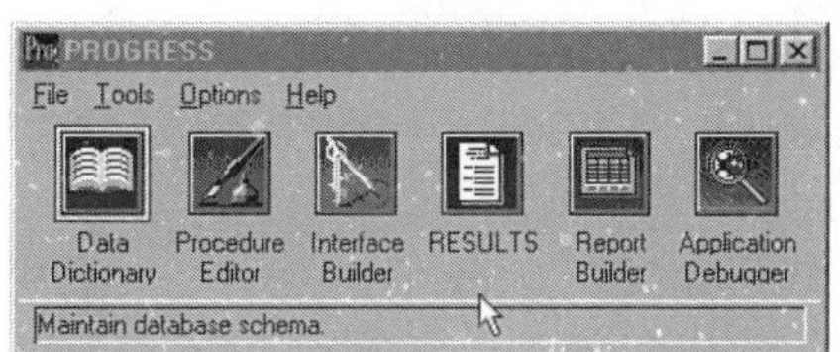

Fig. 1.5

The Application Development Environment (ADE) component desktop.

The PROGRESS desktop is a program invoked by the -p (starting program) parameter in your Windows icon command line. To view an icon's command line, single-click on the icon and press Alt+Enter. Be sure that the text `-p desk.p` appears on the command line after the executable (.exe). This launches the desktop.

The ADE components are as follows:

- *The Data Dictionary* allows for the creation and manipulation of the data structures within databases. This is where you create and modify the definitions for databases, tables, fields, and indexes. The Data Dictionary allows you to create, copy, and manage database connections. Database sequences and triggers are also managed from this tool. For DataServers, the Data Dictionary allows you to create a schema-holder database, which is an empty (no records) database that serves as a road map to the non-PROGRESS database. The Data Dictionary is the primary tool to manage the database aspects of development.
- *The Procedure Editor* is a text editor where you load source code, check syntax, compile, and run the corresponding program. For the experienced PROGRESS developer, the procedure editor takes on increasing value as you use it to customize your application with the 4GL.
- *The User Interface Builder*, otherwise known as the UIB, is a tool that facilitates the creation of user interface objects (windows, dialog boxes, menus, and so on). The UIB generates and manages much of the code involved in the interface development effort. For the experienced developer and novice alike, the UIB tool is central to efficient development efforts. You will explore this leverage and the capability to use the UIB as a meta-tool that you can expand and use to maintain new constructs—in later sections.

- *RESULTS* is a text-oriented report writer. By virtue of being nongraphical, you can easily port its output to PROGRESS-supported TTY environments such as VMS, UNIX, and MS-DOS. The output of a RESULTS session is PROGRESS 4GL code (a .p procedure) that creates the desired report. RESULTS itself is a highly customizable tool. You can include a customized version of RESULTS tailored for the specific end user in any application. This is equivalent to having written and shipped a report writer tool on your own! This book concentrates on the Report Builder, a Windows graphically oriented tool. RESULTS is nonetheless a significant and useful member of the desktop.
- *The Report Builder* is a graphical reporting tool for the Windows environment. The output of a Report Builder session is a Windows style report with Postscript and laser printing capabilities and an on-screen, zoom-enabled view of the report. For most PROGRESS Windows applications, the Report Builder is the report writer of choice. You will use the Report Builder tool in this book to create reports for the sample application.
- *The Application Debugger* is a tool that allows the programmer to view lines of code during execution to locate bugs and general programming oversights. The debugger displays a window independent from the application window. It shows lines of executing code, while sharing control of the program's execution through break points and other advanced diagnostic features.
- *The Translation Manager*, fondly referred to as TranMan by PROGRESS users, allows for the extraction of text strings within a program or set of programs. The TranMan stores these strings in a special database so that a translator (typically a nontechnical person) can translate these text strings to different spoken languages. This allows the translation effort to take place parallel to, but physically separate from, the actual development work.

There are a number of other tools associated with the development environment. Keep in mind that you can also integrate add-on tools with the PROGRESS desktop. This varies with development teams and the scope of their projects. Nevertheless, the Tools menu option displays a complete list of ADE tools (see fig. 1.6) that ship with the PROGRESS full development product (ProVISION).

Fig. 1.6

Tools menu option from the ADE desktop.

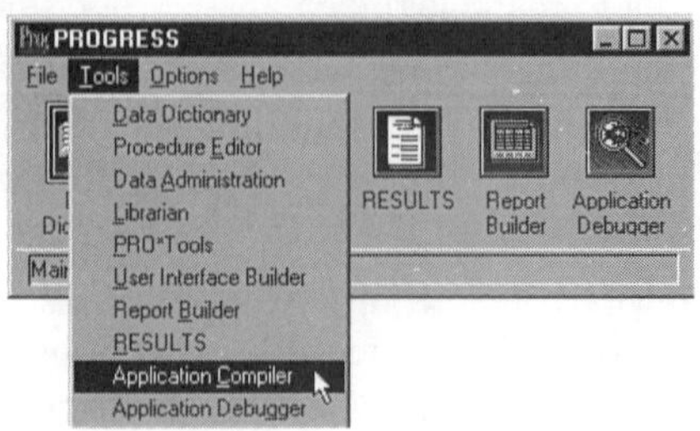

Additional development tools include the following:

- *The Data Administrator* facilitates administration of a database. Database administration through the Administrator encompasses functions such as data and data definitions dump and load, database schema reporting, and DataServer utilities. The Data Administration tool manages database security by defining users and their associated access levels.
- *The Librarian* tool houses commonly used programs, icons, and bitmaps. Each entry in the library is linked to an application object. The Librarian allows you to search, preview, and manage entries. PROGRESS ships the Librarian packed with more than one thousand entries of icons, procedures, and documentation examples. A development team can easily start a new library to house entries unique to its own project. Using the Librarian like this is an excellent way to assist new developers by giving them the capability to view and test individual programs.
- *Application Compiler Tool.* This tool allows for the compilation of single or multiple groups of programs. An average application will have several groupings of programs, including interface screens, reports, and background processes. The compiler tool lets you compile all programs associated with your application in one simple step. You will understand the meaning of a PROGRESS 4GL compile further on in this section.

▸▸ For more information on compiling, see Chapter 2, "Getting Started with ADE Tools." The compiler tool is covered there.

The preceding list comprises the principal components of the ADE. The power of the PROGRESS environment is that its tool set can be expanded. You (that's right, *you*) can create your own tool written in PROGRESS, and add it to the suite. Because PROGRESS is a portable language, your tool will be portable and can be made available to development teams using PROGRESS V8.

The source code to many of the ADE tools listed previously is available to you at no extra cost (we realize how crazy that sounds, but it is true!). Source code to the Dictionary, Librarian, Editor, and many of the common routines used throughout the ADE are all in *your* DLC directory.

The DLC\SRC\... directory structure is as follows:

adecomm\ contains common routines such as color/font selection, portable file find, and many others.

adeedit\ contains source code relative to the PROGRESS Procedure Editor tool.

aderb\ contains the workings of the Report Builder. This tool is the exception, not written in the PROGRESS 4GL (because it was acquired by Progress Software).

proclib\ contains the source code relative to the Librarian. The Librarian is an excellent example of a relatively small tool whose code runs on Motif, Windows, and TTY character mode with no modifications.

prodict\ and adedict\ contain source code relative to the Data Dictionary tool.

prodoc\ contains documentation examples.

prohelp\ contains help examples and help system files.

samples\ and template\ contain sample programs and UIB templates.

Note

These directories are part of the PROGRESS product, not the book's CD.

You have now completed an introduction to the PROGRESS ADE toolset. This high-level view of the ADE should provide the basis for more in-depth experience working closely with the environment.

You are encouraged to peruse Progress Software's documentation on any particular tool not thoroughly described within this text. Progress' documentation is not only award winning, it should serve as a comprehensive guide through some of the tools that are slightly beyond the scope of this book.

Note

For those of you who thrive on hands-on work, you might want to jump to Chapters 2 and 3 for a tour through the ADE. These hands-on chapters will fuse your understanding of the ADE components and their roles. We recommend that you then return to the remainder of this chapter, which covers vital foundation material on the Application Development Model (ADM).

The Application Development Model (ADM) Components

The PROGRESS V8 ADM is a method for creating applications and application components. A common methodology binds the ADE tools and carries the development efforts so as to achieve a correct level of consistency and organization.

As illustrated by figure 1.7, the ADM is a methodology within the development area of PROGRESS. In general, a methodology is a specific, defined set of concepts and rules to perform a task. In this case the task is application development using PROGRESS ADE tools. Without a methodology such as the ADM, different programmers will develop applications in significantly different manners. The ADM, as a standard methodology, is crucial to organized PROGRESS development.

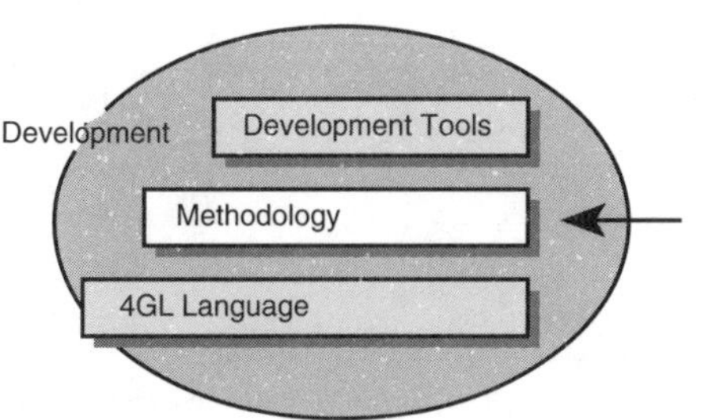

Fig. 1.7

The Methodology section of the development area.

In the executable area, the methodology falls between tools and language as the illustration shows (refer to fig. 1.7). The initial chapters in Part II, "Application Development Model," provide hands-on experience with the model before writing the sample application.

This section introduces the reader to the ADM concepts and to the ADM components. This is done much like the introduction to the ADE in the previous pages, so that you have an overall understanding of what the elements do.

The components covered in this section are as follows:

- Progress SmartObjects
- ADM Message Passing
- UIB Templates

As an ensemble, these components constitute the ADM. This will serve as the basis for further exploration.

Introduction to PROGRESS SmartObjects

The SmartObject is the key component of the model. Before I discuss its specific function, you need to understand where it derives from. Most significant programming and development structures have evolutions that are driven by both theoretical and real-life field experience.

> **Note**
>
> Throughout this text, we refer to PROGRESS SmartObjects (which has a copyright and trademark) simply as SmartObjects to avoid repetition.

Figure 1.8 illustrates the evolution of SmartObjects.

As an introduction to SmartObjects, note that it shares in background from both the object-oriented programming (OOP) concepts (encapsulation, classes, messaging) and the PROGRESS-proven constructs (such as templates and an enormous level of real-life field experience).

Fig. 1.8

The SmartObject evolves!

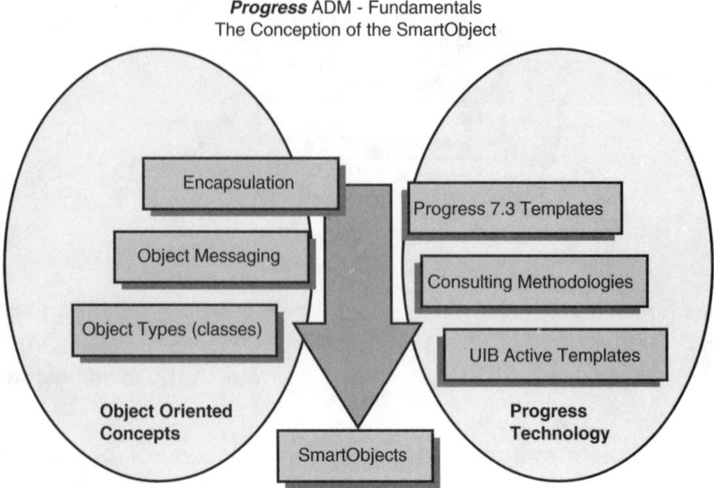

A PROGRESS SmartObject is a subset of an application that stands as a separate entity, contains the necessary functionality to accomplish its specified role, and communicates in a standard, predefined manner with its environment.

In reference to figure 1.8, the definition relates to the object-oriented (OO) world in the following significant ways:

- *Encapsulation.* An OO term referring to an object's capability to house its functionality and data within its confines. Removing an object's dependency on other external constructs allows it to be better maintained, documented, and replaced as an entity. Indeed, without some level of encapsulation, there are not clear and separate entities within a programming effort. In such an environment, maintenance and organization are at a premium. The SmartObject is created with the UIB tool, is called upon by programs at execution time, and is fully self-contained.
- *Object Messaging.* The effect of objects communicating with each other in a predefined and organized manner. Clearly defined object messaging invites development teams to create new kinds of objects that can fit into the message highways. Object messaging combined with encapsulation forms a highly structured and organized environment. SmartObjects communicate with each other using well-defined and standard messaging constructs defined within the Progress ADM.
- *Object Types (Classes).* It is important that objects of significantly different types fit into the model. In most OO models (such as SmallTalk), all objects must be derived from some type. The type of object or *class* determines the object's behavior and function. SmartObjects come in several different types, each performing a specific function in the development of PROGRESS V8 applications. Developers familiar with OO concepts should regard the development of

enhanced or new SmartObjects in much the same way as the development of new object classes.

With this fundamental background for SmartObjects, you can explore them further and note how a SmartObject is at a higher conceptual level then simple OO objects. By this we mean that a SmartObject encapsulates the function of high-level application pieces. This will become evident when SmartObjects are created and studied later in the book.

Chapter 6, "Utilizing Component-Based Development," covers SmartObject encapsulation in greater detail.

The impact of OO programming starts at the simplest level: a newly defined construct with simple function and form (if any at all), along with private and public variables. Such an object forms the foundation of an OO development effort. Larger, more elaborate objects are created from larger and more complex classes in the OO model. The impact of the PROGRESS V8 SmartObject, much like that of PowerBuilder's Data Window and Gupta's Quick Object, is at the application level. A SmartObject is, *at minimum*, a tabular list of records, a series of data input fields, a tab-folder mechanism, and so on. These are high-level constructs compared to minimal C++ classes. Hence, the SmartObject has a more immediate impact on the GUI Client/Server efforts than C++. Because of the surrounding tools, using it does *not* require an understanding of OO concepts.

High-level object orientation of common application components such as lists of records, toolbars, and data views is the strength and leverage of PROGRESS V8 SmartObjects. By way of comparison, Power Builder's Data Windows and Gupta's Quick Objects share in the same philosophy; however, only the Progress SmartObject is fully extendible and based on a 4GL language rather then on a script or pseudo code. As you continue your analysis and work with the PROGRESS SmartObject, you will see how this fact is significant over the long run.

The SmartObject's extendibility and 4GL language foundation give it flexibility and enterprise-wide appeal.

In this section you will learn what types of SmartObjects are built into PROGRESS V8. These components make up part of most applications.

Types of SmartObjects:

- *SmartViewer.* An interface object that displays database fields and other controls for viewing. It has built-in functionality of data saving, new record initialization, and message passing to other object types. (See fig. 1.9.)
- *SmartPanel.* A standard Windows toolbar. Built to communicate messages to related objects that are driven by the panel. If a SmartViewer were a light bulb, the SmartPanel (see fig. 1.10) would be the light switch. The light switch itself has no knowledge of what form of utility it is connected with, and the light bulb cannot determine user input.

Fig. 1.9

SmartViewer example.

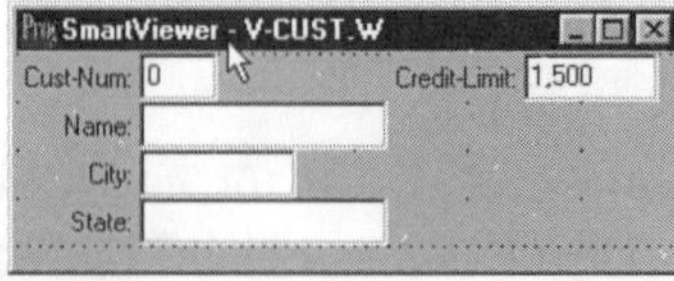

Fig. 1.10

SmartPanel example.

- *SmartBrowser.* A tabular list of records, coming from one or many related tables in a database. A SmartBrowser (see fig. 1.11) has a data query that constitutes a set of records and a visual representation (a browser control).

Fig. 1.11

SmartBrowser example.

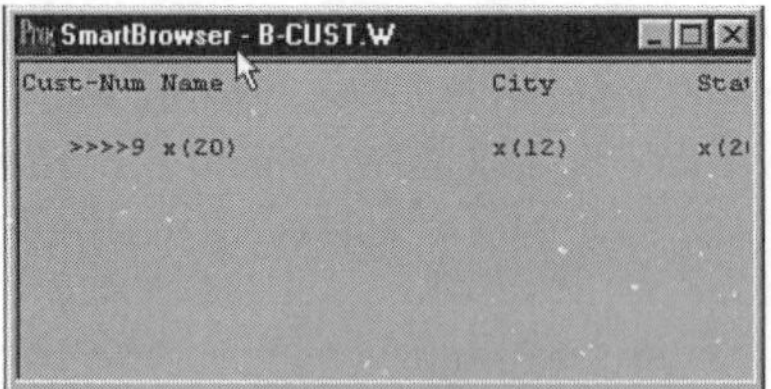

- *SmartQuery.* An object that houses a specific database query or *view*. The SmartQuery has no visual representation of its own (as with the SmartBrowser); it sends and receives records and query commands from other objects. A SmartQuery is typically combined with a SmartViewer and a SmartPanel to make up a typical file maintenance screen (see fig. 1.12).

Fig. 1.12

Smarts in action: Viewer, Panel, and Query involved in a file maintenance screen.

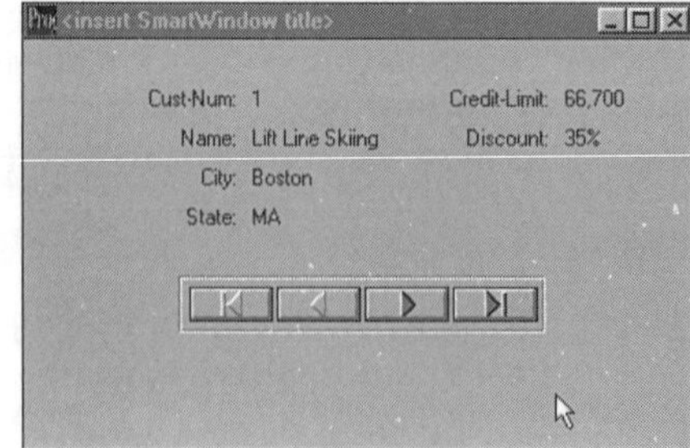

Read on to expand your view of the PROGRESS V8 ADM beyond an introduction to SmartObjects and to discuss message passing.

Understanding ADM Message Passing

As an introduction to PROGRESS ADM message passing, recall that SmartObjects need to communicate with each other in a predefined and relatively organized fashion.

Message passing is a very pervasive phenomenon (see fig. 1.13). It occurs constantly without a conscious decision on your part. For example, examine the trivial case of turning on a light bulb (feel free to try this at home).

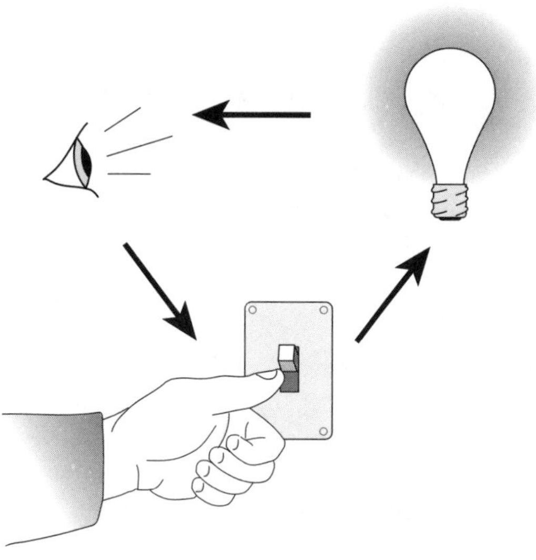
Message Passing - An everyday occurence

Fig. 1.13

Message passing, an everyday occurrence.

1. The eye passes an internal message (from a human body standpoint) to the hand to turn on the light switch.
2. The hand sends an external message to the light switch through simple physical movement of a knob: "switch."
3. The light switch sends an external message to the light bulb through electric impulses: "turn on."
4. The light bulb sends an external message to the eye and the entire room through light waves: "light!"

This example, though simple, is very similar to ADM message passing.

- Messages can often be passed internally within an object. Just as the person in the dark room passed internal messages between eye and hand, a SmartObject can pass messages internally between its data display functional area and its record communication area (for example).
- Messages are often extremely simple. Like a simple movement of a knob, a SmartObject message can be as straightforward as "hide," instructing the object to disappear from sight.
- Messages can be carried over several different media. Various types of messages can utilize different message transport mechanisms. Our example used nerve

cells, electrical impulses, and light waves. SmartObject messages have other unique types of message-transport mechanisms.

- Messages can cascade to multiple related objects. Just as the light from the bulb reaches most of the room, a SmartObject's message can reach many or all of its related objects.

This illuminates the basics of message passing.

Using UIB Templates

The third component of the ADM that we explore at this level is UIB templates. It is important to understand what a UIB template is before exploring the UIB itself.

A template, by definition, is a starting point with built-in functionality and appearance. An MS-Word template, for instance, contains font and margin settings to prepare for a new document built from the template.

A UIB template is an interface entity that has built-in functionality and appearance. Most significantly for your interests, the UIB comes with several templates that constitute the various SmartObject types.

The result of UIB development using a template is a completed SmartObject (see fig. 1.14).

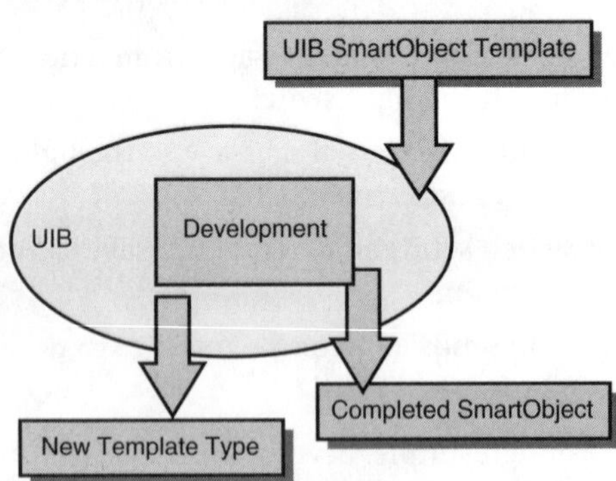

Fig. 1.14

UIB SmartObject templates create SmartObjects.

The reason to mention UIB templates here is to account for where the ADM message passing and general adherence to the ADM comes from in a SmartObject. Functionality such as internal/external messages and other ADM constructs comes from the fact that a SmartObject is created from a UIB template. That template comes preassembled with the necessary functionality.

If SmartObjects were created entirely by the UIB—that is, if they had no true templates—it would be difficult to expand the SmartObject type without changing the UIB itself. Because SmartObjects come from templates, you can change a template and affect all SmartObjects based on that template.

In a manner similar in concept to OO inheritance, a SmartObject type functionality can be altered by changing the template (or class) from which it comes. Because templates are manipulated with the User Interface Builder tool, not with encrypted language or scripts, altering a template is easy.

The ADM components that have been covered in this chapter are as follows:

- PROGRESS SmartObjects
- ADM Message Passing
- UIB Templates

In Parts II and III, you will use these components heavily (although you may not be aware of doing so). This chapter section may serve as a review after you have explored Parts II and III and want to reinforce your overall understanding of the ADM.

Understanding the PROGRESS Database Engine Components

In this section, we review the high level picture of the overall environment and set the stage for an introduction of the database engine components. Refer to figure 1.1 at the start of this chapter for a high-level view of the PROGRESS environment.

The database engine is extremely significant to the performance of the deployed application. Unlike environments that are blind to the data source and rely on external connectivity options for performance and throughput, Progress has developed a robust database engine. Today you can easily find PROGRESS applications attached to PROGRESS databases that are many tens of gigabytes in size and process many millions of transactions per week. Hotel chains, stores, banks, and entire casinos rely on PROGRESS databases and the PROGRESS database engine.

Progress has created an engine on each machine platform for you to store the data in a familiar form and with equal performance-tuning options.

It is important to mention that the physical database is, of course, a matter of disk space of the chosen platform. Typical chosen hardware platforms for databases include most UNIX systems including SCO, Hewlett-Packard, NCR, RS6000, VMS systems, IBM AS400 Servers, and Novell Network Servers. The native PROGRESS database engine performs the same logical functions regardless of platform, and is a unique executable for each platform port. This ensures that the engine takes maximum advantage of the platform on which it is running. A means of freeing memory on VMS will surely not be identical to one on Novell, thus the corresponding database engines are assembled appropriately.

Figure 1.15 outlines the major components of the database engine.

Fig. 1.15

Database engine components.

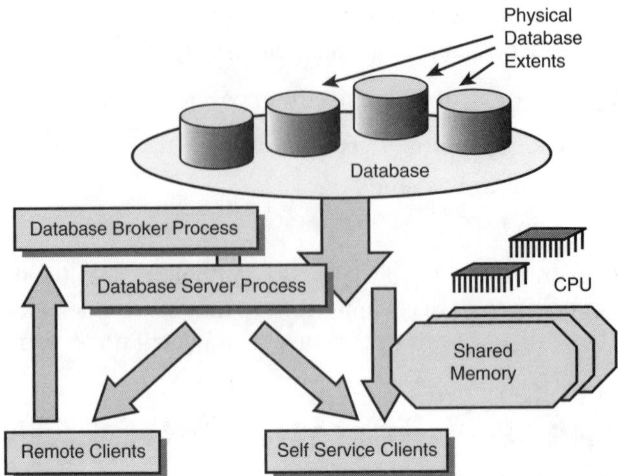

The following is an introduction to the database engine components.

- *Database Extents.* These are separate physical entities, each containing a portion of the entire database, allowing multiple drive spindles to share the burden of accessing huge volumes of data. Simply put, the database can be split into several separate sections of data, each in a database extent. Each extent can reside anywhere on the disk drive structure. In this way, drive spindles, controllers, and other system resources can be used to share the burden of database access.
- *Database.* This logical entity is referred to by each program accessing it. The physical location and configuration of the database itself remains transparent to the code interested in it. In fact, when using DataServers to external databases, even the database *type* (PROGRESS, Oracle, and so on) is transparent to the code.
- *Database Server Process.* The server process serves clients to the database (the users). This includes the local self-serving clients (on the same hardware as the database), and remote (dial-in) clients that may require multiple servers to handle their cumulative requests.
- *Database Broker Process.* The broker process relates to remote clients whose process resides on a system that is separate from the system which contains the broker and server processes. It is responsible for acknowledging their access to the database and starting server processes when necessary. Please note that remote clients are not necessarily "dial-in" clients. For example, two UNIX systems could be connected together and while UNIX system #1 holds the database processes, UNIX system #2 could accept users logging into the database and application.

- *Database Cache.* Database blocks are read into this area of memory and kept there as long as feasible so that subsequent reads of the same data will be memory-based as opposed to disk-based (performance).
- *CPU.* The CPU is heavily involved in facilitating the entire process and is essential to the performance and throughput of systems. The CPU powers the processes of the database server and database broker as well as its normal chores.

The next section discusses DataServers in order to show how you can access non-PROGRESS databases transparently. *Transparently* means that the code would work the same regardless of database used. See figure 1.16.

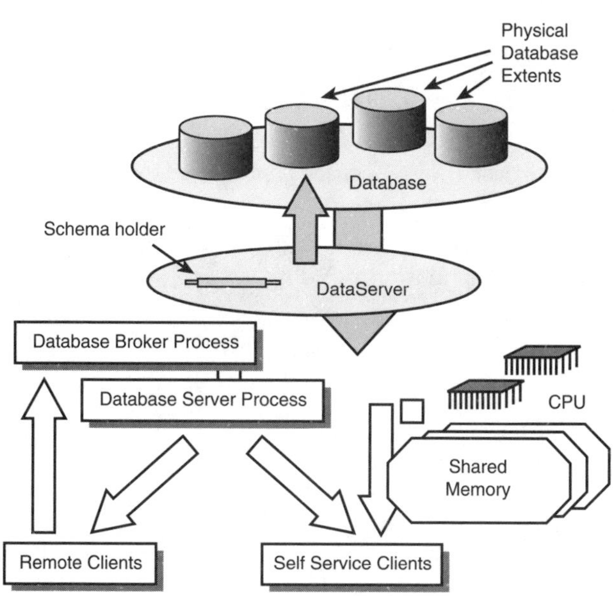

Fig. 1.16

Database engine components combined with the DataServer.

- *Schema Holder.* This is an empty PROGRESS database that maps the fields, tables, indexes, and so on from a PROGRESS format to the external database. Programs connect to the schema holder as if it had data (it physically does not); the DataServer then serves data from the external database to the PROGRESS database engine. It is interesting to note that the PROGRESS DataServer is actually a client of the external database.

You now have the basic database engine information that will allow you to fully comprehend the implication for enterprise-wide application development. The concept of a true database engine is peculiar for some who have been working in environments such as dBASE or Clipper. In such cases, there is no true engine at work; instead, the application executable (.exe) itself contains the mechanisms that fetch and manage data.

From Here...

You are now ready to explore the Application Development Environment. The ADE is divided into two areas of concentration:

- Development Tools: These work with the developer in the creation of executable programs.
- End-User Tools: These are focused on the end user's ability to create reports and are also used for application translation.

The next two chapters provide you with a hands-on introduction to the ADE. A tour through the various ADE tools will expose you to the development environment. Beyond that, you will build a sample application using PROGRESS V8 SmartObjects and the Application Component Environment (ACE).

You can find additional information in the following chapters:

- Chapter 2, "Getting Started with ADE Tools," is a hands-on tour of the ADE tools.
- Chapter 3, "Using ADE End-User Tools," focuses on end-user tools such as report writers and the Database Administration tool.
- Chapter 4, "Introducing PROGRESS Language," teaches you about the PROGRESS 4GL langauge and the rules surrounding it.

CHAPTER 2

Getting Started with ADE Tools

This chapter is a hands-on tour through the Application Development Environment (ADE) that was introduced in Chapter 1, "Introducing PROGRESS." The ADE tools enable the programmer to create programs, windows, databases, translations, triggers, SmartObjects, and more. The ADE tools are the key to programming productivity and consistency. This chapter and Chapter 3 will take you through the use of ADE tools.

Note

If you skipped Chapter 1, we recommend that you review it to provide a strong foundation of terms and concepts.

After reading this chapter, you should be able to do the following:

- Understand the ADE, which will serve as a strong foundation for the rest of your learning and practice
- Use the ADE tools and have a general understanding of their function and purpose
- Perform simple programming tasks
- Understand the details that make development with the ADE tools easier

Voice-of-Experience Movies

See Table G.3 in Appendix G, "Contents of CD," for a list of the Voice-of-Experience files for this chapter.

Accessing the ADE Tools

Figure 2.1 shows the PROGRESS V8 window for the Windows environment. From the desktop icons, you can quickly reach the most frequently used tools within the ADE. This chapter provides a tour of these and other ADE tools.

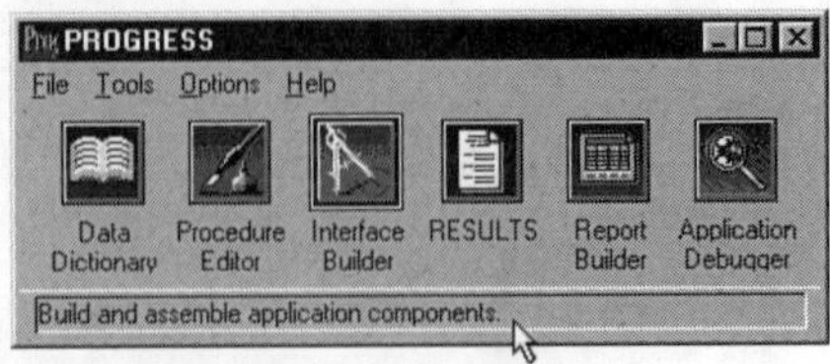

Fig. 2.1

The PROGRESS window.

> **Note**
>
> See the "Installation and Setup" section in Chapter 1 if you don't see the desktop when you double-click the PROGRESS icon.

You can explore each tool in the tour individually; you need not take the entire tour or follow it in sequential order. This way, you can return to this chapter later to examine a specific ADE tool or to review the basics. This chapter covers the *development* portion of the ADE tools, which are used to create and generate code by application developers. The next chapter, "Using ADE End-User Tools," covers the tools that are involved in reporting and translation.

Introduction to Database Tools: Data Dictionary

To enter the dictionary tool, you can click the Data Dictionary button on the desktop, or choose Tools, Data Dictionary from the desktop menu.

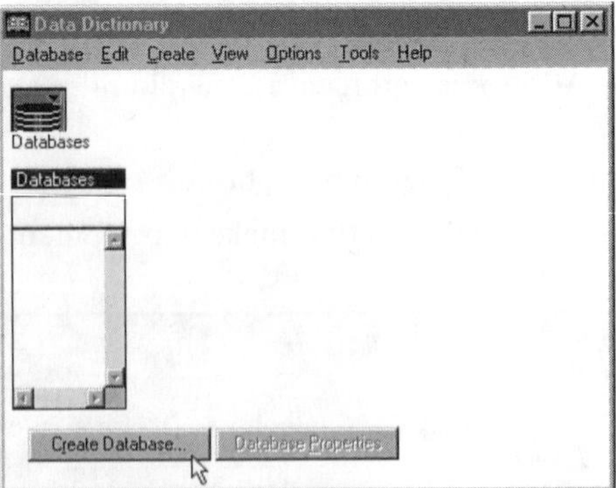

Fig. 2.2

Data Dictionary (no database connections).

Unlike other environments in which the programs themselves handle the connection and disconnection to a database and hold the database schema, PROGRESS has a true database environment. This means that the database and its schema are separate from interface code. You manage the schema through the database tools. You can connect databases from within these tools or at startup. After you connect to a database, it remains connected for the PROGRESS session or until you disconnect it.

To begin the tour of the Data Dictionary, you must do the following:

- Ensure that your working directory path is c:\appdir. Check the properties for your PROGRESS shortcut under Windows 95 to ensure that the working directory is correct.
- Ensure that the sports database is in your working directory. Check the \appdir directory for the file sports.db.

To connect to the sample database, choose Database, Connect from the Dictionary menu, then enter the database physical name (sports), and click OK. The Dictionary loads the database schema (see fig. 2.3). The *database schema* is a data structure that defines all tables, fields, indexes, triggers, and sequences for the database.

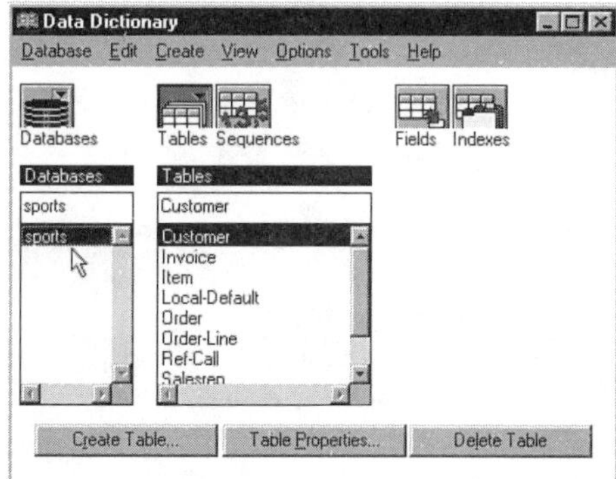

Fig. 2.3

The sports database connected.

PROGRESS uses the following terms to describe a database schema:

- *Database:* An entity containing data and the descriptions of that data.
- *Table:* A logical group of data within a database.
- *Field:* A data element of a certain data type stored within a table. It is also referred to in generic relational terms as a *column*.
- *Index:* An entity that dictates the order in which PROGRESS sorts the records returned from a query.
- *Trigger:* A section of 4GL code stored as an individual program that executes when a particular database event takes place.
- *Sequence:* An entity that keeps a sequential and unique counter for use in a unique field.

To explore the Data Dictionary and see how PROGRESS logically organizes these database elements, click one of the buttons that indicates Tables, Sequences, Fields, or Indexes. As you can see by the positioning of these buttons, Tables and Sequences are elements of the database, whereas Fields and Indexes are elements of a Table. For the next section, click the Fields button to view the fields for the Customer table (see fig. 2.4).

Fig. 2.4

Fields of the table: Customer.

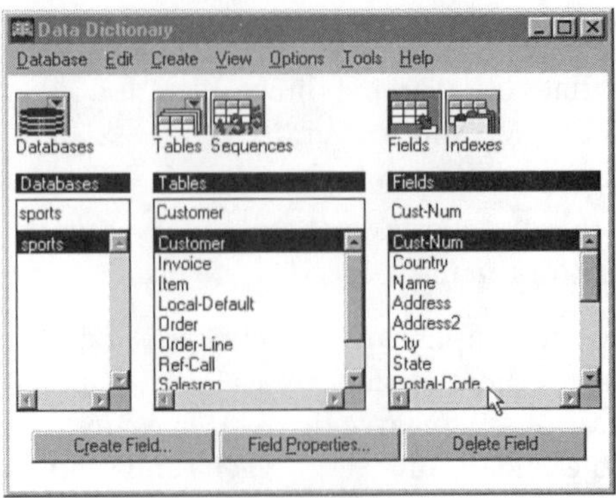

The Fields list scrolls, enabling you to view all the fields in a table.

To view the details of a particular field, double-click the field name from within the Fields list. For now, choose the field properties for Cust-Num (see fig. 2.5).

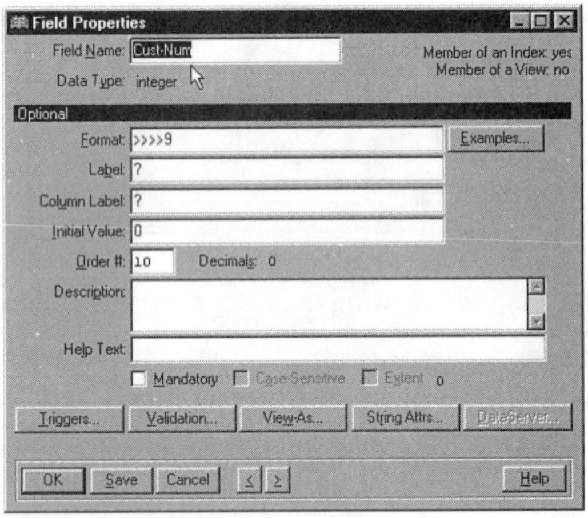

Fig. 2.5

The Customer Number field.

Each field has a variety of properties that specify how it responds to user input, what it looks like when it's displayed, and the parameters for valid data.

In the Field Properties dialog box, notice that the Label and Column Label properties are ?. This indicates that, by default, PROGRESS displays the field name as the Label or Column Label. You can override this setup for any specific instance from within your application.

The customer number field is of data type "integer" and carries a format of >>>>9. The format >>>>9 indicates that PROGRESS displays the value of the field as five integer digits right justified. You can choose Examples to see examples of other integer formats. You can also choose Cancel to return to the dictionary main screen. Choose Indexes from the Data Dictionary main screen to view the table's index structures.

Note

Learn to use either hotkeys or menu items for maneuvering through the tools. When an easy-to-reach button is available for a function, you can infer that you will be using it often!

Choose the field Cust-Num to view its index properties (see fig. 2.6).

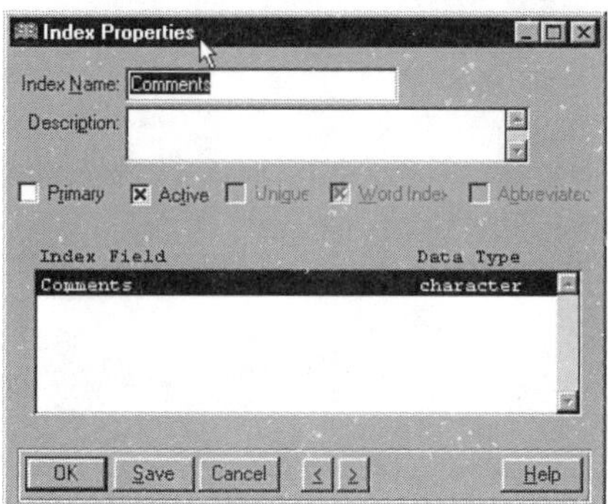

Fig. 2.6

The Index Properties dialog box.

Code that accesses the customer table uses this index. Just as the table of contents in this book enables you to find a chapter quickly because it lists chapters by their numbers, the database index allows the database engine to quickly locate records within a table.

In the Index Properties dialog box, notice that the Primary, Active, and Unique check boxes are checked (even though only Active is enabled). Every table must have a primary key that is used as a default. The primary key must be a unique index to ensure that only one data element exists for the fields specified within the index definition.

The list of index fields in the Index Properties dialog box (see fig. 2.7) shows the table's fields that make up the index. For the Comments index, Comments is the only field used by the index to determine its order.

Notice the A(sc)/D(esc) column in the Index Field list or the Index Properties dialog box. This information determines whether the database returns the requested data in ascending or descending order.

Click the Cancel button to return to the main screen. Now choose the Country-Post index. Notice that it has multiple fields for the Index Field list: Country and Postal-Code (both ascending). This information indicates that, when you're using this index, customer records appear in postal code order within country.

To view a table's properties, choose the Tables button from the Dictionary main screen and choose the Customer table. Most of the information on the Table Properties dialog box, shown in figure 2.7, has to do with elements of the data that you don't usually have to address during application development. The Dump File entry indicates the name of the file that PROGRESS creates when you dump the contents of this table. The Record Size and DataServer Name entries concern DataServer databases.

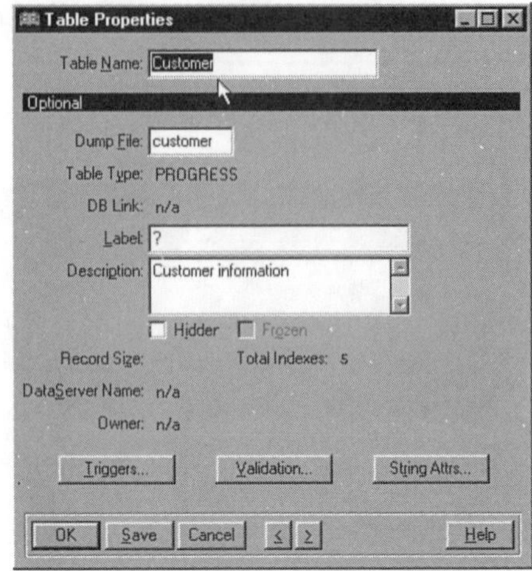

Fig. 2.7

Customer table properties.

You can move forward and backward through the list of tables without leaving this screen by using the < and > buttons on the bottom section of the Table Properties dialog box.

Click the Triggers button to display the Table Triggers screen (see fig. 2.8). In the upper left, you can see the Event drop-down list. This is a list of trigger events that affect a table. You write 4GL code to respond to these events.

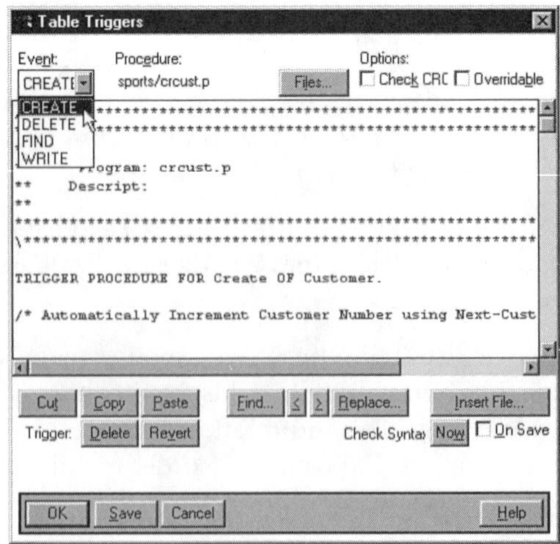

Fig. 2.8

The Table Triggers screen showing the customer Create trigger.

Notice that the procedure name, sports/crcust.p, to the right of the event indicates that the trigger code resides in a separate file. All database triggers are a separate procedure (a .p file).

Note

Within PROGRESS, regardless of the hardware platform, directory, and file entries, use the forward slash (/) for portability. Although the forward slash is *not* valid on all operating systems (MS-DOS and VMS for example), PROGRESS converts it to the appropriate format for the platform. PROGRESS enables you to use the backslash (\) on supported platforms. You will receive errors, however, if you port the work to a platform where the operating system does not support the backslash as the directory delimiter. In addition, do not use drive names but instead refer to directory paths relative to the root or the working directory.

In the example, *sports/* refers to a directory relative to the PROGRESS path. The PROGRESS path is a list of directories that PROGRESS looks through to locate files. This is usually called the PROPATH. In DOS, as with other operating systems, PROPATH is an environment variable. Because the actual *sports.db* database file path name is *\dlc\sports\sports.db,* and because *\dlc* is one of the entries in the PROPATH, the *sports* directory is available for file locations. Notice that you use the backslash (\) to indicate physical DOS file locations, and the forward slash (/) within the PROGRESS environment.

If this convention seems awkward, its purpose is not. If you port this dictionary schema from Windows to UNIX, the trigger procedure still reads sports/crcust.p. Because PROGRESS converts the path for you, you don't have any problems migrating from operating systems.

Click Cancel on the Table Triggers screen and then again on the Table Properties dialog box to go back to the Dictionary main screen.

Choose Database, Disconnect to disconnect from the sports database. Click No if PROGRESS prompts you to save changes.

Notice that you remain in the dictionary with no databases connected. Choose Database, Exit to leave the Data Dictionary tool.

Using Code and Code-Generation Tools

The Procedure Editor and User Interface Builder are considered code and code-generation tools. The User Interface Builder (UIB) is a typical screen painter and rapid application development code generator. It enables the developer to *visually* construct a screen interface, and then it generates the appropriate 4GL code. The strength of this method is that the generated 4GL code is 100 percent PROGRESS 4GL, as if you had typed it in yourself. Most screen paint tools such as PowerBuilder and SQLWindows generate pseudo or script code that you can neither edit nor decipher. The Procedure Editor, as you will see, is a powerful text editor for the PROGRESS development environment.

Entering and Editing Code with Procedure Editor

The PROGRESS Procedure Editor provides the capability to compile programs, insert field and table names, and launch a Debugger tool. The Procedure Editor creates flat ASCII type files. You use it to create PROGRESS programs: .p files and other PROGRESS file types.

To open the Procedure Editor via the desktop, click the Procedure Editor icon or choose Tools, Procedure Editor. The Procedure Editor then appears, as shown in figure 2.9.

Fig. 2.9

The Procedure Editor.

To begin the tour of the Procedure Editor, do the following:

- Ensure that your working directory path is c:\appdir.
- Ensure that the sports database is in your working directory.

Here is a short list of PROGRESS file types. You can view each of these files in the Procedure Editor:

- *.p files.* Files containing PROGRESS 4GL source code. The p stands for procedure.
- *.w files.* Files containing PROGRESS 4GL code generated by the UIB. A .w file typically constitutes a graphical interface program. The w stands for window.
- *.i files.* Files containing PROGRESS 4GL code that will compile into another file. The i stands for include.
- *.ini files.* The PROGRESS.INI file contains PROGRESS environment settings in the Windows environment. The PROGRESS.INI file is in the *dlc\bin* directory.

- *.pf files.* Files contains PROGRESS startup parameters. You specify the file name on the command line. Parameter files are useful if you use numerous startup parameters or if many users use the same parameters.

These files are ASCII files, so you can use *any* text editor to manipulate them.

The PROGRESS Procedure Editor, however, offers a great deal of functionality that makes it much more useful than just a text editor. To see some of this functionality, type the following 4GL code into the Editor:

```
message "Hello World." view-as alert-box.
```

Don't forget the period at the end of the line. You use the period to end all PROGRESS 4GL lines. Press F2 to compile and run your first program. The Compile menu contains the most frequently used functions within the editor: Run, Check Syntax, and Debug.

You can maintain several files concurrently in the Procedure Editor. To create a new file buffer, Choose File, New. In addition to writing source code, you can also run PROGRESS files from the Procedure Editor. Type the following into your new file:

```
run dict.p.
```

Press F2 to compile and run this program. The Data Dictionary tool appears. The dict.p file is the Data Dictionary startup program, so you can run it from the Editor. Remember that the PROGRESS ADE tools are written in the PROGRESS 4GL! Exit the Data Dictionary to continue by choosing File, Exit.

To see the open edit buffers, choose Buffer, List from the Procedure Editor menu. The Open Edit Buffer list shows you all programs that are currently available in the Editor. You can double-click the buffer that you want to view, and you can save buffers that you've modified, which are indicated by an asterisk (*).You can save a buffer to disk by highlighting the buffer and clicking the Save button.

Choose File, New Procedure Window to open a new window with a separate mini-editor. This procedure window does not have the full capabilities of the Procedure Editor, but it is useful for viewing multiple files at the same time on the screen.

You can choose Edit, Insert Fields to insert field names from the Dictionary schema into your code. This capability is extremely useful for commands that encompass many database tables and fields. You also can use the right mouse button to select fields to insert into the editor buffer.

Along with writing and compiling code, you can also connect to a database through the Procedure Editor. Choose File, New to create a new buffer in the editor and type the following:

```
connect \appdir\sports -1.
```

Create another buffer and type the following command:

```
FOR EACH CUSTOMER:
    DISPLAY
```

Now choose Edit, Insert Fields to insert customer fields for display. In the resulting Field Selector dialog box shown in figure 2.10, select the Cust-Num, Name, City, and Phone fields by clicking and using Ctrl+click for each subsequent selection. Click OK to insert the chosen fields into the editor work space. As you can see, inserting fields using this technique relieves you of the burden of typing field names by hand.

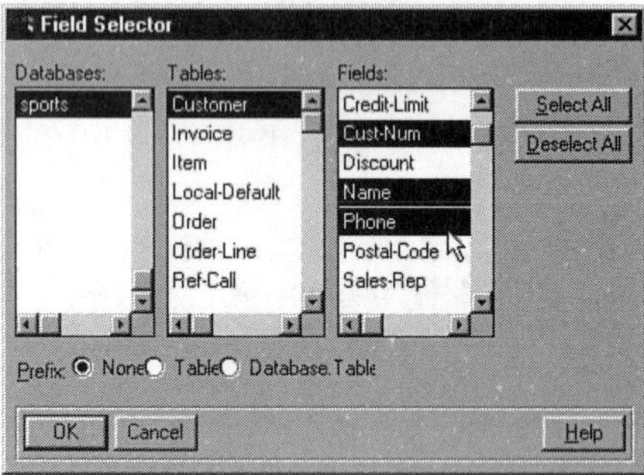

Fig. 2.10

Inserting field names using the Procedure Editor.

Your code now includes the fields for display, and you can run it by pressing F2.

If you want to learn more about any of the PROGRESS keywords in a section of code, you can open a help window for a selected keyword in the Procedure Editor. Double-click the word `display` to highlight it, and then press F1 to launch the Windows Help system.

The Help system contains online PROGRESS documentation for the language, tools, and system administration. You can call the Help system from any of the PROGRESS tools. You can also include help within your own applications.

Now that you've explored the Procedure Editor tool, it's time to take a look at the User Interface Builder (UIB).

Code-Generation Tools: User Interface Builder

The UIB is an extensive tool with great power for the developer. This chapter serves as an introduction. In later chapters, you'll use the UIB to develop an entire application. You use the UIB to "draw" graphical and text-based interfaces. It is also useful for creating common sections of code called "Method Libraries." The UIB takes directions from the developer and generates the necessary code.

To begin the tour of the UIB, you need to have the same working directory and database in place as in the previous sections. Then click the Interface Builder icon on the PROGRESS desktop. The UIB windows, shown in figure 2.11, appear.

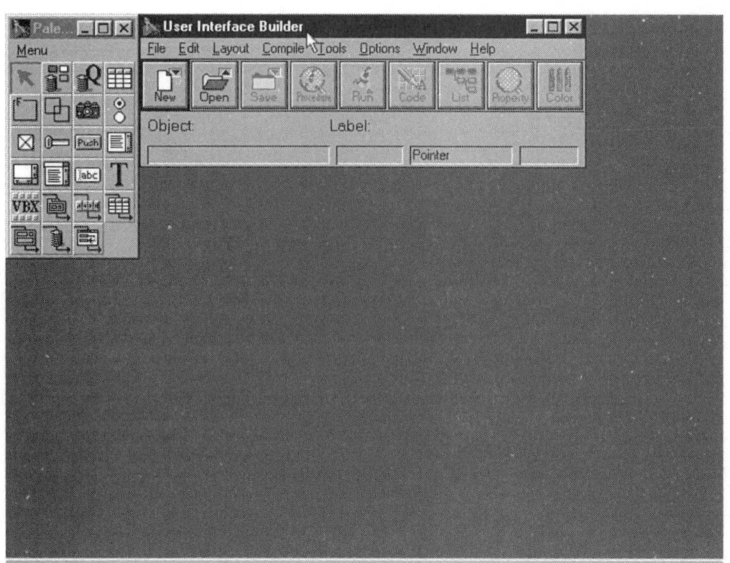

Fig. 2.11

The UIB windows.

If you are not already connected to the sports database, choose Tools, Database Connections. Then enter the database physical name **\appdir\sports** and click OK. Although you don't need a connected database to build applications in the UIB, by connecting, you can work with real data and place fields into the screen interfaces that you create.

Using the UIB, you can create numerous different types of objects and screens to use in your application. To begin creating a new window, click the New icon in the UIB top window. The New dialog box appears with the object selection list, as shown in figure 2.12.

Fig. 2.12

Objects to create using the UIB.

To better understand objects and the UIB, take a look at figure 2.13, which shows the various object groupings:

- *Containers:* Objects designed to hold (or contain) other objects. A typical container is a window or dialog box. Example: SmartWindow.
- *SmartObjects:* Objects that contain specific functionality—user interface as well as logic and data. Example: SmartViewer.
- *Procedures:* Objects that serve as a set of functions and procedures for validation, calculations, and background processes. A procedure typically contains no visual interface elements. Example: an amortization program.

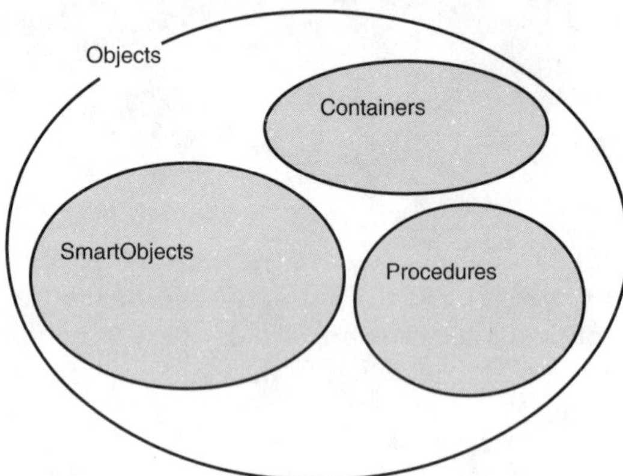

Fig. 2.13

UIB object types.

For this introduction, you will create a simple interface starting with a Window container object. Highlight SmartWindow in the New Object list and click OK. Resize the new window so that it fits comfortably on your screen. Now you can add some simple controls to make your first PROGRESS GUI program.

For the developer new to the UIB, it's a good idea to expand the UIB's toolbar to include labels so that you can tell which icons relate to which objects. To expand the toolbar, choose Menu, Options, Show Labels in the UIB palette (the left window). The labels appear for each of the palette icons. The labels should help you identify objects until you become familiar with them.

The first control that you need in your window is a Browse. The *Browse* is a control that shows a list of records and enables you to scroll through them, like a spreadsheet. Choose the Browse control listed in the Palette dialog box. After you select the Browse control, move your mouse to your working window. The mouse icon changes to a grid-like Browse icon. Click in the general area where you want to place the Browse control.

After you click the location for the Browse, the Query Builder window appears, as shown in figure 2.14. In this window, you can define the Query for the Browse. A *Query* is an entity that specifies which tables, fields, and options PROGRESS uses to retrieve the data.

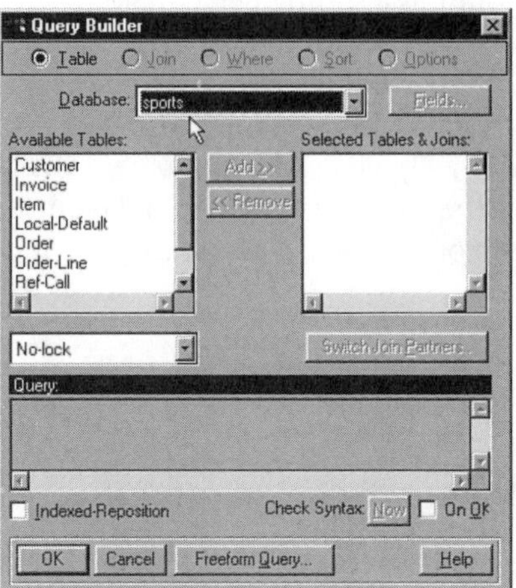

Fig. 2.14

Query Builder visually defines the tables, fields, and options belonging to a Browse.

Double-click Customer in the Available Tables list to add the Customer table to the query. You can select as many related tables as you want (for now, Customer will suffice). Then click the Fields button in the upper-right corner to select the display fields. The Column Editor dialog box appears.

In this dialog box, click Add and double-click the fields Cust-Num, Name, City, and Credit-Limit. Click OK to leave the Multi-Field Selector screen. Click OK to leave the Column Editor and again to leave the Query Builder screen. You are now back to the UIB working area. Adjust the size of the Browse control so that it is wider and appears as shown in figure 2.15.

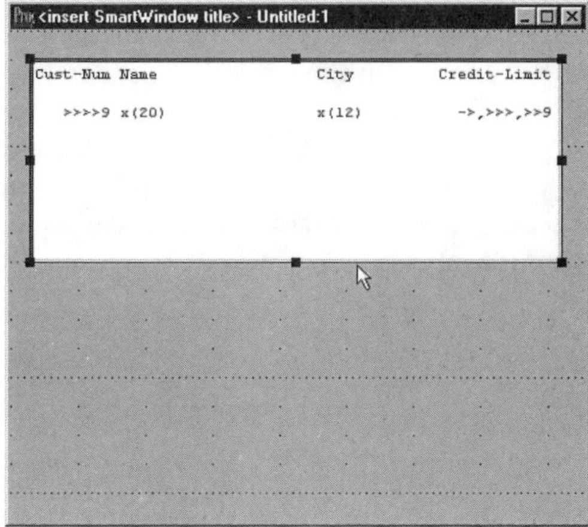

Fig. 2.15

The UIB area with the inserted Browse control.

The control shown in the working window in figure 2.15 is a mock-up of the actual Windows control for the purposes of screen design. Click Run or press F2 to see your Browse in action. Press Escape to return to the working session.

Say that you want to see the discount amount for each displayed customer. A slider control enables you to view the discount as a sliding percentage. Click the slider control in the UIB Palette window. Place the slider in the working window below the Customer Browse. A slider has a default vertical geometry. To change the slider control to horizontal layout, double-click it to open its Property Sheet. Using the Property Sheet shown in figure 2.16, you can quickly view and alter object attributes. Click the Horizontal attribute check box to set the slider to a horizontal layout. Choose OK to exit the Property Sheet, and then use your mouse to adjust the size and position the slider where you want it.

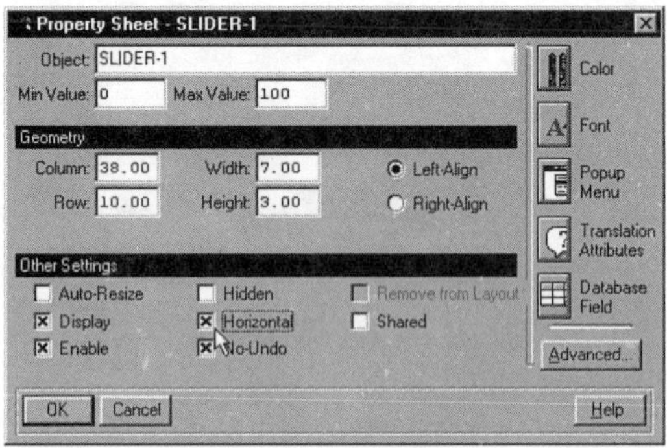

Fig. 2.16

Property Sheet for a slider control.

> **Note**
>
> To view an object's attributes, you can double-click the object or choose the Property button in the UIB toolbar.

The next thing that you need to do is to establish a link between the slider control and the Browse so that, when you see a record in the Browse, the slider displays the appropriate discount amount. To create this link, you use the Browse events `ITERATION-CHANGED` and `ENTRY`. You find these events listed in the UIB's Section Editor. The `ENTRY` event occurs when you first enter the Browse control. You use this event to set the initial value for the discount. The `ITERATION-CHANGED` event executes whenever you select a different record in the Browse; this way, you can keep the discount slide in sync as you view different records.

Click once on the Browse to select it. Click the Code icon on the UIB toolbar. PROGRESS then displays the Section Editor (see fig. 2.17). In this window, you view the code and events associated with your selected object or control.

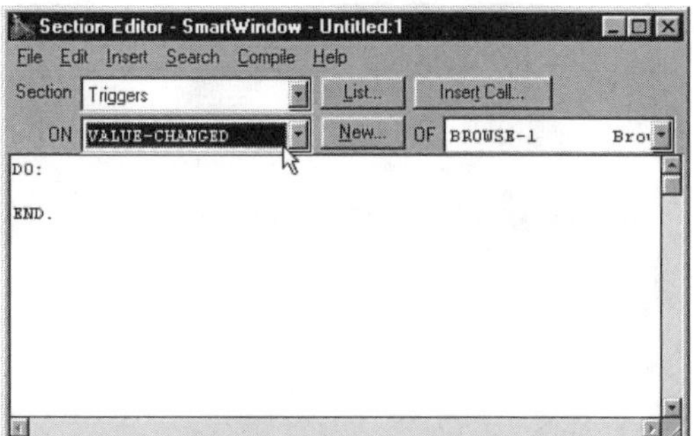

Fig. 2.17

The Section Editor showing code and events related to a control or object.

Because you want to define a new trigger for the Browse, click New. From the Choose Event window, double-click `ENTRY`. Return to the Section Editor and type in the following 4GL code to set the slider's value (on the screen) or "SCREEN-VALUE" to the actual customer's discount:

```
slider-1:SCREEN-VALUE = STRING(customer.discount).
```

The first element, `slider-1`, is the name of your slider (the UIB assigns a default name if you don't specify a name). The `:SCREEN-VALUE` element is an attribute of the slider. It contains the slider's value as it appears on the screen. You use the `STRING()` function to convert the numeric `(customer.discount)` to a string that the `:SCREEN-VALUE` attribute expects. The `SCREEN-VALUE` attribute will always return a Character data type. If you want to check the syntax, press Shift+F2. Or you can choose Compile, Check Syntax to make sure that your syntax is correct.

Tip

You can check the syntax of your program at any time by pressing Shift+F2.

The `customer.discount` field (in `table.field` format) is the discount field of the customer table. When you run the code, PROGRESS displays the discount of the selected Browse record.

Click New and repeat the same process for the event `ITERATION-CHANGED`. This way, you can ensure that with each iteration of the records in the Browse, the slider will display the appropriate discount.

Tip

Choose Copy, Paste to copy sections of code and avoid needless retyping.

Run your program by pressing F2. The slider displays 50 percent as the discount for the first customer in the sports database (see fig. 2.18).

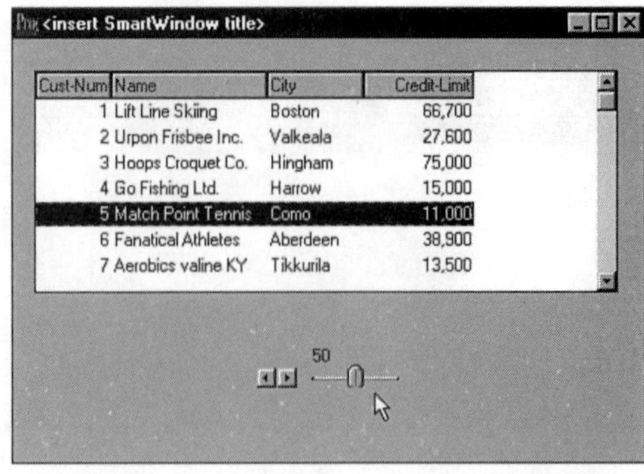

Fig. 2.18

Running the program showing customers and selected customer discount.

Now that you've defined the core logic, you can add the finishing touches. You need an Exit button (pressing Escape to exit is not elegant, and also is a bad habit because, in programs that manage transactions, Escape usually backs out of the transaction). You can also put a label next to the slider indicating its purpose.

To add the Exit button, click Button on the UIB palette and place it to the left of the slider. Click the Attribute button on the UIB toolbar to view the button's attributes. Change the label to **E&xit**, and then click the check mark button.

The `&` in `E&xit` denotes character `x` as a mnemonic. You can then use the mnemonic as a shortcut to the button's functionality by pressing Alt+x. To close the attributes list, double-click the upper-left corner.

Double-click the Button to open its Property Sheet. Toggle the switch Auto-End-Key to on. Auto-End-Key is a function that ends a program when you choose the control. Auto-End-Key is equivalent to pressing Escape and will suffice for now. This technique is not desirable if the program manages transactions, because it can cause the transaction to roll back, instead of ending the program.

After you close the Button Property Sheet, click Text in the UIB palette and place a text control to the immediate left of the slider. This control acts as the slider's label because a slider does not inherently have one. Use the Property Sheet to set the text to **"Discount %"**. Notice that on the UIB toolbar a field displays the label of the selected control. You also could have typed **"Discount %"** in the UIB toolbar, instead of opening the Property Sheet.

Adjust the size of the text control to a satisfactory size, and you're done. Click the List icon in the UIB toolbar. The List Objects screen, shown in figure 2.19, appears and shows all objects on the working window, including the window object itself.

This list gives you quick access to all controls. Double-click the window control and change the title to **Sample Program #1, Chapter 2**. Then click the Save button on the UIB toolbar to save your work. Finally, press F2 to run the completed program (see fig. 2.20).

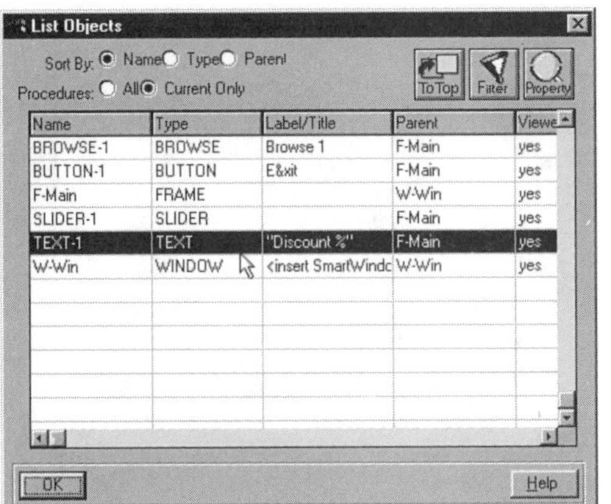

Fig. 2.19

The UIB object list.

> **Note**
>
> Save your work to \appdir\ch02prg1.w. This file also exists on the sample CD in the directory \examples\chap-02. You will use this program later in the ADE tour.

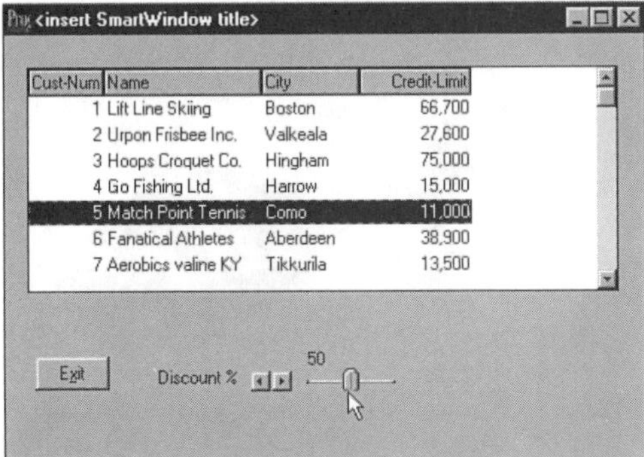

Fig. 2.20

Completed UIB screen.

Now you've completed the introductory tour of the User Interface Builder. You should have the feel of the UIB and what it can do with a relatively simple task. In later chapters, you use the UIB as the primary tool for building your application.

Compiling and Debugging Tools: Compiler Tool

Your tour of the ADE continues with a demonstration of the Compiler tool. Choose Tools, Application Compiler from the desktop to start the Compiler tool, as shown in figure 2.21.

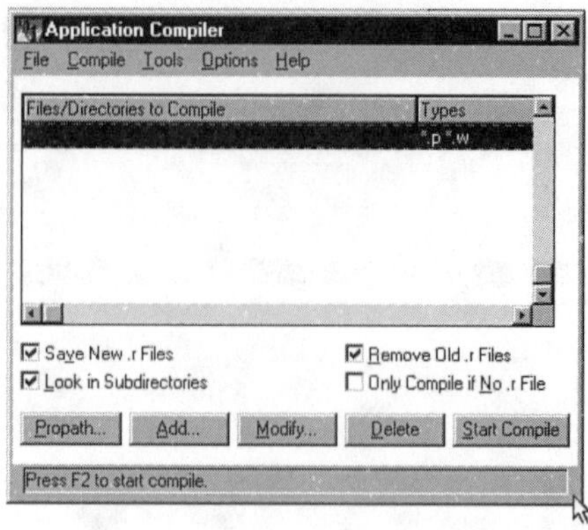

Fig. 2.21

The Compiler tool.

The Compiler tool enables you to compile large numbers of programs located in specific directories. To understand why this is useful, examine what a compiled PROGRESS program looks like. Figure 2.22 shows the evolution from .p file to procedure library.

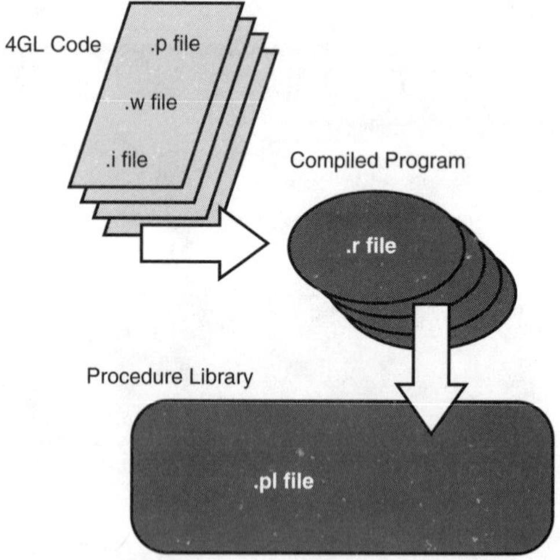

Fig. 2.22

Compiled code evolution.

Code entered by hand or created by a code generator such as the UIB exists in the form of .p, .w, or .i files. The Compiler tool or compile process creates an .r file as a compiled version of these files. The .r compile file not only is in a format that runs quickly (performance), but you can generate an .r for all supported PROGRESS platform types (portability).

You can store a collection of .r files in a procedure library or .pl file. A file appl.pl could contain hundreds of programs that constitute your application. This capability eases deployment and also makes it easier for the interpreter to find files.

In summary, during the development, you create source code and store it as .p, .w, and .i files. During testing, the compile process creates .r files from the source code. This process is called *compile-time*. During deployment, you run the .r files either stand-alone or from within a procedure library (.pl). This process is called *runtime*.

You don't have to precompile your procedures to run them. The interpreter can run the source code within a separate compile-to-.r phase. When it does this, the interpreter must stop and compile each program into memory before executing it. This compiled version of a program in memory is called *session-compile*, named for the fact that it resides in memory only for the duration of the PROGRESS session. After an application is deployed, compiled .r files are available for every program, thus ensuring the highest possible performance.

▶▶ See Chapter 4, "Introducing PROGRESS Language," and Chapter 5, "Further Exploration: Locking, Transactions, and VBXs" for more information about the Compiler tool.

Compiling and Debugging Tools: Debugger

The PROGRESS Debugger is a line debugger. It enables you to view source code during execution, set break points, and view variables. The source code must be available during the debugging session.

To begin the tour of the Debugger, you need to have the same working directory and database in place as in the previous sections and you must Connect to the sports database. Then go through the UIB section of the ADE Tour in this chapter. In this exercise, you will debug the file \appdir\ch02prg1.w. Alternatively, you can load this file from the directory \examples\chap-2 from the sample CD.

The tour of the Debugger tool starts from within the Procedure Editor. You can also call the Debugger from the User Interface Builder.

Click Procedure Editor on the PROGRESS desktop. Choose File, Open and load \appdir\ch02prg1.w. Recall that this program, created earlier in this chapter, shows customers and their discounts.

Choose Compile, Debug from the Procedure Editor menu to launch the Debugger. The debugging process first compiles the code and checks for syntax errors, and then the Debugger opens, displaying the first line of executable code (see fig. 2.23).

You can ignore the file C:\DLC\p18350r.ped (your file name may differ slightly) shown in the top section of the screen. It is a temporary file created for the debugging session. The debugger creates a temporary file of the program you are currently working with so that is does not interfere with the copy of your program in memory.

The arrow pointed at the line `CREATE WIDGET-POOL` shows the first executable line of code. In fact, the first line of code in almost all UIB-generated interfaces is `CREATE WIDGET-POOL`.

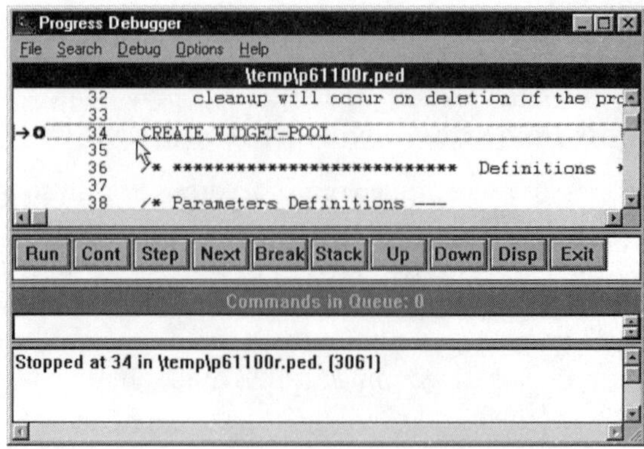

Fig. 2.23

Debugger session running.

Click Next a few times to watch the Debugger proceed through executable lines.

Choose Search, Find Next to locate a section of code for the break point. Search for `ITERATION-CHANGE` by entering **ITERATION-CHANGE** in the Find dialog box's Find What text box. You want to break on each iteration of the Browse in this program. You may recall from the UIB tour that in the event `ITERATION-CHANGED` you synchronized the Browse object with the slider object. By setting a breakpoint on `ITERATION-CHANGE`, you can analyze the program at each new record selected in the Browse.

After closing the search pop-up, click the following line:

```
slider-1:SCREEN-VALUE = STRING(customer.discount)
```

in the PROGRESS Debugger window. Click the Break button marking this line as a break point for the Debugger.

You can now continue running the program until it reaches the break point. Click the Cont button to continue. The program runs and displays customers and the selected customer's discount level.

By clicking a different record in the customer list, you can trip the break point, and the Debugger will reappear. You can now view variable contents by typing commands into the Debugger's command queue window (just below the Debugger buttons). Type **display customer.discount**. PROGRESS accepts the command and displays the discount in the bottom window, as highlighted in figure 2.24. You can also select `customer.discount` by using the mouse and clicking the Display button in the Debugger.

The difference between the Next and Step buttons is that Next goes to the next line of code without stepping through the code within a subprocedure, whereas Step steps into the lines of a subprocedure. Using Step may cause you to enter vast areas of subprocedure code that you know nothing about (if you did not develop them). You may want to use Step to diagnose descendant programs that expect input parameters or those that may be inheriting a transaction from a parent. Use Next for the purpose of introduction.

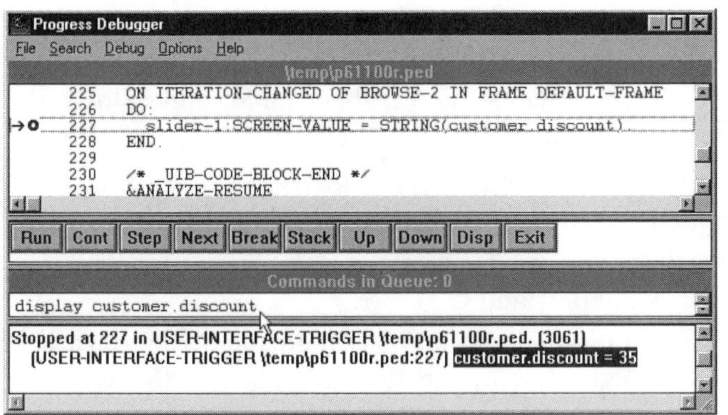

Fig. 2.24

Variable contents shown within the debugging session.

You may continue stepping through the program or exit the Debugger. To exit your program, click the Exit button.

Support Tools: Pro*Tools

ProTools is a set of commonly used tools put together on a toolbar for developer convenience. This introduction gives a brief synopsis of each mini-tool within ProTools.

Choose Tools, PRO*Tools from the PROGRESS desktop to start ProTools. The ProTools toolbar remains available until you either explicitly close it or you end the PROGRESS session.

The simplest way to learn about the contents of the ProTools toolbar is to display the labels for each icon. To do so, click the right mouse button over any of the ProTools icons. Click Menu Bar and then choose File, Labels to show their labels (see fig. 2.25).

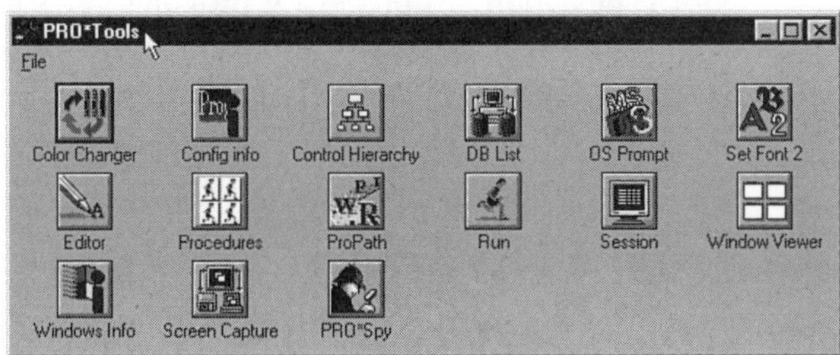

Fig. 2.25

Expanded view of ProTools icons with labels.

The following summarizes each tool within Pro Tools:

- *Color Changer:* Enables you to set the 16 colors (0–15) used by the PROGRESS toolset.
- *Config Info:* Provides PROGRESS configuration information including parameters set from the progress.ini file.

- *Control Hierarchy:* Shows all controls and their hierarchy. Shows the hierarchical relationship among all window controls.
- *DB List:* Shows the connected databases and enables you to connect to additional available databases.
- *OS Prompt:* The DOS prompt window.
- *Set Font 2:* Enables you to set the font quickly for UIB work. (Font 2 is used by the UIB for text.)
- *Editor:* Starts a Procedure Editor window.
- *Procedures:* Shows persistent procedures and their internal procedures. This helps in being able to communicate with the persistent procedures in the session. A *persistent procedure* is a procedure that remains in memory after it has completed execution.
- *ProPath:* Shows the PROPATH entries and enables you to modify them. The PROPATH holds a list of directories that PROGRESS looks through to find programs, icons, and so on.
- *Run:* A run dialog to run a PROGRESS program.
- *Session:* Displays the session attributes such as date format, display type, and so on.
- *Window Viewer:* Displays a list of windows and enables the developer to hide or bring to the top any selected window. This capability aids in the development of multiwindow applications.
- *PRO*Spy:* Monitors and lets you view the message passing between SmartObjects. This tool is important for debugging the messages sent to and from PROGRESS V8 SmartObjects. Refer to Chapter 7, "SmartObject Links and Messages," for more information about message passing.

ProTools contains useful utilities for the development process. It provides quick access to development environment settings such as configuration and fonts. With experience, you will use ProTools often. Look for Progress Software to expand ProTools with each subsequent release.

Miscellaneous Tools: Librarian

The Librarian tool enables you to manage a library of programs, icons, bitmaps, and objects. In fact, you can catalog just about any file within the Librarian.

You can view entries and run PROGRESS programs. You can search for Library entries, and you can even search for text within the entries. The Librarian makes it easy to search for a text string within many programs.

Choose Tools, Librarian from the PROGRESS desktop. The Librarian screen then appears, as shown in figure 2.26.

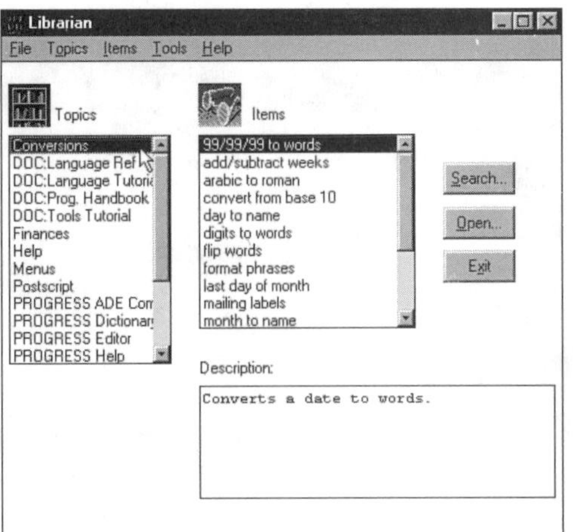

Fig. 2.26

The Librarian tool.

The Librarian takes awhile to load because it contains more than one thousand entries. It includes help files, examples from documentation, and many of the common routines used by the ADE toolset.

> **Note**
>
> Don't let the startup speed of the Librarian tool discourage you. Its slow startup is due to the number of entries it loads by default. You may replace its library cards with your own. The Librarian's cards are stored in \dlc\src\proclib\proclib.dat.

In the Librarian screen, the list on the left shows the library topics (refer to fig. 2.26). The first category is `Conversions`, which is a library of sample conversion programs. The list on the right shows the entries for the selected category. The first entry is `99/99/99 to words`, which is a sample program that converts dates to words. Note the description of the entry in the Description box in the lower-right corner of the screen.

Scroll through the 4GL and highlight a PROGRESS keyword. After you highlight a keyword, click Help to get PROGRESS online help for the word.

> **Note**
>
> The Librarian is an excellent tool for new developers wanting to explore and learn about the team's development environment and common programs.

The Librarian also is a useful tool for cataloging bitmaps and icons. To see how to catalog, scroll down the Topics list on the left and select `Standard Icons`. Then select `admin.bmp` in the Items list (this is the icon for the Database Administrator tool). The Librarian enables you to catalog your images and quickly find the appropriate image for use in GUI interfaces (see fig. 2.27.)

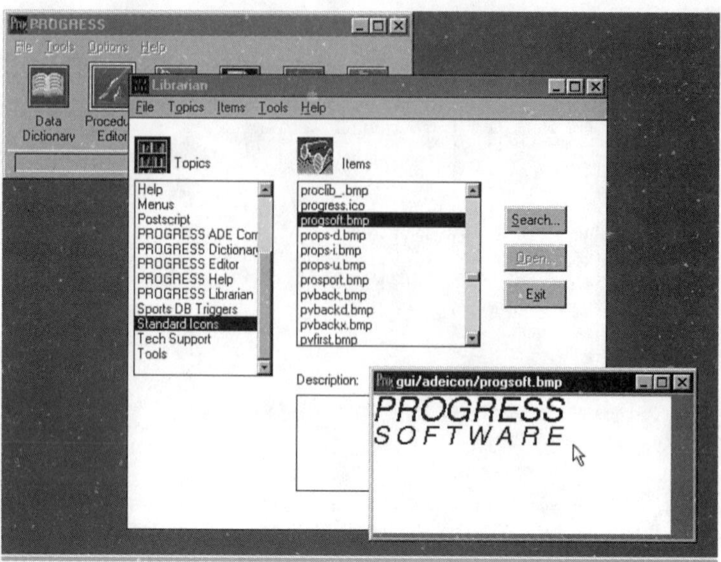

Fig. 2.27

Librarian catalog of images.

In the Topics list, click `Conversions` and then click the Search button. The Search Items dialog box enables you to search through entry names, descriptions, and the entries' contents. Using the analogy of a book library, the ADE Librarian search is equivalent to being able to search on book title, book description, and book contents. Keep in mind that the Librarian does not allow changes to the programs cataloged within it. It is a reference tool, not an authoring tool.

As shown in figure 2.28, we searched for the text SUBSTR in the conversion topics, and the Librarian displayed the list of items that contain that text. The Librarian searches are *not* full work searches, so `SUBSTRING` and `SUBSTRATE` would have been found.

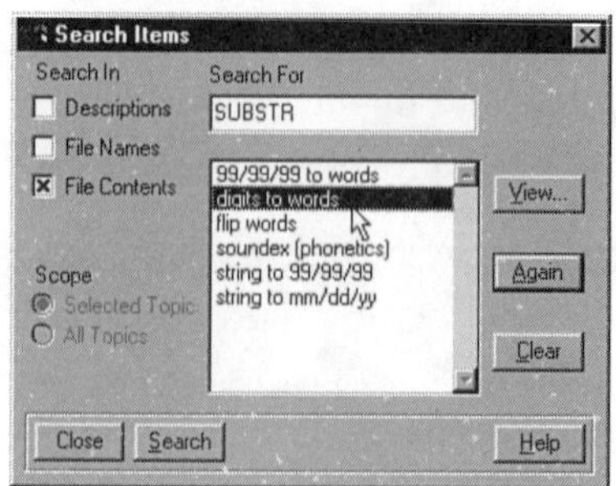

Fig. 2.28

The Search Items dialog box after searching for SUBSTR in the conversion programs.

From Here...

In this chapter, you toured the Application Development Environment development tools.

For more information on related items, refer to the following chapters:

- Chapter 3, "Using ADE End-User Tools." This chapter introduces you to the end-user tools such as report writers and database administration.
- Chapter 4, "Introducing PROGRESS Language." This chapter teaches you the basics of the PROGRESS 4GL.
- Chapter 5, "Further Exploration: Locking, Transactions, and VBXs." This chapter continues the discussion of the 4GL and contains step-by-step examples for using VBXs within PROGRESS screens.

CHAPTER 3

Using ADE End-User Tools

This chapter is a hands-on tour through the Application Development Environment (ADE) End User Tools. It is a continuation of the previous chapter, and you will utilize the reporting tools and translation manager to understand their roles within the overall environment.

Note

If you skipped Chapter 1, we recommend that you review it to provide a strong foundation of terms and concepts.

After reading this chapter, you will be able to do the following:

- Use ADE's end-user tools and have an understanding of their purpose
- Use Report Builder and Results to create PROGESS reports
- Use the Data Administration tool to manage the database structures
- Create reports for database definitions
- Dump and Load database contents and definitions

Voice-of-Experience Movies

See Table G.3 in Appendix G, "Contents of CD," for a list of the Voice-of-Experience files for this chapter.

Accessing the Application Development Environment Tools

Figure 3.1 shows the PROGRESS V8 Desktop for the Windows environment.

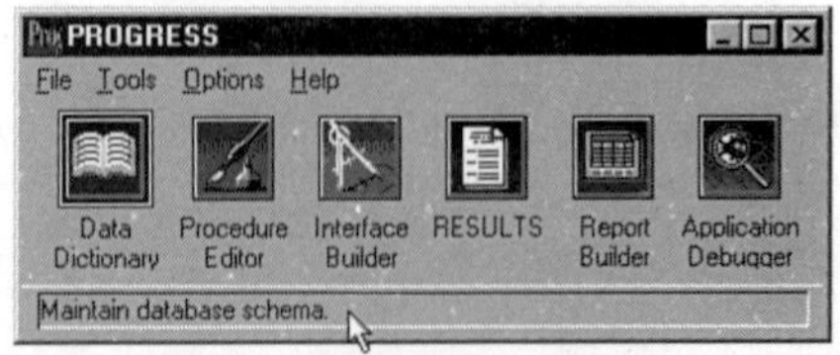

Fig. 3.1

The PROGRESS Desktop.

> **Note**
>
> Check Chapter 1, "Introducing PROGRESS," if you are not able to arrive at the desktop.

From the desktop icons, you can quickly reach the most frequently used tools within the ADE. You will be taking a tour of these and other ADE tools in this chapter.

Each tool in the tour can be explored individually; you need not take the entire tour or follow it in sequential order. This structure allows you to use this chapter for reference; you can return to this chapter for a specific ADE tool or to review the basics.

Using Database Tools: Data Administration

To enter the Data Administration tool, choose Tools, Data Administration from the Desktop menu.

The second tool associated with the database is the Data Administration tool, or "Data Admin." for short. Unlike the other ADE tools, Data Admin. has a plain style and is more of a utility or database workbench. Choose Tools, Data Administration from the desktop menu to enter the Data Administration tool.

To begin the tour of the Data Administration tool:

- Ensure that your working directory path is c:\appdir.
- Ensure that the sports database is in your working directory.

Choose Database, Connect from the main menu. This will bring up the Connect Database dialog box. Enter the database physical name in the Physical Name text box, and click OK. This tells the Data Administration Tool which database to access.

> **Note**
>
> The bottom of the main screen displays the working database. You can connect to more than one database at a time, but you can have only one working database.

The Admin menu, shown in figure 3.2, performs many useful functions.

Under the Admin menu of the Data Administration tool, you have dump and load options for both data and definitions. You can dump or load data out of or into a database. You use this facility to transport a database from one platform to another or to consolidate a database for better performance.

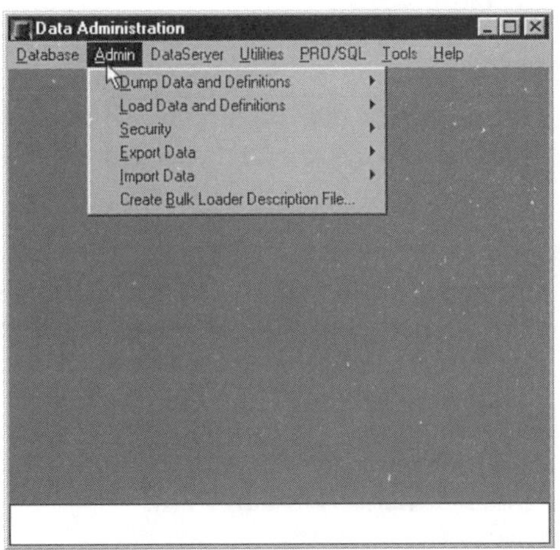

Fig. 3.2

Administration functions.

Transporting a database involves moving both the data definitions and the data from one operating system to another. If the operating systems are the same, you can simply copy the physical database files.

As you can see within the database transport scheme, the files that are transported between platforms are in ASCII format.

The following exercise demonstrates how to move a table (definition and contents) from one database to another. In this particular exercise, the "to" and "from" databases are on the same platform. In practice, the target database may be on any other PROGRESS-compatible platform.

Creating a Data Definitions File

To create a Data Definitions file (.df), use Admin, Dump Data and Definitions, then choose Data Definitions (see fig. 3.3).

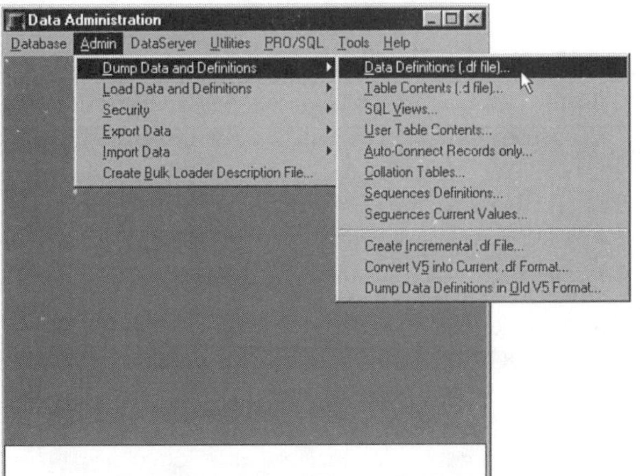

Fig. 3.3

Choosing Data Definitions Dump from the main menu.

Select the customer table for the database dump. A dialog box will show you the default output file, customer.df. Choose OK to continue.

You now have the data definitions file for the customer table. This allows you to define the *structure* of the customer table for another database on any PROGRESS platform.

The data definitions file (.df) is a portable version of your database's structure. This is crucial in situations where you must port a database to a new type of computer (for example, DOS to UNIX) or when you must transmit database structure information in a readable format.

Examine the .df file using the PROGRESS Editor. Note that it is composed of statements for the creation of fields and indexes. The Data Administration tool is capable of reading this file and executing its instructions (see fig. 3.4).

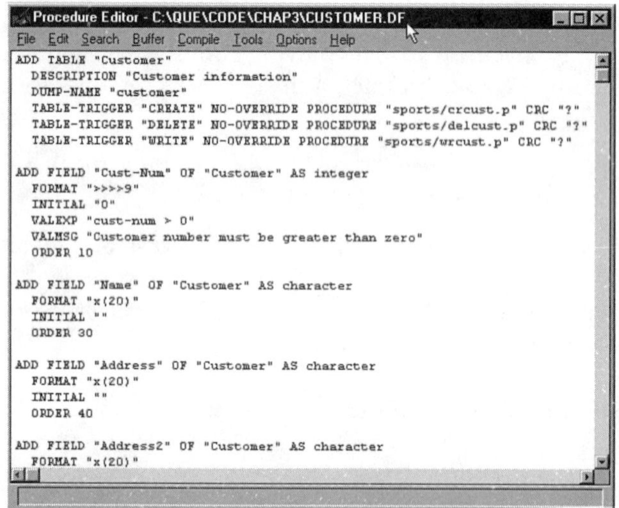

Fig. 3.4

The customer.df file instructions.

Creating an Empty Working Database

You will now use the Data Administration tool to create a new, empty database in which you will construct the customer table. You will use the customer.df file to specify the table's characteristics. The characteristics will be identical to the customer table since this is where the definitions were taken previously. This example highlights how you would easily move a table's definitions from one database to another, regardless of which computer platform they are on.

Return to the Data Administration tool (if you are not already there). Choose Database, Create to establish a new PROGRESS database. Create a database called temp. By omitting a directory name, PROGRESS will place the new database in your working directory.

Note

Do NOT create your new database "temp" within the dlc directory. The dlc directory contains PROGRESS system files. Create a working directory (as explained in Chapter 1, "Introducing PROGRESS") in which all work can be located.

Loading Table Definitions

After you have the target database connected and the data definitions file (.df), you are ready to load the table definition. Be sure you are connected to the temp database (you will see it on the bottom of the Data Admin screen as a connection). If you're not connected, choose Database Connect and select the temp database. By default, your working directory will be the location for the database.

Choose Admin, Load, Data Definitions (.df file). The load file dialog will default using the database name as the prefix (temp.df). This is because you have the table definitions for several tables together. Because you used the name of the single table "customer" in the example, select "customer.df" and choose OK to begin the load process.

The Data Administration tool will show you each table, field, and index name as the names are loaded and will indicate load completion. You now have the table definition loaded into the target database. Remember that the table is *empty*. The data has not been transferred.

To dump and load *data*, repeat the same steps as before, but use Table Contents (.d file). The .d file is a space-delimited list of fields belonging to each record in the table. A .d file contains data for a singular table; therefore, its name implies the table to which it pertains.

As a review, the steps to transfer data and definitions to a target database are as follows:

1. Dump the Data Definitions file (.df) for the tables that you wish to transfer.
2. Dump the Data (.d) for the tables that you wish to transfer. You will create a .d file for each respective table.
3. Create or locate the target database on the target machine.
4. Transfer the .d and .df files using any ASCII transfer protocol from the source to the target machine.
5. Load the .df Data Definitions file on the target.
6. Load the .d Data file(s) on the target.

Tip

You may also use the tool to dump and load a database to accomplish de-fragmentation. Both data and index storage may become fragmented with intensive delete/create-oriented transactions over time. *De-fragmentation* is the process of grouping as much of the physical blocks of data together as possible. This minimizes the disk drive's movement necessary to locate records.

Security Administration

The Security section of the Administration menu serves the various functions of establishing data security for the database. You connected to the sports database with the "blank USERID," as PROGRESS likes to call it. The blank USERID refers to connection to a database with no security. After you establish a user for database security and disallow the blank USERID, the blank USERID is no longer valid and you are bound by the security of the login. To disallow the blank USERID, choose Admin, Security, Disallow Blank Userid Access from the Data Administration main menu. You may restrict reading and writing at various levels in the database.

DataServer Administration

The DataServer menu shows the list of currently supported DataServer databases and their utilities. Recalling the discussion in Chapter 1 regarding external database connections, these DataServers require a *meta-schema* for mapping external structures to a PROGRESS database structure. The DataServer menu manages the schemas and performs specialized functions relative to each DataServer.

In managing the non-PROGRESS databases, the Data Administration tool allows you to associate the foreign database structures (field, table, etc.) with a PROGRESS-equivalent structure. By doing this, each field of a foreign database is associated with a specific meta-schema field in a PROGRESS view of the database. This is necessary for allowing the PROGRESS 4GL to operate seamlessly against the foreign database; in effect the 4GL code believes it is operating against a PROGRESS database since it only sees the meta-schema structure.

The specialized functions available within the DataServer menu include:

- Running ORACLE SQL*Plus
- Importing RMS definitions from CDD/Plus
- Changing the code page for an ODBC schema

Creating Administrative Reports

The Data Admin. tool is capable of reporting on the database definitions and structure. Using your previously created temp database containing the customer table, choose Database, Reports to view the list of choices.

Choose Detail Table to view the details of the customer table. Because customer is the only choice, choose it when the tool prompts you for the specific table name.

Figure 3.5 shows the output to the screen (terminal).

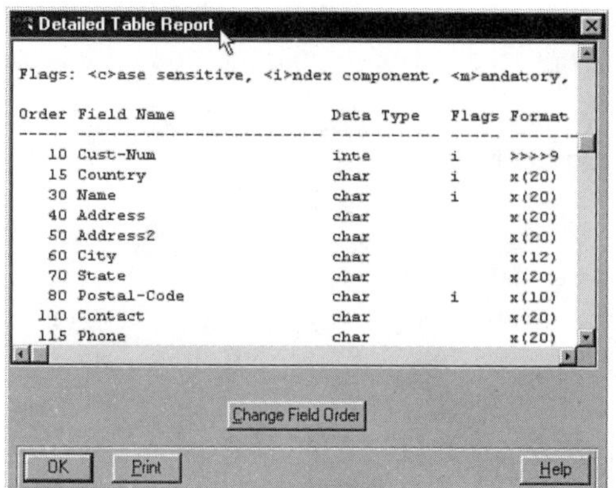

Fig. 3.5

Customer table detail report.

Another useful report is the triggers report. From the same reports menu, choose Trigger (note that there is no accelerator for this menu item). This report shows the database triggers associated with the table (see fig. 3.6).

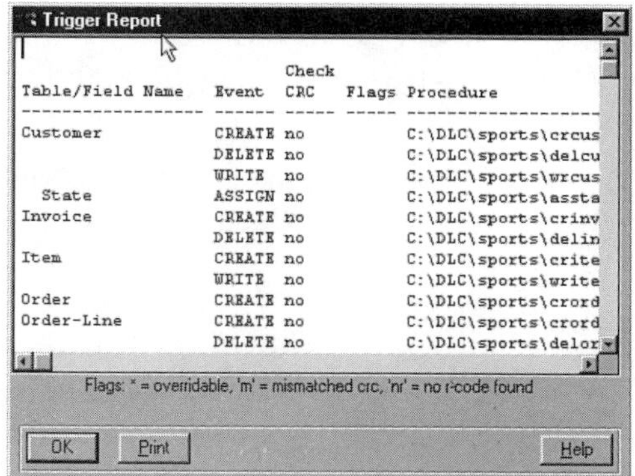

Fig. 3.6

Customer Trigger report showing the triggers defined for each table in the database.

Database triggers are events that *fire* when a certain database action takes place. For example, a `CREATE` database trigger will fire when a record for that table is created. This allows the developer to associate specific code to execute upon the actions on the database tables. There are several possible triggers which can be defined per table, including `CREATE`, `DELETE`, `ASSIGN`.

The triggers report is useful because many times a table will contain several triggers that point to individual programs containing the trigger code. The trigger code is not within the database but is stored in individual program (.p) files. This report helps to identify and locate the associated trigger code.

Loading Data with the Bulkloader Utility

A powerful Data Administration utility is the *Bulkloader*. The loading of ASCII data using the previously described dump and load process can be time-consuming for large tables. The Bulkloader provides a direct and rapid method for loading large quantities of data into tables.

Use the Bulkloader utility to load data when:

1. The load data is greater than 1 megabyte.
2. It is not required to analyze each record as it is being loaded.
3. You would like to load data from the operating system level as opposed to being required to enter the desktop and the Data Administration tool.

To load data into tables using the Bulkloader utility, you must create a Bulkloader file definitions (.fd) file. You do this using the Data Admin. tool.

Choose Admin, Create Bulk Loader Description File and select the desired table(s). This creates a .fd file that tells the Bulkloader utility exactly how to load the data.

On the target database, use the Bulkloader utility with the following syntax (note this is to be given at the DOS prompt):

```
proutil db-name -C BULKLOAD fd-file
```

Replace `db-name` with your database name and `fd-file` with the .fd file created within the Data Admin. tool. Bulkloader is a PROGRESS utility invoked from the operating system.

One of the reasons for the Bulkloader's expediency is the fact that it disables all indexes prior to loading the data. This means you must reactivate the indexes using the command:

```
proutil db-name -C idxbuild
```

> **Note**
>
> You may read information on PROGRESS utilities such as Bulkloader by using PROGRESS' online help facility. Select topics under "System Administration" and "Utilities."

Importing Data

Besides using Bulkloader or Data Load facilities, you may also load data by importing. Choose Admin, Import Data to view the options for importing data.

Knowing the functions of the Data Admin. tool will help you later when you require its functionality. Its capability to facilitate the transfer of table structures aids in the process of deployment to multiple platforms. The data import and bulkload utilities help you in loading data into your databases.

Your familiarity with the Data Administration tool is your entry into PROGRESS database administration and its role in the overall development/deployment cycle.

Using the Results Reporting Tool

Results is one of two PROGRESS report writing tools. A report created with Results is a PROGRESS 4GL program, and Results generates 4GL code. Thus, you can easily port reports to other platforms.

Results produces non-Windows like reports, so it may not be appropriate for Windows-specific environments. The resulting report is straightforward text, no fonts or colors. For standard Windows-style reporting, Report Builder is the appropriate tool. It allows you to use fonts, colors, and laser printers. With PROGRESS, you get a choice of both.

The beauty of Results is that it is highly customizable as a tool. You can therefore customize it and ship it along with your own application. Because Results is written in the PROGRESS 4GL, the possibilities are nearly endless.

To begin the tour of Results:

1. Ensure that your working directory path is c:\appdir.
2. Ensure that the sports database is in your working directory.
3. Ensure that the sports database is connected.
4. Click on the Results icon on the PROGRESS Desktop.

If this is the first time that you're using Results with this database, Results will prompt you to create working files (sports.qc). Upon having created the working files, you see the main screen (see fig. 3.7).

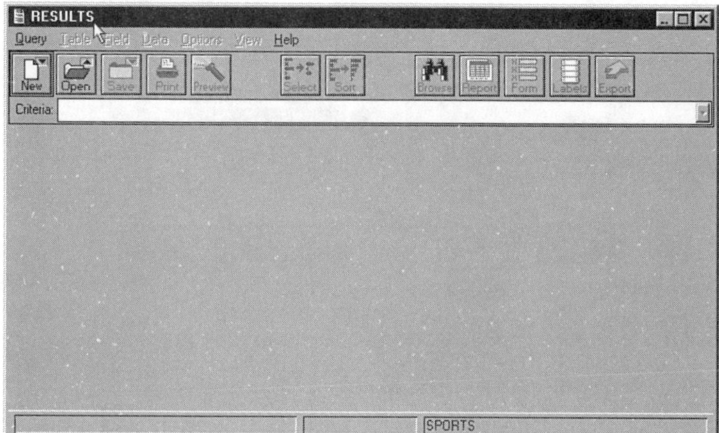

Fig. 3.7

Results main screen.

Tour Objective: For this example, you want to create a report that lists all customers for each sales representative. The list should be broken down by customer city in alphabetical order. Each salesrep customer should appear on a separate sheet of paper, and the report will print by salesrep initials to help distribute the print out. Additionally, the report should total the customers for each rep.

Sounds complicated. With Results, you can accomplish this with nothing but mouse clicks! The generated 4GL code is then usable on all PROGRESS ported platforms.

You begin by starting a New report (click New). Choose the Salesrep and Customer tables in the Add/Remove Tables screen (see fig. 3.8). Be sure to choose Salesrep before Customer so that you achieve the appropriate master/detail relationship.

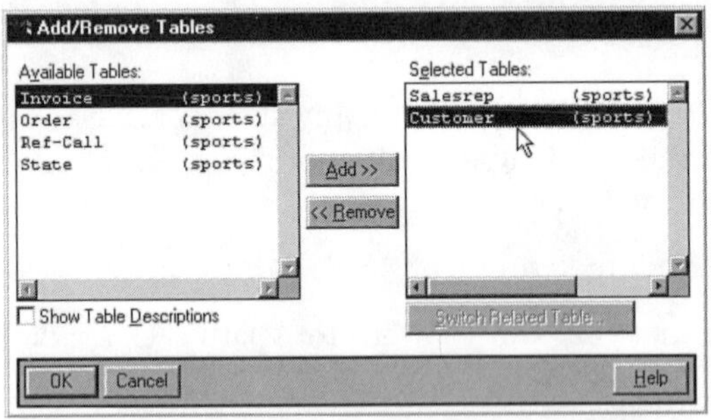

Fig. 3.8

Salesrep and Customer tables chosen for reporting.

Next, choose the fields for reporting in the following order: Rep-Name (scroll to find it in the available fields list), Cust-Num, Name, City, Phone, Credit-Limit. Figure 3.9 shows the fields selected for the report.

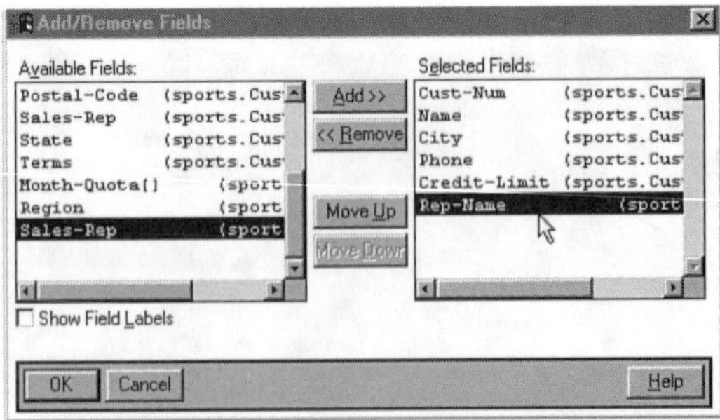

Fig. 3.9

Fields for reporting.

Click OK in the Add/Remove Fields property sheet to return to the main screen.

Results shows you a report view of your chosen tables and fields.

At this point, you can look at several different views of the Salesrep/Customer relationship (from a reporting standpoint, that is). The upper-right side of the Results toolbar presents the five different possible views: Browse, Report, Form, Labels, and

Export. Click each one to explore the outcome, because these are useful views that save time and effort in development.

Return to the report view by clicking the Report button.

Next, you should set the sort criteria for the report. Remember, you want the report sorted by sales rep, and within that by the customer's city. Click on the Sort button in the Results toolbar. The Sort Order Fields screen appears (see fig. 3.10). Choose Sales-Rep (Salesrep table) and City (Customer table) as selected fields.

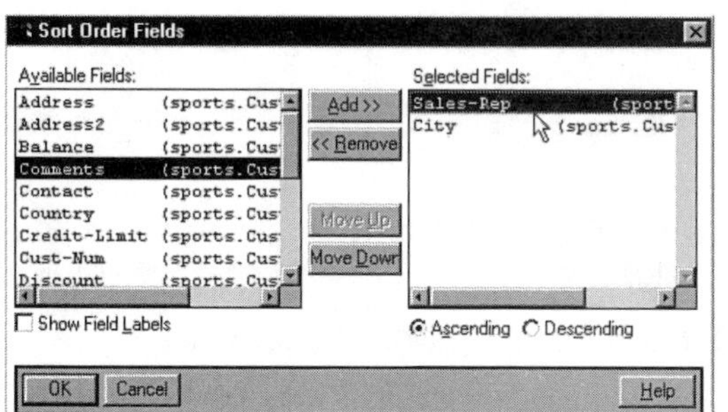

Fig. 3.10

Sort by Sales-Rep and Customer City.

Click OK or press Enter to return to the main screen.

Choose Options, Master-Detail to break out your report by sales rep. The Master-Detail pop-up allows you to choose the relationship between Salesrep and Customer. Double-click on this relationship to continue. This establishes a master-detail relationship between the Salesrep and the customer data elements.

Choose Options, Headers and Footers to set your page headings. The Headers and Footers screen allows you to set all kinds of headers and footers, including group, page, and end-of-report footers. For now, simply set the page heading to show the date and page number.

To do this, click the Center Header button in the Position area of the screen (see the button with the black outline in fig. 3.11). In the Layout area, specify the functions that you want in the header: date and page number.

Double-click {TODAY} and {PAGE} to automatically insert the functions. You can add additional text as shown in figure 3.15 in the "layout" section.

Click OK to return to the main screen.

Note

Notice that the OK button has no hotkey and is not highlighted. The reason for this is that the layout editor uses the Enter key as a regular carriage return for text entry. This is an example of a screen with no default button.

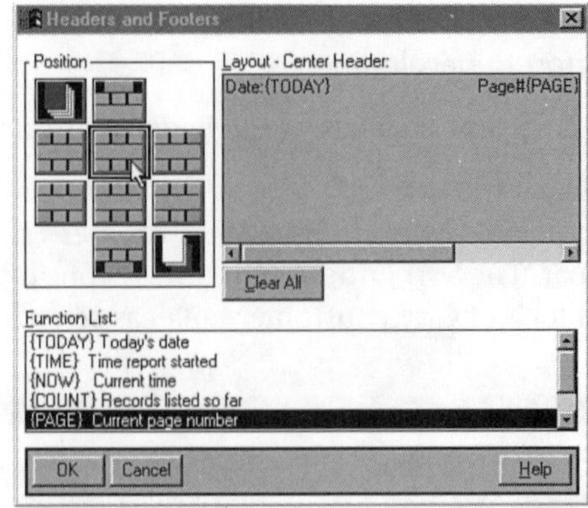

Fig. 3.11

Reporting Headers and Footers.

Next, you need to count the number of customer records per sales rep. You do this by setting an aggregate. Choose Field, Aggregates to establish field aggregates.

In the Field Aggregates screen (see fig. 3.12), click the following:

sports.Customer.Cust-Num for Query Fields (what you want to count)

sports.Salesrep.Sales-Rep for Break-By Fields (the group for which you want the count totaled)

Count aggregate

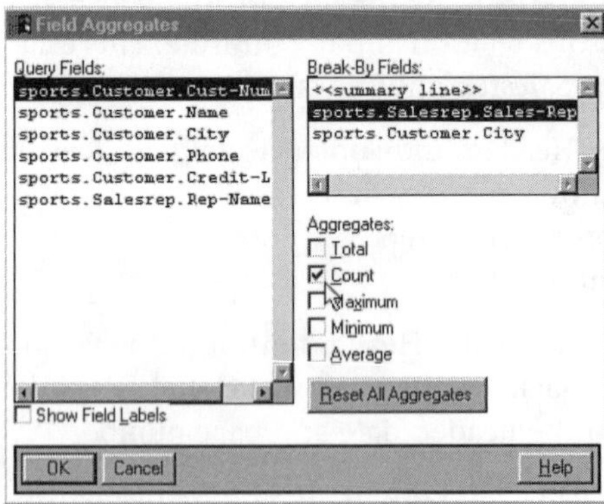

Fig. 3.12

Field aggregates.

Press OK or Enter to return to the main screen.

Click the preview button to view your report.

The only thing missing is the page break between sales reps. Choose Options, Page Break and double-click sports.Salesrep.Sales-Rep to set the correct page break.

You're finished! Click Save to save the report under the name: **Chapter 3: Tour of ADE**.

Results saves reports in a special file that Results interprets as the report list. The file usually has the extension .qd*x*, where *x* is a single-digit numeric (of internal significance only).

Choose Query, Generate to create a 4GL program file for this report. Give it the name **results1.p**.

Later, you can view this file with the Procedure Editor and learn from the generated code. You can also add to this code or seamlessly integrate it into your application.

This concludes the introductory tour of the Results tool.

Reporting Tools: Report Builder

Report Builder (RB) is a Windows-based graphical reporting tool. Its capabilities include the following: PostScript compatibility, report preview with zoom, imbedded graphics, and much more. Although PROGRESS is planning a Report Builder engine for UNIX platforms, currently, RB reports can execute only under Windows.

To begin the tour of Report Builder:

1. Ensure that your working directory path is c:\appdir.
2. Ensure that the sports database is in your working directory.
3. Disconnect from the sports database.

> **Note**
>
> Report Builder will connect to the database by default. To disconnect, go to the Procedure Editor, type **disconnect sports** and press F2. You can also disconnect from the Data Dictionary tool by choosing Database, Disconnect.

Click the Report Builder icon on the PROGRESS Desktop.

Click New to create a new report. The Report Builder prompts you to open a database. Choose your copy of the sports database in the \appdir directory and press Enter.

Choose the customer table and respond Yes to "Create an instant report?"

Choose the fields Cust-Num, Name, City, and Balance for the instant report.

Figure 3.13 shows the instant report with some of the customer fields in place.

What you see is only a format of the report, not a preview of the report printout.

Press the Preview button of the Report Builder toolbar to preview your report. The preview allows you to zoom in and out of the report pages, step through report pages, and print to a printer device.

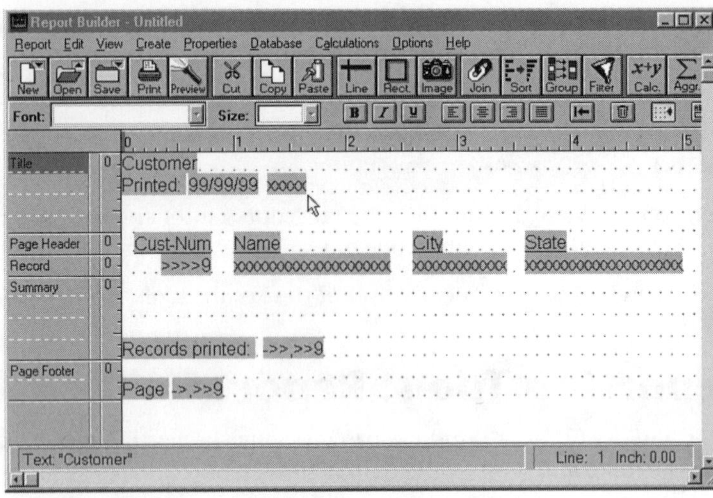

Fig. 3.13

An instant customer report format.

The preview of the report shown in figure 3.14 gives you a graphical representation of the printed report. You have the ability to scroll through the report and to zoom in/out of the text.

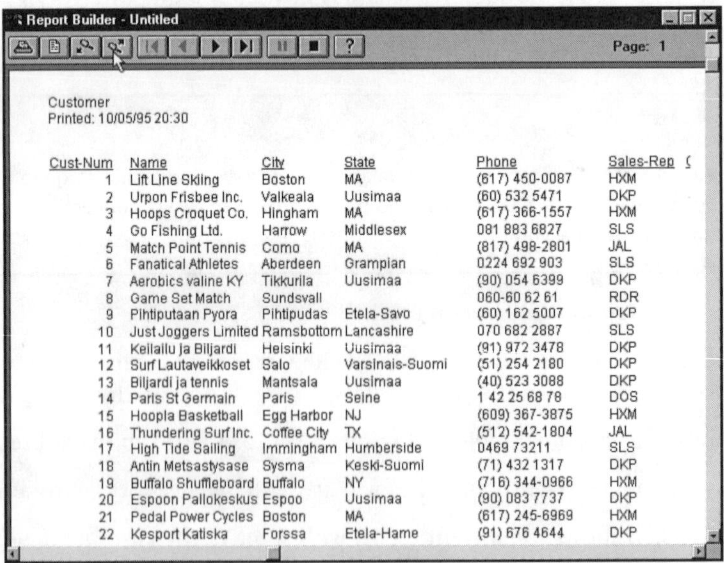

Customer
Printed: 10/05/95 20:30

Cust-Num	Name	City	State	Phone	Sales-Rep
1	Lift Line Skiing	Boston	MA	(617) 450-0087	HXM
2	Urpon Frisbee Inc.	Valkeala	Uusimaa	(60) 532 5471	DKP
3	Hoops Croquet Co.	Hingham	MA	(617) 366-1557	HXM
4	Go Fishing Ltd.	Harrow	Middlesex	081 883 6827	SLS
5	Match Point Tennis	Como	MA	(817) 498-2801	JAL
6	Fanatical Athletes	Aberdeen	Grampian	0224 692 903	SLS
7	Aerobics valine KY	Tikkurila	Uusimaa	(90) 054 6399	DKP
8	Game Set Match	Sundsvall		060-60 62 61	RDR
9	Pihtiputaan Pyora	Pihtipudas	Etela-Savo	(60) 162 5007	DKP
10	Just Joggers Limited	Ramsbottom	Lancashire	070 682 2887	SLS
11	Keilailu ja Biljardi	Helsinki	Uusimaa	(91) 972 3478	DKP
12	Surf Lautaveikkoset	Salo	Varsinais-Suomi	(51) 254 2180	DKP
13	Biljardi ja tennis	Mantsala	Uusimaa	(40) 523 3088	DKP
14	Paris St Germain	Paris	Seine	1 42 25 68 78	DOS
15	Hoopla Basketball	Egg Harbor	NJ	(609) 367-3875	HXM
16	Thundering Surf Inc.	Coffee City	TX	(512) 542-1804	JAL
17	High Tide Sailing	Immingham	Humberside	0469 73211	SLS
18	Antin Metsastysase	Sysma	Keski-Suomi	(71) 432 1317	DKP
19	Buffalo Shuffleboard	Buffalo	NY	(716) 344-0966	HXM
20	Espoon Pallokeskus	Espoo	Uusimaa	(90) 083 7737	DKP
21	Pedal Power Cycles	Boston	MA	(617) 245-6969	HXM
22	Kesport Katiska	Forssa	Etela-Hame	(91) 676 4644	DKP

Fig. 3.14

Preview of customer report.

> **Note**
>
> Click with the magnifying glass on an area to instantly zoom in on that part of the report.

The tasks in this tour are the same as the tasks in the Results section of this chapter. This makes it easier for you to concentrate on the tool rather than the details of the report.

Tour Objective: To create a report that lists all the customers of a sales representative. You want to then sort the list by the customer's city in alphabetical order. Each salesrep report should appear on a separate sheet of paper sorted by salesrep initials to help distribute the printout. Additionally, you want a total number of customers for each rep.

Start a new Report Builder report by pressing the New button on the RB toolbar. Choose the Salesrep table and create an instant report.

Choose the Rep-Name as the only field on the report from the SalesRep table (all other fields come from the customer table).

Choose Database, Group Order to make Sales-Rep a group. This allows you to associate information about the Sales-Rep and apply it as one entity.

The Group Level dialog box shown in figure 3.15 enables you to define a table as a reporting group. Totals, page breaks and aggregates can then be associated with a group.

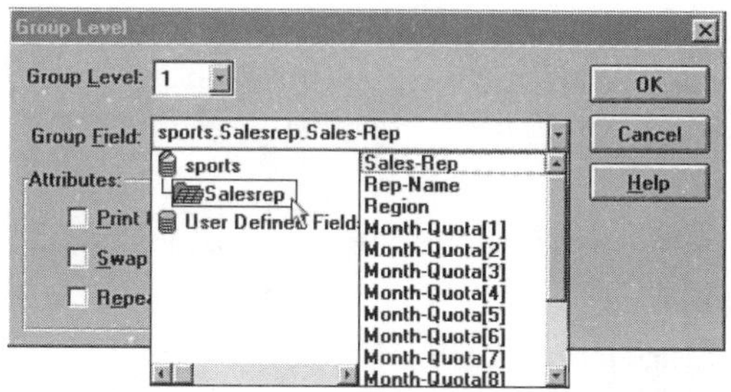

Fig. 3.15

Sales representative grouping.

Next, associate the customer table with the salesrep table to create a join by clicking on the Join button. A *join* is used to associate two related tables. In this case you join sales representatives with customers and thus for every representative read from the database you will be able to read every customer of that representative. The join is simply a mechanism to facilitate and expedite reading records which are related.

Choose the Sales-Rep field in the From Table, Field drop-down list. Choose the Table customer for the To Table and To Table, Field Sales-Rep.

Figure 3.16 shows the sales representative table joined with the customer table.

Click OK to continue. The Joins list screen shows all of the defined joins for this report. Choose Close. Now that you have joined the customer table to the salesrep table, you can insert customer fields into your report.

Fig. 3.16

Salesrep joined with Customer table in the Report Builder join screen.

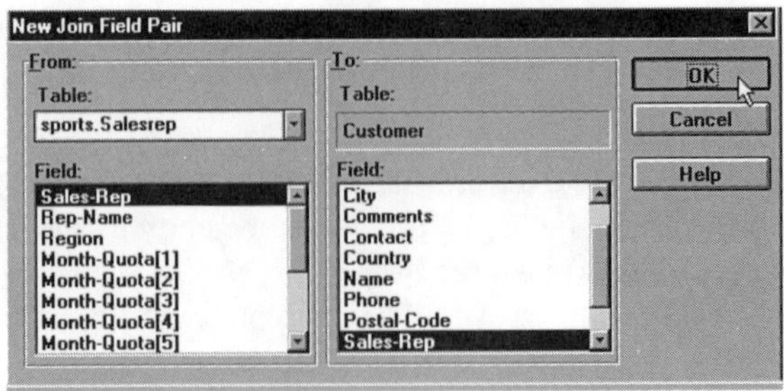

The next step is to insert a new section into the report to group the customer information together. In Report Builder, this is called a band line. A Report Builder band line is a series of rows on a report that show a particular set of information. Identifying a specific set of information with a band line allows you to set attributes and properties for that section of the report.

Choose Create, Band Line. Choose a new type of line and select "1GH-Sales-Rep" to correspond to the first group header for the Sales-Rep grouping.

Move the Rep-Name label and field from the Page Header band line to the newly created band line. To move pieces of the report, first click the desired piece once to select it, and then drag it to the new location.

Click on the 1GH-Sales-Rep band line to select it. Now, press the Ins key on your keyboard to insert new fields. Choose Cust-Num, Name, City, and Credit-Limit. RB places the fields on the band line.

Click Preview to view your report so far. It should show all customers of the first salesrep on the first page.

To place the total number of customers for each salesrep, you need a new band line. A calculated field such as this is also known as an aggregate. Repeat the steps for adding a band line and add the "1GF-Sales-Rep" (Group Footer).

Choose Calculations, Aggregate Field and create an aggregate called cust-count (see fig. 3.17).

Fig. 3.17

Creating an aggregate field.

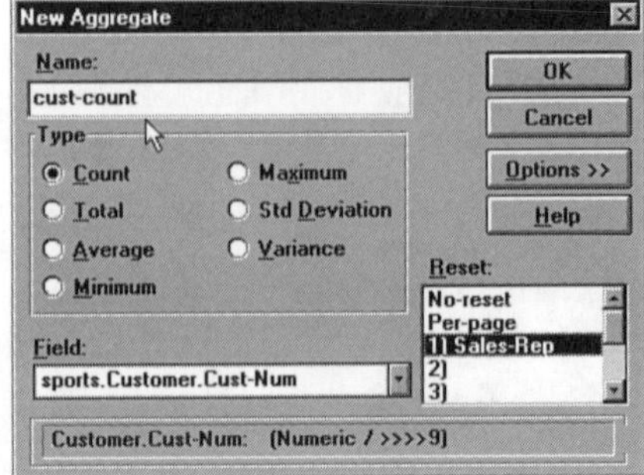

Next, return to the working window and press Ins to insert your new aggregate field: cust-count. Place it in the `1GF-Sales-Rep` band line because you want it to appear in the footer for the sales rep grouping. Add text to the left of the aggregate to indicate its purpose.

Now you're ready to specify the sort order. Remember, you want to sort the report by sales representative and then by the customer's city name alphabetically. Choose Database, Sort Order. Choose the Sales-Rep field first (from the drop-down list), and then the City.

The Sort Order property sheet shown in figure 3.18 enables you to select a sort order for your report.

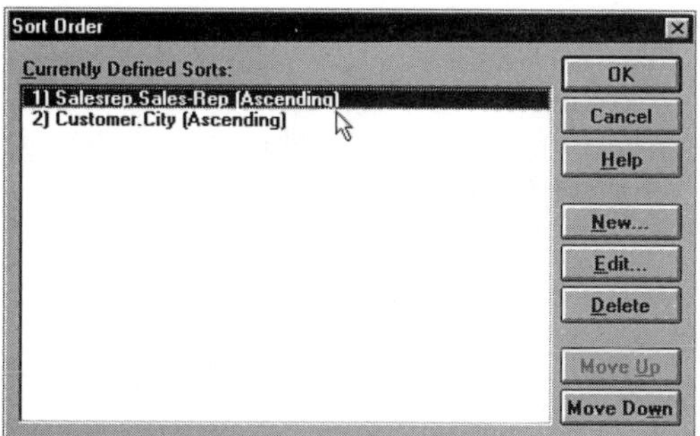

Fig. 3.18

Sort Order screen.

Click Preview to view your finished report. Note the sorting of city within sales representative. Figure 3.19 shows the completed report.

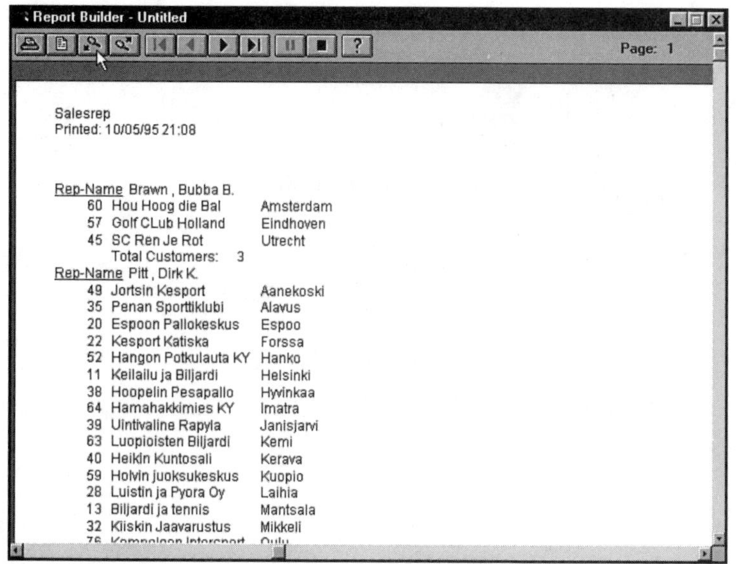

Fig. 3.19

Finished report.

Press the Save button to save the report under the name "Salesrep Customer Report" in the report library.

You have now created a simple yet substantial report in both Results and Report Builder. Later, you'll create more complex reports with more difficult reporting requirements.

Translation Tools: Translation Manager "Tran-Man"

PROGRESS' Visual Translator tool allows you to compile translated versions of your application. This is essential for internationalization and expanding your application to the global markets.

You will find extensive coverage of this tool and internationalization in Part V. Specific coverage of the Visual translator tool is found in Chapters 16, "Preparing for Translation," and 17, "Translating Your Application."

From Here...

Now that you have worked through a hands-on tour of the Application Development Environment, you will continue with a more detailed look at several development constructs.

Learn about the PROGRESS 4GL language in the next chapter, "Introducing PROGRESS Language." It will teach you the language constructs, the basics behind the sports database. You will create a simple file maintenance window and learn how to compile and run your programs.

For more information on related items, refer to the following chapters:

- Chapter 4, "Introducing PROGRESS Language," introduces you to the 4GL language along with its rules and constructs.
- Chapter 5, "Further Exploration: Locking, Transactions, and VBXs," gives you more detail on the 4GL language and takes you through a tour of VBX integration with PROGRESS V8.
- Chapter 16, "Preparing for Translation," introduces you to the Translation Manager.
- Chapter 17, "Translating Your Application" demonstrates the use of the Translation Manager tool for application translations.

CHAPTER 4

Introducing PROGRESS Language

This chapter puts many of the PROGRESS environment constructs together to enhance your skills in developing PROGRESS applications. After your ADE tour in chapters 2 and 3, you are ready to explore the PROGRESS 4GL, database connections, and more.

After reading this chapter, you should be able to do the following:

- Develop simple programs using the PROGRESS 4GL
- Understand the PROGRESS 4GL language rules and constructs
- Understand the PROGRESS 4GL blocking statements and their properties
- Understand the basics of PROGRESS transactions
- Understand how PROGRESS implements the event-driven programming model
- Connect to PROGRESS databases and retrieve records using the 4GL

Voice-of-Experience Movies

See Table G.3 in Appendix G, "Contents of CD," for a list of Voice-of-Experience files for this chapter.

Introduction to the PROGRESS Language

The popularity of fourth-generation languages (4GLs) in the 1980s was the result of many factors. Developers needed a robust language that supported all necessary constructs but was easier to program than existing languages (3GLs such as COBOL, Pascal, or BASIC). The 4GL enables the developer to specify needed functionality in far fewer lines of code than the third-generation languages.

The PROGRESS 4GL line

```
UPDATE customer.
```

creates an updatable view of the customer record, requests a lock from the database engine, and enables the end user to update any fields of the record. In addition to these basic functions, this simple line also takes care of end-user navigation between the fields on the screen (using the mouse or keyboard). If the customer table contains validation, the UPDATE statement automatically adheres to any integrity checks defined in the database. The list of functionality for such a simple 4GL command can be extensive.

The UPDATE 4GL command has the following functionality built into it:

- Displays fields in associated table(s)
- Establishes necessary record locks
- Stores all fields to database upon completion
- Executes code called *schema trigger* defined within the database that responds to specific record activity such as delete or create
- Enables end-user navigation between fields being updated using either the keyboard (Tab key) or the mouse
- Enforces the formats and initial values defined within the database for each field
- Enables execution of field validation

To achieve the same functionality with COBOL, the COBOL developer required several *pages* of code. Depending on the complexity of the table in question, the COBOL scenario could reach 7–10 printed pages of source code.

Each 4GL command can carry extensive functionality that efficiently serves the developer's needs. Usually, a default functionality exists and enhancing the default is easy.

Examine a sample program that will display today's date and the number of days since the first day of 1995. CH04PRG1.p is a simple 4GL program shown in figure 4.1.

Note

If you want to run this program yourself, you can type this simple program into the Procedure Editor, or you can retrieve \examples\chap-04\CH04PRG1.p from the CD (see Appendix G, "Contents of CD").

Figure 4.2 shows the output when this program is run from the Procedure Editor.

The general premise behind the program's construction is as follows:

- A variable will be used to store the number of days since the new year.
- The display of today's date will require a function that provides today's date.
- The calculation of the days since January 1, 1995, will require the use of date calculations.
- The display will mix variables and literal text.

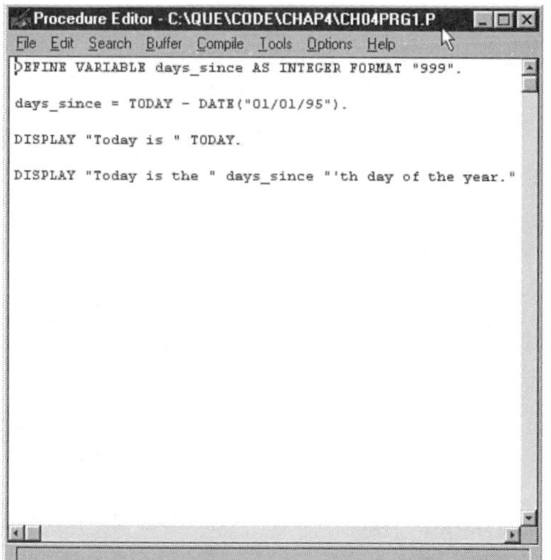

Fig. 4.1

Simple 4GL program.

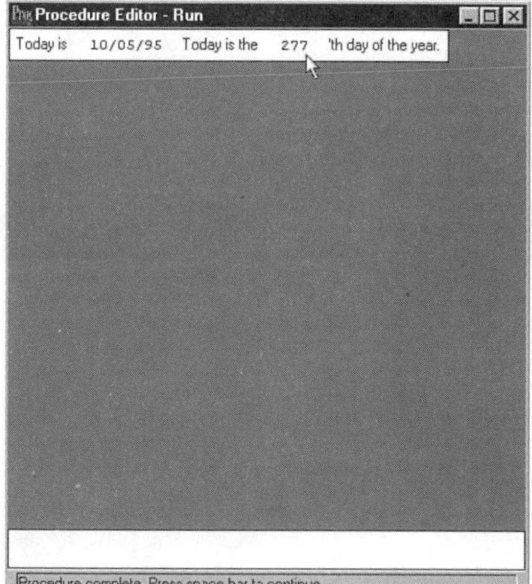

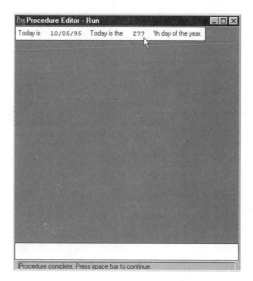

Fig. 4.2

CH04PRG1.p running.

The first line defines an integer variable to hold the days since January 1, 1995:

```
DEFINE VARIABLE days_since AS INTEGER FORMAT "999".
```

Because the largest number of possible days since January 1 of the same year is 365, a format of `"999"` is used. Format `"999"` indicates that three numeric digits will be used to display the number. This number is sufficiently large for any user running the program in 1995–1996.

The next line of code calculates the number of days since January 1, 1995:

```
days_since = TODAY - DATE("01/01/95").
```

The 4GL enables you to perform arithmetic functions using dates. The DATE() function converts a string representation of January 1 into a date format to use in the subtraction. The variable days_since holds the integer result.

The remaining lines of code in CHO4PRG1.p display the dates and calculated days on the screen using the DISPLAY statement:

```
DISPLAY "Today is " TODAY.
DISPLAY "Today is the " days_since "'th day of the year." WITH NO-LABELS.
```

The PROGRESS DISPLAY statement is extremely powerful and has numerous options. The NO-LABELS option prevents column or side labels from being displayed. Note that variables and literal strings can be mixed in the DISPLAY statement.

The period at the end of each PROGRESS 4GL line is mandatory because it indicates the end of a line.

The next example program, CH04PRG2.p, prompts the end user for some information and presents a set of results (see listing 4.1). (You also can find \examples\chap-04\CH04PRG2.p on the CD.) You can look at the program by starting the PROGRESS editor and accessing the file to display it.

Try to read the code for CH04PRG2.p in Listing 4.1 and determine its function by understanding the 4GL language. CH04PRG2.p prompts for the end-user's name and date of birth, and it displays the number of days, hours, and minutes since that day.

Listing 4.1 \examples\chap-04\CH04PRG2.p Prompting for End-User Information

```
DEFINE VARIABLE name AS CHARACTER.
DEFINE VARIABLE dob    AS DATE.

UPDATE name dob WITH SIDE-LABELS FRAME SIMPLE-FRAME.

DISPLAY name ", you have existed for:" SKIP
    TODAY - dob " days" SKIP
    24 * (TODAY - dob) " hours" SKIP
    "and " 60 * 24 * (TODAY - dob) "minutes."
    WITH NO-LABELS FRAME SIMPLE-FRAME-2.
```

Figure 4.3 shows the output when this program is run from the Procedure Editor.

The variable definition lines in CH04PRG2.p are similar to the first sample program (CH04PRG1.p), whereas the UPDATE command is new to this program:

```
UPDATE name dob WITH SIDE-LABELS FRAME SIMPLE-FRAME.
```

This PROGRESS 4GL line presents the user with the variables name and dob of types Character and Date, respectively. The UPDATE command takes care of the data-entry properties of character, date, and all other PROGRESS data types. Invalid dates are automatically trapped by this command.

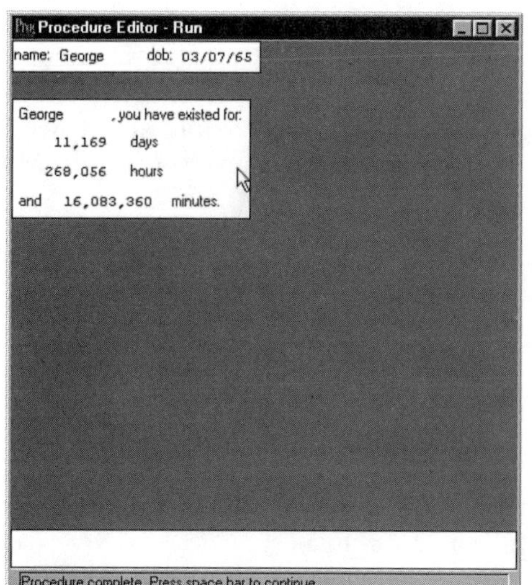

Fig. 4.3

CH04PRG2.p running.

The line `UPDATE name dob.` would have sufficed for the purpose at hand. The example shows some options that are used to improve the on-screen presentation.

The `WITH SIDE-LABELS` option indicates that side labels should be used rather than column labels. This option causes the label to appear on the side of the field.

The `FRAME SIMPLE-FRAME` names the frame in which the information will be presented. This name does not correspond to anything visible in figure 4.3; it is simply an internal name associated with the frame.

Here, PROGRESS 4GL utilized the construct of `FRAME` to aid in data representation. A PROGRESS *frame* is an area on the screen (GUI or TTY) that contains displayed data, text, images, and so on. Each frame has characteristics defined by the program such as side labels, number of display columns, color, font, and many others. If a frame name is not specified, PROGRESS creates a *default* frame with no explicit name.

If you assign a name for the frame, you can add additional displays to that frame in a later section of the program. Assigning a name also enables you to prescribe the frame options separately using the frame's name. The name "SIMPLE-FRAME" is not significant other than being a unique name for the frame.

The last program line

```
WITH NO-LABELS FRAME SIMPLE-FRAME-2.
```

names a new frame `SIMPLE-FRAME-2` and specifies that it should show no labels. If you had omitted this frame phrase and simply indicated `WITH NO-LABELS.`, you would have seen the same result because PROGRESS would have created an unnamed default frame.

From a language standpoint, the PROGRESS 4GL is packed with commands, functions, and features that make your work easier.

The following list contains the character-manipulation *functions* and *statements* available within the PROGRESS 4GL. *Functions* are identified blocks of code that return a value upon executing. *Statements* are identified blocks of code that execute and do not return a value. (These character-manipulation operations are tremendously useful in developing an application; they are listed here to give you a sense of the depth and power of the PROGRESS 4GL.)

`CAPS` function: Capitalizes a string

Example: `cap_string = CAPS("usa").`

Result: `cap_string` contains the string `"USA"`

`ENTRY` function: Returns an entry from a list

Example: `an_entry = ENTRY(1,"Avery,Timmy,Robert").`

Result: `an_entry` contains the string `"Avery"`

`ENTRY` statement: Replaces an entry in a list

Example: `ENTRY(1,a_list) = "ITEM1".`

Result: The first entry of `a_list` is the string `"ITEM1"`

`FILL` function: Creates a fill string

Example: `string_of_spaces = FILL(" ",10).`

Result: `string_of_spaces` contains the string `"          "`

`INDEX` function: Locates an entry in a string

Example: `the_position = INDEX("abcde","c").`

Result: `the_position` contains the integer `3`

`LC` function: Lowercase

Example: `low_string = LC("HOUSE").`

Result: `low_string` contains the string `"house"`

`LEFT-TRIM` function: Trims the left spaces

Example: `trimmed_string = LEFT-TRIM("   Balance").`

Result: `trimmed_string` contains the string `"Balance"`

`LENGTH` function: Returns the length of a string

Example: `the_length = LENGTH("Progress").`

Result: `the_length` contains the integer `8`

`LOOKUP` function: Locates an entry in a list

Example: `the_day = LOOKUP(day_of_weekend,"Saturday,Sunday")`

Result: `the_day` contains either the integer `0`, `1`, or `2` depending on the content of the variable `day_of_weekend`. It contains `0` if the entry is not found.

`NUM-ENTRIES` function: Returns number of entries in a list

Example: `the_entries = NUM-ENTRIES("Joe,Norma,Marc").`

Result: `the_entries` contains the integer `3`

`RIGHT-TRIM` function: Trims right spaces

Example: `trimmed_string = RIGHT-TRIM("Total    ").`

Result: `trimmed_string` contains the string `"Total"`

`R-INDEX` function: Same as `INDEX` but works from the right

`SUBSTITUTE` function: Substitutes within a string

Example: `SUBSTITUTE("&2 comes before &1", "Friday", "Monday").`

Result: Results in the string `"Monday comes before Friday"`

`SUBSTRING` function: Returns a substring

Example: `a_string = SUBSTRING("Monday is OK",1,3).`

Result: `a_string` contains the string `"Mon"`

`SUBSTRING` statement: Replaces a substring

Example: `SUBSTRING("Monday is OK",3) = "Sun".`

Result: Results in the string `"Sunday is OK"`

`TRIM` function: Trims all leading and trailing spaces

Example: `trimmed_string = TRIM("   Sub Total   ").`

Result: `trimmed_string` contains the string `"Sub Total"`

The preceding functions and statements are just for string manipulation! You can use additional options for handling date variables, numerics, delimited lists, database fields, Windows controls, and so on. Choose Help from any of the PROGRESS tools and select the PROGRESS 4GL help topic. You then can explore the more than 350 4GL statements, functions, and phrases available to programmers. It is no wonder that PROGRESS is regarded as a true programmer's language, combining the efficiency of a 4GL and the flexibility of a 3GL.

Many 4GL languages are on the market today. Although they all share some similarities, you will be introduced to many of PROGRESS 4GL's unique features.

Understanding PROGRESS 4GL Coding Syntax Rules

In the following sections, you will learn about the most important coding rules to remember when using the PROGRESS 4GL:

- PROGRESS 4GL is case-insensitive
- Rules for ending a 4GL command

- Rules for multiline 4GL commands
- Abbreviating 4GL commands
- Spacing for arithmetic formulas
- Rules for nested comments

PROGRESS 4GL Is Case-Insensitive

The PROGRESS 4GL is *not* case-sensitive. It does not matter whether you type your variables, commands, or any keywords in upper- or lowercase. String comparisons are also case-insensitive: `"PROGRESS"` is considered equal to the string `"progress"`. A search through the customer table for the first customer whose name begins with `'a'` might return `"ABC Mountain Bikes"`.

Rules for Ending a 4GL Command

All PROGRESS 4GL commands end with a period. The compiler allows the last line of a program to end without a period, however, because the end-of-file pointer supersedes the end of line. You should always use a period at the end of each command even if it is the last line in a program, just to be sure.

Rules for Multiline 4GL Commands

A command can span several lines of text. A carriage return at the end of each line will suffice to indicate continuation. You also can use the tilde character (~) to indicate that the command is continuing on the next line.

Abbreviating 4GL Commands

You can abbreviate most 4GL commands. For example, you can use `DISP` rather than `DISPLAY`. You also can abbreviate most functions. For example, you can use `SUBSTR` rather than `SUBSTRING`. You cannot abbreviate any command or function to fewer than four characters, however. Usually, the limit on minimum abbreviation has to do with specifying enough characters to remove ambiguity for the compiler. `SUBST` could be evaluated as the `SUBSTRING` or `SUBSTITUTE` function; therefore, the abbreviation `SUBST` is not allowed.

You can abbreviate table and field names to one single character as long as it uniquely identifies the entity. For example, `cust.nam` is equivalent to `customer.name` as well as `c.n.`, as long as these abbreviations are unique. Be cautious, however, that a database schema change could occur later on to introduce ambiguity, thus causing the abbreviated field name to no longer be acceptable.

Database names must be given in full; no abbreviations are allowed.

Variable names must be given in full; no abbreviations are allowed.

Spacing for Arithmetic Formulas

The PROGRESS compiler is somewhat sensitive to spacing within a command line. You must be careful when using arithmetic operators and adding spaces around them.

It is a good habit to always place a space before and after any arithmetic operator. Here are a few examples of spacing issues:

`DISPLAY 7-1.` This example has no spaces between the numbers and the period. This lack of spaces results in an error from the compiler because it cannot understand the directive `7-1.`

`DISPLAY 7- 1.` This example has a space separating the `-` and the `1`, but no space appears between the `7` and the `-`. This spacing results in a display of `-7` (negative 7) and `1` separately. The compiler interprets the directive as two separate numbers.

`DISPLAY 7 - 1.` This example has spaces between all elements of the arithmetic operation. It results in a display of `6`.

Other arithmetic operators pose similar constraints.

`DISPLAY 2*(3 + 1).` Results in an error from the compiler.

`DISPLAY 2* (3 + 1).` Results in an error regarding `2*` from the compiler.

`DISPLAY 2 *(3 + 1).` Results in a display of `8`.

`DISPLAY 2 * (3 + 1).` Results in a display of `8`.

Use spaces before and after arithmetic operators. Also use spaces before and after an equal sign (=) in assignments.

In general, you must use a space to separate each word in a command.

Rules for Comments

In the 4GL, you start comments with `/*` and end them with `*/`. Nothing can be placed between the slash (`/`) and the asterisk (`*`). You are allowed to place comments within a line, however, as in the following:

```
DISPLAY "Hello World.".    /* First Program! */
```

A comment can start on one line and end on a later line in the program. Nested comments are allowed.

At this point, you've learned the basic rules of the PROGRESS 4GL. Now consider the PROGRESS 4GL constructs.

Understanding Syntax Rules for PROGRESS 4GL Constructs

Your experience with other 3GL and 4GL languages will facilitate your learning of the PROGRESS 4GL. The constructs presented in this chapter assist you in making the transition to the PROGRESS 4GL syntax and rules.

In this section, you'll explore the various constructs of the PROGRESS language. In many cases, code generation tools such as the User Interface Builder (UIB) will take care of the constructs for you. It is still important, however, to have a fundamental understanding of the generated or programmed code.

In the following sections, you learn about these PROGRESS 4GL constructs:

- Variables
- Delimited Lists
- Blocks
- Frames
- Widgets
- Handles
- Unknown Values
- Preprocessors
- Include Files
- Procedures and Parameters
- Triggers
- `WAIT-FOR`

The implementation of these constructs is unique to the PROGRESS 4GL. You will use these constructs throughout this book and in your PROGRESS 4GL programming experience.

Variables

Variables in the PROGRESS 4GL are similar to variables in other programming languages. Each variable is defined with a specific type, format, and initial attributes.

The variable types are `CHARACTER`, `DATE`, `DECIMAL`, `HANDLE`, `INTEGER`, `LOGICAL`, `MEMPTR`, `RAW`, `RECID`, and `WIDGET-HANDLE`.

Variable Declaration. The definition of an integer may look like the following:

```
DEFINE VARIABLE i-count AS INTEGER.
```

You can abbreviate this definition to the following:

```
DEF VAR i-count AS INT.
```

The variable `i-count` is available for integer storage throughout its scope. A variable's *scope* (the span of code for which it exists) is the trigger, procedure, or program in which it was declared. A variable declared within an internal procedure (described in detail later in this chapter) does not exist outside that procedure.

You can declare variables with initial values, as follows:

```
DEF VAR dt-date AS DATE INITIAL today.
```

Here, the variable `dt-date` initially contains the current date.

There is no practical difference between the variable type `HANDLE` and type `WIDGET-HANDLE`. The reason for the two variable types is for historical compliance with older releases. It is best to use type `HANDLE` for procedure and system handles and use type `WIDGET-HANDLE` or `WIDGET` for pointers to interface controls.

You may often see the `NO-UNDO` clause in a variable declaration:

```
DEF VAR i-total-records AS INT NO-UNDO.
```

This clause immunizes the variable against the effects of the `UNDO` statement, which rolls back the work performed within a transaction. Transaction rollback may affect variables as well as database changes. The `NO-UNDO` separates the variable from the rollback mechanism and thus avoids unnecessary processing. You learn more about transactions in Chapter 5, "Further Exploration: Locking, Transactions, and VBXs."

A powerful construct for declaring variables that will inherit the properties of a database field is the `LIKE` clause, which follows:

```
DEF VAR dt-ship-date LIKE order.ship-date.
```

Here, the variable `dt-ship-date` inherits the properties of the database field `order.ship-date` at the time of compilation. If the database field definition is altered, it will become necessary to recompile the code.

Variable Naming Conventions. You may adopt any variable naming standard that suits your needs and the needs of your development team. One recommended approach is to preface the variable name with an indication of its type, as follows:

CHARACTER	preface with `c-`; example: `c-last-name`
INTEGER	preface with `I-`; example: `i-count`
DECIMAL	preface with `d-`; example: `d-sales-total`
HANDLE	preface with `h-`; example: `h-exit-button`
DATE	preface with `dt-`; example: `dt-ship-date`

Prefacing variables makes it clear, upon reading code, which type a variable belongs to without your having to look at its declaration.

Delimited Lists

A PROGRESS list is a collection of entries in a string separated by a delimiter such as a comma (,). The comma is the default delimiter for lists. You may specify a different delimiter if necessary.

Some examples of list constructs are as follows:

`c-string = "Joseph,Mary,Christopher".` (comma-delimited list of first names)

`c-string = "Smith, Richard¦Dailey, Susan¦Wyles, Anton".` (a pipe-character-delimited (¦) list of full names with a comma separating first and last names)

`c-string = STRING(TODAY) + "," + STRING(TODAY - 7) + "," + STRING(TODAY + 7).` (comma-separated list of dates)

In all cases, the list is represented by a character string. All strings are assigned literally with single or double quotation mark enclosure.

The command

```
c-people = "Chris,John,Lisa,Marie,Bill".
```

assigns the list of names to the character variable `c-people`. To add a new entry to the list, simply append a comma (or the appropriate delimiter) followed by the new entry:

```
c-people = c-people + ",Gerry".
```

You can use functions such as `ENTRY` and `LOOKUP` to manipulate list entries, as in the following example:

```
DISPLAY ENTRY(4,c-people).
```

This command displays `Marie`, the fourth entry in the list of `c-people`.

The list construct is significant because it provides a convenient data-storage mechanism. Interface controls such as combo boxes and selection lists hold their contents in lists. Lists can be used rather than arrays to hold entries of unknown quantity. For example, if there is the possibility of a list of names from 1 to 20 to be stored, storing them in a names list is usually preferable to storing them in an array. The list will save memory because only the actual names needed are stored, whereas the array would require the maximum space, even if it contained only a single entry.

Blocks

A *block* of code in the PROGRESS 4GL is a group of commands enclosed by a block statement that calls for certain properties.

The block statements in PROGRESS are the following:

`DO` statement

`FOR` statement

`ON` statement

`PROCEDURE` statement

`REPEAT` statement

`TRIGGER PROCEDURE` statement

Each block statement has *block properties*. Block properties include record iteration, record locking, record reading, and transactions.

To better understand this concept, look at the following example:

```
DEF VAR I AS INTEGER.
DISPLAY "Block example".

DO i = 1 TO 10:
       FIND NEXT customer.
       DISPLAY name.
END.
```

This code displays the first 10 customer names on the screen.

The DO and END statements define the start and end of a DO block. The DO block has *iteration* properties, so it is usually used for loops. The block automatically loops or iterates until the end is reached in the loop limit.

The FOR block has iteration properties, record reading properties, and much more. Consider this example:

```
FOR EACH customer.
    DISPLAY customer.name.
END.
```

This code displays each customer name. The FOR block automatically reads each sequential record and iterates until the last record of the table.

The REPEAT block has properties similar to the FOR block except that it does not automatically read records. This capability is especially useful when you need the block properties of a FOR EACH block yet do not need next record read properties. Look at the following example:

```
DEF VAR I AS INTEGER.
DISPLAY "Block example".

REPEAT i = 1 TO 10:
       FIND NEXT customer.
       DISPLAY name.
END.
```

This example is similar to the DO block example: the output is identical because the first 10 customer names are displayed. The REPEAT block has other properties that are similar to the FOR block. They include record scope, transactions, and frame scoping.

Table 4.1 lists the block properties and gives a brief description of their purpose.

Table 4.1 Block Properties

Block Properties	Purpose
Iteration	Causes iteration of the block
Record-Scope	Defines the scope of a record buffer
Record-Read	Causes automatic reads of a record
Frame-Scope	Defines the scope of a frame
Transaction	Defines the start and end of a transaction

Some block statements such as REPEAT and FOR have implicit block properties. This means that they have these properties by default. Table 4.2 lists the various implicit block properties.

Table 4.2 Implicit Block Properties

Statement	Implicit Block Properties
REPEAT	Iteration, Record-Scope, Frame-Scope, Transaction
FOR	Iteration, Record-Scope, Record-Read, Frame-Scope, Transaction

The block properties are important because they imply implicit or explicit behavior. The REPEAT block iterates *implicitly,* whereas the DO block iterates *explicitly,* that is, if specifically indicated to do so. The following sections examine each property in greater detail.

Iteration Block Properties. The Iteration block property means that the block iterates automatically as per the block statement. In the case of the DO block, you must explicitly tell it do iterate, as in the following example:

```
DO I = 1 TO 10:
```

For others, such as REPEAT, the iteration is implicit.

Record-Scope Block Properties. The Record-Scope block property means that records accessed within the block are scoped to that block. Record scoping defines the start and end of a record's availability in memory. While a record is scoped, code may access the fields within the record for read or update.

The sample code that follows illustrates an example of record scoping implicitly driven by the FOR block:

```
DISPLAY "Hello World!".

FOR EACH customer WHERE customer.name BEGINS 'a':
    DISPLAY customer.name.
END.

DISPLAY customer.name.
```

The FOR block has implicit record-scoping properties. The customer record is available within the FOR EACH but not outside the block. The DISPLAY customer.name command on the last line results in a "No customer record is available." message at runtime.

You may scope a record to the entire procedure by placing a FIND statement outside the FOR EACH block, as follows:

```
DISPLAY "Hello World!".

FOR EACH customer WHERE customer.name BEGINS 'a':
    DISPLAY customer.name.
END.

FIND FIRST customer.
DISPLAY customer.name.
```

In the preceding examples, all customers whose names begin with *a* are listed. The first customer name then is displayed separately. You effectively have a record scope for customer on the `FOR EACH` and also on the `PROCEDURE because` both have record-scoping block properties.

Blocks such as `DO` may explicitly have record-scoping properties. Look at this example:

```
DO FOR customer.
   FIND FIRST customer.
   DISPLAY name.
END.
```

In the preceding example, the `DO FOR` (buffer) explicitly scopes the customer record to the `DO` block.

It is important to understand record scoping because it plays an important role in determining the length of *record locking*. As you will see later in this chapter and in Chapter 5, "Further Exploration: Locking, Transactions, and VBXs," you can control record locking and transactions by controlling a record's scope.

Record-Read Block Properties. The Record-Read block property implies that with each iteration of the block, a new record will be read according to the directives on the block statement. Consider this example:

```
FOR EACH customer:
    DISPLAY customer.name.
END.
```

Each iteration of the `FOR` block accesses the next customer record. Notice that the `FOR EACH` block is the only block with implicit record-read properties.

Frame-Scope Block Properties. Much like record scoping, frame scope defines the context for a named frame that the program declares within a block. Outside the block in which a frame is declared, the frame no longer exists; the frame no longer has scope. Look at this example:

```
FOR EACH customer:
    DISPLAY customer.name WITH FRAME customer-frame.
END.
DISPLAY "End of loop." WITH FRAME customer-frame.
```

The preceding example results in a compiler error regarding the frame `customer-frame` being referenced outside its scope. The frame is bound by the `FOR` block because the block has frame-scoping properties.

If the preceding example had used a `DO` block rather than a `FOR` block, the frame would have been scoped to the entire procedure, and the error would not have occurred.

Because `FOR EACH` blocks have implicit frame-scoping properties, you will note interesting default behavior with nested `FOR EACH` statements and their output frames, as in the following:

```
FOR EACH customer:
    FOR EACH order WHERE Order.Cust-num = Customer.Cust-num:
```

```
        DISPLAY Customer.cust-num Customer.name Order.order-num
        Order.Order-Date.
    END.
END.
```

Note that, in this example, each list of orders per customer appears in a separate frame. Each iteration of the outer `FOR EACH` block scopes a new frame for display of the records.

Once again, blocks such as `DO` may explicitly scope a frame using the `WITH FRAME` clause, as in this example:

```
DO WITH FRAME cust_frame TITLE "customer".
   FIND FIRST customer.
   DISPLAY name.
END.
```

The explicitly defined frame `"cust_frame"` is scoped to the `DO` block.

Transaction Block Properties. Transaction properties allow a block to start and end a transaction. A *transaction* is a unit of work performed on a database or databases. Records may be modified, created, and/or deleted during the transaction.

The power of transactions is that, prior to their end, they may be retracted. This `UNDO` functionality allows for unlimited numbers of database modifications, additions, and deletions within the confines of a transaction to be undone. In 3GL environments, this functionality was time-consuming and developer-intensive. In PROGRESS 4GL, writing the code is easy and performance is fast.

The following example demonstrates a PROGRESS 4GL transaction:

```
DEF VAR finished AS LOGICAL.

REPEAT WHILE NOT finished:

    FOR EACH customer WHERE name BEGINS "a".
        UPDATE customer.name.
    END.

    UPDATE finished.
END.
```

This simple program updates all the customer names that begin with the letter *a*.

Note the two block structures in the example: a `REPEAT` block and an inner `FOR EACH` block. Both the `REPEAT` and `FOR EACH` blocks have transaction properties. This is important because the work in either transaction may be committed or rolled back. Always keep in mind that the transaction will be started in a block with a transaction property that attempts to alter data in a database.

Given that rule, you can assume that the `FOR EACH` block in the example will start and end transactions, whereas the `REPEAT` block will not because it does not alter data. It does alter the variable `finished`, but no database changes are made.

In the preceding example, a modification to a customer record within the `FOR EACH` block would get written to the database at the end of each `FOR EACH` iteration. There would be no opportunity to UNDO that transaction outside the FOR EACH block because it would have ended there. If you wanted to UNDO the updates to the records with names starting with *a*, the preceding example would not present you with that opportunity, because each individual record update would end a transaction.

If your intent is to be able to undo the modifications to a database after several records are presented, you must expand the scope of the transaction. The following example shows the necessary modifications to the code:

```
DEF VAR finished AS LOGICAL.

REPEAT WHILE NOT finished TRANSACTION: /* Notice Transaction keyword */

    FOR EACH customer WHERE name BEGINS "a".
        UPDATE customer.name.
    END.

    UPDATE finished.
    IF finished THEN UNDO, LEAVE.   /* UNDO transaction */
END.
```

Here, the code explicitly states that the REPEAT block should start a transaction. This causes all the transactions within the FOR EACH block to become sub-transactions of the larger REPEAT block transaction. A *sub-transaction* is simply a transaction within another transaction.

If the end user updates the finished variable with a "yes," the transaction is undone and the block is exited. The changes to all the records updated will be undone. The UNDO and LEAVE statements cause this functionality. The UNDO command causes the rollback of the transaction, whereas the LEAVE command takes execution out of the REPEAT block. Note that UNDO and LEAVE are within the confines of the transaction to be undone. After transactions are ended, they are permanently written to the database.

Transaction properties of a block enable you to specify how a transaction and its sub-transactions will behave. This way, you can precisely define when and how data is written to the database. In Chapter 5, you will explore transactions in greater detail.

Frames

The PROGRESS *frame* is an area on the screen that contains displayed information in the form of data, images, lines, and so on. By naming a frame and assigning it properties, you can have control over the display's fonts, colors, borders, and other attributes. Consider this example:

```
DEFINE VARIABLE c-string AS CHAR FORMAT "x(10)" INIT "Hello World." LABEL
    "Greeting".
DISPLAY c-string"" WITH FRAME test-frame NO-LABELS TITLE "Hello".
```

Here, A frame called test-frame is created with the properties NO-LABELS (do not display labels) and TITLE "Hello" (the title of the frame). Try removing the NO-LABELS clause to show the label of the string ("Greeting"). Now consider the following example:

```
DISPLAY "Hello World." WITH FRAME test-frame TITLE "Hello".
DISPLAY "Good-bye World." WITH FRAME test-frame.
```

Here, the result is that both strings are displayed within the same frame, sharing the same frame title.

Many times, a *default frame* is created by PROGRESS during a display, as it is here:

```
DISPLAY "Hello World".
```

This line causes a default frame to be created for the display. This method is a convenient way to avoid naming frames when it is not necessary.

The frame construct within PROGRESS 4GL is very powerful. You define a frame once, and you can use it (and its properties) throughout the program. You can even share frames between programs and sections of code. See the "Blocks" section earlier in this chapter for further information on frame-scoping properties.

Widgets

A *widget* is a PROGRESS 4GL construct to help manage interface controls. A control can be a fill-in, text, an image, a set of radio buttons, a combo box, or any other interface control either in TTY or GUI display mode.

Each and every interface control can be identified by a widget. Each widget has a widget handle that serves as a pointer (in memory) to the widget and its attributes. See the "Handles" section for more information on handles.

Each widget falls within a widget type: `FILL-IN`, `COMBO-BOX`, `TEXT`, `RADIO-SET`, `IMAGE`, and so on. Each widget within a certain widget type has several attributes and methods. A widget *attribute* is much like a variable or data element. It holds a piece of information that affects the widget's appearance or behavior. Each widget type has numerous attributes. Refer to Appendix A, "Attribute Reference Guide," for a complete list of widget attributes and methods.

In the following example, the fields `customer.name` and `customer.cust-num` have been positioned in a frame on the screen. The code uses widget attributes to alter the fields on the screen.

```
customer.name:SENSITIVE = YES.
customer.cust-num:SENSITIVE = NO.
```

This example enables the name field and disables or grays out the `cust-num` (in GUI mode). The `cust-num is` not modifiable. This is an example of widgets representing data on the screen and the use of attributes to alter the presentation or behavior. In the preceding example, the fill-ins representing `customer.name` and `customer.cust-num` are the widgets, whereas `SENSITIVE` is an attribute.

A widget *method* is much like a function. The method performs a specific action relative to the widget. Like a function, the widget method returns a value indicating success or failure of the method.

In the following example, a button (widget) named BUTTON-1 has been placed on the screen. Say that you want to load an image within the button. You then use the LOAD-IMAGE() method to load the image into the button widget. This means that the button shows the image within itself, like an icon. This example attempts to load the image "happy.bmp" into the button. If it fails to do so, the logical l-success is set to FALSE.

```
DEF VAR l-success AS LOGICAL.
l-success = BUTTON-1:LOAD-IMAGE("happy.bmp").
IF NOT l-success THEN message "Error loading image.".
```

You use the LOAD-IMAGE() method for widgets to execute specific functionality for that widget. Many methods are associated with each type of widget. Refer to Appendix A for a complete list of widget methods and attributes.

The widget construct is extremely powerful in that it enables you to manipulate and alter the controls in the graphical and character interfaces.

Handles

A *handle* provides a pointer to useful variables. Handles are available for system options, session options, and each available widget.

The simplest example of a handle is the handle attribute for a widget, as in the following:

```
DEF VAR handle-1 AS HANDLE.
handle-1 = BUTTON-1:HANDLE.
```

The variable handle-1 or type HANDLE points to the widget BUTTON-1. The purpose is to enable you to manipulate the BUTTON-1 widget indirectly through the handle HANDLE-1.

Many useful handles exist to give you access to system and session attributes. The Clipboard handle is a good example:

```
DISPLAY CLIPBOARD:VALUE.
```

In this example, CLIPBOARD is a system handle that you can use to access the Windows Clipboard.

Another useful system handle is the FILE-INFO handle, as the next example illustrates:

```
FILE-INFO:FILE-NAME = "\autoexec.bat".
DISPLAY FILE-INFO:FULL-PATHNAME FORMAT "x(60)" LABEL "Full Path"
        FILE-INFO:PATHNAME FORMAT "x(60)" LABEL "Path"
        FILE-INFO:FILE-TYPE LABEL "Type"
        WITH FRAME osfile-info SIDE-LABELS TITLE "OS File Info".
```

In this example, the full pathname and file type for the \autoexec.bat file are displayed.

PROGRESS provides many handles for gathering information about the system environment. Table 4.3 lists the various handles.

Table 4.3 Handles Used for System Information

System Handles	Description
CLIPBOARD	Points to the Windows Clipboard
COLOR-TABLE	Allows reading and setting color table entries
COMPILER	Allows access to compiler attributes
DEBUGGER	Allows for launching debugger actions
ERROR-STATUS	Allows access to error information for the last encountered error
FILE-INFO	Points to attributes for a given file
FONT-TABLE	Allows access to attributes in the current font table
LAST-EVENT	Points to attributes relative to the last event
RCODE-INFO	Allows access to attributes of a given .r compiled program
SESSION	Allows access session attributes

Unknown Values

The *unknown value* is a PROGRESS construct that enables you to store a ? into any variable or data field. The ? or unknown value indicates that no data has been assigned to the variable. The unknown value can be useful for cases in which a value must be provided for a variable and you must check to see that something has been entered.

```
DEFINE VARIABLE finished AS LOGICAL INITIAL ?.

REPEAT WHILE finished = ?:
    UPDATE finished.
    IF finished = ? THEN DISPLAY "You must respond with yes or no.".
END.
```

This example keeps prompting the user for a reply until the user responds with yes or no.

Because you are interested in the difference between a value of yes, no, or no entered value, the unknown value can be useful. Without the unknown value, the variable finished would have the default initial value of no. It would be difficult to determine whether a value of no had actually been entered, or whether it was just the original default for the logical variable.

Use of the unknown value is common with mandatory database fields. The question mark (?) appears in the data field to indicate no value or unknown value.

Preprocessors

PROGRESS *preprocessors* are powerful constructs for efficient coding. Preprocessors are similar to C macros; they allow program-wide macro substitution. Look at this example:

```
&SCOPED-DEFINE table  customer
&SCOPED-DEFINE fields cust-num name phone

FOR EACH {&table}:
    DISPLAY {&fields}.
END.
```

Both `table` and `fields` are preprocessors and can be used as substitutes for the actual `table` and `fields` literals. Preprocessors can greatly simplify your coding and allow a single piece of code to become effective toward several different tables. The compiler replaces the preprocessors accordingly at compile-time.

Preprocessors are important because they allow large sections of code to be compiled against various different options. You can make a program that maintains a customer table maintain a different table by simply changing the references to `customer` and its `fields` to preprocessors. After the preprocessors are defined for the new table and its fields, the corresponding compiled code is a file maintenance program for the table.

You will see extensive use of preprocessors by the UIB. Preprocessors are easy to spot because they are always enclosed by curly brackets ({}) and preceded by an ampersand (&). For example, `{&frame-name}` contains the name of the frame. Table 4.4 lists a few commonly used UIB-maintained preprocessors.

Table 4.4 A Sampling of UIB-Maintained Preprocessors

Preprocessor Name	Description
`{&browse-name}`	The first browser defined in the frame
`{&displayed-fields}`	Fields displayed
`{&enabled-fields}`	Enabled fields
`{&fields-in-query-{&browse-name}}`	Fields in the query for the browser defined in `{&browse-name}`
`{&first-table-in-query-{&browse-name}}`	Name of first table in the browser defined in `{&browse-name}`
`{&open-query-{&browse-name}}`	The code for the `OPEN QUERY` statement of `{&browse-name}`
`{&UIB_is_running}`	Indicates if the program is being run from the UIB

Include Files

Include files are a fundamental construct within the PROGRESS 4GL. They allow for modularity, code reuse, and ease of maintenance. An *include file* is simply a section of code stored in a separate file and included in a program at compile-time.

Following is the include file `for-each.i`:

```
/* for-each.i */
FOR EACH {&table}:
    DISPLAY {&fields}.
END.
```

This example displays all the fields specified with the `{&fields}` preprocessor for the table specified with the `{&table}` preprocessor.

The following program example can make use of the `for-each.i` include file as follows:

```
{for-each.i
     &table  = "customer"
     &fields = "cust-num name phone"}
```

Here, the compiler inserts the code for the include file `for-each.i` and passes the `table` and `fields` parameters as replacements to the preprocessors within the include file. The result is that the customer number, name, and phone are displayed for each record in the customer table.

You will notice many include files within UIB-generated programs. An include file reference is always enclosed within curly brackets and by convention has a file-name extension of .i for include.

Procedures and Parameters

A PROGRESS *procedure* can be a stand-alone program or an internal procedure defined within a program. In either case, the procedure has a unique name and may require parameters for input, output, or input-output (both).

You declare an internal procedure using the PROCEDURE statement as follows:

```
PROCEDURE compute-date.
```

Parameters allow data to be passed into and out of the procedure. The following example is a procedure to compute the number of days between two given dates:

```
PROCEDURE compute-date.
   DEFINE INPUT PARAMETER dt-from-date AS DATE.
   DEFINE INPUT PARAMETER dt-to-date AS DATE.
   DEFINE OUTPUT PARAMETER i-delta AS INT.
   i-delta = dt-to-date - dt-from-date.
END.
```

The procedure is invoked as in the following example:

```
DEF VAR i-days AS INT.
RUN compute-date (INPUT DATE("01/01/95"), INPUT today, OUTPUT i-days).
```

Keep in mind that the order, type, and orientation (input, output, or input-output) of the parameters in the RUN statement must match identically their definition within the procedure.

Triggers

Triggers are sections of code that execute upon a specific condition at runtime. These conditions are called *events*. You will see many examples of triggers throughout PROGRESS 4GL code. You can declare the following types of triggers within the PROGRESS 4GL environment:

- *Widget Trigger.* This section of code executes upon a widget event. Each widget (interface control) may have several triggers associated with it. Examples of widget events include CHOOSE (for buttons), ENTRY (for fill-ins), and VALUE-CHANGED (for radio sets). The code associated with the trigger is placed within the widget trigger definition. The following is an example of a trigger to execute upon choosing a button:

```
ON CHOOSE OF button-1:
    MESSAGE "You have clicked on the button.".
END.
```

- *Database Trigger.* This program (.p) executes upon a database table event. Each table may have database triggers defined for CREATE, DELETE, ASSIGN, and so on. The actual code for the database trigger is not stored within the database but rather is in a separate .p file. This example declares code to execute upon the creation of new customer records:

```
TRIGGER PROCEDURE FOR Create OF Customer.
    /* insert additional code here to execute upon write of customer table */
END.
```

See Chapter 2, "Getting Started with ADE Tools," for more detailed information on declaring database triggers.

- *Session Trigger.* Similar to the widget trigger, a session trigger uses the ON {event} OF {object-name} syntax, but it pertains to database tables. You can thus associate the CREATE, DELETE, or any other table event to a section of code to invoke. Unlike the Database trigger, however, the invoked code in the session trigger is not pointed to by the database; it is unique to the program defining the trigger. The following example sends a message when a customer record is deleted:

```
ON DELETE OF customer DO:
    message "You have deleted a customer record.".
END.
```

PROGRESS 4GL triggers define the actions taken within the event-driven model. As events fire, triggers associated with the events cause code to be invoked. The event-driven model implies that event triggers will be defined and that a central waiting point will exist from which events are processed.

WAIT-FOR

If you are a 3GL programmer, you are probably familiar with the *procedural* programming model. In the procedural model, each statement is executed sequentially until the end of the program is reached. Loops and GOTOs force the execution stream to specific areas of the code. As you will see, the event-driven model is organized quite differently.

The WAIT-FOR statement is central to the event-driven model supported by the PROGRESS 4GL. After the WAIT-FOR is encountered, all event processing is enabled, and triggers are ready to be fired based on end-user actions.

In Listing 4.2, the sample program \examples\chap-04\CH04PRG3.p, taken from PROGRESS' online help example, shows the function of the WAIT-FOR and demonstrates PROGRESS's event-driven model. This sample program shows variable and trigger definition, frame definitions, and the use of WAIT-FOR as the event-processing statement.

Listing 4.2 \examples\chap-04\CH04PRG3.p—Function of the WAIT-FOR

```
DEFINE BUTTON more-button LABEL "MORE". /* define the button widgets...*/
DEFINE BUTTON next-button LABEL "NEXT".

FORM customer.cust-num customer.name more-button next-button
    WITH FRAME brief.  /* define the brief information frame */

FORM customer EXCEPT cust-num name
    WITH FRAME full.   /* define the full record frame */

ON CHOOSE OF more-button       /* the trigger for the more button */
   DISPLAY customer EXCEPT cust-num name WITH FRAME full.

ON CHOOSE OF next-button       /* the trigger for the next button */
   DO:
      HIDE FRAME full.
      FIND NEXT customer NO-ERROR.
      IF AVAILABLE customer
      THEN DISPLAY customer.cust-num customer.name WITH FRAME brief.
   END.

FIND FIRST customer.   /* initialization */
DISPLAY customer.cust-num customer.name WITH FRAME brief.

ENABLE more-button next-button WITH FRAME brief.

WAIT-FOR WINDOW-CLOSE OF CURRENT-WINDOW FOCUS more-button.
```

Notice the sequence of definitions in the event-driven model shown in this listing:

1. The interface is defined (frame definitions).
2. The triggers are defined for the interface.

3. The interface is initialized (display, enable, and so on.)
4. The `WAIT-FOR` begins the event-driven processing.

The program does not end until the user closes the window by double-clicking in its upper-left corner, which causes the `WAIT-FOR` to end. If you add a `"PAUSE."` command directly before the `WAIT-FOR`, the program will run, but no events will be processed because the `WAIT-FOR` is the event-processing mechanism within the PROGRESS 4GL. You will find a `WAIT-FOR` in all UIB-generated programs.

The PROGRESS 4GL supports both the *procedural* and *event-driven* models of programming. The event-driven model shown in Listing 4.2 is perfect for graphical applications, whereas the procedural is still utilized with legacy code for TTY applications.

Querying the Sports Database

In this section, you learn about the sports database connection. This information will prepare you for the simple queries section that follows. The sports database contains customer records and sales information for a retail store.

To begin this section, you must

- Set your working directory (chapter 1) to c:\appdir
- Copy the sample sports database into your working directory (chapter 1).

To connect to the sports database and prepare for executing some simple queries, start the Procedure Editor and type the following:

```
connect \appdir\sports -1.
```

The `-1` indicates that you are connecting in single-user mode.

Creating Simple Data Requests

After you connect to the sports database, clear the editor buffer or choose File, New from the Editor menu to start a new program. Then type in the following code:

```
FOR EACH customer BY customer.name:
    DISPLAY customer.name city phone.
END.
```

Run the program by pressing F2. Then you can view the list shown in figure 4.4.

This set of commands to list customers by name is straightforward. You also can use Structured Query Language (SQL) statements to query a database. *SQL* is an industry standard set of statements used to query relational databases. Most programming environments that contend with database access offer SQL syntax compatibility. The PROGRESS 4GL complies to the SQL standards and at the same time provides its own set of robust database access statements.

Fig. 4.4

Each customer name and phone number listed by name.

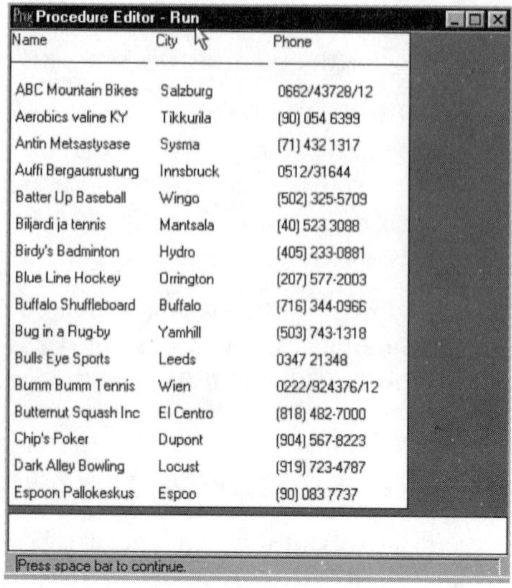

Consider this example of using SQL statements to access the data:

```
SELECT name, city, phone FROM customer ORDER BY name.
```

You can join tables during a query using SQL or the PROGRESS query language constructs, as follows:

```
SELECT cust-num, name, sales-rep, balance
       FROM customer WHERE balance > All
              (SELECT balance FROM customer WHERE sales-rep = "JAL")
       ORDER BY balance DESC.
```

This SQL example displays all customers with balances greater than any customer belonging to `sales-rep "JAL"`. See figure 4.5.

Fig. 4.5

SQL query example.

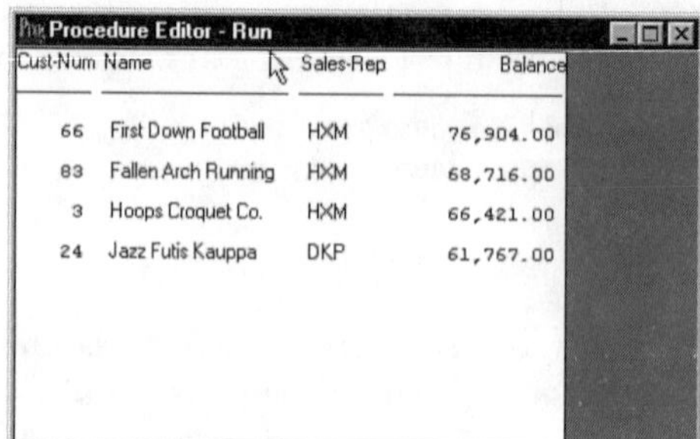

Here are the differences between SQL and the native PROGRESS database access statements:

SQL Database Access (Advantages):

- Uses recognizable industry-standard syntax
- Complies with ANSI SQL rules and constructs

SQL Database Access (Disadvantages):

- May not take advantage of database-specific functions; for example: PROGRESS word indexes
- May not perform optimally for a given database engine
- Lowest common denominator approach because it must function on all databases that support SQL

PROGRESS 4GL Database Access (Advantages):

- Maximum performance against PROGRESS databases
- Maximum optimization for PROGRESS databases
- Takes advantage of all PROGRESS database features

PROGRESS 4GL Database Access (Disadvantages):

- Not an industry-standard syntax

The most significant difference between using the PROGRESS 4GL and SQL syntax is the way in which they are oriented toward data retrieval. Whereas SQL is oriented toward retrieving a *set* or *collection* of records that meets the specified criteria, the PROGRESS 4GL is oriented toward individual records.

To pursue this difference more closely, examine the `FOR EACH` (PROGRESS 4GL) versus the `SELECT` (SQL) statement.

Database Access Using PROGRESS 4GL `FOR EACH`:

```
FOR EACH customer:
    DISPLAY customer.name.
END.
```

Database Access Using SQL `SELECT`:

```
SELECT customer.name FROM customer.
```

In the `FOR EACH` example, each record is dealt with individually; as the programmer, you can manipulate each customer within the `FOR EACH` block. In the `SELECT` example, the set of customer records is returned as a collection of records. You cannot manipulate each record as the `SELECT` statement retrieves it.

This is not to say that SQL denies programmers the ability to work with individual records within a set. It is simply a case of which way the language is oriented. The PROGRESS 4GL contains an extremely powerful database query capability, which goes above and beyond the aim of SQL and is specifically targeted for access to PROGRESS databases.

If you are comfortable with SQL statements, you can use equivalent SQL statements in this section to accomplish the sample queries. It is strongly recommended that you reach a proficient level with the PROGRESS 4GL in addition to SQL language, because it is more directly aimed at the PROGRESS development environment.

For the rest of this section, you will not be using SQL syntax. The sample queries will use the PROGRESS 4GL language to illustrate its syntax.

Joins are a necessity in any program that combines data from separate database tables. A simple example of customer order records follows:

```
FOR EACH customer, EACH order OF customer:
    DISPLAY Customer.cust-num Customer.name Order.order-num.
END.
```

PROGRESS iterates within the `FOR EACH` block and the inner `EACH` order loop automatically. PROGRESS also automatically joins the customer and order tables by looking for a common, indexed field—in this case, `cust-num`. So, this example shows each order number for each customer.

For a join to take place automatically, both tables must have a common field of the same name, type, and format. Also, the field on the related table (in the preceding example, this is `Order.Cust-num`) must be uniquely indexed.

If the two tables do not meet the join criteria, you can still join them by forcing a join clause like the one in the next example. This capability is useful for situations where no unique index for the common field exists in the related table. Be aware that joining tables without properly defined indexes may be time-consuming because the related table may be read sequentially (in the worst case).

```
FOR EACH customer:
    EACH order WHERE Order.Cust-num = Customer.Cust-num:
        DISPLAY Customer.cust-num Customer.name Order.order-num
        Order.Order-Date.
    END.
END.
```

Note the `WHERE` clause on the `FOR EACH` block indicating the basis for the two-table join. Note also that if `Order.Cust-num` is not a unique key for the order table, the order records are read sequentially to locate the orders that meet the `WHERE` clause.

As long as you design your database properly, you can join several tables simultaneously with little effort. The following example shows a join among three tables: customer, order, and order-line.

```
FOR EACH customer, EACH order OF customer, EACH order-line OF order:
    DISPLAY Order.cust-num Order.ship-date qty.
END.
```

The order-line table is joined with the order table, which is joined with the customer table to display order lines for orders of customers.

The `FOR EACH` phrase has powerful sorting functionality. Sorts can be requested of any tables used for the query. The following example shows the `BY` clause used to specify the order in which records are displayed:

```
FOR EACH customer, EACH order OF customer,
    EACH order-line OF order, item OF order-line
    BY promise-date BY customer.cust-num BY line-num:
         DISPLAY promise-date customer.cust-num
                 order.order-num line-num item.item-num item-name.
END.
```

This example displays order and item fields while sorting by fields in customer, order, and order-line tables.

Querying for Database Schema Information

In addition to queries against actual data in a database, you may also find it useful to query against the database schema information. PROGRESS stores the schema structure of a database (the fields, tables, index information, and so on) in a set of system tables. These schema information tables are called the *meta-schema*.

Consider the following example:

```
FOR EACH _file:
    DISPLAY _File._File-name.
END.
```

Figure 4.6 lists all the files in the database schema and meta-schema. A simple join displays all fields associated with a file, as in the following example:

```
FIND _File WHERE _File-name = "customer".
FOR EACH _field OF _File:
    DISPLAY _Field._Field-Name.
END.
```

Figure 4.7 lists fields belonging to the customer table. In this manner, you may access the full data dictionary schema for any connected database from within your PROGRESS 4GL programs.

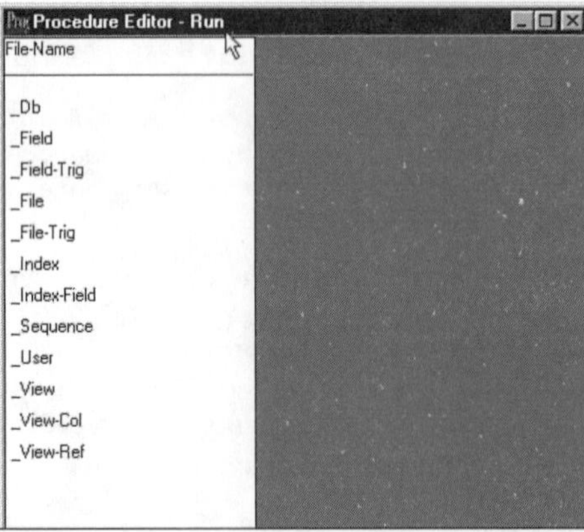

Fig. 4.6

Listing of sports database meta-schema.

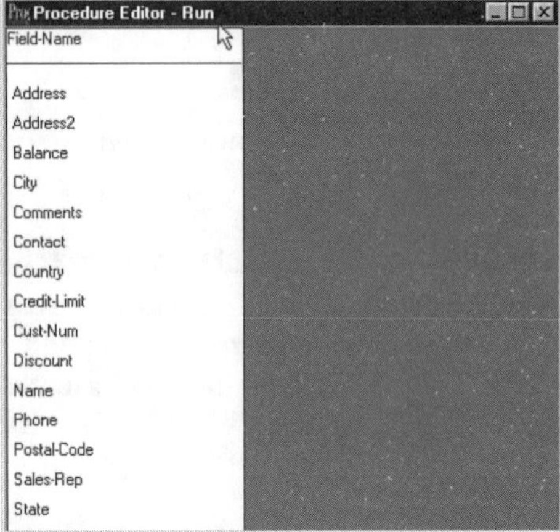

Fig. 4.7

Listing of sports database meta-schema: customer fields.

Although I do not recommend that you alter the Data Dictionary schema through programming such as this, it is possible to do so. You must be careful to not violate database integrity—for example, deleting a field while leaving active indexes that utilize such a field.

Many useful utilities have been written with the PROGRESS 4GL to manage and report on the database schema information.

From Here...

The contents of this chapter will serve as a review for you after completing the book. The foundation material and discussion of PROGRESS 4GL constructs are central to your understanding of the material that follows in this book.

For more information on related items, refer to the following chapters:

- Chapter 5, "Further Exploration: Locking, Transactions, and VBXs." This chapter gives you more detail on the 4GL language and takes you through a tour of VBX integration with PROGRESS V8.
- Chapter 22, "PROGRESS Programming Tips." This chapter gives you the expert tips and tricks to maximize the power of the PROGRESS 4GL and increase your productivity.
- Appendix F, "Structure of .w Files." This appendix explains the organization of a UIB-created .w file. You will learn how preprocessors and UIB-generated code combine to make a completed .w program.

CHAPTER 5

Further Exploration: Locking, Transactions, and VBXs

This chapter explores many of the concepts covered in Chapter 4, "Introducing PROGRESS Language," in greater depth. The principles of record locking and transaction scoping are vital to your enterprise application. This chapter also covers other topics such as the integration of VBX (Visual Basic eXtensions) controls in your version 8 GUI screen. Examples of different VBXs included in V8 and the CD show off the power of these prepackaged components.

After reading this chapter, you should be able to:

- Understand record locking principles
- Understand `NO-LOCK`, `SHARE-LOCK`, and `EXCLUSIVE-LOCK` statements and their behavior
- Understand the principles of transaction scoping and the use of the before-image file (.bi)
- Understand subtransactions and the use of the local before-image file (.lbi)
- Use the compiler listing option to examine block structures in 4GL code
- Integrate VBXs into your PROGRESS code

Voice-of-Experience Movies

See Table G.3 in Appendix G, "Contents of CD," for a list of the Voice-of-Experience files for this chapter.

Review of Record and Transaction Scope

In Chapter 4, you learned that certain blocks in the PROGRESS 4GL have record- and transaction-scoping properties. The blocks scope the record being accessed, thereby defining the record's availability in memory. If records are changed or exclusively locked with the block, a transaction will be assigned to the block marking the start and end of a database transaction or subtraction.

The purpose of record scope is to define the area of code in which a record buffer is available. PROGRESS 4GL commands act upon the record for the duration of the record's scope.

The purpose of transaction scope is to define the area of code in which a transaction starts and ends. Locks established during a transaction are not released until the transaction ends.

One important purpose of record and transaction scoping is to enable the *compiler* to define the *duration* of locks applied to database *records*.

Examine the three key words in the preceding definition:

- *Compiler*. It is the blocks in your 4GL code that determine the record and transaction scope, and thus the type and length of record locking that will transpire at run-time.
- *Duration*. Because you do not explicitly tell the database engine to start and stop holding a record lock, the scope of the record and transaction serves that function. Your understanding of record scope as well as transaction scope will allow you to effectively manage the duration of record locking.
- *Records*. In multi-user mode, databases are not locked, tables are not locked, and individual fields are not locked. Under normal circumstances (see following note), locking applies only to records. Other database engines lock tables or *pages* of records, which can create serious bottlenecks in multi-user mode.

Note

Advanced PROGRESS developers will note that when using the Data Dictionary, a SCHEMA-LOCK is established that locks every user out of the database until the schema changes are completed.

To begin this section, you must set your working directory to c:\appdir and have copied the sample sports database into your working directory (see Chapter 1, "Introducing PROGRESS," for details).

To connect to the sports database and prepare for executing some simple queries, start the Procedure Editor and type:

```
connect \appdir\sports -1.
```

The -1 indicates that you are connecting in single-ser mode. Then, type the following 4GL program into a new editor buffer:

```
message "Hello World.".

for each customer:
   display name.
end.
```

Save the program as \appdir\scope.p using File, Save As from the PROGRESS Editor.

Assuming that this program is run by itself (not from another program that had transactions started already), we can determine its record-locking properties. The program uses the `FOR` block to display each customer's name. Because the `FOR` block has record scoping properties, any locks established within the `FOR` block will be released at the end of iteration of the block.

Before worrying too much about what kind of lock you are going to hold for the customer records within the `FOR EACH`, examine the listing of this program's compile to see what the scope of the record is.

In a new editor buffer, type the following line followed by F2 (Run):

```
compile \appdir\scope.p listing \appdir\scope.lis
```

This launches the compiler for the program scope.p and produces a compiler listing for you. You may view the resulting compiler listing, scope.lis, using the procedure editor:

```
scope.lis (compiler listing)

\appdir\scope.p                              06/30/95 07:15:13   PROGRESS(R)
Page 1

{} Line Blk
-- ---- --
      1     message "Hello World.".
      2
      3   1 for each customer:
      4   1    display name.
      5   1 end.


\appdir\scope.p                              06/30/95 07:15:13   PROGRESS(R)
Page 2

     File Name       Line Blk. Type Tran            Blk. Label
-------------------- ---- --------- ---- -------------------------------
\appdir\scope.p         0 Procedure No
\appdir\scope.p         3 For       No
    Buffers: sports.Customer
    Frames:  Unnamed
```

The source code listing shows the `FOR` block with a series of `1` marks. Marks of `2`, `3`, and beyond would indicate nested block structures, as you will see later.

On page 2, all blocks are listed:

```
\appdir\scope.p         0 Procedure No
```

This indicates that there is a `PROCEDURE` block (a default for all programs) that is *not* a transaction (the `NO` appears under the `Tran` column of the report). Also, the `PROCEDURE` block begins at line 0 of the listing.

```
\appdir\scope.p         3 For       No
    Buffers: sports.Customer
    Frames:  Unnamed
```

This indicates that there is a `FOR` block (due to the `FOR EACH` statement) that is also *not* a transaction (you will see why later in this section) and starts at line 3 of the listing.

The `FOR` block scopes the buffer sports.Customer as indicated by the compiler listing. It also scopes the `Un-named` frame because I did not name a frame for the `DISPLAY` statement (see Chapter 4, "Introducing PROGRESS Language," regarding frame scoping). Frame scoping has no bearing on record locks, so we will not treat it further in this chapter.

The significance of this listing is that it tells you that records from sports.customer will be scoped to the `FOR` block. This means that locks applied to these records will not be released and will be held *until the block iterates or ends*. The use of compile listing is essential to the analysis of a program and its record and transaction characteristics.

Tip

The `compile listing` feature can be used to learn a great deal about record locking and transactions. You can develop any valid PROGRESS 4GL program, and view its record- and transaction-scoping properties using the compiler's listing option as demonstrated in this chapter. Try it!

As you learned in Chapter 4 and was illustrated in the previous example, the `FOR EACH` block has record scope properties. With more experience, you will learn that the `FOR EACH` block establishes a *weak scope* on the record. This means that the scope will be expanded beyond the `FOR EACH` block if the record is accessed beyond the block's boundaries.

Scope.p line 2 could be changed to contain the statement: `FIND FIRST customer.` This would access the record outside of the `FOR EACH` block, thus scoping the record to the procedure. Try making this alteration and viewing the new compile listing.

Note

By establishing a *strong scope* with blocks such as `DO FOR` and `REPEAT FOR`, you can be sure that the record scope will be confined. Use of the `FOR EACH` block will cause records to be *weak scoped*; the record scope may expand to the largest block that accesses the record.

Tip

Using `compile listing` against variations of code is a great way to master the concepts presented in this chapter.

Introduction to Record Lock Types

As record locks are established, PROGRESS denotes precisely what type of record lock is in place to determine the multi-user access restrictions. The common record lock types are NO-LOCK, SHARE-LOCK, and EXCLUSIVE-LOCK (listed in order of multi-user restrictions). Other uncommon and rarely seen locks such as LIMBO-LOCK are not relevant to this level of discussion on record locking, and will not play a significant role in your development efforts.

In a multi-user system using shared memory, such as VMS or UNIX, you may monitor the locking using Progress' PROMON utility. This utility is included with the product and it allows you to view locks as they are established.

> **Note**
>
> Advanced PROGRESS developers will note that a LIMBO-LOCK denotes a record that is within transaction scope, yet no longer within the record scope of the process that exclusively locked it. Otherwise it is functionally similar to an EXCLUSIVE-LOCK.

The three major types of record locks are described in the following sections.

NO-LOCK

NO-LOCK records are available for all to access. Any records that the user has security privileges to are available for access via a NO-LOCK.

The NO-LOCK option for record access implies that there is no intent on modifying any part of the record or deleting it.

Because NO-LOCK records can be viewed at any time, it is mathematically possible that part of the NO-LOCK records that you access are simultaneously being updated by the database engine. This can happen if a series of NO-LOCK customer records are being read at the same instant that another user is updating his or her account balance. Although this may occur only rarely, the user may read some updated customer records along with other nonupdated records. This phenomenon is referred to as a *dirty read*. As the name implies, part of the records read is dirty from partial updates to the database.

> **Note**
>
> Advanced PROGRESS developers will note that NO-LOCK access to a record causes an extremely brief lock of type NO-LOCK on the record. This is placed for the split second during which the database engine is reading the record, so that potential record updates are not taking place simultaneously.

SHARE-LOCK

A SHARE-LOCK record is locked to the extent that other users may also lock the record, but only if those locks are also shared. Many users may have a shared lock on the same database record at the same time. None of them may upgrade the record lock to EXCLUSIVE unless they remain the only user with a SHARE lock on that record.

The SHARE-LOCK option is the default for all record access commands except for queries (OPEN QUERY statement, which by default is NO-LOCK). The SHARE-LOCK option for record access implies that there is *possible* intent of updating the record.

As you learned in Chapter 4, the intent of updating a record will cause the compiler to scope a transaction block if a transaction is not already active. Reading a record with SHARE-LOCK does *not* cause a transaction block to be defined. You must show the compiler intent of modifying the record by using an assignment command that would effectively alter a field or fields.

The next step ultimately from SHARE-LOCK is to establish an EXCLUSIVE lock on the record in order to modify it. Any SHARE-LOCK record will upgrade to EXCLUSIVE-LOCK once the data is to updated. This upgrade is only possible if no other SHARE or EXCLUSIVE level locks exist for the record.

If two users are both trying to upgrade to EXCLUSIVE-LOCK at the same time, they may end up waiting on each other indefinitely because neither will release or upgrade. This scenario is affectionately called a "deadly-embrace" by PROGRESS developers. It is easily solved by incorporating a check of what level of lock is held and returning control to the user.

EXCLUSIVE-LOCK

An EXCLUSIVE-LOCK record is a record that is not available for any other SHARE or EXCLUSIVE locking. The record may be read with NO-LOCK at any time.

The EXCLUSIVE-LOCK option for record access dictates that you have intent of updating the record. The compiler will form a transaction scope around the exclusively locked record, and it is assumed that the record will change. Of course, it is up to the 4GL code that you write to determine whether or not any data does indeed change.

Note

Advanced PROGRESS developers will note that it is most efficient to establish an EXCLUSIVE-LOCK on records which *will* be modified. This avoids the effort to upgrade the lock from SHARE-LOCK. Also records that are not modified should be read with NO-LOCK for maximum efficiency.

You have seen record scope as it relates to a record's availability in memory, and transaction scope as it relates to record changes. Transaction and record scope are interrelated. The two scope types play as an ensemble within the confines of your application code and its attempts to read/modify records. Next you will examine more examples of record locking.

Examining Record-Locking Examples

In the example of scope.p, each customer record is accessed with a `SHARE-LOCK` (the default). The `SHARE-LOCK` is established at the `FOR EACH` statement for a customer record, and is held until the iteration of the `FOR EACH` onto another customer record. Thus, only one customer record is held in the prescribed lock at any given moment.

Prior to and beyond the `FOR` block (in scope.p), no customer records are available (assuming that it was not called by another program with customer record scoped). That is, no customer records are scoped and thus no customer records are locked.

Record Locking Scenario: Record and Transaction Scope Are Equivalent

Examine another example of record scoping. In the program scope2.p that follows, you'll find the first customer record and update the city field. The user is then prompted with a message to continue.

scope2.p

```
def var ans as logical.

find first customer.
customer.city = "Boston".

message "Click to continue..." view-as alert-box update ans.
```

The program displays nothing during execution except for the alert box prompting the user to continue.

After saving the program as scope2.p, type the compiler command in a new editor buffer:

```
compile \appdir\scope2.p listing \appdir\scope2.lis
```

Scope2.lis (compile listing)

```
\appdir\scope2.p                        06/30/95 08:04:31   PROGRESS(R)
Page 1

{} Line Blk
-- ---- ---
      1     def var ans as logical.
      2
      3     find first customer.
      4     customer.city = "Boston".
      5
      6     message "Click to continue..." view-as alert-box update ans.
```

```
\appdir\scope2.p                          06/30/95 08:04:31   PROGRESS(R)
Page 2

     File Name       Line Blk. Type Tran            Blk. Label
-------------------- ---- --------- ---- -------------------------------
\appdir\scope2.p        0 Procedure Yes
    Buffers: sports.Customer
```

Note that on page 2 the PROCEDURE block is scoping the sports.Customer records starting on line 0.

Note also that the compiler has determined that the PROCEDURE block is a transaction (the Yes under the Tran column of the report). This is *not* because of the find first statement, which defaults to SHARE-LOCK access. It is due to the assignment of the customer.city field within the block.

Not assigning the customer.city field and finding the first record with EXCLUSIVE-LOCK would also have forced the compiler to label the PROCEDURE block as a transaction. This is because use of EXCLUSIVE-LOCK implies record modifications.

At the time of the FIND FIRST record access, the record is read with SHARE-LOCK (the default). The assignment of customer.city forces the lock to upgrade to EXCLUSIVE-LOCK.

Because the customer record is scoped to the entire procedure and because the transaction is also scoped to the procedure, the exclusive record lock will not be released until the procedure ends. This is the simplest case, where record scope and transaction scope are equivalent.

Although the scope2.p example is a small procedure, imagine if this were a large program with many pages of code and many control statements such as MESSAGE that give the end user control of program execution. Records could be locked exclusively for extended periods of time, forcing other users to wait or be blocked from access.

Record Locking Scenario: Transaction Scope Lies Within the Record Scope

Another example shows the case when a transaction is scoped *within* a record's scope. As with the earlier examples, simply type the program into the PROGRESS Editor.

scope3.p

```
find first customer.

do transaction:
   find first order of customer exclusive-lock.
   message "Click to Continue" view-as alert-box.
end.

message "Outside of Transaction" view-as alert-box.
```

The compile listing of scope3.p shows that the `PROCEDURE` block is the scope for the customer record (because of the `find first customer`). It also shows that the `DO` block is the scope of the transaction (because of the explicit `TRANSACTION` clause on the `DO` statement).

Scope3.lis (compile listing)

```
\appdir\scope3.p                       10/24/95 22:41:39   PROGRESS(R)
Page 1

{} Line Blk
-- ---- ---
      1     find first customer.
      2
      3   1 do transaction:
      4   1    find first order of customer exclusive-lock.
      5   1    message "Click to Continue" view-as alert-box.
      6     end.
      7
      8     message "Outside of Transaction" view-as alert-box.
      8


\appdir\scope3.p                       10/24/95 22:41:39   PROGRESS(R)
Page 2

     File Name       Line Blk. Type Tran            Blk. Label
-------------------- ---- --------- ---- -------------------------------
\appdir\scope3.p        0 Procedure No
    Buffers: sports.Order
             sports.Customer

\appdir\scope3.p        3 Do        Yes
```

In this case, the customer record is scoped to the entire procedure and the transaction is scoped to the `DO TRANSACTION` block. The exclusive record lock will be released when the `DO` block ends. At that point, since it will still remain scoped, it will be downgraded to a `SHARE-LOCK`. Upon the end of the record scope (the end of the procedure block) the record will be released.

Once a transaction ends, if a record is still scoped, the lock will be downgraded to `SHARE-LOCK`. At this point, you use the `RELEASE` statement to remove the lock entirely and release the record.

In scope3.p, inserting a `RELEASE customer` statement on line 7 would release the record and its lock. This is useful because the user could sit on the "Outside of Transaction" alert box for hours while the `SHARE-LOCK` remained active on the customer record!

> **Note**
>
> The RELEASE statement has no effect when used within a transaction. The locks cannot be given up until the transaction ends. The RELEASE statement is effective in releasing records outside of a transaction while they remain scoped. Expert PROGRESS developers use this to minimize record contention.

Record Locking Scenario: Record Scope Lies Within the Transaction Scope

In this final example, you see the reverse condition from the previous example. In this case, the scope of a record lies within the confines of a transaction. The sample code follows:

scope4.p

```
FIND FIRST customer.
customer.name = "Lift Line Skiing".

FOR EACH order OF customer:
    order.ship-date = today.
    MESSAGE "Changing Order Date" view-as alert-box.
END.
MESSAGE "Outside of Order Scope" view-as alert-box.
```

The compile listing shows that the scope of the Order record is the FOR EACH block. The transaction starts with the assignment of the customer name at the top of the program. Thus the Order record scope will end while a transaction is active. As usual, compile the program with the listing option to produce the following output:

```
\appdir\scope4.p                        10/24/95 23:06:37   PROGRESS(R)
Page 1

{} Line Blk
-- ---- ---
      1     FIND FIRST customer.
      2     customer.name = "Lift Line Skiing".
      3
      4   1 FOR EACH order OF customer:
      5   1     order.ship-date = today.
      6   1     MESSAGE "Changing Order Date" view-as alert-box.
      7     END.
      8     MESSAGE "Outside of Order Scope" view-as alert-box.
      9
      9


\appdir\scope4.p                        10/24/95 23:06:37   PROGRESS(R)
Page 2
```

```
     File Name       Line Blk. Type Tran            Blk. Label
-------------------- ---- --------- ---- -------------------------------
\appdir\scope4.p        0 Procedure Yes
    Buffers: sports.Customer

\appdir\scope4.p        4 For       Yes
    Buffers: sports.Order
```

Because locks are not released until the transaction ends, the Order record locks (one for each order of customer) are not released until the end of the procedure. This is very significant, often a transaction may be already active from a calling program. The records scoped in the called program, as is the case with scope4.p, will establish locks and those locks will linger through the end of the transaction.

This is the reason that your understanding of Progress database record locks is important. Your ability to use the compile listing option to examine the record and transaction scope and determine the length of record locking will greatly assist you. After all, your application will not serve the end users well if most records are locked exclusively for long periods of time.

Let's review the significance of record and transaction scoping:

The purpose of record and transaction scope is for the *compiler* to define the *duration* of locks applied to database *records*.

Now review some of the most important points from this section:

- Record scope, in conjunction with transaction scope, dictates the duration of record locks.
- Record buffer scope and transaction scope are both determined at compile time by the PROGRESS compiler. Although it is possible to outline which areas of code are scoped, the exact order of when a transaction will start/end and when records will be released depends on the sequence of events at run-time.
- The compiler listing option exposes record scoping for you to examine easily and accurately. The compiler listing is an extremely powerful tool for learning and establishing proper record and transaction scoping.
- The record lock types are `NO-LOCK`, `SHARE-LOCK`, and `EXCLUSIVE-LOCK`. `SHARE-LOCK` is the default for record access (except for `QUERY`, where `NO-LOCK` is assumed).
- The PROGRESS compiler may implicitly upgrade or downgrade record locks, according to the 4GL statements. An exclusive lock may be requested for a record that is being modified, even though the 4GL code did not specify that the record be accessed with `EXCLUSIVE-LOCK`. Likewise, an exclusive lock may be downgraded at the end of a record scope if a transaction is still active.
- Record locking and transaction scoping are related in that a record must have established a lock in order for the transaction to function. As a result, the record lock will persist until the latter of the scope of that particular record or until the end of the transaction scope.

Understanding Record-Locking Mechanics

As a program is running, the Progress database engine registers the user as having connected to database(s) accessed by the program. Within an active transaction, as records are locked with the `NO-LOCK`, `SHARE-LOCK`, and `EXCLUSIVE-LOCK`, the database engine keeps track of the locks held. The database engine maintains a list of locked records (shared or exclusive) in a *lock table*. As users attempt to establish a `SHARE` or `EXCLUSIVE` lock, the lock table is searched for other users with locks on the record.

Establishing and upgrading locks can take time and slow down a program. This is why the `NO-LOCK` option is recommended on all record access statements when you have no intent of modifying the record. This is also why the `EXCLUSIVE-LOCK` option is recommended when you are fairly certain that the record will be modifying. By specifying `EXCLUSIVE-LOCK`, you avoid the expense of upgrading the lock from `SHARE-LOCK`, as was the case in the scope2.p example.

The size of the lock table is driven by a database start-up parameter `"-L"`. If the lock table is not large enough, the database engine may not be able to hold enough locks for the number of users running the application concurrently. Use PROGRESS' *System Administration Manual* for guidelines on setting the Lock Table size for your database.

Working with Database Transactions

A database transaction is a finite unit of work that takes place either in its entirety or not at all. If the system crashes in the midst of the transaction, for example, all work will be reversed and the database will be returned to the exact state of the start of the transaction.

In this section, you will study the mechanics of a PROGRESS transaction. In the spirit of reinforcing your skills with the compile listing, you will review more transaction-scoping examples. Note that the examples in this section will be presented directly as compiler listing and will avoid listing source code for the sake of being to the point.

Imagine a transaction with the following components:

1. Delete Customer Record
2. Delete Orders Associated with Customer
3. Update Accounting Tables

If the system crashes immediately after step 1 and the steps are not reversed, the database would contain orders with no corresponding customer data. Such "orphan" records would cause serious problems in the database. By using a transaction, you ensure that all or none of the changes are effectively brought to bear on the physical database.

Examine figure 5.1, which shows the anatomy of a typical transaction.

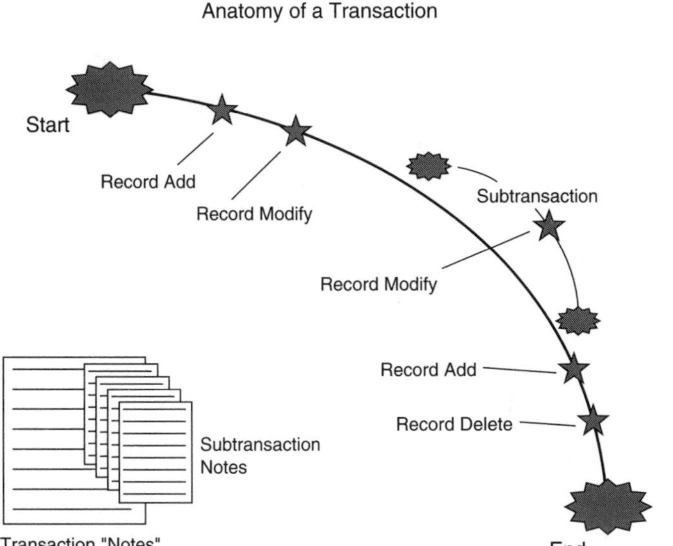

Fig. 5.1

Anatomy of a database transaction.

Note that only one transaction may be active at a time for each PROGRESS session/ client process.

During the transaction, record modifications, creations, and deletions are written to the transaction notes file, which keeps track of the changes to the database. For the PROGRESS database, the transaction notes are written to a file with extension *.bi*, the *b*efore *i*mage file. The before image file (.bi) is stored on the server system, along with the database itself (this is a distinguishing factor for client/server environments).

A *subtransaction* is a unit of database work that takes place while a transaction is already active. Subtransaction notes are written to the local before image file with prefix *lbi*; for example, lbi29304. The 29304 is an arbitrary unique identifier established for the subtransaction.

Additionally, the lbi files keeps notes of variables which may need to be rolled back along with an `UNDO` statement. The lbi is also used to keep notes for work done against foreign (non-PROGRESS) databases.

Note

Using `NO-UNDO` in your variable declarations will avoid the overhead of writing local before image (lbi) notes when the variable is altered. Unless you require the variable to roll back along with the database, the `NO-UNDO` clause should be used.

These lbi files are physically stored on the client machine (in the case of client/server). There should be an lbi file per user using the database.

The reasons for keeping notes of the transaction's database changes are as follows:

- If the transaction is rolled back, the notes in the lbi and bi files are used to return the database in its original pre-transaction state.
- If the transaction is committed, the notes are used to make the database changes permanently.
- If the database is recovered after a system crash, the bi notes will be used to properly recover the database.

Keep in mind that, during a transaction, modified records are locked exclusively. Because of the exclusive locks, no other users can make modifications to the altered records. An after image note (changed record) may not be written to the before image file until an `EXCLUSIVE` lock has been attained. If the record is still share or exclusively locked, this will not occur.

Transaction Example: Transaction Scoped to Procedure

The following example highlights how you can attain greater control of a program's transaction. You are given the compiler listings, so there is no need to type the program in, unless you want to.

Scope5.lis (compile listing)

```
\appdir\scope5.p                          06/30/95 08:04:31   PROGRESS(R)
Page 1

{} Line Blk
-- ---- ---
      1     def var ans as logical.
      2
      3     find first customer.
      4     customer.city = "Boston".
      5
      6     message "Click to continue..." view-as alert-box update ans.

\appdir\scope5.p                          06/30/95 08:04:31   PROGRESS(R)
Page 2

     File Name       Line Blk. Type Tran            Blk. Label
-------------------- ---- --------- ---- --------------------------------
\appdir\scope5.p        0 Procedure Yes
    Buffers: sports.Customer
```

The compiler recognizes the entire procedure as a transaction block. This is because there is no block structure such as `FOR` or `REPEAT`, and the `customer.city` field is modified.

The transaction spans the entire procedure; therefore, the exclusive lock associated with the first customer is held until the end of the program.

Transaction Example: Transaction Scoped to `DO` Block

To reduce the duration of the lock, a transaction block can be placed in order to explicitly define the scope. Once again, you are presented with the compile listing, there is no need to type or load this short program.

Scope6.lis (compile listing)

```
\appdir\scope6.p                          07/07/95 22:48:53   PROGRESS(R)
Page 1

{} Line Blk
-- ---- ---
      1     def var ans as logical.
      2
      3   1 DO TRANSACTION:
      4   1    find first customer.
      5   1    customer.city = "Boston".
      6     END.
      7
      8     message "Click to continue..." view-as alert-box update ans.


\appdir\scope6.p                          07/07/95 22:48:53   PROGRESS(R)
Page 2

     File Name       Line Blk. Type Tran            Blk. Label
-------------------- ---- --------- ---- -------------------------------
\appdir\scope6.p        0 Procedure No
    Buffers: sports.Customer

\appdir\scope3.p        3 Do        Yes
```

Note the effects of the `DO TRANSACTION` block.

1. The transaction is limited to the `DO TRANSACTION` block; the customer record is exclusively locked only until the `END` of the `DO` block.
2. The scope of the customer buffer is the entire procedure. This is because the `DO` block does not have record scoping properties by default. A `REPEAT` or `FOR` block would have scoped the record buffer. (Use of `FOR EACH` to limit scope is shown in the next example.)
3. The lock on customer will be downgraded at the end of the transaction to `SHARE-LOCK`. The customer record is still available after the transaction with `SHARE-LOCK` access.

Transaction Example: Transaction Scoped to `FOR EACH` Block

Examine scope7.lis compile listing as another example of transaction control.

In scope7.p, each customer record of each order record is updated to be located in Boston.

Because of the `FOR` block and the intent to modify records within the block, the compiler will label the `FOR` block as a transaction. The `FOR` block has record scoping properties, so the `ORDER` and `CUSTOMER` buffers are scoped to the block.

Scope7.lis (compile listing)

```
\appdir\scope7.p                          07/07/95 23:01:37   PROGRESS(R)
Page 1

{} Line Blk
-- ---- ---
      1     def var ans as logical.
      2
      3   1 FOR EACH ORDER:
      4   1    find first customer of order.
      5   1    customer.city = "Boston".
      6     END.
      7
      8     message "Click to continue..." view-as alert-box update ans.

\appdir\scope7.p                          07/07/95 23:01:37   PROGRESS(R)
Page 2

     File Name       Line Blk. Type Tran            Blk. Label
-------------------- ---- --------- ---- -------------------------------
\appdir\scope7.p        0 Procedure No
\appdir\scope7.p        3 For       Yes
    Buffers: sports.Customer
             sports.Order
```

By using the compile listing (using the listing option of the compile command), you are now able to determine:

1. The record scope for all buffers in your program
2. The transaction start/end points
3. Subtransactions
4. The length of record locks held within a transaction
5. The areas of your code where a transaction lies within a record scope, where record locks will be downgraded as in sample scope3.p
6. The areas of your code where a record scope lies within a transaction, where record locks will remain in place until the end of the transaction. This was demonstrated in scope4.p

VBX Integration

PROGRESS Version 8 provides support for VBX (Visual Basic eXtension) components. These Windows-based components, added through the UIB, provide a rich set of graphical controls that provide features and functions not found in the built-in set of PROGRESS controls. The addition of VBX controls to your Windows application will provide competitive advantage to your product.

VBXs, as well as SmartObjects, bring the component theme to the PROGRESS V8 environment. Unlike SmartObjects, VBXs are not portable to non-Windows platforms. VBX technology is currently limited to platforms that run 16-bit applications, such as Windows 3.1 and 95.

> **Note**
>
> VBXs are for Windows deployment only. Be sure to determine which platforms your PROGRESS-based application will be deployed prior to choosing to integrate VBXs.

A VBX is a graphical Windows control that you have purchased or constructed. Since no development environment can be expected to provide *all* possible controls, VBXs can be an important addition to your control palette.

The following controls are supplied as part of PROGRESS V8 and can easily be added through VBX integration:

- *PSSpin.* A Spinbox control
- *PSTimer.* Returns an event after a specified interval expires
- *PSOle2.* Provides an OLE container to link or embed information from other applications
- *PSCombo.* A Combobox control

Other controls you will find on the CD-ROM are:

- *CSCalndr.* A calendar control from Crescent Software
- *CSMeter.* A meter control from Crescent Software
- *Graphx.* A graphing control from Bits Per Second and distributed by Matrix Link
- *MsgFilter.* A Windows message filter from Maximize Software
- *SaxTab.* A tab folder from Sax Software
- *SaxComm.* A communications package from Sax Software

VBX controls are available from various sources. Crescent is one of the largest providers of VBX controls.

Getting Started

Think of a VBX control as a native control (those that come with V8). A VBX control has properties, events, and methods. As you will see in the following section, VBX integration is not difficult; the VBX is used much like a native control.

If you use a PROGRESS VBX control or purchase a VBX control and add it to your application, you can freely distribute that VBX to your customer. In fact, you must add the VBX to your distribution medium and include the VBX as part of your installation process. You cannot assume that your customer has any VBX controls!

Most VBX controls that you will purchase will have a license (.lic) file. The license file allows you to add VBX controls into your application at design time. The license file can *never* be distributed, as this allows a programmer to use the VBX in design mode.

> **Note**
>
> If you are running Windows 3.x, you must have SHARE.EXE loaded.

The Control-Container

V8 has introduced a new built-in, the control-container. This built-in holds the VBX control, much like the image built-in holds a bitmap. The control-container is the "glue" that binds the PROGRESS environment with the VBX control. Some of the responsibilities of the control-container are as follows:

- Defines the position, size, sensitivity, and visibility of the control
- Implements `GET-CHAR-PROPERTY` and `SET-PROPERTY` as methods to access properties of a VBX
- Supports PROGRESS events such as `ENTER` and `LEAVE`
- Provides support to handle the events of a VBX

For each VBX control you add to your application there is a control-container. However, for the most part, you think of them as one entity.

VBX Example

This example of VBX integration shows the use of a spin control and a timer control. The user will be able to "spin" through dates and to see the current time.

A spin control allows the user to spin through a set of values until the desired value appears. A spin control works by clicking one of its buttons and keeping the button pushed as the control spins through the values. Achieving this functionality, in PROGRESS, without the spin control is rather difficult and cumbersome. As you will see, the PSSpin.vbx makes the task easy.

The second control that you will use in this example is `PSTimer`. This VBX provides events to your application after a specified timer interval expires.

PSSpin.vbx, PSTimer.vbx, and Progress.lic are provided by Progress and should be placed in your windows\system directory during installation.

Adding the Spin Box. You will start the example by adding the controls needed to display and change the date.

1. From the UIB, create a new object by clicking on the New button on the UIB main window.

2. Choose DIALOG from the new object list. We will use the dialog for simplicity in this example.
3. Insert a fill-in control, and position it toward the upper-left portion of the dialog box.
4. Change the object name from `fill-in-1` to **`display-date`,** and its label to **`Date`**.
5. Choose the VBX icon in the UIB palette. A dialog box appears with the list of VBX controls that are available in your environment. Figure 5.2 shows the VBX picker (your list may vary).

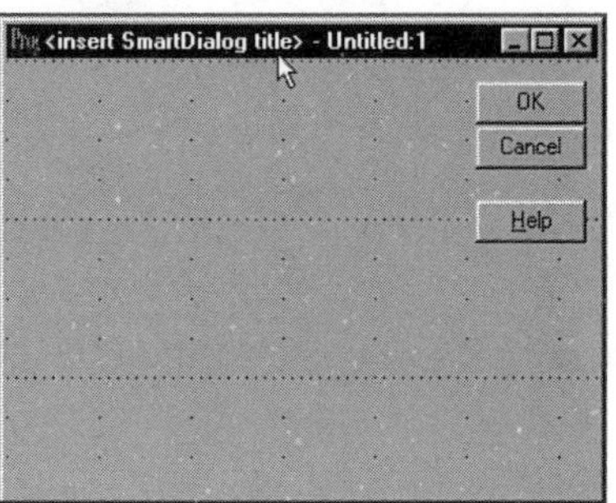

Fig. 5.2

The VBX picker dialog box.

6. Select PSSpin.vbx from the list of VBX controls and click OK.
7. At this time, `PSSpin` checks to see if you have a license to use it. If you have a license to use `PSSpin`, you can now add it to your interface.
8. Move the cursor (which is now VBX) to the right of the display-date and click. The `PSSpin` VBX is placed on the screen.
9. Change the name of the spin control from `hc_PSSpin` to **`my-spinner`**.
10. Position and size the control so it appears integrated with display-date. Figure 5.3 shows the addition.

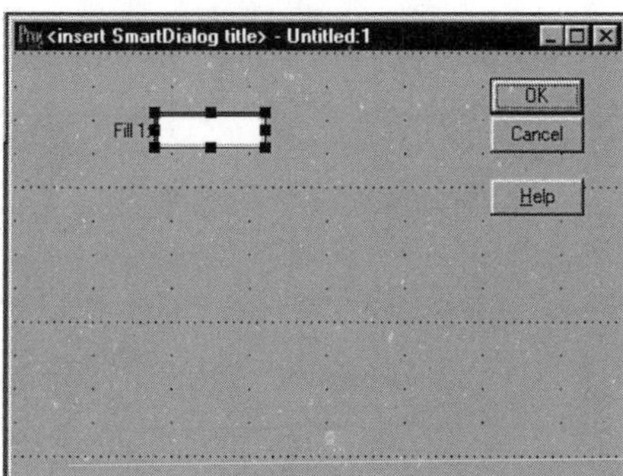

Fig. 5.3

The spin VBX integrated with the interface.

Changing Properties of a VBX Control. Each VBX defines a unique set of properties. The number of properties depends upon the complexity of the VBX. In the UIB, you can change the properties of a VBX control with the VBX Properties Window.

1. Double-click on my-spinner.
2. Click on the SpinRate property, change the value from 10 to 30, and close the property window. When run, this spinbox will *try* to spin 30 times per second.

Adding Event Procedures. Next, you need to program the event procedures for `SpinUp`, `SpinDown`, and `KeyDown`. These are three of the events that are defined by `PSSpin`. Like properties, each VBX control defines its own set of events.

An event generated by VBX control is processed like PROGRESS events; Each event is added to the PROGRESS event queue and handled in order.

However, there are important differences:

- Unlike PROGRESS events, VBX events can pass parameters.
- VBX events are not handled by TRIGGER syntax; instead, VBX events use internal procedure syntax.

Intuitively, handling VBX events is no different than handling PROGRESS events. VBX events are programmed using the Section Editor.

1. Click on my-spinner to select it. Click on the Code button in the UIB main window to start the Section Editor.
2. Click New. A dialog box appears with a list of the events the `PSSpin` control supports.

   The PROGRESS events are listed, first followed by the events defined by the VBX. These events are prefixed with `VBX`. Figure 5.4 shows this.

> **Note**
>
> The contents of the event list will be different for each VBX. When the event list is displayed the UIB asks for the events defined by the VBX.

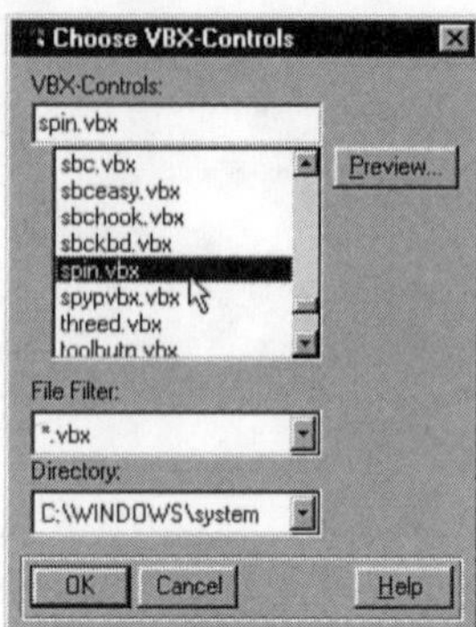

Fig. 5.4

The Choose Event dialog box.

3. Since we want to increment the date when the user clicks on the up arrow of the spinner, choose VBX.SPINUP from the list and choose OK. The section changes to the default code for the spinup event, as shown in figure 5.5.

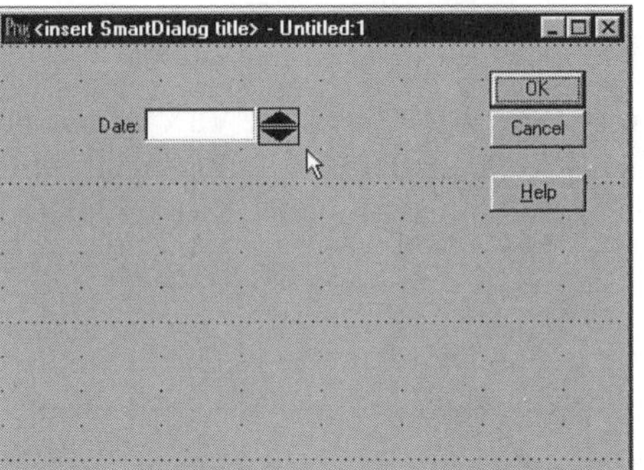

Fig. 5.5

The default code section for the `Spinup` event.

> **Note**
>
> In the .w file, VBX event handlers are defined with *internal procedure* syntax with the following naming convention:
>
> ```
> <control-container name>.<event name>
> ```

4. Bump the date up by 1. Before the `END PROCEDURE` statement, add the following code to the event procedure:

```
display-date:SCREEN-VALUE IN FRAME {&FRAME-NAME} =
    STRING(DATE(display-date:SCREEN-VALUE) + 1).
```

5. We need to add an event for spindown. Repeat steps 2 and 3, choosing VBX.SPINDOWN instead of VBX.SPINUP. Add the following code to bump the date down by 1:

```
display-date:SCREEN-VALUE IN FRAME {&FRAME-NAME} =
    STRING(DATE(display-date:SCREEN-VALUE) - 1).
```

> **Tip**
>
> The event-processing model is different for VBX controls. Unlike PROGRESS, which distributes the events to the built-ins, VBX controls process events and distributes them back to Progress.
>
> This difference is especially visible when working with keystrokes, especially the standard keystrokes. You will have to transform key events to PROGRESS events. If you choose not to trap keystrokes, if a VBX control has focus, then standard PROGRESS behavior for keystrokes will not work. On <key> ANYWHERE triggers will not fire.

The third event you will handle is the `PSSpin` box's `KEYDOWN` event. This event is generated whenever a user releases a key. You will make the escape and F2 keys work as expected.

6. Add an event procedure for VBX.KEYDOWN. Follow steps 2 and 3, choosing VBX.KEYDOWN instead of VBX.SPINUP. The UIB has added two parameters to the code section.

   When creating *any* event procedure the UIB asks the VBX if there are any parameters for the event. If there are parameters, the UIB generates the proper syntax. This makes add event handlers easy for you. You don't have to always have the documentation of the VBX handy to know which events take what parameters.

7. Add the following code to event procedure. It checks for the ASCII values of the escape and F2 key and applies the corresponding PROGRESS events.

```
IF nKeyCode = 27 THEN APPLY "END-ERROR" TO SELF. /* ESC */
ELSE IF nKeyCode = 113 THEN APPLY "GO" TO SELF.  /* F2  */
```

   The last thing you have to do before running the program is to initialize the date.

8. Since you are working with a dialog box, the place to initialize the date field is in the main code block. From the section editor, choose Main Block from the Section drop-down combo box.

9. After the `RUN enable_UI.` line, add:

```
display-date:SCREEN-VALUE = STRING(TODAY).
```

10. Click and hold onto the up arrow of the spin box. The date will increment into the future until you release the mouse button. Click and hold on the down arrow. The date will decrement until you release the button.

11. Return to the design window by pressing the ESC or F2 key. Since my-spinner has focus, the `KEYDOWN` event will be fired.

Adding a Timer. In this part of the example, you will add the `PSTimer` control to your interface. You will learn how to set a property of a VBX at runtime.

As you will see, this control is different from the spinbox. The `PSTimer` provides a *service* and does not have any runtime visualization. If a visualization is needed, as in this example, you have to provide it. The service `PSTimer` provides is to continuously provide events after an interval you specify expires.

1. Add another fill-in control to the interface. Place it underneath the date fill-in. Change the name of the new fill-in to **display-time** and its label to **Time**.
2. Move the mouse over the VBX icon in the tool palette. Use the right mouse button to drop the custom menu. Choose `PSTimer` from the list.
3. Now move into the design window and add the timer control. You do not have to worry about the position or size of this VBX control.
4. Change the name of the timer control to **my-timer** (see fig. 5.6).

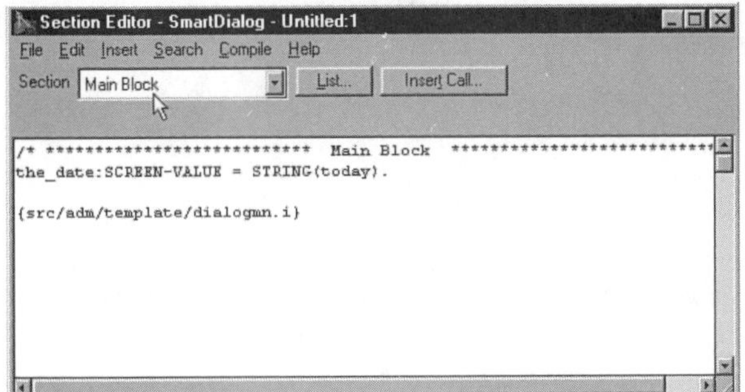

Fig. 5.6

The interface after the timer control is added.

5. You have to program an event handler for my-timer. Select my-timer and open the section editor.
6. Choose New and select VBX. In the section editor, create an event handler for VBX.TICK.
7. When my-timer expires, you will display the current time. Add the following code before the `END PROCEDURE`:

```
DEFINE VARIABLE s AS LOGICAL NO-UNDO.
display-time:SCREEN-VALUE IN FRAME {&FRAME-NAME} = STRING(TIME,
"HH:MM:SS":U).
```

Tip

`PSTimer` is not an interrupt timer. That is, it does not interrupt your program when the interval expires. Instead, `PSTimer` queues a timer event on the event queue. This event will be processed in turn.

You have programmed what you want to do when the timer expires. But you still need to start the timer. You will have `my-timer` generate events every 1000 milliseconds (one second).

8. In the section editor, change to the main code block section.

Tip

When you are not working with SmartObjects and you need to initialize a VBX control, you initialize it after the `enable_UI` statement. Unlike built-in controls, the VBX is not ready for use until after it has been enabled.

9. *After* the enable_UI statement, start `my-timer`:

```
DEFINE VARIABLE s AS LOGICAL NO-UNDO.
s = my-timer:SET-PROPERTY("Interval":U, 1000).
```

> **Tip**
>
> If you need the `PSTimer` control to be a "one-shot" timer, set the interval to 0 at the beginning of the tick event handler.

10. Run the example.

Now the example has a running clock. Notice that the `PSTimer` control is not displayed. By default, the UIB doesn't display "service only" controls.

You have completed the VBX integration example.

The .wbx File

VBX controls contain information and data structures that cannot be stored in the .w file. Therefore, the UIB saves this information into a *binary file* with default extension .wbx.

The binary file holds the design time information about the VBX controls that are included in your application. The file is created by the UIB when the .w file is saved. During execution, the information in the binary file is loaded into the VBX controls.

When the VBX control is loaded from the binary file, the control is displayed in the state in which the control was last saved. In code, you can now change any runtime properties of the VBX control. However, these runtime changes cannot be folded back into the binary file. A binary file can only be saved by the UIB while designing the interface.

> **Tip**
>
> PROGRESS searches the PROPATH for the binary file. If you need the binary file relative to the PROPATH, you can change where the binary file is found by the .w. Choose the Procedure icon from the toolbar. Change the VBX binary property to the new name.

There is one binary file for each .w file that has VBX controls. If your application has five .w files with VBX controls there will be five .wbx files.

When you remove the last VBX control from an interface and save the .w file, the UIB deletes the corresponding binary file.

The binary file is not r-code—it should not be confused with the r-file. The binary file is a separate file, and it must be shipped with your application.

Deploying an Application with a VBX Control

To deploy your VBX-enhanced application, you need to distribute these additional files:

- All .wbx files.
- .vbx files, as well as any additional files and DLLs. The documentation of the VBX control will provide the information you need to properly distribute the VBX control.

You will have to distribute a Progress.ini file. It must have the following line in the [Startup] section:

```
AllowDesignMode=no
```

Without this line, PROGRESS initializes itself to check license files when a VBX control is used. Since license files are not needed for distribution, you must tell PROGRESS not to check for them.

And as a reminder, usually you must never distribute the license file (.LIC) of the VBX control. It violates your license agreement.

Properties

As you have seen in the example, each VBX has its own set of properties. The UIB provides access to the properties in design mode with the VBX Property Window. During runtime, the 4GL provides support to *set* as well as to *get* VBX properties.

At runtime, PROGRESS provides the `GET-CHAR-PROP` method to get the value of a VBX property. This method returns the current value of the property as a character value. You will have to convert the string to the correct datatype. For example, if you wanted to increase of the `SpinRate` of my-spinner you would add the following:

```
DEFINE VARIABLE spin-rate AS INTEGER NO-UNDO.
DEFINE VARIABLE s         AS LOGICAL NO-UNDO.
spin-rate = INT(my-spinner:GET-CHAR-PROP("SpinRate":U)) + 5.
s = my-spinner:SET-PROP("SpinRate":U, spin-rate).
```

Here are some questions to keep in mind when working with properties:

1. Do you need a PROGRESS property or a VBX property?

   Properties such as `X`, `Y`, `WIDTH`, `HEIGHT`, `HIDDEN`, `SENSITIVE` are PROGRESS properties and use the `<variable-name>:<property-name>` syntax.

2. What flavor is the VBX property? Read/write in Design time? R/W Runtime only? R/W in design time and only readable at runtime? Is it an array property?

   You will need to refer to the documentation of the VBX to learn the proper use of its properties. Design-time-only properties can only be set using the VBX property window.

   If the VBX property is an array property, then use variations on the property methods:

   ```
   <vbx-name>:SET-PROP("<prop-name>", <index>, <value>)
   <vbx-name>:GET-CHAR-PROP("<prop-name>", <index>)
   ```

Tip

Color properties of VBX controls use RGB values, not PROGRESS color mapping. At runtime, if you need to change a color property, you will need to provide an integer RGB color number.

The experts have provided an RGB macro to make it easy to set the value of color properties. The function is located in SAMPLES\SOURCE\RGB.I.

3. The spelling of VBX properties is checked at runtime, not at compile time. Spelling errors will not be caught until you try to run your application and execute the code.
4. The VBX property name itself can never be translated. It is a constant. To reduce the task of translating your application you should make all references to VBX properties untranslatable.

From Here...

You have now learned a lot more about PROGRESS transactions and record locking. You have also explored the opportunities of integrating VBXs into the PROGRESS 4GL.

For more information on related items, refer to the following chapters:

- Chapter 21, "Making the Most of the Application Component Environmnent," shows you how to integrate a VBX into a SmartObject.
- Chapter 22, "PROGRESS Programming Tips," teaches you the programming tips used by PROGRESS V8 experts.

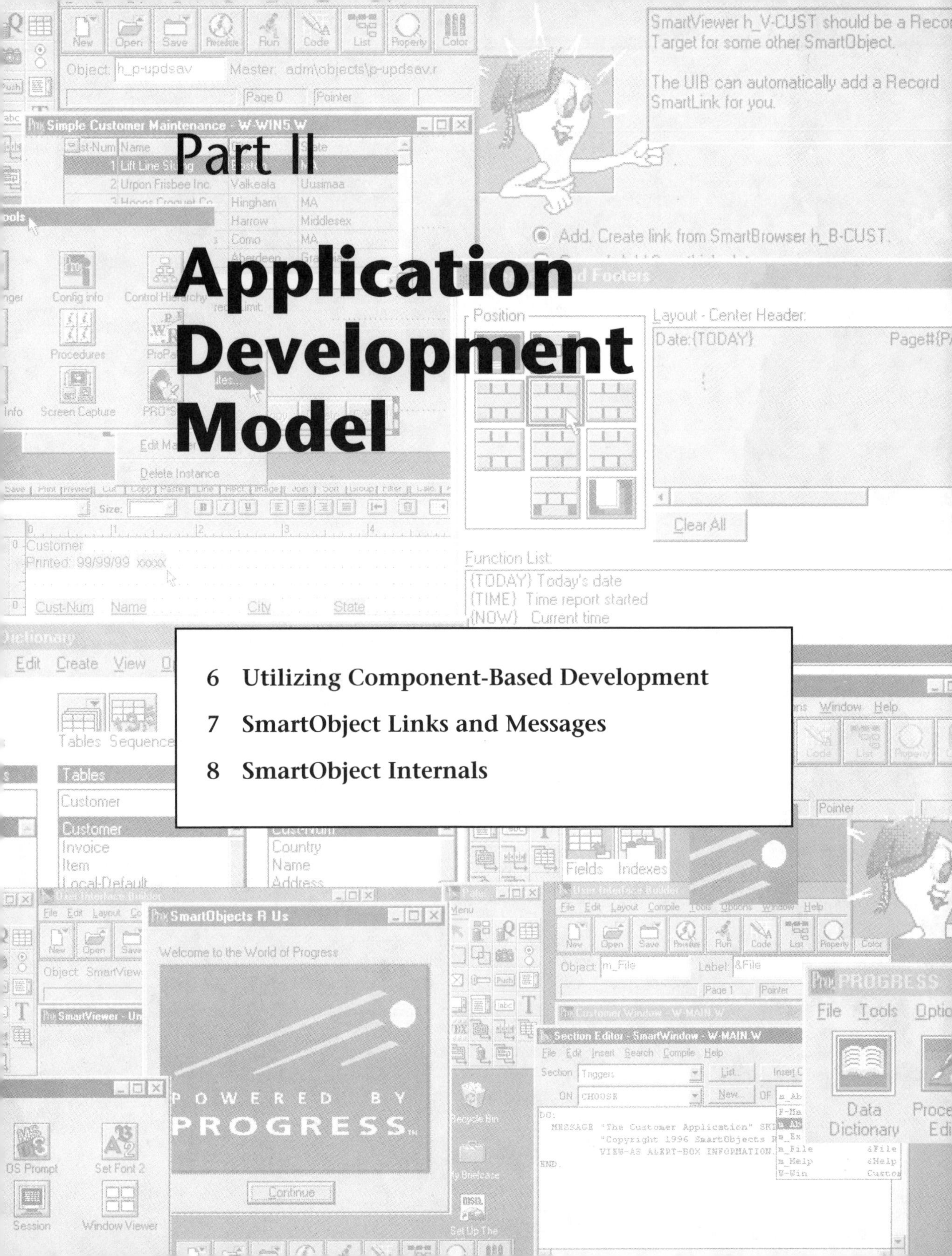

Part II

Application Development Model

SmartViewer h_V-CUST should be a R
Target for some other SmartObject.
The UIB can automatically add a Rec
SmartLink for you.
Add. Create link from SmartBrowser h_B-CUST.
Object: h_p-updsav
Master: adm\objects\p-updsav.r
Simple Customer Maintenance - W-WIN5.W
PRO*Tools
Config info
Control Hierarchy
Procedures
ProPath
Screen Capture
PRO*Spy
Edit Master
Delete Instance
Headers and Footers
Position
Layout - Center Header:
Date:{TODAY}
Clear All
Function List:
{TODAY} Today's date
{TIME} Time report started
{NOW} Current time
{COUNT} Records listed so far
{PAGE} Current page number
Customer
Printed: 99/99/99
Cust-Num
Name
City
State
User Interface Builder
File Edit Layout Compile Tools Options Window Help
Tables
Sequences
Fields
Indexes
Customer
Invoice
Item
Local-Default
Cust-Num
Country
Name
Address
SmartObjects R Us
Welcome to the World of Progress
POWERED BY
PROGRESS
Continue
Section Editor - SmartWindow - W-MAIN.W
Section Triggers
ON CHOOSE
OS Prompt
Set Font 2
Session
Window Viewer
Data Dictionary

CHAPTER 6

Utilizing Component-Based Development

The Application Development Model (ADM), from an architecture and engineering level, views application development as both evolutionary and component based. In this chapter, you'll explore briefly what this means and how it affects your development process.

You will create several basic SmartObjects and learn the term SmartObject *Master*. You will connect the new SmartObjects to produce functional interfaces. You will also see firsthand how the components are scalable.

After reading this chapter, you should be able to:

- Understand the importance of a component-based approach to development
- Understand the various phases of evolution that bring a development team from complete chaos/disorganization to order and efficiency
- Learn how V8 SmartObjects are able to leverage your development efforts
- Understand project management issues relative to the GUI paradigm and component-based development
- Build and connect SmartObjects to create functional interfaces
- Understand why tab folder screens are becoming very popular in today's graphical interfaces
- Understand the use of the UIB under V8 and component-based development

Voice-of-Experience Movies

See Table G.3 in Appendix G, "Contents of CD," for a list of the Voice-of-Experience files for this chapter.

The ADM and SmartObjects: Evolutionary and Component-Based

What is meant by evolutionary and component-based?

Evolutionary means that sections of the application (modules) can begin as highly segmented/modal and *evolve* into complex/modeless interfaces. A *segmented interface* is one that is composed of several relatively simple screens. A *modal interface* is one that does not allow the user to perform tasks outside the interface. In contrast, a *complex/modeless interface* is one that contains many complex objects and allows the user to perform tasks outside the interface.

Component-based means that reusable objects are the key to maintenance and productivity. Components have a progressively beneficial affect on productivity as the development team gains experience. Segmenting your application into components also helps to keep your code organized.

> **Note**
>
> This chapter is of special interest for project managers and project leaders interested in ADM development efforts. Chapter 12, "Introduction to User Interface Design," also focuses on project planning topics.

Understanding an Evolutionary and Component-Based Process

You will study closely the evolutionary process behind a development team's entry into new GUI technology. GUI client/server is a new paradigm that may cause a paradigm-shift shock for many developers.

The significance of this evolutionary profile is that it highlights the significance of the V8 ADM and how it evolved.

The typical evolution of experience using the graphical model involves the following issues:

- Early work done by developers new to the environment is almost always discarded as experience increases. Such "experimentation" increases overall development costs significantly.
- The incapacity of noncomponent-based solutions to scale gracefully results in flawed time estimates and project timelines.
- Developers concentrating on user interfaces should be somewhat isolated from the background tasks (transaction processing, calculations, and so on). Both productivity and quality are improved by better insulating the interface from background processing.

You will examine the evolution of the development process. The analogy of an automobile manufacturing plant will be used to highlight certain facets of the methodology at each phase. You will explore analogies built from the inefficiencies and evolution of the model automobile plant. Exploring these concepts will help you understand the basis behind the V8 Application Development Model.

Pre-Evolution Phase

During this phase, developers are lacking any sort of programming standards or structure. Having recently emerged from training courses, the developers are very much in an exploration mode and are repeating the same mistakes as others.

In this phase, there is little or no sharing of code, complete lack of consistency, and a strong desire to reinvent the wheel.

In the graphical environment, new developers have the tendency to concentrate their efforts on the exciting portions of the interface while ignoring the mundane yet critical elements. While the developers concentrate on "fancy" issues of consistency, productivity and basic functionality are side-stepped. Such distracted developers focus their early attentions on such things as dynamic menus, multidocument interfaces, and drag-and-drop techniques.

The best early investment of development time is instead spent on the foundation of the application: templates and objects.

Here's a pre-evolution phase analogy:

- *Description.* In this phase, the manufacturing plant consists of workers or groups of workers building cars from the ground up without effective use of preexisting or predesigned parts.
- *Output.* Each car looks and drives differently. Quality is highly dependent on worker skill and individual worker talent.
- *Productivity.* Productivity is low; creativity rules the factory. Serious productivity is lost while trying to adhere to standards.

Early Evolution Phase

During this phase, a common set of templates begins to emerge and take hold. The team realizes that the work of a few engineering-oriented developers can enhance the productivity of the rest of the team.

Figure 6.1 illustrates some typical templates created in this phase. These few templates brought forth relatively simple interfaces with deep functionality behind the scenes. Many areas of an application can be addressed with such templates.

Early in the development evolution, windows are seen as separate functional components. In the pre-V8 environment, PROGRESS 7.3A templates are often used as the building blocks for record look-ups and file maintenance screen types.

This level of granularity (at the window level) becomes inefficient as the development complexity increases.

At this phase of the evolution, many separate windows are required for an application, yet developers new to the GUI/Event Driven model are able to become successful using a small set of templates.

Fig. 6.1

Early evolution in GUI development: Windows as separate components of an application.

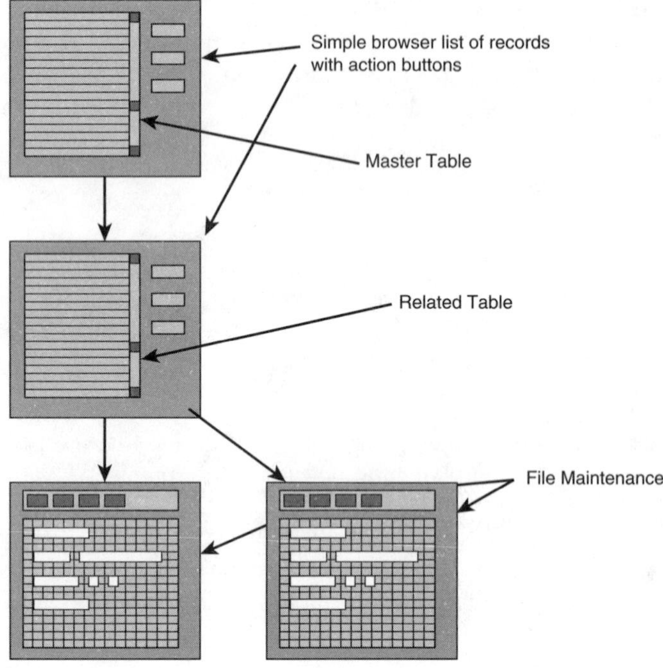

The screen types at this stage could be simply:

- Browser
- File Maintenance
- Menu

Experiences with early versions of the PROGRESS GUI releases involved the development of templates for the preceding three screen types. After high-quality templates were in place, developers could create the associated screen types with relative ease.

Although no one is suggesting that applications built in this manner are consistent with today's GUIs, entire applications *could* be deployed using this scheme. If 60 to 80 percent of an application could follow this route, you could enjoy substantial productivity gains early in the development cycle.

Here's an early evolution phase analogy:

- *Description.* In this phase, the manufacturing plant builds a few types of cars. Few options are available for each type. A functional sedan, minivan, and sports car may be the car types built. Variations and new models are expensive to manufacture, and suffer from quality and productivity problems.

- *Output.* Each type of car is consistent. Variations and extra options must be added during the later phases of production. This means that if many cars require a sunroof, the effort will be duplicated. The plant is ill prepared to produce a new type of automobile quickly.
- *Productivity.* Productivity is high for the standard car type supported by the plant. As consumer demand calls for options and variations, productivity and quality suffer.

Further in the Development Evolution

A reasonable level of complexity beyond the early stages of development is one that begins to combine common reusable objects.

Consider, for example, the combination browser and data fields screen shown in figure 6.2.

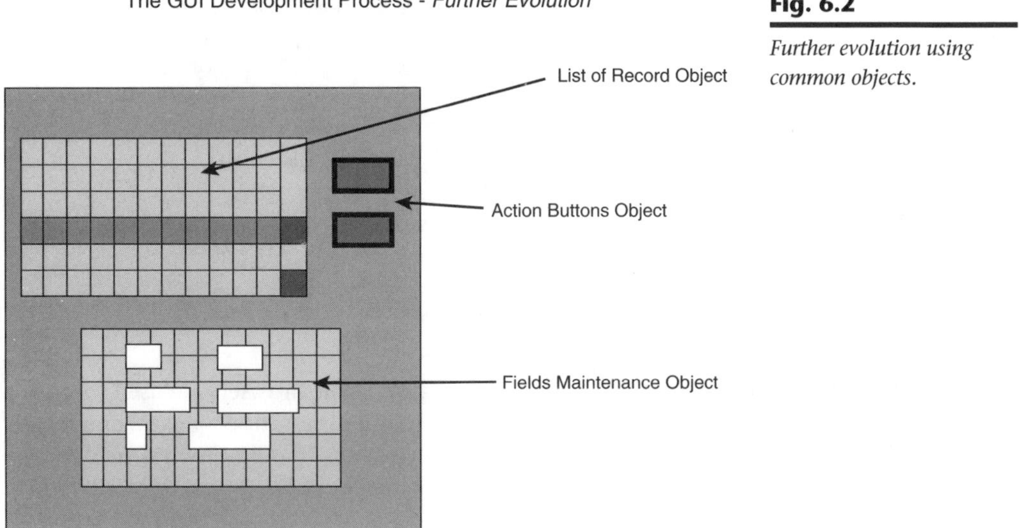

Fig. 6.2

Further evolution using common objects.

In figure 6.2, encapsulated objects are not yet being combined to form a complex screen. The screen here is a template created for the purpose of browser/data fields combination.

This is an extremely common screen type where one window performs both the record positioning functions as well as the data manipulation. This screen type could readily be created using one of the 7.3A templates. It is important to consider and outline other possible screen types at this phase of the evolution.

It is valuable to study some examples of templates that combined two or more specific functions (example: browser and viewer). The terms "browser" and "viewer" are simply descriptive in this context. Later in this chapter, you will see how V8

SmartObjects, such as SmartBrowser and SmartViewer, emerged from these early concepts.

The following is a list of templates that effectively contained multiple functions merged together.

Template screen types:

- *Browser/viewer combination.* In figure 6.3, the browser + viewer screen allows a list of records to be viewed while certain fields are presented for update. This was handy for modifying records quickly.

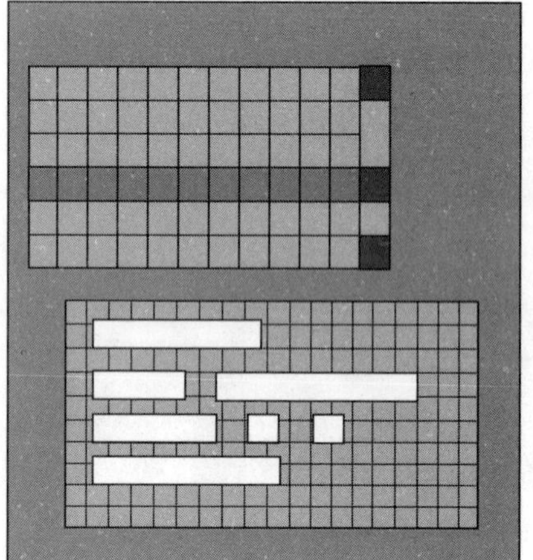
The GUI Development Process - *Further Evolution*
Browser +Viewer Combination

Fig. 6.3

Browser + viewer combination (same as previous figure).

- *Multiple synchronized browsers.* In figure 6.4, multiple browsers are used to show lists of records for related tables. This was useful for locating a record or a related record, such as an order of a customer. The interface would then proceed to another template in order to either view the detail of the record or modify it.
- *Toolbar connected to viewer.* In figure 6.5, a toolbar is connected to a viewer. The toolbar typically provides record navigation functionality (first, last, previous, next). This was used to navigate through records while being able to see each field separately. This was an alternative to the browser that presents data in a tabular fashion.

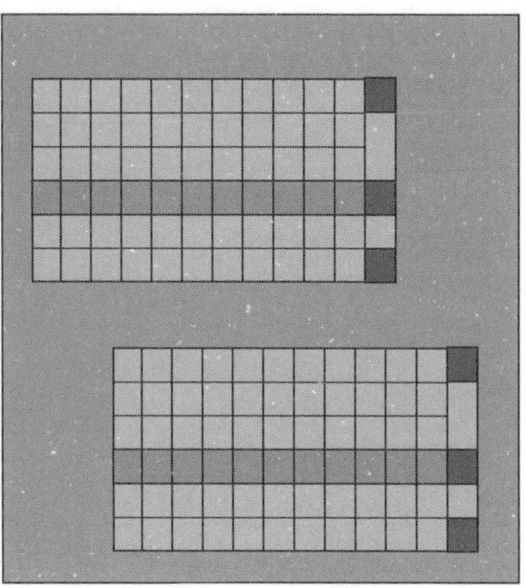
The GUI Development Process - *Further Evolution*
Multiple Synchronized Browsers

Fig. 6.4

Multiple synchronized browsers.

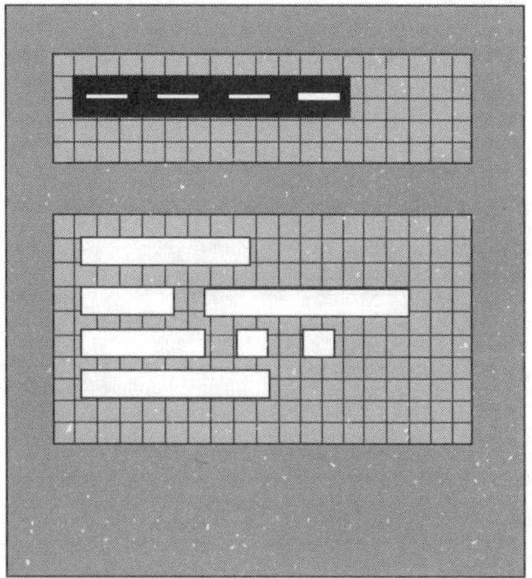
The GUI Development Process - *Further Evolution*
Toolbar +Viewer

Fig. 6.5

Toolbar connected to viewer.

- *Toolbar connected to viewer with associated browser.* In figure 6.6, the toolbar + viewer + browser allows for a list of records with certain updatable fields and a toolbar providing data manipulation functions (save, undo, clear). This was used in cases where relational data was viewed at the same time as the master record if the relation was open for record update.

Fig. 6.6

Toolbar connected to viewer with associated browser.

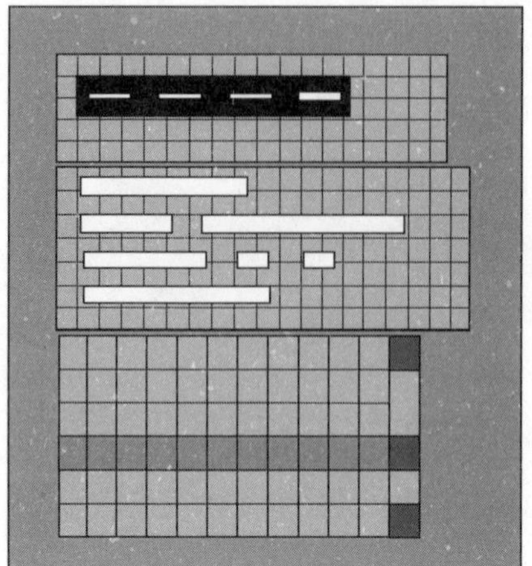
The GUI Development Process - *Further Evolution*
Toolbar +Viewer + Broswer

■ *Toolbar connected to viewer with associated toolbar+viewer combination.* In figure 6.7, the combination of toolbar and viewer allows the end-user to step through one set of records while independently stepping through a related set of records.

Fig. 6.7

Multiple toolbar + viewer combinations.

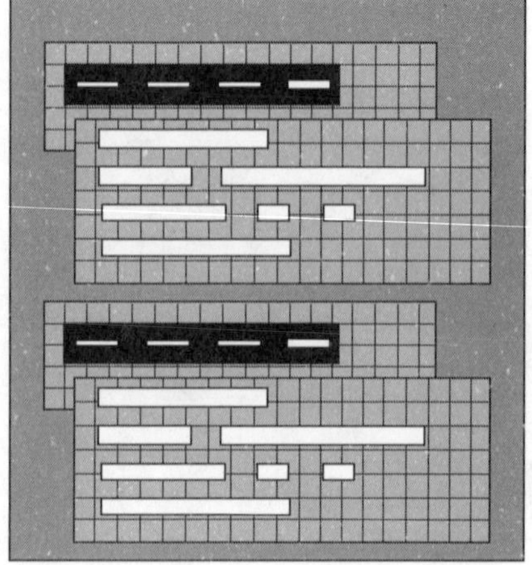
The GUI Development Process - *Further Evolution*
Multiple Toolbar +Viewer Combination

The screen types at this level of evolution are finite, yet numerous. Imagine how many possible combinations you could reach for the average-sized application. There are far too many to be covered by templates at the window level. This is precisely why organization and reusability at the *window* level is limiting. Most applications are *not* made of 3 to 5 types of screens (in the literal sense).

By using SmartObjects and component-based development, you can create and support the exponentially greater number of screen types needed.

At this stage in the evolution, an application requiring 50 significantly different screen types would require 50 templates. It would be preferable to create many of the 50 variations by combining available objects.

Put in different terms, with 5 to 8 objects combined in various permutations, one could construct the 50 unique screens necessary.

Here's an intermediate evolution phase analogy:

- *Description.* In this phase, the manufacturing plant is able to produce several different models. Several different assembly lines create the multitude of car types with high productivity. Variations and options are addressed by a multitude of automobile assembly lines.
- *Output.* Many different models are built with quality and productivity. There is some exchange of parts, such as steering wheels and tires. Other essential parts are specific to model types.
- *Productivity.* Productivity is high. New automobile types can be designed by separate teams that understand the construction process. The factory is able to support the multitude of assembly lines necessary to manufacture the diverse set of automobiles required. The plant is not necessarily maximizing the reuse of parts from one car type to another. Also, significant new car types still require their own assembly line.

Using the Latest Evolution: SmartObjects

The latest evolution in the Progress development methodology is *SmartObjects.* SmartObjects provide the reusable objects from which all of the screen types can be constructed. *SmartBrowsers* present lists of records in tabular form. *SmartViewers* show details of a record and allow for data entry. *SmartPanels* provide the toolbars to drive the interfaces. The many types of SmartObjects and their purposes are discussed in this chapter and in Chapters 7 and 8.

Consider the various stages of evolution presented in the last few pages. What does the SmartObject technology mean in terms of the automobile analogy?

Here's an advanced evolution phase analogy:

- *Description.* In this evolution phase,the automobile plant is able to create a tremendous number of different cars with varying options and variations. Essential parts can be readily interchanged while assuring compliance with standards.
- *Output.* Cars are produced with a high level of customization. A minivan can be manufactured with a sports car engine, station wagon wheels, and sedan interior. The resulting car is easily customized and maintainable at the repair shop.

The repair shop can replace the engine with any other available engine that complies to the standards. The owner can easily swap steering wheels, tires, or windows simply by replacing them with other compliant parts. The plant can sell its parts with confidence that other plants using the same process will be able to use the parts seamlessly.

- *Productivity*. Productivity is extremely high. Quality is based on the quality of each component rather than the experience of the constructor. Less-skilled laborers are used on the factory assembly line, whereas higher-skilled workers assure the quality of the components. Components are purchased from other companies to save money and attain a best-of-breed end product. New types of automobiles and *vehicles* can be modeled, tested, and produced by combining different components together.

Summary of the Different Evolutions of Development

In summary, you can make the following observations about the evolutionary stages of GUI Client/Server development using PROGRESS V8 SmartObjects.

- Even novice developers can begin by using simple templates to create functional windows. Many templates are provided by PROGRESS as part of the product.
- Sections of a standard user interface, such as the toolbar, call for a reusable and modular approach. A simple SmartObject, such as the SmartPanel (toolbar), can satisfy this requirement easily. Because the toolbar SmartObject does not relate to a query or present data directly, it does not involve the complex messaging requirements of other SmartObjects.
- Sections of the application are created, and commonly used browsers or groups of data fields are identified. Such common browsers and data field groups are turned into SmartBrowsers and SmartViewers.
- As experience increases within the development team, SmartObjects are used to create more versatile interfaces, such as folders and paging systems.

When you start with SmartObjects, you are already far in the evolutionary process of GUI development. A developer fresh out of SmartObject training who creates SmartPanels and SmartViewers during the first week is highly productive. Such SmartObjects do not get thrown away after the developer becomes more experienced; the SmartObjects scale gracefully through the development process as the complexity increases.

You will notice that a SmartPanel or SmartViewer created for a very simple file maintenance window, such as the one in figure 6.5, will also be used within complex folder systems. The object is not copied; it is reused.

Change to a SmartObject constitutes a change in that object everywhere it has been used, automatically.

The ADM, from an architecture and engineering level, views application development as both evolutionary and component based. It will help you if you keep that view in mind as you proceed through an in-depth tour of the ADM in the next chapters.

The ADM saves development time and money by:

- Saving maintenance effort
- Streamlining the Quality Assurance (testing) effort
- Improving quality of product
- Improving scalability

Creating the Components with SmartObject Masters

Now you'll take a look at how SmartObjects are put together to form a functional screen. You will first build some simple SmartObjects and then connect them to form functional interfaces. Many of the details of SmartObject assembly, construction, and communication will be covered in further chapters.

To begin this section, you must:

- Have set your working directory (see Chapter 1, "Introducing PROGRESS") to c:\appdir.
- Have copied the sample sports database into your working directory.
- Have connected to the sports database.

A *SmartObject Master* is an instance of a SmartObject. One type of SmartObject is the SmartViewer. The SmartViewer displays database fields from particular tables. A *SmartViewer Master* is a specific SmartViewer that has been created for the customer table, for example.

A summary of "SmartObject" terms follows:

- *SmartObject.* A general term applied to PROGRESS V8 reusable components and the technologies within; for example: Customer SmartViewer.
- *SmartObject Master.* A specific SmartObject instance; for example: Customer SmartViewer Master, Order SmartQuery Master.
- *SmartObject Template.* The starting point for the creation of a SmartObject Master. To create the Customer SmartViewer, begin with the SmartViewer template in the UIB. If you alter the template, all subsequently created masters will inherit the template's characteristics.

To summarize, the term SmartObject is common throughout the V8 ADM, along with the term SmartObject Master implying a specific instance and SmartObject Template pointing to the SmartObject's class.

Given this prescribed PROGRESS terminology, this book will typically refer to a SmartObject Master as simply a "SmartObject." For example, Customer SmartViewer will be used to imply the SmartViewer Master for Customer.

You will create four SmartObject Masters in this chapter:

- Customer SmartViewer
- Customer SmartBrowser
- Order SmartViewer
- Order of Customer SmartQuery

UIB Font Settings

Before you begin building these SmartObjects, you should change certain settings in progress.ini to change the fonts used within the PROGRESS environment. It is strongly suggested (not mandatory), that you do this simply so that the screen shots will match what you see on your screen. If you are using a SuperVGA monitor, you can skip this step as your screen will look similar and have similar proportions. Please skip this if you aren't using Windows 95.

By using size 8 fonts such as Courier New and MS Sans Serif, you will have greater screen real estate to work with. Because Windows 95 is predominantly using MS Sans Serif 8 point, the UIB will fit better into the desktop environment.

> **Note**
>
> Before proceeding, make a copy of your progress.ini file before editing it in order to be able to restore it later.

To open an editor window from the UIB, choose Tools, New Procedure Window.

Open the file \dlc\bin\progress.ini in the PROGRESS editor. Change the `DefaultFont` and `DefaultFixedFont` (see fig. 6.8).

Fig. 6.8

Progress.ini default font changes.

Next, alter the font list section, which is 2-3 pages into the .ini file. Alter Font 0 and Font 1 to use Courier New and MS Sans Serif, respectively (see fig. 6.9).

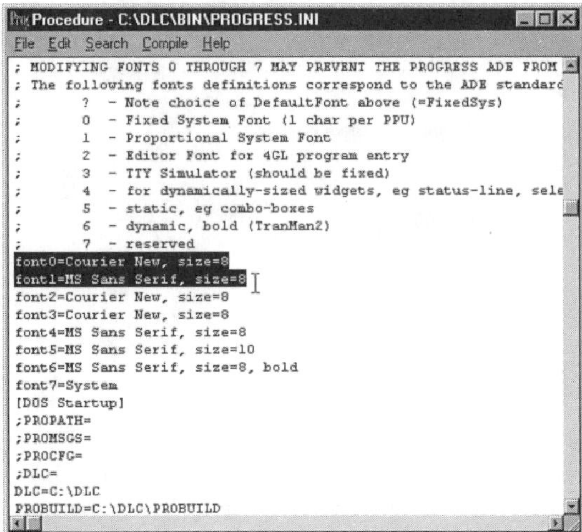

Fig. 6.9

Changing the font properties.

After changing progress.ini, you must exit and return to PROGRESS for the changes to take effect. You are now ready to use the PROGRESS environment using the newly selected fonts. PROGRESS uses fonts 0, 1, and the "default" fonts listed in progress.ini for the ADE tools. PROGRESS does not warrant that the tools will be geometrically correct while using *any* font, so be cautious.

> **Note**
>
> Before the changes to progress.ini take effect, you must restart your PROGRESS session.

Exit PROGRESS and return to the UIB to begin creating this chapter's SmartObjects. Be sure to connect to the sports database as usual.

Creating a Customer SmartViewer

The first SmartObject that you will create is a SmartViewer. The SmartViewer presents data by field, usually for data entry. The SmartViewer is the object of choice when displaying or altering data to be presented in nontabular form.

From the UIB's main window, click the New button to create a new object. The New Object list appears, as shown in figure 6.10.

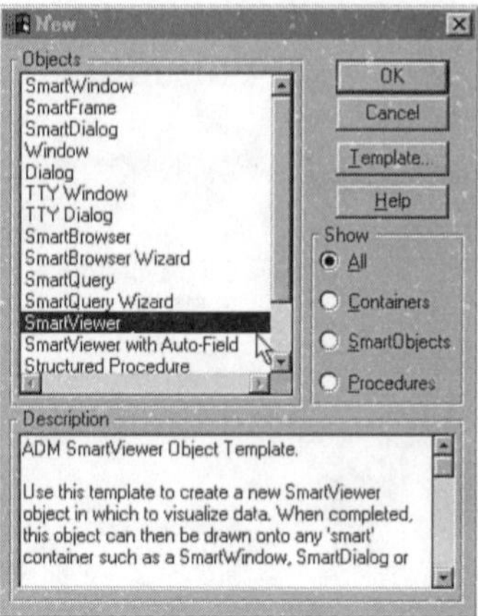

Fig. 6.10

Selecting a new type of object.

Choose SmartViewer to create a new instance or SmartObject Master for Customer.

▶▶ See Chapter 8, "SmartObject Internals," for information on how the UIB generates the list of possible new object types. You will need this when creating your own SmartObject type (template).

After selecting SmartViewer as your new object type, you will be presented with an untitled SmartViewer template. Here you may place database fields and any of the many controls available on the palette.

For this SmartObject, you will click the db-fields button on the palette to select database fields. See the pointer in figure 6.11 for the location of the db-fields icon.

Tip

You may choose Menu, Options, Show Labels from the palette menu to easily view the names of each object on the palette.

Having selected the db-fields icon, position the mouse cursor over the new SmartViewer and click to insert db-fields.

Select the customer table within the Table Selector dialog box and choose the fields: `cust-num`, `state`, `city`, `discount`, `credit-limit`, as shown in figure 6.12.

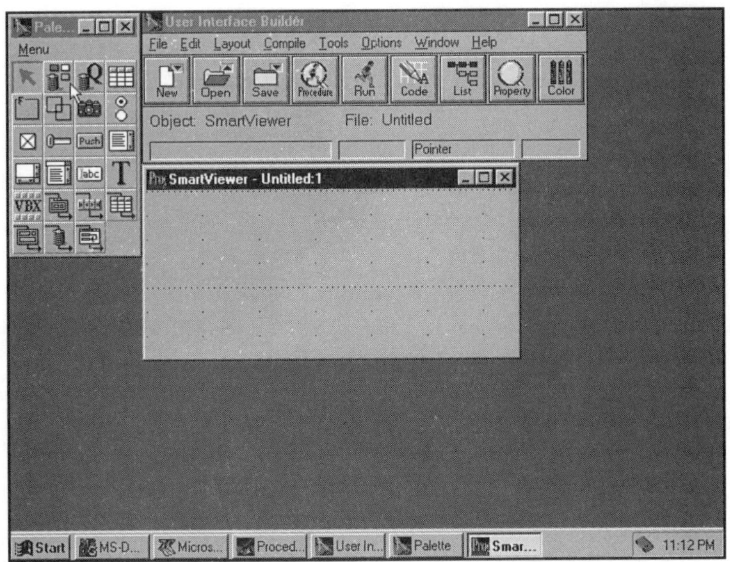

Fig. 6.11

The SmartViewer untitled template.

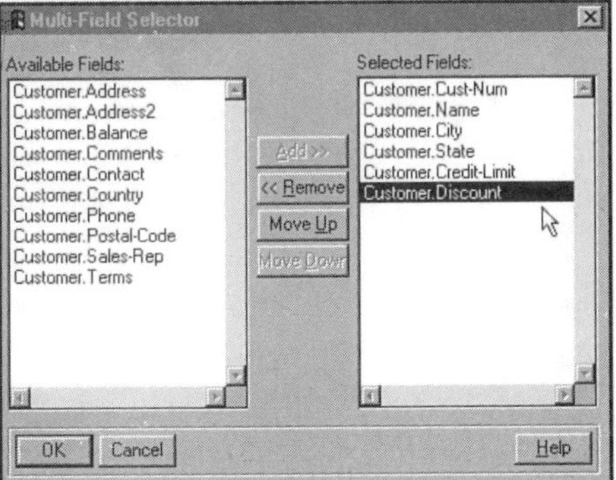

Fig. 6.12

Fields for the customer SmartViewer.

The UIB will position the fields in some best-guess location within the SmartViewer. Relocate the fields as shown in figure 6.13.

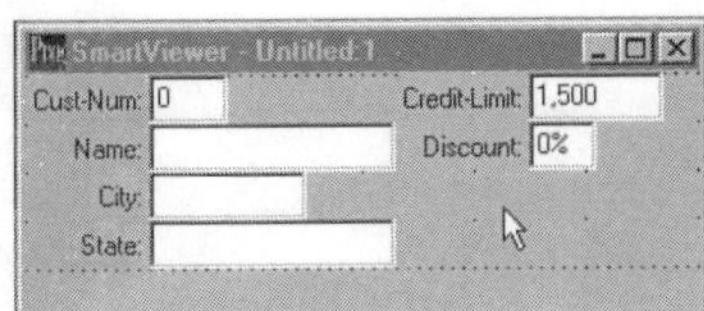

Fig. 6.13

Placement of customer fields.

You have completed the SmartViewer component. It is capable of displaying the chosen customer fields and storing them to the database if necessary. Save the SmartViewer as \appdir\v-cust.w.

You will notice that the UIB will show, in its main window status bar, "Saving" and "Compiling." The UIB will, by default, compile the SmartObject Masters to be able to run them quickly. You will find v-cust.w (the source code) and v-cust.r (the compiled code).

Creating an Order SmartViewer

Repeat the steps to create an Order SmartViewer. This is an instance or SmartObject Master for fields in the Order table.

Click New in the UIB main window to view the New Object selection list. Unlike the previous example, select SmartViewer with Auto Field. The Auto-Field feature automatically prompts you for the fields to use within the SmartObject.

Choose the Order fields: `order-num`, `order-date`, `promise-date`, `ship-date`, `terms`. Organize the fields so that they appear as shown in figure 6.14.

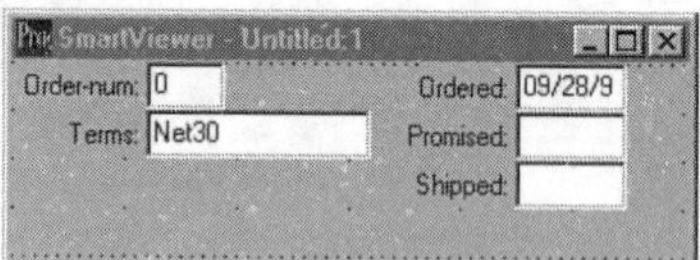

Fig. 6.14

The Order fields should look like this.

SmartViewer fields begin in the upper-left corner of the SmartViewer. This is because the SmartViewer is a component. It will eventually be placed within a window along with other components. There should not be any wasted space in the SmartViewer perimeter.

Save the Order SmartViewer as \appdir\v-order.w.

Creating a Customer SmartBrowser

Next, you will create a SmartBrowser Master for Customer. A SmartBrowser presents a list of records from a table or series of joined tables. The SmartBrowser is the object of choice for manipulating a tabular list of records and for record searches.

From the UIB's main window, click the New button to create a new object. Select SmartBrowser Wizard.

> **Tip**
>
> Wizards take the developer step-by-step through the creation of a SmartObject. You will find details on Wizards and their construction in Chapter 19, "Using Active Templates."

The Wizard will take you through the steps for creating your new SmartBrowser Master. Figure 6.15 shows the external tables (page 2) of the Wizard.

External tables are necessary when a SmartObject is dependent on external objects for data. In this case, the Customer SmartBrowser shows customer records from the customer table—no need for external table references.

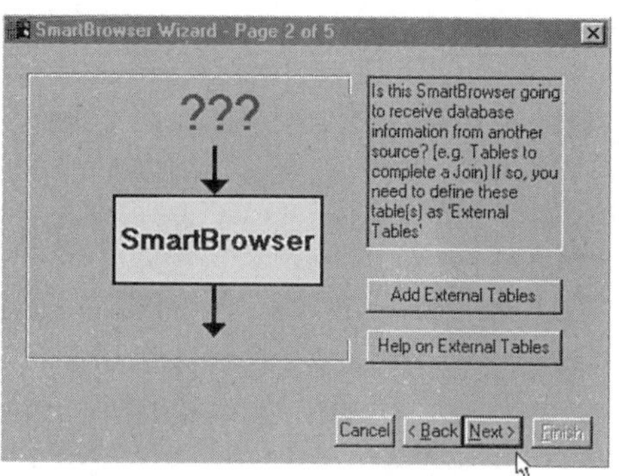

Fig. 6.15

The Wizard's External Table page.

The Wizard's page 3 shows the query for the SmartBrowser. Each SmartBrowser is associated with a query. The query dictates which records are shown, as well as the order in which they are presented.

Click Define Query and select the customer table for the query.

Proceeding to page 4 of the Wizard, you are prompted for Fields to display. Click Add Fields. Select the fields `cust-num`, `name`, `city`, `state`, and `phone` from the add fields selection screen.

Click OK to proceed to the last page of the Wizard, which congratulates you on the completion of the SmartBrowser.

Now that the SmartBrowser is completed, press F2 to test-run it. SmartObjects, such as the SmartBrowser, that are not dependent on external data sources can be tested as stand-alone objects.

Figure 6.16 shows the SmartBrowser running in a test window.

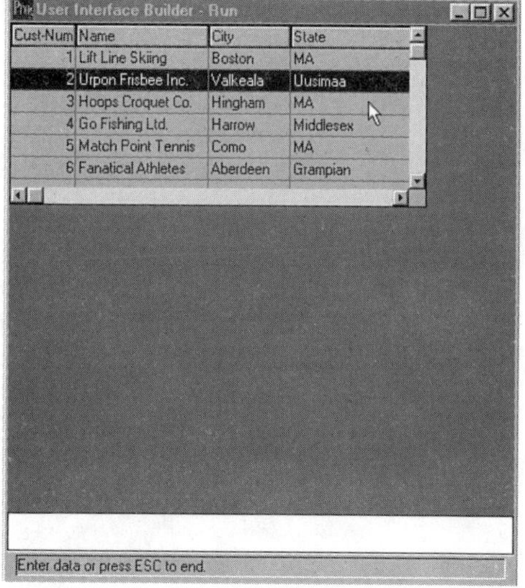

Fig. 6.16

The Customer SmartBrowser running.

Save your SmartBrowser as \appdir\b-cust.w.

Creating a SmartQuery for Orders Records of Customer

Next, you will create a SmartQuery for Orders of Customer. The intent is to display order records for a given customer. In this case, customer will be an external table. This will allow the SmartQuery to receive messages telling it which customer to show records for. You will learn about messages in great detail in Chapter 7, "SmartObject Links and Messages."

From the UIB's main window, click the New button to create a new object. Select SmartQuery Wizard.

On page 2 of the SmartQuery Wizard, click Add External Tables and select Customer.

Next, you will define the actual query for the SmartQuery. Click Define Query and add the Order Table so that the list appears as shown in figure 6.17.

Fig. 6.17

Tables selected for the query.

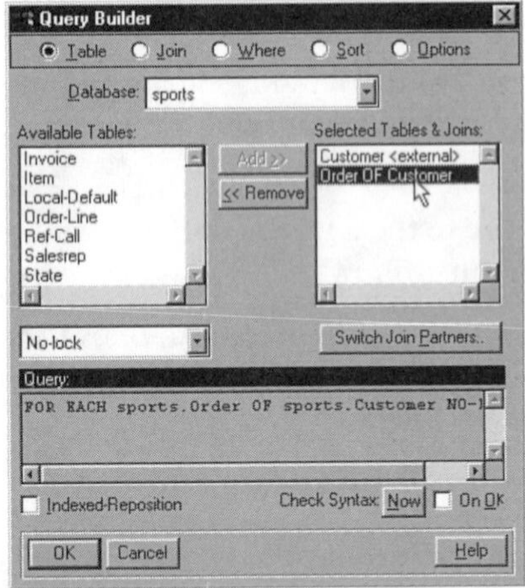

Notice that customer was labeled as "external." This is because you designated the customer table as an external table in page 2 of the Wizard.

Save your SmartQuery as \appdir\q-ordofc.w.

You have completed the construction of the SmartObject for this chapter. Next you will connect the SmartObjects to form functional interfaces. You did not need to know the design for the interfaces in order to construct the components. PROGRESS SmartObjects are ready to be "plugged" together and communicate effectively.

In Chapter 7, "SmartObject Links and Messages," you will learn about how the SmartObjects communicate and function together.

Connecting the Components

In this section, you'll connect your SmartObjects together to form a simple file maintenance screen and a more complex folder tab interface. As promised earlier in this chapter, the complexity of the overall interface does not affect the individual SmartObjects. The *same* SmartObjects will be used for the simple and complex interfaces.

Because it is often helpful to see the end product before building it, figure 6.18 shows the simple customer maintenance screen.

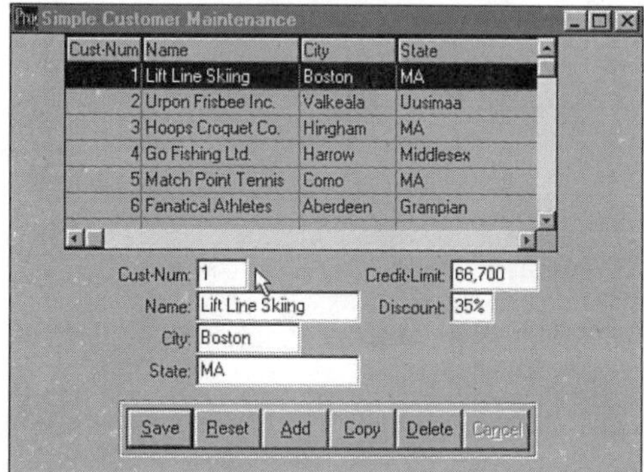

Fig. 6.18

The customer maintenance screen.

The customer SmartBrowser and SmartViewer are connected along with a SmartPanel, which directs the maintenance functions. You will no doubt require a screen such as this for a significant percentage of your working tables.

Tip

In Chapter 21, "Making the Most of the Application Component Environment," you will learn how to parameterize your screens so that they can use various SmartObjects defined at runtime. This means that you will have one screen, such as the Customer maintenance example above, that may be used as maintenance for several tables.

The next interface is significantly more complex. It presents a folder tab allowing the user to view customers and orders. Figure 6.19 shows the interface with customer tab active.

This allows the user to view customer information and to scroll through customer records using the browser in the upper section of the screen. Notice the Customer SmartBrowser and SmartViewer connected.

Figure 6.20 shows the second tab with Order SmartViewer and a SmartPanel to allow the user to navigate through the orders of the given customer.

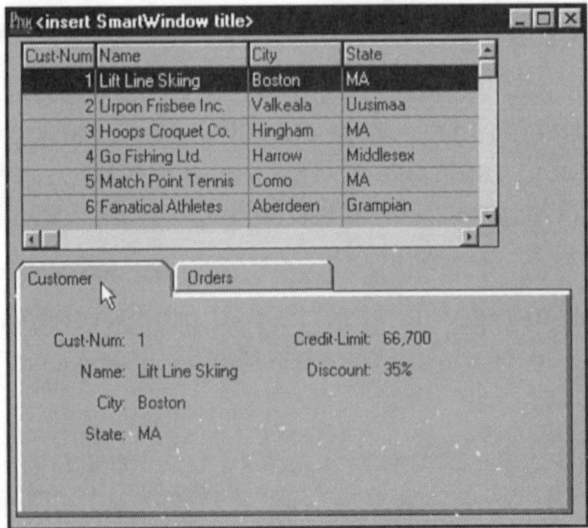

Fig. 6.19

The customer folder tab interface.

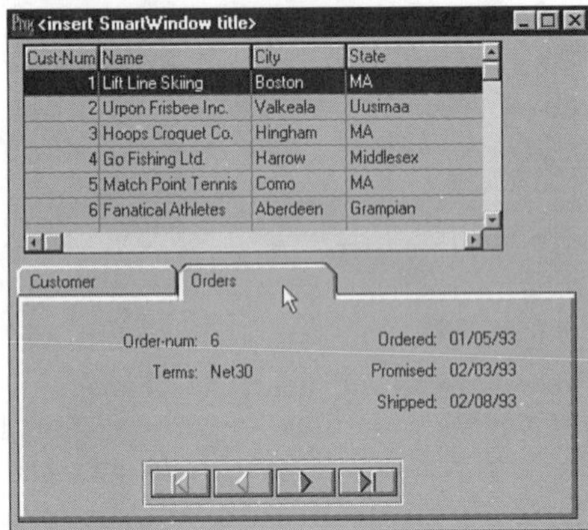

Fig. 6.20

The second tab of the interface.

In the later example, the SmartObjects or components used are the same as in the first example. It is simply a matter of arranging them and connecting them in a different fashion.

You have seen how the tab-folder interface allows the developer to build an interface that presents a great deal of information on one screen. The tab-folder approach is the best approach when you have several related SmartObjects that can be placed on the same window and are best viewed as pages of information.

In the remaining section of this chapter, you will see how these screens are built using the SmartObjects created earlier.

Creating the Customer Maintenance Screen

The customer maintenance screen is comprised of three SmartObjects:

- Customer SmartBrowser
- Customer SmartViewer
- Save SmartPanel

The trick is to connect these three objects so that they communicate effectively. Most SmartObjects receive and/or send messages. In Chapter 7, "SmartObject Links and Messages," you will learn exactly how these messages travel.

1. Click New to create a new object.

   This time, you will be creating a SmartWindow. The SmartWindow is a special type of SmartObject called a *container*. Containers are SmartObjects that contain other SmartObjects.

2. Select new SmartWindow. It will start as shown in figure 6.21.

   Notice the Cue Card explaining the function and construction of a SmartWindow.

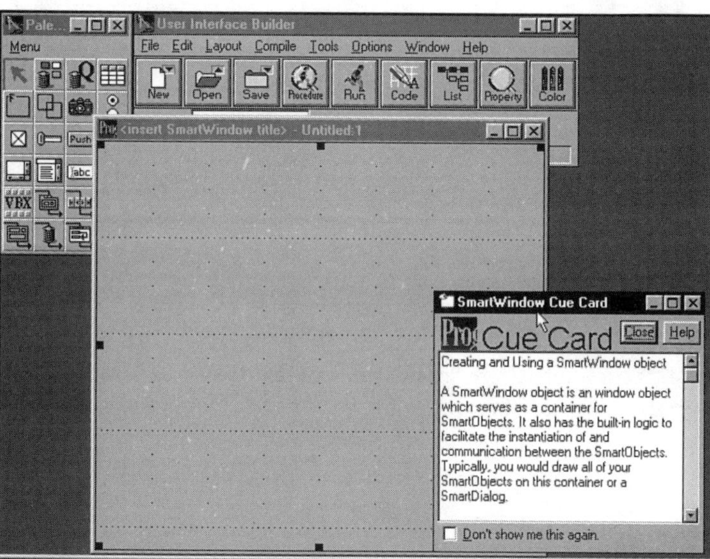

Fig. 6.21

The new SmartWindow with SmartWindow Cue Card.

Tip

In Chapter 19, you will learn how active templates are used to drive the SmartObject Cue Cards. The Cue Cards can help you create helpful new SmartObject types.

Note

It helps to click within the SmartWindow and select its frame before placing SmartObjects within it. This ensures that SmartObjects are placed on *top* of the SmartWindow's frame.

You are now ready to place your SmartObjects into the SmartWindow:

1. Click the SmartBrowser icon as pointed to in figure 6.22. Unless you are already connected to the sports database, you will be prompted to connect. Connect to your sports database.

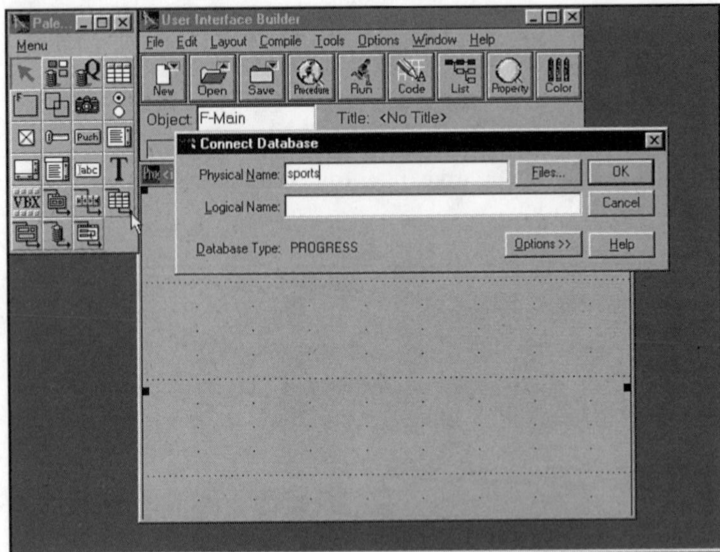

Fig. 6.22

Connecting to sports while selecting a SmartBrowser.

After the database has connected, the SmartBrowser selection process continues. The Choose SmartBrowser dialog box prompts you for SmartBrowsers in the working directory.

2. Click Browse to find the SmartBrowser b-cust.w where you saved it last.

> **Tip**
>
> In Chapter 8, "SmartObject Internals," you will learn how the SmartObject directories can be organized. The Choose SmartObject dialogs of the UIB can point to your working development directories to allow you to locate objects quickly.

3. After b-cust.w is selected, click in the SmartWindow to place it as shown in figure 6.23.
4. Repeat the process for the customer SmartViewer. If you cannot locate the SmartViewer icon within the UIB palette, choose Menu, Options, Show Labels. This will expand the palette to make it easier to learn the palette icons.
5. Choose the Customer SmartViewer v-cust.w and place it below the Smart Browser. Before positioning the SmartObject, the UIB will prompt you to *link* the SmartObjects, as shown figure 6.24.

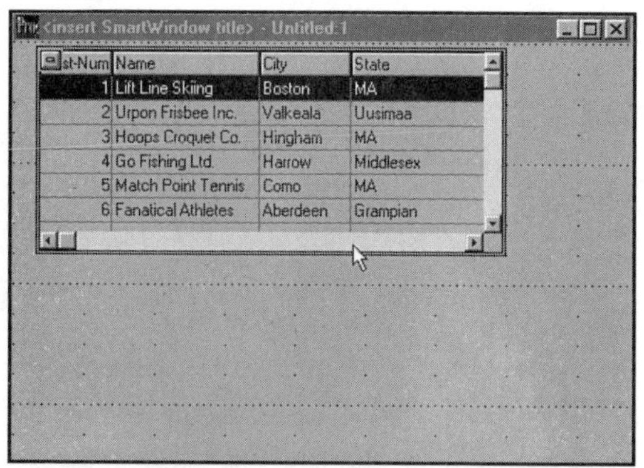

Fig. 6.23

The SmartBrowser placed within the SmartWindow.

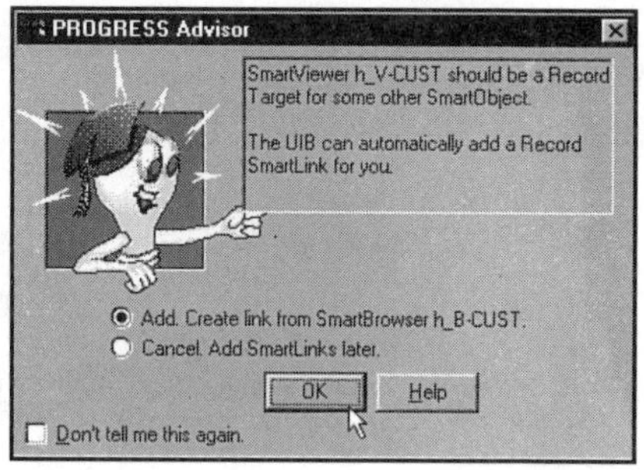

Fig. 6.24

The UIB's Link Advisor in action. You are prompted for the link between the Customer SmartBrowser and SmartViewer.

6. Choose the default option as shown and click OK. The two SmartObjects are now connected. This will allow the SmartBrowser to send records to the SmartViewer.

▸▸ In Chapter 7, "SmartObject Links and Messages," you will explore the details of how SmartObjects communicate.

The last SmartObject you need is the SmartPanel. You need a SmartPanel that allows the user to maintain the customer records. Functions such as save, delete, and copy should appear on the panel.

1. Click the SmartPanel icon on the palette. Choose p-updsav.w.

   The SmartPanel list shows the SmartPanels provided with PROGRESS V8. Each serves a unique function. (Chapter 9, "A Sample GUI Application," explores the available SmartPanels further.)

2. The UIB's Link Advisor prompts you for a link between the SmartPanel and the SmartViewer. Choose the default link, and the SmartPanel will send messages to the customer SmartViewer.

3. Press F2 to run the customer file maintenance screen. The SmartObjects work seamlessly together to produce a functional screen. Save the window as \appdir\w-win1.w.

Next you will compose a more complex interface using tab folders.

Creating the Tab Folder Screen

Here's how you create a Tab folder screen:

1. Click New to start a new SmartWindow. Much like the last example, the SmartWindow will be the container for your tab folder interface.
2. Click the SmartFolder icon and position the folder as shown in figure 6.25. Resize the SmartWindow and SmartFolder as shown in order to have adequate room.

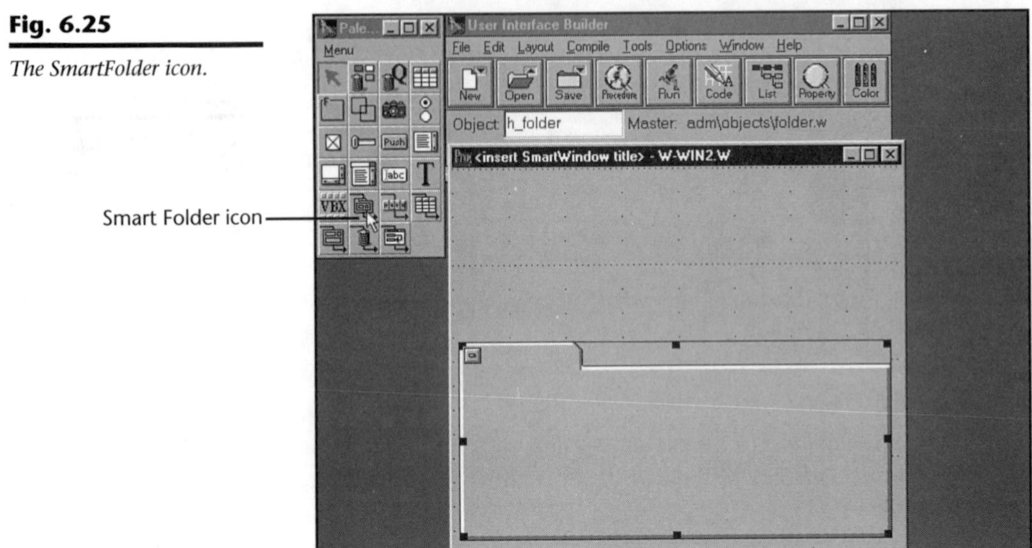

Fig. 6.25

The SmartFolder icon.

You will place the Customer SmartBrowser above the folder. The folder will have two tabs. The first tab will present the Customer SmartViewer. The second tab will present the Order SmartViewer and the navigation SmartPanel. This will allow the user to view customer records as well as related orders on the same screen.

You will learn more about folder screens and their workings in Chapter 8, "SmartObject Internals," and Chapter 10, "Connecting the Components."

For this exercise, choose default links for the Link Advisor. The instructions will be slightly abbreviated because the steps have been presented for the last example.

Place the customer SmartBrowser above the SmartFolder as shown in figure 6.26.

The next step is to place SmartObjects within page 1 of the SmartWindow. All SmartWindows are capable of managing multiple pages of SmartObjects.

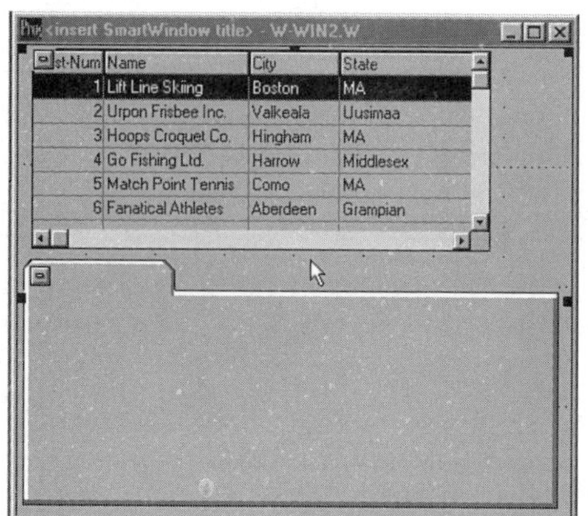

Fig. 6.26

The SmartBrowser placed above the SmartFolder.

▶▶ Chapter 10, "Connecting the Components," shows you much more on pages and Tab folders.

A quick way to select which page to place SmartObjects in is to double-click within the page area of the UIB's main window (it should indicate "Page 0"). Place the customer SmartViewer within page 1, as shown in figure 6.27.

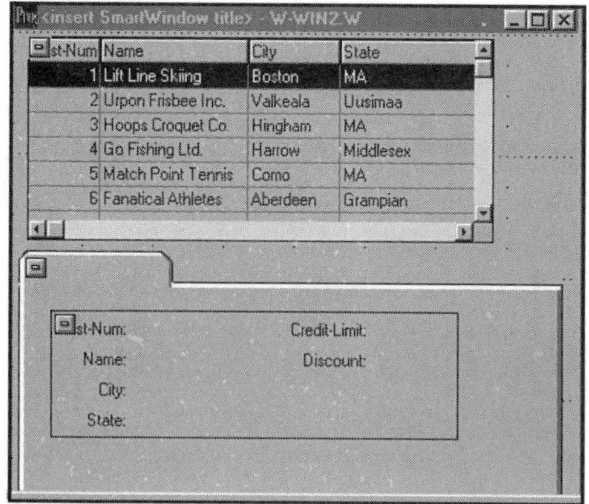

Fig. 6.27

The SmartViewer on page 1.

Double-click on the page area to set page 2. Place the SmartQuery q-ordofc.w within the SmartFolder. Place the Order SmartViewer v-order.w on page 2 also. Upon placing the SmartQuery, the Link Advisor will present you with two viable options to connect the query with a record source. Choose the default choice that connects the Order SmartViewer with the Customer SmartBrowser.

> **Note**
>
> Although the SmartObjects for each page were placed within the confines of the SmartFolder, this does not mean that the SmartFolder parents the SmartObjects. The SmartWindow contains the SmartObjects, whereas the SmartFolder determines which page is shown.

Press F2 to run the tab folder interface. Click the tabs to switch pages. An interface may have several tabs with several SmartObjects placed throughout the pages.

In Chapter 8, "SmartObject Internals," the mechanics behind SmartObject pages will be explored further.

You have now completed the chapter on SmartObjects. You have explored the theory behind SmartObjects and component-based development, and you have put it to good use in the examples.

Both screens and all the contained SmartObjects were created without *any code*. In what other development environment can you create interfaces such as these without any code at all? Notice that the SmartObjects could have been created separately, by different programmers in different locations.

Save the tab-folder window as \appdir\w-winZ.w using File, Save As.

From Here...

In this chapter you learned the evolutionary phases of a development team striving for ultimate efficiency and productivity. You began working with V8's SmartObject technology. You put together components to create working interfaces, without writing code. You even created tab-folder interfaces like those popularized by Windows 95. These allow you to place many pages of information on a single screen.

In the next chapter, you will learn about SmartObject links and messages. The links and messages between SmartObjects are essential to the encapsulation and organization of your development efforts.

For more information, see the following chapters:

- Chapter 7, "SmartObject Links and Messages," explores SmartObject communication in greater depth and detail.
- Chapter 8, "SmartObject Internals," brings you inside the mechanics of the SmartObjects. Learn what lies under the hood.
- Chapter 9, "A Sample GUI Application," discusses many of the topics covered in this chapter in much greater detail. In the later section on the sample application, you will put your V8 skills to further use.
- Chapter 10, "Connecting the Components," shows you more detail on linking SmartObjects together to form a working interface.

CHAPTER 7

SmartObject Links and Messages

SmartObjects depend completely on their links to other objects and the messages passed through those links. Without links and messages, the SmartObjects would not function together.

In this chapter, you will learn about the essential elements of linking the SmartObjects together and the messages passed through those links. You may use predefined links with which the ADM is familiar, or create your own *new links* that carry unique messages.

After reading this chapter, you will be able to:

- Understand how links work and are established
- Understand how messages are passed between SmartObjects
- Use `dispatch` and `notify` to send messages
- Explain the different methods used to launch messages
- Understand how to define new link types to customize the ADM communication channels
- Understand the power of SmartObject *State Messages*

Voice-of-Experience Movies

See Table G.3 in Appendix G, "Contents of CD," for a list of the Voice-of-Experience files for this chapter.

Understanding Encapsulation of Objects

As discussed in Chapter 1, "Introducing PROGRESS," encapsulation is a means to a highly organized development effort. By encapsulating objects, the developer assures that the object will be as follows:

- Self contained
- Able to be maintained as a single unit of work

- Largely unaffected by changes outside of itself
- Highly reusable
- Easily swapped with another compatible object

In the customer file maintenance screen presented in the last chapter, each SmartObject was encapsulated.

The SmartObjects were created independently. The order of their development was of no importance. The SmartObjects do not interact with their surroundings besides the messages they receive through the links.

Understanding the value of encapsulation leads the developer to learn more about links. The SmartObjects make use of links that PROGRESS calls *SmartLinks*. In this book I often refer to them simply as *links*.

Setting Up SmartLinks

In Chapter 1, the analogy of a light switch was used to illustrate message passing. Using that example, you imagine a link between the light switch and the light bulb. The link enabled the transmission of messages *from* the light switch *to* the light bulb.

Fig. 7.1

The light switch to light bulb link.

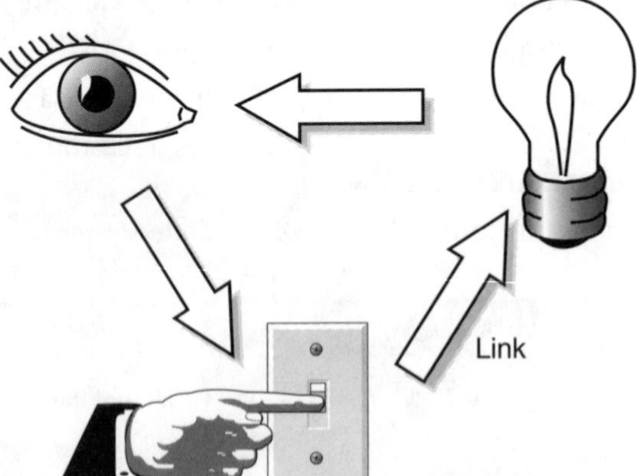

In this case, the light switch is the link *source*, whereas the light bulb is the link *target*.

The following definitions apply:

- *Link Source:* The SmartObject that sends messages into the link.
- *Link Target:* The SmartObject that receives messages from the link.

In the example, imagine a unique *link type* between the two objects. This link type sends messages such as ON or OFF. If a link existed between the eye and the light bulb, it would send messages such as SEE-LIGHT and MEASURE-BRIGHTNESS, for example.

Each link type has an associated name. The link between light switch and light bulb could be called INTENSITY. This allows you to name and identify links between objects. There is no implicit correlation between a link name and the messages that can traverse through it.

If you replaced a light switch with a dimmer switch, the dimmer and light bulb would still be connected through the INTENSITY link as before. The dimmer would send different messages to the light bulb because its functionality is more complex.

If you replaced a light bulb with a radio, the dimmer switch would send messages through the same INTENSITY link to drive the volume of the radio.

As you can see, SmartLinks are passageways between objects without regard to the specific messages that travel across. The name of the link is significant in that it states the general connectivity implied. If the link described in this example were called ON-OFF it would be misleading for any *source* objects other than those with only two possible messages (On and Off, 0 and 1, and so on).

Using Links Between SmartObjects

Links exist between SmartObjects in the same way as they were imagined in the preceding example. SmartObject Links, or SmartLinks, have names and the UIB is capable of alerting the developer of implicit links that should be placed between SmartObjects.

In figure 7.2, the UIB's Link Advisor is prompting the developer to establish a link between the Customer SmartBrowser and the Customer SmartViewer.

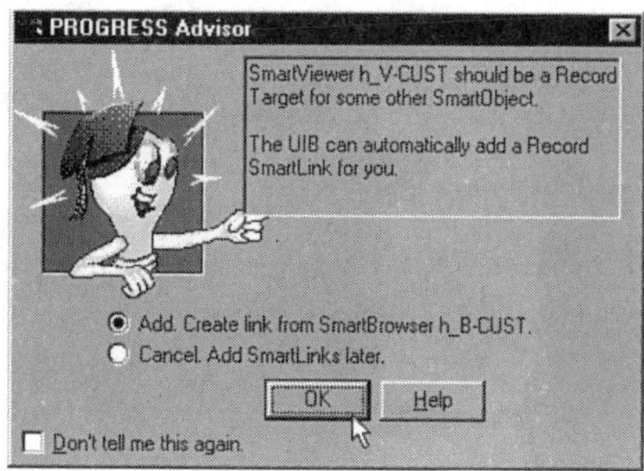

Fig. 7.2

The Link Advisor.

The advisor states quite clearly in its text:

```
SmartViewer h_V-CUST should be a Record Target for some other SmartObject.
The UIB can automatically add a Record SmartLink for you.
```

It suggests establishing a record link between the SmartBrowser `b-cust` and the SmartViewer `v-cust`. The *Record* Link is a specific type of link that is associated with messages carrying records. By being linked with a Record Link, the SmartViewer will receive the current customer record from the SmartBrowser and thus be able to display it.

Remembering the terms listed previously, the SmartBrowser is the *record source*; it is the source for the link and the source of messages through that link.

The SmartViewer, as pointed out by the Advisor, is the *record target* and will receive messages through the record link.

How does the Link Advisor or the UIB know that the SmartViewer is a record target? Inside each SmartObject template, the possible source and target link types are listed. Each SmartObject is thus predisposed to a set list of possible source and target possibilities.

Tip

In Chapter 8, "SmartObject Internals," you will learn precisely how the source and target link types are defined within a SmartObject's template.

Not only does the UIB know that the SmartViewer is a possible target of the link type "record," it also knows that the SmartViewer is dependent on a record source for customer records. This is because the SmartViewer has customer as an external table. Although you never explicitly defined customer as an external table, the SmartViewer automatically defined it upon the addition of customer fields within the SmartViewer.

You will recall that the Orders of Customer SmartQuery has an external table of customer as well. The Link Advisor would prompt the developer for a record source if the SmartQuery q-ordofc is placed in a container that has a record source for customer. Such a source could be the customer SmartBrowser.

Returning to the earlier analogy, the addition of another light would prompt the developer (or, in this case, the interior designer) for a possible INTENSITY source for the new light. It would possibly default to the light switch for the INTENSITY source.

Otherwise, if you added a television object, you would likely *not* be prompted for the light switch as the INTENSITY source. The television would not be associated with link types of INTENSITY because televisions are controlled by remotes and are sent entirely different messages.

In the customer file maintenance screen shown in the previous chapter, the SmartPanel is linked to the Customer SmartViewer using a different link type called `TABLEIO`. The `TABLEIO` link connects objects that are intended to pass messages pertaining to maintenance functions. Such functions include new, copy, delete, undo, commit, and others generally associated with table input/output.

The following is a review of the links in the customer maintenance screen.

- The SmartBrowser is a record source.
- The SmartViewer is a record target.
- A SmartLink exists between the SmartBrowser and the SmartViewer so that messages pertaining to the customer can be passed.
- The SmartPanel is a `TABLEIO` source.
- The SmartViewer is a `TABLEIO` target.
- A SmartLink exists between the SmartPanel and the SmartViewer so that messages pertaining to `TABLEIO` can be passed.

As a general rule, a SmartObject that acts as a target of any type of link is capable of acting upon the messages *received*. Thus, a SmartViewer should be able to display a record after it receives it. Also, the same SmartViewer is able to save or delete a record if given such a directive.

Tip

By understanding the functions necessary for a *target* SmartObject, you can deduce what functionality lies encapsulated within the object. Appendix B, "SmartObject Method Reference," lists all ADM events contained within the SmartObjects.

It is true that the SmartPanel itself knows nothing about customer records. It is not capable of saving the currently displayed customer record. It simply sends the message "save" through the `TABLEIO` link.

Setting Up Links to Multiple Targets

A SmartObject can be a source to several targets. This is very useful because you often will have the need to associate a source SmartObject with several targets.

In this section, you will create a new SmartViewer to display the customer comments field. This is a typical example of a SmartViewer that is highly reusable because you may require customer comments to appear in several screens. By encapsulating the functions associated with altering a customer's comments into an individual SmartObject, you increase organization and reusability.

To begin this section, you must:

- Have set your working directory (Chapter 1) to c:\appdir.
- Have copied the sample sports database into your working directory.
- Have started the PROGRESS User Interface Builder Tool.
- Have connected to the sports database.

Click New on the UIB main window. Select SmartViewer and add the customer.comments database field as shown in figure 7.3. You should also add a text widget to provide a label for the customer comments widget.

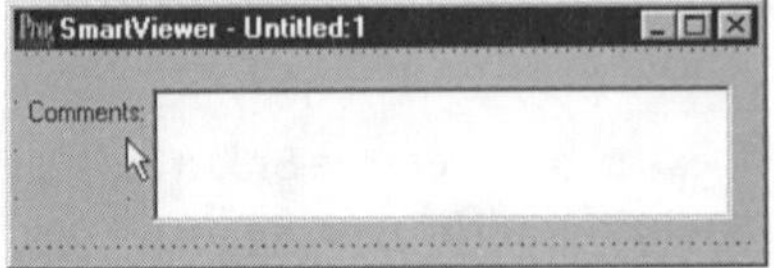

Fig. 7.3

The Customer Comments SmartViewer.

> **Note**
>
> Note that a text control "Comments:" was added to the left of the comments field. The comments field is viewed as an editor control because it is defined in the database that way.

Choose File, Save to save the new SmartViewer as \appdir\v-cmnts.w.

Open the window created in Chapter 6, "Utilizing Component-Based Development," saved as w-win1.w. You will insert the new SmartViewer into the window under the Customer SmartViewer. Expand the window as shown in figure 7.4. The Link Advisor will prompt you for a record *source* for the Customer Comments SmartViewer.

For this example, choose the SmartBrowser as the record source to demonstrate multiple targets.

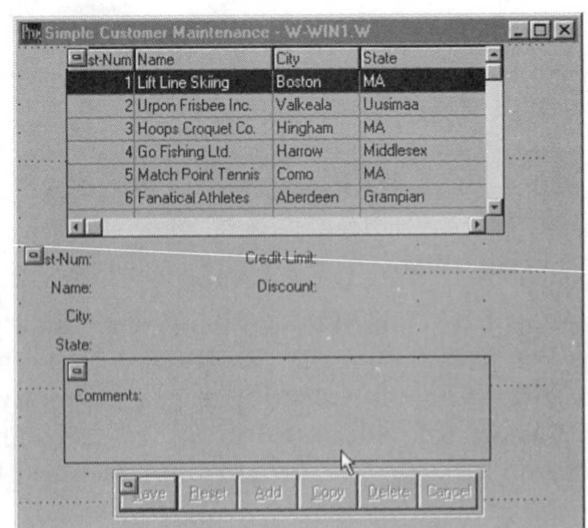

Fig. 7.4

The Customer Comments SmartViewer inserted into the customer maintenance screen.

Run the new maintenance screen by pressing F2. You will notice several characteristics of the resulting interface and the SmartObjects within:

- The Comment SmartViewer is not enabled.
- The file maintenance functions apply only to the Customer SmartViewer (because it is the only object linked to the Panel).

The running customer maintenance screen appears in figure 7.5.

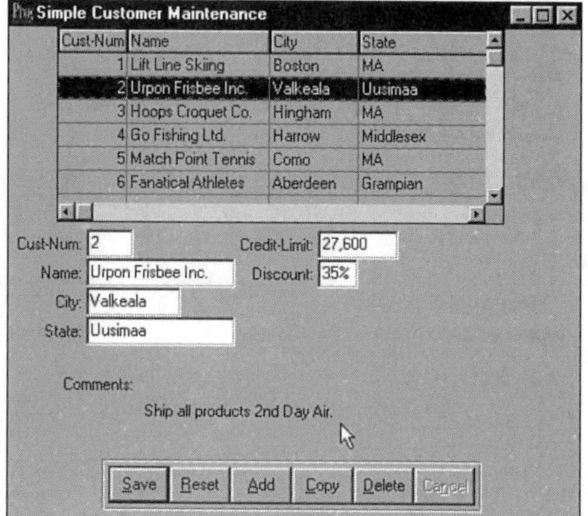

Fig. 7.6

The Customer Maintenance screen with the additional viewer.

The reason for the preceding characteristics is the communication between the panel and its targets. The panel sends messages to its targets, thereby enabling and disabling them. In general, a SmartViewer not connected to a SmartPanel will not be enabled for data entry. This is the case with your new Comments SmartViewer.

Nonetheless, the SmartBrowser has multiple targets for the link type record. You could easily have linked the SmartViewer for customer with the Comments SmartViewer as presented by the Link Advisor. It would have worked equally well. Often, you will find multiple source and target possibilities.

Tip

In Chapter 8, "SmartObject Internals," you will learn how a SmartLink source is capable of sending messages to multiple targets. You will also understand where the links are defined at runtime.

Using File, Save in the UIB, save your new customer maintenance window as \appdir\w-win3.w.

It is important to understand that the links defined during the component connections are stored within the SmartContainer (in this case,the SmartWindow). At execution time, the SmartWindow launches each SmartObject and then instructs these objects on their respective sources and targets. More detail on this subject in Chapter 8.

ADM Predefined Link Types

Within the ADM, several link types are prebuilt into every SmartObject. The suite of ADM SmartObjects shipped with V8 is prepackaged to send and receive ADM link messages.

The ADM predefined link types are like standard house wiring. Your home is prewired to accept outlets, phone connections, and door bells. Understanding this wiring allows you to connect electrical devices without much effort. It is important to remember that you can add new wiring and devices as well.

Table 7.1 shows the ADM predefined SmartLink types.

Table 7.1 ADM Predefined Link Types

ADM Link Type	Messages
RECORD	Record information
NAVIGATION	Navigation messages: Next, Prev, and soon
TABLEIO	Maintenance messages: Save, Copy, and so on
STATE	State information: No Record, Update Mode and so on
GROUP-ASSIGN	Messages grouping TABLEIO targets
CONTAINER	Container messages: View, Hide, and so on
PAGE	Messages from paging object; for example, folder
PAGE*n*	Messages to all SmartObjects in page *n*
(USER DEFINED)	Messages defined by developers

Table 7.2 shows an example source and target for the ADM link types. This is not a complete list of *all* possible sources and targets. Chapter 8 discusses how to determine all target and source combinations.

Table 7.2 ADM Predefined Link Type Examples

ADM Link Type	Possible Source	Target
RECORD	SmartBrowser	SmartViewer
The SmartBrowser sends the current record to the SmartViewer for display and possibly for maintenance.		
NAVIGATION	SmartPanel	SmartQuery
The SmartPanel (for example, p-navico) sends messages to reposition the query (for example next, prev, first, last).		
TABLEIO	SmartPanel	SmartViewer
The SmartPanel (for example, p-updsav) sends messages to manipulate the record within the SmartViewer (example save, undo, delete, copy).		
STATE	SmartViewer	SmartPanel
The SmartViewer sends a message about its state to the SmartPanel (for example, updating-record).		

ADM Link Type	Possible Source	Target
GROUP-ASSIGN	SmartViewer	SmartViewer
The SmartViewer sends maintenance messages (from TABLEIO) along to the target SmartViewer so that both viewers respond in tandem.		
CONTAINER	SmartWindow	SmartBrowser
The SmartWindow sends container messages (for example, hide, view, initialize) to the SmartBrowser. If the SmartWindow is hidden, the contained SmartBrowser is also hidden.		
PAGE	SmartFolder	SmartWindow
The SmartWindow receives messages from the SmartFolder indicating which page to display.		
PAGEn	SmartWindow	SmartViewer
The SmartViewer receives messages from the SmartWindow as the pages are selected (for example, hide, view).		

In Chapter 8, you will discover many of the messages that travel along these predefined links. You will learn how the ADM determines which links a message will traverse through, and under which circumstances.

Now that you understand the various possible link types, you will examine how to maintain these link connections with the UIB.

Managing Links with the UIB

You can manage links with the UIB without the Link Advisor. Remember that the Link Advisor activates only when SmartObjects are added. If you wanted to change the links for SmartObjects already placed into a SmartWindow you would need to alter their SmartLinks.

To alter SmartLinks, click the Ventilator button on any SmartObject within the window. Clicking the SmartViewer Ventilator produces the list shown in figure 7.6.

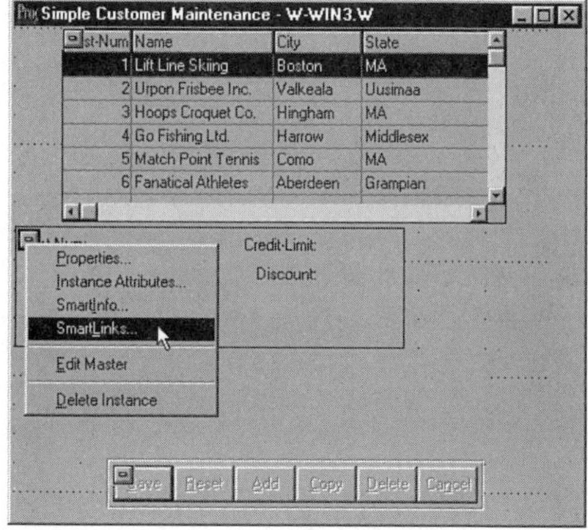

Fig. 7.6

The Ventilator button on the SmartObject produces a pull-down menu.

Choose SmartLinks to view all SmartLinks associated with the SmartObject or the window at large.

Click the radio set option, All Links, to view all links active within the SmartWindow. The SmartLinks window appears showing the SmartLinks defined for the interface.

From this screen, you can easily remove and add SmartLinks between existing SmartObjects. Click Add to view the Add a SmartLink screen (see fig. 7.7). Select the SmartBrowser on the leftmost list of possible *sources*. The possible link types are listed: `RECORD`, `STATE`, and `NEW`.

Fig. 7.7

The addition of a SmartLink.

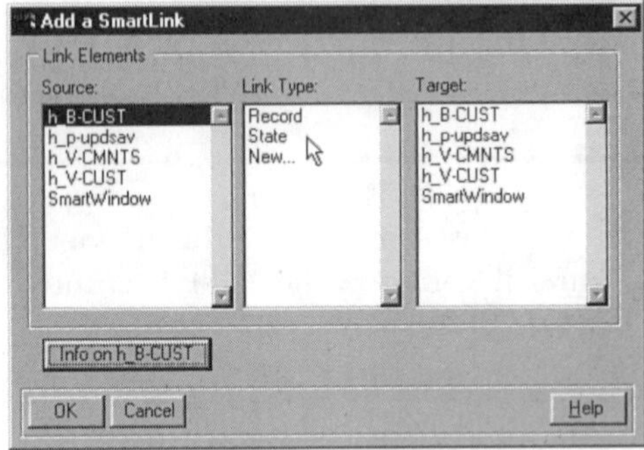

You have already experimented with the `RECORD` link type. The STATE link type is for messages indicating an object's *state*. The name of an object's state usually indicates the object's present action; for example, the state new-record indicates that the object is creating a new record. More information on states and state messages will be covered later in the chapter.

The `NEW` link type implies that you may want to add a new link type to connect SmartObjects. You may connect two SmartObjects with a new link type called `RECID`, which allows messages passing record `RECID`s, for example.

Tip

In Chapter 8, you will experiment with a new link type and send messages along the new link.

Click the Info on h_B-CUST button to view more detail regarding the SmartBrowser and its links. The SmartInfo windows will be displayed giving you information about the h_B-CUST source (see fig. 7.8). Note that h_B-CUST is simply a name given to the SmartBrowser. The h_ indicates that it is stored as a *handle,* similar to a pointer.

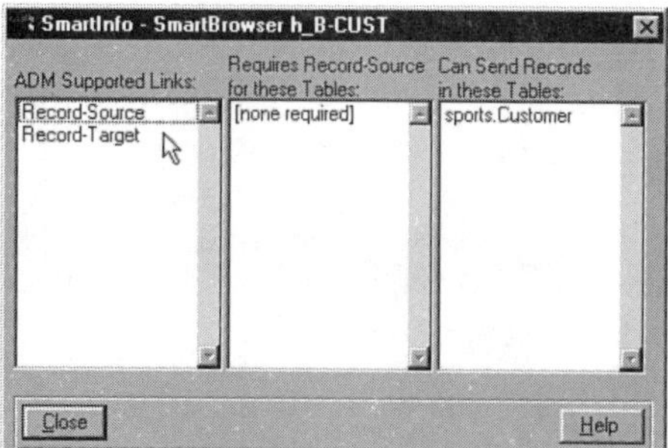

Fig. 7.8

The SmartLinks info screen.

> **Note**
>
> You may also access the SmartLinks by clicking Procedure in the UIB main window, and by clicking SmartLinks within the Procedure dialog.

Notice the sections displayed in the information screen:

- ADM Supported Links: Record Source, Record Target
- No Record Sources Required
- Can Send Customer Records

This tells the developer (and the UIB itself) the SmartLinks that are available to and from the SmartObject. In this case the SmartBrowser h_B-CUST can be a record source and a record target. This means that it can send records and receive records. No record sources are required since the SmartBrowser h_B-CUST has no external tables defined for it. The SmartInfor screen specifically states that records of type Customer can be sent by this SmartBrowser.

Examine the info screen for the other SmartObjects on the window to learn more about them.

Introduction to SmartObject Messages

You will now explore the world of SmartObject messages. Messages travel along SmartLinks. As discussed in the previous section, messages may travel along any link; in fact, all links are capable of transferring any message. In reality, however, each link has a list of messages that are likely to be found along its path. This helps organize the sometimes complex link and messaging structure.

An example of messages is the doorbell in your home. The doorbell is connected to a ringing device via electrical wires. Similar to the light switch and light bulb, these electrical wires are capable of carrying electrical signals of any kind (within reason, of course). The link between the doorbell and ringer may be called the BELL link. As you recall, the light switch link was called INTENSITY. Imagine also another link connecting intercom units in the home: INTERCOM.

Table 7.3 shows possible messages across the imaginary link types.

Table 7.3 Links and Messages

Link Type	Messages
BELL (door bell to ringer)	RING
INTENSITY (light switch to bulb)	BRIGHTER
	DARKER
INTERCOM (intercom to intercom)	SPEAK
	RECEIVE
	ATTENTION
	CHECK-STATUS

The physical electrical *wires* between these devices represent the *links*. You could certainly connect the door bell with an intercom. The message "RING" would be sent across the link; the target intercom would not respond to the message.

Similar to the preceding example, the ADM and the UIB will not prevent you from linking inappropriate devices together. The SmartObjects will simply send and receive messages without knowing who is on the other end of the link. Messages will be acted upon only if the receiving SmartObject is capable of responding.

You will learn that sending a message to a SmartObject that is not capable of responding *will not produce an error message*. This allows you greater overall flexibility in your component construction.

Note

SmartObjects will not produce an error message when unknown messages are sent to them. This is important to remember when debugging your programs since a spelling mistake in the name of a message could cause a problem without much notice.

Thus, messages usually follow along a prescribed link type.

Anatomy of a SmartObject Message

In this section, you will learn:

- How to compose a SmartObject message
- The various ways to send the message
- Naming conventions

A SmartObject message consists of the following parts:

1. The Link type across which the message will traverse
2. The message name; for example, "RING"
3. The method with which the message will be transmitted

Some of the parts listed here are often optional. It is important to understand the default as well as extended functionality built into messaging.

Using Notify to Send Messages

For a real example for SmartObject messaging, recall the page 2 object in Chapter 6's tab folder example. Load the tab-folder window using File, Open. Load the file saved in chapter 6 \appdir\w-win2.w. You can find this program on the CD in \examples\chap-06.

The SmartPanel is the `NAVIGATION` Source, whereas the SmartQuery is the `NAVIGATION` Target. As shown in figure 7.9, the `NAVIGATION` link is established so that the SmartPanel can send messages directly to the SmartQuery.

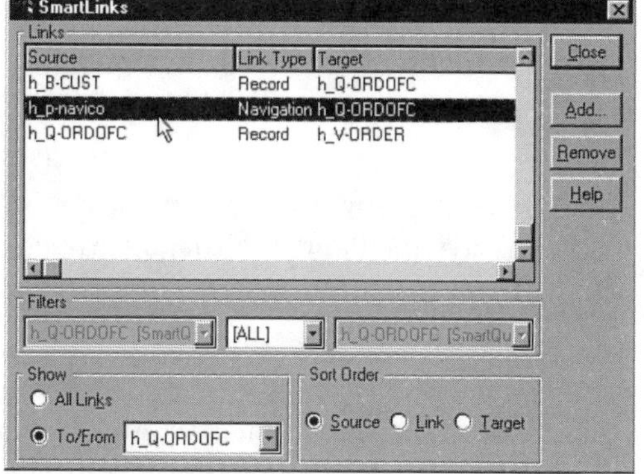

Fig. 7.9

Tab folder page 2 showing SmartQuery, SmartPanel, and SmartLinks dialog.

The SmartPanel p-navico is designed to send the following messages to its targets:

- `get-next`
- `get-prev`
- `get-first`
- `get-last`

Using the UIB's procedure window, you will examine the actual message passing code within the SmartPanel.

Choose Tools, New Procedure Window to start the Procedure Window. Open the file \dlc\src\adm\objects\p-navico.w, the navigation palette.

Locate the trigger for the button, `Btn-Next`. This is the code that sends the "next" message to all SmartPanel targets (if any).

The code follows:

```
ON CHOOSE OF Btn-Next IN FRAME Panel-Frame /* Next */
DO:
  RUN notify IN THIS-PROCEDURE (IF first-on-left THEN 'get-next':U
                                                  ELSE 'get-prev':U).
END.
```

The navigation SmartPanel is designed to allow the buttons to be reversed. Usually, the first record button is on the left. In certain international applications, the first record button should be on the right; the buttons are reversed. The variable *first-on-left* determines the orientation. Here, you assume that *first-on-left* is TRUE.

The essential statement for the message is as follows:

```
RUN notify IN THIS-PROCEDURE ('get-next':U).
```

The general syntax for the notify statement is as follows:

```
RUN notify [IN {procedure-handle}] ('{message-name}[,{link-names}]':U).
```

`notify` is an internal procedure found in all SmartObjects. It is used to send messages to a SmartObject's *targets*. Examine the structure of the `notify` statement carefully. The `IN {procedure-handle}` clause is optional. If omitted, `notify` will run in the SmartObject itself (a typical scenario).

In certain cases, it may be convenient to run `notify` from within another SmartObject. This is possible only if you have the handle to that SmartObject. Later in this chapter, you will learn how state messages return the target object's handle.

The `{message-name}` indicates the message to be sent. In the example, the message name is `get-next`. In all cases with ADM predefined links, the message name is related to the method within the target SmartObject. The SmartQuery contains a method called `adm-get-next`, which is called when the get-next message is sent. The exception to this is messages of type **STATE** where the message name is simply the name of the state.

▶▶ See Chapter 8 to learn how the ADM determines which method is called when ADM messages are sent between SmartObjects.

Continuing with the syntax analysis, the `{link-names}` clause is optional. You will find that ADM messages such as get-next travel along a predefined set of link types. In this case, the default link type is `NAVIGATION-TARGET`. The message `get-next` travels to the SmartObject's `NAVIGATION` target; the SmartQuery, for example.

The `:U` indicates that the string containing the message and link names is not to be translated by the translation manager tool.

Given the described syntax, the following statement:

```
RUN notify IN THIS-PROCEDURE ('get-next':U).
```

or, more simply:

```
RUN notify ('get-next':U).
```

will effectively send the "get-next" message to all of the SmartObject's targets of the NAVIGATION link.

It would also be valid to use the following statement:

```
RUN notify ('get-next,NAVIGATION-TARGET':U).
```

You may also provide a list of links such as 'get-next,NAVIGATION-TARGET,RECORD-TARGET' or use 'get-next,*' to transmit the message across all links!

This illustrates the various flavors and flexibility within the notify statement. Remember that all SmartObjects contain the notify internal procedure. This is because all SmartObjects inherit the functionality contained within the Method Library *smart.i*. This method library contains internal procedures such as notify.

You have learned that notify is used to send messages across the SmartLinks. Another mechanism exists to send messages more locally, used when a SmartObject is to send a message to itself or to one specific SmartObject whose handle is known.

Using Dispatch to Send Messages

dispatch is used to send messages to a SmartObject whose handle is known. Typically, this is used to send a message within a SmartObject. To understand the importance of dispatch, examine its function and syntax.

dispatch is found throughout all SmartObject method libraries. An example of dispatch is found within \dlc\src\adm\method\query.i. Following the examples used in the discussion on notify, focus your attention on the procedure adm-get-next. You will recall that this is the internal procedure called upon receiving the message 'get-next'.

In adm-get-next, if it becomes necessary to get the last record (if no next record is available, for example), the following statement executes:

```
RUN dispatch IN THIS-PROCEDURE ('get-last':U).
```

The general syntax for the dispatch statement is as follows:

```
RUN dispatch [IN {procedure-handle}] ('{message-name}':U).
```

Dispatch is an internal procedure found in all SmartObjects. It is used to send messages to a specific SmartObject pointed to by the procedure handle that dispatch is called in.

As with the structure of notify, dispatch will default the procedure-handle to THIS-PROCEDURE; that is, the SmartObject itself. As with the notify statement, the message name is related to the name of the internal procedure called as a result of the message.

The message `'get-last'` eventually causes the procedure `adm-get-next` to be called.

`Dispatch` determines whether the target SmartObject contains a *standard* version of the message. The standard version is prefixed by `adm-`. The standard method for `get-next` is `adm-get-next`. `Dispatch` then looks for a *local* version of the message prefixed by `local-`. Thus, the developer can program an internal procedure in the SmartQuery named `local-get-next` that will execute in place of `adm-get-next`.

The capability to run either the local or the standard method is the reason that `dispatch` is used, even in cases in which the method is called within the same SmartObject. You might ask: Why not use the simple `RUN` statement to call an internal procedure? The reason is so that local methods will be executed properly.

Creating Local Methods

Local methods defined within SmartObjects allow the programmer to add to the SmartObject's standard behavior. As you learned in the previous section, notify will look for a `local-` method prior to running an `adm-` method. Next, you will create a local `get-next` method and add to the standard behavior of the `get-next` method. This new code will be invoked when the SmartObject receives the `get-next` message.

Continuing your work upon \appdir\w-win2.w you will need to select the second page and create a new method for the SmartQuery. Using the second page of the tab folder window, click the ventilator button for the SmartQuery, as shown in figure 7.10. Clicking on the ventilator assures that the SmartObject is selected and highlighted.

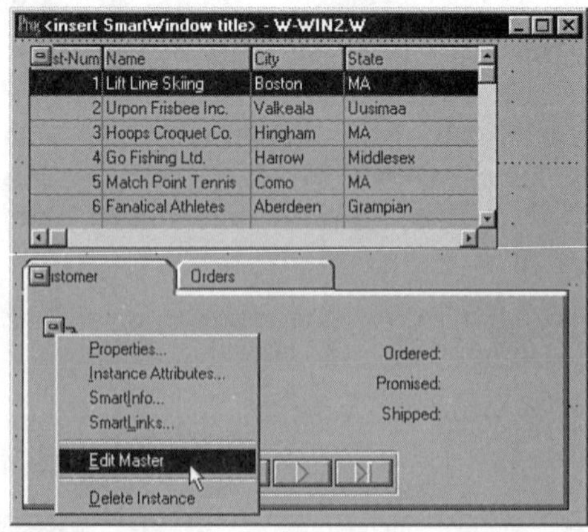

Fig. 7.10

Tab folder page 2 SmartQuery ventilator.

To add a method to the SmartQuery, you must edit the SmartObject's Master. Select Edit Master to load the SmartQuery master: q-ordofc.w in the UIB. You now have the ability to edit the SmartObject Master for the SmartQuery. Any changes made here will automatically be inherited by all other instances of the SmartQuery. This means that if you have used the SmartQuery `q-ordofc` in 10 SmartWindows, they would all upgrade immediately based on your changes to the master.

After the SmartQuery is loaded, click within it and click the Code button in the UIB main window to view the Section Editor (see fig. 7.11).

In the Section Editor, choose the Procedures section.

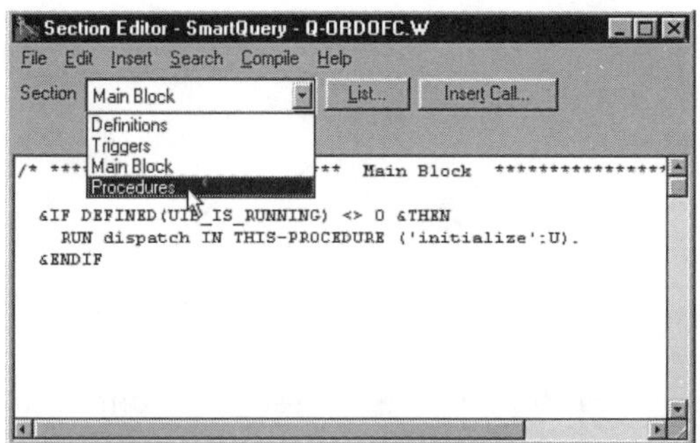

Fig. 7.11

The procedures section of the SmartQuery in the Section Editor.

Choose New to create a new procedure. Choose Local ADM Event to create the `local-get-next` method.

Note the code within `local-get-next` prepared for the developer upon creation of the new method.

```
/* Code placed here will execute PRIOR to standard behavior. */

  /* Dispatch standard ADM method.                             */
  RUN dispatch IN THIS-PROCEDURE ( INPUT 'get-next':U ) .

  /* Code placed here will execute AFTER standard behavior.    */
```

You have the opportunity to place code prior to the *standard* event (`get-next`) or after. By adding a simple alert box, you can test the functionality of the local event.

```
/* Code placed here will execute PRIOR to standard behavior. */
  MESSAGE 'Getting Next Record' VIEW-AS ALERT-BOX.

  /* Dispatch standard ADM method.                             */
  RUN dispatch IN THIS-PROCEDURE ( INPUT 'get-next':U ) .

  /* Code placed here will execute AFTER standard behavior.    */
```

This will cause a message to appear before the SmartQuery fetches the next record. You may place more significant code in a similar fashion.

Save the SmartQuery and run the tab folder window once again. Select page 2 and scroll through a customer's orders. The SmartPanel will send the `'get-next'` message to the SmartQuery (see fig. 7.12).

Fig. 7.12

The events and messages of the SmartPanel's `'get-next'`.

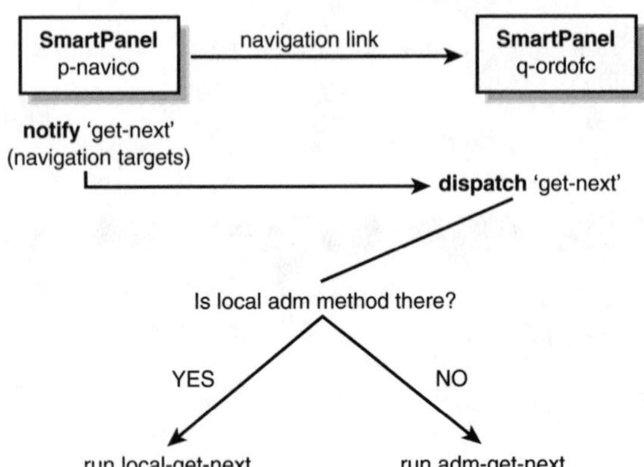

Experiment with defining various local ADM events. The Section Editor lists all possible ADM events that you can localize. As you learn more about local ADM events, remember the function of `dispatch` in calling the local or standard ADM events.

In the previous sections, you have learned:

> `notify` is used when a SmartObject wants to send a message across a specific link type to its targets. In using `notify`, the SmartObject is launching messages to its targets. Multiple links can be specified.
>
> `dispatch` is used when a SmartObject wants to send a message to a specific SmartObject *and* there is a need to check for *standard* or *local* events within the target.
>
> `{message-name}` used within `dispatch` or `notify` is the name of the event to call. In the case of a standard event, the prefix `adm-` is added. In the case of a local event, the prefix `local-` as added. A message name of `'get-next'` will run `adm-get-next` or `local-get-next`.
>
> `{link-name}` used within notify is the name of the specific link destination within a link type. Examples: `RECORD-TARGET`, `NAVIGATION-TARGET`, `NAVIGATION-SOURCE`. If the link is one of the predefined ADM links the ADM will default the link destination accordingly.

▶▶ Chapter 8 "SmartObject Internals," covers messaging and ADM links in greater detail.

Defining a SmartObject's Status with State Messages

State messages are messages passed along specific link types to convey a status of SmartObjects. It is often useful for a SmartObject to send out a state message letting any interested objects know that it has reached a particular status or state. For many objects in the design phases, you may design a State Transition Diagram (STD) that shows the various states the object might be in.

A television VCR, for example, can be in one of several states: OFF, ON, RECORD, PLAYBACK, PROGRAM, and so on. A SmartViewer may also transition through states such as `RECORD-AVAILABLE`, `NO-RECORD-AVAILABLE`, `NEW-RECORD`, and so on.

Tip

State messages allow for a high degree of encapsulation and keep your SmartObjects very organized.

Many state messages are part of the functional ADM. The standard SmartObjects send state messages that make part of the ADM's standard events. The event `'get-next'` is built into a SmartQuery and thus is part of standard events.

When a SmartViewer is showing no record, it sends a state message to any SmartPanel that is a source of `TABLEIO`. This allows the SmartPanel to gray out certain buttons that are not applicable if no record is available. Because this is standard behavior for ADM SmartPanel and SmartViewer, the state message travels along standard ADM links such as those listed in the previous links section. Chapter 8 covers the path of standard ADM state messages.

Any messages that are not part of the standard ADM functionality travel along links of type STATE. You will have a requirement to pass messages between SmartObjects in this manner.

In this section, you will add to the customer file maintenance window created in Chapter 6 (w-win1.w). You will use a state message between two SmartViewers. The result will be a customer file maintenance with a new SmartViewer showing a "Balance Details" button. This button will be used to show specifics pertaining to a customer's balance.

In this case, there is a requirement to have a SmartViewer whose purpose is to receive state messages of 'balance' and 'no-balance'. Upon receiving these messages, the button within the SmartViewer will enable or disable and the SmartViewer will cause the state source object to show its credit available.

The `balance` SmartViewer can be used along with any SmartObject that shows a balance and sends state messages of 'balance' or 'no-balance'. The `balance` SmartViewer is highly reusable and although it is relatively simple in this example, it could contain much more functionality in a true application.

Creating the New Balance SmartViewer

Create a new SmartViewer by clicking New and selecting SmartViewer in the new object dialog. The SmartViewer will contain a single button within it labeled Balance Details as shown in figure 7.13.

Fig. 7.13

The balance SmartViewer.

In order to respond to a state message, you need to alter the procedure `state-changed` in the Section Editor.

The `state-changed` procedure handles any new states sent to the SmartObject. The code handles either state `"balance"` or `"no-balance"` that will be received from the customer SmartViewer.

```
WHEN "balance" THEN DO:
     h_caller = p-issuer-hdl.
     BUTTON-1:SENSITIVE IN FRAME {&FRAME-NAME} = YES.
     END.
  WHEN "no-balance" THEN DO:
     BUTTON-1:SENSITIVE = NO.
     END.
```

Note that the first reference of `BUTTON-1` requires an `IN FRAME {&FRAME-NAME}` clause to specify which frame the button is in.

The variable `h_caller` is a handle that you will define in the Definitions section. It is set to the parameter `p-issuer-hdl`, which is the passed procedure handle for the object sending the state message.

> **Note**
>
> Objects receiving state messages in state-changed always have the handle of the SmartObject that sent the state message. The handle is in the input parameter `p-issuer-hdl`.

Click Definitions while remaining in the Section Editor and add the local variable as shown in figure 7.14.

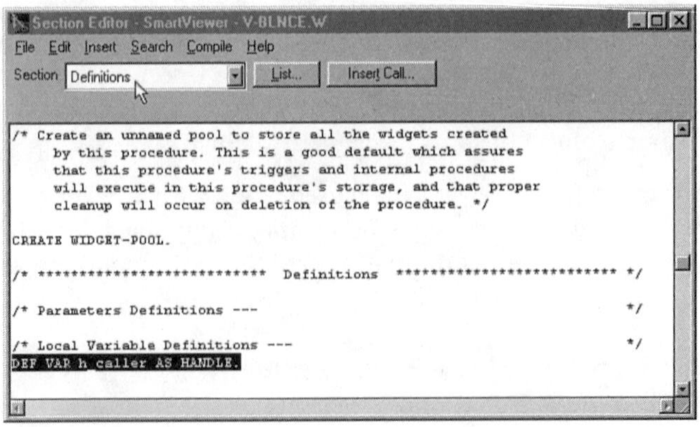

Fig. 7.14

The variable `h_caller` defined as a handle in the Definitions section of the Section Editor.

```
Section Editor - SmartViewer - V-BLNCE.W
File  Edit  Insert  Search  Compile  Help
Section  Definitions   List...   Insert Call...

/* Create an unnamed pool to store all the widgets created
     by this procedure. This is a good default which assures
     that this procedure's triggers and internal procedures
     will execute in this procedure's storage, and that proper
     cleanup will occur on deletion of the procedure. */

CREATE WIDGET-POOL.

/* ***************************  Definitions  ************************** */

/* Parameters Definitions ---                                           */

/* Local Variable Definitions ---                                       */
DEF VAR h_caller AS HANDLE.
```

Finally, you must add a CHOOSE trigger for the button. Upon clicking the button, the SmartViewer will run a procedure within the SmartViewer that sent the message. The purpose of this procedure is to show balance. It will be called `show_balance`.

Use the Section Editor to add a trigger for CHOOSE of the button. The trigger code is as follows:

```
RUN show_balance IN h_caller.
```

Save the new SmartViewer as \appdir\v-blnce.w.

Modifying the Customer SmartViewer

Next, you must open the original customer SmartViewer, v-cust.w, and modify it to send the appropriate state message regarding the customer's balance. Also, an internal procedure is required to show the available credit.

To send the state message of `"balance"` or `"no-balance"`, you must locate an appropriate *local* ADM event for the task. Because the ADM method `"display-fields"` is called as the SmartViewer displays a new record, it would be an opportune location to send the state messages.

Create a local ADM event called `"local-display-fields"` using the Section Editor. Select Procedures and click New. The select Local ADM Event will be displayed.

Add code to send the appropriate state messages. The `local-display-fields` will be as follows:

```
/* Code placed here will execute PRIOR to standard behavior. */

  /* Dispatch standard ADM method.                             */
  RUN dispatch IN THIS-PROCEDURE ( INPUT "display-fields":U ) .

  /* Code placed here will execute AFTER standard behavior.    */
IF AVAILABLE customer AND
   customer.balance > 0 THEN RUN new-state ("balance":U).
                        ELSE RUN new-state ("no-balance":U).
```

The last three lines of code send the appropriate state messages in case of balance.

The general syntax for the new-state statement is as follows:

```
RUN new-state [IN {procedure-handle}] ("'{state}[,{link-names}]"':U).
```

The optional `{link-name}` clause allows you to specify link types other than `STATE` that the state will pass through. This may be a comma-separated list, as was the case with the `notify` and `dispatch` statements.

Finally, you need to program the internal procedure `show_balance`, which will show the balance information if necessary.

Use the Section Editor to add a new procedure `show_balance`. The code for the procedure is simply:

```
message "Customer Credit Available:"
        STRING(customer.credit-limit - customer.balance,"$>>>,>>9.99").
```

Save the customer SmartViewer. You are now ready to put the new components together again.

Putting the Components Together with State Link

Edit the customer maintenance screen (w-win1.w) by adding the balance SmartViewer (v-blnce.w) as shown in figure 7.15.

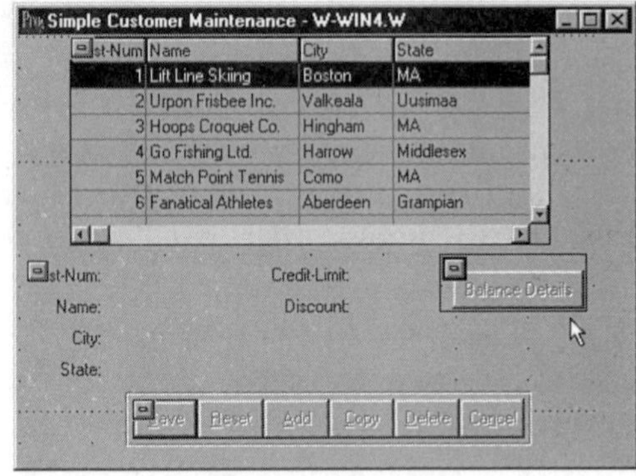

Fig. 7.15

The customer SmartViewer and the balance SmartViewer together on the customer maintenance screen.

Add a state link by clicking on the ventilator of either SmartViewer and selecting SmartLinks. Add a state link between the customer and balance SmartViewers as shown in figure 7.16.

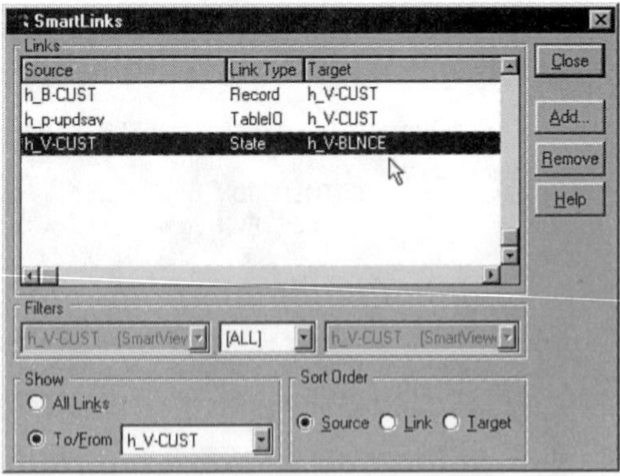

Fig. 7.16

The state link added between the SmartViewers.

Run the window by clicking F2. You will notice that the balance button enables and disables according to the customer balance. Clicking the balance button causes a credit available message to appear.

The `balance` SmartViewer is a classic example of state messages at work. The `balance` SmartViewer does not require any knowledge of the customer record; it requires only a message regarding the existence of a balance. The SmartViewer could be used in several different scenarios.

Save the Program using File, Save.

From Here...

In this chapter you learned the important role of encapsulation toward organized programming. You explored how ADM events use the SmartLinks to send messages between SmartObjects linked together. The dispatch and notify commands were explained and you learned about state messages.

For more information on related items, refer to the following chapters:

- Chapter 8, "SmartObject Internals," discusses the internal workings of SmartObjects and SmartLinks. Learn the code behind the ADM's functionality.
- Chapter 21, "Making the Most of the Application Component Environment," explores ways of maximizing the V8 environment.

CHAPTER 8

SmartObject Internals

This chapter takes you on an in-depth tour of the ADM internals. Step-by-step instructions demonstrate how you can view *all* of the source code that enabled SmartObjects to function.

In Chapter 6, "Utilizing Component-Based Development," you learned the theory and techniques involved in creating and connecting SmartObjects. In Chapter 7, "SmartObject Links and Messages," you discovered the power of SmartLinks and encapsulated objects. Now you will explore the internal workings of the Application Development Model.

Voice-of-Experience Movies

See Table G.3 in Appendix G, "Contents of CD," for a list of Voice-of-Experience files for this chapter.

The distinguishing factor for PROGRESS' V8, setting it apart from the competition, is the fact that it works by using PROGRESS code. Unlike other development environments whose inner workings are either proprietary or written in C, PROGRESS uses its 4GL for the ADM's internals. This allows the developer an unparalleled level of flexibility and options.

After reading this chapter, you should be able to do the following:

- Identify and understand the files associated with the ADM's functions
- Understand ADM Method Libraries and their location
- Know how to customize an ADM Method without changing the Progress-installed Method Libraries
- Know how to work with SmartObject templates
- Understand the effect of paging on ADM links
- Understand the workings of the ADM Broker
- Establish a new link type for messages

- Create SmartLinks dynamically
- Understand SmartObject attributes
- Customize the SmartObject instance attributes sheet

Locating Significant Application Development Model Files

This section describes the location and purpose of ADM files. This will help you customize and extend the model for your development requirements. Remember, the PROGRESS environment is written in the PROGRESS 4GL.

In describing the layout of ADM files, you will examine the ADM's directory structure.

ADM Directory Structure

Throughout this chapter, the Progress-installed main directory is assumed to be \DLC. \DLC is the default directory for installation. You may, of course, install PROGRESS on a different directory during the installation process.

Under the PROGRESS main directory (assumed here to be \DLC), the ADM files are located in two subdirectories:

1. \dlc\gui\adm for executable (.r) files
2. \dlc\src\adm for source (.w,.p,.i) files

> **Note**
>
> Throughout this chapter, you will see the backslash (\) being used for directory structures *except* where directory structures are shown from within PROGRESS code. PROGRESS uses the forward slash (/) for compatibility.

The ADM source directory contains numerous subdirectories which contain the working code for SmartObjects. The following table shows the name and contents of the source subdirectories.

Table 8.1 ADM Source Code Subdirectories

Subdirectory	Content
Method	Method Libraries and significant includes
Objects	SmartPanels, SmartFolder, and Broker
Samples	Sample SmartObjects
Support	Wizards, Instance Attribute Dialogs
Template	SmartObject Templates and low-level include files

Accessing the SmartObject Customer (.cst) File

When choosing New from the UIB main window, you are presented with a list of possible new objects. The list is comprised of SmartContainers, SmartObjects, and others. Where does this list come from?

The objects managed by the UIB in the palette are stored in two files in the \dlc\src\template directory:

- progress.cst, which contains definitions for the non-Smart objects on the palette
- smart.cst, which contains definitions for the SmartObjects

Using the UIB's Procedure Window, choose Tools, New Procedure Window and load the file \dlc\src\template\smart.cst, as shown in figure 8.1.

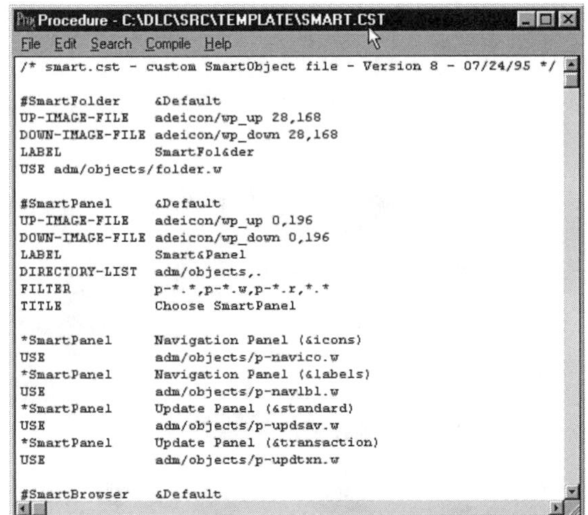


```
/* smart.cst - custom SmartObject file - Version 8 - 07/24/95 */

#SmartFolder     &Default
UP-IMAGE-FILE    adeicon/wp_up 28,168
DOWN-IMAGE-FILE  adeicon/wp_down 28,168
LABEL            SmartFol&der
USE adm/objects/folder.w

#SmartPanel      &Default
UP-IMAGE-FILE    adeicon/wp_up 0,196
DOWN-IMAGE-FILE  adeicon/wp_down 0,196
LABEL            Smart&Panel
DIRECTORY-LIST   adm/objects,.
FILTER           p-*.*,p-*.w,p-*.r,*.*
TITLE            Choose SmartPanel

*SmartPanel      Navigation Panel (&icons)
USE              adm/objects/p-navico.w
*SmartPanel      Navigation Panel (&labels)
USE              adm/objects/p-navlbl.w
*SmartPanel      Update Panel (&standard)
USE              adm/objects/p-updsav.w
*SmartPanel      Update Panel (&transaction)
USE              adm/objects/p-updtxn.w

#SmartBrowser    &Default
```

Fig. 8.1

Viewing smart.cst from a Procedure Window.

The .cst file contains definitions for all palette controls. Here you will find the information that the UIB uses to determine which SmartObjects are available, which templates are used, and so on.

See Chapter 20, "Extending the Development Tools," for more information on the UIB Object Palette and the .cst files.

SmartObject Templates

In Chapter 6, you learned about SmartObject Masters and SmartObject Templates. A SmartObject template is the starting point for a new SmartObject Master. The template is the *mold*; any objects created from the mold will start off with its characteristics. Any changes to the template have an impact on objects created only *after* the template is changed.

In the smart.cst file, you will find the following lines describing the SmartViewer:

```
*NEW-SMARTOBJECT Smart&Viewer
TYPE             SmartViewer
NEW-TEMPLATE     src/adm/template/viewer.w

*NEW-SMARTOBJECT Smart&Viewer with Auto-Field
TYPE             SmartViewer
NEW-TEMPLATE     src/adm/template/vieweraf.w
```

These describe the New SmartViewer and the possible templates. In the case of a regular SmartViewer (no Auto-Field option), the template shown is src/adm/template/viewer.w. In Chapter 4, "Introducing PROGRESS Language," you learned that PROGRESS often uses the forward slash (/) for compatibility with different operating systems.

The file \dlc\src\adm\template\viewer.w is the template used for new SmartViewers with no Auto-Field.

Open the SmartViewer template using the UIB File, Open.

After the template is loaded, click Procedure to view the Procedure Settings, as shown in figure 8.2.

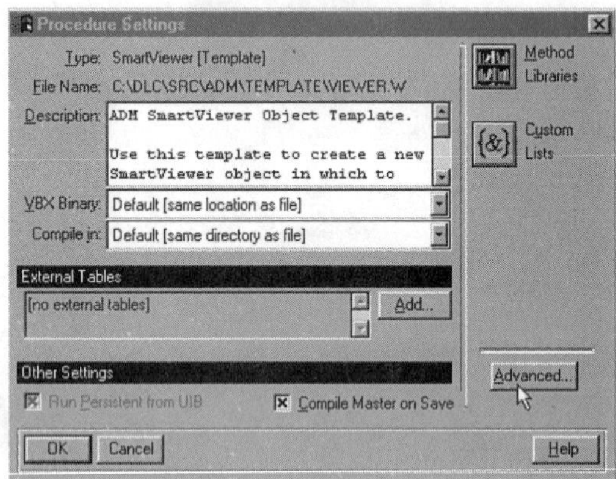

Fig. 8.2

The SmartViewer Template's Procedure Settings window.

Any changes done to the description, Method Libraries (which are discussed further on in this chapter), and Custom Lists will affect any subsequently created SmartViewers. Keep in mind that the Auto-Field SmartViewer template, vieweraf.w, would require changes as well. The Auto-Field SmartViewer template brings forward the field selection dialog to help in creating the SmartViewer (see fig. 8.3). It is a slightly different template although its ultimate purpose is equal. Changes to the SmartViewer template `viewer.w` need to be applied to the Auto-Field SmartViewer template `vieweraf.w` as well.

Click Advanced to view the Advanced Procedure Settings.

The following settings are available in the Advanced Procedure Settings. Note that most of the settings are read-only for the SmartViewer; the settings would be enabled for a newly defined template.

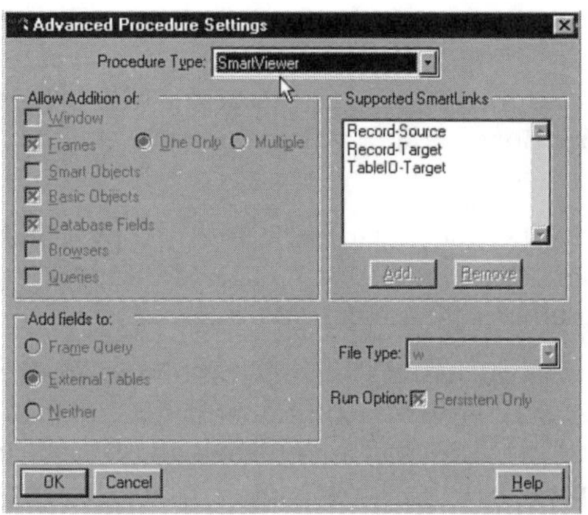

Fig. 8.3

SmartViewer Advanced Procedure Settings.

The following is a summary of the different sections on the Advanced Procedure Settings dailog box. Each section contains several individual settings:

- *Section "Allow Addition of:."* Controls that are allowed within the SmartObject type are listed. Note that Basic Objects are the window controls such as radio-set, buttons, text, and so on.
- *Section "Supported SmartLinks."* This list determines which SmartLinks will be supported by the SmartObject type.
- *Section "Add Fields to:."* This determines the automatic behavior upon adding a database field. Each added field may add to the tables in the external tables list by choosing External Tables. Alternatively, fields may add to the Frame's Query by choosing Frame Query. Neither indicates that additional fields do not automatically set the Frame Query or the external tables list.

The file type determines the default extension. This is useful in the remote case that a new SmartObject template is intended for nonvisual purposes, in which case the extension would be .p. An example of this would be a SmartObject which calculates amortization as a background process. It might be called `amort.p` rather than `amort.w` since .w is typically used for window interfaces.

Special ADM Objects: SmartPanel and SmartFolder

The SmartPanel and SmartFolder are specialized SmartObjects that do not have templates and do not produce SmartObject Masters. Every SmartFolder used throughout an application is running the same SmartFolder object `folder.w`. Likewise, every instance of a SmartPanel is running one of the SmartPanels available with V8 `p-navico.w`, `p-updsav.w`, and the rest.

This section focuses on these non-template SmartObjects so you can understand how to work with them effectively. You will learn where the code is stored for these objects and how to compile it following any changes.

Open the folder by choosing File, Open in the UIB. Load the folder using the file \dlc\src\adm\objects\folder.w. The folder adjusts itself at design and at runtime to show the tabs and resize itself. The folder appears as a rectangle with an edge giving it a 3-D look. The actual tabs are positioned and drawn dynamically at design time and runtime.

It is unlikely that you will need to alter the folder, but you may copy it and create a different SmartContainer with similar functionality. A tab folder with tabs on the right or bottom edge might be useful for your application.

The SmartPanels also do not have templates. If your application requires a new SmartPanel, it is necessary for you to copy an existing SmartPanel and make the required changes. It is important to recognize that SmartPanels and SmartFolders only exist as a single instance, used throughout an application. This means that you need only alter or customize the single instance of the SmartFolder or SmartPanel.

You may open the SmartPanels using the UIB. Their locations are as follows:

\dlc\src\adm\objects\

p-navico.w	Navigation using icons
p-navlbl.w	Navigation using labels
p-updsav.w	Update/Save, Short Transaction
p-updtxn.w	Update with Long Transaction

Remember that with all of these nontemplate SmartObjects—the SmartFolder and SmartPanel—the compiled .r code is not in the same directory as the source.

You will need to place any newly compiled .r files for standard SmartFolder or SmartPanels in the directory \dlc\gui\adm\objects.

You are now able to identify the SmartPanels and the SmartFolder objects. These SmartObjects will be extremely common throughout your application so it is important to understand how they are invoked.

ADM Method Libraries

Each SmartObject points to several include files which provide its functionality. These include files are called Method Libraries in the context of SmartObjects and the ADM. The UIB allows you to manage the Method Libraries for each type of SmartObject. The Method Libraries provide each SmartObject type with its core methods; for example, SmartViewers get their data access methods from the Method Library called `record.i`.

Method libraries contain standard, inherited functionality within a SmartObject. Changing the code within a Method Library causes all SmartObjects of that class to reflect the change upon recompile. This makes the Method Libraries an extremely powerful way to organize your code.

Load the SmartViewer template into the UIB as in the previous example. Click Procedures, then OK, and Method Libraries to view the Method Libraries that make up part of the SmartViewer (see fig. 8.4).

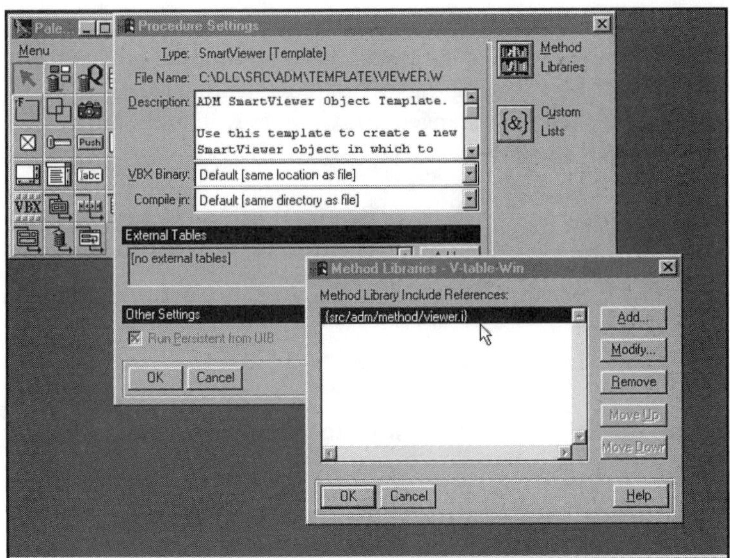

Fig. 8.4

SmartViewer Method Libraries.

The Method Library `viewer.i` contains all the methods necessary for a SmartViewer. See Appendix B, "SmartObject Method Reference," for a reference on ADM Methods and Events.

All Method Library include files are stored in the directory \dlc\src\adm\method. Load viewer.i into a Procedure Window and you will notice that it contains references to other include files:

```
{src/adm/method/smart.i}
{src/adm/method/record.i}
{src/adm/method/tableio.i}
```

These include files contain the lower-level functions present in various SmartObjects. Remember that many of the methods found within are prefixed with `adm-`; these are standard `adm` methods as discussed in the previous chapter:

- `smart.i`. Contains functions essential to all SmartObjects. Basic functions such as hide, destroy, and communications are found here.
- `record.i`. Contains functions relative to records management. Functions such as `display-fields` and `open-query` are found here.
- `tableio.i`. Contains functions used for table maintenance such as save, delete, and copy.

An example of a commonly used method is `adm-display-fields`. This method is found within `record.i` and is inherited by all SmartViewers and SmartBrowsers.

It is *extremely likely* that a development team will require a change (even if minor) to a method such as `adm-display-fields`. A change may be required to customize or improve the given functionality of a SmartObject.

Customizing Your ADM Methods

Progress understands that teams will want to customize ADM methods. It is essential that methods be customized *without* changing the original include files (Method Libraries). If the original include files were changed, the changes would have to be re-established upon installing new versions of PROGRESS.

Tip

SmartObject methods must be customized without changing the original PROGRESS supplied include files. This will ensure that subsequent PROGRESS installs will not overwrite your modifications.

Some less desirable options available to a team wanting to customize ADM methods are as follows:

1. Edit the actual include files in the \dlc directories.

   This is not recommended because new versions of PROGRESS would overwrite the changed methods. It would also be difficult to restore the originals if needed.

2. Copy the include files into a working area and set PROPATH so that the working area precedes the \dlc area.

   This is not recommended because you may need to alter very few methods, whereas an include file may contain many. It will also make it difficult to accept a new release of the ADM.

3. Remove the reference to the original Method Library and insert a new library under a custom name.

   This is also not recommended for reasons similar to #1 and #2.

The best solution has been provided for by Progress' ADM team. Examine the header of a method such as `adm-display-fields` in `record.i` using a Procedure Window or editor.

```
&IF DEFINED(EXCLUDE-adm-display-fields) = 0 &THEN

&ANALYZE-SUSPEND _UIB-CODE-BLOCK
_PROCEDURE adm-display-fields Method-Library
PROCEDURE adm-display-fields :
/*-----------------------------------------------------
  Purpose:     Displays the fields in the current record.
  Parameters:  <none>
  Notes:
-------C---------------------------------------------*/
```

The top line is most important. Note that it would not be visible if the library had been loaded by choosing the UIB File, Open.

If the preprocessor `EXCLUDE-adm-display-fields` is defined anywhere in your development environment, the `adm-display-fields` in the standard Method Library is ignored.

To expose a new, customized version of `adm-display-fields`, create a new include file called **`custom.i`**. Insert the `EXCLUDE` preprocessor for any and all methods that you wish to customize, followed by the new methods.

```
&SCOPED-DEFINE EXCLUDE-adm-display-fields

&ANALYZE-SUSPEND _UIB-CODE-BLOCK
_PROCEDURE adm-display-fields Method-Library
PROCEDURE adm-display-fields :
/*---------------------------------------------------
  Purpose:     Custom version of adm-display-fields.
  Parameters:  <none>
  Notes:       Customized for Project X
---------------------------------------------------*/
/* insert custom code for display-fields here...   */
RETURN.
END PROCEDURE.

/* _UIB-CODE-BLOCK-END */
```

You may build this custom include file with the UIB by creating a New Method Library. Place the `&SCOP EXCLUDE-` definitions in the Definitions Section and create each method using New Procedure. It is recommended that the UIB be used to create and maintain Method Libraries.

After your custom Method Library is ready, you may insert it *above* the standard Method Library in the UIB shown in figure 8.5.

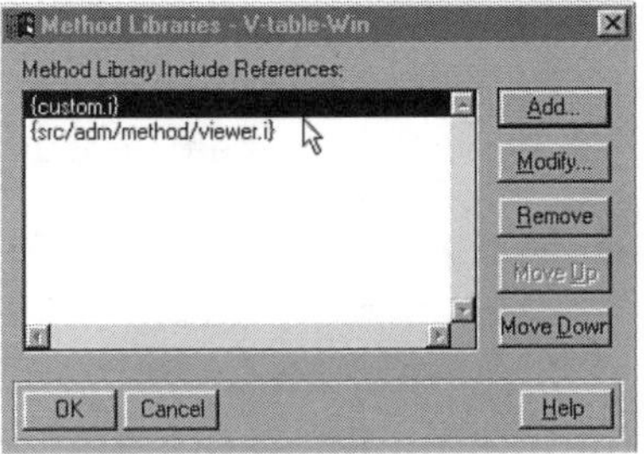

Fig. 8.5

SmartViewer with Custom Method Libraries.

You may now recompile all SmartObjects that use this Method Library, and your custom methods will be in place. The size of the resulting compiles will not increase because the standard method library is *completely ignored* by the compiler! In this fashion, you are well prepared for new releases of PROGRESS and for customizations to the standard methods.

Accessing a SmartObject's Attributes

In the object-oriented world, an object class consists of private and public *methods* and private and public *data*. A SmartObject's public data consists of variables that are stored within and are accessible by outside objects. Each SmartObject's public data should be declared and maintained through the use of SmartObject *attributes*.

You may view a SmartObject's *instance attributes* by clicking the ventilator (the top left corner or the object) and selecting instance attributes as shown in figure 8.6.

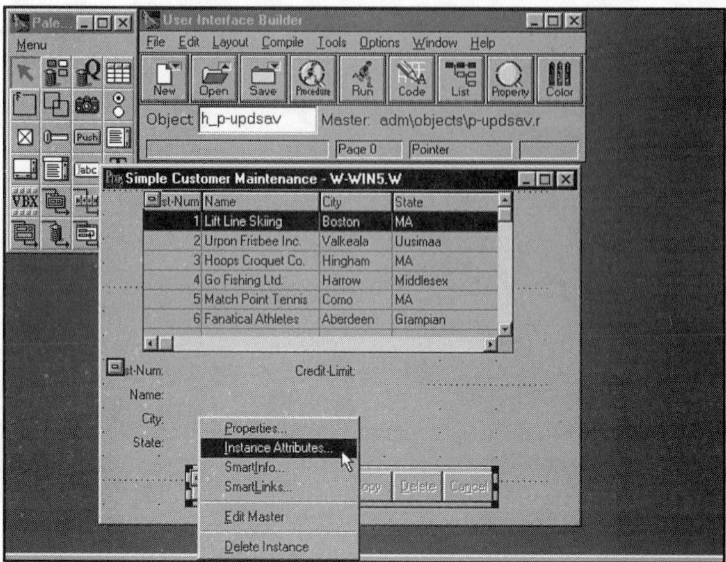

Fig. 8.6

SmartPanel instance attributes selection.

Each instance of a SmartObject may have a unique set of values stored in its attributes. Attribute sets may vary between SmartObject types.

In the case of the SmartPanel, the attributes consist of edge-pixels (the thickness of the panel's edge), behavior of the Add button (single or multiple adds), and the function of the Save button (`save` or `update`) shown in figure 8.7.

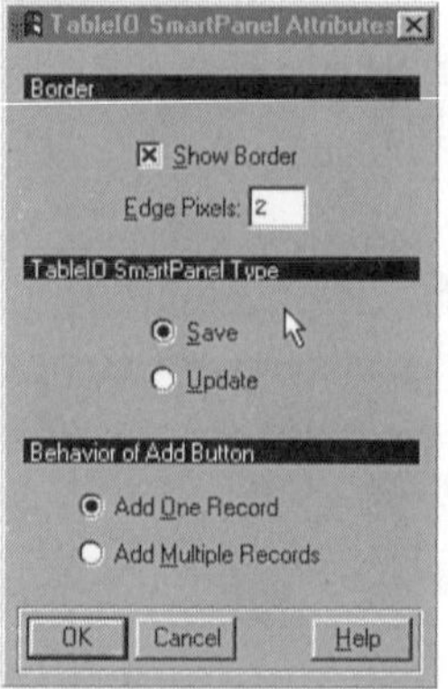

Fig. 8.7

SmartPanel Instance Attributes dialog.

In Chapter 20, "Extending the Development Tools," you study an example of a simple attribute editor screen to maintain a SmartObject's attributes at design time.

Setting SmartObject Attributes

In this section you study SmartObject attributes. As a SmartObject is placed into a SmartWindow, it becomes an instance of the SmartObject. Each instance can have unique attributes which tailor its appearance and behavior.

To illustrate this, consider a SmartViewer which shows employee information: name, start date, title, and salary. For certain instances of the employee SmartViewer, you may want to hide the salary field. You could therefore define an attribute called `show-salary` to manage the visibility of salary in the SmartViewer. This section introduces you to SmartObject attributes and the flexibility they bring forth.

The code shown in this section is to prepare you for an attribute exercise further on in the chapter. There is no need to type the code or run it just yet.

To set a SmartObject attribute, use the statement `set-attribute-list`, which carries the syntax:

```
run set-attribute-list [in {procedure-handle}]
('{attribute-name}={attribute-value}':U).
```

The `in {procedure-handle}` clause is optional and used only for setting attributes in objects whose handle is known.

For example, to set an attribute called `'bgcolor'` whose value sets the background color of a SmartObject:

```
run set-attribute-list ('bgcolor=11').
```

To set an attribute called `'balance'` whose value is the customer balance:

```
run set-attribute-list ('balance=' + STRING(customer.balance)).
```

The input parameter sent is always one string with an equal sign (=) separating the attribute name from the value.

To retrieve an attribute, use the command `get-attribute` with the following syntax:

```
run get-attribute in {procedure-handle}] ('{attribute-name}':U).
```

The value of the attribute will be found in `RETURN-VALUE`, which contains return values from a procedure. `RETURN-VALUE` is a string and contains `""` (empty) if the attribute is not valid.

Next, let's use SmartObject attributes to enhance an earlier sample program.

Attributes in Action

A strong example of SmartObject attributes is the customer maintenance screen used in Chapter 7, w-win4.w, and shown in figure 8.8.

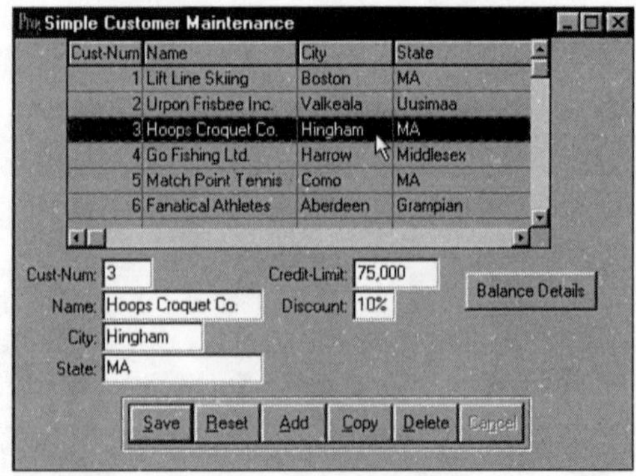

Fig. 8.8

w-win4.w customer maintenance screen.

You will recall that the balance button is a separate SmartViewer that receives state messages from the Customer SmartViewer. The Balance button, when selected, calls an internal procedure inside of the Customer SmartViewer whose handle is known from the state message.

It would be organized for the balance button trigger to simply *get* the attribute of `'balance'` from the Customer SmartViewer and display it. It makes more sense for the procedure `show_balance` to exist within the Balance SmartViewer rather than the Customer SmartViewer. After all, the Customer SmartViewer does not concern itself with a customer's outstanding balance.

Now edit the Master for the Customer SmartViewer `v-cust.w` by clicking the SmartViewer's ventilator and selecting Edit Master. Click Code to enter the SmartViewer's Section Editor and select the procedure `local-display-fields`.

Remember, `local-display-fields` is a local method used to perform functions at the time of displaying the customer fields. Change it to read as follows:

```
/* Code placed here will execute PRIOR to standard behavior. */

  /* Dispatch standard ADM method.                              */
  RUN dispatch IN THIS-PROCEDURE ( INPUT 'display-fields':U ) .

  /* Code placed here will execute AFTER standard behavior.    */
IF AVAILABLE customer AND
   customer.balance > 0 THEN RUN new-state ('balance':U).
                        ELSE RUN new-state ('no-balance':U).

IF AVAILABLE customer THEN
   RUN set-attribute-list ('balance=' +
                 STRING(customer.balance)).
```

In addition to running `new-state` (as it did before), the attribute `'balance'` is set accordingly, using `set-attribute-list`.

Edit the Master for the Balance SmartViewer `v-blnce.w` by clicking the SmartViewer's ventilator and selecting Edit Master. Click Code to enter the SmartViewer's Section Editor and select the `CHOOSE` trigger for the button.

Change the code as follows:

```
DO:
DEF VAR d_balance AS DECIMAL.
  RUN get-attribute IN h_caller ('balance').
  IF RETURN-VALUE NE "" THEN DO:
      d_balance = DEC(RETURN-VALUE).
      message "Customer remaining credit is "
            STRING(d_balance,"$>>>,>>9.99").
  END.
END.
```

The trigger is capable of retrieving the balance as an attribute of the external SmartViewer. Note that the `RETURN-VALUE` (a string) is converted to a decimal using the `DEC()` function, and then converted to a string with the proper format.

Be sure to save the SmartViewers before testing the maintenance screen. It will work the same from the user's perspective.

In the above code the Balance SmartViewer was altered so that it could determine if a balance existed. The `balance` attribute is a way for the Customer SmartViewer to communicate its balance setting. It can be said that, through the use of attributes, it is better organized.

Attribute Storage in the SmartContainer

You may wonder, where are the instance attributes stored? Unlike the newly defined attributes in the last example, the instance attributes must be contained in the SmartContainer.

Each SmartContainer with SmartObjects in it contains a link of objects and their attributes. This allows the SmartContainer to start each of its SmartObjects with their unique instance attributes.

Load the window w-win4.w into a Procedure Window (choose Tools, New Procedure Window), shown in figure 8.9, and search for the ADM method `adm-create-objects`. It is here that the container creates its SmartObjects and initializes them. Part of the initialization process is to transfer the instance attributes, of which only the container is aware.

The SmartPanel's instance attributes are sent from the container to its newly created SmartPanel.

```
INPUT  'SmartPanelType = Save,
            Edge-Pixels = 2,
            AddFunction = One-Record':U ,
```

You may be beginning to understand how you will be able to set your own custom attributes at initialization. You can create a local ADM event called `local-create-objects` where additional instance attributes are sent. Chapter 20 covers this some more.

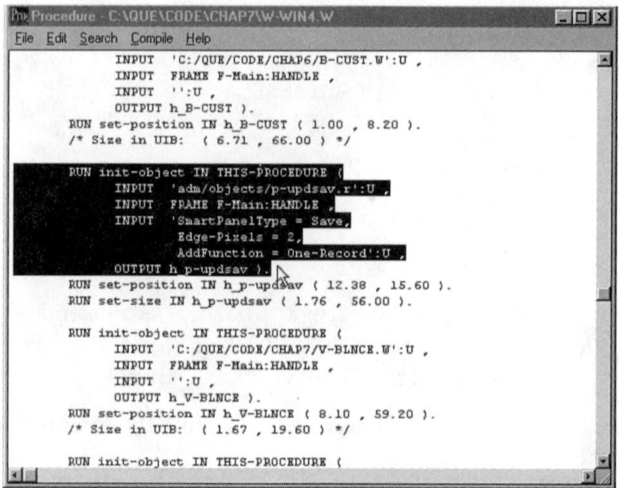

Fig. 8.9

w-win4.w code viewer in the Procedure Window; `adm-create-objects` *method.*

Managing Links and Messages with ADM Broker

You learned about SmartLinks and messages in Chapter 7. This section discusses an internal process that governs and manages links and messages of all SmartObjects: the ADM Broker. The Broker manages all links and messages for SmartObjects within an application. If multiple SmartWindows are running simultaneously, *one* broker manages all links and messages.

Broker Functionality

The Broker starts as a persistent procedure upon the start of the first SmartContainer. It remains active until that SmartContainer ends.

Figure 8.10 shows the broker as it relays messages to a container's objects. The significant functions of the broker are:

- Keeps a temporary table (memory based) of all links for all SmartObjects that have been initialized
- Manages the traffic of messages to and from SmartObjects
- Is responsible for the operation of the `notify` method
- Holds code related to SmartLinks that otherwise would need to exist within each SmartObject

The last point is significant because the code to manage SmartLinks, if it resided within each SmartObject, would cause an increase in size of approximately 20 percent.

The ADM ***BROKER***

BROKER

- SmartLinks Storage
- Messaging Code
-Links Management

dispatch ('row-available')

dispatch ('row-available')

notify ('row-available')

SmartViewer

SmartBrowser

SmartViewer

Record Links

Fig. 8.10

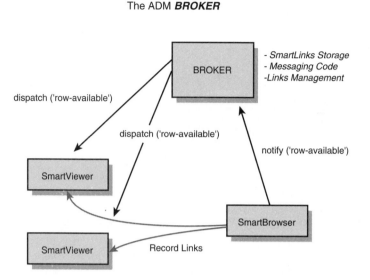

The ADM Broker relative to a SmartContainer's objects.

Note that, in the diagram, the Broker runs `dispatch` to send messages to each individual SmartObject target. `notify` is actually an instruction to the Broker, whereas `dispatch` is an instruction to a SmartObject.

You may load the Broker program into the UIB by opening \dlc\src\adm\objects\broker.p by choosing File, Open (see fig. 8.11). The Section Editor reveals several internal procedures vital to the Broker's function.

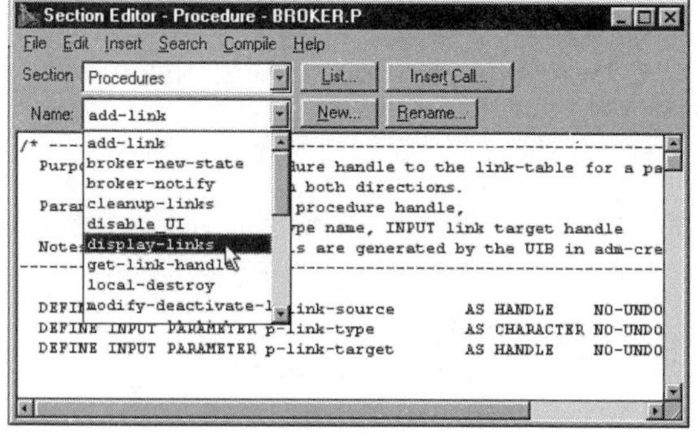

Fig. 8.11

The Broker's internal procedures.

Using the Display-Links Procedure

The selected procedure is `display-links`. If called at runtime, this Broker procedure will display all links. All SmartObjects have the handle for the ADM Broker that can be used to execute Broker procedures. The Broker handle is `adm-broker-hdl`. If you wish to display all links at runtime for testing purposes, you may place the code:

```
run display-links in ADM-BROKER-HDL.
```

Also, in the Broker's Definitions Section you will find the definition for the SmartLinks temp table.

```
DEFINE TEMP-TABLE adm-link-table NO-UNDO
    FIELD link-type  AS CHARACTER
    FIELD link-source AS HANDLE
    FIELD link-target AS HANDLE
    FIELD link-active AS LOGICAL
    INDEX link-type IS PRIMARY link-type link-active
    INDEX link-source link-source link-type link-active
    INDEX link-target link-target link-type link-active.
```

At any given time, this temp table will contain all SmartLinks for as many containers as are running.

Defining the Broker Notify Paths

The Broker controls all messages passed between SmartObjects. ADM messages travel through *default* ADM Link paths. That is, an ADM message such as `row-available` will automatically travel to `RECORD-TARGET`. The Broker manages this through variables called `adm-notify-methods` and `adm-notify-links`.

Select the Definitions Section in the Broker code. You will see the definitions as follows:

```
DEFINE VARIABLE adm-notify-methods AS CHARACTER INIT
"exit,initialize,hide,view,~
enable,row-available,destroy,get-first,~
get-prev,get-next,get-last,open-query,~
add-record,update-record,copy-record,delete-record,~
reposition-query,reset-record,cancel-record":U NO-UNDO.

DEFINE VARIABLE adm-notify-links AS CHARACTER INIT
"CONTAINER-SOURCE,CONTAINER-TARGET,CONTAINER-TARGET,CONTAINER-TARGET,~
CONTAINER-TARGET,RECORD-TARGET,CONTAINER-TARGET,NAVIGATION-TARGET,~
NAVIGATION-TARGET,NAVIGATION-TARGET,NAVIGATION-TARGET,RECORD-SOURCE,~
TABLEIO-TARGET,TABLEIO-TARGET,TABLEIO-TARGET,TABLEIO-TARGET,~
RECORD-SOURCE,TABLEIO-TARGET,TABLEIO-TARGET":U NO-UNDO.
```

Each variable is a comma-delimited list. The method `row-available` is item #6 in the `adm-notify-methods` list. The sixth item of `adm-notify-links` is `RECORD-TARGET`.

Thus, the ADM Broker is programmed to send any `row-available` ADM messages to a SmartObjects `RECORD-TARGET`. A SmartBrowser can execute the statement:

```
run notify ('row-available').
```

and the Broker will know to send messages to all SmartObjects that are targets of link type **RECORD**.

This enables you to determine the default links used by ADM messages. You may, as an expert, add ADM messages which have default links of their own by customizing the broker. The broker is like a telephone operator for all calls between the SmartObjects at runtime.

Broker State Messages Paths

As discussed in Chapter 7, the broker manages all state messages passed within the ADM standard methods. The Broker contains a list of state messages that will travel along standard ADM links. The Broker manages this through the variables `adm-state-names` and `adm-state-links`.

In the Definitions Section again:

```
DEFINE VARIABLE adm-state-names AS CHARACTER INIT
"link-changed,record-available,no-record-available,~
update,update-complete,first-record,last-record,only-record,not-first-or-last,~
delete-complete":U NO-UNDO.

DEFINE VARIABLE adm-state-links AS CHARACTER INIT
"*;TABLEIO-SOURCE,NAVIGATION-SOURCE;TABLEIO-SOURCE,NAVIGATION-SOURCE;~
TABLEIO-TARGET,RECORD-SOURCE,NAVIGATION-SOURCE;~
TABLEIO-TARGET,TABLEIO-SOURCE,RECORD-SOURCE,NAVIGATION-SOURCE;~
NAVIGATION-SOURCE;NAVIGATION-SOURCE;NAVIGATION-SOURCE;NAVIGATION-SOURCE;~
RECORD-SOURCE":U NO-UNDO.
```

The message `record-available` is the second item in the list `adm-state-names`. The second item in `adm-state-links` is `TABLEIO-SOURCE`. Thus, when a SmartViewer has no record, the `TABLEIO-SOURCE` SmartPanel will receive the message and be able to gray-out the appropriate buttons.

Note that the asterisk (*) can be used to wildcard link types as is the case with the state message `link-changed`.

Dispatch: dispatch-qualifier, dispatch-errors

In Chapter 7, you learned that the `dispatch` command is given to run an ADM method. Recall that `dispatch` will run a *local* ADM event if it exists, or a *standard* ADM event. For the method `display-fields`, `dispatch` would look for `local-display-fields` and `adm-display-fields`.

It may be useful to add a custom prefix for ADM methods. The preprocessor `ADM-DISPATCH-QUALIFIER` can be used to establish a custom prefix. `dispatch` will look for the customer prefix *after* the local prefix and *before* the standard.

The code that follows could be placed into a customer Method Library called custom.i to establish a custom prefix called `custom`.

```
&SCOP ADM-DISPATCH-QUALIFIER custom
```

You will be required to position the custom Method Library high in the Method Library list for a SmartObject in order for the preprocessor to take effect. Using `dispatch` under this scenario would cause a search for `local-{method-name}`, then `custom-{method-name}`, and finally `adm-{method-name}`.

Another preprocessor, `ADM-SHOW-DISPATCH-ERRORS`, can be used to trap errors during `dispatch`. Normally, `dispatch` will execute an internal procedure with the `NO-ERROR` option. This means that the statement:

```
run dispatch ('dispay-fields').
/* notice missing 'l' in display-fields */
```

would *not* return an error, whereas the procedure `adm-dispay-fields` would not be found.

Although this can be stressful when debugging a program with `dispatch` statements, it also allows SmartObjects to send messages to SmartObjects that do not have the required methods. This is valuable because there may be several targets, only some of which need to respond to a message.

To turn error processing on during a debugging session, you may define the preprocessor `ADM-SHOW-DISPATCH-ERRORS`.

```
&SCOP ADM-SHOW-DISPATCH-ERRORS
```

This preprocessor is placed in any SmartObject for which you would like to see error messages during `dispatch`. You may place the preprocessor in a Method Library placed high on the Method Library list.

The method `show-errors` will be run if `dispatch` is unable to locate the given method. Using the previous example, `dispatch ('dispay-fields')` would cause `show-errors` to execute where the developer may place debugging statements. This is extremely valuable for trapping `dispatch` errors caused by misspelled method names!

The ADM Broker is a powerful mechanism used in managing and organizing the messages and links. I encourage you to study the Broker to fully understand the SmartObject messaging internals. The ADM Broker is at the heart of all messages between SmartObjects.

Use caution when you make changes to the Broker. If changes are made, as in the case of the SmartFolder, be sure to place the compiled .r in \dlc\gui\adm\objects directory. Better still, place the compile Broker in your own directory that falls ahead of \dlc in the PROPATH.

Setting Up Advanced Links

Chapter 7 gave you the tour of SmartLinks and messaging. In this section, you will create a new link type and use it with the customer maintenance screen example. You will also learn how SmartLinks can be established dynamically by looking internally to the way links are created.

Establishing a New Link Type

In the customer maintenance screen used in Chapter 7 and this chapter (refer to fig. 8.8), the Customer SmartViewer and the Balance SmartViewer communicate. The Balance SmartViewer wants to tell the Customer SmartViewer to display information on remaining credit.

The example in this chapter had you sending a state message and using the `get-attribute` statement to retrieve the customer's balance. In this section, you will define a new link between the two SmartObjects and send a message across the new link to get to the result.

A synopsis of what you are about to do:

1. Establish a new link called 'Balance' between the SmartViewers.
2. Program the Balance button to `notify` all `BALANCE-SOURCE` SmartObjects of a message called `show_balance`.

Because the procedure `show_balance` already exists in the customer SmartViewer from Chapter 6, that will work for this example.

Load the customer maintenance screen w-win4.w from your work in either this chapter *or* Chapter 7. The changes made in this chapter will not affect the example here.

Edit the SmartLinks for the balance SmartViewer so that they appear as shown in figure 8.12. Select New as the link type and enter **Balance** as the link name. This establishes a new link type to connect the objects. Link names are not case-sensitive.

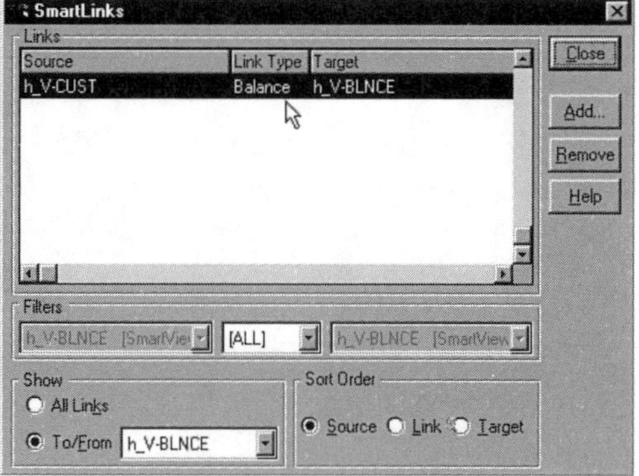

Fig. 8.12

The Balance SmartViewer connected via the Balance link.

In this scenario, the Customer SmartViewer will be the `BALANCE-SOURCE`, whereas the Balance SmartViewer will be the `BALANCE-TARGET` of any messages sent across the new link.

Modify the trigger code for the balance button as follows:

```
DO:
run notify ('shw_balance,BALANCE-SOURCE':U).
END.
```

That is it! The trigger will cause a notification of all `BALANCE` sources with the message `show_balance`. Because the internal procedure `show_balance` exists within the Customer SmartViewer, it will work perfectly.

The tremendous advantage to this technique is that if the Balance SmartViewer was linked with 'Balance' to several other objects, they could all respond!

Creating Dynamic Links

So far you have seen how SmartLinks are established at design time, using the UIB. This is not always possible; sometimes SmartLinks must be established at runtime.

Regardless of which link types are used, it may be necessary to establish a SmartLink at runtime. You may only know about the SmartLink while the programs are running. Perhaps the exact type of link is stored in a database somewhere. There are many possible scenarios in which links need to be created dynamically. One common example is when you have two separate SmartWindows that need to communicate with each other.

The following example shows two SmartWindows communicating with each other (see fig. 8.13). Customer records are sent across a RECORD link, which was established at runtime.

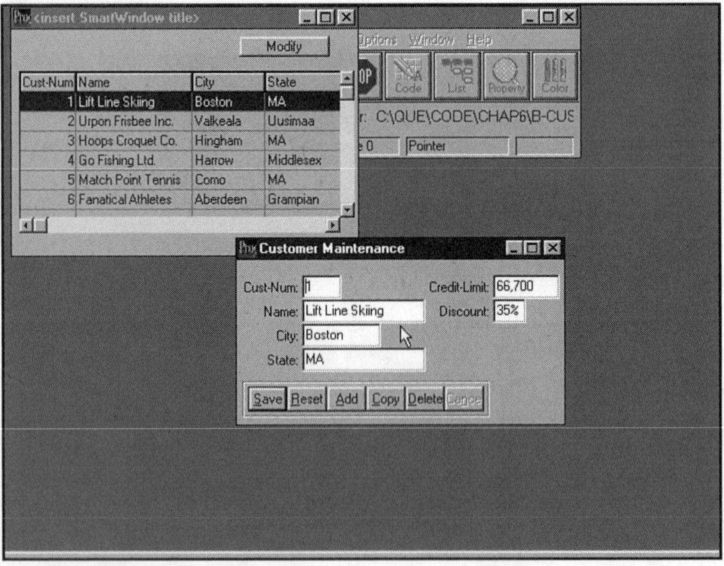

Fig. 8.13

Two connected SmartWindows via RECORD link.

As the customer records are perused in the browser, the separate SmartWindow presents the Customer record and allows the user to maintain it. It is as if the SmartBrowser in the upper window were linked via record link to the SmartViewer in the lower window. How can this be? The UIB can link SmartObjects only within the same window.

The trick is to establish the record link immediately after running the second window. Examine the trigger code for the Modify button in the first window:

```
DO:
DEF VAR h-popup AS HANDLE NO-UNDO.

  run appdir\w-cust.w persistent set h-popup.
  /* Links to SmartWindow */
  RUN add-link IN adm-broker-hdl ( h_b-cust , 'Record':U , h-popup ).
  RUN dispatch IN h-popup ("initialize").
END.
```

The second pop-up window, w-cust.w, is run `persistent` so that it stays in memory and returns to the caller. The `add-link` method is called *in the Broker* to establish a link of type `RECORD` between the SmartBrowser and the new SmartWindow. Finally, `initialize` is dispatched in the new SmartWindow to bring it into view and initialize it.

You may create the second SmartWindow following the abbreviated steps:

1. Create New SmartWindow.
2. Insert the Customer SmartViewer v-cust.w from the Chapter 6 exercises.
3. Insert the SmartPanel p-updsav.w to accept the default link to the SmartViewer.
4. Establish a `RECORD` link between the SmartWindow and the SmartViewer.
5. Save as w-cust.w.

This allows the SmartWindow to pass messages through to its SmartViewer. The calling program need only establish a link to the SmartWindow. Because there is no way for the calling program to know what receiving object *might* reside within, this is a powerful technique.

This type of linking is called *pass-thru links*. A SmartContainer passes links through to its SmartObjects.

You may create the first calling SmartWindow following the abbreviated steps:

1. Create New SmartWindow.
2. Insert the Customer SmartBrowser b-cust.w from the Chapter 6 exercises.
3. Add a button with label Modify and the trigger code shown above (same as the Modify button used in the last example).

When running this example, note that you are allowed to launch several pop-up windows, each of which will link to the calling program. You may have multiple pop-up windows showing the customer record.

Another equally common scenario is when a SmartWindow needs to call a SmartDialog and establish a similar link. The difference is that a SmartDialog is *modal;* it does not return to the caller until it is finished.

Because of its modality, the SmartDialog will require that the SmartLink be established from within. In order for the SmartDialog to know the handle of the SmartBrowser, you will pass the handle as a parameter.

Create the SmartDialog using the same steps for creating the second SmartWindow, except use SmartDialog as the container. Remember to create a `RECORD` link between the SmartDialog and its SmartViewer just as you did for the SmartWindow.

The following code within the SmartDialog method `local-initialize` will establish the link.

```
/* Code placed here will execute PRIOR to standard behavior. */
  RUN add-link IN adm-broker-hdl
( h_source , 'Record':U , THIS-PROCEDURE ).

  /* Dispatch standard ADM method.                             */
  RUN dispatch IN THIS-PROCEDURE ( INPUT 'initialize':U ) .

  /* Code placed here will execute AFTER standard behavior.    */
```

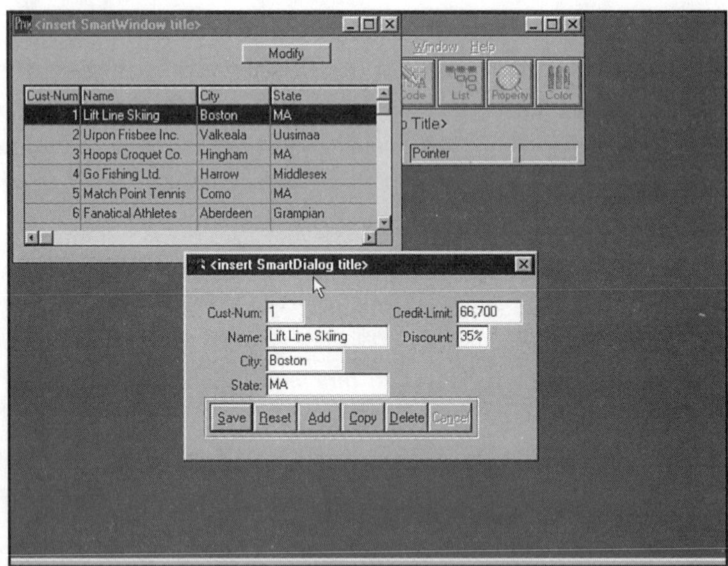

Fig. 8.14

The SmartWindow to SmartDialog example.

The handle `h_source` is an input parameter defined in the Definitions Section of the SmartDialog:

```
DEF INPUT PARAMETER h_source AS HANDLE.
```

The calling SmartWindow's trigger should be altered to run the SmartDialog and pass the SmartBrowser's handle:

```
DO:
  run \appdir\d-cust.w (h_b-cust).
END.
```

You now have working experience with dynamic SmartLinks. The examples of SmartWindow and SmartDialog pop-ups are common, as you will surely find with your development efforts.

In this chapter you explored the inner workings of the ADM and SmartObjects. You learned the significance of Method Libraries and where they are located in the DLC directory. The ability to have instance-specific attributes was demonstrated. You also learned how to define SmartLinks dynamically at runtime.

From Here...

This concludes Part II, "Application Development Model." The next chapters will take you through the development of a sample application. You will put many of the techniques learned in this part to good use.

Be sure to check out Part VI, "Tips from the Pros," with even more in-depth information about the ADM and the PROGRESS environment.

- Chapter 19, "Using Active Templates," shows you how to bring your SmartObject templates alive to make SmartObject development even more productive.
- Chapter 20, "Extending the Development Tools," shows you more about customizing your development environment.
- Chapter 21, "Making the Most of the Application Component Environment," shows you the tips the experts use to maximize V8.
- Chapter 22, "PROGRESS Programming Tips," shares the programming tips from the pros. Learn how to make the most of the PROGRESS environment.

Part III

Creating a Sample Application

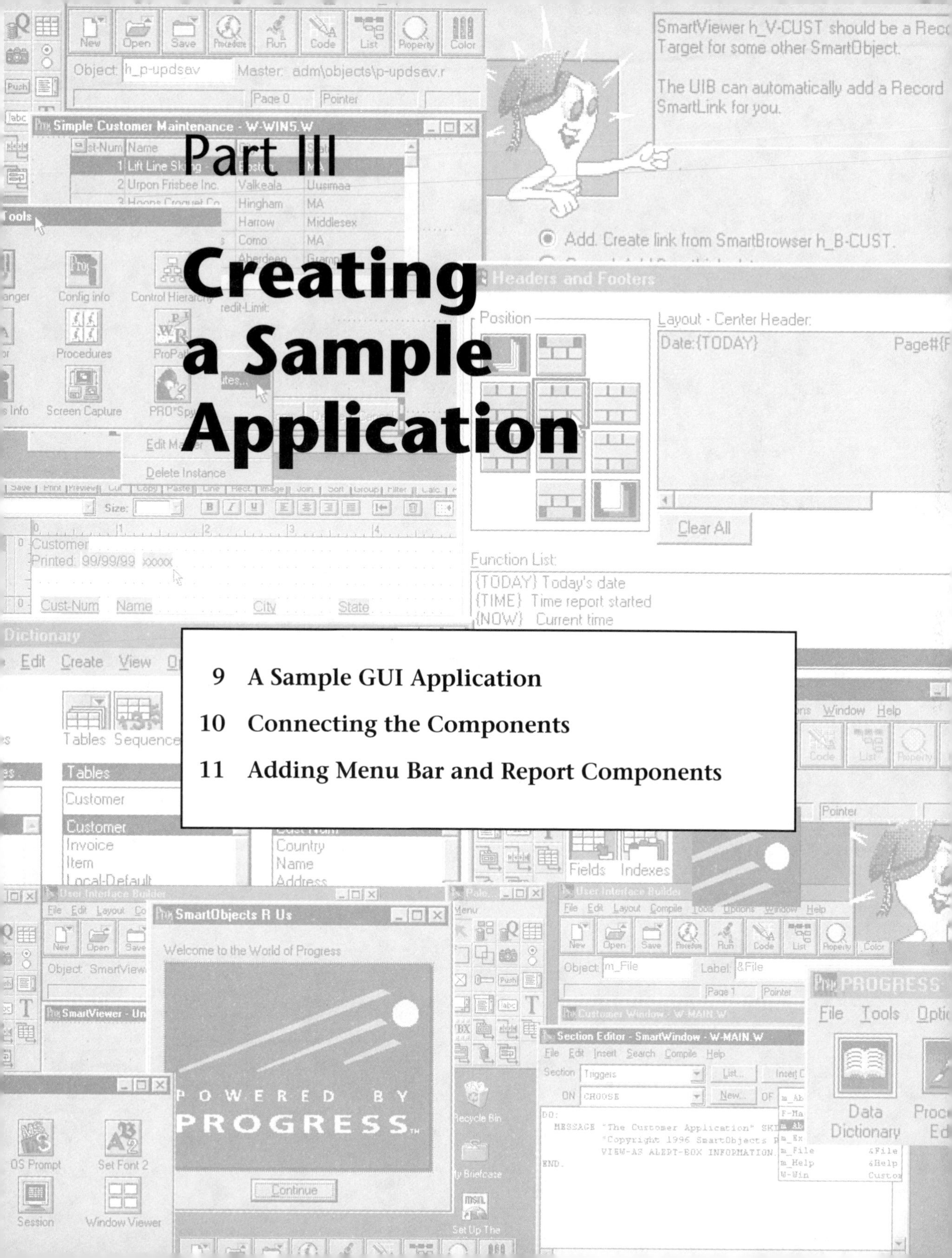

SmartViewer h_V-CUST should be a Re
Target for some other SmartObject.
The UIB can automatically add a Recor
SmartLink for you.
Add. Create link from SmartBrowser h_B-CUST.
Object: h_p-updsav
Master: adm\objects\p-updsav.r
Simple Customer Maintenance - W-WIN5.W
Name
City
State
1 Lift Line Skiing
Boston
MA
2 Urpon Frisbee Inc.
Valkeala
Uusimaa
Hingham
Harrow
Middlesex
Como
Aberdeen
Grampian
Changer
Config info
Control Hierarchy
Procedures
ProPath
Screen Capture
PRO*Spy
Edit Master
Delete Instance
Headers and Footers
Position
Layout - Center Header:
Date:{TODAY}
Clear All
Function List:
{TODAY} Today's date
{TIME} Time report started
{NOW} Current time
{COUNT} Records listed so far
{PAGE} Current page number
Customer
Printed: 99/99/99
Cust-Num
Name
City
State
Edit
Create
View
Options
Tools
Help
Tables
Sequences
Fields
Indexes
Customer
Invoice
Item
Cust-Num
Name
User Interface Builder
File
Edit
Layout
Compile
Tools
Options
Window
Help
New
Open
Save
Run
Code
List
Property
Color
Object:
Label:
Pointer
SmartObjects R Us
Welcome to the World of Progress
POWERED BY
PROGRESS
Continue
OS Prompt
Set Font 2
Session
Window Viewer
Recycle Bin
My Briefcase
Object: m_File
Label: &File
Page 1
Section Editor - SmartWindow - W-MAIN.W
Section
Triggers
ON
CHOOSE
List...
New...
DO:
MESSAGE "The Customer Application"
"Copyright 1996 SmartObjects
VIEW-AS ALERT-BOX INFORMATION.
END.
PROGRESS
File
Tools
Data Dictionary

CHAPTER 9

A Sample GUI Application

This chapter describes the sample application that you will be constructing in the chapters that make up this section. The sample application has been designed to give you hands-on experience with the User Interface Builder (UIB), the Application Development Model (ADM), and various other areas of the PROGRESS V8 environment.

The sample application uses the sports database that comes with PROGRESS V8. This database contains data relative to a sporting goods store. The sports database is a good choice for the sample application because you need not create it or any sample data.

If you would like practice using the Data Dictionary tool, you may create a database similar in design to sports and use it against the sample application.

This chapter also takes you through the creation of each SmartObject needed for the sample application.

> **Note**
>
> It is recommended that you proceed sequentially through this chapter and chapters 10 and 11 because some of the material will be presented early on and won't be repeated.

After reading this chapter, you should be able to:

- Understand the design of the sample application that will be built in the chapters of Part III
- Understand the tables and relations in the sports database as they relate to the sample application
- Understand how to catalog necessary components needed for a development effort
- Create a component list for your own application
- Expand your understanding of SmartObjects
- Understand how each of the SmartObjects is created

- Create SmartObjects for your own applications
- Understand more of the details of using PROGRESS V8 to develop applications

Voice-of-Experience Movies

See Table G.3 in Appendix G, "Contents of CD," for a list of the Voice-of-Experience files for this chapter.

Phases of Component-Based Development

An analysis of the phases for component-based development reveals advantages of the component-based approach.

In a development methodology that does not use objects or components the focus is on individual *programs*. Component-based development focuses on *components*, separate and highly organized pieces of the application.

The overall phases of component-based development that will be highlighted in this part of the book are:

- Design the application.
- Identify components necessary to meet application design.
- Build each component. Components are built separately. The sequence of components built is of little importance.
- Connect components together.

Follow these steps in this chapter and the subsequent two chapters for the sample application.

Designing a Sporting Goods Store Application

This sample application will have real world functionality and design requirements. The following list is a good example of real world requirements and what we are requesting for our sample application:

- Use a graphical user interface (GUI) compatible with Windows 95.
- Use an event-driven paradigm to allow end-user to be "in control" of the application.
- Allow for multi-user access to the application data.
- Develop application using component-based development resulting in manageable and reusable application components.
- Use minimum network traffic in a networked environment.
- Handle database integrity issues in case of system crash.

Fortunately, PROGRESS will take care of many of the real world requirements. Also, PROGRESS will allow you to deploy your application on multiple platforms and operating systems.

For the functions of the application, you have the following requirements:

- Show customer detail information such as name, address, city, and so on
- Allow for modification, creation, and deletion of a customer record
- Search for customers in the database using wildcards (for example, use *J* for any customers whose names contain J) and using partial keys (for example, use Jo for any customers whose names begin with Jo)
- Show orders and order lines for any customer, which allows the user to view all orders placed by a customer with information about the order and its detail
- Show the salesrep for the customer so that the user knows which sales person is responsible for the customer account

Figure 9.1 shows the functional layout of the Sporting Goods application. The relationships between functional areas of the application are represented as a diagram.

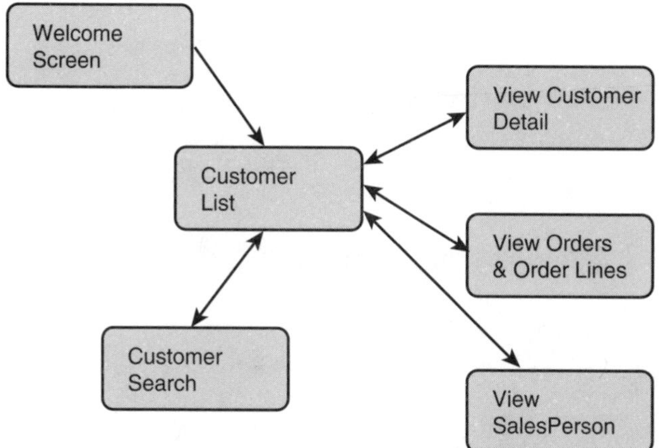

Fig. 9.1

Functional layout of Sporting Goods application.

You will add reports and extra functionality later in chapter 11. At this point, you've seen the overall design for the sample application.

Reviewing the Database Design

First, you will study the design of the tables used in the sample application. The relationships for these tables are explored prior to beginning the sample application work.

The tables involved in the sample application are all from the sports database:

- Customer
- Order

- Order-line
- Salesrep

The relationships among these tables are shown in figure 9.2.

The relationships in this model work as follows:

- A customer has zero or many orders
- A customer has one sales person
- An order has one or many order lines
- A customer has one sales rep

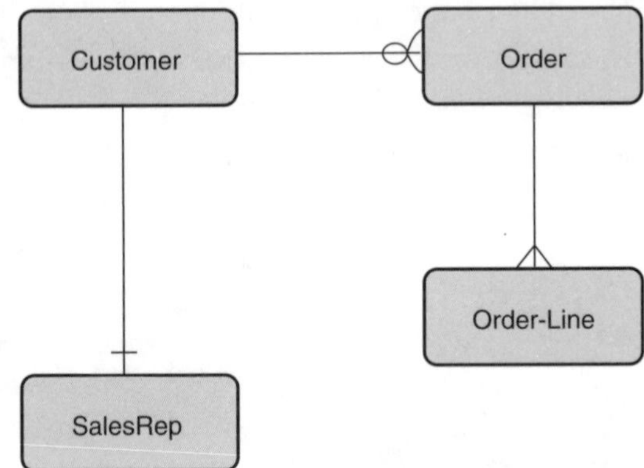

Fig. 9.2

Database design for sample application.

Identifying the Components: The Design Phase

In the component design phase of the design process, you identify which components will be necessary. This phase would normally take place following the user interface design phase (see Chapter 12, "Introduction to User Interface Design," on this subject). By utilizing the paper modeling approach to UI design, the components necessary are more easily identified because, in most cases, each individual paper model represents a component.

For this sample application, you will not construct a paper model, which would be impractical to present in book form. You will identify the components based on the requirements and data model. Understanding the paper design techniques highlighted in Chapter 12 can dramatically improve your interface design, as you will learn.

Here is a review of the requirements and components:

- Customer Information Requirement Criteria:

  Requirement: Show customer detail information such as name, address, city, and so on.

Components: Customer SmartViewer, Customer SmartBrowse

- Record Modifications Requirement Criteria:

  Requirement: Allow for modification, creation and deletion of a customer record.

  Components: SmartPanel with `Update`, `Delete`, `Copy`, and so on

- Customer Search Requirement Criteria:

  Requirement: Search for customers in the database using wildcards (for example, *J* for any customers whose names contain J) and using partial keys (for example, Jo for any customers whose names begin with Jo).

  Components: Customer search screen (window or dialog)

- Related Tables Requirement Criteria:

  Requirement: Show orders and order lines for any customer. This allows the user to view all orders placed by a customer with information about the order and its detail.

  Components: Order SmartBrowse, Order Line SmartBrowse

- Salesrep Display Requirement Criteria:

  Requirement: Show the salesrep for the customer so that the user knows which salesperson is responsible for the customer account.

  Components: Salesrep SmartViewer

Component Lists

Table 9.1 lists the components needed for the sample application and the database tables that they are associated with.

Table 9.1 Identified Components

Database Table	Components Identified
Customer	Viewer, Browse, Panel, Search screen
Order	Browse
OrderLine	Browse
SalesRep	Viewer

Be sure that you have a source of records for every instance of a viewer component. In the preceding list, for example, the Customer viewer has an associated customer browse component. The role of the browse (or the query) component is to make records available to other components. The salesrep viewer has no source of records. You need either a browser or a query component relative to salesrep records.

In this case, because you do not need to present a SmartBrowser of sales representatives, a SmartQuery for the SalesRep table will work nicely.

You also need a welcome screen. This will not be associated with any table or table(s), but you will include it as a component.

Table 9.2 Identified Components

Database Table	Components Identified
Customer	Viewer, Browse, Panel, Search screen
Order	Browse
OrderLine	Browse
SalesRep	Viewer, Query
(N/A)	Welcome Screen

Listing components by object type as shown in Table 9.3 may be very valuable to the development effort. Remember that your development project will most likely span many times the number of objects used in this small sample application. Although these simple tables may seem trivial for the sample application, they will be significant for a real project. Listing components will assist project managers with function point analysis and the identification of reusable components.

The table display, again arranged by component type:

Table 9.3 Identified Components by Object Type

Object Type	Instance
Viewer	Customer, Salesrep
Browse	Customer, Order, OrderLine
Query	Salesrep
Panel	(Record Update)
Custom	Customer Search Screen, Welcome Screen

Note that the welcome screen and the customer search dialog are custom built and not associated with any object type. The intent is to build them without Smart Object technology. Both interfaces will be called by SmartObjects but will not be SmartObjects themselves (see Chapter 11, "Adding Menu Bar and Report Components"). The welcome screen and customer search screen will be built on the basic Window and dialog box templates.

When Smarts Are Not a Necessity

With experience, the developer can find a clear path toward deciding whether an interface object should or should not be SmartObject based.

Tip

One appropriate guideline in deciding that an interface object will *not* be a SmartObject is if the object has no data elements and is not going to interact with other components with messages. One example of this is the sample application welcome screen. Its functionality is not based on SmartObjects if it communicates via *runtime parameters* or *shared variables,* instead of using calling ADM events and methods.

See the "Why Not Use a SmartDialog?" section in Chapter 11 for an additional discussion on this topic.

The welcome screen has no data elements, and it will be used only once in the application. Even if an object is invoked from several areas of the application, it may still not need to be reusable.

The toolbar (SmartPanel) is an example of an object with no data elements, but which needs to communicate with other SmartObjects using ADM messages.

The customer search dialog box is an example of an object whose functionality is totally self-contained and whose communication with the outside world is not through ADM messages. A SmartObject will call the dialog box, but the dialog box will then become the sole input device for the user. When the search dialog is finished, it will dismiss itself and return control to the SmartObject that called it.

The search screen is based on a browse, and it does use PROGRESS' database access capabilities, but it does not communicate with any SmartObjects except through input/output parameters. This is not to say that the dialog is not a reusable object. It can be used anytime you need to search for a particular record. It is just that the functionality is separate from SmartObjects and their interobject communication.

If interactive searches in persistent windows were needed throughout the application, then these windows would have to continuously communicate with any active SmartObject. A persistent search window could not be a self-contained object programmed in an *ad hoc* matter. In this environment, a new SmartObject type should be constructed. The new SmartObject type (for example, a SmartSearch object) would probably be built from the SmartBrowse template because the two have similar features.

It is certainly possible that the customer search screen be added to the basic SmartBrowser. If you have many areas of your application that require search capability, however, it would be smarter (no pun intended) to create a SmartSearch object type. In Chapter 11, you will build the customer search screen as a non-SmartObject.

> **Tip**
>
> An object for your application may come from one of three sources: 1) A standard ADM SmartObject template, 2) A new developer-defined SmartObject template or 3) non-SmartObject-based source code or template.

You are now ready to build the necessary objects. In the next section, you will proceed through a step-by-step guide to creating the SmartObjects necessary for your sample application.

In Chapter 10, "Connecting the Components," these objects will be combined in a single multipage SmartWindow.

Finally, in Chapter 11, you will see how to add some finishing touches to your application. It will be at this point, when you build the custom Welcome and Search screens, that you will see how to combine SmartObjects with custom-built components.

Creating Your SmartObjects

To begin this section, you must:

- Set your working directory (see Chapter 1, "Introducing PROGRESS") to c:\appdir.
- Copy the sample sports database into your working directory.
- Connect to the sports database using the Data Dictionary, the Procedure Editor, or the UIB tool (see Chapter 2, "Getting Started with ADE Tools").

In the previous chapter, you created a list of objects needed for the sample application by object type. Refer to Table 9.3 for the list of components by object type.

Begin by creating the SmartViewers for both the Customer and Salesrep tables.

Choose Tools, User Interface Builder from the PROGRESS desktop. The UIB will present the main toolbar and palette, as shown in figure 9.3.

> **Tip**
>
> Before beginning with the UIB, be sure to set the fonts in progress.ini in order to maximize your working area. See the section "UIB Font Settings" in Chapter 6 for a step-by-step explanation. If you are *not* using Windows 95 or if you wish to continue with the default font settings, please disregard this tip.

Creating the Customer SmartViewer

The SmartViewers needed are Customer and Salesrep. Click the New button in the UIB main window to create a new SmartViewer.

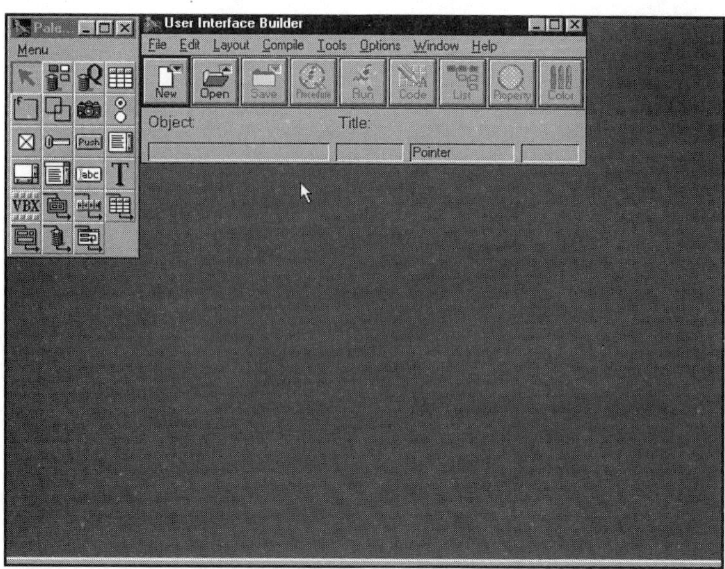

Fig. 9.3

The UIB Main window and palette.

Choose SmartViewer from the objects list. An empty SmartViewer appears at a default size. Note the window in which the SmartViewer resides. This window is for design-time only; at runtime, the SmartViewer will be a frame. Most SmartObjects consist of PROGRESS frames; this is because the UIB requires at least a frame in which to place widgets.

> **Note**
>
> It is helpful to remember that non-container SmartObjects (SmartViewer, SmartBrowser, SmartPanel, etc.) consist of PROGRESS frames. A frame holds the widgets of the SmartObject. The window that appears to contain the SmartObjects while in UIB design mode is only for design mode.

Click the database fields icon on the UIB's palette (shown with the pointer in the next figure). The Multi-Field Selector dialog box will be displayed. Select the following fields for the customer viewer: cust-num, name, city, state, credit-limit.

Figure 9.4 shows the selected fields from the customer table.

Click OK to insert the fields onto your new SmartViewer. Arrange the fields similarly to the arrangement shown in figure 9.5. But first, here are some tips on cosmetics work in the UIB:

- Double-click a control to bring up its property sheet.
- Use the label area in the UIB main window to set a control's label quickly.
- Select multiple widgets by clicking with the Ctrl key held down. Color can be set for multiple widgets by pressing the Color button in the UIB main window.

- You may select several controls simultaneously for movement by clicking while pressing the Ctrl key.

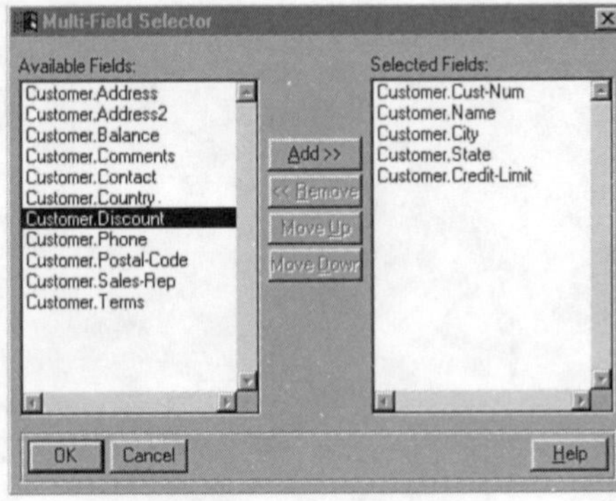

Fig. 9.4

The fields chosen for the customer viewer.

Fig. 9.5

The customer fields arranged nicely in the SmartViewer.

Next, you will need to disable the customer number field because it is the unique key to the customer table. Users cannot change the customer number field of a customer record in this sample application.

Double-click on the Cust-Num field to view its property sheet. Click off the Enabled toggle box to disable the fill-in. Figure 9.6 shows the Enabled toggle box in the property sheet in the Off state.

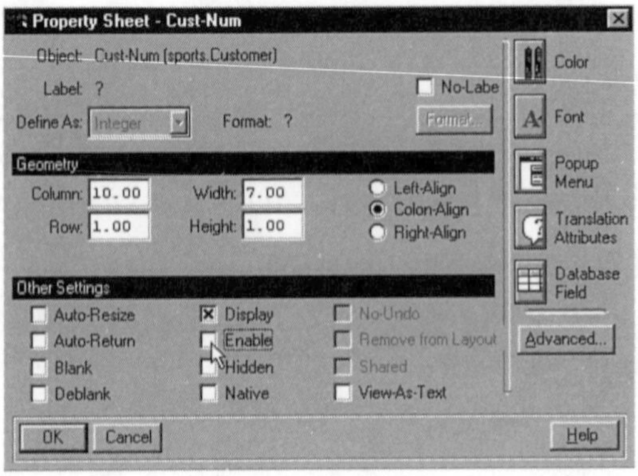

Fig. 9.6

The property sheet for the disabled fill-in for customer number.

> **Note**
>
> SmartObjects created for the sample application may overwrite SmartObjects created in earlier chapters in your working directory. If you have an interest in keeping previously created SmartObjects, be sure to copy them into a separate directory before continuing.

You have completed the customer viewer. Save your work to the samples directory in your appdir working directory. Make sure that the SmartViewer is named `v-cust.w` in the \appdir directory.

After saving the SmartViewer, you will notice both `v-cust.w` and `v-cust.r` in the sample subdirectory. This is because, by default, the UIB compiles SmartObjects at save time. You may change this default (at the object level) by clicking the Procedure button in the UIB main window and checking off the Compile on Save toggle box. It is recommended that the compile option be left ON for the sample application.

Creating the SalesRep SmartViewer

The next viewer that you will create shows fields for the SalesRep table.

> **Note**
>
> Because the steps are similar, the instructions for creating the SalesRep SmartViewer are an abbreviated version of the preceding instructions for the Customer SmartViewer.

Click the New button in the UIB main window to create a new SmartViewer. Choose SmartViewer.

Click the database fields icon on the UIB's palette. You will select the following fields for the salesrep viewer: Rep-Name, Sales-Rep, Region.

Arrange the fields similar to the arrangement shown in figure 9.7.

Fig. 9.7

The fields chosen for the SalesRep viewer.

According to the application design, the fields for the salesrep will not be modifiable by the end user. For this reason, there is no need to set the primary key (`Sales-Rep`) field as disabled.

You have completed the salesrep viewer. Save the SmartViewer as `v-salrep.w` in your appdir working directory.

You now have the two SmartViewers necessary for the sample application: `v-cust.w` and `v-salrep.w`.

Summary of the Development Steps for SmartViewers

Note the following about your work so far in the sample application:

- You have not typed any code.
- The SmartViewers that you have created are prepackaged and ready for table modification, field navigation, object messaging, and many other features! (See Chapter 6 for more information about component-based development.)
- The SmartViewers were created with no knowledge of the rest of the application or even the objects that they will reside in and communicate with (see Chapter 6 for more information about encapsulation).
- As the developer of the SmartViewers, you did not need PROGRESS 4GL experience or even significant programming experience. Anyone on the development team can be chartered with basic SmartObject building tasks.

You will now create the SmartBrowsers necessary for the sample application.

Creating Your SmartBrowsers

Now that you have your SmartViewer developed to perform the functions of displaying customer data, let's create SmartBrowsers to present lists of database records.

The SmartBrowsers needed are Customer, Order, and Order Line.

Creating the Customer SmartBrowser

Click the New button in the UIB main window and create a new SmartBrowser by selecting SmartBrowser Wizard from the object list. The Wizard will step you through the query and fields selection process (which you would otherwise reach through the property sheet).

On page 2 of the SmartBrowser Wizard, when you are prompted for external tables, choose Next to proceed to the next page. The customer SmartBrowser has no external tables. You will learn about external tables when building the next SmartBrowsers, Order, and Order Line.

On page 3 of the SmartBrowser Wizard, press the Define Query button.

Add the Customer table to the query by selecting Customer in the tables list and clicking the Add>> button on the Query Builder dialog box shown in figure 9.8. You may also double-click on Customer to achieve the same result.

Choose OK to return to the SmartBrowser Wizard and proceed to the next screen, Fields to Display. Click the Add Fields button to view the Column Editor window of the UIB.

Click the Add button, as shown in figure 9.9, to add fields to the browser.

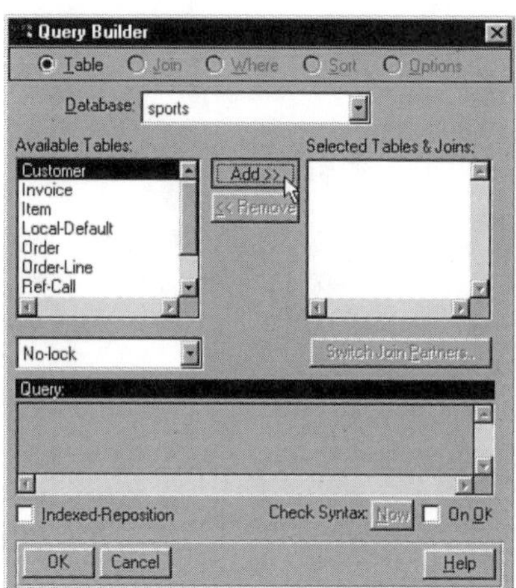

Fig. 9.8

Adding customer to the query definition.

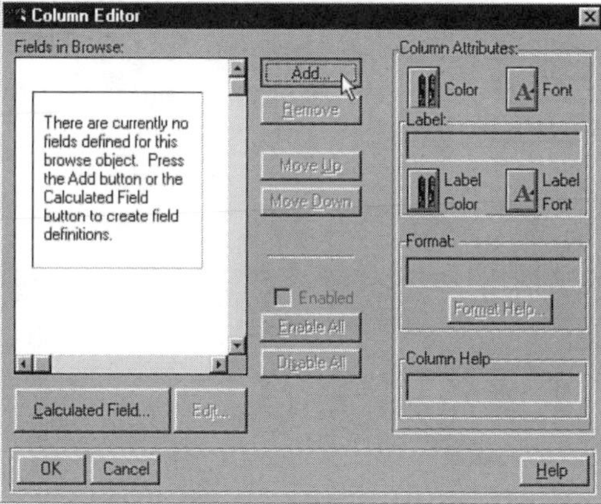

Fig. 9.9

Adding fields to the SmartBrowser.

Choose only the `customer.name` field for this SmartBrowser. After returning to the Wizard, you will proceed to the next screen, and the SmartBrowser Wizard will be finished.

Arrange the SmartBrowser so that it appears as shown in figure 9.10. This browser will need to be tall and thin to fit the main window of your sample application. The size of the browser should be about 25 columns by 10.5 lines as indicated in the browser's property sheet.

To change the width and height of the SmartBrowser, double-click in the browser control and set its geometry using the Property Sheet. Of course, you can also resize the browser with the mouse.

Remember that the SmartBrowser object is really a basic PROGRESS browser object inside a frame. If you are having difficulties resizing the browser itself, first resize the frame (by dragging the design window larger). Then you will be able to resize the browse control.

Fig. 9.10

The SmartBrowser arranged for height.

As was the case with the SmartViewers, the design window containing the SmartBrowser is used by the UIB only at design time. At runtime, only the frame and its contents will be presented.

You have completed the customer SmartBrowser. Save your work to your *appdir* working directory. Save the SmartBrowser as `b-cust.w` in the \appdir directory.

Next you will create the SmartBrowser for Order. Although the following two SmartBrowsers are created in much the same way as the Customer SmartBrowsers, they do have external table definitions that deserve special attention.

Creating the Order SmartBrowser

> **Note**
>
> The step-by-step instructions for creating the Order and Order Line SmartBrowsers are an abbreviated version of the preceding instructions for the Customer SmartBrowser. Pay special attention to the process of defining external tables.

1. Click the New button in the UIB main window and create a new SmartBrowser by selecting SmartBrowser Wizard from the object list.
2. On page 2 of the SmartBrowser Wizard, when you are prompted for external tables, choose Next to proceed to the next page. For this example, you will define external tables as the last step.
3. On page 3, press the Define Query button.
4. Add the order table to the query by selecting order in the tables list and clicking on the Add>> button.
5. Choose OK to return to the SmartBrowser Wizard, and proceed to the next screen, Fields to Display.
6. Click the Add Fields button to view the Column Editor window of the UIB.
7. Click the Add button to add fields to the browser.
8. Choose the Order-num, Order-Date, Promise-Date, Ship-Date, and Carrier fields for this SmartBrowser.

After returning to the Wizard, you will proceed to the next screen, and the SmartBrowser Wizard will be finished.

Arrange the SmartBrowser so that it appears as in figure 9.11. This browser will be wide and shallow to fit the main window of your sample application.

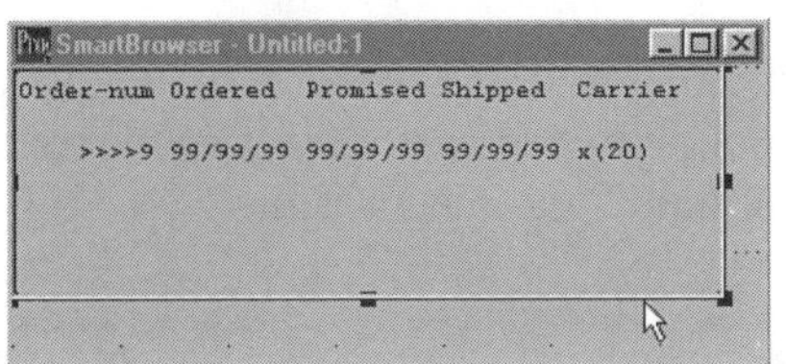

Fig. 9.11

The SmartBrowser arranged for width.

The Order-Num column is taking too much room because of the label Order Num.; the order number field is considerably less wide than its label. Change the column label to No. in the Column Editor dialog box by double-clicking within the browser and choosing the Fields button in the property sheet.

Change the label to No. on the Column Editor dialog box, as shown in figure 9.12.

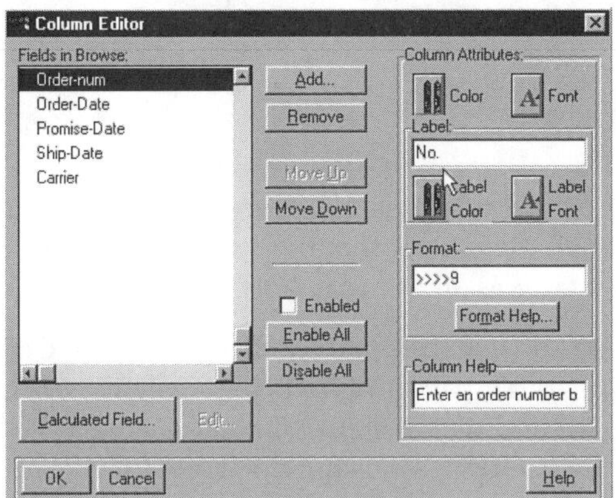

Fig. 9.12

The Order Number label changed in the browser fields window.

Next, you must specify an external table for the Order SmartBrowser. In its present form, the Order SmartBrowser would query the records in the Order table, yet would not know that only the orders for a given customer should be in the query.

The appropriate query for the Order SmartBrowser is as follows:

```
FOR EACH order OF customer.
```

By defining the join in the Order SmartBrowser, it will communicate with a customer record source (SmartBrowse, SmartQuery).

By defining customer as an external table, the Order SmartBrowser will expect customer records to be passed via object messaging.

Tip

By looking at your database design (ER diagram), you can easily determine where external tables are necessary for SmartObjects. A SmartObject associated with a table that is the dependent in a one-to-one or one-to-many relationship will likely need an external table defined.

To specify an external table, click the Procedure button in the UIB main window. Choose Add and double-click customer to add customer as an external table. The Procedure Settings windows should appear as in figure 9.13.

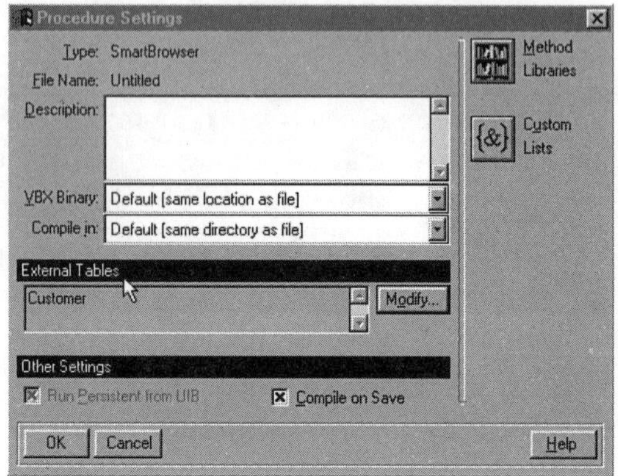

Fig. 9.13

The Procedure Settings window showing customer as an external table.

Now that Customer is referenced as an external table, you must redefine the query to include the Customer, Order join. Remember that the query was defined originally prior to defining the Customer table as an external table.

Double-click within the browser to view the property sheet. Click the Query button to view the Query Builder window. What you must do here to redefine the query is to remove Order from the tables list and then add it again. Once added, the UIB assumes that it is to be joined with the customer table. Naturally it would have been more practical to define Customer as an external table from the start. This example highlights how to redefine queries using the UIB.

The Query Builder window should appear as shown in figure 9.14.

The Wizard expedites the selection of external tables, queries, and fields for the SmartBrowser.

You have completed the Order SmartBrowser. Save the SmartBrowser as `b-order.w` in your *appdir* working directory.

Next you will create the SmartBrowser for Order Line.

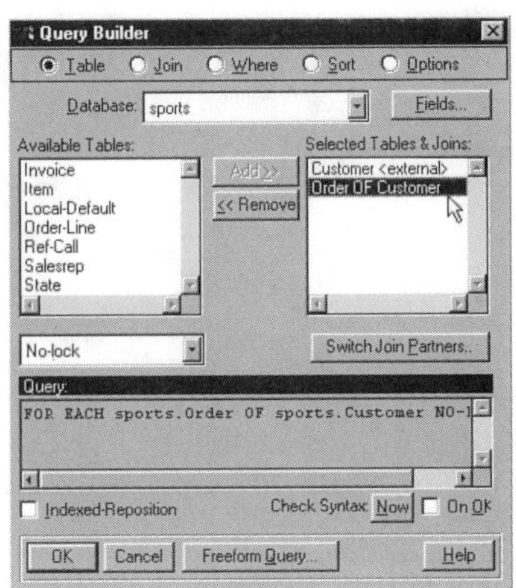

Fig. 9.14

The Query Builder window showing the customer, order join.

Creating the Order Line SmartBrowser

Click the New button in the UIB main window and create a new SmartBrowser by selecting SmartBrowser Wizard from the object list.

On Page 2 of the SmartBrowser Wizard, you will be prompted for external tables. According to the sports database design, the Order Line table is dependent on the Order table. Choose the Order table as external and proceed to the next page.

> **Tip**
>
> In this case, you are using the SmartBrowser Wizard to specify external tables before specifying the query. This is a much easier approach than that taken in the Order SmartBrowser case described previously. In the Order SmartBrowser you built, you defined the query *and then added the external table.*

On Page 3, press the Define Query button.

Add the order line and item tables to the query by selecting `Order Line` and `Item` in the tables list and clicking the Add>> button. Automatic joins between `Order`, `Order Line`, and `Item` are created by the Query Builder screen.

Choose OK to return to the SmartBrowser Wizard and proceed to the next screen, Fields to Display. Click the Add Fields button to view the Column Editor window of the UIB. Click the Add button to add fields to the browser.

Choose the `Item.Item-num`, `Item.Item-name`, `Order-line.qty`, `Order-line.price` fields for this SmartBrowser.

Figure 9.15 shows the fields for the Order Line browser.

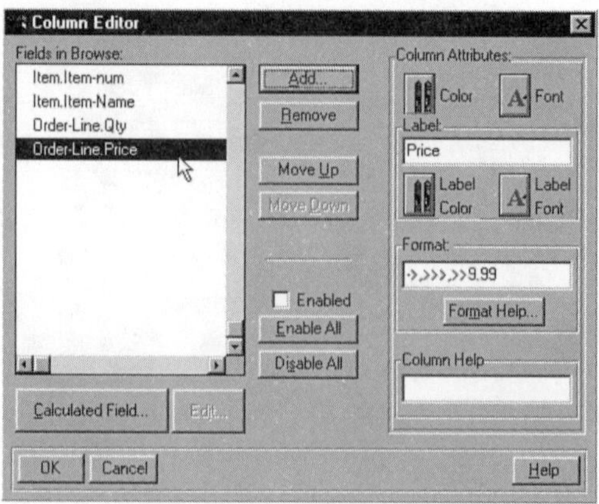

Fig. 9.15

The Column Editor dialog showing the chosen fields.

After returning to the Wizard, you will proceed to the next screen and the SmartBrowser Wizard will be finished.

Arrange the SmartBrowser so that it appears as shown in figure 9.16. This browser will be wide and shallow like the Order SmartBrowser.

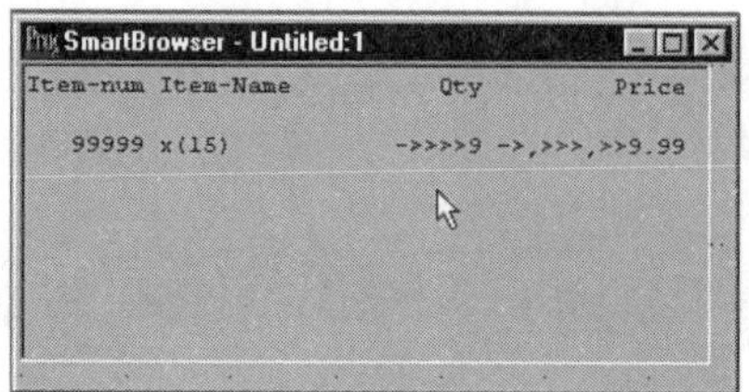

Fig. 9.16

The SmartBrowser arranged for width.

You have completed the Order Line SmartBrowser. Save your work in your *appdir* working directory. Save the SmartBrowser as `b-ordln.w` in your *appdir* working directory.

You will now create a SmartQuery to connect Customers and Salesreps. A *SmartQuery* is much like a SmartBrowser with no visualization. That is to say that a SmartQuery acts as a record source but does not, in and of itself, display anything.

Creating Your SmartQuery

The SmartQuery for Salesrep is needed to provide records to the Salesrep Viewer object. Every SmartViewer must have a record source. Record sources are typically SmartBrowsers or SmartQueries. In this particular case, there was no need to view the list of sales representatives with a browser. The Salesrep SmartQuery will join Customer and Salesrep records and will be a record source for any Salesrep viewer object.

Choose New from the UIB main window and select SmartQuery Wizard. On Page 2 of the SmartQuery Wizard, select external table: Customer.

Page 3 of the Wizard specifies the query. The query must join customer and salesrep tables, as shown in figure 9.17.

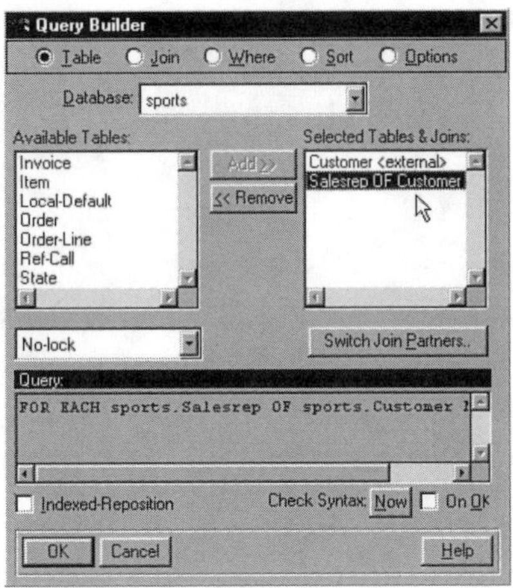

Fig. 9.17

The Query Builder window showing a join between customer and salesrep tables for the salesrep SmartQuery.

The resulting SmartQuery is visualized at design time, as shown in figure 9.18. The SmartQuery is shown at design time as a Q. The SmartQuery's position on the screen is not important since it does not visualize at runtime. At runtime, the SmartQuery is invisible while it provides a record source for other SmartObjects.

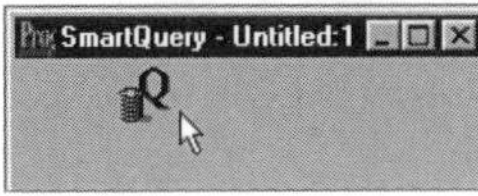

Fig. 9.18

The visual design-time SmartQuery.

You have completed the Salesrep SmartQuery. Save the SmartQuery as `q-salrep.w` in your *appdir* working directory.

Creating Your SmartPanel

SmartPanels are the objects with the highest reusability factor. It is unlikely that you will need to create many different types of SmartPanels throughout your application. PROGRESS V8 provides you with several SmartPanels (also called toolbars), as shown in figure 9.19.

The SmartPanels can be found in the directory DLC\src\adm\objects (where DLC is the PROGRESS installation root directory). These SmartPanels are listed in Table 9.4.

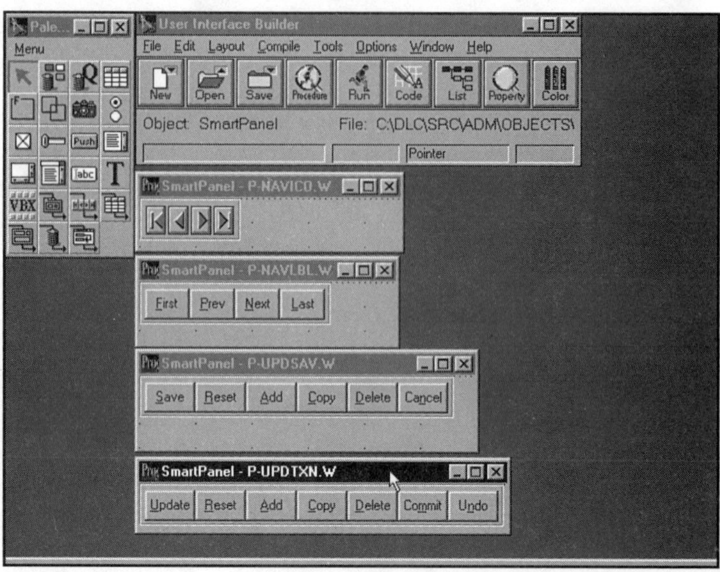

Fig. 9.19

Several SmartPanels provided with PROGRESS V8.

Table 9.4 SmartPanel Instances Provided with PROGRESS V8

SmartPanel Name	Description
`p-navico.w`	For record navigation, icon based
`p-navlbl.w`	For record navigation, text based
`p-updsav.w`	For record update, text based
`p-updtxn.w`	For record update with transaction, text based

SmartPanels have no direct association with data; therefore, they can be highly generic like those listed in the previous table.

You will utilize `p-updsav.w` as the SmartPanel for the sample application. It will allow you to modify the record presented in the Customer SmartViewer. You need only to connect a SmartLink from the SmartPanel to the appropriate SmartViewer.

Managing the transaction as it relates to customer record changes is not necessary for the sample application. For this reason, you will use `p-updsav` rather than `p-updtxn`. The SmartPanel `p-updsav` will manage database updates while not worrying about the management of a large transaction.

From Here...

The next step is to connect all of the components together with SmartLinks. The SmartObjects created in this chapter emphasize that you can create application components without typing any code. Most of the SmartObject's functionality is inherited within their templates and Method Libraries. Also keep in mind that the SmartObjects created for the sample application could have been created by different developers, at different times, and in different cities. Component-based development with SmartObjects is highly organized and productive!

In the next chapter you will connect all of the components that you built. This is a very exciting step in the development process.

It is important to recognize that in a truly component-based development process, the component build phase and the component connect phase are separate. The next chapter concentrates on this point further.

Note

Using SmartObject component-based development, components are built prior to being connected. This means that your development project can be segmented into two distinct phases: *build* and *connect*.

For more information on related items, refer to the following chapters:

- Chapter 10, "Connecting the Components," shows you how to use SmartLinks to connect built components.
- Chapter 11, "Adding Menu Bar and Report Components," completes the sample application.

CHAPTER 10

Connecting the Components

This chapter takes you through the connection of the SmartObject components you built in Chapter 9, "A Sample GUI Application." As you learned in the preceding chapter, in a truly component-based development process, the component build phase and the component connect phase are separate. The components are built independently of how they will be pieced together to form the final application.

After reading this chapter, you should be able to do the following:

- Understand the importance of SmartContainers
- Understand how SmartObjects are connected
- Create container objects for your applications
- Understand how container "pages" work
- Have a deeper understanding of message passing and object communications
- Use the PRO*Spy tool to debug the object messages as they occur
- Understand more of the fine details of using PROGRESS V8 to develop applications

Voice-of-Experience Movies

See Table G.3 in Appendix G, "Contents of CD," for a list of the Voice-of-Experience files for this chapter.

Reviewing the Sample Application

In the preceding chapter, you created the objects for the sample application. The components are listed by object type in the table 10.1.

Table 10.1 Identified Components by Object Type

Object Type	Instance
Viewer	Customer, Salesrep
Browse	Customer, Order, OrderLine
Query	Salesrep
Panel	(Record Update)

The resulting objects created in Chapter 9 are shown in Table 10.2.

Table 10.2 Objects

Description	Master File Name
Customer browse	`b-cust.w`
Customer detail viewer	`v-cust.w`
Orders browse	`b-order.w`
Order Line browse	`b-ordln.w`
Salesman viewer	`v-salrep.w`
Salesman query	`q-salrep.w`
Update Panel	`DLC\gui\adm\objects\p-updsav.w`

Each of these SmartObjects (except the Update Panel) should now exist in your appdir directory (that is, c:\appdir). You should have two copies of each file: source code, ending with the .w extension, and compiled r-code, ending with the .r extension.

To begin this section, you must first do the following:

- Set your working directory (see Chapter 1, "Introducing PROGRESS") to c:\appdir
- Copy the sample sports database into your working directory (chapter 1)
- Complete Chapter 9 and have all the SmartObjects listed previously. You can copy them from the CD. See Appendix G, "Contents of CD," for a complete listing of CD contents.
- Connect to the sports database using the Data Dictionary, the Procedure Editor, or the UIB tool (see Chapter 2, "Getting Started with ADE Tools").

Creating the Sample Application's Main Window

In this chapter, you will create the main window of the sample application, which will contain the SmartObjects and drive the sporting goods store interface. You will learn how container objects such as SmartFolder and SmartWindow play an important role in the application framework.

You will create the main window in phases, each getting you progressively closer to what the final screen should look like. Following these real-life steps in putting the main screen together will help you build your own applications.

Creating the Container Object

For your sporting goods store application, the main screen will be a window containing the SmartObjects designed in Chapter 9.

According to the specification, the application must show the following information:

- Customer Data (with the capability to modify)
- Orders and order line data for the customer
- Salesrep for the customer

For this reason, you need to be able to switch the main screen among the three pages listed here. This function of paging is inherent within the SmartWindow container, as you will see in this chapter.

Begin by creating the container window. Click the New button in the UIB main window. The New Object screen shows the list of object types. Double-click on SmartWindow as shown in figure 10.1.

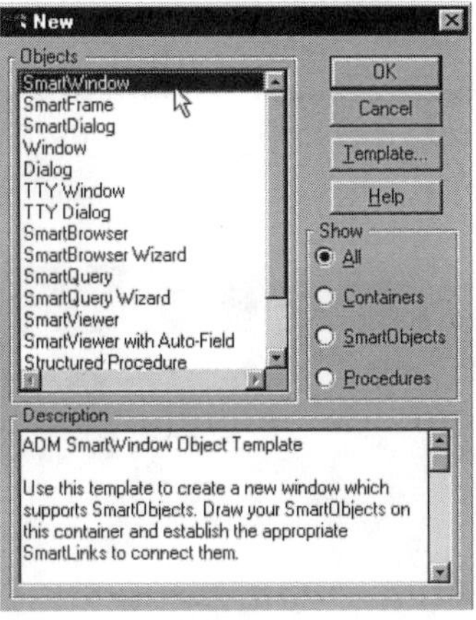

Fig. 10.1

Creating a new SmartWindow.

A cue card then appears, giving you instructions for the SmartWindow. Cue cards can be helpful for the novice V8 developer. Close the cue card after reading it for information on SmartWindow containers.

▶▶ See Chapter 19, "Using Active Templates," to learn how to define your own cue cards.

The SmartWindow should then appear as shown in figure 10.2. Note the selected frame that exists within the SmartWindow object. In Chapter 9, you learned that SmartObjects were based on PROGRESS frames: SmartBrowsers and SmartViewers. These objects are created in the UIB in their own *design window*. This design window, however, really represents the frame inside a SmartObject. Generally, growing the design window causes the frame to grow.

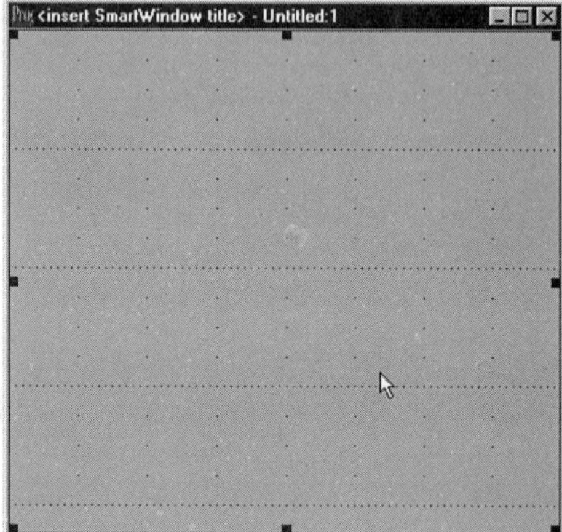

Fig. 10.2

The frame within the SmartWindow.

For SmartWindows, as the name implies, the window is a significant part of the object. Technically, the frame of the SmartWindow is needed if non-SmartObject controls (buttons, fill-ins, and so on) will be placed directly within the SmartWindow. The SmartWindow's frame can also be used as the parent for SmartObjects. SmartObjects can also parent directly to the window without the intervening frame object. In practice, however, there are some very good reasons for keeping the frame within the SmartWindow (shown selected in fig. 10.2).

Tip

You should always parent SmartObjects in a SmartWindow to the default frame in that window for the following three reasons:

- You can tab between fields in different SmartObjects only if the objects share a common *frame* parent.
- The mnemonic shortcut keys (for example, Alt+X) do not work between SmartObjects that are not in the same frame.
- Controlling the overlapping of SmartObjects is easier if they parent to a single frame.

After you have created the new SmartWindow, you are ready to begin creating your interface.

Resize the window and frame to the appropriate size (large enough to hold the SmartObjects that you plan to place inside). To help you with this task, you can follow these instructions:

1. View the Property Sheet for the frame (within the window) by double-clicking within the frame area.
2. In the Geometry Section of the Property Sheet, set the width and height to 75 by 13, as shown in figure 10.3. The geometry units in this case are character units.
3. To view the Property Sheet for the window, press Ctrl and click within the frame at the same time. This selects the window. Click the Property button in the UIB main window to view the Property Sheet for the window.
4. Repeat Step 2 to set the window's geometry.

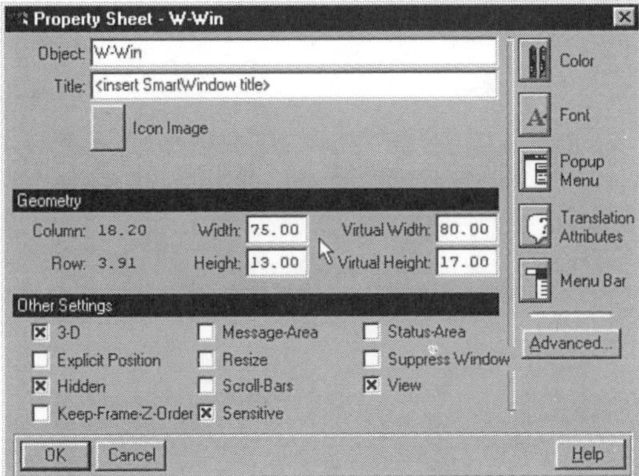

Fig. 10.3

Setting the geometry for the window.

You now have a container object for the main window. Next, you will begin placing components within the container window and linking them together.

Connecting the Sample Application Components

Now you're ready to step through the design of each page of the main window. You will design the following pages using the UIB:

- Page 0 containing Customer SmartBrowser
- Page 1 containing Customer SmartViewer and Update SmartPanel
- Page 2 containing Order and Order Line SmartBrowsers
- Page 3 containing Salesrep SmartViewer

Placing the SmartBrowser on the Initial Page

You begin by placing the Customer SmartBrowser (`b-cust.w`) into the container. Click the SmartBrowser icon on the UIB palette. The Choose SmartBrowser window appears.

If you have set up your environment correctly, all the SmartBrowsers that you created in Chapter 9 should show in the list for the current working directory.

Tip

If the SmartBrowser search dialog box does not show SmartBrowser objects in your working directory, be sure to set your Windows 95 working directory to \appdir to view the list of SmartObjects.

Using the SmartBrowser button on the UIB's Object Palette, you can select from the SmartBrowsers that you have already created. Note that the .w and .r files are listed. After you locate the file `b-cust.w`, click OK. Then you can place the SmartBrowser anywhere within your new SmartWindow. Figure 10.4 shows the SmartBrowser icon over the design window. This indicates that you are allowed to drop the object onto your working area. Now drop the SmartBrowser into the SmartWindow by clicking in the desired location.

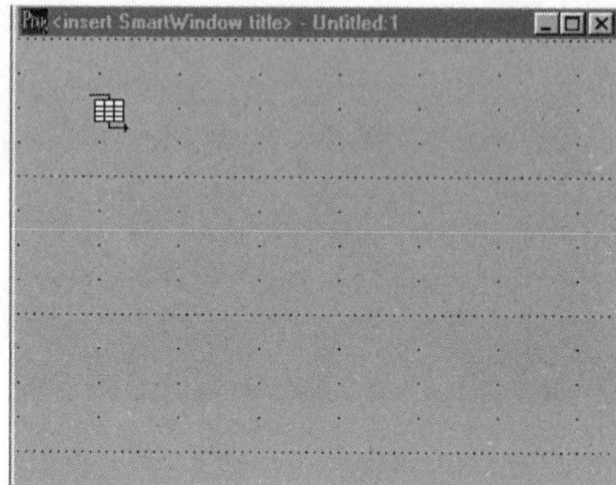

Fig. 10.4

The icon indicates that you are about to place a SmartBrowser object.

Click the Run button on the UIB main window to view your SmartBrowser in action. The SmartBrowser for Customer is fully functional within the SmartWindow (see fig. 10.5). It has no objects with which to communicate—yet.

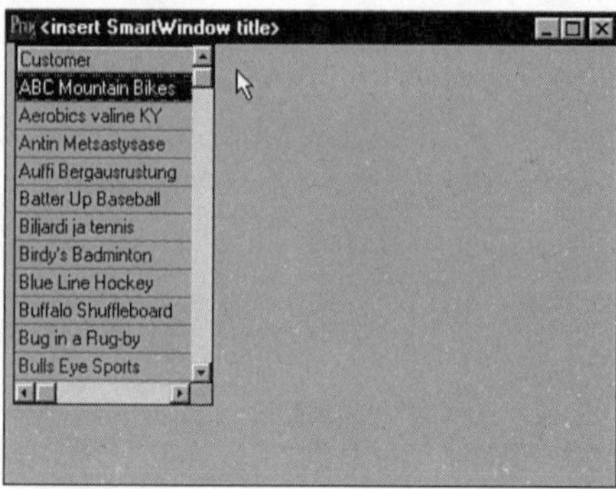

Fig. 10.5

The running window with SmartBrowser for Customer records.

Placing the Customer Viewer on the First Page

Next, you can indicate to the UIB that you will be designing the contents of Page 1 (Customer viewer). Remember that you want three separate, independently viewed pages of information for each customer in the list.

Page 0 is the default design and startup page. The SmartObjects on Page 0 are always visible at runtime. The SmartObjects on pages 1 through *x* are visible only when their page is selected for viewing.

To indicate to the UIB that you want to design Page 1, choose Edit, Goto Page from the UIB's menu. The resulting Goto Page dialog box prompts you for the page to design. Enter **1** in the Display Page Number text box.

> **Tip**
>
> If you double-click on the page number in the UIB main window status area, you can open the Edit, Goto Page dialog box. This option is available only on SmartContainers that support paging.

The SmartObjects that you insert now will be presented in page 1 of the container.

Think of a SmartContainer (such as your SmartWindow) as a layered circuit board. A multilayered circuit board has a main board where the most essential elements (chips) are placed. The circuit board also has one or more additional sub-boards, or layers, that contain additional circuitry. The chips on all the sub-boards and main board can communicate together.

Having selected Page 1 for design (which should be reflected by "Page 1" in the UIB main window status area), you can now insert the Customer viewer. Click the SmartViewer icon on the UIB palette. Locate the file `v-cust.w` and place it next to the Customer SmartBrowser. The PROGRESS Advisor then prompts you for automatic creation of a SmartLink.

Choose OK to accept the Record SmartLink between the two SmartObjects as prescribed by the Advisor. Any time that you insert a SmartObject that serves as a record destination for a particular table, the Advisor will prompt you to establish a record link to that object from a record source.

Next, you can run your interface as it stands so far to see the two SmartObjects working together. First, you must instruct the UIB that you want to start the interface on Page 1 of your design. This will bring up the Customer SmartViewer (Page 1) at the start of the application.

To indicate Page 1 startup, click on the Procedure Settings button (or choose Tools, Procedure Settings) in the UIB main window. The Pages dialog box then appears, as shown in figure 10.6. Click the Page button.

Tip

You can also use the Pages dialog box to move SmartObjects from one page to another. This capability is particularly useful if you are augmenting a simple window to have multiple pages (and you need to move some SmartObjects from page 0 to page 1), or if you accidentally add a SmartObject to the wrong page.

Moving a SmartObject between pages is always better than deleting it on one page and then adding it on another. Deleting the object deletes all its properties and links. You will have to re-create them when you add the object again. Moving the object between pages retains all useful information and settings.

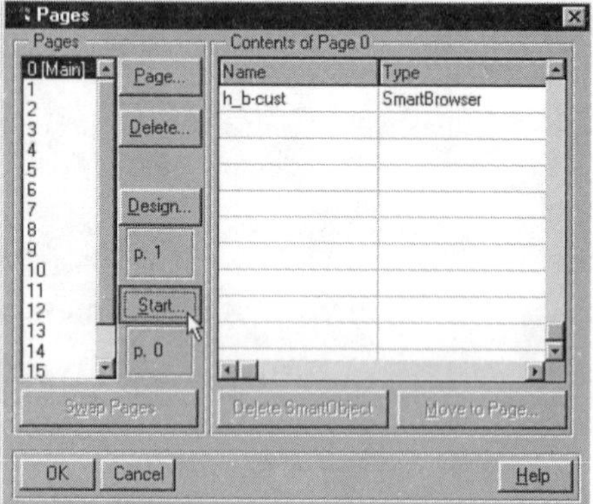

Fig. 10.6

Setting the pages in the Pages dialog box.

In the Pages section of the Pages dialog box, set the Start Page to 1. This setting makes Page 1 of your SmartWindow visible when you start the application.

Click the Run button or press F2 to run your main window in its current state. Your window should look something like figure 10.7.

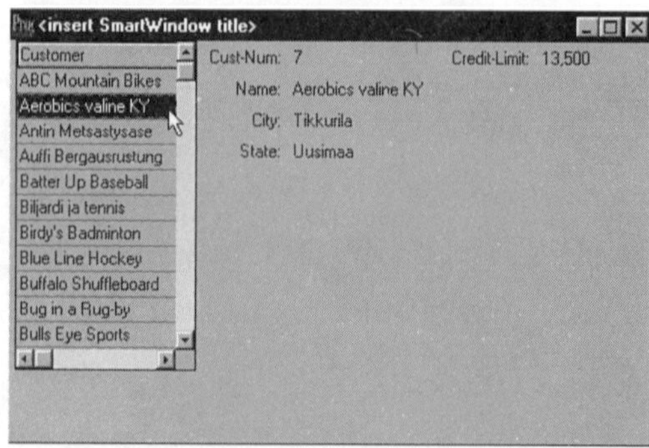

Fig. 10.7

Your functional interface so far: Customer list and details.

Save your work in a separate file named `w-msging.w` in your appdir working directory. You will use this file later to explore message passing.

Also, save your work to the file `w-main.w` in the same directory using File, Save As.

Note the following points at this stage of the construction process:

- The Record SmartLink between the Customer Browse object and the Customer Viewer object passes records from source to target, keeping both in sync.
- The SmartWindow container simply contains the objects. They are not copied into the window. Each SmartObject is truly independent. Each SmartObject is a true component.
- The UIB's Advisors aid you in the connectivity between components when their relationship seems obvious.
- You have not typed any 4GL code to build any of these objects.

You will be placing the update panel into page 1 along with the Customer SmartViewer later in this chapter. Now you'll continue with the design for pages 2 and 3 of the SmartWindow.

Placing the Order SmartBrowsers on the Second Page

To set the design to page 2, double-click on the Page # in the UIB main window status area (as you did in the preceding section). Set the Page # to **2**. You will be inserting the Order and Order Line SmartBrowsers into this page.

Click the SmartBrowser icon on the UIB palette. Select the `b-order.w` file in your sample directory. The Advisor asks you about the possible SmartLinks that make sense at this juncture.

The choices presented by the Advisor are as follows:

- Record Link from SmartBrowser `h_b-cust.w`
- Record Link from SmartViewer `h_v-cust.w`

The `h_` in the SmartObject names is simply used to construct a name for the *handle* that points to the SmartObjects. `h_b-cust` is a *handle* to your Customer SmartBrowser.

Choose the first option for Customer SmartBrowser as the record source (that is, `h_b-cust`).

The Advisor presents you with these options because either the SmartBrowser or the SmartViewer for Customer may serve as a record source for the Order SmartBrowser.

To help illustrate this point further, double-click in the newly positioned Order SmartBrowser to bring up its Property Sheet. As shown in the figure 10.8, the SmartObject's Property Sheet enables you to view the object's SmartLinks and SmartInfo. Click the SmartInfo icon.

The SmartInfo screen then appears, showing you the object's capabilities in terms of supported ADM links, record sources, and target possibilities (see fig. 10.9).

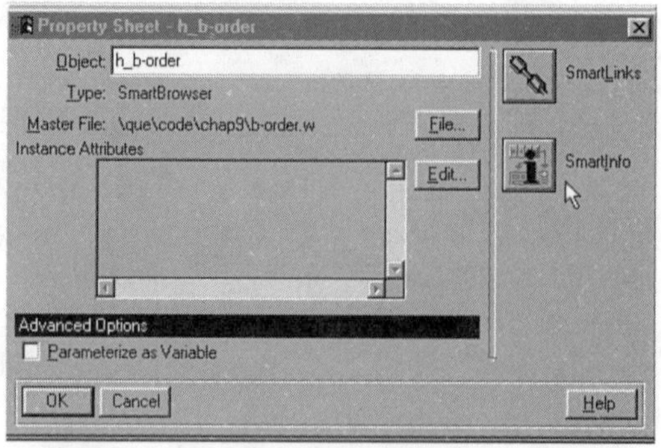

Fig. 10.8

The SmartObject's Property Sheet.

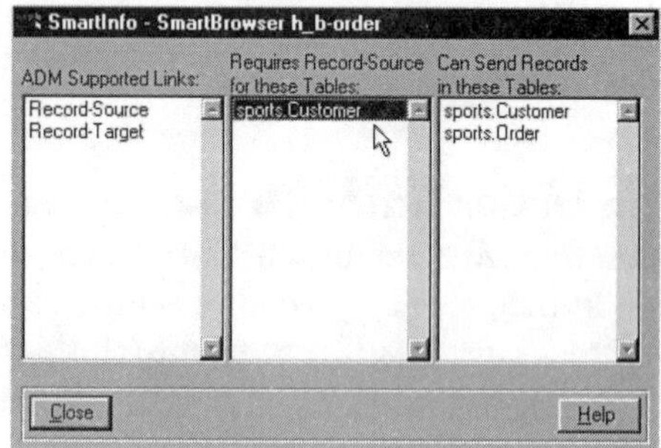

Fig. 10.9

The SmartObject's SmartInfo screen.

Note that the `h_b-order` object (a SmartBrowser for orders) requires a record source for the Customer table. Why is this? The answer is that you specified Customer as an *external table* when creating it in Chapter 9. The object contains a query that is a join of Customer and Order.

Note also that the SmartInfo screen indicates that the object can send records of Customer and Order. That will help you in connecting the Order Line SmartBrowser because it demands a record source for Order (Order is an external table).

Next, add the Order Line SmartBrowser that will receive records from the Order SmartBrowser. Click the SmartBrowser icon on the UIB palette and select the master file, `b-ordln.w`. Position the Order Line SmartBrowser directly below the Order SmartBrowser. The PROGRESS Advisor appears.

Choose the default option to establish a record source of Order SmartBrowser. The Order SmartBrowser provides Order records to the Order Line SmartBrowser that has Order as an external table (as you specified in chapter 9). Position your SmartObjects for Page 2, as shown in figure 10.10.

Save your work again to the file `w-main.w` in your working appdir directory.

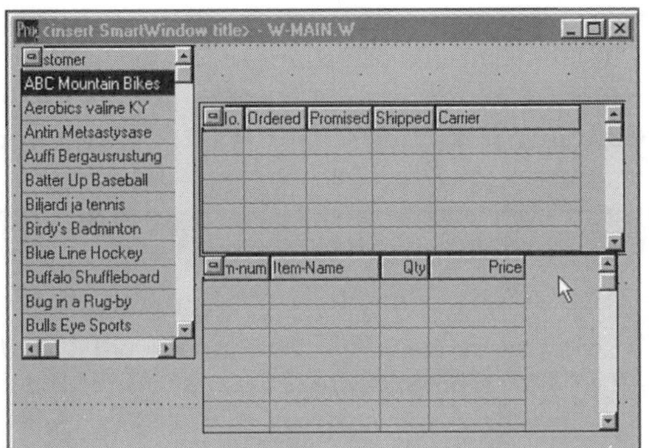

Fig. 10.10

Page 2 SmartObjects positioned.

> **Note**
>
> If you try to run your window at this stage, you will see only Page 1's SmartObjects. This happens because no mechanism exists yet to switch the interface to show page 2. You will create that mechanism later.

Placing the SalesRep Viewer and SmartQuery on the Third Page

To set the design to Page 3, double-click the Page # in the UIB main window status area. Set the Page # to **3**. You will insert the SalesRep Viewer and SmartQuery into this page.

Click the SmartQuery icon on the UIB palette and select the query that you built earlier in Chapter 9: `q-salrep.w`. The SmartQuery is not a visible object; you can place it anywhere in the window area. Figure 10.11 shows the SmartLinks Advisor for the SmartQuery.

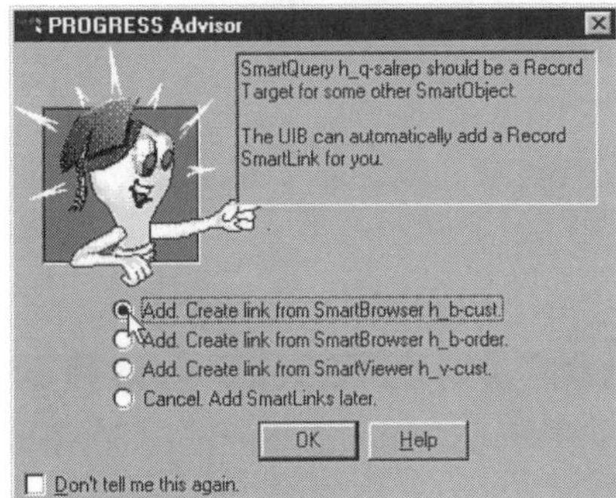

Fig. 10.11

SmartLinks for the SmartQuery.

Note the long list of possible record sources for the SalesRep SmartQuery. The SmartQuery that you built in Chapter 9 specified Customer as an external table. The Advisor is indicating that several possible sources exist for the record source. Choose the option that points to the Customer SmartBrowser, `h_b-cust`, for the record source.

> **Note**
>
> When you are presented with choices for SmartLink record sources, it is recommended that you choose the most direct source. Choosing the Customer SmartViewer as a record source for the SalesRep SmartQuery is indirect. The Customer SmartBrowser is the most *direct* record source in this example.

Now that you have a SalesRep record source in the form of the SalesRep SmartQuery, you're ready to insert the SalesRep SmartViewer into Page 3.

Click the SmartViewer icon on the UIB palette and select the file `v-salrep.w` (which you created in Chapter 9). Position the SalesRep viewer as shown in figure 10.12. The PROGRESS Advisor, as you may have been able to predict, appears, indicating that the SmartQuery is an excellent record source for SalesRep records. Choose the default option presented by the Advisor.

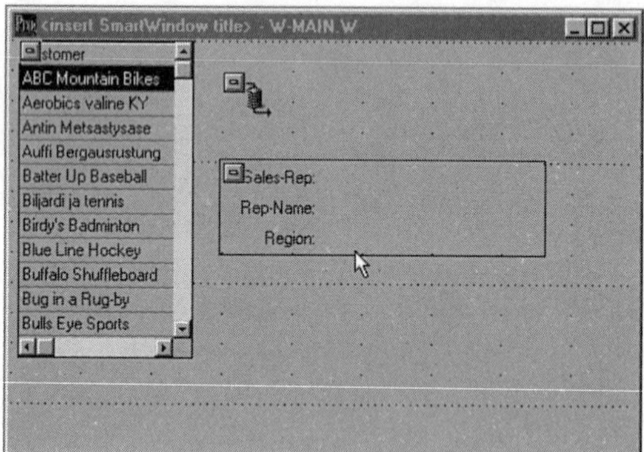

Fig. 10.12

The Page 3 SmartViewer for SalesRep along with the SmartQuery.

Now you have completed placing the objects for Page 3 of your main window interface. Save your work once again to the file `w-main.w` in your working appdir directory.

Installing Page-Management Control

Page-management control is an important part of your interface construction. Page management is simply a mechanism that selects a visualized page. In the sample application main window, you have specified three pages. When running the main window, you can view only Page 1, which you specified as the startup page.

Ultimately, for your main window, you will place a tab folder object to manage the pages for you and provide a Windows 95 look to the interface. For now, you will use a simple radio set to manage the viewed page.

Be sure to set the Page # to 0 because it is the place where you want the page control (the radio set). To do this, double-click on the Page # area of the UIB main window's status area. Enter **0** as the page number when prompted by the Goto Page dialog box.

Click the radio set icon on the UIB palette. Then place the radio set in the upper-middle area of the window (see fig. 10.13).

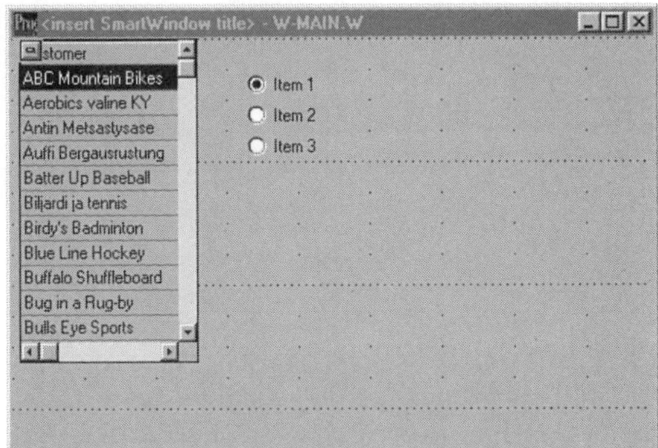

Fig. 10.13

A radio set placed into Page 0 to control the page during runtime.

As you can see, the radio set is named with `Item 1`, `Item 2`, and so on, as the radio set choices. Double-click the radio set to view its Property Sheet. The Property Sheet `RADIO SET-1` then appears, as shown in figure 10.14. Set the buttons list as shown in the figure, and click the Horizontal property to align the radio set lengthwise.

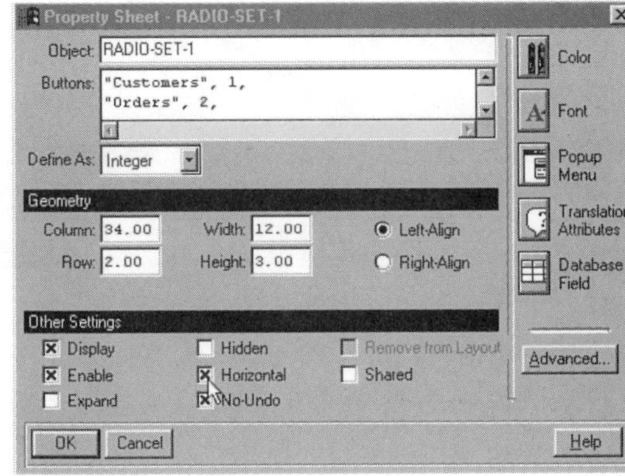

Fig. 10.14

The Property Sheet for the paging radio set.

Note the item list specified as follows:

```
"Customer", 1, "Orders", 2, "Salesrep", 3
```

This list is a grouping of labels and their corresponding values. A selection of `"Customer"` would return a value of 1 (integer) for the radio set. This capability will come in handy when you're managing the page numbers because the radio set values correspond to the pages on the window.

Stretch the radio set out so that it appears as shown in figure 10.15.

Fig. 10.15

The radio set positioned within the window.

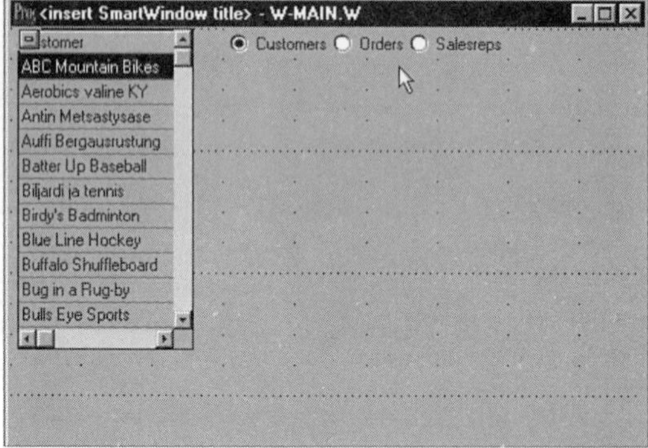

Earlier in this chapter, you read about the SmartWindow containing a frame. The frame of the SmartWindow is needed only if non-SmartObject controls (buttons, fill-ins, and so on) will be placed directly on the SmartWindow.

In this case, you are placing a non-SmartObject, the radio set, onto the frame. You cannot place a control such as a radio set directly onto a window; it must reside on a frame.

To make the radio set functional, you need to program its `VALUE-CHANGED` trigger. Click the radio set to select it, and click the Code button in the UIB main window. Figure 10.16 shows the code that you need to enter into the Section Editor for the `VALUE-CHANGED` trigger of the radio set.

Fig. 10.16

The Section Editor showing the `VALUE-CHANGED` trigger for the radio set.

Section Editor - SmartWindow - W-MAIN.W

File Edit Insert Search Compile Help

Section: Triggers | List... | Insert Call...

ON: VALUE-CHANGED | New... | OF: RADIO-SET-1

```
DO:
  ASSIGN {&SELF-NAME}.
  RUN select-page ({&SELF-NAME}).
END.
```

The trigger code is very simple and is repeated here along with an analysis of the commands:

```
ASSIGN {&SELF-NAME}.
RUN select-page ({&SELF-NAME}).
```

Tip

A radio set to select pages has been provided by PROGRESS as a *custom object*. If you click with the right mouse button on the Radio Set icon in the Object Palette, you will see a Select Page option. This option sets the UIB so that the next radio set will automatically be created with the correct data type and trigger code to select pages.

You can find additional information on creating your own custom objects in Chapter 21, "Making the Most of the Application Component Environment."

`{&SELF-NAME}` is a common preprocessor that you can use to substitute for a control's name. The control name for the radio set happens to be `radio-set-1`. The use of the preprocessor ensures that the code is valid for any control regardless of name.

The `ASSIGN {&SELF-NAME}.` command is interpreted by the compiler as `ASSIGN radio-set-1.`. This assigns the screen value of the radio set to the radio set variable.

The `RUN select-page {&SELF-NAME}).` command runs the procedure `select-page` (inherent within any SmartWindow object) to set the viewing page. The page will be set to the value within the radio set variable (1, 2, or 3).

Now close the Section Editor window and run the main window by pressing F2. Figure 10.17 shows a radio set manipulating the multiple pages of the SmartWindow.

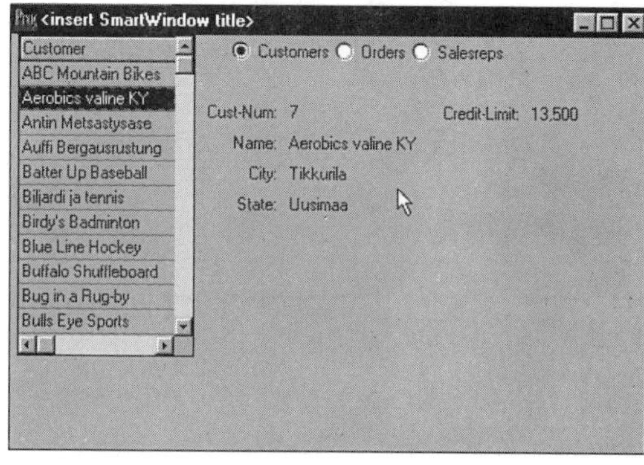

Fig. 10.17

The interface with a radio set to manage the pages. Page 1 is shown.

While the window is running, use the radio set buttons to view the three different pages of the main window. Save your work once again to the file `w-main.w` in your working appdir directory.

You will now replace the radio set with a more elegant tab folder control paging mechanism. Tab folders are prominent in Windows 95 interfaces. They allow one window to contain many pages. Examine the Windows 95 Display Properties window for a good example of a tab folder interface (see fig. 10.18).

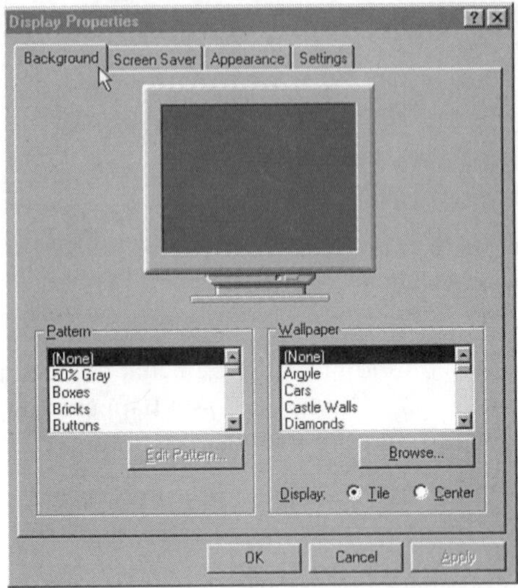

Fig. 10.18

The Windows 95 Display Properties window tab folders.

PROGRESS V8 enables you to design such tab folder interfaces effortlessly using the SmartFolder object. You will now alter your radio set controlled interface by inserting a folder object. The folder object will control the pages just as the radio set has.

Select the radio set by clicking it once. Press the Del key to remove it (and its trigger code). While you're on Page 0, insert a SmartFolder by clicking the SmartFolder icon in the UIB palette. Position the SmartFolder to the right of the Customer SmartBrowser.

The PROGRESS Advisor pops up, prompting you to accept a SmartLink for Page Source. Accept the default option for Page Source.

Just as the Customer SmartBrowser was a *Record* source for the Customer SmartViewer, the SmartFolder (generic) is a *Page* source for the SmartWindow container. That is, the SmartFolder is a *source* of page management for the SmartWindow that displays the various designed pages.

Following are analogies of the record source and record target to help make the point clear:

- A SmartBrowser or SmartQuery is a record source for SmartViewers. The record source sends records to the target so that the target can display the appropriate data.
- A SmartFolder is a page source for SmartWindows. The page source sends page numbers to the target so that it can display the appropriate page.

What you learned about Record SmartLinks helps you to understand the other link types such as Page SmartLinks. See Chapter 7, "SmartObject Links and Messages," for more information on SmartLinks.

Resize the SmartFolder as shown in figure 10.19. Select all three pages to be sure that the SmartObjects within each page fit comfortably within the SmartFolder. Because the SmartFolder is on Page 0, you can resize it while viewing any of the design pages. (The approximate size is 50 columns by 10.5 rows.)

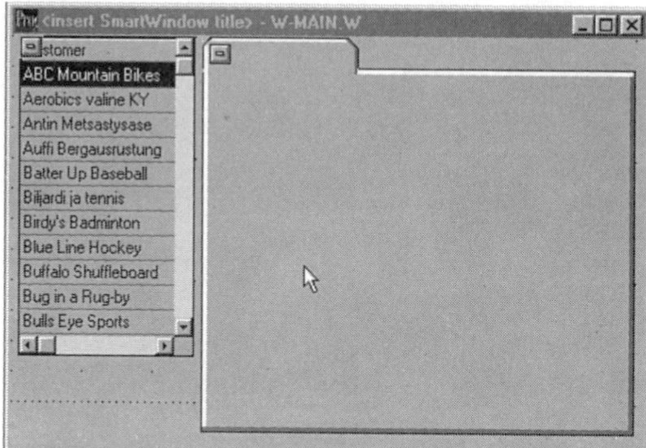

Fig. 10.19

The SmartFolder resized appropriately.

Now you must establish the SmartFolder's tab labels. Three tabs are necessary to manage the three design pages. Double-click the SmartFolder to view its Property Sheet. Choose Edit to edit its Instance Attributes. Figure 10.20 shows the SmartFolder Attributes dialog box set for three tab labels.

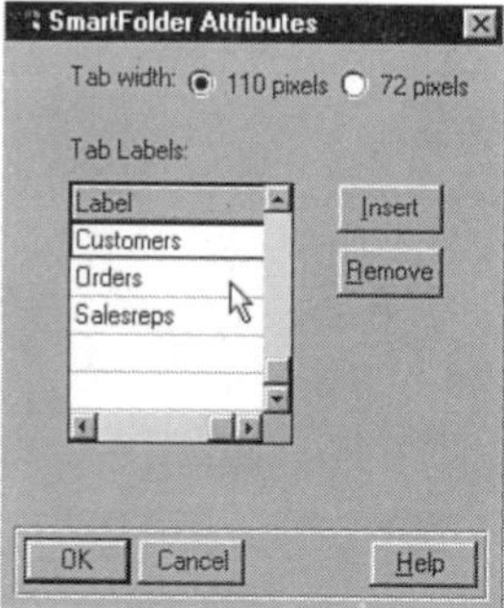

Fig. 10.20

The Tab Labels for the SmartFolder are Customers, Orders, and Salesreps.

Run the window by pressing F2. The window is now fully functional with the tabs. Page 1 is shown in figure 10.21. You can click the various tabs to view different pages.

Now you have a folder tab interface with several pages of SmartObjects. With PROGRESS V8, you can develop folder interfaces with very few lines of code. The folder object is provided with V8 as a page-management object. At the time of the printing of this book, several third-party vendors have probably begun selling alternative paging objects. See Appendix G, "Contents of CD," for a list of vendors who have supplied samples for the CD.

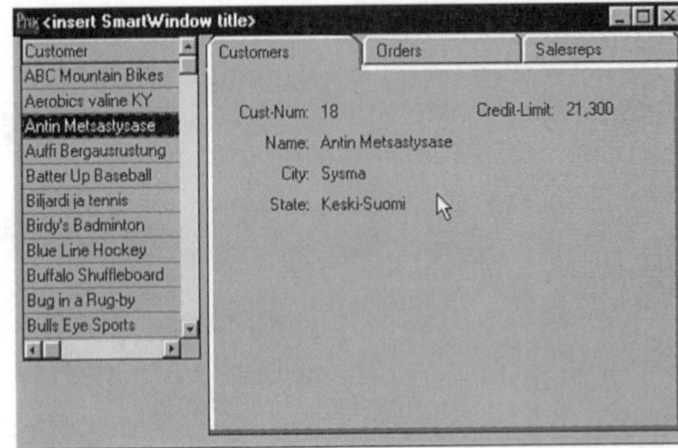

Fig. 10.21

The functional interface. Page 1 is shown.

Installing the SmartPanel

You have not yet placed one of the components: the SmartPanel `p-updsav.w`. The specification for the sample application called for the capability to modify Customer detail. You must insert the SmartPanel into page 1, which contains the Customer SmartViewer.

Select page 1 as your design page by double-clicking the Page # in the UIB main window status area and entering **1** as the page number. Then click the SmartPanel icon on the UIB palette, choose `p-updsav`, and position the panel below the Customer SmartViewer.

As you might expect, the Advisor prompts you for a possible source for the `TABLEIO` SmartLink. The SmartPanel is a `TABLEIO` source for any SmartObject with a Record Source. The possible `TABLEIO` targets are the objects you have positioned that have record sources.

The appropriate target for the `TABLEIO` is the SmartViewer for Customer because it is the SmartObject that you want the SmartPanel (toolbar) to control. The data in the Customer SmartViewer is what you intend to modify.

Choose `h_v-cust` for the `TABLEIO` target (the `h_` is part of the handle name).

> **Note**
>
> When you're thinking about SmartLinks, always think in terms of *source* and *target* for the messages that will travel through the link. See Chapter 7 for explanations of links and messages.

Your window is now able to update the Customer fields presented in the Customer SmartViewer. Figure 10.22 shows the design window with Page 1.

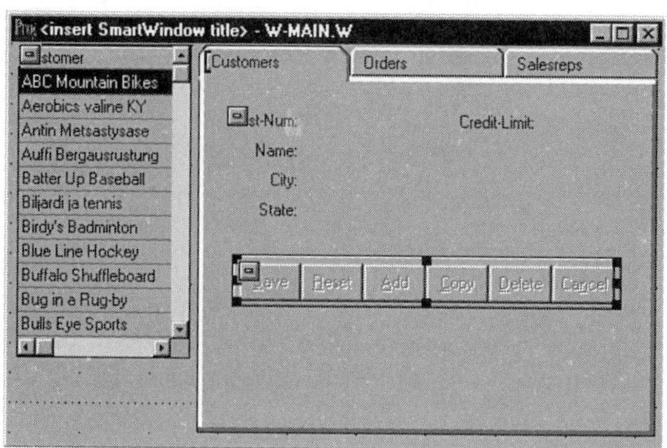

Fig. 10.22

The functional interface with SmartPanel. Page 1 is shown.

Save your work once again to the file `w-main.w` in your working appdir directory. Now you have completed the main window of the sample application.

Message Passing and Object Links

This section summarizes what you've seen with regards to object links. Several SmartLinks were established during your assembly of the main window. All were proposed by the Advisor while you inserted SmartObjects into the window.

You can view this collection of SmartLinks for your main window. To do so, click the Procedure button on the UIB main window to open the Procedure Settings window. Then click the SmartLinks icon. The SmartLinks dialog box then appears, showing all the SmartLinks for this window (see fig. 10.23).

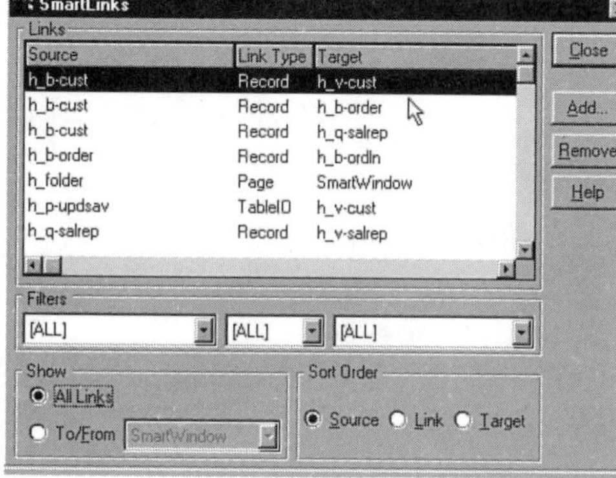

Fig. 10.23

The SmartLinks dialog box.

The SmartLinks are initially listed by *source*. For added clarity, Table 10.3 lists the SmartLinks shown in the SmartLinks dialog box.

Table 10.3 SmartLinks

Source	Link Type	Target
b-cust	Record	q-slsrep
b-cust	Record	b-order
b-cust	Record	v-cust
b-order	Record	b-ordln
folder	Page	SmartWindow
p-updsav	TABLEIO	v-cust
q-slsrep1	Record	v-salrep

If you superimpose the Record SmartLinks on top of the database design for the sample application, you can see the relationship between database design and record links (see fig. 10.24).

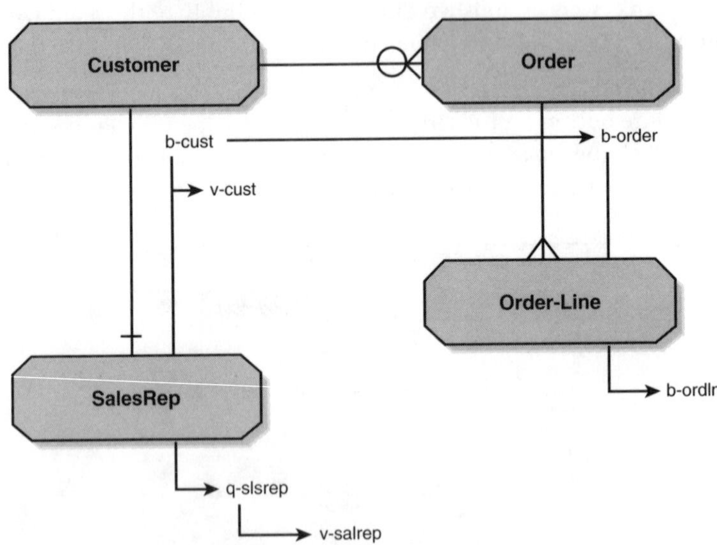

Fig. 10.24

Database Design and Record SmartLinks superimposed.

Each table relationship has a corresponding Record SmartLink. The relationship between Customer and SalesRep has a corresponding Record SmartLink between the *source* (Customer SmartBrowser) and the *target* (SalesRep SmartQuery).

Within each table in the database design, you may have more than one SmartObject with Record SmartLink connections. In the sample application, the SalesRep table has a SmartQuery that acts as the record source to the target SmartViewer for SalesRep.

Note

You may be able to determine much of your Record SmartLinks before any assembly process takes place, simply by examining your database design ER diagrams. Drawing expected SmartLinks during design time can help you determine the complete list of SmartObjects necessary.

Continuing to look at the last table, in addition to the RecordSmartLinks, you also notice a Page SmartLink between the SmartFolder and the SmartWindow. This allows the SmartFolder to pass a message regarding which page to display to the SmartWindow. In the sample build, you created a radio set that instructed the SmartWindow which page to view by using the `select-page` procedure. The SmartFolder is simply a more sophisticated and smart way of doing the same thing.

Also in the list of SmartLinks shown in Table 10.3 is the TABLEIO SmartLink connecting the SmartPanel and the Customer SmartViewer. This allows the SmartPanel to send messages regarding record update to the SmartViewer.

You now have working experience with SmartLinks and message passing. How can you detect which messages are being passed between SmartObjects at runtime?

Testing the Links

Understanding the SmartLinks between SmartObjects requires a higher level of understanding than that of the actual ADM events that fire as a result of the SmartLinks. Figure 10.25 shows how SmartLinks are related to ADM events within linked SmartObjects.

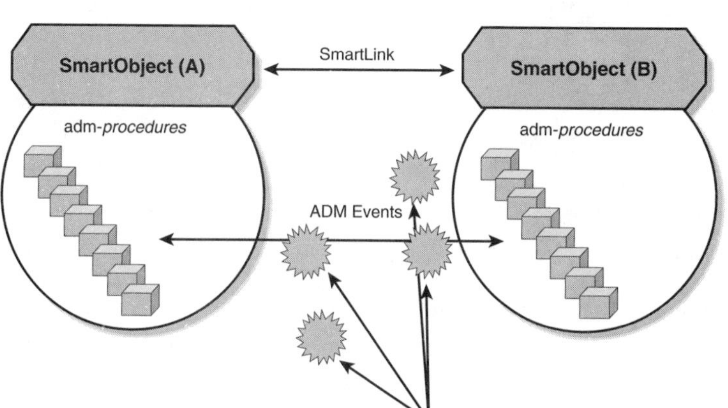

Fig. 10.25

SmartLinks and ADM events.

By virtue of two SmartObjects being linked via a specified SmartLink and SmartLink type (Record, TABLEIO, Page, and so on), ADM events will fire given the appropriate triggers.

> **Note**
>
> Understanding ADM events is essential to becoming an experienced PROGRESS V8 developer. Appendix B, "SmartObject Method Reference," provides a list of ADM methods for PROGRESS-supplied SmartObjects.

Using the PRO*Spy Tool

The PRO*Spy tool comes with PROGRESS V8. Its purpose is to show SmartObject messages at runtime. By viewing SmartObject messages, you can debug an application's SmartLinks and alter message paths to improve efficiency.

A network analyzer may be attached to a network wire to show the packets sent across the network during activity. Similarly, the PRO*Spy tool shows the messages across SmartLinks during activity.

In this section, you will study the output of PRO*Spy as it examines the ADM events firing in an early version of the sample application window. You will use PRO*Spy to analyze the events of the window named `w-msging.w`, which you saved earlier in the samples directory.

Choose Tools, Pro*Tools to start the Pro*Tools window from the UIB. Figure 10.26 shows the Pro*Tools window launched from the UIB.

Fig. 10.26

*Pro*Tools and the UIB window.*

Click the PRO*Spy icon. Locate the file `w-msging.w` so that the PRO*Spy tool can start it. Figure 10.27 shows PRO*Spy having started the window containing the Customer SmartBrowse and SmartViewer.

Click a different customer record in the Customer browser (any customer will do). This way, you can force the two objects to communicate and several ADM events to fire. Remember, the two objects are connected through a Record SmartLink. In figure 10.28, you see the ADM events that PRO*Spy intercepted.

The ADM events are listed as follows:

```
b-cust.w :adm-row-changed : smartbrowser
b-cust.w :notify: row-available : smartbrowser
v-cust.w :adm-row-available : smartviewer
v-cust.w :get-attribute: fields-enabled=no : smartviewer
v-cust.w :adm-display-fields : smartviewer
v-cust.w :notify: row-available : smartviewer
```

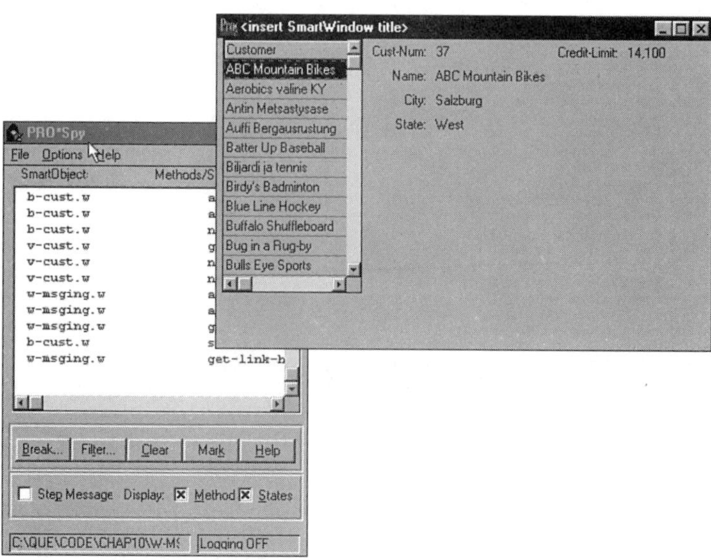

Fig. 10.27

*PRO*Spy and* `w-msging.w`*.*

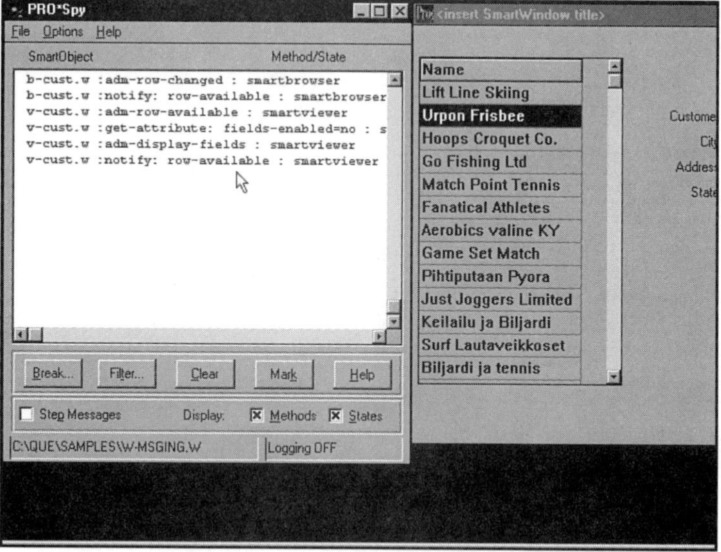

Fig. 10.28

*PRO*Spy showing ADM events for record changed.*

The details of each ADM event are covered in Appendix G, "Contents of CD." The point of this exercise in this section of the chapter is to illustrate that SmartLinks encompass ADM events that fire with SmartObjects.

Note the following ADM events that fired within the SmartBrowser in the PRO*Spy session:

- `adm-row-changed`
- `adm-row-available (notify)`

Here are the events within the SmartViewer:

- `adm-row-available`
- `adm-display-fields`
- `adm-row-available (notify)`

From Here...

In this chapter, you learned how to connect SmartObjects together. You have studied the role of SmartContainers such as the SmartWindow and its paging capabilities. The PRO*Spy tool shows you which messages are sent and received while the application runs. At this point, you have gained an appreciation for the connecting phase of component-based development.

Now that you have completed putting the components together for the main window, you continue with the finishing touches in the next chapter. You will create the non-SmartObject components such as the Welcome screen and the Customer Find dialog box. You also will create ReportBuilder reports for the sample application and prepare the application for deployment.

For more information on related items, refer to the following chapters:

- Chapter 7, "SmartObject Links and Messages." This chapter provides a review of ADM events and firing methods (`notify` and `dispatch`).
- Chapter 8, "SmartObject Internals." This chapter provides a review of the code behind SmartObject functionality.
- Chapter 21, "Making the Most of the Application Component Environment." Read this chapter for directions on creating new SmartLink types.
- Appendix B, "SmartObject Method Reference." This appendix lists all SmartObject methods invoked through ADM messages.

CHAPTER 11

Adding Menu Bar and Report Components

This chapter takes you through the final steps needed to create the sample application that was described in Chapter 9, "A Sample GUI Application."

In the previous two chapters you have seen how to create components of your application based on the SmartObject technology. However, as you build applications there is often the need to go beyond this technology and add custom objects and components. Writing these additional components will require you to use much more of the PROGRESS 4GL.

The focus of this chapter is to show you how to create your own custom components and merge these with a SmartObject application. While there are many things that you might like to do to enhance an application, this chapter will show how to build the following typical components:

Voice-of-Experience Movies

See Table G.3 in Appendix G, "Contents of CD," for a list of Voice of Experience files fo this chapter.

- Menu Bar: Simple File and Help menus will be added to the main application window.
- Secondary Windows: A "Welcome" window will greet users before they get to the main application window.
- Dialog boxes: A dialog box that allows users to search for customers by name or by country will be added to the customer SmartBrowser.
- Reports: Two simple reports will be created using the Progress Report Builder.

After reading this chapter, you should be able to:

- Use the UIB to add a Menu Bar to a SmartWindow
- Use the UIB's Code Section Editor to attach "trigger" code to objects
- Create components of an application that are not based on SmartObjects

- Call these components from a "Smart" application
- Create reports using the Progress Report Builder

What You Need to Start This Chapter

This chapter assumes that you have performed several functions discussed in the previous chapters. In order to begin this section, you need to have the following:

- Set your working directory (see Chapter 1, "Introducing Progress") to c:\appdir.
- Copied the sample sports database into your working directory (Chapter 1).
- Connected to the sports database using the Data Dictionary, the Procedure Editor, or the UIB tool (Chapter 2, "Getting Started with ADE Tools").
- Started the UIB.
- Completed the sample application components from the section in Chapter 9 entitled "Developing SmartObjects," and the section in Chapter 10 entitled "Connecting the Components." These SmartObject components comprise the sample application that you will be extending in this chapter.

In Chapters 9 and 10, you created the basic SmartObject components for this sample application. These components are listed in Table 11.1.

Table 11.1 Previously Created Sample Application Components

Description	Master File Name
Customer browse	b-cust.w
Customer detail viewer	v-cust.w
Orders browse	b-order.w
Order Line browse	b-ordln.w
Salesman viewer	v-salrep.w
Salesman query	q-salrep.w
Main Window	w-main.w

Each of these SmartObjects should now exist in your working appdir directory (that is, c:\appdir).

What You Will Add in This Chapter

In this chapter, you will add some final touches to the Main Window, and create some new, custom-built components. In particular, you will

- Add a simple Menu Bar to the Main Window.
- Add a Welcome, or "splash," screen to the application (that is, a screen that comes up when the user starts up the application).

- Add a search dialog called from the customer SmartBrowser (b-cust.w) that allows the user to search for a particular customer by country or by name.
- Create a library of database reports using the Progress Report Builder.

Adding a Menu Bar

In this section, you will learn how to add a menu bar to a window. The menu you create will be very simple:

- a File menu, with the single option Exit
- a Help menu, which brings up an About box

In building this simple component, you will not only be extending the sample application, but you will also be familiarizing yourself with the UIB's Code Section Editor.

Unlike the SmartObjects that you built in Chapter 9, the components that you will build in this chapter are all built from scratch. You will have to add code to each object before they will perform any useful function. The more complex the function, the more difficult the coding will be.

This section will start with the simple case of adding a menu bar. The first step will be to open your main application window in the UIB. This file was created in your working appdir directory in Chapter 10, under the name w-main.w. Figure 11.1 shows the UIB with the Main Window opened.

A copy of the w-main.w, with all the changes added in this chapter, can be found on the CD-ROM in \examples\chap-11\w-main.w.

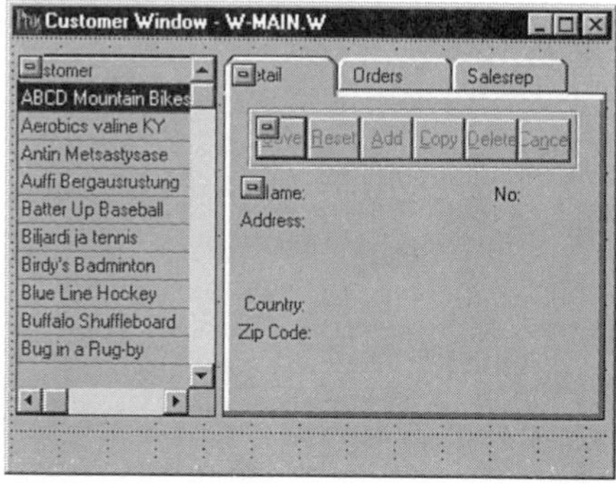

Fig. 11.1

Open your Main Window, w-main.w, in the UIB.

Menus and menu items are really their own class of objects. However, the User Interface Builder treats menus as a property of the object they are associated with. To add the menu bar, you will need to go to the Property Sheet for the window.

1. Make sure that the current object (displayed in the UIB's Main Window) is the window and not the frame.

2. Click the Property button (or use the Tools, Property Sheet menu item). Be careful that the frame in the window is not the current object, or you will go to the Frame Property Sheet, instead of the Window.

> **Tip**
>
> Use the Tools, List Objects menu (Ctrl+L) to get to the Property Sheet of any object that you are having trouble selecting directly.
>
> It is always hard to select objects that are covered by other objects, such as the window under the default frame. The List Objects dialog box lets you choose any object as the UIB's current object.

3. Click the Menu Bar button in the Window Property Sheet, shown in figure 11.2. This will bring up the Menu Bar Property Sheet, where you will be able to define the contents of the menu bar.

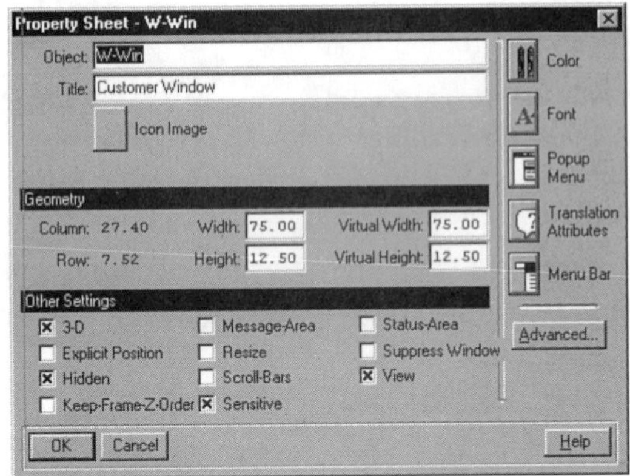

Fig. 11.2

Menu bars and pop-up menus are accessible from the Property Sheet of their owner.

Once the menu bar Property Sheet comes up, you will want to add the menu-bar elements. Figure 11.3 shows the completed menu bar in the Property Sheet.

The fastest way to enter a menu is to enter the Label field for the menu elements, one by one. There are a few tips that will help you enter these menus:

- Use & before the characters that should be underlined as mnemonics in the menu (for example, typing **E&xit** will create a menu item, Exit).
- Names for each menu element are automatically generated based on the label that you enter (for example, typing **E&xit** will make a variable name, `m_exit`).
- You can override the default variable name by typing over it.
- You can change the level of the menu (to make a submenu or menu item) by using the >> and << buttons.
- Clicking Enter in the label field automatically creates a new menu element with the same indenting.

> **Tip**
>
> The Alt+<arrow keys> are a shortcut to using the Up, Down, >> and << buttons. For example, Alt+→ is the fastest way to demote a menu element to the next level.

1. Entering the following keystrokes will create the correct menus:

   &File<Enter>
   <Alt+ →>**E&xit**<Enter>
   <Alt+ ←>**&Help**<Enter>
   <Alt+ →>**&About**...<Enter>

   You should have now created four menu elements, with object names: `m_file`, `m_exit`, `m_help`, and `m_about`. These names are important because you will be attaching triggers to these objects in the UIB's Code Section Editor.

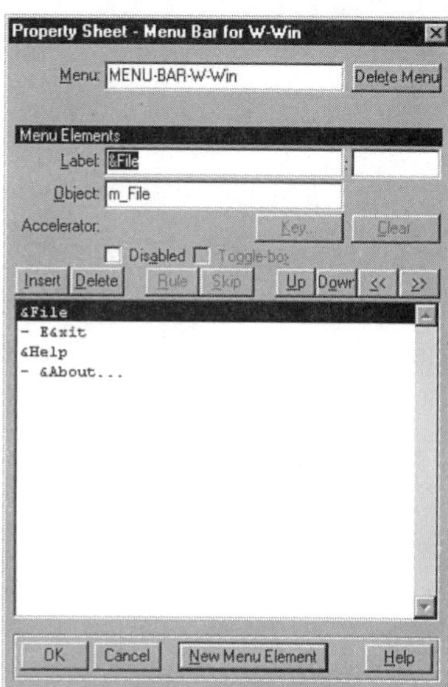

Fig. 11.3

Menu Bar Property Sheet showing the completed menu bar for the sample application main window.

2. Click OK in all the dialog boxes and Property Sheets until you return to the UIB's Main Window. Your application window should now be displayed with the menu added (as in fig. 11.4).

You can choose each menu and menu item in your window. If you select a menu item, it will become the current object in the UIB's Main Window. Once it is the current object in the UIB, you can attach trigger code to it.

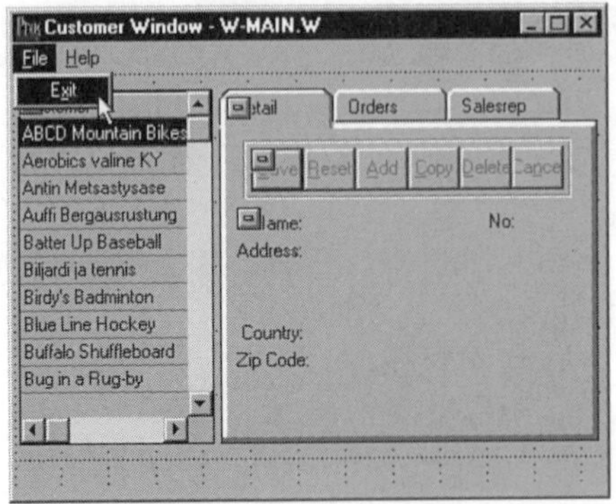

Fig. 11.4

Main application window with the addition of a menu bar. You can select individual menu items even when the UIB is active.

1. Choose File, Exit on the w-main.w window.

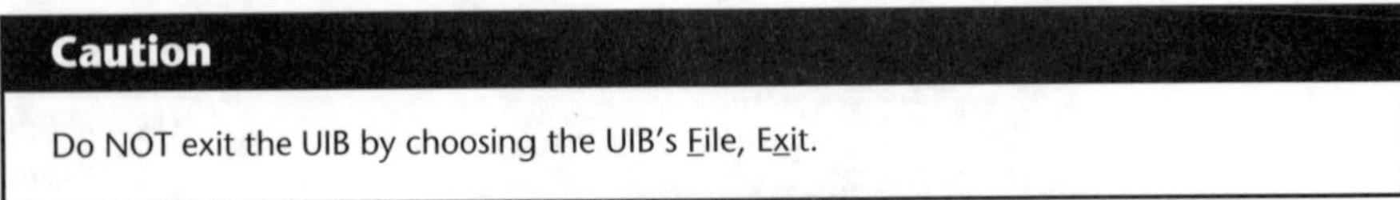

Caution

Do NOT exit the UIB by choosing the UIB's File, Exit.

2. Once this is the current object, press the Code button on the UIB's Main Window (or choose Window, Code Section Editor). This will bring up the UIB's Code Section Editor.

   The Code Section Editor is the place where you can write the specific instructions on object triggers. Because the UIB was focused on your object, `m_exit`, the section editor should already have selected the `CHOOSE` trigger for this object. Figure 11.5 shows the trigger code that you should write in the section editor.

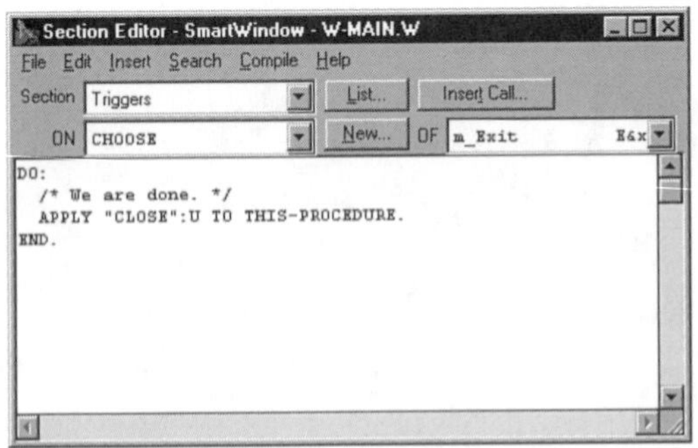

Fig. 11.5

The UIB Code Section Editor showing the code for the `CHOOSE` trigger on the `m_Exit` menu item.

3. Add the following code for the `ON CHOOSE OF` trigger on the `Exit` menu item, `m_exit`.

```
DO:
  /* We are done. */
  APPLY "CLOSE":U TO THIS-PROCEDURE.
END.
```

Otherwise many entry-level readers will find this frustrating.

Note

You do not need to have the `ON CHOOSE OF m_exit` in your code. The UIB takes care of this line. You need to enter only the `DO:...END.` block. The UIB also initializes the trigger with the `DO:` and the `END`. You do not need to enter these again.

This trigger tells PROGRESS to `CLOSE` the procedure where the trigger is defined. This procedure is your main application window, w-main.w.

You can now add a simple trigger to the About menu item. The name of this object is `m_About`. You can use the combo box of object names to change to the `m_About` object.

The code that you should write on the `CHOOSE` trigger of `m_About` is going to use PROGRESS' built-in alert box. The `MESSAGE` statement, with the `VIEW-AS ALERT-BOX INFORMATION` option, displays your text in a standard alert box.

Tip

You should use the `MESSAGE...VIEW-AS ALERT-BOX...` to display any message where you want the user to respond by clicking OK.

PROGRESS supports the following styles of alert box: `MESSAGE`, `INFORMATION`, `QUESTION`, `WARNING`, and `ERROR`.

The code to write for the About box will use the alert box to show a simple dialog. You should add the following code to the `ON CHOOSE OF` trigger for the `m_About` menu item.

```
DO:
  MESSAGE "The Customer Application" SKIP
          "Copyright 1996 SmartObjects R Us"
          VIEW-AS ALERT-BOX INFORMATION.
END.
```

At this point, save your file (as w-main.w). You can also run it, or use Compile, Check Syntax (Shift+F2) to check your code.

Tip

The UIB provides two levels of syntax checking: one for individual code blocks, and one for the file as a whole. If you choose Compile, Check Syntax on the UIB's Main Window, then you will check the whole file. The menu item in the Code Section Editor applies to the current code block.

(continues)

(continued)

If you check the whole file then there is a chance that the compiler could give an error and drop you in an altogether different section of code. This is especially true if some sections have missing or mismatched comments symbols, END statements, quotes, or periods.

Checking syntax from the Code Section Editor generally provides the most useful error messages.

Adding the Welcome Screen

The next component that you will build is the "Welcome," or *splash*, screen. This is a window that will come up when a user starts up your application. The window will splash your welcome message (and copyright notice) across the screen. The splash screen will stay up until the user presses a Continue button.

Figure 11.6 shows the Welcome screen that you will be creating.

Fig. 11.6

A welcome window splashes your copyright notice across the screen at startup.

A complete copy of the source code for this screen can be found on the CD-ROM in \examples\chap-11\splash.w.

This Welcome screen will be entirely custom coded. It will not utilize any SmartObject technology. Although you could build it as a SmartObject, there is really no particular benefit to doing so.

SmartObjects are designed to make it easy for you to build components of a database application that can communicate in a structured manner. The Welcome screen does not display any database fields, nor does it need to communicate with the rest of the application. Once it has done its job (and the user clicks Continue), it can go away. There is really no other function of the window.

The first step will be to create a new basic window. In the previous chapter, you learned how to use the File, New dialog. You can also use the right mouse button on the New button in the UIB Main Window as a shortcut to create a new window.

To create a new basic window:

1. Click with the right mouse button on the New button.
2. Choose the Window option. This will create a basic window, with a default frame.
3. Double-click on the frame in the window to bring up the Frame Property Sheet.
4. In the Property Sheet, set the size of the frame 55 columns by 12 rows.
5. When you have set the property sheet as shown in figure 11.7, you can click the OK button to accept your changes.

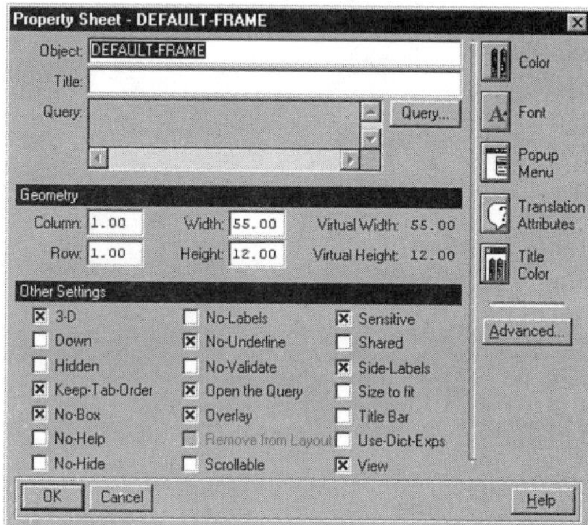

Fig. 11.7

Frame Property Sheet with changes needed for the Welcome screen.

Now that the frame has been resized, you can double-click in the window (outside the frame area) to bring up the Window Property Sheet. Make the following changes:

1. Set both the virtual size and viewport size to the same size as the frame.

> **Tip**
>
> If you type the new sizes into the Virtual Width and Virtual Height, the viewport Height and Width fields will automatically change when you tab out of the fields.
>
> This behavior occurs any time the virtual size is reduced below the viewport size.

2. Change the Title of the window to **SmartObjects R Us**.
3. When you have set the Property Sheet, you can click the OK button to accept your changes.

You are now ready to add new objects to your Welcome screen:

1. Select the Text icon on the UIB Object Palette and add a text object to the window.

2. Add a Button object.
3. Add an Image object.
4. Resize each object until your design window looks approximately like the one shown in figure 11.8.

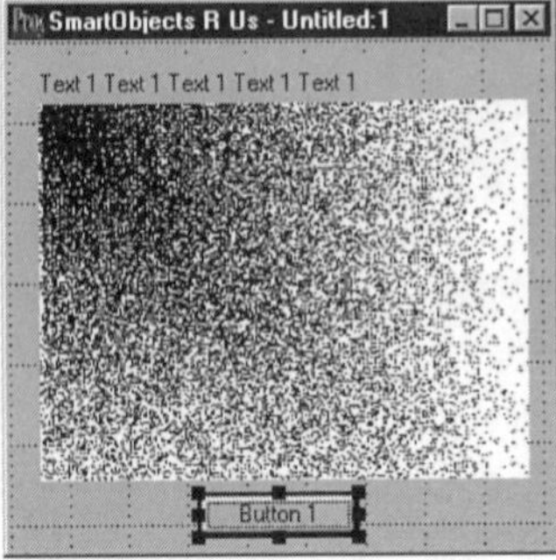

Fig. 11.8

Welcome screen after adding Text, Image, and Button objects.

You can use the fill-in fields in the UIB Main Window to change the text in the Button and Text objects.

1. Change the Text object to read **Welcome to the World of PROGRESS**.
2. Change the label on the button to **&Continue**.

The next step will be to add the image file to the Image object.

1. Double-click the image to bring up the Image Property Sheet.
2. Click the Image button. This brings up the Image Files dialog shown in figure 11.9.

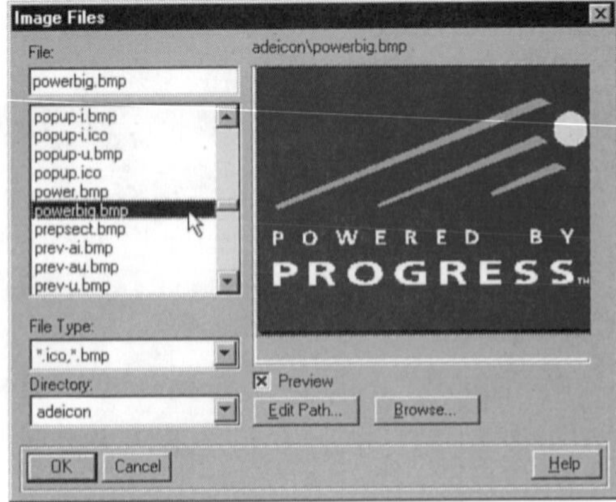

Fig. 11.9

The Image Files dialog lets you preview and select image files.

3. Select the powerbig.bmp image in the adeicon directory.
4. Press OK in the Image Files dialog and the Image Property Sheet.

5. When you return to the design window, resize and reposition the image and button until everything is visible and in position (refer to fig. 11.7).

There is only one remaining task needed to complete the Welcome screen. You will need to add code to the Continue button that dismisses the splash screen.

1. Select the Continue button and bring up the Code Section Editor.
2. Add the following code to the `ON CHOOSE OF` trigger on the button, `Button-1`. (This will be the same code that you added to the File, Exit menu item in w-main.w earlier in this chapter.)

```
DO:
  /* Dismiss the Splash Screen. */
  APPLY "CLOSE":U TO THIS-PROCEDURE.
END.
```

3. At this point, you can run your Welcome screen. You can see that it stays visible until the user either clicks the Continue button or closes the window using the System menu item, Close.
4. You have completed the Welcome screen. Save the window as splash.w in your appdir working directory.

You must now incorporate the Welcome screen into the sample application.

1. Open the main window of the sample application, w-main.w.
2. Bring up the Code Section Editor and change to the Main Block section.
3. Add a line to run splash.w, as in figure 11.10. Using the `PERSISTENT` option on the `RUN` statement allows the user to view the main window before dismissing the splash screen. If you want to ensure that the user first responds to the splash screen, remove the `PERSISTENT` keyword.

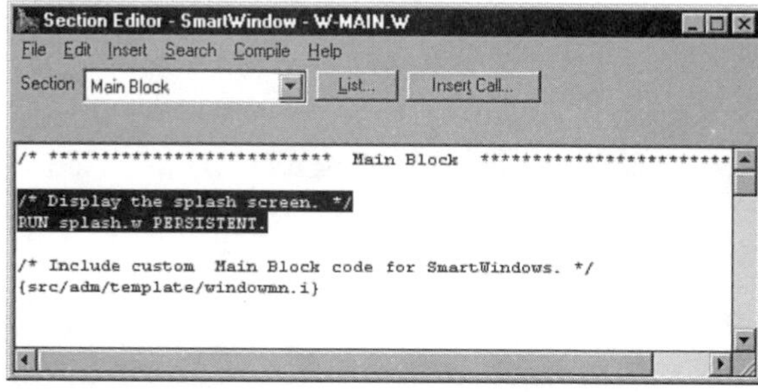

Fig. 11.10

Add a statement to run the Welcome screen in the Main Block.

4. Save your changes to w-main.w by clicking the Save button.
5. Click the Run button on the UIB Main Window. Note how the Welcome screen comes up first.
6. Choose File, Exit to close your application.

Building a Customer Search Screen

The final component of the sample application that will be built in the UIB is the Customer Search Screen. This screen will be a dialog box in which the user can select a customer from a browse. This browse can be restricted to show all the customers in a given country, or all customers whose names match a given filter (for example, Name Filter `L*` will be all customers whose names begin with *L*). Figure 11.11 shows this search dialog.

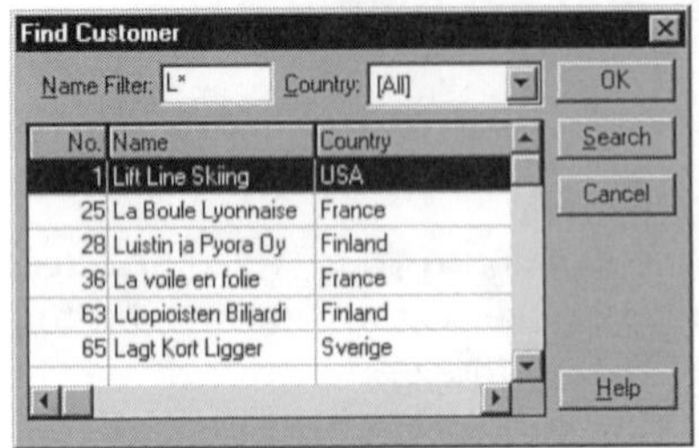

Fig. 11.11

Find Customer dialog.

A complete copy of the source code for this screen can be found on the CD-ROM in \examples\chap-11\findcust.w.

This dialog will be created from a basic dialog box, with standard OK, Cancel, and Help buttons. You will place a browse object in the dialog box to display customers. A fill-in field will show the current name filter (for example, `L*`), and a combo box will list all valid countries in the database. All the logic and behavior of this dialog will have to be custom coded.

In building this dialog box, you will learn some additional techniques about the Progress environment, including

- How to call a dialog box with parameters from a SmartObject
- How to use the Where Builder to create complex queries
- How to populate a combo box or selection list based on values in a database

Why Not Use a SmartDialog?

This dialog box could also have been created with a SmartDialog containing a SmartBrowser. Custom code would still have to be written, most notably to add the search criteria for name and country to the SmartBrowser. Localized methods would also have to be added to facilitate the passing of data between the SmartDialog and the SmartBrowser.

There would also be certain advantages to using SmartObject technology, including

- *Full Functionality*. All the capabilities of SmartObjects would be available in the search dialog. Record passing from the SmartBrowser to related SmartObjects could be easily supported. Navigation and Record Update capabilities could be added.

- *Reusability*. The SmartObjects used in this dialog could be reused independently in other parts of the application. The SmartBrowser could be reused outside of the SmartDialog.
- *Maintainability*. Using standard SmartObject technology is almost always going to be easier to maintain than custom-coded components. This is especially true on projects with numerous programmers or long service lives. In both cases, the maintenance programmer may not be the same as the original developer.

There would also be disadvantages to using SmartObjects to develop the Customer Search Dialog.

- *Code Size*. You would need two SmartObjects (a SmartBrowser and a SmartDialog) to replace the single basic dialog. In addition, the SmartObjects would contain all the normal SmartObject code for functions that are not needed in this particular application.
- *Excessive Structure*. Developing this search dialog is going to involve writing custom code, even if SmartObjects are used. If you program with SmartObjects, you need to structure all this code in terms of SmartObject methods and links. For a simple application such as the Customer Search Dialog, this structure could be overkill.

So, should SmartObjects be used for this dialog box?

The answer depends on whether you believe the benefits of SmartObject technology exceeds the cost. If the dialog were more complex, if it had more browses, or if it needed to do record updating, then SmartObjects probably should be used.

For the case of simple dialogs in which the user is asked to choose one option, or where information is only being displayed (and not updated), then it is reasonable to rely on custom dialog boxes. Also remember that any dialog box is inherently a reusable object in its own right. It can be called from anywhere in your application, by any component that knows its calling convention.

Creating the Customer Search Dialog

In creating the search dialog, the broad outline of steps to follow are: (1) create a simple dialog; (2) add basic objects; (3) add logic to objects; and (4) connect this to the rest of the application.

You begin by creating a basic (not Smart) dialog box

1. Click the New button on the UIB's Main Window and select the basic Dialog option (see fig. 11.12).
2. Double-click on the new dialog box to bring up its Property Sheet. Change the Title to Find Customer. Click OK to accept this change.
3. Click the Help button in the new dialog box. Choose the UIB command Edit, Duplicate. This will create a button exactly the same size and location as the existing Help button, but with the following object name: `Btn-Help-2`.

Fig. 11.12

Select the basic dialog from the list of File, New options.

4. Using the fill-in fields in the UIB's Main Window, change the object name to `Btn_Search`, and the label to `&Search`.
5. Widen the dialog box by dragging the right edge farther to the right.
6. Move the buttons until they approximate the spacing shown in figure 11.13.
7. Select the Fill-in icon from the UIB Palette and click in the dialog box to create a new fill-in.
8. Using the UIB's Main Window, change the object name of the fill-in to `srch_name`, and the label to `Name &Filter`.
9. Initialize the `srch_name` field to *. Do this by double-clicking on the `srch_name` fill-in to bring up its Property Sheet. Click the Advanced button and enter the character * into the Initial Value field. Click OK to the design window.
10. Repeat the process to create a combo box named `srch_country`, with the label `&Country`.
11. Position all the objects until you have a screen that is similar to figure 11.13.

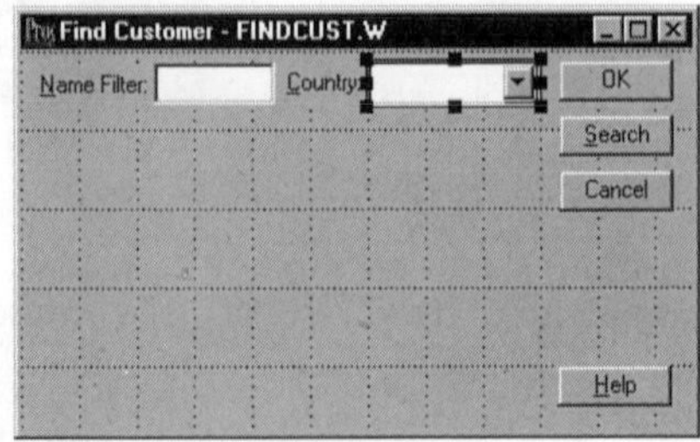

Fig. 11.13

The Search dialog under development. All fields and buttons have been added and sized.

At this point, the Browse Object is the only remaining user interface element to add. You will set up this browse object using the same Query Builder that you used to build the SmartBrowser components for the sample application. In this example, however, the query will be more complex.

Using the WHERE Clause

In the previous examples, the queries that you built were simple requests that found all records in a table (for example, FOR EACH customer), or were simple joins or two tables (for example, FOR EACH order OF customer). In this search dialog, the simple FOR EACH must be augmented by a WHERE clause. The WHERE clause will specify two conditions:

- Find customers where the customer's name matches the value in the srch_name field.
- Find customers from the country shown in the srch_country combo box, with an option to show customers in all countries.

The PROGRESS code to represent this query is as follows:

```
FOR EACH sports.Customer
WHERE
     (Customer.Name MATCHES srch_name)
  AND
     (Customer.Country eq srch_country OR srch_country eq "[All]")
```

Note that you need to explicitly handle the special case when srch_country equals "[All]". This variable is a combo box that shows all valid countries in the database, plus one catch-all value of "[All]". (You will see how the list of countries is created later in this chapter.)

The preceding expression also uses the MATCHES function. The MATCHES function is used by PROGRESS to handle pattern matching. For example, testing for a MATCH of A* returns true if the expression begins with A; *A* matches any string containing A; and * matches all strings.

The quotation marks above are a necessary part of the PROGRESS syntax. More information on the MATCHES function is available in the PROGRESS Language Reference. For comparison, you may also want to look up the BEGINS and the CONTAINS functions. These functions are more efficient on large databases, although they are more limited in the kinds of searches they support.

You can add this WHERE clause in the UIB's Query Builder. The *Query Builder* allows you to create and modify the components of a PROGRESS query. You can add the browse object to the screen, and access the Query Builder as follows.

1. Choose the Browse icon on the UIB's Object Palette. Click and drag out an area where you want the Browse to be.
2. When you release the mouse button after drawing, the UIB will immediately bring up the Query Builder on the Tables page. Select Customer from the Available Tables, and then click the Add>> button.

3. In the radio set at the top of the Query Builder, select the Where button. Enter the `WHERE` clause into the Where Criteria, as shown in figure 11.14. (Do not enter the word *WHERE* in this field.)

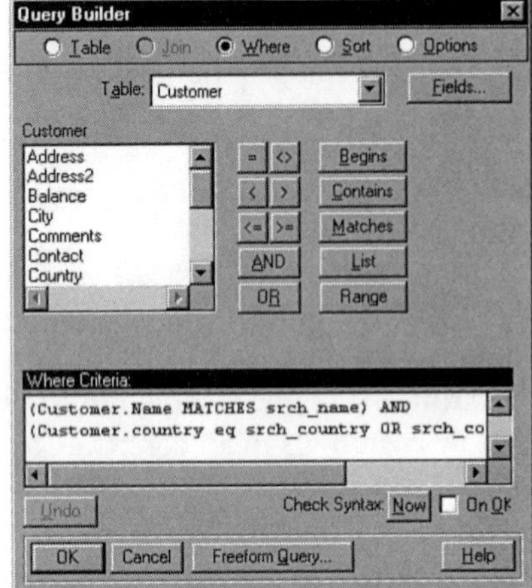

Fig. 11.14

The Where section of the Query Builder lets you enter complex selection criteria.

4. Click the Now button to check the syntax of the code. The syntax should be correct.
5. Click the Fields button near the top-right corner of the Query Builder to bring up the Column Editor.
6. Click the Add button in the Column Editor and add the three customer fields: `Cust-Num`, `Name`, and `Country`.
7. Click OK on both the Column Editor and in the Query Builder to return to your design window.
8. You are now finished designing the user interface of the Customer Search dialog. Save the dialog as `findcust.w` in your working *appdir* directory.

Initializing the Search Dialog Box

With the user interface finished, the next step will be to add the code that will make the search dialog functional. Three tasks need to be coded:

- Initializing the `srch_country` combo box
- Reopening the browse query when the user changes the search criteria
- Returning the value of the customer record selected to the calling program

The following steps will initialize the combo box:

1. Click the Code button on the UIB's Main Window to bring up the UIB's Code Section Editor.
2. Change to the Main Block section. Add the following code that will run an internal procedure to look through all existing customer records and add each

country to the list in the combo-box. Note: this run statement must follow the code that parents the dialog box to the active window. That is, the line that sets `FRAME {&FRAME-NAME}:PARENT= ACTIVE-WINDOW.`

```
/* ***************************  Main Block
*************************** */

/* Parent the dialog-box to the ACTIVE-WINDOW, if there is no parent.
*/
IF VALID-HANDLE(ACTIVE-WINDOW) AND FRAME {&FRAME-NAME}:PARENT eq ?
THEN FRAME {&FRAME-NAME}:PARENT = ACTIVE-WINDOW.

/* Fill the combo-box of valid countries. */
RUN find-all-countries.
```

3. You must now define the `find-all-countries` procedure. Change to the Procedures section and press the New button. Create a new procedure named `find-all-countries`, and add the following code.

Listing 11.1 `find-all-countries` in examples\chap11\findcust.w

```
/*-----------------------------------------------------------
  Purpose:     Find every country (alphabetically)
               and fill the LIST-ITEMS
               of the srch_country combo-box.
  Parameters:  <none>
-----------------------------------------------------------*/
  DEFINE VAR result AS LOGICAL NO-UNDO.

  DO WITH FRAME {&FRAME-NAME}:
    /* All lists start with "[All]". */
    ASSIGN srch_country:LIST-ITEMS = "[All]"
           srch_country:SCREEN-VALUE = "[All]"
           srch_country = "[All]"
           .
    FOR EACH customer BREAK BY country:
      IF FIRST-OF (country) THEN result
         = srch_country:ADD-LAST(customer.country).
    END.
  END.
END PROCEDURE.
```

The `find-all-countries` procedure first adds the default value of `"[All]"` to the drop-down list in the combo box. The `srch_country` variable is also set to this value. The procedure then loops through all the customers ordered by their country field (that is, `FOR EACH customer BREAK BY country`).

The `BREAK BY` keywords allow you to test for the first (and last) of any break group. In this case, every time a new country group is started (that is, `FIRST-OF (country)`), the country name is added to the list. This code guarantees that all countries used in the database are added to the `srch_country` combo box, in ascending alphabetic order.

Opening the Search Dialog Box

Next, you will want to add the code that will reopen the query. You will want to call this code when the user clicks the Search button, presses the Enter key in either `srch_name` field, or changes the `srch_country` combo box.

1. Click the Code button on the UIB's Main Window to bring up the UIB's Code Section Editor.
2. Change to the Triggers section. Change to the `CHOOSE` trigger on `Btn_Search`.
3. Enter the code as shown in figure 11.15. Note that you are actually entering code for a series of triggers into the single section. This code will be stored with the Search button, but it will fire on all three events.

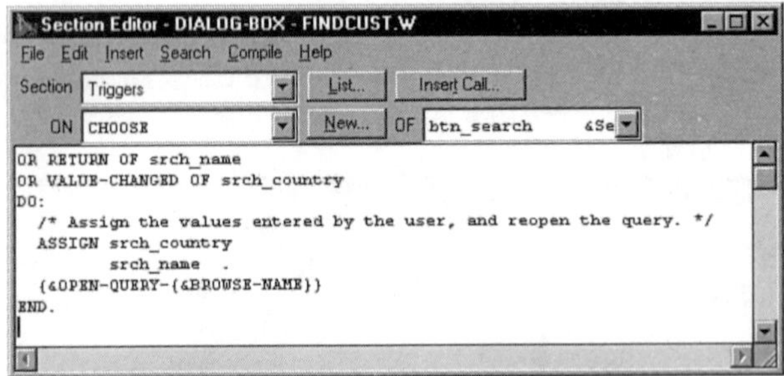

Fig. 11.15

Code to reopen the query when the user changes the search criteria.

At this point, your dialog box is functional. You can run it and enter new name criteria, or change the country and the selected countries will change. There is only one step remaining. You need to define parameters so that the dialog box will be able to pass the result back to the calling program.

Defining Output Parameters

You should define two output parameters: a `ROWID` of the selected record, and a logical parameter to tell the calling program whether the user clicked OK or Cancel in the dialog box. There will be no input parameters.

The steps to follow are quite simple:

1. Return to the Code Section Editor and change to the Definitions section. Modify the code to define the input parameters as follows:

Listing 11.2 Definitions section in \examples\chap-11\findcust.w

```
/*------------------------------------------------------------------

  File: findcust.w
  Description: Returns a customer ROWID
  based on user-defined search criteria.
  Input Parameters:
      <none>
  Output Parameters:
      prCustomer - the ROWID of the selected customer record
```

```
      pOK         - TRUE if user OK's the dialog, FALSE if they Cancel.
---------------------------------------------------------------*/

/* ************************  Definitions  *********************** */

/* Parameters Definitions ---                                   */
&IF DEFINED(UIB_is_Running) eq 0 &THEN
DEFINE OUTPUT PARAMETER prCustomer AS ROWID NO-UNDO.
DEFINE OUTPUT PARAMETER pOK        AS LOGICAL NO-UNDO.
&ELSE
/* Test parameters - to enable running from inside the UIB. */
DEFINE VAR prCustomer AS ROWID NO-UNDO.
DEFINE VAR pOK        AS LOGICAL NO-UNDO.
&ENDIF
```

2. Go to the Main Block and add code after the WAIT-FOR statement. This code will be executed only if the user executes a PROGRESS GO. (GO is the PROGRESS equivalent of the OK button. Pressing the Enter key in a dialog box, or clicking the OK button, will issue the PROGRESS GO event.) When the user performs a GO, this code will assign the two output parameters.

Listing 11.3 Main code block in \examples\chap-11\findcust.w

```
/* ************************  Main Block  *********************** */

/* Parent the dialog-box to the ACTIVE-WINDOW,
   if there is no parent.   */
IF VALID-HANDLE(ACTIVE-WINDOW) AND FRAME {&FRAME-NAME}:PARENT eq ?
THEN FRAME {&FRAME-NAME}:PARENT = ACTIVE-WINDOW.

/* Fill the combo-box of valid countries. */
RUN find-all-countries.

/* Now enable the interface and wait for the exit condition.        */
/* (NOTE: handle ERROR and END-KEY so cleanup code will always fire. */
MAIN-BLOCK:
DO ON ERROR   UNDO MAIN-BLOCK, LEAVE MAIN-BLOCK
   ON END-KEY UNDO MAIN-BLOCK, LEAVE MAIN-BLOCK:
  RUN enable_UI.
  WAIT-FOR GO OF FRAME {&FRAME-NAME}.

  /* If we get this far, the user pressed OK. */
  /* See if there is a valid choice. */
  IF AVAILABLE customer
  THEN ASSIGN prCustomer = ROWID(customer)
              pOK        = YES.
  ELSE ASSIGN prCustomer = ?
              pOK        = NO.
END.
RUN disable_UI.
```

3. You can now test your dialog box (by running it). After you are satisfied, save it (as findcust.w) in your working appdir directory.

You probably noticed that the prCustomer and pOK parameters seemed to be defined twice in the Definitions section. A problem with developing procedure that takes parameters is that they are hard to test directly from the UIB or the Procedure Editor. You normally cannot run a procedure that requires parameters unless you run it from some other program.

The UIB gets around this problem by allowing you to write code two ways: once as it really will perform in operation, and once as it will be run while testing from the UIB. The UIB defines a preprocessor variable called `UIB_is_Running`. This variable is defined only in code under development and being run directly from the UIB.

In the definition section of `findcust.w`, you used this preprocessor variable to define the parameters as local variables when being run from the UIB.

```
/* Parameters Definitions ---                                    */
&IF DEFINED(UIB_is_Running) eq 0 &THEN
DEFINE OUTPUT PARAMETER prCustomer AS ROWID NO-UNDO.
DEFINE OUTPUT PARAMETER pOK        AS LOGICAL NO-UNDO.
&ELSE
/* Test parameters - to enable running from inside the UIB. */
DEFINE VAR prCustomer AS ROWID NO-UNDO.
DEFINE VAR pOK        AS LOGICAL NO-UNDO.
&ENDIF
```

Tip

When defining a procedure with parameters in the UIB, you should use the preprocessor variable `UIB_is_Running` to allow the procedure to be run from inside the UIB.

Calling the Search Dialog Box

Now that you have created the Customer Search dialog, you must add code in the sample application to call this dialog.

A copy of the `b-cust.w`, with all the changes added in this chapter, can be found on the CD-ROM in \examples\chap-11\b-cust.w.

1. Open the main window of your application: `w-main.w`.
2. Use the right mouse button on the customer SmartBrowser in the window. Choose the Edit Master option. This will open the file `b-cust.w`.
3. When `b-cust.w` comes into the UIB, grab the customer SmartBrowser and move it up about a row and a half vertically. This will open up some room to add a new button.
4. Select the Button icon on the UIB's Object Palette and draw a button immediately under the browse (see fig. 11.16).

Fig. 11.16

The customer SmartBrowser can be extended to make room for a new button.

5. In the UIB Main Window, change the object name to `btn_find` and change its label to **Fi&nd Customer**.
6. Click the Code button while this button is still selected. This will bring up the Section Editor for the CHOOSE trigger on the button. Type the following code as the `ON CHOOSE OF Btn_Find` code block:

Listing L.4 `ON CHOOSE OF Btn_Find` in \examples\chap-11\b-cust.w

```
DO:
 DEF VAR rID AS ROWID NO-UNDO.
 DEF VAR lOK AS LOGICAL NO-UNDO.

 RUN findcust.w (OUTPUT rID, OUTPUT lOK).
 IF lOK THEN DO:
   /* Set the BROWSE widget so it doesn't
      scroll unless it has to. */
   lOK = {&BROWSE-NAME}:SET-REPOSITIONED-ROW
           (MAX (1, {&BROWSE-NAME}:FOCUSED-ROW),
            'CONDITIONAL').
   /* Reset the line in the browse, and then
      notify all other RECORD-TARGETS of the
      event. */
   REPOSITION {&BROWSE-NAME} TO ROWID rID.
   RUN dispatch ('row-changed').
 END.
END.
```

6. Save the changes to b-cust.w in your working appdir directory.

If you now run your application, you will be able to press the Find Customer button to bring up the Customer Search dialog. Whatever customer is selected in the dialog will become the current customer in the SmartBrowser when you press OK.

Creating Printed Reports

A final component of any application is the printed reports. Progress offers three distinct methods of producing printed reports:

- The PROGRESS 4GL
- Progress RESULTS
- Progress Report Builder

The PROGRESS 4GL contains many functions for writing directly to files or to printers. The basic element of a screen in PROGRESS is the `FRAME` object. Frames can be defined for a printer, with special page-top, page-bottom, and iterating block sections. The `DISPLAY` keyword works the same sending data to a printer-based frame as to a screen-based frame.

Progress RESULTS is a user-friendly front-end to the PROGRESS 4GL. It allows a developer to create an end-user application geared toward browsing through a database. Users can use both custom and predefined reports that take advantage of the PROGRESS 4GL.

There is one major limitation to both the PROGRESS 4GL and to RESULTS (which uses that 4GL and therefore inherits it limitations). The reports you generate are based on code that writes sequentially to an output stream, character by character. As such, you are really limited to using a single, fixed-width font. This means that you cannot have graphics, bold titles, or any of the fancy presentation elements that your users would expect in their reports.

In the past, experienced PROGRESS programmers who wanted fancy reports had to generate raw PostScript, or other page description code, directly. However, this was a laborious and error-prone process.

The solution to this problem is the Progress Report Builder.

Progress Report Builder

The Report Builder is a fully functional reporting tool. It supports fonts, images, print preview, mailing labels, and everything that a sophisticated user would expect.

The Report Builder is one of the few tools supplied by Progress that is *not* written in the PROGRESS 4GL. Because it is a separate program, you need to be aware of a few issues:

- The Report Builder runs only on Microsoft Windows. (Progress will soon release runtime versions of the Report Builder, however, that will be able to print reports built in Windows on other platforms, including OSF/Motif and UNIX.)
- The Report Builder must have its own connection to the database. This is fine in a multi-user environment, but if you have only a single-user license, then a single database cannot be simultaneously connected to a running PROGRESS application *and* the Report Builder.

- The language used by the Report Builder to create relationships between tables and calculated fields is only a subset of the PROGRESS 4GL.
- The Report Builder does not store each report as an individual file. In the Report Builder, you create a report library (which can contain one or more individual reports). This is different from the UIB, where you create a separate disk file (.w) for each screen in your application.

Sample Reports

This section creates a report library for the sample application. This library will contain a few reports that parallel the screens you have developed for the sample application.

A completed version of the report library created in this section can be found on the CD-ROM in \examples\chap-11\reports.prl.

To start the Report Builder, follow these steps:

1. Close all open SmartObject windows in the UIB.
2. Disconnect the sports database from your PROGRESS session (unless you are using a separate multiuser database server). You can disconnect either by selecting the Tools, Database Connections option in the UIB, or by using the DB List tool from PRO*Tools.
3. Use the Tools, Report Builder menu item to bring up the Report Builder. You might like to first close the UIB and PRO*Tools, and run the Report Builder from the PROGRESS Desktop.
4. The first time the Report Builder comes up you will be presented with a splash screen. Take the default action and close the startup dialog. You will now see the Report Builder main screen, as shown in figure 11.17.

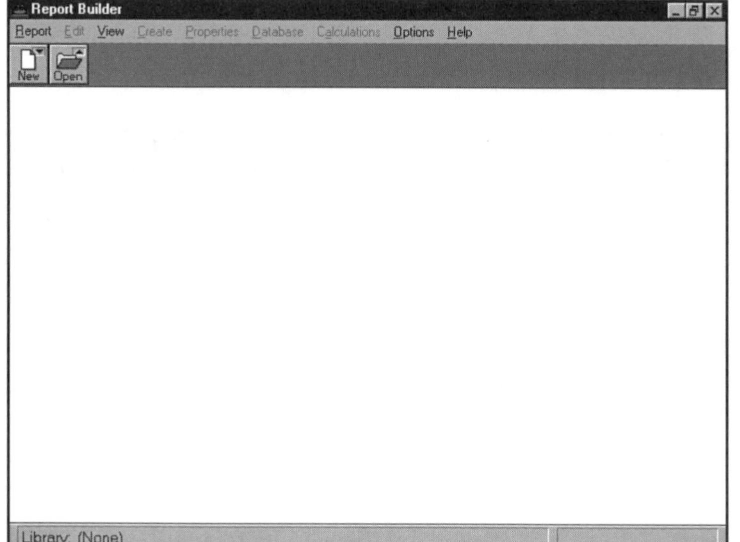

Fig. 11.17

The Report Builder main screen.

Note

Going into the Report Builder from the PROGRESS tools will retain all the default directory settings.

If you decide to go directly into the Report Builder from the Window's desktop, you will need to set the working directory to c:\appdir. Otherwise, the Report Builder will have trouble locating your database.

To change the working directory you will need to select the icon for the Report Builder on the MicroSoft Windows desktop, and edit the properties for this program item. You will need to change the working directory so that Windows knows the path to start in.

When you create a new report in the Report Builder, it will automatically lead you through the necessary steps. To create a simple customer report, follow these steps:

1. Click the New button on the toolbar.
2. When prompted for the database name, connect to the sports database.
3. You will be immediately prompted for a Database Table to use for your first report. Choose the Customer table (see fig. 11.18). The dialog in figure 11.18 is different from the dialog you used to select database tables and fields in the rest of the PROGRESS tool set.

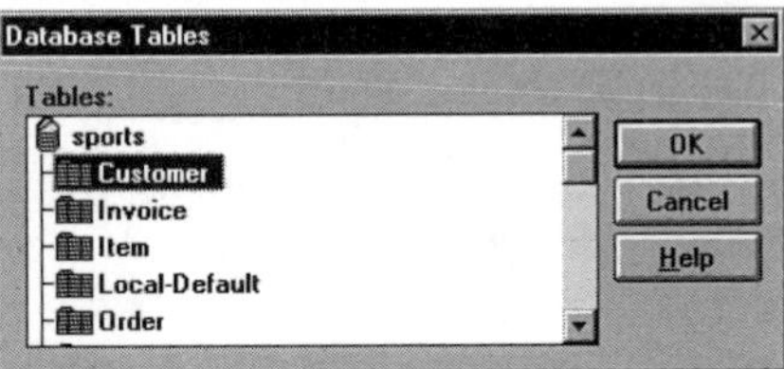

Fig. 11.18

The Report Builder contains a hierarchical outline of your database.

4. You will next be asked whether you want to create New Report using an Instant Layout. Click Yes. This will bring up the Instant Layout Fields dialog.

Tip

The fastest, and safest, way to create a new report is to use the Instant Layout feature. Once the layout is created, you can change it any way you want. This is always easier than trying to create a layout from scratch.

5. Select the following fields from the customer table: `Cust-Num`, `Name`, `Address`, `Address2`, `City`, `State`, `Postal-Code`, `Country`, and `Phone`. This will create a tabular layout similar to figure 11.19, with all the fields lined up in one row.

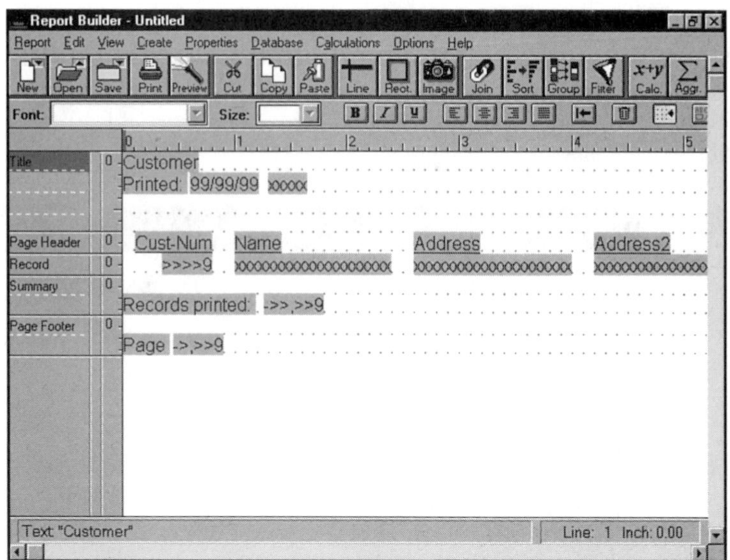

Fig. 11.19

The instant layout defaults to a table with one row per record.

There are a few important points to note about layouts in the Report Builder.

- The basic elements of a report layout are the *bands*. Each line of the report is in a band. These bands are grouped by type. Figure 11.20 shows a layout with four band lines in the Title, a single Page Header band, a single Record band, and two bands each for the Summary and Page Footer group.
- Different types of bands are repeated at different intervals. For example, the title bands will appear once per report. The Page Header and Page Footer will appear once per page. The Record band will be repeated once for each record.
- Bands can be selected by clicking on the title margin at the left of the report. You can create, delete, or change the properties of selected bands.

The report you have created is ready to run. To preview it, press the Preview button on the toolbar. As with most graphic applications, you can scroll through the Print Preview, or zoom in and out. Closing the Print Preview window returns to you to the Report Builder layout window.

You may have noticed in the Print Preview that some of the fields were not visible. Both Country and Phone Number did not fit on the default page. If you scroll the layout window, you will see that these fields are on the layout, but beyond the right edge of the page (indicated by the letter *R* in the ruler).

To make the fields all fit on one page, you will need to adjust the layout. The following steps show how to stack the various address fields into a single block.

1. You will need to add more Record bands in order to hold the stacked address. Click on the label of the Record band to select it. Then choose Create, Band Line.

2. Create three (3) Record Band lines below the current line.
3. Move the `Address2`, `City`, `State`, `Postal-Code`, and `Country` fields to be under the Address (see fig. 11.20). You move fields in the Report Builder by clicking and dragging them to their new position. Note that as you move fields, the associated label *does not move.*

> **Tip**
>
> If you cannot tell which field is which, you can change the Report Builder to view field names instead of input masks.
>
> Choose View, Field Names from the Report Builder menu bar. This value can be toggled back and forth as necessary.

4. Delete the labels for `Address2`, `City`, `State`, and `Postal-Code` from the Page Header band. To delete a label, just click on it to select it. Then press the Delete key.

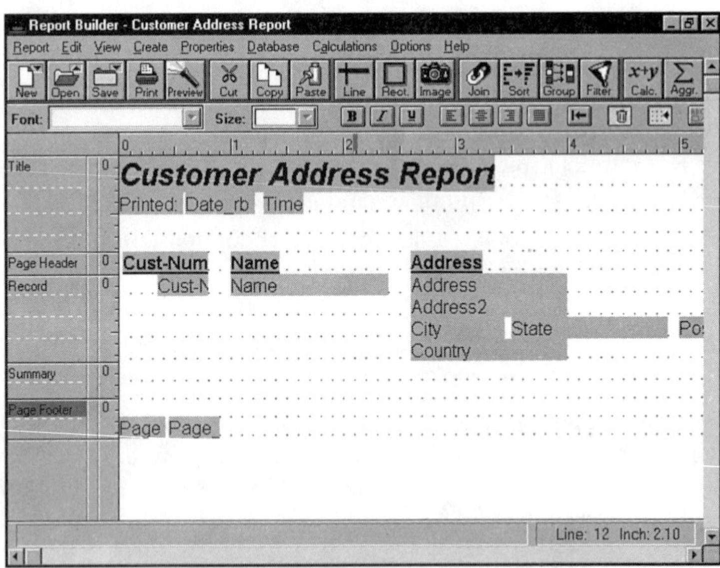

Fig. 11.20

New layout showing Field Names.

5. Move the Phone field to the left until it falls within the boundaries of the page.
6. Change the font of all the labels to be bold. You change the properties of a field by selecting it, and then choosing Properties, Font (or by using the buttons in the Format toolbar).
7. Change the title of the report from Customer to Customer Address Report. To edit text, first highlight it and then choose Properties, Edit In-Place (F2).

8. Change the font of the title to be 20-point, bold, italic by choosing Properties, Font.
9. You can now preview your report by pressing the Preview button.

When you preview the report, pay particular attention to multiple line addresses. Not all customer records have both an `Address` and an `Address2` field. In the preview, however, you will see that there are no blank lines. The Report Builder does not, by default, print blank bands. This is obviously a time- and paper-saving feature.

You may have also noted that the Title band automatically grew when you changed the font to 20 point. Again, the Report Builder is trying to be sensible in its defaults. You can change these defaults by double-clicking on the label of a band to bring up its Property Sheet.

You are now ready to save your report. Remember that the Report Builder stores multiple reports in a single Report Library. This feature allows the Report Builder to store all database connection information and defaults only once (for the entire library). You are also allowed to create long descriptive report names within the library, instead of being limited to file names supported by your operating system.

To save the reports:

1. Choose File, Save.
2. When prompted for a new library name, create a library, `reports.prl`, in your working appdir directory.
3. You will then be prompted for the name of the report itself. Call this report the **Customer Address Report**.

Using Merge and Calculated Fields in Your Report

If you print or preview this report, you may notice that the `City`, `State`, and `Postal-Code` fields are not displayed very aesthetically. There is lots of white space between the fields, especially if the `State` string is short.

One way of dealing with this is to change the properties of the `State` and `Postal-Code` field to Merge Left. Double-clicking on these fields will bring up a Property Sheet where you can set this property (by pressing the Merge button).

Another way to fix this layout issue is to create a calculated field that merges the individual fields into a single new value. Follow these steps to create a calculated field:

1. Click the Calc button on the Report Builder toolbar.
2. Press the New button. This will bring up the Edit Calculation dialog.
3. You must give the calculated field a unique name. Type **CityStateCode** as the Calculated Field Name (see fig. 11.21).
4. Enter the following expression in the Expression box:

```
City + ", " + State + "  " + Postal-Code
```

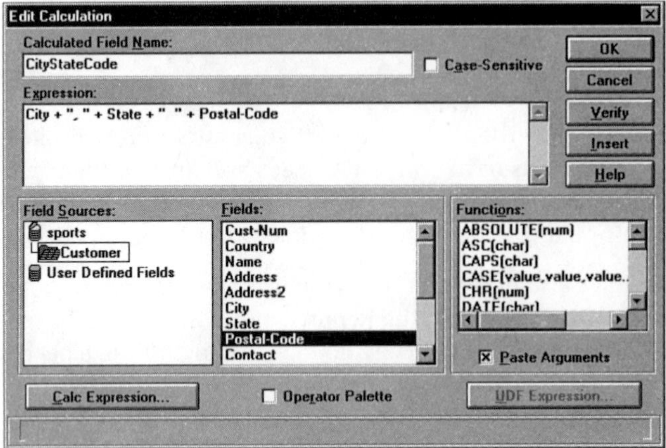

Fig. 11.21

Calculated Fields can be created in the Report Builder.

4. Return to the Customer Address Report by clicking OK in the New Calculation dialog, and Close in the Calculated Fields dialog.
5. Delete the `City`, `State`, and `Postal-Code` fields from the layout. You will do this the same way you deleted the labels above. Simply select the fields and press the Delete key.
6. Now insert the new calculated field. To insert a field, simply right-mouse click at the location you want to create the field. This will bring up the Insert Field window (see fig. 11.22).

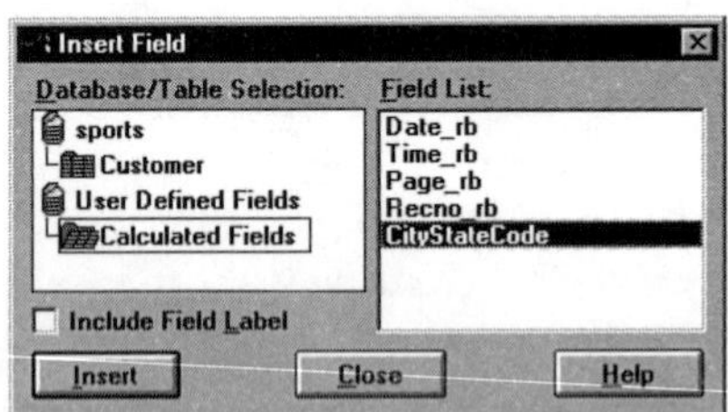

Fig. 11.22

The Insert Field window lets you insert one or more fields.

7. Expand the User-Defined Fields and choose the CityStateCode Calculated Field. Press the Insert button, and then Close the window.
8. Double-click on the `CityStateCode` field to bring up its Property Sheet.
9. Change the format to **X(50)**.
10. Preview your report. Then, save it with your changes.

Using Joins and Groups in Your Reports

The preceding example shows how to create a report from data in one table. However, that will only be an option in the simplest of cases. In most situations, your reports will be much more complicated. An invoice, for example, will contain information about a customer, an order, and probably a sales representative. This data will come from many tables in your database. In addition, each order is going to cover many ordered items. You will want group each item on a separate line within the bigger report.

In this final section, you will learn how to create such a report that joins two tables and prints data in nested groups. In particular, you will build a report that shows Orders, by Customer.

1. Choose Report, Close to close the Customer Address Report that you have been working on.
2. Click the New button on the toolbar.
3. Create a new instant report showing only the `Cust-Num` and `Name` fields from the Customer table.

You have now created a simple report that is very similar to the one you built in the last example. The next step will be to add fields from another table. This cannot be done until you have told the Report Builder how to connect, or join, the two tables. In the UIB, these joins came for free. In the Report Builder, you will have to explicitly create the joins.

1. Click on the Join button on the Report Builder toolbar.
2. Click in the Join To Table combo box and select the Order table from the sports database.
3. Click the New Field Pair button. Join the two tables using the `Cust-Num` field in both tables. This creates a join for all Orders associated with a particular `Customer.Cust-Num`. Figure 11.23 shows the New Join dialog box set up for this join.

   Be very careful to ensure that you have used the `Cust-Num` fields in both tables for your join. It is very common for developers to accidently select fields that really have nothing in common. Even though the report will compile, the output will be nonsense. For example, it is legal to create a join where the customer ZIP code equals the quantity ordered. Both may be integer values, but the query is meaningless.
4. You can now add records from the Order table. Click in the Record band using the right mouse button to bring up the Insert Field window.
5. Click the Insert Field Label toggle box. This will add the column labels to the Page Header band for each field added.
6. Insert the following Order fields: `Order-Num`, `Carrier`, `Order-Date`, and `Ship-Date`.

You may have noted that the New Join dialog supports a variety of *Join Types*. These are represented in the radio set at the bottom of the dialog.

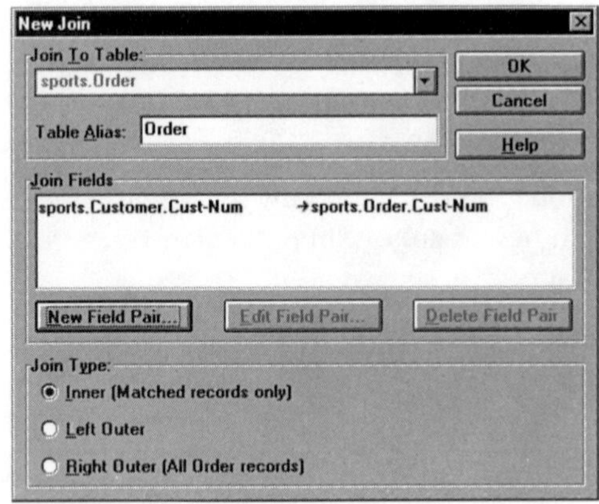

Fig. 11.23

The New Join dialog box showing a join between the Customer and Order tables.

Three standard join types are supported:

- *Inner Join.* Records are not shown unless both tables used in the join have valid records. In this example, the join is between customers and orders. If there are customers without any orders, then these customers will not appear in the join.

  This type of join is the default.

- *Left Outer Join.* The primary table will still be shown, even if there are no matching records in the secondary table. You would choose this option if you wanted to see customers that had no orders. In this case, the report will blank out any fields depending on the order table.

- *Right Outer Join.* The secondary table will be shown, even if there are no matching records in the primary table.

  This type of join is very uncommon. In this example, a right outer join would find orders where there were no customers, which is a situation that would never exist unless there was a problem with the database.

At this point, you are ready to return to the Report Builder design window. Click OK in the New Join dialog. Then Close the Joins dialog box.

At this point, you could preview your report. If you did, you would see that every line of the report contained the Customer fields as well as the Order fields. This is not exactly what you want. What you want is to show the Customer fields once, followed by all the Orders for that Customer. Only then would you move on to the next Customer.

You will now need to create a group based on Order, and add a Group Header band to show the information common to the group.

1. Click on the Group button in the Report Builder toolbar. This brings up the Group Order dialog.
2. Click on the New button to bring up the Group Level dialog.
3. As shown in figure 11.24, set the Group Field for Group Level 1 to `sports.Customer.Cust-Num`.

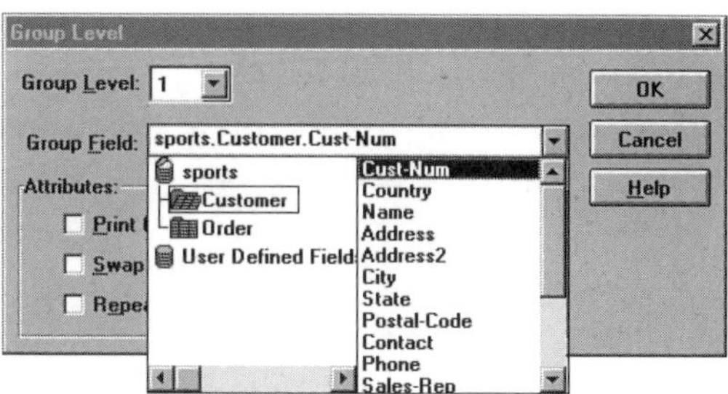

Fig. 11.24

The Group Level dialog lets you organize the levels in a report that shows fields from multiple tables.

4. Return to the Report Builder main window and choose Create, Band Line to add a two-line group header.
5. In the Create Band Line dialog box, indicate that you want to create two (2) new lines.
6. Press the Different Type radio button. In the combo box, choose the type `1GH - Cust-Num`. This creates a Group Header for the `Cust-Num` group you just created.

The next step will be to move the customer fields to the Group Header band and rearrange the layout. Figure 11.25 shows the final layout.

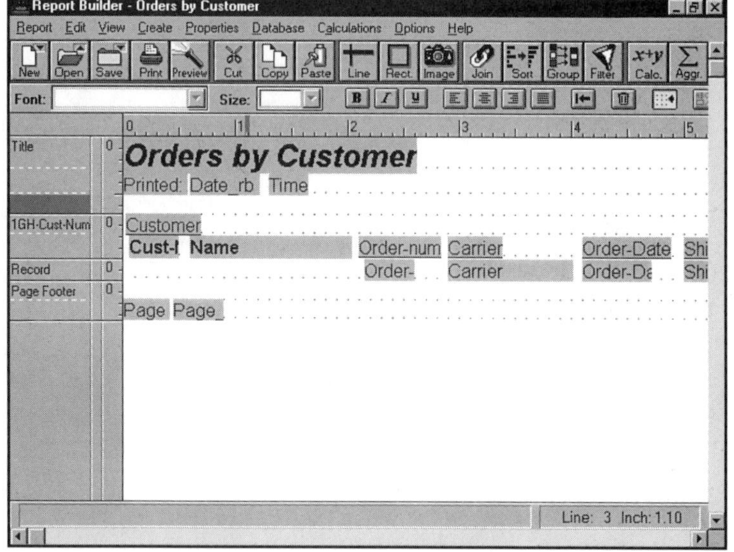

Fig. 11.25

The final layout of the Orders by Customer report.

The steps to create this layout are as follows:

1. Move the Customer fields to the the `1GH-Cust-Num` band.
2. Make these fields bold.
3. Move the Labels from the Page Header band into the `1GH-Cust-Num` band.
4. Rearrange all the fields horizontally until there is no overlap.

5. Delete the bands that are no longer needed, including: `Page Header`, both `Summary Bands`, and the bottom band.
6. Change the text in the title from Customer to **Orders by Customer**. Make the text 20 point, bold, italics.
7. Press the Preview button to view the report. Notice that the customer information is presented only once per block.
8. Close the Print Preview window and return to the Report Builder.
9. Choose Report, Save to save the report. You will not be asked for a Library name this time. Just enter the new report name: **Orders by Customer**.
10. Choose Report, Exit to exit the Report Builder.

Congratulations, you have just finished creating a Report Library using the PROGRESS Report Builder. Whenever you open up this library, the Report Builder will automatically try to connect to the same database environment with which it was created.

The Report Builder can be used stand-alone or called from inside your PROGRESS applications. It is the most convenient way to generate aesthetically pleasing and useful reports for your applications.

From Here...

In these last four chapters you have seen how to contruct a simple application using SmartObjects and your own custom components. There are a few points to consider.

- You have had to type lots of code to develop your own custom components in this chapter.
- These custom components had only very limited functionality. There are clearly many ways in which you could extend the menu bar, Welcome screen, and search dialog box. All these extensions will take more coding.
- Compare this to the SmartObjects created in the previous chapters in which you created components with extensive functionality with no coding.

The next chapters in this book will leave the sample application behind. These chapters instead focus on application design in general. The next chapter looks at user interface design and describes some issues and techniques for producing the usable applications. This is followed by a chapter on database design.

Some of these chapters are far less PROGRESS-specific than much of this book. As you read about the issues of user interface and database design, however, consider the general lessons in terms of the specific sample application that you have just created. Think about what was right, and what was wrong, in the work you have completed.

- Chapter 12, "Introduction to User Interface Design." This provides an overview of how to build a successful user interface.
- Chapter 13, "Understanding Database Design." This chapter exposes you to issues in structuring your database efficiently.

- Chapter 21, "Making the Most of the Application Component Environment." This chapter lists some of the best ways to use SmartObjects and the PROGRESS tools.
- Chapter 22, "PROGRESS Programming Tips." This chapter lists some of the issues and tricks of using the PROGRESS 4GL.

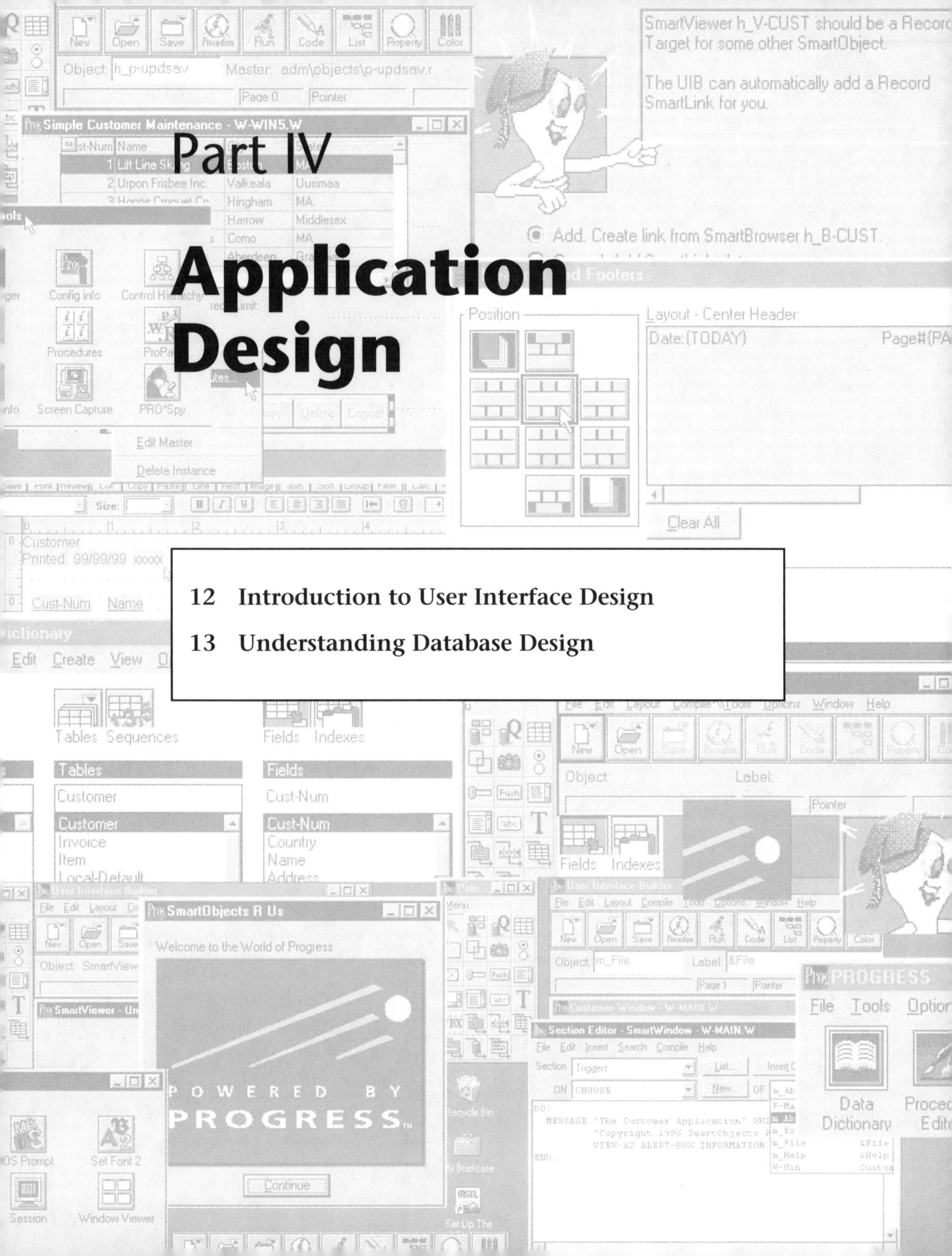

Part IV

Application Design

12 **Introduction to User Interface Design**

13 **Understanding Database Design**

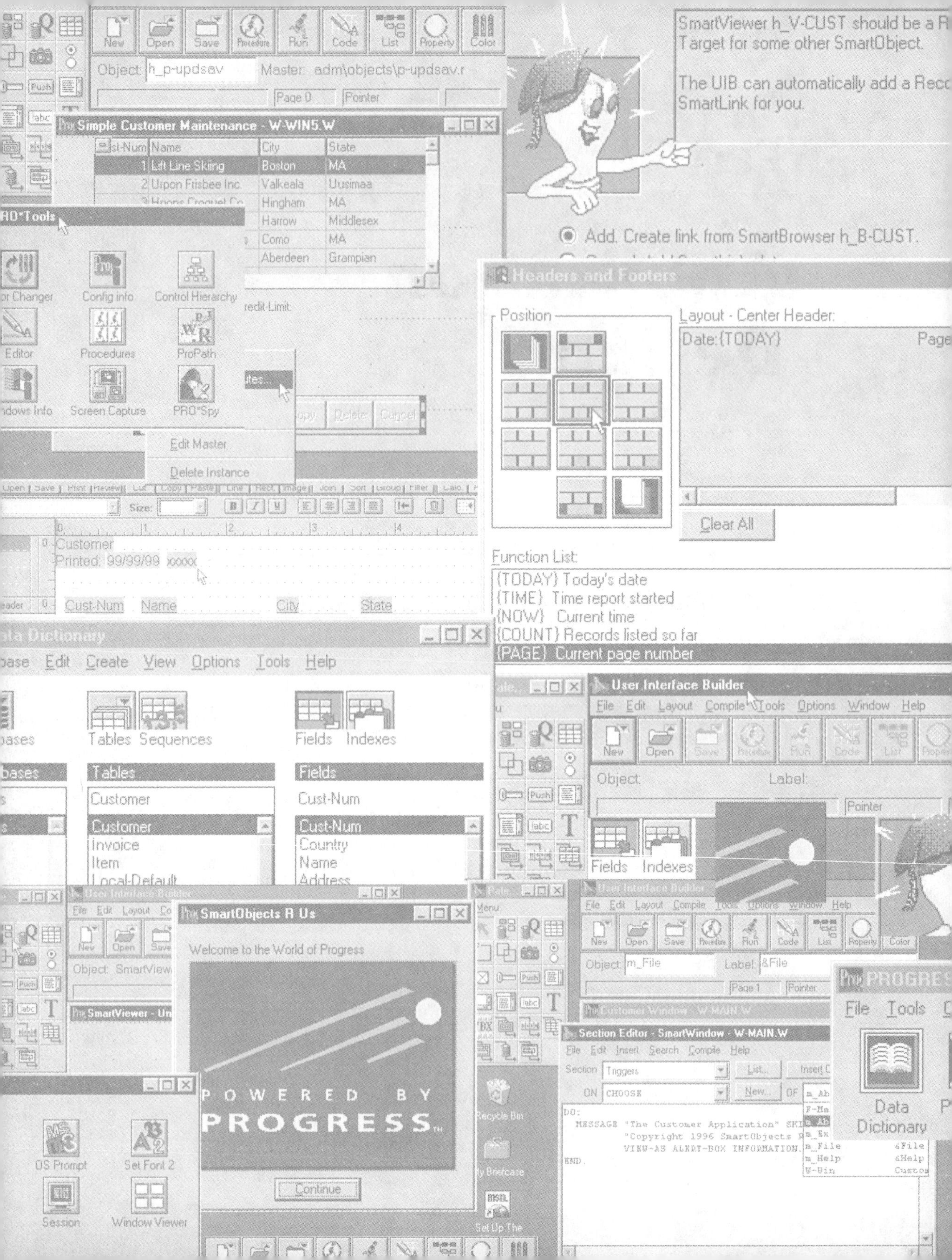
New
Open
Save
Procedure
Run
Code
List
Property
Color
Object: h_p-updsav
Master: adm\objects\p-updsav.r
Page 0
Pointer
SmartViewer h_V-CUST should be a R
Target for some other SmartObject.
The UIB can automatically add a Reco
SmartLink for you.
Add. Create link from SmartBrowser h_B-CUST.
Simple Customer Maintenance - W-WIN5.W
Name
City
State
1 Lift Line Skiing
Boston
MA
2 Urpon Frisbee Inc.
Valkeala
Uusimaa
Hingham
MA
Harrow
Middlesex
Como
MA
Aberdeen
Grampian
PRO*Tools
Config info
Control Hierarchy
Editor
Procedures
ProPath
Screen Capture
PRO*Spy
Edit Master
Delete Instance
Headers and Footers
Position
Layout - Center Header:
Date:{TODAY}
Clear All
Function List:
{TODAY} Today's date
{TIME} Time report started
{NOW} Current time
{COUNT} Records listed so far
{PAGE} Current page number
Size:
Customer
Printed: 99/99/99
Cust-Num
Name
City
State
Edit
Create
View
Options
Tools
Help
Tables
Sequences
Fields
Indexes
Tables
Fields
Customer
Cust-Num
Customer
Invoice
Item
Cust-Num
Country
Name
User Interface Builder
File
Edit
Layout
Compile
Tools
Options
Window
Help
New
Open
Object:
Label:
Pointer
Fields
Indexes
SmartObjects R Us
Welcome to the World of Progress
POWERED BY
PROGRESS
Continue
Object: m_File
Label: &File
Page 1
Pointer
Section Editor - SmartWindow - W-MAIN.W
File
Edit
Insert
Search
Compile
Help
Section
Triggers
List...
ON
CHOOSE
New...
OF
DO:
MESSAGE "The Customer Application"
"Copyright 1996 SmartObjects
VIEW-AS ALERT-BOX INFORMATION.
END.
m_File
&File
m_Help
&Help
Data Dictionary
File
Tools
OS Prompt
Set Font 2
Session
Window Viewer
Recycle Bin
Set Up The

CHAPTER 12

Introduction to User Interface Design

What is user interface design? Most of us recognize the importance of planning the design of a house, a car, a database, and so on. What are the important issues in the design of software user interfaces?

In this chapter, I will explore some of the issues in user interface design:

- What constitutes an effective design?
- How do you get feedback on the design, and from whom?
- How will you know that the design is acceptable?
- What is the output of the design—the end product of the design effort?
- What elements of the design do you want feedback on?
- What are the steps in the design process?
- How do you integrate the design and review process into project plans and timelines?

This chapter explores the many answers to each of these questions. You will investigate the science of designing effective user interfaces and why it is important to the overall GUI development process.

PROGRESS uses paper prototyping techniques for the interface design of such tools as the User Interface Builder for V8. The PROGRESS Software consulting group has also used these techniques with client development efforts. You will explore paper prototyping and its role within the overall design process.

After reading this chapter, you should be able to:

- Understand the iterative development process
- Understand paper prototyping techniques
- See how rapid prototyping plays a significant role in getting the design completed correctly
- Understand the tremendous importance and benefits of usability testing
- Consider the end user's perspective of the GUI

- Compare delivery of systems with and without user feedback on the interface design
- Understand the guidelines behind SmartObject work estimating

Creating an Effective User Interface

Many developers consider a user interface (UI) effective when it has met the specification requirements of the program's functional specifications and when the interface follows a proper style guide. Others think of an effective UI simply as a screen with the appropriate Windows controls that lead to an attractive ensemble. Neither of these attitudes results in a truly effective user interface.

The effective user interface must be tested, and then tested again with real end users. It may require several cycles of testing and revision. The effective user interface design process must include a conduit for end user feedback.

To be effective, it is necessary to have a plan for the interface design process. The design team can then follow the plan and understand the milestones associated with it.

One plan and process that has been highly successful (especially with object-oriented development projects) is the iterative process. In this process, you are able to test several rounds of interface prototypes with end users. I will explore the significance of the iterative development process next.

Introduction to the Iterative Development Process

The iterative development process rotates around the four corners of any design process:

- Plan
- Implement
- Measure
- Learn

As figure 12.1 implies, this review process should occur frequently in order to get the most from it. This is due to the simple fact that more iterations of planning and learning allow you to better refine the interface.

Table 12.1 shows the iterative process phases for the house project, an ineffective software project, and our proposed effective software project.

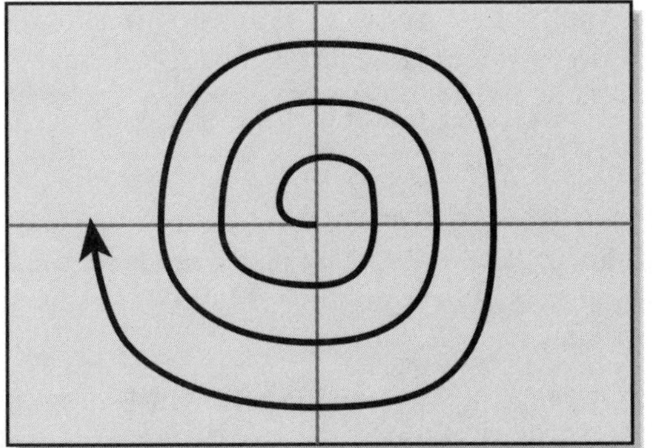
Iterative Development

Fig. 12.1

The iterative development process.

Table 12.1 Iterative Process Phases for House Project

Phase	House Project	Ineffective Software Project	Effective Software Project
Plan	Determines specifications, shows pictures	Determines specifications	Determines specifications
Implement	Constructs foamboard model	Creates product	Designs prototype
Measure	Buyer reviews model	Beta test	User reviews prototype
Learn	Make changes to model	Very minor revisions	Revise prototype
	Returns to planning phase, refining details	No opportunity for further refinement	Returns to planning phase, refining details

In the *planning* phase, you create an interface design in a form that can be presented to end users. This does not require you to actually produce the finished, working interface; a prototype would work nicely at this stage.

In the *implement* phase, you present an interface prototype to the end users in order to receive feedback on the design. In today's development process, this implementation phase is almost always interpreted as the beta release. Such late-stage attempts at gathering feedback are usually ineffective, however, because they are too late. A prototype could be reviewed by end users much earlier, allowing more effective implementation.

In the *measure* phase, the team assesses what was learned from the implementation phase. You are not able to measure much if the process is not conducive to user feedback. Obviously, in simply describing the interface design verbally to an end user, one may get some feedback. The point, however, is to be able to measure the effectiveness of an implementation to a large extent before proceeding.

In the *learn* phase, the team refines its understanding of the end user's needs, which leads to an improved future implementation.

If you substitute the word *implementation* with *produce complete application*, you see the typical and unfortunate development scenario. A team plans, produces the application, measures the application's success in beta, and learns from its mistakes. Just in time for version 2.0 of the application!

If the implementation could be greatly simplified and involved little or no programming, things would be different. Feedback could be obtained much earlier, allowing for multiple cycles of implementation, measurement, and refinement. This results in a far superior interface design.

In this chapter you will see how the paper prototyping method is supportive of the iterative process and allows rapid movement among the four phases.

Tools for the Iterative Process

The tools used in the iterative process involve rapid prototyping and usability testing. The rapid prototyping techniques and tools are used in the planning and implementation phases. The usability testing techniques facilitate the measuring and learning phases.

Figure 12.2 highlights the iterative development process.

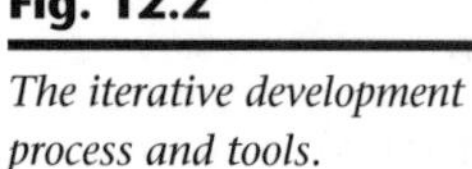

Fig. 12.2

The iterative development process and tools.

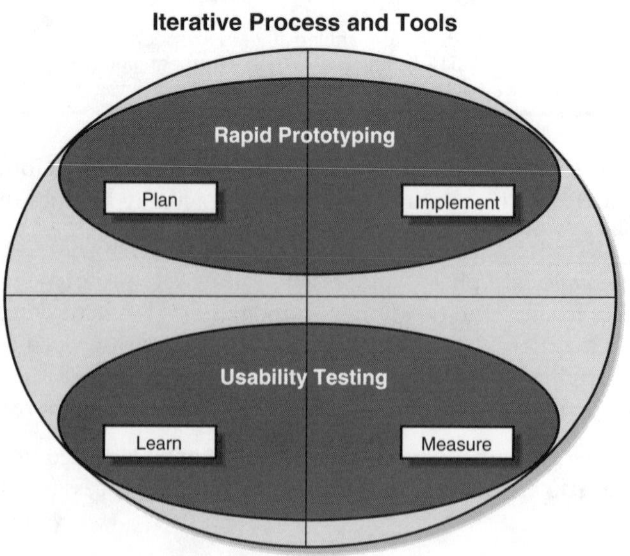

The keys to effective prototyping are that it involves minimal effort and it allows many team members to participate. We will demonstrate how paper prototyping techniques can accomplish these goals.

Usability testing involves putting the paper prototype in front of end users in a structured way so that you can measure their responses. The measurement and learning phases are driven by usability testing.

Using Paper Prototyping

Architects use paper and cardboard building models. Automobile manufacturers use clay models. Aeronautical engineers use wind tunnels. The reasons for these is that the developers, architects, car makers, and aeronautical engineers want end user feedback from home buyers, drivers, and pilots. They want this feedback quickly and inexpensively. They need the feedback over several iterations of models.

The analogy carries to programmers and end users. Interface developers using paper prototyping will deliver a superior product—at least as superiority is measured by more satisfied end users!

The concept behind paper prototyping is very straightforward. Create a paper representation of each SmartObject (with the exception of SmartQueries, which are not visible). Create a paper model of the SmartContainers that hold the window or dialog for each screen. Combine the pieces of paper to present a prototype of the screen at startup and be prepared to maneuver the pieces to emulate the screen changes as the users operate on the paper models.

Many developers and designers reading this book are wondering what is wrong with their expensive design tools. There is nothing wrong with today's design tools. Paper modeling is often overlooked as an important tool in and of itself for designing interfaces. Capturing end user interface requirements through paper modeling is used in countless popular application design efforts, both large and small.

Figure 12.3 shows the ingredients of paper prototyping.

One of the important factors in emulating a working screen is sample data. This is the case with electronic prototypes as well. This can be taken care of with transparencies with sample data that can easily be overlaid on top of the paper objects. Realistic sample data is crucial to the user evaluating the clarity and usefulness of the design.

Paper prototyping concepts:

- Use a separate piece of paper for each SmartObject.
- Use a larger piece of paper for the Window and Dialog containers.
- Prepare transparencies for prototype sample data.
- Be prepared to simulate most of the possible permutations possible in a usability test.
- Use common sense.
- Be creative!

Fig. 12.3

The paper prototyping materials.

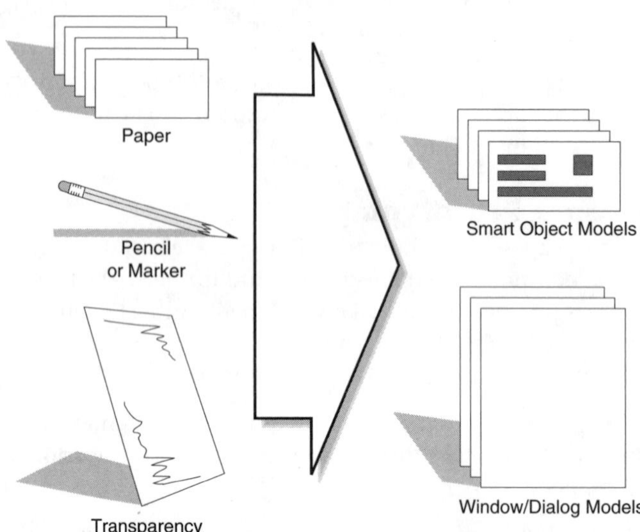

Give yourself time to experiment with paper prototyping. Item four in the previous bulleted list can be most difficult for prototypers with little time or experience. To cover *most* possible permutations requires extensive preparation. The fact is that doing so with an electronic prototype would be even more difficult. If you have designed a script for users to follow, it will help you to be prepared for their likely actions. Anticipate that they will click in the wrong places, or attempt to type the wrong sort of data.

In using your creativity, remember the following paper prototyping techniques:

- Use colored transparency pieces to simulate grayed-out text, buttons, or menu items
- Use transparencies to show sample data in browsers and viewers
- Use separate pieces of paper for drag-and-drop objects

Remember, you can simulate practically anything in paper prototyping.

An additional consideration is that paper prototyping does not require computer experience. This means that anyone who understands the application requirements can be involved. The fact that the prototype can be ripped, crumpled, and thrown into a bucket means people should be less defensive about negative feedback. The ability to create the prototype quickly, without extensive development effort, also reduces people's sensitivity to criticism.

Note

With extensive electronic prototypes, end users may be reluctant to provide negative feedback. Using the paper model, encourage end users to throw away pieces that do not work effectively! Bring a wastebasket with the model. Be prepared to create new objects to place them into the paper prototype and ask the user's opinion.

What are the pros and cons of paper prototyping compared with electronic prototyping?

Paper prototyping and electronic prototyping pros and cons are shown in table 12.2.

Table 12.2 Pros and Cons of Paper Prototyping and Electronic Prototyping

Advantage/ Disadvantage	Paper Prototyping	Electronic Prototyping
Advantages	Conveys product "feel" well. Can be created quickly, with little expense. Can utilize nontechnical staff.	Can provide a polished, more true "look."
Disadvantages	Does only an average job at portraying "look" of application. May artificially draw user's attention to things brought out by the paper model.	Can provide a polished, more true "look." Uses lots of development time and funds. May inhibit user's criticisms.

Consider the importance of look versus feel of an application. The look is the impression of the application upon the end user's eyes. The feel is a different issue; it is the flow and movement of the application. Developers tend to give greater importance to the interface look.

From a cost/benefit standpoint, the feel of an application is much more expensive to alter and change after completion. An incorrect feel of an application can greatly affect the usability and end user satisfaction. I don't mean to imply here that appearance issues are unimportant. It is rare that deficiencies in the look will render an application unusable, however.

Paper prototyping allows you to tackle the feel interface issues as soon as possible. This is one major benefit of the paper prototype.

A newsletter provided to application partners by PROGRESS Software talked about paper prototyping. The essence of the article was, "Everything you needed to know about interface design you learned in kindergarten." Paper, scissors, markers, and tape. Give it a try.

Remember that the paper model supports the *plan* and *implement* phases of the iterative process. By definition, both planning and implementation take place rapidly with paper prototyping. After you become comfortable with the process, paper modeling is not time consuming.

Implementing Usability Testing

Remember from figure 12.2 that usability testing techniques involve putting the paper prototype in front of end users. Usability testing facilitates the measurement and learning phases.

Without effective usability testing, the paper models would serve little purpose.

Usability Testing Concepts

This section highlights the steps involved in usability testing. Be sure to study and prepare each step carefully.

- Be sure to have a reasonable amount of prepared object paper models before starting tests.

Remember that you need paper model objects for each screen involved in usability testing. You also will need sample data on transparencies that fit on top of the object models. You may restrict usability testing to a particular module or limited set of screens. Don't wait until you believe that you have *everything* modeled before trying a usability test. In fact, the feedback from testing a single module can help you learn and better plan other modules.

- Run through mock tests yourself with developers to check for completeness.

Give yourself a task associated with the screen being modeled and try accomplishing the task. See the "Rules for Usability Tests" section later for rules on the session. You will most likely notice that you are missing certain objects or sample data.

- Let the end users schedule when they will participate.

Do not force this exercise on the end users. Let them know in advance that their time is needed for the usability test and invite them to schedule a convenient time. Let them know that they need no advance preparation; you will explain the details at the time of the exercise.

- Prepare the end users for the exercise. Let them know that this is their chance to provide input in the design process.

Don't ignore psychology and its impact on this process. Let the end users know that this is *not a test of them* but rather a test of the design. It is their chance to help you identify the flaws in the design! Explain to them the rules of the exercise and how it will benefit the resulting deployed application.

- Prepare a clear and written script of tasks that the end users will attempt using the model.

Choose tasks related to each screen or set of screens and create a script indicating the steps necessary. The script should give them a functional task to perform, not a series of keystrokes or mouse clicks. It should provide them with the sample data that they should use for this task. (This way, you can have the transparencies prepared in advance, and the user can maintain focus on the product, not the data.) See figure 12.4.

It is often beneficial to identify the person(s) who will champion your development project from the end-user perspective and involve them in the script development. Be sure to educate them thoroughly on the process. The sooner real "ownership" takes place, the better for the overall success of the project.

Sample Script – Usability Testing

Script # ___________ Date: ___________
For Module: ___________

Description: For a given customer and order #, add an order line for a given order item.

Details:

Customer: Dan Reynolds
Order #: 3056
New Item: Water Pump – Small

Fig. 12.4

A sample script for usability testing: adding an order line.

Note that the customer name rather than the customer ID or customer number is given. This will test the interface's ability to allow search on name. The same is true for an item where the item ID will need to be gathered by the end user through the interface.

In certain cases in which the end user works from a pre-set form containing data to be entered, you may present the script with a filled-out form. This better simulates the real-world scenario.

Rules for Usability Tests

The rules for the usability tests are extremely important. Guidelines for usability testing ensure a productive and meaningful session for designers and testers.

Rules for usability tests using paper prototypes:

- End users will use their finger as a mouse click and are encouraged to talk out loud about what they are thinking during the exercise. Often, it helps to have two end users work together to motivate the open speech.

- Be sure that all materials are ready for the test.
- Have one member of the design team assigned to silently take notes of the exercise. Alternatively, audio tape or video tape the tests to review later.
- One or more members of the design team should simulate the computer by presenting new screens, pop-ups, and sample data as the end users use the model.
- Avoid having too many members of the design team watching; this might intimidate the users.
- All design team members should be completely silent during each scripted session. Unless your application will be giving voice instructions, this is the only way to effectively simulate the end user's environment.
- If the end user gets completely stuck somewhere, be prepared to abort the test and go on to another one.

The following could serve as an agenda for conducting a usability test with end users.

Usability test agenda:

- Welcome tester(s) and describe the session objectives.
- Introduce the design team members.
- Have the tester(s) introduce themselves and describe their job function relative to the software being reviewed.
- Show a sample session using design team members and a sample script. Point out the desire to have end users vocalize their thoughts and the purpose of the script.
- Explain the rules of the usability test.
- Re-emphasize that the test is designed to identify shortcomings in the model. The end user can do nothing wrong in this scenario.

The typical set of notes gathered during a usability session may look like the following (using the script example from fig. 12.4):

- User had difficulty getting from main screen to customer maintenance; button choice not clear enough.
- Table look up was confusing; too many clicks needed; user got lost.
- User clicked once on browser list rather than double-clicking.
- Not clear to the user whether order item added was saved to the database. No confirmation.
- Script did not ask user to return to main screen; may need to enhance script for next session.

The value of simple findings such as those listed here is incredible. The struggles of the end user noticed at this stage in the design will easily lead to improvements in the final product for this module and others. Feedback and modification can be done cheaply, before major development and documentation investments have been made. Note that some of the comments come only from watching the end user very attentively during the session.

After the user has completed a script, go on to the next script either for the same screen(s) or a different set. If a review of the difficulties and feedback is desired, do so and record the comments on video or paper.

For the design records, place a copy of the script, paper models, and all notes in a folder labeled with the date and session for future review.

> **Note**
>
> Organizing the script, models, and notes of a usability test can provide valuable design information for other design team members, or for teams designing future releases.

If you are not satisfied with the success of an interface model during the usability test, change it and try again. If the same end users are used for the ensuing test, they will feel part of the team. They will feel that they have provided feedback and it has been used.

If all this feeling of design involvement is a new thing for your end users, be prepared for compliments and positive feedback about the process. See figure 12.5.

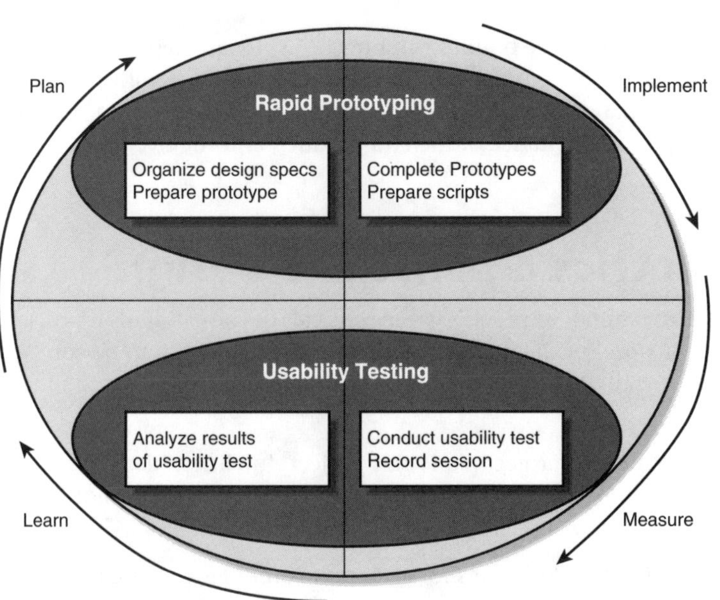

Fig. 12.5

The paper prototyping process, with tools and tasks associated with each step of the process.

The results of this process are outstanding. End users feel part of the design effort. They feel that their feedback is taken seriously and not defensively. The process can iterate or loop relatively rapidly because it does not involve complex computer work or detailed art work. With each iteration, the design improves. Ultimately, the customers will be more satisfied with the product.

Some design teams proceed to develop a set of screens after usability test results are satisfactory. These developed screens are then put to the same tests as the paper models, with the same scripts. Here the team views firsthand the effectiveness of its paper design process. The team will notice which areas are better modeled by paper and which are exaggerated or minimized.

Understanding the Psychological Perspectives

In countless uses of paper prototyping and usability testing in the real world of interface design, there is a set of reoccurring themes.

- The end users feel part of the design team.
- The designers are less defensive about their work.
- The iterative process exposes end users to designers in organized and repeated sessions. This greatly enhances the rapport between the two groups.
- Developers will be more confident about the interface designs and the need for certain interface pieces.
- End users will be less inclined to provide negative feedback at deployment time because they are part of the design. The application, in its real form, will be given a fair chance.

It pays to return to the analogy of the building architect. A software designer, just like an architect, uses models to obtain customer feedback. This makes a significant difference in the quality of the final product. You will notice the positive effect on the design process, the end user's acceptance of the end product, and the overall end product quality.

Applying Metrics against the Design

For project managers, the estimation process is very critical. In the estimation process, you estimate the units of work for the quantity and complexity of work to be completed. The word *estimate* is the key, because it is only an educated guess of the time needed.

Well-prepared estimates turn into project plans and project timelines. Many software products in the market today help project managers prepare timelines and monitor accomplishments.

The process of estimating follows. Estimates for each task combine to create a project plan or schedule.

- Interface design
- Catalog of interfaces required (UI units)
- Catalog of objects needed for each UI unit
- Metrics worksheet to generate estimate per UI unit
- Estimate of work for all interface units
- Project timeline, project plan worksheets

Using a Metrics Worksheet

You are now focusing on item four, the metrics worksheet. A worksheet is created for each UI unit to help you estimate the work required. The total required for all units can easily be determined by looking at the collection of metrics worksheets (see fig. 12.6).

> **Note**
>
> The metrics worksheet is available on the CD as examples\chap-12\metrics.xls. This can be opened using most spreadsheets.

File Edit View Insert Format Tools Data Window Help

	A	B	C	D	E	F	G	H	I
1	*Metrics Worksheet*								
2	*Functional Area Information*								
3	*Functional Area*								
4	*Logical Unit Of Work*								
5	*LUW Description*								
6									
7	*Base Man Hours*								
8	*Component/Process*	Cntr	View	Qry	Brw	Pnl	Fldr	Weight	Hours
9									
10									
11									
12									
13									
14									
15									
16									
17									
18									
19									
20									
21									

Metrics Worksheet

Fig. 12.6

A metrics worksheet to facilitate the estimation process.

Each user interface unit (UI) will have an associated metrics worksheet. I will analyze the various parts of the worksheet.

Functional Area Information

The functional area is typically the module or set of programs in which this unit of work resides. For a tax table maintenance program, for example, the functional area may be Table Maintenance.

The functional area is significant because it will allow you to estimate by module or group of programs (see fig. 12.7).

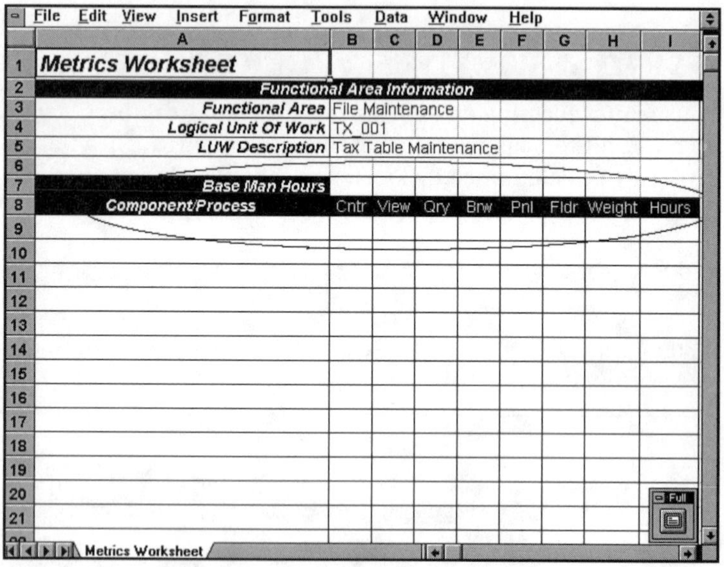

File Edit View Insert Format Tools Data Window Help

	A	B	C	D	E	F	G	H	I
1	Metrics Worksheet								
2	Functional Area Information								
3	Functional Area	File Maintenance							
4	Logical Unit Of Work	TX_001							
5	LUW Description	Tax Table Maintenance							
6									
7	Base Man Hours								
8	Component/Process	Cntr	View	Qry	Brw	Pnl	Fldr	Weight	Hours

Metrics Worksheet

Fig. 12.7

Functional Area Information section of metrics worksheet.

Logical Unit of Work

Many times, a unit of work code name serves as a convenient handle for project documents such as timelines. The handle can use one of many naming styles such as *xxx-nnn*, where *xxx* represents the functional area and *nnn* is a unique numeric. I encourage you to decide upon a naming convention for logical units and be consistent.

Logical Unit of Work Description

The Logical Unit of Work description describes the LUW, for example: Tax Table File Maintenance.

Base Man Hours

The Base Man hours row describes the hours typically associated with each type of component, as shown in Table 12.3 and figure 12.8.

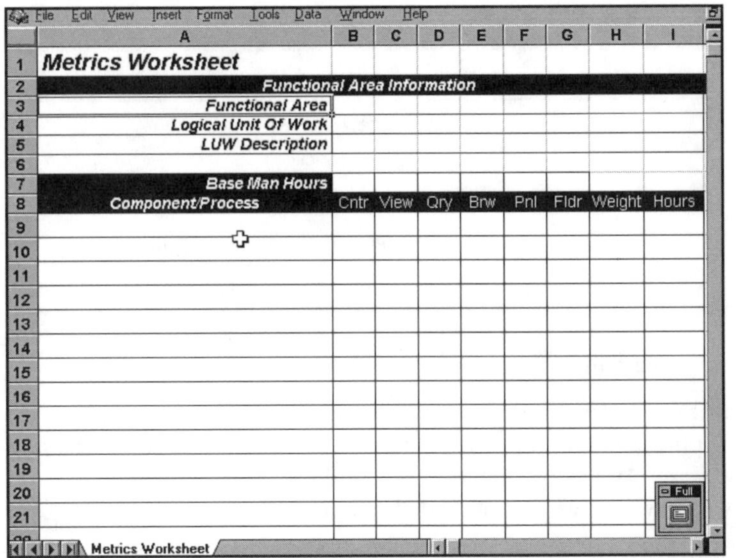

Fig. 12.8

Base Man Hours/ Components section of metrics worksheet.

Table 12.3 Component Types

Component Type Code	Components
CNTR	(Containers: SmartWindow, SmartDialog, SmartFrame)
View	(SmartViewer)
Qry	(SmartQuery)
Brw	(SmartBrowser)
Pnl	(SmartPanel)
Fldr	(SmartFolder)

Each type of component carries associated base hours. Each type of component's base hours indicates its effort relative to a general unit of work. The unit of work number is not related to a direct number of hours but simply a relative unit for the purpose of estimation.

The base hours for each component is typically as follows in table 12.4.

Table 12.4 Objects and Base Man Hours

Object Type	Base Man Hours	Abbreviation
SmartContainer		CNTR
SmartWindow	1	
SmartDialog	1	
SmartFrame	1	

(continues)

Table 12.4 Continued

Object Type	Base Man Hours	Abbreviation
SmartViewer	3	View
SmartQuery	1	Qry
SmartBrowser	2	Brw
SmartPanel	1	Pnl
SmartFolder	2	Fldr

I will explore each component and the reasoning behind the hours estimates.

SmartContainers: SmartWindow, SmartFrame, SmartDialog. These container objects serve the basic purpose of holding other SmartObjects. The SmartContainers provide the Window, Frame, or Dialog that will surround the interface. These SmartContainers have a low relative unit of work measurement.

SmartContainers (with the exception of SmartFolders, which are estimated separately) very rarely contain application logic or complex calculations.

SmartFolder. The SmartFolder container presents pages of objects using a folder interface common throughout Windows 95. There can be significant logic behind the definition of each page. This is especially true when folder pages get defined at runtime based on data.

SmartFolders carry higher relative base hours than the other SmartContainers.

SmartViewer. Although many SmartViewers will be simple and not time consuming to create, the SmartViewer can become quite complex. Significant application logic, validation, and calculations can contribute to the SmartViewer's complexity.

SmartViewers carry high relative base hours but must be carefully measured for estimated complexity, as you will see in the section concerning weight that follows.

SmartBrowser. SmartBrowsers contain a browse control and a query. Although this presents a relatively simple effort, many SmartBrowsers contain more than a browse. It is common for a SmartBrowser to contain a fill-in field and buttons to facilitate query search.

SmartBrowsers carry medium level base hours and are rated in large part by weight.

SmartPanel. SmartPanels are collections of controls that drive other SmartObjects within the interface. SmartPanels rarely if ever contain application logic, validation, or calculations.

SmartPanels carry low base hours and are rarely complex.

SmartQuery. SmartQueries are not visible. They contain a query that defines tables, joins, and selection criteria. Most queries are simple and can readily be defined by combining the needs of the interface and the database design. Therefore, query has relatively low base hours.

Weight

Perhaps the most important data element in the worksheet for estimates is the weight column. Estimated hours are calculated as follows:

BASE HOURS × WEIGHT

This implies that a high weight factor with low base hours will take about the same amount of time as a low weight and high base hours. The weight factor has a wider range and is highly dependent on the quality of the paper design because this demonstrates relative complexity.

I will review each object type and its weight factors. This is meant as a set of guidelines, not an absolute set of estimation numbers for *your* project.

SmartViewer. Relative Weight Range: 1 through 15.

Simplest Scenario: A SmartViewer associated with one table displaying a limited number of database fields with little business logic and few pop-ups or lookup fields. (Relative weight of 1)

Complexity Factors:

- Association with multiple tables
- Significant business logic requirements
- Significant number of pop-ups, lookup fields, or calculated fields
- Large number of fields making for screen layout challenges

SmartContainer. Relative Weight Range: 1 through 5.

Simplest Scenario: A SmartContainer housing few noncontainer-based objects and no controls or extra functionality within itself.

Complexity Factors:

- Association with container type objects such as SmartFolders
- Inclusion of frames, fill-ins, buttons, and so on within the container
- Significant business logic built into the container
- Complex menu associated with the window in a container (Window type)

SmartBrowser. Relative Weight Range: 1 through 3.

Simplest Scenario: A SmartBrowser associated with one table displaying a limited number of database fields with little business logic. (Relative weight of 1)

Complexity Factors:

- Association with multiple tables
- Significant business logic requirements
- Significant number of driver controls driving the browse query

SmartFolder. Relative Weight Range: 1 through 3.

Simplest Scenario: A three-page tab folder with no dynamic creation of additional tabs and little messaging with the associated objects. (Relative weight of 1)

Complexity Factors:

- Dynamic creation of tabs
- Significant messaging between SmartFolder and other objects (particularly State Messaging)

SmartPanel. Relative Weight Range: 1 through 3.

Simplest Scenario: A simple navigation toolbar. (Relative weight of 1)

Complexity Factors:

- Large number of buttons and images
- A toolbar containing other toolbars within it
- Significant messaging between toolbar and other objects (particularly State Messaging)

Background and Calculation Factors

There are other significant factors that affect work estimates. Background processes and complex calculations are good examples. The metrics worksheet can be adapted to fit those objects if necessary.

You may use the metrics worksheet to estimate the work involved in creating the SmartObjects. This coupled with a work estimate for all other processes can result in the complete estimate.

Don't forget testing, redesign, documentation, and deployment efforts in the overall estimate. Also, do not overlook end user training. Time and resource requirements for end user training can be quite substantial.

Impact of Reusability

As your application development effort gains momentum, many SmartObjects will exist in your libraries. A catalog of such SmartObjects containing name, function, messaging options, and so on is extremely valuable. It will enable developers to take advantage of work done and tested, and will minimize the frequency with which you reinvent the wheel.

For estimating additional development efforts that make use of existing SmartObjects, you should include the existing SmartObjects in the metrics worksheet with a weight factor of 0.5 or 0.25. Zero should not be used because there is usually some work involved in resizing or positioning a SmartObject.

From Here...

Your use of the paper prototyping, usability testing, and metrics worksheet should greatly enhance your design efforts. In this chapter you learned the principles and steps involved in paper modeling. You explored the psychological impact of getting end users involved from the design phase in a real modeling exercise.

For more information on related items, refer to the following chapter:

- Chapter 13, "Understanding Database Design," outlines the basics behind database design and highlights database design skills that are essential to a successful development effort.

CHAPTER 13

Understanding Database Design

This chapter will introduce you to the principles and concepts of database design. You will study the rules of database normalization and entity relationship diagrams. By maximizing the effectiveness of your database you will increase the performance and overall quality of your application. As database design is absolutely crucial in the development of business applications, this chapter is devoted exclusively to this subject.

After reading this chapter, you should be able to do the following:

- Understand the fundamental concepts of database design
- Normalize a set of data to maximize the effectiveness of the database design
- Understand Entity Relationship diagramming to clearly define and present the database structures

Database Design Concepts

Like all Relational DataBase Management Systems (RDBMS), the Progress database follows the *relational* model. Other database models include *network* model and *hierarchical* model, neither of which will be discussed further in this text. The relational model is most frequently applied in client-server applications.

The relational database model is a tabular representation of the data using rows and columns. The term *rows* is used to represent records within a table, whereas *columns* relates to the fields within a record.

The following attributes pertain to this discussion of relational database models. You will need to understand the terms defined in the next sections in order to follow the discussion further on in this chapter.

Definition: Columns

The following points pertain to table columns.

- Represent fields in a table
- Also referred to as fields and attributes

Fig. 13.1

Relational model as a tabular list of rows and columns of data.

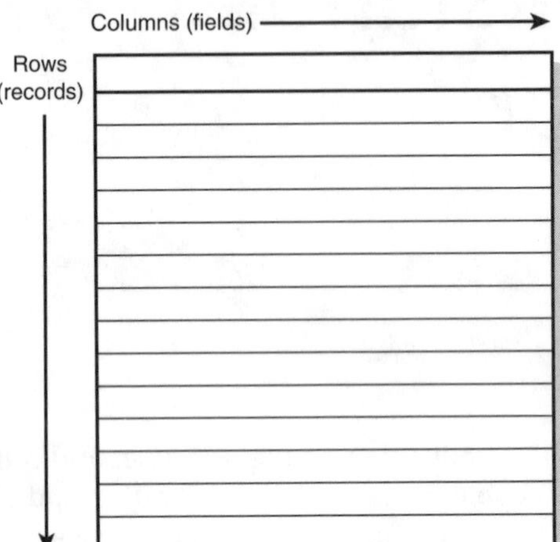

- Each column has a range or set of possible valid values. This is often referred to as the column *domain*. Columns are homogeneous such that all entries in any column are all of the same type.
- Examples of columns or fields: `Cust-num`, `Cust-Name`, `Order-Date`
- A column includes similar data for various records; for example, the cust-num for every customer

Definition: Rows

The following points pertain to table rows.

- Represent records in a table
- Also referred to as records and tuples
- The order of records is not important; a separate index structure will define the order of records
- Examples of rows or records: Customer record, SalesRep record, Invoice record
- A row includes all the fields of data related to a single record; for example, `cust-id`, `cust-address`, `cust-name`

Definition: Repeating Attributes

The following points pertain to repeating attributes.

- A set of fields that repeat within a record
- Also referred to as array of fields and field extents
- Example of Repeating Attributes: Sales-Quota[1..12],12 monthly sales quotas for a sales rep

Definition: Database Relations

The following points pertain to database relations.

- A two-dimensional representation of the columns in a row, a listing of all the fields for a given record
- Also referred to as Record Structure, Record Schema, and Record Definition
- In the notation, the key field is shown underlined; the name of the relation is shown outside parenthesis
- Examples of relations: `STUDENT` (***`Student_ID`***, `Name`, `YOG`) `ORDER-LINE` (***`Cust-Num`***, ***`Order-Num`***, ***`Line-Num`***, ***`Item-ID`***)

Definition: Index Keys

The following definition pertains to index keys.

- An attribute (field) or attributes that are part of an index and determine order, uniqueness, or both. Order is important for reporting, sorting, and tabulation. Uniqueness is important for quick record searches and identification. A table may have many keys defined for it, each meeting the preceding key definition.

Definition: Candidate Keys

The following definition pertains to candidate keys.

- An attribute or set of attributes that uniquely identifies a row and is nonredundant.

Definition: Primary Keys

The following definition pertains to primary keys.

- A candidate key that is chosen to identify a record when no other key is explicitly chosen.

Definition: Sample Record Set

The following definition pertains to sample record set.

- A list of sample records that meet the integrity rules for the table. Used as examples or illustrations. Also known as an *instance.*

Definition: Functional Dependence

The following definition pertains to functional dependence.

- In a relation, a field (A) is functionally dependent on field (B) if the value of (B) determines the value of (A). A field (A) is functionally dependent on a set of fields (Bx) if (A) is functionally dependent on the entire (Bx) but not functionally dependent on any individual field in (Bx).

Example:

From the sports database, you will notice the customer records (first six records shown in Table 13.1).

Table 13.1 Customer Records

Cust-Num	Name	City
1	Lift Line Skiing	Boston
2	Urpon Frisbee	Valkeala
3	Hoops Croquet Co.	Hingham
4	Go Fishing Ltd	Harrow
5	Match Point Tennis	Como
6	Fanatical Athletes	Aberdeen

The relation here is `CUSTOMER` (***`Cust-Num`***, `Name`, `City`).

The columns are `cust-num`, `name`, and `city`.

Each row is a Customer record.

There are no repeating attributes (see SalesRep table for an example of repeating field: Month-Quota[12]).

The primary key for this table is `Cust-Num`. This establishes uniqueness for the customer number and sets the order of records in cases in which another key is not explicitly chosen. An alternate, nonprimary key of *name* could be used if necessary. By examining the instance (sample records), you can determine which functional dependencies exist:

```
Cust-Num -> Name
```

Given any customer number, you can determine the customer name. Name is functionally dependent on customer number.

```
Cust-Num -> City
```

Given any customer number, you can determine the city. City is functionally dependent on customer number.

```
City -> Name
```

Given a city, you cannot determine the name. Name is not functionally dependent on city.

These concepts are important because they will help you clearly define relations and structures for the database that you are designing. Such structures will need to be well planned and organized to maximize the effectiveness of the queries and requests against the data.

Introduction to Database Normalization

One of the essential elements of database design is *normalization*. Normalization is a process by which the structure of the columns, rows, and relations is altered to maximize efficiency and effectiveness.

In this section, you will explore various levels of normalization. The levels covered here are first, second, and third normal form. The rules for normalization at the different levels are given with a corresponding example.

First Normal Form

This is the minimum level of normalization. Some database designs do not reach this level with certain tables. We explore this in more detail.

Definition: A record design is in first normal form if there are no repeating groups.

Example 1: Repeating Groups and First Normal Form

Table 13.2 Student Records

Student	Name	Class1	Class2	Class3
1	John Smith	Biology 2	Chemistry1	English Lit
2	Kathy Lane	Physics I	CPU Design	Calculus
3	Rich O'Reilly	Physics I	Calculus	
4	Robert Fays	Compilers	Data Structures	
5	Charles Chu	Data Struc	Database I	Compilers
6		Tricia Barkley Accounting	Economics	English Lit

In this design, you have the relation:

```
STUDENT(stud_ID, name, class1, class2, class3)
```

Assume that the student ID is the primary key. In this example, the fields `class1`, `class2`, `class3` are considered repeating fields.

The repeating group of `class1`, `class2`, and `class3` means that this design is *not* in first normal form. Some practical reasons that this design would be relatively weak are as follows:

1. To change the name of a class, all student records must be checked for possible update.
2. Any queries on classes must query the `class1`, `class2`, and `class3` fields separately.
3. Any index fields on classes must include the separate `class1`, `class2`, `class3` fields.

4. To associate more than three classes with a student, the database design will need to change!
5. Blank or empty class field entries will have to be read and processed even though they provide no data.

This relation is not a strong design. Accessing information in a database designed like this would be slow and difficult.

A better design would be in the first normal form:

```
STUDENT(stud_ID, name)
ENROLLMENT(stud_ID, class)
```

With the relations given here, `STUDENT` and `ENROLLMENT`, the weaknesses exhibited by the example are removed. Access would be faster and easier. Modification would be much simpler.

The new relations (in first normal form) would arrange the sample data as follows. Table 13.3 lists the records within the student table.

Table 13.3 Student Table

Student	Name
1	John Smith
2	Kathy Lane
3	Rich O'Reilly
4	Robert Fays
5	Charles Chu
6	Tricia Barkley

Table 13.4 Enrollment Table

Student	Class
1	Biology 2
1	Chemistry 1
1	English Literature
2	Intro to Physics
2	CPU Design
...	...

Second Normal Form

This level of normalization takes the database design slightly further. Fields (attributes) dependent on a part of the primary key are identified.

Definition: A database design having second normal form must meet the rules for first normal form AND:

1. No nonkey fields are functionally dependent on an individual field in the primary key.

   OR (exception #1)

2. Only one field is involved in the primary key.

   OR (exception #2)

3. There are no nonkey fields.

Example 2: Low Normalization and Second Normal Form

Table 13.5 Customer Records

Cust-Num	Order-Num	Order-Date	Cust-Name
1	1	03/05/95	Lift Line Skiing
2	1	02/12/94	Urpon Frisbee
2	2	12/03/95	Urpon Frisbee
2	3	05/01/95	Urpon Frisbee
3	1	04/07/95	Hoops Croquet Co.
4	1	10/12/94	Go Fishing Ltd
5	1	01/03/95	Match Point Tennis
6	1	02/09/95	Fanatical Athletes

In this design, there is the relation:

```
ORDER(Cust-Num, Order-Num, Order-date, Cust-Name)
```

Assume that the set of (`Cust-Num`, `Order-Num`) is the primary key. This multifield key is essential because both customer number and order number are necessary to ensure uniqueness. This design is not second normal form.

Some practical reasons that this design would be relatively weak are as follows:

1. The customer name is repeated for each order of that customer, which increases data storage requirements.
2. A change in a customer's name would force a read for possible update on the entire table, causing slow access.
3. An insert of a new row (record) into this table forces a query for customer name from a related table, slowing performance.

4. Database integrity could be jeopardized if modifications or deletions to the customer table are made without regard to the customer name field in this table.

This design of this relation could be improved.

In violation of the second normal form rule, note that in the following relation (which was shown previously):

ORDER(***Cust-Num***, ***Order-Num***, Order-date, Cust-Name)

`Cust-Name` is functionally dependent on `Cust-Num`. Given any customer number, the customer name can be derived. Thus, customer name is functionally dependent on a field of the primary key set. Check the second normal form definition to understand why this makes the relation only first normal form.

A better design would be in second normal form:

CUSTOMER(***Cust-Num***, Cust-Name)
ORDER(***Cust-Num***, ***Order-Num***, Order-date)

The new relations (in second normal form) would arrange the sample data as shown in Table 13.6.

Table 13.6 Customer Table

Cust-Num	Cust-Name
1	Lift Line Skiing
2	Urpon Frisbee
3	Hoops Croquet Co.
4	Go Fishing Ltd
5	Match Point Tennis
6	Fanatical Athletes

Table 13.7 Order Table

Cust-Num	Order-Num	Order-Date
1	1	03/05/95
2	1	02/12/94
2	2	12/03/95
2	3	05/01/95
3	1	04/07/95
4	1	10/12/94
5	1	01/03/95
6	1	02/09/95

You may notice that because the customer name is not repeated, fewer total characters (bytes) are stored in this second normal form. One of the advantages of normalization is effective database storage.

Third Normal Form

This level of normalization takes the database design further again.

Definition. A database design having third normal must meet the rules of second normal form AND:

- Must not contain any pair of nonkey fields being functionally dependent.

This means that if a third normal form relation exists as R(`a`,`b`,c,d) where (a,b) is the primary key then the pair of attributes (c,d) and (d,c) are not functionally dependent. This means that given the value for (c), (d) may not be derived, and vice versa.

Table 13.8 shows Example 3: Low Normalization and Third Normal Form.

Table 13.8 Student Records

Student	Name	Class1	Major
1	John Smith	Biology 2	Medical Science
2	Kathy Lane	Intro to Physics	Physics
3	Rich O'Reilly	Intro to Physics	Engineering
4	Robert Fays	Compiler Theory	Computer Science
4	Robert Fays	Data Structures	Computer Science
6	Tricia Barkley	Accounting	Business

In this design, you have the relation:

```
STUDENT(stud_ID, name, class, major)
```

The above relation is assuming that the student ID is the primary key.

Some practical reasons that this design would be relatively weak are as follows:

1. To change the name of a class or major, all student records must be checked for possible update.
2. To associate a class with a different or new major, all student records must be checked for possible update.
3. A name change for a student will cause multiple records to be read and modified.
4. The name of the student must be repeated for each class that the student is registered for.
5. The `student_ID` field cannot be unique in this relation because a student can have multiple class registrations (example: student #4).

This relation is not a strong design. It would be cumbersome, slow, and difficult to maintain.

A stronger, third normal form design would encompass:

```
STUDENT(Student_ID, Name)
CLASS(Class_ID, Class_Name)
MAJOR(Major_ID, Major_Name)
ENROLLMENT(Student_ID, Class_ID)
STUDENT-MAJOR(Student_ID, Major_ID)
```

It is essential for you to understand the process by which you arrived at the preceding third normal form design for the example. I'll break down the iterative process, which brings us to the third normal form solution.

Step 1, the initial relation:

```
STUDENT(Student_ID, Name, class, major)
```

For Step 2, because (`class, major`) are functionally dependent, we remove both from the relation creating new relations. This is done to avoid repeating the class name and major for every enrollment record. This reduces data storage requirements. We now have:

```
STUDENT(Student_ID, Name)
CLASS(Class_ID, Class_Name)
MAJOR(Major_ID, Major_Name)
ENROLLMENT(Student_ID, Class_ID)
```

Both Major and Class Identifiers (`ID`) are designed to minimize repeated name storage; the names are stored once. The issue at this stage is that there is no longer a connection between a student and his or her major. You cannot determine a student's major.

For Step 3, we must add another relation:

```
STUDENT-MAJOR(Student_ID, Major_ID)
```

So, now you have a third normal form design for storing data on student enrollment, classes, and majors.

Here is another example illustrating third normal form.

Table 13.9 shows Example 4: Low Normalization and Third Normal Form.

Table 13.9 Customer Records

Cust-Num	Order-Num	Line-Num	Item ID	Description
1	1	1	102	Aluminum Baseball Bat
2	1	1	205	Catcher's Glove
2	1	2	215	Sports Sox
2	2	1	560	Misc. Tennis Equip.
3	1	1	301	Golf Balls - 24 pack

Cust-Num	Order-Num	Line-Num	Item ID	Description
3	1	2	309	Gloves - Golfing
3	2	1	215	Sports Sox
3	2	2	342	Ladies Apparel - Golf

In this design, you have the relation:

```
Order-Line(Cust-Num, Order-Num, Line-Num, Item-ID, Item-Desc)
```

The above relation assumes that the set of (Cust-Num, Order-Num, Line-Num) is the primary key. This multifield key is essential beecause both customer number, order number, and order line number are necessary to ensure uniqueness.

Some practical reasons why this design would be relatively weak are as follows:

1. The item description is repeated for each order and order line of each customer, which increases data storage requirements.
2. A change in an item's description would force a read for possible update on the entire table, causing slow performance.
3. An insert of a new row (record) into this table forces a query for item description from a related table.
4. Database integrity could be jeopardized if modifications or deletions to the item table are made without regard to the item description field in this table.

This design of this relation could be improved.

Notice that the relation is in second normal form: none of the nonkey fields are functionally dependent on any field in the primary key.

Yet the relation (from the preceding example):

```
ORDER-LINE(Cust-Num, Order-Num, Line-Num, Item-ID, Item-Desc)
```

does not reach third normal form. Why not?

Item description can be derived given any item ID. Because these are both nonkey fields, the relation is weak.

The design in third normal form could be:

```
ORDER-LINE(Cust-Num, Order-Num, Line-Num, Item_ID)
ITEM(Item_ID, Item-Desc)
```

The rules for normalization go beyond even third normal formal. Fourth and fifth normal form rules exist. Even *relation calculus* can be applied to a design to maximize its effectiveness and efficiency. This mathematical adaptation to the normalization challenge allows for the rules to be defined in nonabstract terms. For practical purposes, third normal form design gives a good level of efficiency in data storage and access speed. It is seldom necessary to go to further levels of normalization.

Database Denormalization

You must take care not to overnormalize your database design. Just as proper normalization creates faster and more efficient storage, too much normalization can lead to unwanted cycles or disk reads to get the data you need.

For example, the student enrollment could include data to keep track of the major abbreviation. This would satisfy the need to store an abbreviation (for example, "CS") for a given major (for example, "Computer Science").

In third normal form:

```
STUDENT(Student_ID, Name)
CLASS(Class_ID, Class_Name)
MAJOR(Major_ID, Major_Name)
MAJOR-ABBREV(Major_ID, Abbrev)
ENROLLMENT(Student_ID, Class_ID)
STUDENT-MAJOR(Student_ID, Major_ID)
```

It can easily be argued that this design is overnormalized. The abbreviation is a short character string of data and it will not likely be changed for the life of a major. The need for a `Major` abbreviation is almost always preceded by the read for the `Major` itself. Thus, the abbreviation would be better placed in the `Major` relation.

```
STUDENT(Student_ID, Name)
CLASS(Class_ID, Class_Name)
MAJOR(Major_ID, Major_Name, Abbrev)
ENROLLMENT(Student_ID, Class_ID)
STUDENT-MAJOR(Student_ID, Major_ID)
```

The preceding set of relations would be reduced to second normal form because the nonkey fields `Major_Name` and `Major_Abbrev` are functionally dependent. For most queries and lookups on the database, this design would be preferable.

In general, you may follow these guidelines for normalization/denormalization:

- Normalize your database design to third normal form.
- Identify data fields that, due to their nature, could best be paired with fields in other relations.
- Denormalize to maximize efficiency given the real-world nature of your data.
- Make sure that the denormalization will result in less complex query code, less disk access to get common data, or both.

Normalizing to an extent that is blind to the nature of your data is not a strong choice. Thus, it is essential that the database designer(s) understand the true nature of the data to be stored and how it will be used.

Entity-Relationship Diagrams

Entity-relationship (ER) diagrams allow the logical representation of your databases to be drawn. This provides a convenient reference to relationships among fields and tables.

Many variations of ER diagramming styles exist, each having unique merits and drawbacks. Software is available to aid in this phase of the design process.

One commonly used ER notation shows the various database tables and their relations using the shapes shown in figure 13.2.

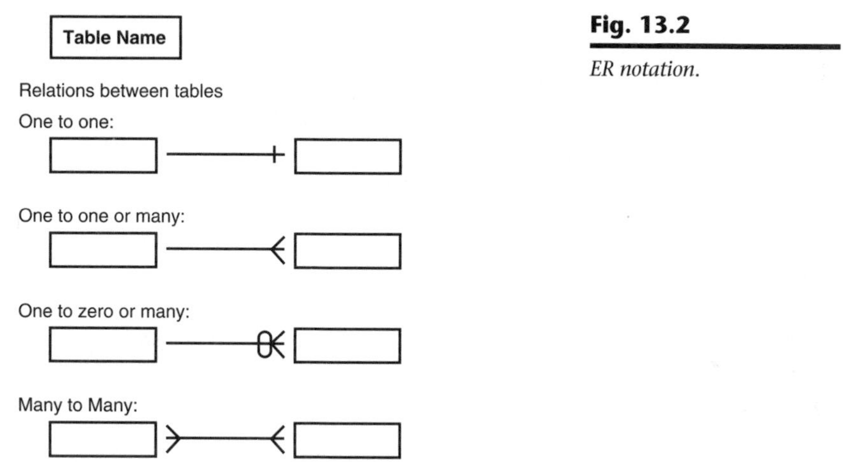

Fig. 13.2

ER notation.

Using this notation, the following relations can be represented as an example:

```
STUDENT(Student_ID, Name)
CLASS(Class_ID, Class_Name)
MAJOR(Major_ID, Major_Name, Abbrev)
ENROLLMENT(Student_ID, Class_ID)
STUDENT-MAJOR(Student_ID, Major_ID)
```

This can be read as follows:

- A student is enrolled for no classes, one class, or many classes.
- A class has many enrollments (assuming that a class would not be given for one or no students).
- A class has one major associated with it.

Some notations show the fields, keys, and relations along with the diagram. This can come in handy with large designs for which a separate list of field names and relations may be hard to follow.

Fig. 13.3

ER notation.

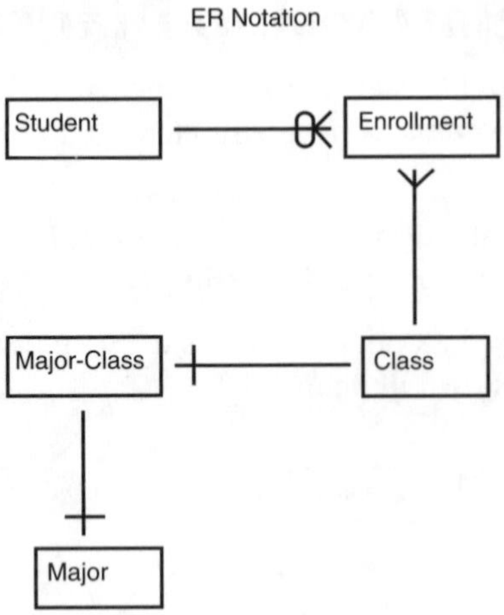

ER Notation

Student

Enrollment

Major-Class

Class

Major

A good indication that your database design is strong is the use of verbs between ER diagram boxes. Try using verbs to describe the relationships you have defined, example:

> A student *may have* an enrollment.
>
> A class *has* many enrollments.

Fig. 13.4

ER notation.

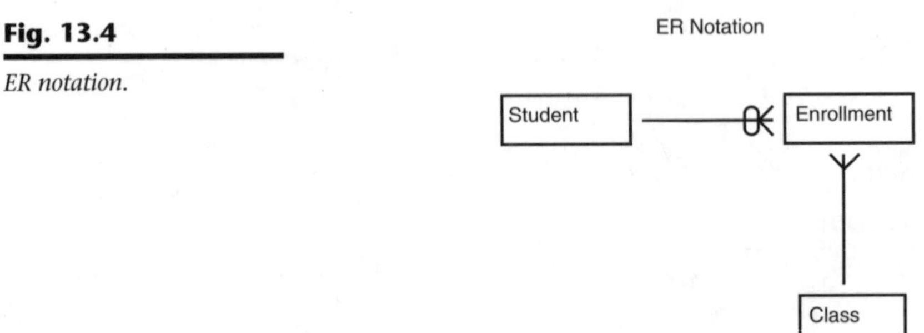

This technique may help you understand the nature of your relations and the way they will work with your developed application.

Transforming Logical Model to Physical Model

The logical database model includes the normalized list of relations, a list of attributes (fields) for each table in the database, and entity-relationship diagrams.

The physical model is created using the Progress Data Dictionary tool (see Chapter 2, "Getting Started with ADE Tools") by creating tables, fields and indexes.

For a relation such as the example used earlier:

```
STUDENT(Student_ID, Name)
CLASS(Class_ID, Class_Name)
MAJOR(Major_ID, Major_Name, Abbrev)
ENROLLMENT(Student_ID, Class_ID)
STUDENT-MAJOR(Student_ID, Major_ID)
```

you would need to create the tables: `STUDENT`, `CLASS`, `MAJOR`, `ENROLLMENT`, `MAJOR-CLASS`. Each would have the fields listed within the relation parentheses.

At least one index would need to be created to carry the primary key. Because PROGRESS allows you to define many indexes for a table, it is important to understand the impact of indexes associated with a table.

The reasons for creating indexes are as follows:

- To establish uniqueness
- To set an order for record retrieval
- To enable you to join tables quickly given common key field
- To provide fast access to records pointed to by index

The impact of additional indexes:

- Additional processing and disk access for each row insert and deletion.
- Additional disk space taken up by index data. Although the data for each index entry is compressed, there can be a substantial percentage of database disk space taken up by the index.

You must consider the trade-offs regarding adding indexes to your physical database model. Performance and disk space are ultimately at stake.

From Here...

Now you have the ability to create properly normalized database design and represent them in diagram form. The proper database design approach saves time and effort in the development phase to an exponential degree. Apply these techniques for your next application development effort.

For more information on related items, refer to the following chapters:

- Chapter 2, "Getting Started with ADE Tools," discusses the Data Dictionary tool used to define new database.
- Chapter 12, "Introduction to User Interface Design," covers the design of interfaces using paper modeling techniques.

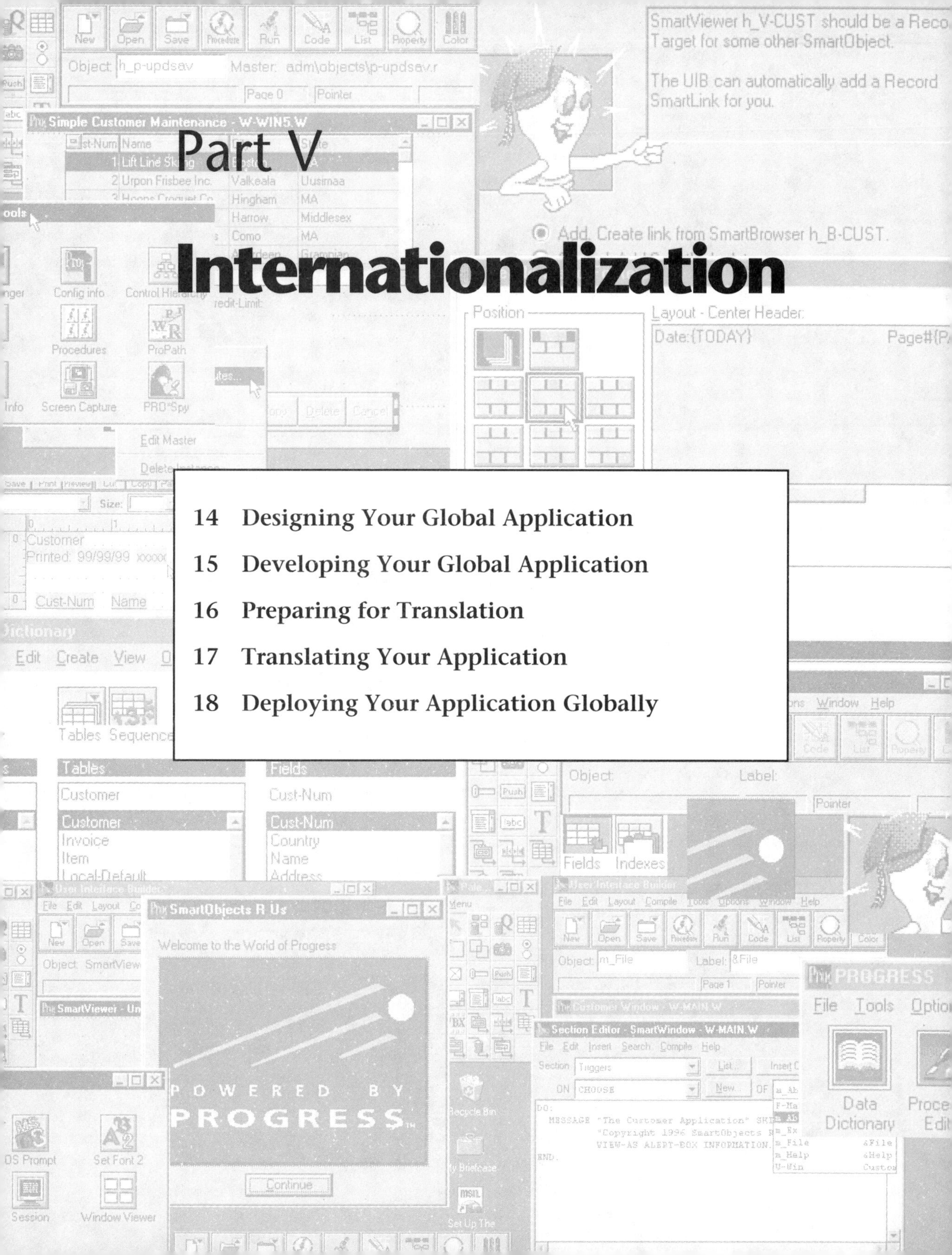

Part V

Internationalization

SmartViewer h_V-CUST should be a Record Target for some other SmartObject.
The UIB can automatically add a Record SmartLink for you.
Add. Create link from SmartBrowser h_B-CUST.
New
Open
Save
Procedure
Run
Code
List
Property
Color
Object: h_p-updsav
Master: adm\objects\p-updsav.r
Page 0
Pointer
Simple Customer Maintenance - W-WIN5.W
Name
City
State
1 Lift Line Skiing
Boston
MA
2 Urpon Frisbee Inc.
Valkeala
Uusimaa
Hingham
MA
Harrow
Middlesex
Como
MA
Aberdeen
Grampian
Config info
Control Hierarchy
Procedures
ProPath
Screen Capture
PRO*Spy
Edit Master
Delete Instance
Headers and Footers
Position
Layout - Center Header:
Date: {TODAY}
Clear All
Function List:
{TODAY} Today's date
{TIME} Time report started
{NOW} Current time
{COUNT} Records listed so far
{PAGE} Current page number
Customer
Printed: 99/99/99
Cust-Num
Name
City
State
Edit
Create
View
Options
Tools
Help
Tables
Sequences
Fields
Indexes
Customer
Invoice
Item
Local-Default
Cust-Num
Country
Name
Address
User Interface Builder
File
Edit
Layout
Compile
Tools
Options
Window
Help
Object:
Label:
Pointer
SmartObjects R Us
Welcome to the World of Progress
POWERED BY
PROGRESS
Continue
OS Prompt
Set Font 2
Session
Window Viewer
Object: m_File
Label: &File
Page 1
Section Editor - SmartWindow - W-MAIN.W
Section
Triggers
ON
CHOOSE
Data
Dictionary
Recycle Bin
My Briefcase

CHAPTER 14

Designing Your Global Application

A growing number of companies are recognizing the importance of "internationalizing" their applications to serve global markets. These companies look to Application Development Environment vendors such as Progress Software to provide a platform and toolset to support their global development efforts.

In this chapter you will learn:

- The importance of making your applications internationalized
- Why internationalization will be a requirement for all applications in the future
- User interface issues to consider as you design a global application
- Technical considerations to keep in mind as you design a global application

Why Is Internationalization Important?

You may be asking yourself, "Why should I develop a global application?" There are good reasons for developing an internationalized software program, whether you are a small development shop or a multinational corporation.

Say that you are a small- to medium-sized software development company, developing and marketing your own application. To start with the basics, "going global" can increase your revenues. Think how difficult and expensive it would be to gain a five percent market share in an already cramped domestic software market. Now, imagine that you could keep the same market share but increase the market *size* by 100-fold. That is what "going global" can do for you. As an example, the Japanese market for software is estimated to be anywhere from 50 to 90 percent the size of the U.S. market. The European Community market is equally large. Introducing your software into these markets opens up large new revenue opportunities.

For example, consider Progress Software. Progress was founded in 1982, and began shipping product domestically and internationally in 1984. By the end of 1987, when Progress opened its first international subsidiary, total revenue for the company was about $6 million in U.S. dollars, 15 percent of which was from international sales. The next year, and every year since 1987, international revenue has made up more than half the total annual revenue of the company, as figure 14.1 shows.

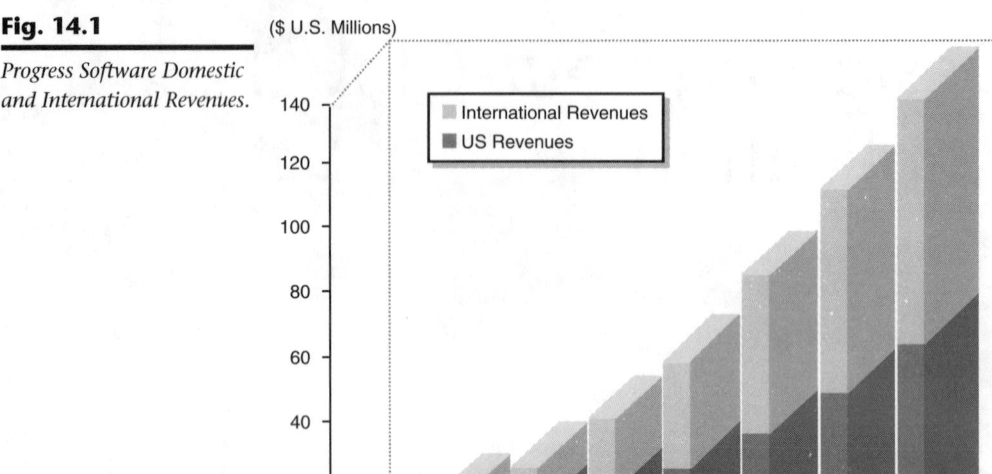

Fig. 14.1

Progress Software Domestic and International Revenues.

Internationalization Starts a Positive Cycle of Growth

Selling your product into additional markets allows you to sell more product. More copies of your product sold results in a reduced cost per unit sold (given fixed overhead in your organization). A reduced cost per unit sold allows you to reduce your price, or to offer better discounts to your dealers, distributors, and/or customers. This makes you more competitive, and perhaps allows you to take further action to promote your product and increase sales. Thus, the cycle of increasing revenue and market share begins.

Still not convinced that it is worth it? You'd better be sure that your competition isn't going global, or you will be facing reduced prices from your competition.

Balancing Out Economic Cycles

Almost every company that sells domestically has a slow period. In the U.S. and in much of Europe, this can be January ("this year's budget is not approved yet, and we bought everything we needed at the end of last year"), July, and August (vacation season). But in other parts of the world, these months are strong selling months (July and August are winter months in Australia, so they are not popular vacation months, and are therefore good months for sales). Selling into varied international markets smoothes out the slow months in your revenue stream.

Additionally, not all economies expand (or contract) at the same rate. Not all countries are in a recession at the same time. Recently, for example, European economies were still slow, whereas the U.S. economy was beginning to rebound, and the Southeast Asian economies were booming. If you are unfortunate enough to be based in a country or region with a slow economy, it can be a relief to be selling into other regions with growing and thriving economies.

Internationalization Improves Your Product

There are more benefits to internationalizing your software and marketing it globally. When more users use your product, you will receive more input on product enhancements and features. Your product becomes more competitive in Country A because of a feature that you implemented for Country B.

Also, perceived limitations in your product in one country might not be limitations at all in another country, and since competition varies from one country to another, a competitor could be exploiting a weakness in your product in one country, but that competitor may not be present in another country.

Internationalize Up Front in Product Design

Perhaps you are thinking, "Well, I'll just develop for my domestic market now, but I'll go back and localize my software later if the market opportunity presents itself." You would not be alone in thinking this way. There are several flaws in this approach, however.

Presume that you developed your product for your domestic market only. After the code was written, you put it through significant testing and documentation, and released it. It is now four years later, and you wish to create the Chinese version of your application. Your engineers (who may be new employees) must revisit four-year-old code, make potentially destabilizing changes to it, rebuild it, and then you must test both the Chinese *and* domestic versions. You will test the former to see whether it works, and you will test the latter to see that it has not been broken by your changes. You will probably be required to re-release both versions. The costs of doing all of this are very high: engineering resources, test resources, product quality risks, documentation resources, customer updates, and support. It would have been easier and less costly to internationalize the software during its creation.

Another approach might be to make a copy of your application, and create a Chinese version out of that copy. The impact and risk to the original version is lower, and you will have to test only the new Chinese version. The problem with this approach is that you now have two versions of your source code. When you fix a bug, you must now fix it in two places. Furthermore, in cases where functionality had to take a different direction in order to accommodate the new language, you may have to fix the same bug in two different ways. This increases the cost and complexity of testing and support. The problem continues to get worse if you support four, five, or six different languages (versions) of your product. Again, it would have been easier and cheaper to internationalize the software during its creation, and to have one version of software which can support multiple languages.

The two preceding approaches are referred to as *retrofitting* software—the engineer's bane. Few engineers enjoy revisiting old code in order to squeeze what are effectively bugfixes into it; they'd much rather design and implement new features. The approach superior to retrofitting software, internationalizing the software from the start, is called *enabling* the software. You are enabling one set of source code to support multiple languages up front.

Selling Globally Requires Internationalization

People will want to run your application in their native language. They will want fields to sort appropriately for their alphabet. They will want local currency format, numeric formats, date formats, and other culturally specific features. The best, most cost-efficient way to provide these capabilities is to enable your application to support a variety of cultural requirements as you develop the software; that is, to internationalize your software by design.

Multinational Companies Already Know This

If you develop for a large multinational company, or if you sell software to one, you already know the importance of internationalized applications. The savvy, forward-looking multinational company wants to standardize on one application (or suite of applications) worldwide. This greatly facilitates exchange of information between and among offices, and it reduces company-wide support costs. It also allows the company to hire local personnel without paying a premium for multilingual proficiency.

Each application must be capable of being run by people speaking English, French, Spanish, Swedish, Turkish, Russian, Chinese, Japanese, Thai, and so on, and they will want to run the application in their native language, following local conventions. Their work will also be less error-prone if they are working in their native language. Internationalization is an absolute necessity for companies operating worldwide.

Definition of Internationalization Terms

People often confuse internationalization with localization and translation. The following terms will be used throughout the rest of this section.

> *Internationalization:* To design your software in such a way that it can easily support other cultural requirements such as different alphabets, different alphabetic sorting, different date formats, translations of user interface elements (buttons, menus, dialogs, and so on). You are not actually providing those alphabets and translations at this stage. Rather, you are enabling your software to support them.
>
> *Localization:* The actual act of tailoring a piece of software for a specific country, language, or market. Localization would include choosing and incorporating a specific date format, a particular currency, choosing the appropriate character set, and collation.
>
> *Translation:* Most people assume that internationalization is simply translation. In fact, translation is only a part of the process. For software, translation means rendering system messages, buttons, menu items, labels, help, and all (or most) user interface tokens into the local language.

Internationalization Is a Requirement for the Future

As the world gets smaller through technical breakthroughs in communication, the need to exchange data in a multiplicity of languages has grown. And although distant areas of the world are now more closely linked, this does not mean that the world is becoming more homogenous. In fact, the opposite is the case. The number of countries in the world is actually increasing. After World War II, there were approximately 80 countries in the world. Today, there are approximately 180! And there are more than 1,500 different spoken languages today.

More People with Less Education Are Using Computers

More important, technical breakthroughs have made software available to a class of people with less education than before. Ten years ago, most people who worked with software had college educations (and a fair chance at having learned some level of English). Today, retail applications and personal computers are being used by people who may have never completed a secondary education. Chances are, high school students in Beijing or Prague or Bangkok do not speak English, but they might be operating a computer terminal. Your software must speak *their* language—they don't speak yours.

Software Is Being Developed in Every Language

It could be claimed that English language software has been an accepted standard worldwide for decades. This is partly due to the U.S. dominance of the software market in the 1960s, 1970s, and 1980s. Software development, however, is now taking place worldwide in a variety of languages. You will be competing against local developers providing their software in their native language. If native software is easier to use, this will be a competitive advantage. In addition, major software companies such as Lotus and Microsoft release their products in a variety of languages, making local language a requirement for entry into almost any large international market. The "bar is being raised" for companies to provide more national language support than before.

Designing Your Global Application

As stated above, if you spend more effort during the design phase of an application, you will spend far less effort retrofitting internationalization after the application has been developed and released. This chapter will touch on major areas of international application design.

Dozens of books have been written on internationalizing software. Many of these references may be found in Appendix D, "Internationalization." This chapter does not aim to provide as much information as those volumes. Rather, the aim here is to cover the basic areas that would be of interest and concern to a typical application developer using PROGRESS.

This discussion is divided into two sections: user interface considerations and technical considerations. The former is concerned with the way your program and its data is presented to the program user. The latter covers the technical details that you will address while developing the application.

User Interface Considerations for Global Applications

Topics will be covered in the following areas:

- Icon design
- Screen Layout
- Culturally specific fields and values
- Color and sound
- Designing for translatability

Icon Design

If you wish to design an application with culturally acceptable images (icons, graphics, artwork, and so on), there are two approaches that you can take: provide country-specific icons for each market that you wish to enter, or design one set of icons that are culture neutral. Although the latter will probably result in less effort and support, it may not always be possible. There may be times when an icon is so perfectly appropriate for one culture that you will want to use it. In this case, you would have a specific icon for one country, and one or more corresponding icons for the rest of the world.

Assume that you would like to design and support culture-neutral icons. Here are some hints to follow.

Use Objects That Are Universal

Avoid unfamiliar objects; that is, make sure that any object you portray in an icon would be recognizable in another culture. For example, mailboxes and telephones do not look the same in different countries.

Avoid Puns That Don't Translate

It is always a temptation to use wordplay in user interface design. The problem with puns, however, is that they are not always understood when translated. A very familiar example is the Run icon. In some Norton Desktop programs (and in PROGRESS), this is an image of a man running. Unfortunately, some languages don't have the concept of starting a program by *running* it. Their concept may be *executing* it, *launching* it, or *initiating* it. The play on the word *run* may not mean anything to them.

Avoid the Use of Body Parts as Images

Almost every culture is sensitive to a particular part of the human body, and that particular body part varies from culture to culture. Here are some examples:

- A pointing hand (index finger extended) means "you're crazy" in Italy, and is considered rude in much of the Middle East and Asia.
- An uplifted hand (as in waving good-bye, or stop) is a direct insult in Greece, and would also be offensive in many Southeast Asian countries, where showing the bottom of one's hand is dirty and offensive.
- A picture of an eyeball is offensive in the Middle East, where pointing to your eye may mean that someone is not to be trusted.
- Displaying bare anatomy can be offensive in many cultures where skin should not show.

Avoid the Use of Animals

Different animals are sacred in different cultures, and animals may represent different meanings in different cultures. For example, cows are sacred in India, so displaying a cow in an icon may carry more meaning than you intended. An owl is considered wise in Europe and America, but is considered a foolish, brutal bird in Taiwan.

Avoid Sports References

Unless the sport is universal, you should avoid references to specific sports. Although it's tempting to refer to a "home run" or a "touchdown" if you are American, these sporting achievements may mean nothing to people who are not fans of baseball or American football. As a counter-example, is it good to "bowl clean" in cricket, or would you rather "hit a six"? Is it good to be "in your pocket" in golf? Did you have a good day if you went "love and love" in tennis, or would you rather be "double bageled"? (Answer: To be "bowled clean" in cricket is analogous to striking out in baseball; to "hit a six" is analogous to a grand slam. You are having a bad day if you are "in your pocket" in golf. If you beat your opponent "love and love" in tennis, you won 6-0, 6-0. Your opponent was "double bageled.")

If you really need to use a sports reference, try using a sport that would be recognized worldwide, such as a sport traditionally included in the Olympics ("win the race," "jump the farthest," and so on).

Avoid Regionally Specific Images

A prime example of this is displaying a world map in an icon. It is always interesting to international travelers to watch the evening news or weather broadcast in another country, and to see that particular country located at the center of the world. In Saudi Arabia, the center of the world map is the Arab Peninsula. In Japan, the Island of Honshu is in the center of the map. In Russia, Eastern Europe (and specifically Moscow) is centered.

If you are an American company trying to establish a global presence, and trying to demonstrate that you are not seeking international business as an afterthought, then you should avoid placing the United States in the center of your world icon.

When designing the opening screen for Translation Manager 2.0, Progress Software chose a different approach. We added a level of abstraction to a world image by displaying a map projection rather than a globe, thus de-emphasizing any specific center in a direct reference to the world. This can be seen in figure 14.2.

Translation Manager
Version 2

Fig. 14.2

Translation Manager 2.0 opening screen.

The Different Meanings of Numbers

The number 13 is almost universally viewed as an unlucky number. In fact, most buildings do not have a floor numbered 13. Floors are numbered 10, 11, 12, 14, 15, and so on. In Asia, the number 4 is also an unlucky number. In many buildings in Asia, the floors are labeled 1, 2, 3, F, 5, 6 or 1, 2, 3, 3b, 5, 6, and so on. When selecting the numbers of product revisions, be cautious with these "magic" numbers.

Avoid Religious and Superstitious Symbols

Crosses and stars have a wide selection of religious, superstitious, and taboo meanings around the world. Take care to avoid their use.

Screen Layout

There are many issues to remember related to screen layout when creating your global application. The following sections cover some of the items to keep in mind as you design your application screens.

Display Resolution and Color Depth

Every computer user today knows that display screens come in a wide variety of resolutions and color depths. For example, the following resolutions are in use today:

Standard	Resolution
CGA:	80 x 24 (characters)
EGA:	320 x 200 (pixels)
VGA:	640 x 480
SuperVGA:	800 x 600
Hi Resolution:	1024 x 768
Very Hi Resolution:	1280 x 1024

Standard	Resolution
Ultra High Resolution:	1600 x 1200
Super High Resolution:	2048 x 2048 and above

Each of these resolutions may also be configurable at a wide range of color depth, depending on the graphics display adapter in use:

Black and White	Colors	Bits of Color
black and white		1 bit
4 grayscales		2 bits
16 grayscales	16	4 bits
256 grayscales	256	8 bits
64K grayscales	64K	16 bits
"true color"	16.7 million	24 bits

The key point here is that when you are ready to deploy your application in the field, the target systems can have a wide variety of resolutions and color depth. You should be cautious not to design your application to run on a single specific resolution, or on a small subset of the configuration options; you will limit your market.

Internationally, there are other screen configurations. The NEC PC has historically been the most popular PC in Japan. For years, the default resolution has been 640 × 400, not 480. This means that there are 80 "missing" pixels vertically. Depending on your screen design, this means that you could be missing the bottom two rows of your display screen. This would not be good if you use the bottom two rows for user input or warning messages! If you wish to design an application that will run in the most resolutions, you should consider designing your screens to be a little smaller than a VGA screen.

Input Method Editors

If you are targeting your application for China, Japan, Korea, or Taiwan, there is another consideration for screen layout: the space taken by Asian Input Method Editors. Chinese, Japanese, and Korean character sets contain thousands and thousands of unique characters. It would be virtually impossible to fit all of these characters on a single keyboard (though it *has* been tried in the past). In order to input these thousands of characters, system developers have provided intelligent software interfaces or "input method editors" that allow users to generate the characters in a variety of ways. One method, for example, enables users to type the phonetic representation of the desired character or word. The input method editor will analyze the phonetic input and prompt the user with all of the characters that sound like the input.

These input method editors can take up one or more lines at the bottom of the screen (see fig. 14.3), so again, be careful about filling an entire screen with your application.

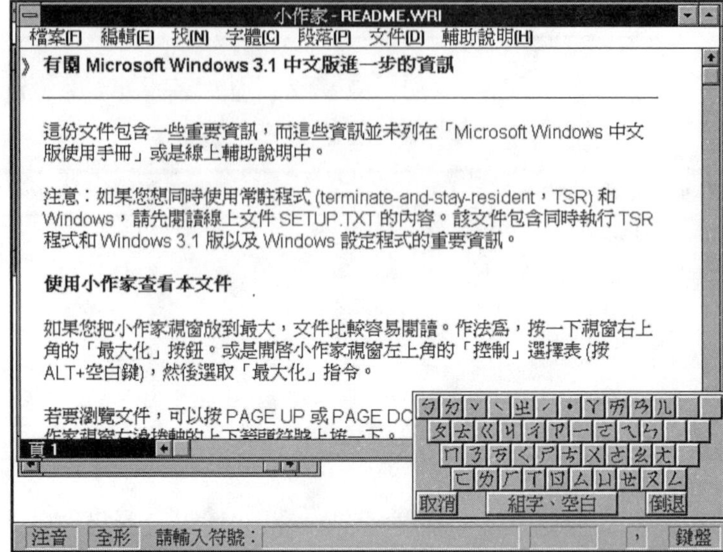

Fig. 14.3

The traditional Chinese input method editor.

This is the input method editor integrated in Microsoft's Traditional Chinese Edition of Windows 3.1. Note that the input method editor takes up a full row across the bottom, as well as the space for a mock Bopomofo keyboard in the right hand corner (more on Bopomofo later).

Don't Clutter Dialog Boxes

When you overfill a dialog box with input values and prompts, it can be very difficult for users to follow and understand. This difficulty is exacerbated if your dialog is in the user's second or third language. Take care to design clean dialogs with ample white space. There are two benefits: first, the user will not get confused as easily with your dialog; second, you will be preparing for an easier translation effort. More on this later.

Do Not Assume That Eye Movement Is Left to Right

Arabic, Persian, and Hebrew read from right to left and top to bottom. Japanese, Chinese, and Korean can read left to right and top to bottom, but they can also read top to bottom, right to left. When designing screens, do not assume that people will always interpret the left side prompts as fields to be filled first. If displaying your process graphically, take care that Arabic and Hebrew users don't run your process backwards!

Culturally Specific Fields and Values

Here are some further culturally variant issues to consider when designing an application:

Date and Time Formats

The order of day, month, and year will vary from country to country. For example:

4 p.m. on July 15, 1995 would be represented as:

> 7/15/95, 4:00 PM in the United States
>
> 15.7.95, 16.00 or 15-7-95, 16.00 in France
>
> 1995/7/15, 1600 or 7/7/15, 1600 in Japan (see the "Calendars" section that follows)

The order of the values as well as the separation characters may vary from country to country.

Calendars

Not every culture works with the western, Gregorian calendar. Though most will recognize dates in this format, certain cultures will prefer to use their local calendar. In many countries, government agencies will require official documents to be in their local calendar. For example,

The year 1995 in the Western Hemisphere is

> 2538 in Thailand (the Buddhist year)
>
> Heisei 7 in Japan (the Emperor date)

Likewise, "weekend" can mean many different days, depending on the culture. It is not always Saturday and Sunday. If you plan to incorporate a weekend feature in your application, this should also be configurable. The same holds true for work weeks and work hours. This would be important if you are designing a Human Resource Management package, for example.

> **Note**
>
> The mention of Human Resource packages leads to another point. Laws, codes, and procedures vary from country to country. If you are designing an application, such as Human Resources Management or Tax Management, it would be wise to provide entrypoints in your application so that you can plug in alternate rules (or entire programs) applicable to your destination country.

Numeric Formats

The symbol that separates the digits into groups of thousands and the symbol that is used to represent the decimal separator can change as well. The comma is not always a thousands separator and the period is not always a decimal separator.

For example, the number 12,345.67 in the United States could be represented as:

12.345,67 in Germany (period, then comma)

12 345,67 in France (space, then comma)

12'345.67 in Switzerland (apostrophe, then period)

12.345,67 or 12.345$67 in Portugal (period, then comma or dollar sign)

Rounding Rules

The rules for rounding a number up or down also vary from culture to culture. Take care not to hard-code specific assumptions about how numbers are rounded. Rather, make the rounding rules flexible and tailorable. Some of the references in Appendix D, "Internationalization," will list various rounding rules by country.

Currency Formats

Obviously, the numeric format differences listed previously will be reflected in currency input and display. But beyond this, the length and placement of the currency symbol itself can vary.

The amount $12,345.67 in the U.S. might have as a counterpart:

12.345,67 DM	in Germany
12 345 FF 67	in France
12.345$67 Esc	in Portugal

Also take into consideration currency length. Although the format xxx,xxx,xxx.xx might seem adequate to hold large numbers, there are currencies for which this is not the case. In Turkey, for example, where, as of this writing, the Turkish Lira is trading at approximately 30,000 TL to the U.S. dollar, a business dinner can cost more than 10,000,000 TL. Imagine what a car, a computer, or a house can cost.

Never assume specific currency formats when designing and developing an application for international use.

Phone Number Formats

When designing input screens, you should be prepared for variably formatted fields. Phone number fields are good examples. Here are some sample phone numbers of Progress Software subsidiary and distributor offices around the world (country code in brackets):

U.S.A.:	[1] (617) 280-4000
Austria:	[43] 1 696 603
Belgium:	[32] 2 716.04.20
France:	[33] 1.4116.1600 or [33] 1 41.16.16.00
Japan:	[81] 3 3584 5211
Spain:	[34] 1 307 77 14
U.K.:	[44] 1256 816668

Australia:	[61] 3 9 885 0544
Lebanon:	[961] 1 348235
China:	[86] 18315-522

As you can see, there are a variety of groupings and separators. Take care not to hard-code a specific pattern.

Address Formats

The format of addresses can vary as much as the formats for telephone numbers. Another interesting point about addresses is that the order of address components can vary. In most of the western hemisphere, addresses will start with the most specific component of the address and get larger. For example, if you wanted to address a letter to the Managing Director of the Progress Software U.K. office, you would write:

Mr. James Bush
Progress Software Ltd.
The Square
Basing View
Basingstoke
Hampshire
England SK4 IBS

Addresses in England follow the order Name, House Name, Street, Region of City, City, County, Country, Postal Code.

In some countries, however, the address components are in the opposite order, from big to small. Russia, Japan, and Egypt are three examples. If you are Japanese and you wanted to address a letter to the Managing Director of the Progress Software Japan office, you would write (presumably in Japanese):

Japan
107 Tokyo
Minato-ku
Akasaka 3-11-3
Akasaka Nakagawa Bldg, 5F
Progress Software KK
Kumagai-san* 　　　　* "-san" = "Mr."

Color and Sound

When designing a user interface, it is important to be sensitive to the use of color. Color can carry inherent meaning and, like everything else, that meaning will vary from culture to culture.

For example, in North America and Western Europe, the color red is associated with danger. In China and much of Asia, red is associated with marriage. Whereas white implies purity in the West, it is more closely associated with death in the East.

When designing pop-up screens and dialogs, the choice of color should be configurable. A red screen signaling a warning in the U.S. may not be as effective in China.

Sound can also be a useful tool in designing an application, but it also brings certain challenges cross-culturally. A warning siren for one culture may not be recognizable to another culture. Police sirens and fire sirens vary from country to country.

Finally, there are some cultures in which the use of sound may not be appropriate at all. In Japan, for example, offices are typically arranged to have many desks in a large open area. In Japanese culture, confrontation and public embarrassment are to be avoided. If you design an application in which a screen beep indicates that your user has made a mistake, this will be embarrassing for him or her when they are working in front of dozens of peers. In this case, the use of sound is inappropriate.

Designing for Translatability

Chances are that you will want to translate your application for use in another country. Chapters 16 and 17 cover the use of Translation Manager and Visual Translator for doing this. Before you use these tools, however, there are some design hints that will make the translation job easier.

Leave Room for Text Expansions

It is good practice to avoid cluttered dialogs in user interface design. Leaving a good amount of white space in a screen will result in a simpler dialog to follow. A cluttered dialog can make your application difficult to use.

There is another good reason to leave white space. If you plan to translate your application, you should be aware that translations can often be far longer than the original text phrase. This is particularly true when translating from English to European languages. When designing your screen, you should leave enough room between objects to allow them to grow upon translation.

The following table has been widely used to anticipate text growth on translating from English to a European language:

English Message	European Language
Up to 10 characters	Add 101–200 percent
11–20 characters	Add 81–100 percent
21–30 characters	Add 61–80 percent
31–50 characters	Add 41–60 percent
51–70 characters	Add 31–40 percent
More than 70 characters	Add 30 percent

Obviously, there are always exceptions to this rule, but used as a guideline, this table can save you reengineering work later. A good practice is to contact a translation firm in your target country to learn from its experience what your text growth requirements will be to translate from your native language to the local language.

> **Note**
>
> Incidentally, the preceding table is used by Translation Manager 2.0 for default text growth expansion. Translation Manager is discussed in detail in Chapter 16, "Preparing for Translation," and Chapter 17, "Translating Your Application."

Leave Room for Text Expansion in Objects

Objects within a screen should also accommodate text growth during translations. For example, if you have text on a button, you should leave space for that text to grow, yet still fit on the button. Because button text tends to be a single word, you should consider leaving space twice as long as the original text on the button.

Use Familiar Terms

Microsoft Windows has become the dominant desktop interface in the world today. Most people have become familiar with the standard menu items in Windows-based applications. Rather than choose new terms and names for menu items, your application will be more intuitive for Windows users if you use the same or similar terms where they make sense. For example:

The File Menu:	New
	Open
	Close
	Save
	Save As
	...
	Exit
The Edit Menu:	Undo
	Repeat
	Cut
	Copy
	Paste
	Paste Special
	Clear
	Find
	Replace
	Goto

These menus are quite well known and appear in the same order in a variety of international Microsoft Windows versions. Providing the same interface to your users will save them training time and make your application more intuitive.

Tip

An added bonus to using Microsoft terms in your interface is that your translation effort can be much easier when using Translation Manager 2.0. Translation Manager incorporates the Microsoft Language Glossaries for more than a dozen languages. These glossaries have the translations that Microsoft has used to translate those same menus. If you've used the same terms as Microsoft, then you will be prompted by Translation Manager with the same translations they used—again, making your application more intuitive for speakers of other languages.

Do Not Piece Together Phrases

It is a frequent temptation to break messages up into subcomponents and then to piece together specific user messages at runtime. Although this would be a logical technique for a programmer, it is a terrible idea to the translator for a number of reasons:

- The translator will be faced with many pieces of a phrase, but will not know how they relate to each other.
- The order of grammatical components varies from language to language. For example, English and Chinese sentences are normally formed as noun-verb-object. In Korean and Japanese, sentences are normally formed as noun-object-verb. If you hard-code your language order, no translation can be correct.
- The gender and number of the constituent parts of a message can affect other parts of the message. There will be no association after the parts are separated for translation.

As a rule, you should form complete sentences and messages in your code. Though it may seem to create redundant data, it will be far more beneficial when you must do translations. Also as a rule, messages and warning should be as concise and short as possible.

Design: Technical Considerations

The previous section covered the user interface issues in designing an application. This section will concentrate more on the underlying techniques and requirements at the code level.

Because most applications center around the input, manipulation, and management of data, this is where most of the technical considerations apply. Specifically, the management of character data requires some care. You can get into trouble if you hard-code assumptions about the following:

- What it means to be alphabetic
- Uppercasing and lowercasing
- Character sizes and representations
- Character ordering

Each of these considerations will be examined in the sections that follow.

Distinguishing Alphabetic Characters from Nonalphabetic Characters

In developing applications, it will often be necessary to distinguish alphabetic characters (letters) from nonalphabetic characters (numbers, symbols, and so forth). For example, you might want to ensure that the characters input for a person's last name and city are purely alphabetic.

Asked what is alphabetic, an English speaker would probably give the quick answer that it is any character between a and z (or A and Z). In fact, they might code something like this in their program:

```
If "A" <= char <= "Z" or "a" <= char <= "z", then char is alphabetic.
```

But other languages have more characters.

It is time again to define some terms. These terms will help the discussion of issues related to alphabets:

- *Character Set*: This refers, basically, to all of the alphabetic characters, numbers, punctuation, and symbols that you use to read and write your language. For example, the English character set would be all the characters and symbols used to write English (abcd...1234...!@#$%^&&...and so on).
- *Codepage*: A specific assignment of numeric values to every character within a character set. In most codepages, for example, the character A is given the value 65, B is 66, C is 67.

Chapter 18, "Deploying Your Application Globally," will go into far greater detail on character sets and collations.

Take a look at codepage 1252, also referred to as "Latin 1." This is the codepage used by Microsoft Windows for North America, Latin America, and Western Europe (see fig. 14.4). It is also virtually identical to codepage ISO8859-1, the codepage for UNIX in the same regions, and the default codepage for PROGRESS.

As seen in this character map, the second and third rows contain the characters that you would associate with the English language, but the sixth and seventh rows contain a great many more characters that *are also* alphabetic. The assumption that all alphabetic characters fall between A and Z is false. When developing your application to manage alphabetic text, you should keep this in mind.

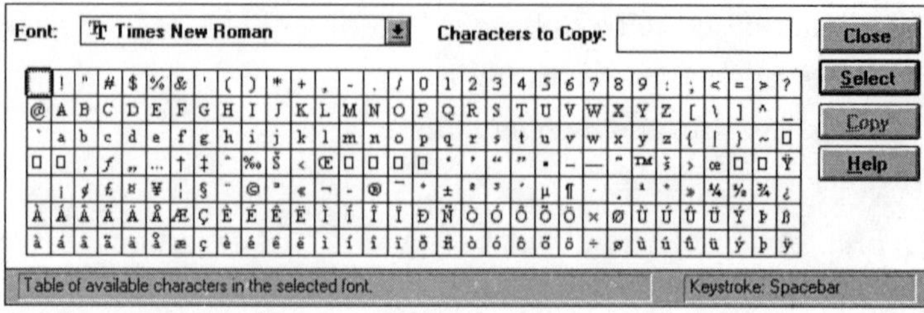

Fig. 14.4

The 1252 codepage, as represented by Microsoft Windows Character Map utility.

Uppercasing and Lowercasing

Referring back to the 1252 codepage, note that capital A is 32 characters before lowercase A. Likewise, little z is 32 characters after capital Z. Almost every programmer has at some time noticed this, and has designed logic into his software that looks like the following:

```
/* to capitalize a character, subtract 32 */
upperchar = lowerchar - 32;
/* to lowercase a character, add 32 */
lowerchar = upperchar + 32;
```

This rule would apply correctly to the basic English characters, and would even apply correctly to many of the extended characters found in the sixth and seventh row of this codepage. It is not always true, however:

> The German character "ß" (sharp-s) is another form of "ss," and has no upper- or lowercase concept. It is the upper- and lowercase of itself. If you subtracted 32 from the character to get its uppercase value, the result would be "¿," which is incorrect. If you added 32 to get its lowercase value, the results would be "ÿ," which is also incorrect.
>
> The character "ÿ" (value 255) is the lowercase for character "Ÿ" (value 159), so again, your algorithm would generate incorrect results. If you subtracted 32 from "Ÿ," the result would be a nonprinting character. If you added 32 to "ÿ," you would have character 287, which is an invalid character value.

Your algorithm broke down for only a few characters in the 1252 codepage, so you might be inclined to assume that it is mostly true, and you might write special cases into your algorithm for the few characters where it doesn't work. But before you do that, take a look at some other character sets and codepages to see whether you will get into trouble when you try to run your program internationally.

Suppose that you plan to sell your application in Moscow. Take a look at the character set and the Microsoft Windows codepage for Cyrillic, the alphabet for Russia (see fig. 14.5). It is codepage 1251.

Again, looking at this codepage, the English alphabet looks the same, but you would have problems with ÿ and a few others as well. There are also some problems with a couple of Cyrillic characters.

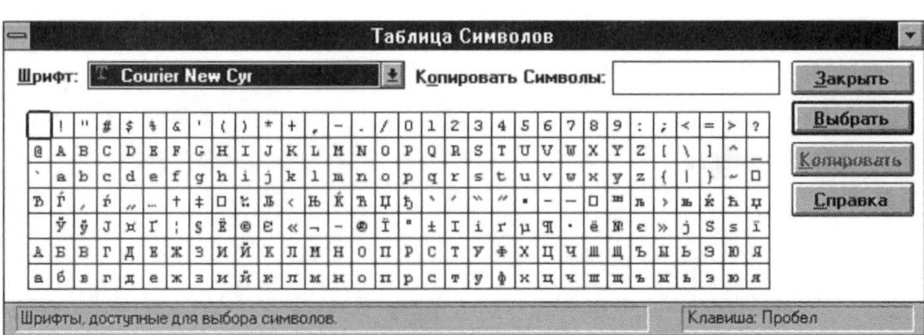

Fig. 14.5

Microsoft Windows Character Map for Russian codepage 1251.

Suppose that you hope to sell your application in Tel Aviv. Take a look at the Hebrew character set and codepage 1255 (see fig. 14.6).

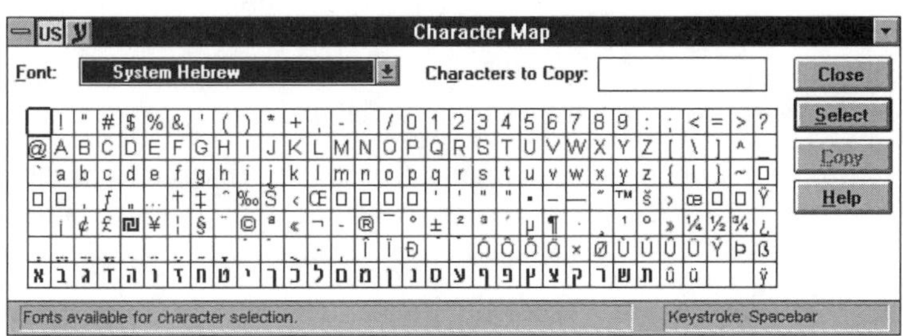

Fig. 14.6

Microsoft Windows Character Map for Hebrew codepage 1255.

You will have definite problems with your algorithm when it comes to the Hebrew characters, because there are *no* upper- or lowercase characters for any of the characters in the Hebrew alphabet.

Finally, suppose that you have an opportunity to sell your application to a company in Riyadh. What does the Arabic alphabet and codepage 1256 look like (see fig. 14.7)?

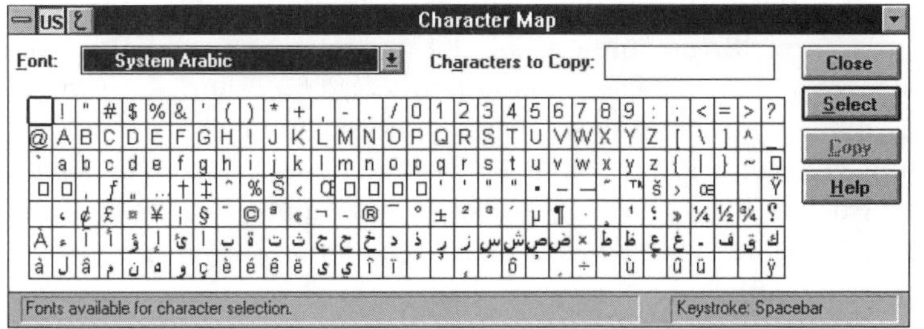

Fig. 14.7

Microsoft Windows Character Map for Arabic codepage 1256.

Here again, there are no upper- or lowercase values for the Arabic alphabet. In fact, your algorithm effectively keeps you from selling your application in either Israel or Saudi Arabia.

Any assumption about upper- and lowercasing fails in many more places than you might have originally assumed. You would spend considerable time allowing for "special cases."

Your conclusion should be that you should omit any uppercase or lowercase assumptions from your code, and rely on PROGRESS to handle this for you.

Character Sizes and Representations: Chinese, Japanese, and Korean Characters

You've seen that assumptions about the specific value or attributes of characters can cause trouble when you run your application in another language. Your new knowledge will help you avoid coding problems in your application as you are developing it, rather than after you've tried running it at a potential customer's site.

Say that you'd like to sell your application in Japan and China. Are there any other assumptions about characters that you still hold, which could cause trouble later? In fact, there are. Again, however, a little knowledge during the design phase will greatly simplify your work in the development and deployment phases. If you enable your application to support Chinese and Japanese up front, getting your programs to run when you are ready to sell in Japan and China will be much easier.

The alphabets shown previously are relatively small collections of characters. In fact, all of the characters needed for a particular character set can fit in a 256-entry table, and each character can be represented by a single byte.

Chinese, Japanese, and Korean alphabets, however, are made up of thousands of characters. It is not possible to store thousands of unique values in a single byte. To do this, you will need two bytes. These characters, as stored in two bytes, are called *double-byte characters*.

Double-byte character sets and their support are not difficult to understand once you know the basics. The following definitions will make the discussion easier to follow. Here are definitions for some more terms: *double-byte character sets*, *double-byte enablement*, *lead bytes*, and *trail bytes*.

> *Double-Byte Character Set*: A double-byte character set contains all the characters and symbols used for writing Chinese, or all the characters and symbols used for writing Japanese, or all the characters and symbols used for writing Korean. There is not a double-byte character set that contains Chinese, Japanese, and Korean in a single character set. A double-byte character set can contain single-byte characters (such as the alphabetic characters and numbers in the English character set), and double-byte characters (storing a Chinese or Japanese or Korean character in two bytes).
>
> *Lead Byte:* The first byte of a double-byte character.
>
> *Trail Byte:* The second byte of a double-byte character.
>
> *Double-Byte Enablement:* To write your application so that it can properly handle both single- and double-byte characters.

Before you get into the programming details about double-byte character sets, take a guided tour of those character sets.

Understanding Chinese Text Characters

Chinese characters are grouped into three categories: Pinyin, Bopomofo, and Hanzi.

- Pinyin and Bopomofo characters are simple characters used to represent phonemes. There are 63 of these.
- The characters that most people associate with Chinese characters are referred to as "Hanzi" characters, literally, "characters of the people."

There are actually two Chinese character sets: Traditional Chinese, and Simplified Chinese.

- Traditional Chinese contains tens of thousands of characters and is the Chinese used in Taiwan (Republic of China).
- Simplified Chinese contains fewer characters than Traditional Chinese (though is still contains thousands of characters) and many of the characters are drawn with fewer strokes, hence "simplified." Simplified Chinese is used in Mainland China (People's Republic of China).

Microsoft Windows uses codepage BIG-5 for Traditional Chinese, and GB2312 for Simplified Chinese. BIG-5 includes more than 13,000 characters. GB2312 includes approximately 7,500 characters. (GB is short for Guo Biao, Chinese for "National Standard"). GB2312 also includes some Greek and Russian Cyrillic characters. Extensions from third-party companies are available for BIG-5, which also add Greek and Cyrillic character support in the codepage.

Take a look at the Character Map for Traditional Chinese codepage BIG-5, as shown in figure 14.8.

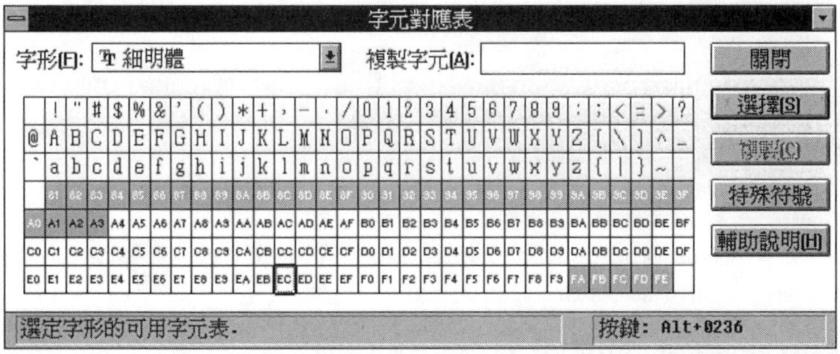

Fig. 14.8

Microsoft Windows Character Map for BIG-5.

You'll notice that English characters are included in the BIG-5 codepage. In fact, the first 128 characters of BIG-5 are identical to the first 128 characters of ISO8859-1 and codepage 1252, and they are single-byte characters. Starting at location number 81 hex (as seen in the character map), the hexadecimal value of the byte is displayed rather than a specific character. The gray hexadecimal values are invalid values for lead bytes; white hexadecimal values indicated are valid lead bytes of double-byte characters. It is not a good assumption that if a byte has one of these valid values, that it is a lead byte. As you will see, the range for trail bytes may overlap with the range for lead bytes. A byte containing a valid lead byte value *may* be a lead byte; it could also be a trail byte.

Look at one of these valid lead bytes and see what would happen given a variety of trail byte values. Again using Microsoft's Character Map, if you click on a valid lead byte, a new table appears with all of the double-byte characters which could have this value for a lead byte (see fig. 14.9). In this case, look at the lead byte EC:

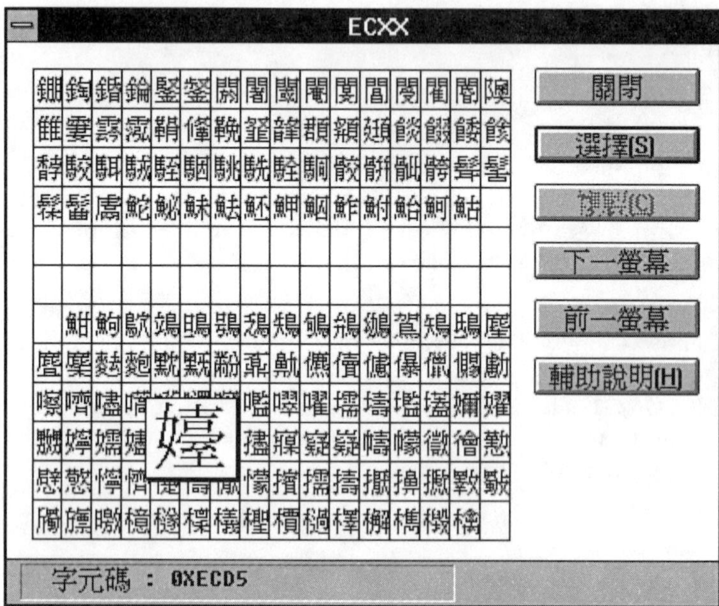

Fig. 14.9

Microsoft Character Map displaying all double-byte characters that have EC as a lead byte.

As the map shows, there are many Chinese characters that could have lead byte EC. You look at one example here with a lead byte of EC and trail byte of D5. This is the character Ta'i.

Understanding Japanese Text Characters

The Japanese character set is also made up of thousands of characters. These are organized into four categories of alphabets or syllabaries:

- Romaji—Roman characters (A through Z, a through z)
- Katakana—Characters that represent syllables (for example, ka, ta, na, su, and so on). Katakana characters are used to phonetically spell out words of non-Japanese origin. There are 56 basic katakana characters, and 86 total when including accented katakana.
- Hiragana—Also characters that represent syllables, but Hiragana characters are used to phonetically spell out words of Japanese origin. There are 56 basic hiragana characters, and 83 total when including accented hiragana.

- Kanji—Kanji characters are pictographic characters derived long ago from Chinese characters. There are also many new Kanji characters that are uniquely Japanese.

Microsoft Windows uses the codepage Shift-JIS to represent the Japanese character set. There are approximately 6,400 Kanji characters in Shift-JIS. (JIS stands for Japanese Industrial Standard.)

The Shift-JIS codepage includes some number of Greek and Russian Cyrillic characters as well.

Take a look at the organization of Shift-JIS shown in figure 14.10.

Fig. 14.10

Character Map for Shift-JIS Japanese character set.

As you can see by looking at the beginning of the codepage, the English characters are found first. In fact, this is the same encoding of the first 128 characters of ISO8859-1 for these single-byte characters.

Further down, you see katakana characters—single-byte katakana characters. You've selected one: character 200 (ne).

Looking further down the codepage in figure 14.11, you come upon the basic English characters again, except that this time they are *double-byte* versions of the English characters (Romaji). Also further down, you see double-byte hiragana characters, and a little further down, you see double-byte katakana characters.

Going even further into the codepage, you see the Kanji section of the double-byte character set (see fig. 14.12), and select one character, lead byte EE, trail byte 92.

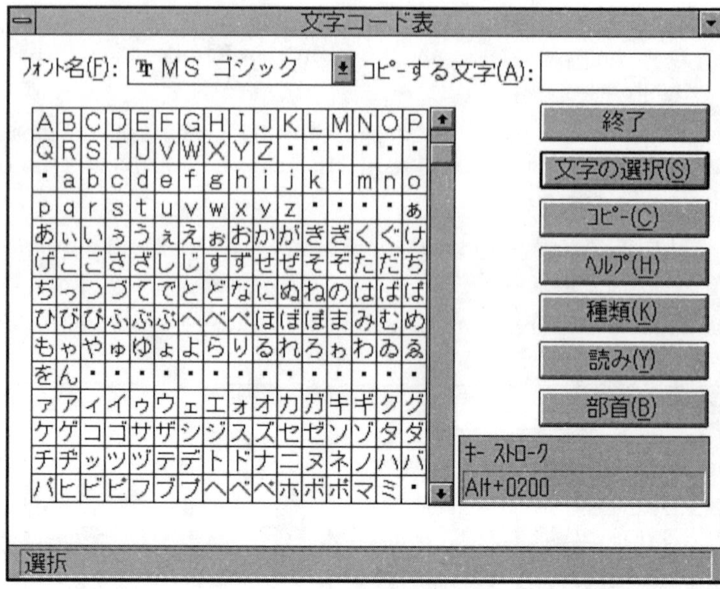

Fig. 14.11

Double-byte Romaji, Hiragana, Katakana.

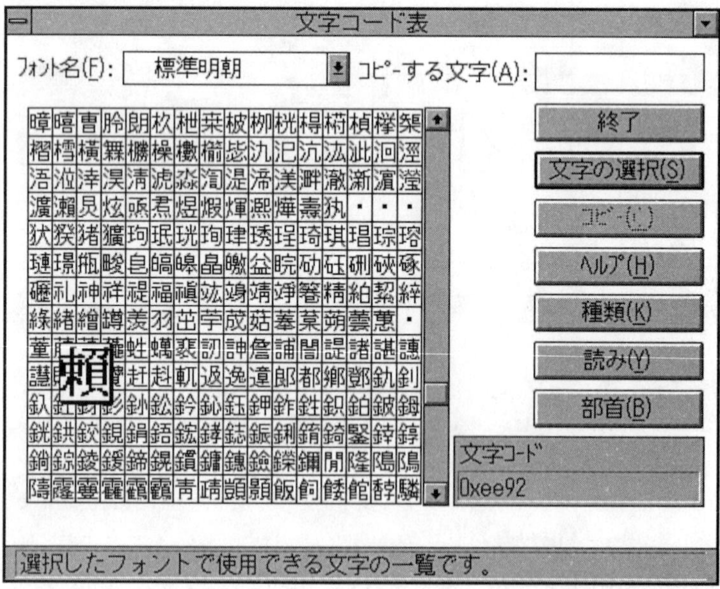

Fig. 14.12

Kanji portion from Shift-JIS codepage.

As you look at these double-byte character sets, it may seem a daunting task to develop software that can handle this many characters. In fact, using the double-byte enabled version of PROGRESS, it can be quite simple.

Before you read about the techniques for developing a double-byte enabled application, take a look at the last language requiring a double-byte character set: Korean.

Understanding Korean Text Characters

The Korean character set is again composed of a few different alphabets. To begin with, the Roman characters can again be found at the beginning of the codepage.

Korean characters are grouped into two sets: Hangul-based characters and Hanja-based characters.

- Hangul—In the year 1446 during the reign of King Sejong, he and his scholars derived an alphabet to simplify their writing. This alphabet, made of 28 characters, is still in use today, and is only slightly modified from its original design.
- Hanja—The Koreans also make use of Chinese characters. These characters carry meanings similar to their original Chinese, and can require as many as 30 strokes to render the characters.

Take a look at the Korean Character set, using the Character Map utility in the Microsoft Windows Hangul Edition (see fig. 14.13). This is codepage KSC5601 (KS is an abbreviation of Korean Standard). KSC5601 also contains Greek and Russian Cyrillic characters, as well as Japanese Katakana and Hiragana.

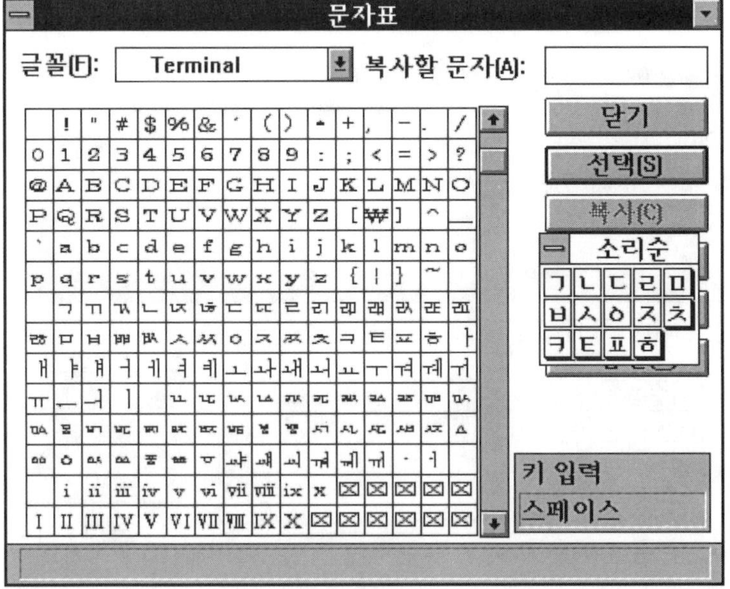

Fig. 14.13

Korean base codepage—KSC5601.

Again, the basic Roman characters make up the first 128 characters of the codepage (single byte). Following those, you find the primitive elements used in forming the Hangul character set. There are 94 of these.

Figure 14.14 shows the Korean characters found farther down the codepage:

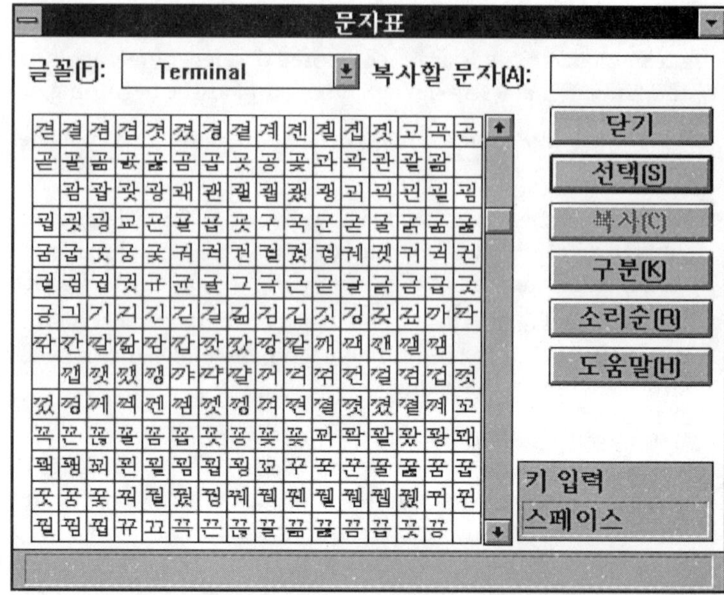

Fig. 14.14

Hangul composed characters.

Here you see the Hangul parts pieced together into syllables. Many of these combinations are senseless, but the codepage holds together logically. There are approximately 2,400 of these combined Hangul elements.

Finally, in figure 14.15, you see the later values of the KSC5601 codepage, the Hanja characters:

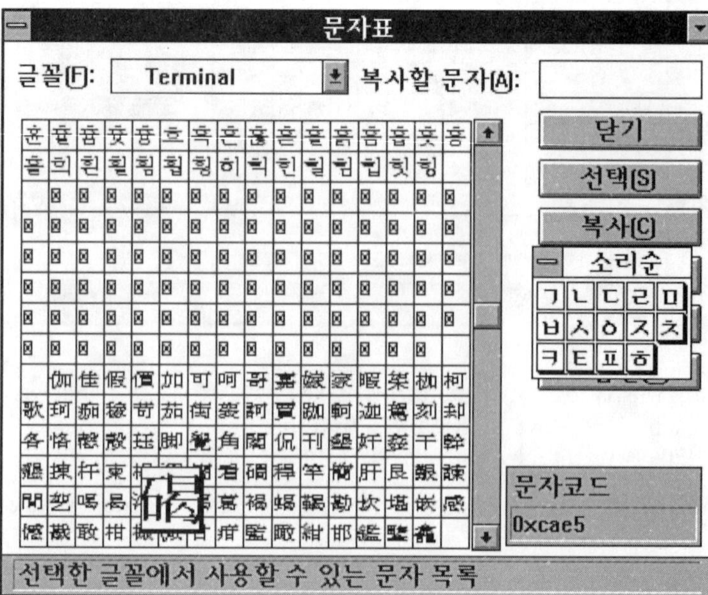

Fig. 14.15

Korean Hanja characters.

These characters, also derived long ago from Chinese characters, are used mostly with historic documents and with official correspondence. There are approximately 5,000 of these Hanja characters.

Proper Handling of Double-Byte Characters

Now that you've seen the various double-byte codepages, you can summarize some basic observations and rules about working with double-byte data:

- Double-byte character sets are made up of single- and double-byte characters; that is, a character can be one or two bytes long.
- Strings of characters may be all single byte, all double byte, or mixed single and double byte.
- A byte's numeric value will determine whether it is capable of being a lead byte or a trail byte of a double-byte character. Its position in the string will determine its actual usage.
- Looking at a solitary byte, it is not always possible to determine whether it is a single-byte character, a lead byte, or a trail byte, because the ranges of valid values for trail bytes overlap those of single bytes and lead bytes.

This leads you to follow the following rules about handling double-byte character sets:

1. An application should never split a double-byte character, because the result would be two new single-byte characters, or could piece together brand new (unintentional) double-byte characters. In either case, the results would be garbage.
2. An application should never assume that the length of a character is one byte, and should never assume that a single character will take one screen position.
3. An application should never assume that the length of a character is two bytes, and should never assume that a single character will take two screen positions.
4. Applications should work in terms of characters, not in terms of bytes, unless the developer has a reason for explicitly knowing the storage length of a string of characters.
5. Applications should take care when examining a single byte, because it could be part of a double-byte character.
6. Applications should take great care when performing a specific operation on a byte.

Note

An example for rules 5 and 6: if you decide to replace bytes containing " \" with the " /" (if, for example, you were converting a filename from DOS to UNIX), this could be dangerous. If you hit a double-byte character whose trail byte just happened to be " \," you are really corrupting a double-byte character, not replacing a legitimate " \."

Fortunately, there are mechanisms in Double Byte Enabled PROGRESS to help an application developer follow these rules. These mechanisms are documented in the next chapter, "Developing Your Global Application."

Character Ordering

Now that you have completely rid your application of all assumptions about the representation of characters, you can look at how they are ordered.

Everyone knows that A comes before B, which comes before C, and so on. If you looked at codepage 1252 values, you would say that "character number 65 comes before character number 66, which comes before character number 67, so the lower the value, the earlier in the alphabet it comes." But this is not always true.

Take a look at some alphabetic orderings for languages that use the 1252 codepage:

English:

ABCDEFGHIJKLMNOPQRSTUVWXYZ

German:

AÄBCDEFGHIJKLMNOÖPQRSßTUÜVWXYZ

Swedish and Finnish:

ABCDEFGHIJKLMNOPQRSTUVWXYZÅÄÖ

Danish and Norwegian:

ABCDEFGHIJKLMNOPQRSTUVWX(Y=Ü)ZÆØÅ

The point here is that you should not make any assumptions about the alphabetic ordering of characters based on their actual placement in the codepage (that is, their numeric value). You should rely on PROGRESS to manage the alphabetic ordering for a given codepage.

Character ordering is important for more than sorting names in reports. Databases are indexed, searches are performed, and queries are resolved using character ordering. If a character ordering is incorrect (or culturally inconsistent), the application will appear to be malfunctioning.

The details of how PROGRESS does this are covered in more detail in Chapter 18, "Deploying Your Application Globally."

From Here...

Given the points brought out in this chapter, you have a lot to consider when designing your application. There have been a lot of *watch out for*'s and *don't do*'s, and so on. This can seem like a big burden now, but as most people have learned when trying to sell an existing application abroad, it is better to know the issues during the design phase than when a potential sale has gone sour during the deployment phase.

For more information related to topics in this chapter, refer to the following:

- Chapter 15, "Developing Your Global Application," builds on the information in this chapter. It will cover the *here's how to*'s and *do*'s when developing an application in the PROGRESS environment.
- Chapter 16, "Preparing for Translation," covers the steps to perform at the start of developing your application to make it easy to translate.
- Chapter 17, "Translating Your Application," covers the steps and hands-on information to convert your PROGRESS application to another language.
- Chapter 18, "Deploying Your Application Globally," covers how to get your application to run in all global environments.

CHAPTER 15

Developing Your Global Application

Many articles on internationalization focus on what *not* to do, and spend very little time explaining *what* to do or *how* to do it. You're shown the dangers and pitfalls, but are given no help in avoiding them.

Like those articles, Chapter 14 listed many issues that should be considered while designing an international application, but did very little to tell you how to solve the problems. That is the purpose of this chapter. Now that you know what some of the problems are, you will learn how to solve those problems in the Progress environment.

In this chapter, you learn the following:

- What PROGRESS startup configuration parameters are available to handle cultural differences, and how they affect the code you write
- The PROGRESS 4GL functions which can be used to write culturally neutral programs
- How to write double-byte enabled code for supporting Chinese, Japanese, and Korean character sets
- The location and content of a variety of files included with PROGRESS to facilitate localization

This chapter is organized in five sections. Each section covers a major area of internationalization support in PROGRESS. Using the functions described and following the examples given will help you to develop internationalized applications. The major sections are:

1. *PROGRESS International Startup Parameters*—This section covers the PROGRESS functions which can be used to solve issues with numeric format, day/month/year order, and alternate calendars. Startup parameters provide powerful support for internationalization, simply by using the correct commands when beginning a PROGRESS session.
2. *PROGRESS Internationally-oriented 4GL Functions*—This section summarizes the PROGRESS 4GL functions which can be used when developing internationalized software.

3. *Double-Byte Enablement in PROGRESS*—This section discusses the issues and solutions in developing double-byte enabled software. Software which properly handles Chinese, Japanese, and Korean characters (double-byte characters sets) is referred to as double-byte enabled.
4. *Other PROGRESS International Support Files*—This section describes a collection of support files which will help with managing collations and code pages for a variety of countries and languages. Many of the files used internally by PROGRESS have also been translated, localized, and built into the product. This section explains how and where to access these files.
5. *Implementation Techniques*—Having reviewed all of the available functions and parameters in the preceding sections, this final section provides techniques and practical approaches for implementing applications that must be deployed across a variety of cultures, countries, and languages.

The syntax and technical details for the first three sections are fully documented in the *PROGRESS Programming Handbook*, the *PROGRESS Language References*, the *System Administration Guide*, and the *Double-Byte Enabled PROGRESS* manual, and the discussion here is not meant to duplicate or replace that documentation. These sections will simply gather together the various components useful for internationalization, and explain them in better context.

The fifth section contains new information and techniques not found in current PROGRESS documentation.

PROGRESS International Startup Parameters

As mentioned in Chapter 14, "Designing Your Global Application," there are a number of culturally-specific conventions which impact the way your software interfaces with the user. You've seen that date formats can vary from country to country, and that even numeric formats can be culturally variant.

You could write many lines of code in all of your applications to account for these differences in format, but this would be a waste of your time and resources. You should look to your development environment vendor to provide the mechanisms to help you.

There are a number of parameters which can be specified on the PROGRESS startup line, and which alter the behavior of the PROGRESS environment. They are described in this section.

You can add these startup parameters to the PROGRESS command line (the Command line in the Microsoft Windows Program Item Properties dialog), or else you can put them in the STARTUP.PF file. For example, if your command line for PROGRESS is:

```
_prowin.exe -p _desk.p
```

adding the European startup parameter would be done with:

```
_prowin.exe -p _desk.p -E
```

-E European Numeric Format Parameter

When you use the "European Format" startup parameter, the thousands separator in numbers will be changed from , (comma) to . (period), and the decimal separator will be changed from . (period) to , (comma) throughout the PROGRESS environment.

Example:

```
_prowin.exe -p _desk.p -E
```

-d (mdy, dmy, ymd, and so on) Date Format Parameter

You can use the Date Format startup parameter to specify a different ordering for day, month, and year in date formats throughout PROGRESS. For example, if you set the parameter -d to dmy, then dates will input and display as day, followed by month, followed by year.

Example:

```
_prowin.exe -p _desk.p -d dmy
```

-yy {xxxx} Century Parameter

The Century Parameter allows you to specify a different century basis (other than the default of 1900). If you wanted the century (the first two digits of a four-digit year) to start with 25 for Thailand, you would set the Century Parameter as follows:

Example:

```
_prowin.exe -p _desk.p -yy 2500
```

Note

The Century Parameter may seem to be useful only to international audiences where the date is based on a different era. Don't forget that you are less than a decade from the year 2000, and the Century Parameter will be useful for everyone!

Using Internationally Oriented PROGRESS Functions

Again, you could write many lines of code in all of your applications to handle the specific requirements of each country and language you wish to support, but this would be a waste of your time and resources. You should look to your development environment vendor to provide a programming language which includes support for this functionality.

There are a number of PROGRESS 4GL functions that can make the effort of internationalization much easier. They are described in the following sections.

FORMAT Phrase

The FORMAT phrase is one of the most powerful and complicated mechanisms in PROGRESS. FORMAT phrases are pieces of other 4GL statements, such as DEFINE VARIABLE and DISPLAY, and in the area of internationalization, they can be very useful. They can be used for formatting currency, digit grouping, dates, and so on. Format phrases are used to set up display and input characteristics, and can be composed of a variety of data types:

- CHARACTER x(8)

  Example: DEFINE VARIABLE N AS CHARACTER FORMAT "x(25)"

- DATE 99/99/99

  This default says display the digits as:

  two numbers "/" two numbers "/" two numbers.

  Other values could be:

  99-99-99 (separate the numeric field with "-")

  99.99.99 (separate the numeric field with ".")

  999999 (display six digits with no separation)

  99999999 (display eight digits with no separation)

  Example: DEFINE VAR DT AS DATE FORMAT "99-99/99"

> **Note**
>
> This sets only the numeric representation, not the order of Day, Month, or Year. Those are set independently with the -d startup parameter.

- DECIMAL ->>,>>9.99 (the default)

  \- says replace with a minus sign if negative, null if not

  \> says replace with a digit if not a leading 0

  9 says replace with a digit, including when 0

  , is the thousands separator

  . is the decimal separator

- INTEGER ->,>>>,>>9
- LOGICAL yes/no

  We could change this to another language

  Example: DEF VAR L AS LOGICAL FORMAT LOGICAL "OUI/NON"

A program example will show the power of the startup parameters and use of the FORMAT Phrase. The PROGRESS 4GL program, CURRENCY.P, is a simple program which demonstrates how dates and numbers can be varied with the FORMAT phrase and the PROGRESS startup parameters -E and -d.

Assume you desired a numeric format that had four digits before the decimal and three digits after the decimal. You could specify:

```
DEFINE VARIABLE NUM1 AS DECIMAL FORMAT "(>>,>>>9.999)"
```

In the FORMAT phrase above, the parentheses will display only if the value is negative, > will be replaced with a digit if there is one, and 9 will be replaced with a 0 or a digit if there is one. The , stands for the thousands separator and the . stands for the decimal separator.

Here is the program listing for CURRENCY.P:

```
/* currency.p */
DEFINE VARIABLE test1 AS DECIMAL FORMAT "(9999,999) YEN" NO-UNDO.
DEFINE VARIABLE test2 AS DECIMAL FORMAT "(9999.999) Rubles" NO-UNDO.
REPEAT:
    SET test1 LABEL "Yen"    COLON 10 SKIP WITH SIDE-LABELS.
    SET test2 LABEL "Rubles" COLON 10 SKIP (1).
END.
```

In this example, a 4 x 3 decimal format is specified and being used for currency representation. Note that the Yen currency contains the thousands separator, and the Rubles currency contains the decimal separator. When you run this program using PROGRESS default parameters (, = thousands; . is decimal), there is different behavior for the two numeric separators.

More interesting, the behavior will change depending on whether you have started up PROGRESS in the default (American) mode, or the European Mode (with -E). The different behavior is described in the following sections, and it will demonstrate the power of the startup parameters.

Running CURRENCY.P Using the American Numeric Format

When running CURRENCY.P with the default PROGRESS numeric defaults, Yen displays as a fill-in field as ",", and Ruble displays as a fill-in field as ".". As you type digits in the test1 fill-in field, the Yen field fills in from right to left, and fills in beyond the ",".

As you type digits in the test2 fill-in field, the Rubles field fills in from right to left to the left of the decimal, but you must press . to fill in to the right of the decimal, and it now fills in left to right.

This is expected behavior in the U.S.

Running CURRENCY.P Using the European Numeric Format

If you had started PROGRESS with the -E ("European Format") option, different behavior would take place.

When running CURRENCY.P with the European numeric format, Yen displays as a fill-in field as ".", and Ruble displays as a fill-in field as "," (note the difference from the American example above).

As you type in digits in the `test1` fill-in field, the `Yen` field fills in from right to left, and fills in beyond the ".".

As you type in digits in the `test2` fill-in field, the `Rubles` field fills in from right to left to the left of the comma decimal separator, but you must press "," (again, note the difference from the American format) to fill in to the right of the decimal, and it now fills in left to right.

International FORMAT Attributes

The `FORMAT` phrase has more attributes which reflect the internationalization built into the PROGRESS environment. Again, without this built-in behavior, you would have to write code to handle country-specific cases.

When defining the `FORMAT` phrase, there are special symbols which are used to specify the valid data which can fill those fields. They are:

`FORMAT` Attribute (!) represents a letter (uppercased):

This attribute will use the ISALPHA table in the codepage definition to ensure that all alphabetic characters within a codepage qualify. Furthermore, it will then use the `UPPERCASE-TABLE` to properly uppercase every alphabetic character to its proper uppercase value.

`FORMAT` Attribute (A) represents a letter (upper- or lowercase):

This attribute will use the ISALPHA table in the codepage definition to ensure that all alphabetic characters within a codepage qualify.

`FORMAT` Attribute (N) represents a digit or letter:

This attribute will use the ISALPHA table in the codepage definition, as well as the digits 0–9, to restrict the user's input to an alphanumeric value.

Note

Non-roman digits are not currently interpreted as digits. Examples of these are the Thai digits, the Hebrew digits, and the Hindi digits found in Thai, Hebrew, and Arabic and Persian codepages, respectively.

Also, the double-byte representation of digits is not currently interpreted as digits. Double-byte character sets contain single-byte and double-byte versions of digits. Only the single-byte versions may be included in a `FORMAT` statement.

Finally, double-byte characters require two positions in a `FORMAT` phrase. That is, `FORMAT "AAAA"` could store four single-byte characters or two double-byte characters.

DATE, TODAY, DAY, WEEKDAY, MONTH, YEAR 4GL Functions

As was discussed in Chapter 14, "Designing Your Global Application," it would be wrong to assume that there is a specific order of days, months, and years in a date string. If you designed a program which parsed a string representing a date, you would run into trouble with date order in various countries.

Example: Suppose you wrote a program to parse a character string being passed to you, and that all you could be sure of is that the numbers were separated by "/." If you were passed the string "11/10/12," how would you interpret it?

If your program made the American assumption that the numbers before the first "/" were the month, that the numbers between the two "/" were the day, and that the numbers after the second "/" were the year, you would conclude that the date was November 10, 1912. However, if your program made the French assumption that they went day, month, year, then the date would be 11 October 1912. Only one can be correct.

The problem gets more complicated when you must perform operations on the dates, such as calculating the number of days between two dates.

There is a potential to write a great amount of code to resolve this issue. Fortunately for you, PROGRESS already contains that code.

Dates are stored in PROGRESS in an internal format, and displayed in a user-definable order and format. Calculations against those dates are done using the internal format.

Here are the PROGRESS 4GL Keywords for proper date handling:

- `DATE (month, day, year)`—Returns a date in internal storage format, of the day specified by month, day, and year; or
- `DATE (string)`—Returns a date in internal storage format, given a string. That string must be in the same order representation as used with the -d startup parameter in order for the function to work correctly.
- `TODAY`—Returns the current system date in internal storage format.
- `DAY (date)`—Converts an internally stored date value to the day of the month (1 through 31).
- `WEEKDAY (date)`—Converts an internally stored date value to the day of the week (1 through 7).
- `MONTH (date)`—Converts an internally stored date value to the month of the year (1 through 12).
- `YEAR (date)`—Converts an internally stored data value to the year value (4 digits).

Example: Date Handling with `DATES.P`. Take a look at how these functions work. The program DATES.P inputs a date, and then breaks it into its components:

```
/* Dates.p */
DEFINE VARIABLE date1 AS DATE       LABEL "Date" FORMAT "99/99.99" NO-UNDO.
DEFINE VARIABLE theday AS INTEGER   LABEL "Day"     NO-UNDO.
DEFINE VARIABLE themonth AS INTEGER LABEL "Month"   NO-UNDO.
```

```
DEFINE VARIABLE theyear AS INTEGER  LABEL "Year"    NO-UNDO.
DEFINE VARIABLE thewkday AS INTEGER LABEL "Weekday" NO-UNDO.

DISPLAY SESSION:DATE-FORMAT       LABEL "Session:Date-Format"
        TODAY FORMAT "9999-99.99" LABEL "Today"
        TIME                      LABEL "Time (raw)"
        STRING(TIME, "HH:MM:SS")  LABEL "Time".
REPEAT:
   DEFINE FRAME a
      date1
      theday themonth theyear thewkday
      WITH  8 DOWN.
   SET date1 WITH FRAME a.
   ASSIGN theday = DAY(date1)
          themonth = MONTH(date1)
          theyear = YEAR(date1)
          thewkday = WEEKDAY(date1).
   DISPLAY theday themonth theyear thewkday WITH FRAME a.
END.
```

Comments:

1. If you run PROGRESS with default settings, the date format is mm/dd/yy.
2. PROGRESS will issue the error `The month of a date must be between 1 and 12` if you try to input anything else when it is expecting a month. PROGRESS will issue the error `day in month is invalid` if you try to input a bad day when it is expecting a day.
3. The default century is 1900, and 19 is assumed to be the first two digits of the century when you input a two-digit year. If you have set the format to input a 4-digit year, you can enter any 4 digits. For example, you could change the format in the statement

   ```
   DEFINE VARIABLE date1 AS DATE LABEL "Date" format "99-99-9999"
   ```

4. You can also change the format of the date separators. The characters . and / are also valid. In fact, you can mix and match these characters and set a date of 99.99/9999 if you wish. No other date separation characters are valid, however.

Alternate formats:

- If you set the `-d` startup parameter to ymd, then your program will be expecting that years are entered before months and days. All the day and month validation will take place on the appropriate fields automatically.
- If you did set the `-d` startup parameter to ymd, then your 4-digit year format as mentioned above in comment 3 would also have to change. You would need to set it to the following:

  ```
  DEFINE VARIABLE date1 AS DATE LABEL "Date" FORMAT "9999-99-99"
  ```

- If you set the `-yy` century startup parameter to another value, PROGRESS will then assume that the first two digits of a four-digit year are the `yy` values. In Chapter 14, "Designing Your Global Application," it was mentioned that the

Thai Buddhist year is 543 years more than the Gregorian (western) year. To better support the Buddhist calendar, you would start PROGRESS with `-yy 2500`. Now when you input a year of 32, PROGRESS saves it as 2532. This setting would automatically assign years between 2500 and 2599 (again, if the input format is 9999 for a year, you can override all four digits). Incidentally, if you had set the `-yy` options to `2540`, then PROGRESS would automatically assign years between 2540 and 2639, thus giving you more control over the century range.

> **Note**
>
> These functions assume a Gregorian calendar, and do not currently support Hebrew or Muslim 13-month calendars. In order to support these other calendars, it would be possible to write a 4GL procedure that accepts the internal date value as input, and outputs a string with the appropriate Hebrew or Muslim date.

V

Internationalization

TIME

As was also mentioned in Chapter 14, "Designing Your Global Application," time formats vary from country to country. Similarly to dates, it would be a mistake to code specific assumptions about the formats of time display and input.

The PROGRESS environment once again provides functions which easily manage time for you. They are:

`TIME`—Returns the number of seconds elapsed since 00:00:00 (midnight). As such, it is format independent.

To format a time according to local conventions, you would use the `FORMAT STRING` function as follows:

`FORMAT STRING (source, format)`—If source is an integer, and the format begins `"HH:MM"` or `"HH:MM:SS"`, then `FORMAT STRING` assumes that the source value is the value as used by `TIME`. It will then convert the output string to a time format. If there is an "a" or "A" in the format string as well, then AM and PM time formats are used.

> **Note**
>
> If you omit the ":", PROGRESS will not interpret the strings as an hours:minutes:seconds designator.

> **Tip**
>
> Separators other than ":" between hours, minutes, and seconds are not supported. To output a time format such as 1700, it is necessary to write a special 4GL procedure with which you would reformat the numeric display.
>
> The code to display time using HHMM format is simply as follows:
>
> ```
> REPLACE( STRING(TIME, "HH:MM") ,":", "")
> ```
>
> The `STRING` function converts the time to hours and minutes. The resulting string has the colons (:) replaced with the NULL character. This allows you to display `1730` rather than `17:30`.

CAPS and LC

As you have learned from Chapter 14, there is no simple algorithm for calculating the uppercase or lowercase value of a character. Different character sets, different character set encodings (codepages), and different languages have unique rules for determining what is the upper- or lowercase of an individual character.

PROGRESS provides two functions which will return the correct upper- and lowercase values for an inputted character. These functions take note of the specific character set and codepage being used, and return the correct character.

Example:

```
newstring = LC (oldstring)
newstring = CAPS (oldstring)
```

These functions use the character set definition found in the codepage in use at the time (the `-cpinternal` codepage). For more details on codepages and PROGRESS codepage startup parameters, see Chapter 18, "Deploying Your Global Application."

Example: CAPS-LC.P—Proper Upper- and Lowercasing for Western Europe. The following program, CAPS-LC.P will uppercase and lowercase four strings containing a variety of characters.

```
/* caps-lc.p */
DEF VAR string1 AS CHAR INIT "ABCDEFGHIJKLMNOPQRSTUVWXYZ".
DEF VAR string2 AS CHAR INIT "abcdefghijklmnopqrstuvwxyz".
DEF VAR string3 AS CHAR INIT "ÀÁÂÃÄÅÆÇÈÉÊËÌÍÎÏÐÑÒÓÔÕÖxØÙÚÛÜYÞß".
DEF VAR string4 AS CHAR INIT "àáâãäåæçèéêëìíîïðñòóôõö÷øùúûüyþÿ".

DISPLAY
  "CAPS" AT ROW 1 COLUMN 1
  CAPS (string1) FORMAT "x(35)" AT 1
  CAPS (string2) FORMAT "x(35)" AT 1
  CAPS (string3) FORMAT "x(35)" AT 1
  CAPS (string4) FORMAT "x(35)" AT 1
  "LC"  AT ROW 1 COLUMN 40
  LC (string1) FORMAT "x(35)" AT 40
```

```
  LC (string2) FORMAT "x(35)" AT 40
  LC (string3) FORMAT "x(35)" AT 40
  LC (string4) FORMAT "x(35)" AT 40
  WITH NO-LABELS.
```

When you run this program, all characters (including the extended characters beyond the basic ASCII alphabet) are properly upper- and lowercased. Using the default upper- and lowercase rules for PROGRESS, the results will be:

```
CAPS


ABCDEFGHIJKLMNOPQRSTUVWXYZ
ABCDEFGHIJKLMNOPQRSTUVWXYZ
ÀÁÂÃÄÅÆÇÈÉÊËÌÍÎÏÐÑÒÓÔÕÖ×ØÙÚÛÜÝÞß
ÀÁÂÃÄÅÆÇÈÉÊËÌÍÎÏÐÑÒÓÔÕÖ÷ØÙÚÛÜÝÞŸ


LC


abcdefghijklmnopqrstuvwxyz
abcdefghijklmnopqrstuvwxyz
àáâãäåæçèéêëìíîïðñòóôõö×øùúûüýþß
àáâãäåæçèéêëìíîïðñòóôõö÷øùúûüýþÿ
```

Example 2: RUS-CPLC.P—Proper Upper- and Lowercasing for Russia. This is a similar program to CAPS-LC.P above, except that the strings have been initialized with Russian Cyrillic Data. The program is listed in figure 15.1.

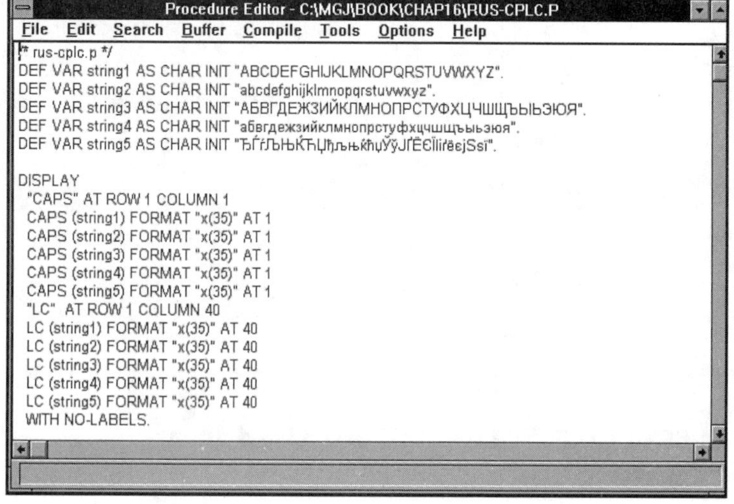

```
Procedure Editor - C:\MGJ\BOOK\CHAP16\RUS-CPLC.P
File  Edit  Search  Buffer  Compile  Tools  Options  Help
/* rus-cplc.p */
DEF VAR string1 AS CHAR INIT "ABCDEFGHIJKLMNOPQRSTUVWXYZ".
DEF VAR string2 AS CHAR INIT "abcdefghijklmnopqrstuvwxyz".
DEF VAR string3 AS CHAR INIT "АБВГДЕЖЗИЙКЛМНОПРСТУФХЦЧШЩЪЫЬЭЮЯ".
DEF VAR string4 AS CHAR INIT "абвгдежзийклмнопрстуфхцчшщъыьэюя".
DEF VAR string5 AS CHAR INIT "ЂЃѓЉЊЌЋЏђљњќћџЎўЈҐЁЄЇІіґёєјЅѕї".

DISPLAY
 "CAPS" AT ROW 1 COLUMN 1
 CAPS (string1) FORMAT "x(35)" AT 1
 CAPS (string2) FORMAT "x(35)" AT 1
 CAPS (string3) FORMAT "x(35)" AT 1
 CAPS (string4) FORMAT "x(35)" AT 1
 CAPS (string5) FORMAT "x(35)" AT 1
 "LC"  AT ROW 1 COLUMN 40
 LC (string1) FORMAT "x(35)" AT 40
 LC (string2) FORMAT "x(35)" AT 40
 LC (string3) FORMAT "x(35)" AT 40
 LC (string4) FORMAT "x(35)" AT 40
 LC (string5) FORMAT "x(35)" AT 40
 WITH NO-LABELS.
```

Fig. 15.1

RUS-CPLC.P Program testing Russian Cyrillic uppercase/lowercase

When this program is run under the Russian edition of Microsoft Windows, the correct upper- and lowercasing for the Cyrillic characters takes place, as shown in figure

15.2. This is driven by a different codepage definition and a set of Russian upper/lowercase rules, all specified to PROGRESS at startup time. See Chapter 18, "Deploying Your Application Globally," to see how this is done.

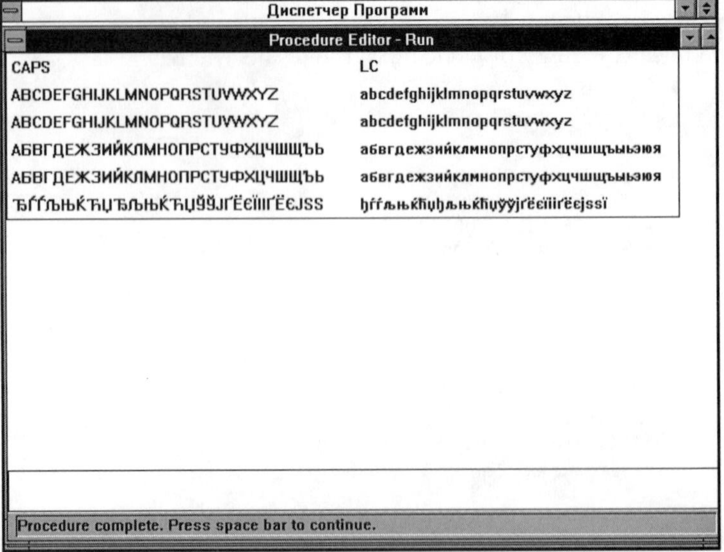

Fig. 15.2

Russian Cyrillic characters properly uppercased and lowercased.

Tip

If you want the PROGRESS Editor tools to use a different font that supports extended characters, you will have to change Font 2.

Font 2 is the font used by the Procedure Window, the Procedure Editor, and the UIB's Code Section Editor.

You can change Font 2 using the "Set Font 2" application available in PRO*Tools.

You can also type the following line and run it from the editor directly:

```
SYSTEM-DIALOG FONT 2
```

If you want to permanently change the definition of Font 2, then you will have to edit your PROGRESS.INI file.

MESSAGE and SUBSTITUTE 4GL Functions Used in an International Context

The MESSAGE function is another very powerful and intricate 4GL function. It can be used to display messages in an alert box (GUI applications) or in a message area (Character mode applications).

Almost every application will display messages of some sort to the user. You have learned earlier in Chapter 14 that building messages from smaller message components is not a good idea. When the messages must be translated, the components will not fit together well, depending on the language and its grammar. As a rule, you should construct whole, complete messages.

There are cases, however, where you can carefully construct compound messages. Of particular interest with MESSAGE is the SUBSTITUTE function. Used in conjunction, they can be effective when piecing together messages that are to be translated.

Syntax:

```
SUBSTITUTE (base-string, expression, [expression...])
```

Example:

You could build a message from three components as follows. &1 and &2 are arguments to the message statement.

```
DISPLAY MESSAGE SUBSTITUTE ("There were &1 tables in &2 databases",
    table-num, db-num).
```

If this were translated into French, one possibility would be:

```
MESSAGE SUBSTITUTE ("Dans &2 bases-des-données, il y a &1 tables")
```

The reversed arguments are correctly handled by the SUBSTITUTE command.

Note

MESSAGE SUBSTITUTE cannot be used for all cases because there may still be some impact on translation beyond grammatical order (gender, number, and so on), but there are times when this can come in handy.

INPUT, OUTPUT, INPUT-OUTPUT, and CODEPAGE-CONVERT

As was discussed earlier in this chapter (in the CAPS and LC section), as well as in Chapter 14, "Designing Your Global Application," codepages vary from one operating system to another, and from one computer platform to another. As a reminder, codepages are specific numeric assignments for each character used in your language's character set.

It is important to be able to transfer data between PROGRESS and external sources, such as files, input devices, and databases. The PROGRESS INPUT and OUTPUT statements provide this capability. As we have seen, those files and external devices may originate on systems which use different codepages for representing your character set. It is necessary, therefore, for these functions to support the mapping of character data from one codepage to another.

These PROGRESS 4GL statements all support this codepage conversion.

`CODEPAGE-CONVERT (source-string, target-codepage, source-codepage)`

`CODEPAGE-CONVERT` converts a string from one codepage to another. It is not necessary for `target-codepage` or `source-codepage` to be the current codepage.

> **Note**
>
> These codepages must be found in your CONVMAP.CP file. PROGRESS looks for the codepage definitions in CONVMAP.CP, then loads the codepage mapping table into memory to perform this function. See Chapter 18, "Deploying Your Application Globally," for more information on codepages.

`INPUT`, `OUTPUT`, and `INPUT-OUTPUT`

This is a very powerful and robust set of functions. There are dozens of parameters that can be specified with these commands, all of which are covered in depth in the *PROGRESS Language References*. There are codepage-related parameters, however, that are interesting to internationalization. The commands are grouped together here for convenience.

- `INPUT FROM ... CONVERT TARGET target-cp SOURCE source-cp`

  Specifies a new input stream. You can specify that a codepage conversion other than the default should take place. By default, `INPUT FROM` will convert data from the `-cpstream` codepage to the `-cpinternal` codepage.

- `INPUT FROM ... NO-CONVERT`

  `NO-CONVERT` specifies that the default codepage conversion should not take place (from `-cpstream` to `-cpinternal`); no conversion should be performed at all.

- `INPUT THROUGH ... CONVERT TARGET target-cp SOURCE source-cp`

  Use the output from a UNIX program as input to the current program. You can specify that a codepage conversion other than the default should take place. By default, `INPUT THROUGH` will convert data from the `-cpstream` codepage to the `-cpinternal` codepage.

- `INPUT THROUGH ... NO-CONVERT`

  `NO-CONVERT` specifies that the default codepage conversion should not take place (from `-cpstream` to `-cpinternal`), and that no conversion should be performed at all.

- `INPUT-OUTPUT THROUGH ... CONVERT TARGET target-cp SOURCE source-cp`

  Starts a UNIX program that will provide all input to the current program, as well as accept all output. You can specify that a codepage conversion other than the default should take place. By default, when accepting data, PROGRESS will convert data from the `-cpstream` codepage to the `-cpinternal` codepage, and when outputting data, will perform the reverse mapping.

- `INPUT-OUTPUT THROUGH ... NO-CONVERT`

  `NO-CONVERT` specifies that the default codepage conversion should not take place (from `-cpstream` to `-cpinternal`), and that no conversion should be performed.

- `OUTPUT THROUGH ... CONVERT TARGET target-cp SOURCE source-cp`

  When outputting to a new destination (such as a UNIX process), you can specify that a conversion should take place on the data between what a designated (and presumable current) codepage is and what the desired destination codepage should be. The default is to convert data from the `-cpinternal` codepage to the `-cpstream` codepage.

- `OUTPUT THROUGH ... NO-CONVERT`

  `NO-CONVERT` specifies that the default conversion should not take place, and that no conversion should be performed.

- `OUTPUT TO ... CONVERT TARGET target-cp SOURCE source-cp`

  Specifies a new output stream. Again, you can specify that a codepage conversion other than the default should take place. By default, `OUTPUT TO` will convert data from the `-cpinternal` codepage to the `-cpstream` codepage.

- `OUTPUT TO ... NO-CONVERT`

  `NO-CONVERT` specified that the default conversion should not take place, and that no conversion should be performed.

> **Note**
>
> Codepage conversion between double-byte character set codepages (Japanese/Shift-JIS, Korean/KSC5601, Simplified Chinese/GB2312, and Traditional Chinese/BIG-5) is not possible, nor is conversion between a double-byte character set and a single-byte character set (for example, Japanese/Shift-JIS and Arabic/1256).

Additionally, the following functions are affected by PROGRESS Codepage Startup parameters, discussed in detail in Chapter 18, "Deploying Your Application Globally."

`EXPORT` and `IMPORT` Functions in an International Context

The `EXPORT` and `IMPORT` functions allow you to write and read data between PROGRESS and an external file. That external source may have different formats for numbers and dates, so it is important to understand how PROGRESS must handle those different formats.

As was discussed briefly in Chapter 14, "Designing Your Global Application," various operating systems and languages can be represented by different codepages (encodings for their character sets). The details about codepages and their management will be covered in Chapter 18, "Deploying Your Application Globally," but codepage-specific behavior will be included here for completeness.

`EXPORT` will convert data into standard character data, and write it to a named stream. `EXPORT` will output that data in the `-cpstream` default format. Furthermore, it will follow the settings for `-yy`, `-d`, and `-E` startup parameters; that is, it will output four-digit years using the century setting (the first two digits of the year), the date ordering format (day/month/year, and so on), and with the thousands and decimal separators as specified by the presence of absence of the -E parameter.

IMPORT will read character data from a named stream and convert it to data that could be stored in PROGRESS records. Typically, IMPORT reads in data that was created with the PROGRESS EXPORT function. IMPORT will read that character data in the -cpstream codepage and convert it to the -cpinternal codepage. Furthermore, it will assume that the character data format conforms to the settings for -yy, -d, and -E startup parameters; that is, it will assume and create four-digit years using the century setting (the first two digits of the year), the date ordering format (day/month/year, and so on), and will try to interpret numeric data following the convention for thousands separators and decimal separators, as specified by the -E parameter.

Programming for a Double-Byte Character Set

As covered in Chapter 14, "Designing Your Global Application," Chinese, Japanese, and Korean alphabets contain tens of thousands of characters. This many characters cannot be represented by a single byte. In fact, each character requires two bytes to represent it. For this reason, programs which can handle characters which are made of two bytes are called "double-byte enabled" programs.

Double-Byte Enabled PROGRESS (DBE PROGRESS) provides a complete development environment that is double-byte-character-set-aware. That is, when a double-byte character is encountered by PROGRESS, it is dealt with properly. This means the following:

- Lead bytes and trail bytes are not mistaken for other single-byte characters when viewing a string
- Double-byte characters wrap correctly at the end of lines
- Double-byte characters are input and displayed as a single entity
- Double-byte characters collate correctly
- Double-byte characters properly upper- and lowercase correctly
- A trail byte is never separated from its lead byte
- A lead byte always carries its trail byte with it

To ensure that the double-byte characters are managed properly as described above, Progress provides a Double-Byte Supplement to the base product. This Double-Byte Supplement updates some of the PROGRESS program components to add this knowledge of double-byte character sets. When using Double-Byte Enabled PROGRESS, the 4GL functions which manipulate character data will be aware of the special handling required by that data.

PROGRESS Double-Byte Functions

The following PROGRESS 4GL functions have extra knowledge of double-byte character handling in the double-byte enabled version of PROGRESS. Used properly, these functions will allow the programmer to develop software which will properly work with character strings containing Chinese, Japanese, and Korean data, as well as strings which contain or mix in single-byte data.

LENGTH *(string, type)*

You use the LENGTH function to determine the length of a string. For example, if you wanted to know how long a customer's last name is, you would use the LENGTH function. If the customer's last name was in Korean, containing double-byte characters, the LENGTH function should behave properly.

LENGTH returns the length of a string, and does so one of two ways. If type = "RAW", then LENGTH returns the length of a string in bytes. If type = "CHARACTER", then LENGTH returns the length of a string in whole characters. The default is for LENGTH to return the "CHARACTER" length. On single-byte systems, or with single-byte data, this will be equivalent to "RAW". With Double-Byte Enabled PROGRESS and double-byte data, this will most likely be different.

OVERLAY *(target, position, length, type)*

This function is used to replace a group of characters in a string with another group of characters. It is possible that these two groups of characters will be different lengths. Although this function is rarely used in the Progress community, it would be useful, for example, if you needed to do wholesale substitutions in previously-stored fields in a database.

As you can imagine, since you can replace some characters with some other characters, this function must be very aware of double-byte characters in order to avoid corrupting any of them when the substitution takes place.

This is one of the most complicated text-processing statements in the PROGRESS language, and shows the value of having an application environment that is double-byte enabled to its core. The type parameter indicates whether the position and length parameters are to operate in bytes or whole characters. As with the LENGTH function, if type is "RAW", it instructs PROGRESS to operate in bytes. If type is "CHARACTER", then PROGRESS will operate in whole characters.

In "CHARACTER" mode, when a single-byte character is to overlay a double byte character, great care is taken not to leave orphan lead or trail bytes behind. When a double-byte character is to overlay a single-byte character, great care is taken to overlay only one whole character by one whole character, and to shift the other characters right. In "RAW" mode, a simple byte-level overlay takes place, and data could be incorrectly written. The default is "CHARACTER" mode.

SUBSTRING *(source, position, length, type)*

SUBSTRING extracts a portion of a character string. It is useful when breaking up a string. If, for example, you wished to extract a person's first initial from their first name, you would use `SUBSTRING`. If that person's first name were in Chinese, Japanese, or Korean, it would be important to extract the entire first character, not just the first byte of the character. This is why `SUBSTRING` has been double-byte enabled.

The parameter type can have one of three values: `"CHARACTER"`, `"RAW"`, and `"FIXED"`. If `type` is `"CHARACTER"`, then `position` and `length` are to operate on whole characters. If `type` is `"RAW"`, then `position` and `length` are to operate at the byte level. If `type` is `"FIXED"`, however, then `position` should operate in character units, `length` should be in bytes, but only whole characters are to be returned. This means that if the substring returned, given the length, would have split a double-byte character, then one less byte is returned so that orphan lead bytes or trail bytes are not returned with the substring.

> **Note**
>
> The `FIXED` parameter only works when SUBSTRING is being called as a function, not when it is being used as a statement.

Additionally, there is a 4GL function that is helpful when parsing through raw data. This is described in the following section.

IS-LEAD-BYTE

There are times when a program needs to parse through data one byte at a time, such as when it is looking for "special characters." If, for example, you wrote a program which turned a DOS file name into a UNIX file name, your program would probably scan through the string byte-by-byte looking for a "\", to be replaced by a "/". As you read in Chapter 14, "Designing Your Global Application," if "\" is a trail byte, then replacing it would effectively corrupt a double-byte character. You can determine whether a specific byte is potentially part of a double-byte character by using `IS-LEAD-BYTE`.

The `IS-LEAD-BYTE` function may be used to determine whether a given byte is possibly the first byte of a double-byte character. If the byte is a valid lead byte value, it returns YES; otherwise, it returns NO. Because lead and trail byte ranges have some overlap, the simple fact that a byte *could* be a lead byte does not absolutely mean that it is a lead byte. It could also be a valid trail byte. When a byte returns a YES `IS-LEAD-BYTE` value, you must look at the bytes surrounding it to determine whether it is in fact the first byte of a double-byte character.

Double-Byte-Sensitive 4GL Functions

The following 4GL functions are sensitive to double-byte characters. That is to say, it is not necessary to specify any kind of `"RAW"` or `"CHARACTER"` parameter to the functions; they will simply work correctly on double-byte data, transparently to your application logic.

LASTKEY

The LASTKEY function is used to examine keyboard input character-by-character. It might be used to immediately check and verify data being entered as being valid data.

The LASTKEY function is double-byte enabled. It will hold a value read by READKEY only after the Chinese, Japanese, or Korean Input Method Editor places a double-byte character into the keyboard buffer. It returns only the value of the character in the buffer—not all the keystrokes that may be necessary to define a double-byte character in the Input Method Editor itself. With double-byte characters, LASTKEY will hold a value between 1 and 65,535 (2 bytes = 16 bits; 2**16 is 65,536).

READKEY

The READKEY function is used to read a single character being input from the keyboard.

The READKEY function is double-byte enabled. It will read a value only after the Chinese, Japanese, or Korean Input Method Editor places a double-byte character into the keyboard buffer. It returns only the value of the character in the buffer—not all the keystrokes that may be necessary to define a double-byte character in the Input Method Editor itself. With double-byte characters, READKEY will return a value between 1 and 65,535.

ASC *(char)*

The ASC function converts a character to its numeric value in the current codepage. It could be used, for example to generate and validate checksums.

With single-byte characters, ASC returns a value between 0 and 255. When ASC is performed on a double-byte character, it returns a value between 256 and 65,535.

CHR *(int)*

The CHR function returns the character represented by a numeric value in the current codepage. This might be useful when converting binary data from an external source to its representative text.

In single-byte PROGRESS, CHR accepts a value between 0 and 255 and returns the character. In Double-Byte Enabled PROGRESS, if CHR is handed a value between 0 and 255, it will still return the single-byte character. If it is handed a value between 256 and 65,535, however, it will check to see whether the first byte of the integer value could be a valid lead byte. If so, it returns (displays) a double-byte character. If not, it returns a null string.

Following are other 4GL functions that are double-byte aware. They are documented in the Command Reference, and their specific double-byte behavior is documented in Double-Byte Enabled PROGRESS.

```
APPLY
BEGINS
ENCODE
```

```
ENTRY
FILL
INDEX
LOOKUP
MATCHES
NUM-ENTRIES
R-INDEX
SUBSTITUTE
```

Double-Byte Startup Aid

There is also a startup option that is helpful when developing applications that will operate on double-byte character sets.

```
-CHECKDBE
```

This PROGRESS startup parameter instructs the compiler to warn the developer whenever the `SUBSTRING`, `LENGTH`, or `OVERLAY` commands are used without explicitly specifying `"CHARACTER"`, `"RAW"`, or `"FIXED"`. This reminds developers to carefully examine whether they wish to be working in raw bytes, or with whole characters (there are cases for both).

Double-Byte Enabled Coding Examples

The *Double-Byte Enabled PROGRESS Manual* and the *Command Reference* explain in detail how specific 4GL functions operate on double-byte data. More complex examples are available from Progress on proper double-byte program development.

Since you may be new to this concept, what follows are two examples in which double-byte characters are incorrectly handled on a single-byte system, and in which they properly behave on a double-byte system.

The first example (see fig. 15.3) shows incorrect editing of double-byte characters on a system that is not double-byte enabled. In this example, a user had input four Traditional Chinese characters in the Big-5 codepage, using the Input Method Editor which is built into Chinese Microsoft Windows.

The first line in figure 15.3 displays the characters correctly. It is not unusual that double-byte characters might display correctly on a single-byte system. Many people have been fooled into thinking that single-byte applications actually support double-byte data because they can do this.

The second line shows a user attempting to highlight a double-byte character, but only one of the two bytes is highlighted. This is because the cursor logic knows nothing about double-byte characters.

The third line shows the result of deleting one byte of a double-byte character. A single-byte system is unaware of the link between the two bytes of a double-byte character, and will blindly split the two, thus creating a new (garbage) character.

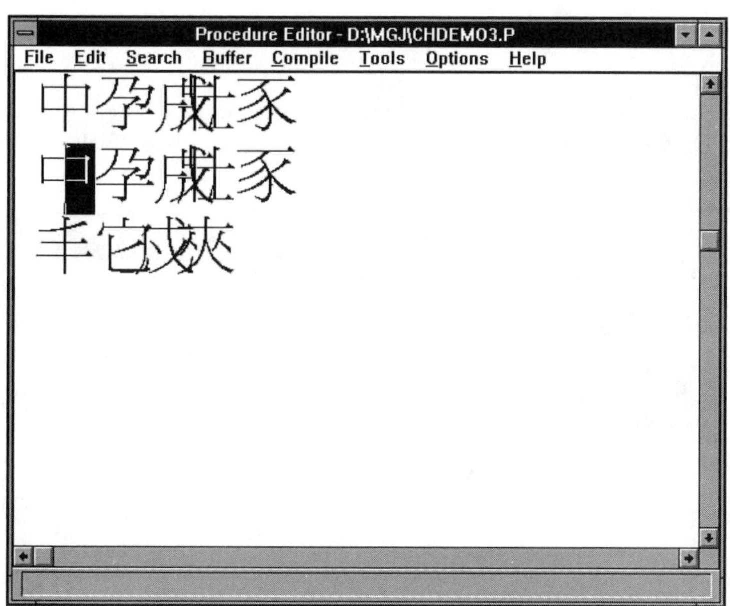

Fig. 15.3

Improper editing of double-byte characters with a single-byte editor.

In figure 15.4, now the other byte of that double-byte character will be deleted.

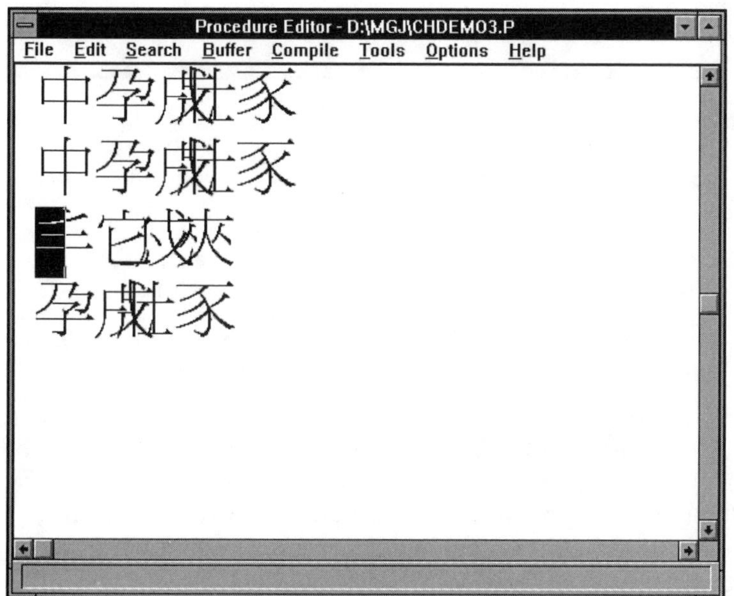

Fig 15.4

A second deletion appears to correct the problem.

This fourth line in figure 15.4 shows the result of deleting the second byte, which had been left behind. The result appears to be correct, though it was necessary to press two deletes to remove one character. This is not very user-friendly behavior, but it appears to work. This would not be acceptable behavior for experienced users of double-byte enabled applications.

In figure 15.5, here are some double-byte characters being edited on a system that is double-byte aware. In this case, it is the Procedure Editor in Double-Byte Enabled PROGRESS.

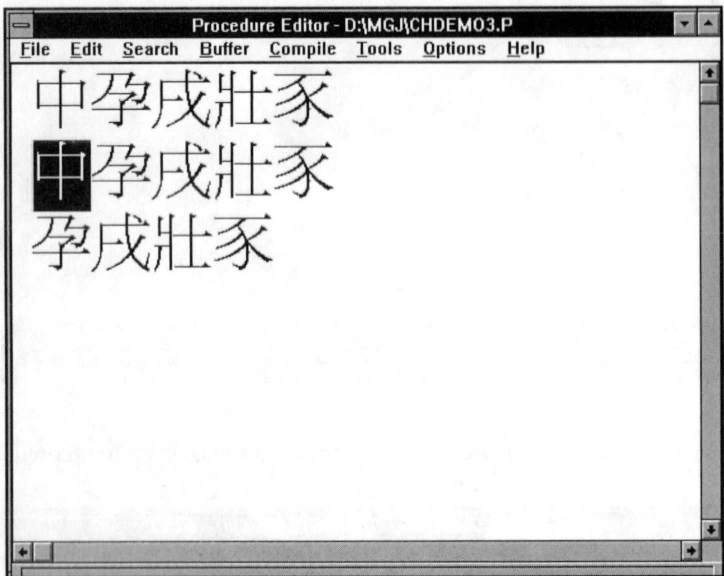

Fig. 15.5

Proper editing of double-byte characters by the Double-Byte Enabled PROGRESS Procedure Editor.

As seen in the example, an entire double-byte character is recognized and highlighted by the cursor. When a backspace or delete takes place, the entire double-byte character is deleted, never leaving behind lead or trail bytes. This is proper behavior.

Take another example. Say that you wish to take a substring from a larger string. For example, suppose you wish to extract the first character of someone's first name.

As said before, the `SUBSTRING` function in PROGRESS supports either `"RAW"` operation (byte-by-byte) or `"CHARACTER"` operation (operating only on whole characters).

The following 4GL program tests substringing running on the single-byte version of PROGRESS (demonstrating what all single-byte applications would do). It will then be run on the double-byte version of PROGRESS, demonstrating proper behavior for double-byte enabled application environments. This program, CHDEMO1.P, may only be run on the Traditional Chinese version of Microsoft Windows, where the font support for Chinese exists. Unless you have this version of Windows, you will not be able to try this program. The figure shows the source code from within the PROGRESS Procedure Editor, running on Traditional Chinese Windows.

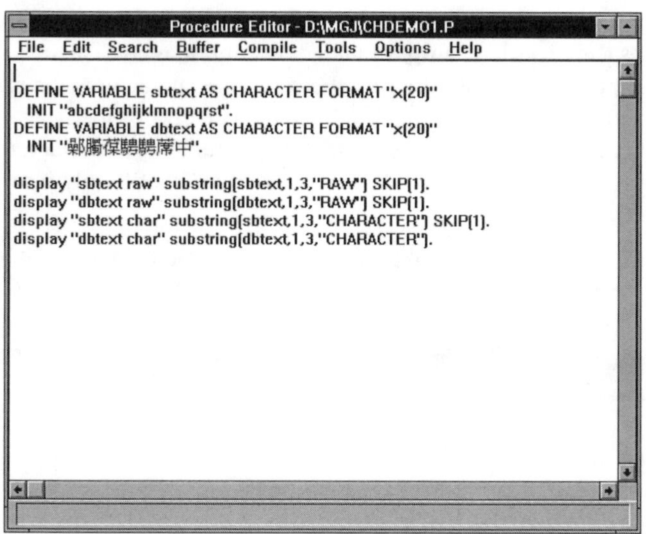

Fig. 15.6

4GL procedure to test single- and double-byte substrings.

This simple procedure will take the first three units of a string of single-byte characters and the first three units of a string of double-byte characters. In the first case, units will be `"RAW"` characters (as specified to the `SUBSTRING` function), and in the second case, units will be specified as `"CHARACTER"` as specified to the `SUBSTRING` function.

Figure 15.7 shows the result of running the program on single-byte PROGRESS.

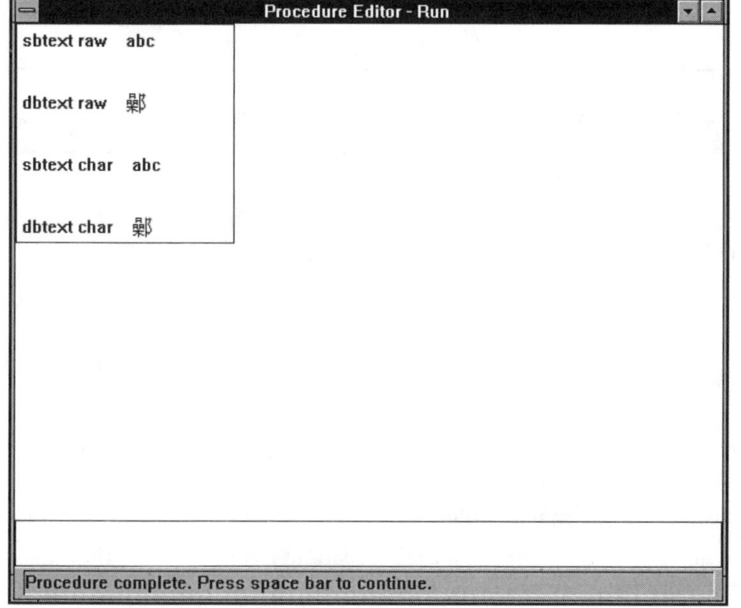

Fig. 15.7

Running CHDEMO1.P on a single-byte version of PROGRESS.

Looking at the result in figure 15.7, when operating on single-byte data, single-byte enabled PROGRESS does the expected thing. In fact, `"RAW"` mode is equivalent to `"CHARACTER"` mode using the `SUBSTRING` function, because one character is the same size as one byte. On double-byte data, single-byte PROGRESS works properly again when using the `"RAW"` parameter: it returns only one valid double-byte character (two bytes of the three). But when asked to return three "characters," it still only returns three bytes, and returns bad results.

Now take a look in figure 15.8 at what Double-Byte Enabled PROGRESS does when running CHDEMO1.P.

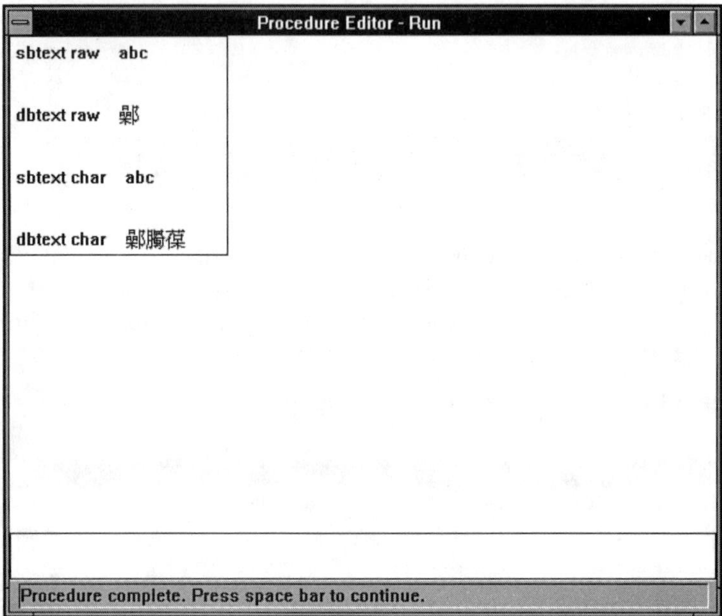

Fig. 15.8

Running CHDEMO1.P on a double-byte version of PROGRESS.

In this example, the `"RAW"` cases are the same, as expected, and the `"CHARACTER"` case operating on single-byte data also behaves as expected. But the `"CHARACTER"` operation on double-byte data now returns (correctly) three whole double-byte characters (6 bytes).

There are many more examples of where single-byte systems fail on double-byte data, including:

- Searching for a specific character, such as *, \, ?, and so on, which could be trail bytes of double-byte characters
- Sorting data using a single-byte enabled sort
- Running programs (such as compilers) that are single-byte only, and that delimit certain strings and keywords by special (single-byte) characters that may be trail bytes of double-byte characters

As you evaluate development environments for writing applications which may be deployed in China, Japan, Korea, or Taiwan, it is extremely important to verify from the vendors that their products are double-byte enabled, and that you can develop double-byte enabled code with them.

International Development Support Files

There are a number of other files and programs that are shipped in the International Supplement to the base PROGRESS product. These files are helpful in international development. Most of these may be found in the $DLC\PROLANG (or $dlc/prolang on UNIX systems) directory, under subdirectories for individual countries. For example, support files for Korea may be found in the directory $DLC\PROLANG\KOR.

The following sections cover some of the supplemental items provided to assist you with international development.

Textless Icons

The default PROGRESS icons contain English captions, written right on the icon. For non-English speaking users, this text can be distracting.

Each PROGRESS icon with text integrated in the image is also available in a "textless" form. These icons may be found in the directory $dlc\gui\adeicon\textless.

If a user wishes to run PROGRESS with icons devoid of English text, the textless icons should be used.

`PROMSGS` Translations

The PROGRESS program communicates to programmers and end users through a group of messages called `PROMSGS`. These messages display warnings and information, such as: `file xxx not found` in the PROGRESS Procedure Editor, and `cannot understand line xxx after yyyyy` in the PROGRESS Compiler.

PROGRESS system and error messages, numbering over 4,000, have been translated to more than two dozen languages. A `PROMSGS` file can be found in the language-specific subdirectory of $dlc\prolang. For example, the Czech `PROMSGS` may be found in the $dlc/prolang/cze directory.

Empty Databases

As of Version 7, and in Version 8, all databases are labeled with the codepage of the data they contain, and all databases include the collation table that was used to build the indexes. As will be discussed in more detail in Chapter 18, "Deploying Your Application Globally," different codepages and languages collate differently. For each major codepage family, an empty database exists as a quick start for creating new databases with culturally correct codepage and collation.

.df Files

.df files are PROGRESS database schema dump files which may be loaded into other databases to transfer schema information. Progress Software ships .df files that contain alternate collations. It is possible to change the codepage and collation of an existing database by loading a new .df containing the new collation tables and codepage name, and then rebuilding the indexes of that database. .df files exist for each major language family and codepage, and can also be found in a \prolang subdirectory.

International STARTUP.PF Files

STARTUP.PF is a file for which PROGRESS will search while initializing. In this file, you can specify parameters for modifying run-time behavior, as if you had added them to the startup command line. For example, you can place the `-E` and `-d` parameters (as discussed above for European format numbers and variable date ordering) in this file.

For each language, a STARTUP.PF file exists in a subdirectory of $dlc\prolang. This STARTUP.PF file has optional values for `-cpinternal` and `-cpstream` for each codepage of that language family, as well as the assumed `-E` and `-d` settings. The startup parameters `-cpinternal` and `-cpstream` control codepage mapping, and are fully documented in Chapter 18, "Deploying Your Application Globally."

> **Note**
>
> There is also a special version of a PROGRESS file which is shipped specifically for Japanese systems: PROGRESS.INI. The PROGRESS.INI for Japanese PROGRESS contains different font definitions than with other versions of PROGRESS, and may be found in $DLC\PROLANG\JPN.

Using Global Implementation Techniques

The information above covers the details of working with currency formats, date formats, and other culturally-specific fields. It is not clear, yet, how all of these functions fit together in an overall programming approach.

This section provides a couple of examples of how real programs could be written to handle issues of internationalization.

Supporting International Currency and Date Formats

If you are developing an application that is going to be deployed in a number of different environments, you will be faced with the problem of changing date and currency formats at each installation.

Although you could edit the source file and recompile it for each country, a superior solution is to dynamically change formats of certain fields based on certain global variables.

Here is an example which does this. The name of the program is I18N.P. In this programming example, there are two global variables defined:

```
DEF NEW GLOBAL SHARED VARIABLE g-currency-format AS CHAR NO-UNDO
    INITIAL "(9,999.999) YEN".
DEF NEW GLOBAL SHARED VARIABLE g-date-format     AS CHAR NO-UNDO
    INITIAL "99.99.99".
```

These variables need to be set based on user preferences, or country-specific information, when your application starts up. You could store the values based on user settings stored in a database, or on settings in the PROGRESS.INI file. The choice depends on your specific requirements.

Here are the basic steps that the example procedure will follow:

1. It makes sure that the routine is called correctly by checking the input parameters.
2. It looks at each object in the current frame and verifies its format and data type.
3. If the object is displaying a `DECIMAL` value, and if it seems to be showing a currency value, then the program changes the format to `g-currency-format`.

> **Note**
>
> In this sample program, currency fields are identified as those fields beginning with "$". This test could change based on your own identifier.

4. If the object is displaying a `DATE` value, then the program changes the format to `g-date-format`.
5. The program then checks whether there is another object in the frame, and if so, it goes to the next object. This continues until no more objects are in the frame.

This code is implemented as I18N.P:

```
/* -------------------------------------------------------
  File: i18n.p

  Description: Set the values for standard date and currency
  format, stored in the global variables:
     g-currency-format
     g-date-format
  If these are set to ?, then the format will not be changed
  dynamically.

  This routine should be called PRIOR to the DISPLAY of any data,
  and preferably prior to viewing the frame.

  Calling:
      RUN i18n.p (INPUT FRAME {&FRAME-NAME}:CURRENT-ITERATION))

  Input Parameters:
    ph_fldgrp - (HANDLE) Handle of the field-group
                of a Progress Frame.
```

```
-------------------------------------------------------- */
DEF INPUT PARAMETER ph_fldgrp AS HANDLE NO-UNDO.

/* ******** Global Variables ************** */
/* These can be set in another procedure.   */
DEF NEW GLOBAL SHARED VARIABLE g-currency-format AS CHAR NO-UNDO
    INITIAL "(9,999.999) YEN".
DEF NEW GLOBAL SHARED VARIABLE g-date-format     AS CHAR NO-UNDO
    INITIAL "99.99.99".

/* ***** Local Variables ****** */
DEF VAR h AS HANDLE NO-UNDO.

/* Check that there is something to do - i.e. that at least one
   of the formats is not UNKNOWN. */
IF g-currency-format eq ? AND g-date-format eq ? THEN RETURN.

/* Make sure we have a field group. If the user
   passed in a FRAME, then use the current iteration
   of that frame. Otherwise report an error. */
IF ph_fldgrp:TYPE eq "FRAME":U THEN
  ph_fldgrp = ph_fldgrp:CURRENT-ITERATION.
ELSE IF ph_fldgrp:TYPE ne "FIELD-GROUP":U THEN DO:
  MESSAGE "i18n.p expects a field-group."
          VIEW-AS ALERT-BOX ERROR.
  RETURN.
END.

/* Walk the widget tree of the field group and swap
   the position of labels with the associated object. */
h = ph_fldgrp:FIRST-CHILD.
DO WHILE VALID-HANDLE (h):
  /* Does the object have a valid side-label? */
  IF CAN-SET (h, "FORMAT":U) THEN DO:
    /* Change Currency on decimal fill-ins, if necessary. */
    IF h:DATA-TYPE eq "DECIMAL":U AND h:FORMAT BEGINS "$":U
       AND g-currency-format ne ?
    THEN h:FORMAT = g-currency-format.
    /* Change dates, if necessary. */
    IF h:DATA-TYPE eq "DATE":U AND g-date-format ne ?
    THEN h:FORMAT = g-date-format.
  END.

  /* Check the next widget. */
  h = h:NEXT-SIBLING.
END.
```

The preceding program dynamically changes the objects in a frame, allowing culturally dependent fields to be changed to their proper display form at runtime.

For more information on dynamically changing objects at runtime, see Chapter 22, "PROGRESS Programming Tips." This chapter describes more of the issues involved in dynamically changing object attributes. The process of "walking the widget tree" is also discussed more there. A further example is given in Chapter 22 that describes these concepts in terms of moving labels to the right-side of fill-in fields, useful in countries that display data from right to left, such as Saudi Arabia and Israel.

Alternate Layouts by Country

Another item that you will find yourself wanting to change on a country-by-country or locale-by-locale basis are the layout of screens that display address and telephone number information.

Different countries have different address schemes, as discussed in Chapter 14, "Designing Your Global Application." There are three approaches that you may consider taking in order to handle this problem:

1. *Display Data into an Editor.* Perhaps the easiest solution is to merge all the address fields into a single string and display this in an editor object. This is only an acceptable solution if you are displaying the data, however.
2. *Multi-layout in the UIB.* The Progress User Interface Builder (UIB) supports a multi-layout feature. Within a single file, you can create different named layouts. Each layout could be country specific, and you could switch between layouts at runtime.
3. *Use Directories for Country-Specific Files.* If you have many differences in layout for objects such as the SmartViewer or SmartBrowsers, it may be easier to create multiple copies of some files and store them in different directories: one directory per country. You could then use PROPATH (Progress' file search algorithm) or your own deployment system to make sure that a Dutch user used the files in the Dutch directory, and a Japanese user used the Japan directory, and so on, to find the SmartObjects.

From Here...

A lot of information has been covered in this chapter. You have reviewed the parameters which may be specified at startup time to change the behavior of internationally-sensitive fields. You have reviewed a number of 4GL statements and functions which may be used to develop international code. You have been introduced to the double-byte enabled functions in PROGRESS, and have seen when double-byte data is correctly and incorrectly handled. Finally, you have seen programming examples using some of those features.

Again, detailed syntax for the functions, statements, and startup parameters may be found in standard PROGRESS programming documentation.

Following the guidelines from Chapter 15, "Developing Your Global Application," and using the functions and parameters documented here, your application should be pretty well internationalized.

You are now ready to move on to the next step in the process of designing, developing, and releasing a global application.:

- Chapter 16, "Preparing for Translation," will explain the use of the PROGRESS Translation Manager to prepare your application for sending to a translator for translation.
- Chapter 17, "Translating Your Application," continues where Chapter 16 left off, and explains how the PROGRESS Visual Translator can be used to translate PROGRESS 4GL code.
- Chapter 18, "Deploying Your Application Globally," will cover the last steps in actually installing and running your international application throughout the world. It discusses the remaining issues to be addressed, and how the PROGRESS environment addresses them.
- Chapter 22, "PROGRESS Programming Tips," will tell you more about dynamically changing objects, as was done in the I18N.P example above.

CHAPTER 16

Preparing for Translation

You've now designed and written your application to be capable of being deployed in other countries.

Through the use of PROGRESS 4GL functions such as `DATE`, `DAY`, `MONTH`, `YEAR`, `FORMAT`, `CAPS`, `LC`, `IS-LEAD-BYTE`, and so on, you have safeguarded the software from different countries' date formats and character set specifics. It will be much easier to deploy your application internationally because you planned for it up front.

In your UI design, you avoided culturally specific objects (or else you isolated them for ease of replacement or localization). You also made sure that you left room for translations in case they expand, and you avoided piecing together application messages. These were all good things to do. These techniques were outlined in Chapter 15.

Voice-of-Experience Movies

See Table G.3 in Appendix G, "Contents of CD," for a list of the Voice-of-Experience files for this chapter.

What's left is to translate your application. You could do this by revisiting the source code and pulling out all phrases that would require translation, but this retrofitting would be a large effort, and it would be dangerous to code stability. Alternatively, you could make a copy of the source code and simply translate all the phrases in place, but the result would be a new set of application source code for each language, and that would be a support nightmare.

The best way for you to translate the application is, in fact, to use Translation Manager 2.0, a new product in PROGRESS Version 8.

This chapter introduces you to the process and tools used to translate a PROGRESS application. It covers:

- The basic process used to translate software (regardless of the application environment)

- The components of the PROGRESS Translation Management System, and how those components match the general translation process
- The steps to be followed in the PROGRESS Translation Management System to: (1) prepare software for translation, (2) translate the software, and (3) merge the translations back into the software
- Actually preparing a sample application for translation using Translation Manager

Introduction to Translation Manager 2.0

Translation Manager 2.0 refers to two products: Translation Manager and Visual Translator. Their descriptions will follow. Since most application developers are unfamiliar with the general process of translating software, however, it is useful to review the process typically used in the industry. This is the process designed into Translation Manager 2.0 for doing translations.

The Translation Process

There are two key people in the translation process: the project manager and the translator. Figure 16.1 illustrates their responsibilities.

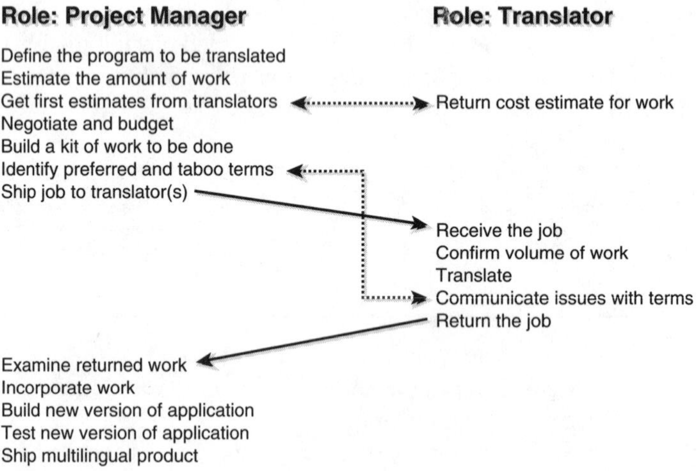
Role: Project Manager
Role: Translator
Define the program to be translated
Estimate the amount of work
Get first estimates from translators
Return cost estimate for work
Negotiate and budget
Build a kit of work to be done
Identify preferred and taboo terms
Ship job to translator(s)
Receive the job
Confirm volume of work
Translate
Communicate issues with terms
Return the job
Examine returned work
Incorporate work
Build new version of application
Test new version of application
Ship multilingual product

Fig. 16.1

Roles of the project manager and the translator.

The project manager and the translator have two very different roles, and two different skill sets.

Project Manager Responsibilities

The project manager may be managing a translation project in-house with the company's own group of translators, or may be managing a variety of third-party translators, many of them thousands of miles away. Either way, the project manager is responsible for:

- *Planning and estimating:* The project manager is responsible for estimating the volume of translation necessary, determining the number of languages to be targeted, forecasting the cost of these translations, and budgeting the effort with senior management.
- *Preparation for translation:* The project manager must gather together the source code for translation. This requires working with developers to know when the code is stable enough for translation. The project manager will also define a glossary of terms to be used by the translator when translating. Some of these terms are company-standard translations for product components. Others may be derived from a glossary of the translations used previously in hardcopy documentation or other technical publications. After all of these materials are gathered together, the project manager will build a kit to be sent out to each translator.
- *Managing the translation:* The project manager will build and send translation kits out to translators. He or she may also purchase additional software for performing and testing the translations. When issues come up with the kit (questionable terms, specific translations, schedules, and so on), the project manager must also step in.
- *Consolidating the returned translations:* The project manager is responsible for receiving the kits back from the translator(s) and incorporating the translations into the product. He or she will probably coordinate the quality assurance of the resultant product, and the deployment of a multilingual version of the application.
- *Adherence to tasks and budget:* The project manager is also responsible for ensuring that the translators provide complete translations on time and within budget.

The project manager may not be multilingual, but he or she will have fairly high technical skills in order to manage the collection of source code and the merging of translations with it.

Translator Responsibilities

The translator may or may not work for the same company as the project manager. He or she is obviously responsible for doing the translations. The translator may already have a set glossary of terms to use for doing the translation, and will want to import it into the translation process.

The translator is responsible for:

- *Receiving the translation job:* The translator will receive the kit, install necessary software, and prepare the kit on the system for translation.
- *Translating:* Obviously, the translator is responsible for doing the translations.
- *Tracking time and effort:* The translator is also responsible for tracking the billable time spent doing the translation and for producing status reports for management and for the customer.

- *Delivering the translations:* The translator must return the completed work to the project manager.

He or she will probably be PC-literate, but probably will not be proficient in the application to be translated. Obviously, the translator should be multilingual, and will typically have *native* fluency in the target translation language, with *acquired* fluency in the source language.

Now, let's see how the Translation Manager products match up to those roles in Translation Manager product terms (see fig. 16.2).

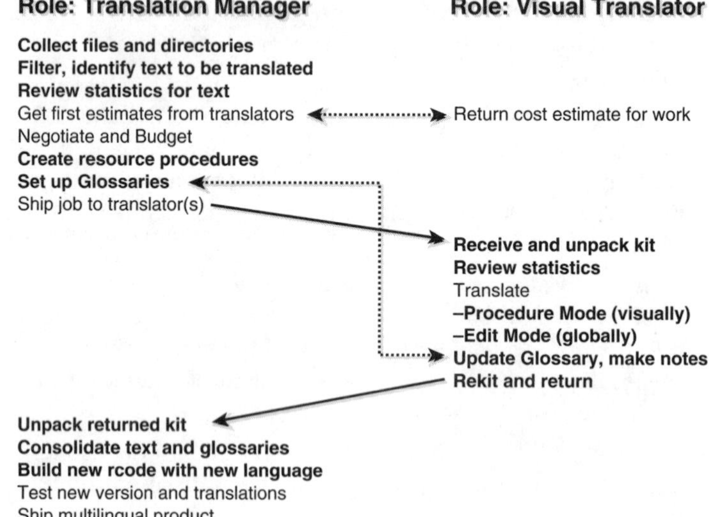
Role: Translation Manager
Role: Visual Translator
Collect files and directories
Filter, identify text to be translated
Review statistics for text
Get first estimates from translators
Return cost estimate for work
Negotiate and Budget
Create resource procedures
Set up Glossaries
Ship job to translator(s)
Receive and unpack kit
Review statistics
Translate
–Procedure Mode (visually)
–Edit Mode (globally)
Update Glossary, make notes
Rekit and return
Unpack returned kit
Consolidate text and glossaries
Build new rcode with new language
Test new version and translations
Ship multilingual product

Fig. 16.2

The Translation Manager and Visual Translator process.

Translating an Application: The Process from Start to Finish

This chapter and the next chapter introduce you to the Translation Manager products. One of the best ways to learn is by example, so these chapters take you through the process of translating the SmartObjects R Us customer application. For simplicity, you will take the simplest path through the products, accepting most of the defaults.

You will perform the following steps to create a multilingual application. Basically, you (1) prepare your application for translation, (2) translate it, and (3) consolidate the translations into your original application. More specific instructions about the phases and steps you take follow.

Preparing for Translation: Translation Manager

In the first phase of the process, the project manager prepares the source files for translation and gathers together all components that the translator needs in order to do the translation. Using Translation Manager, you:

1. Begin a new translation project.
2. Identify all the procedures for that project.
3. Extract the text to be translated.
4. Create resource procedures for that project.
5. Build or import a translation glossary.
6. View the statistical details for this project.
7. Bundle everything together into a kit for the translator.

Translating the Application: Visual Translator

In the second phase of the process, the translator takes the materials sent by the project manager, translates them, and returns them. Using Visual Translator to do this, you:

1. Unpack or open the kit.
2. Add to the translation glossary.
3. Translate all the resource procedures, using either Visual Mode or Edit Mode.
4. View the statistics.
5. Bundle and return the kit to the Project Manager.

Consolidating the Translations: Translation Manager

In the third and final phase of the process, the project manager takes the materials returned from the translator, scans the work for completeness and accuracy, and then merges (or consolidates) the translations with the application. Again using Translation Manager, you:

1. Unpack the kit.
2. Consolidate the translations.
3. Compile the program, now with translations.

By the time the final step is complete, the multilingual application is ready to deploy.

You're ready to begin. In this chapter, you're the project manager, putting together a kit of the SmartObjects R Us application to send to translators.

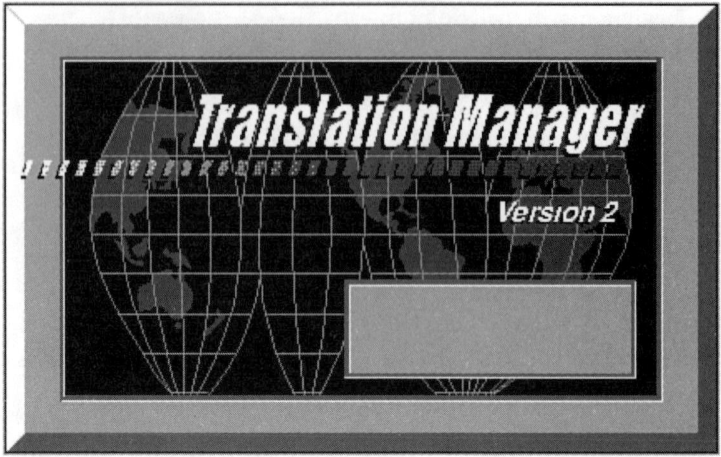

Fig. 16.3

Welcome to Translation Manager 2.0.

Translation Manager: Preparing for Translation

You start with the first phase of the process: preparing the application for translation. This involves gathering together all the source for the application, extracting the phrases to be translated from that source, incorporating a preferred set of pretranslated terms (if available), and bundling all materials together into a kit to send to the translator.

Starting the Translation Manager

You start Translation Project Manager by clicking the Translation Manager icon found in the PROGRESS Desktop, or by selecting it from the Tools menu from any PROGRESS application. Upon invoking the program, you enter the folder-based interface with the following screen:

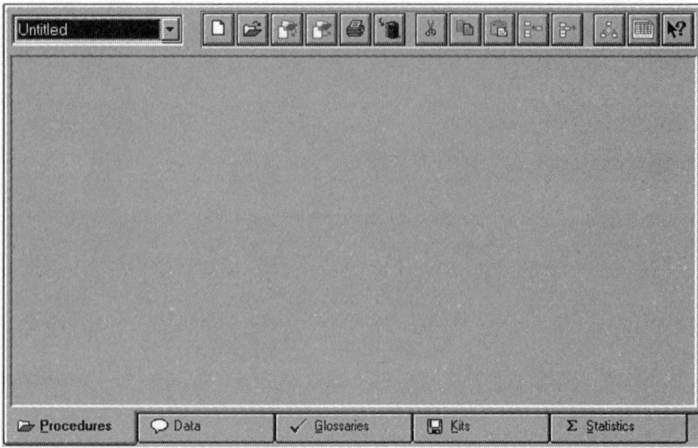

Fig. 16.4

Translation Manager opening screen.

There are five tab folders that are the interface to Translation Manager. The project manager uses this program for outbound work (building the kit and sending it to the translator), and inbound work (receiving the finished work from the translators and using the translations during the consolidation and compilation phase). The five tab folders are used for the tasks described in the following sections.

Procedures

Outbound—This tab controls the management of the PROGRESS procedures being added or removed from a kit.

Inbound—This tab is where the translator's returned work is used to create a multilingual version of the application by the project manager.

Data

This tab controls the extraction of text phrases to be translated from the identified procedures. Within this tab, the project manager also has control over the filters used to extract the text phrases. Resource procedures used by the Visual Translator are also created here.

Glossaries

This tab controls the creation of glossaries to be sent to the translator for use. In this folder, glossaries may be input by hand, and external glossaries may be imported into Translation Manager (including the many Microsoft Language Glossaries packaged with Translation Manager).

Kits

Outbound—This tab is used for bundling the translation kit into a form convenient for sending to the translator.

Inbound—This tab is used for consolidating the returned kit from the translator back into the translation project database. It's here that the project manager receives updates and resolves discrepancies in translations.

Within this kit dialog, it's also possible to invoke compression software to reduce the volume of data (the size of kits) being sent to and received from the translator.

Statistics

This tab is extremely helpful to the project manager. Data gathered during the kit building and data extraction phases is displayed here. The project manager can use this information for estimating the volume, effort, and cost for translations.

Following the display order of these five tab folders, you will walk through the process of generating a kit for translation.

Translation Manager comes up in the Procedures Tab by default. This is where you will start.

Building a New Project: Procedures Tab

You are creating a new translation project, so you select the File, New menu option, and fill in the New Project creation dialog, as shown in figure 16.5.

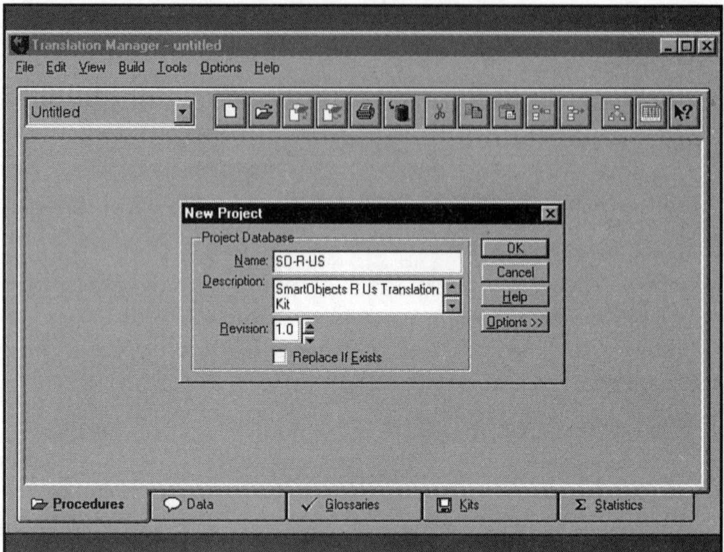

Fig. 16.5

Creating a new translation project.

Name the project SO-R-US. The project name must be limited to eight characters, because the name will be used to create databases and support files.

The default Revision for a new project is 1.0. You can assign a different number (useful if this project is for an updated version of the application), but because this is a new project and product, 1.0 is fine. The revision is used to track changes and iterations to the translation process.

Finally, there is a Replace If Exists toggle. The default is not to overwrite existing projects and databases.

You are now presented with the Procedure template. It will be empty to start.

Identify All the Procedures for the Project

Working in this tab, you can begin to add PROGRESS code modules to the translation kit. Click on the Add button to start the process. There are two choices for adding code: file by file, or by directory.

In this case, you will add an entire directory. The application files are stored in c:\appdir, and the dialog box appears as in figure 16.6.

Translation Manager will search for all modules with standard PROGRESS code extensions, namely .P and .W. If you follow a different naming convention for source files, you can add your file naming extensions to the search criteria.

Translation Manager will search for and add all the files in the directory as specified, and will summarize its finding in an Information window. In this case, Translation Manager found 9 procedures.

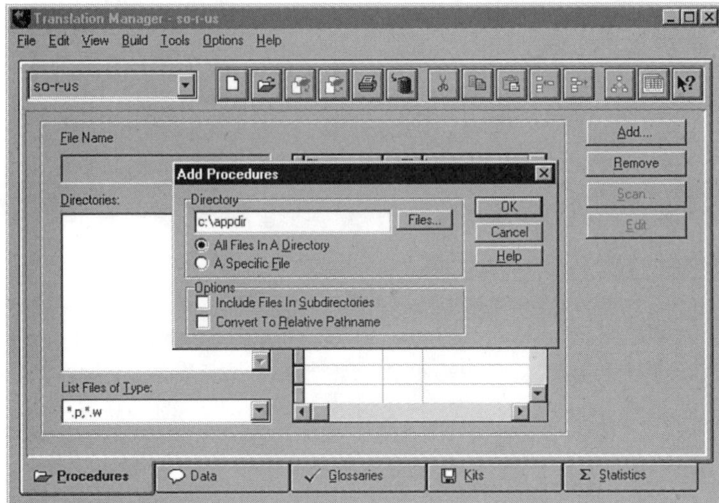

Fig. 16.6

Adding procedures to the project.

Now your procedure list is filled with all of the modules that comprise the SmartObjects R Us application, as seen in figure 16.7.

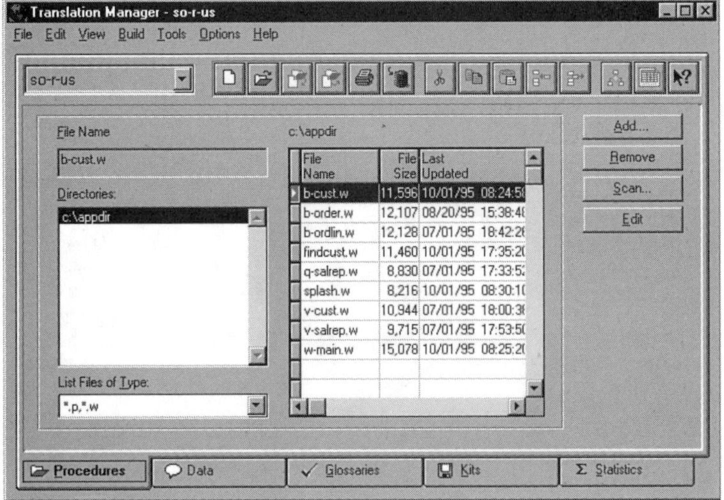

Fig. 16.7

The application modules to be translated in this translation project.

At this point, you could continue adding more modules, or you could remove specific modules already extracted. It is now time to gather the text phrases to be translated by extracting them from the procedures you just identified. To do this, you move on to the Data tab.

Extract the Text to be Translated

When you move into the Data tab, you are presented with an empty template for displaying the phrases to be translated.

You click on the Extract button to begin extracting the phrases from the procedures added to the project.

> **Tip**
>
> It really makes no difference whether you click the Extract button or the Filters button above it.
>
> No filters have been defined yet for controlling the extraction. Filters specify which text phrases from certain 4GL commands are to be extracted and which ones are to be ignored. An advanced user might actually click on the Filters button first to tailor the filters for extraction.
>
> After advanced users have achieved the proper filter settings for their coding style, they will probably use the same filter settings (stored in an .xrf file named <projname>.xrf) for each translation project, and advanced users would also skip over the Filters button as well.

The Extract dialog is shown in figure 16.8.

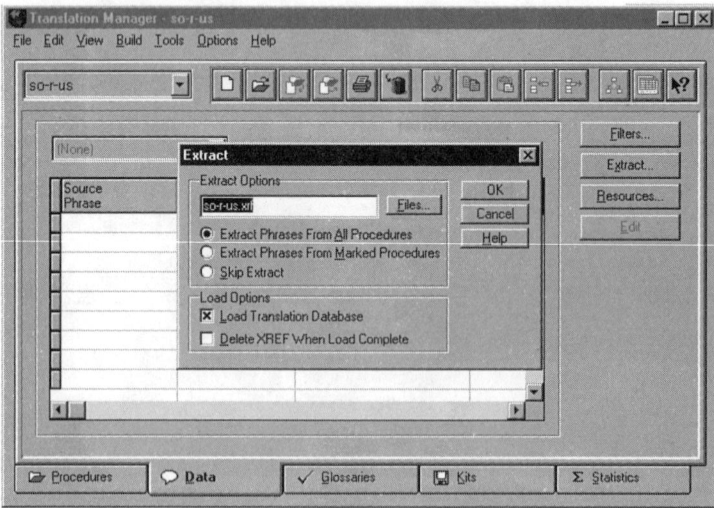

Fig. 16.8

Extract dialog in the Data tab.

When you click the Extract button for the first time, Translation Manager brings up the Filter Wizard, a simple mechanism for seeing and possibly modifying the default filters chosen for extracting phrases. Text phrases are found in many 4GL statements, from MESSAGES to FORMATS to INPUTS, and so on. Many of these text phrases are not necessary for translation. The filtering mechanism allows you to ignore those phrases when building a kit for the translator. The first of 12 Filter Wizard screens is shown in figure 16.9.

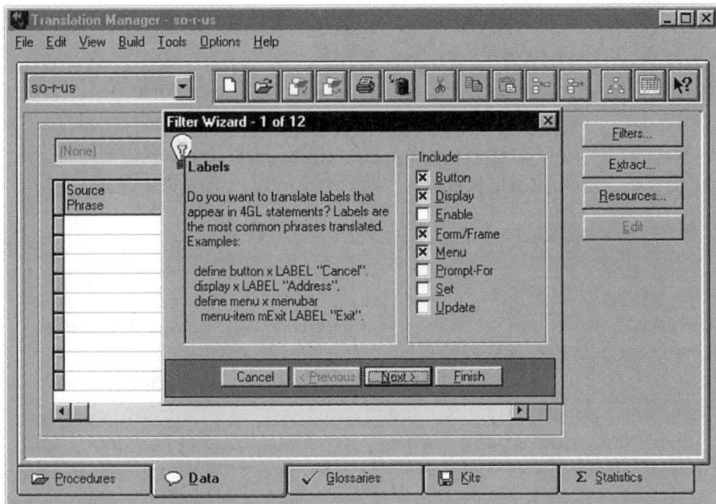

Fig. 16.9

The Filter Wizard opening screen.

The Filter Wizard has 12 screens that allow you to change the filter settings. Because this is your first time through the process, you will not change any settings and you will retain all the defaults. You can either step through the filter settings to see the choices, or you can click the Finish button to skip through the Wizard. Either way, at the final Filter Wizard screen, you will click on the Apply button, and you will be accepting the default choices offered and adding filter settings to the project database, as shown in figure 16.10.

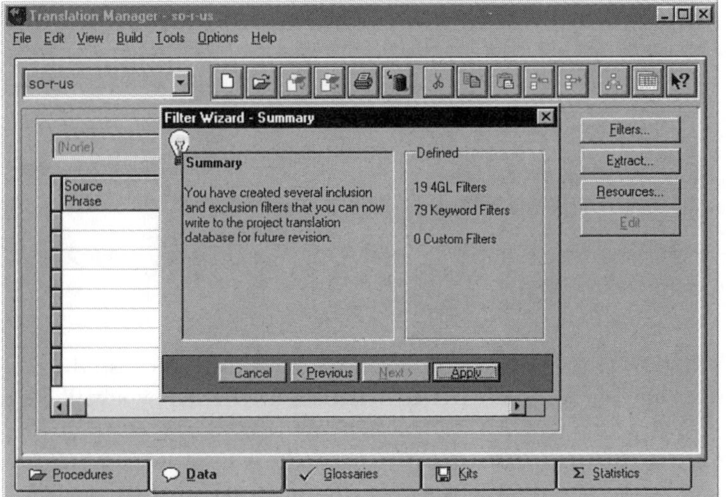

Fig. 16.10

Final screen for Filter Wizard.

V

Internationalization

Note

All of the 4GL keywords and default filter settings are listed in Appendix D, "Internationalization."

Having selected and applied filter choices to the project, you return to the Extract dialog. You have control over how many steps the extraction process should do right now. Extraction actually involves compiling all of the source procedures to extract the strings into a Translation Manager specific string xref file, applying the filters to all the phrases found, and then adding the selected ones to the project database.

Note

Actually, this is not completely accurate. Translation Manager will, in some cases, add strings into the project database that are supposedly filtered off. This is to enable Visual Translator to visualize the procedures as closely as possible. Although a particular text phrase is not to be translated, it may play a role in the look and feel of the dialog being translated, and you will want to see it. Take, for example, your company name, "SmartObjects R Us." This string could be filtered as "don't translate," but it is still brought along in the project database.

You choose to do the entire process in one step, and leave the default toggles to extract the phrases and load the translation database.

Tip

In the Extract dialog, there's a toggle giving you control over whether Translation Manager should delete the xref file once the extraction is complete. If you want to examine the Translation Manager string xref file, you should accept the default, retaining the xref file.

The string xref file is *not* the same file as the compiler xref file. The string xref file contains very detailed, specific information about the strings in your procedures. This information was not added to the compiler xref file, in order to avoid adding confusion to it. Many people examine that file and have built analysis programs around that file; changing it would have had negative side effects.

The Translation Manager string xref file is named <projname>.xrf, though you can override that name in the Extract dialog. You can also create it when compiling a file directly by adding the STRING-XREF <filename> directive to the compiler statement.

This string xref file can be rather large and, in most cases, you'll choose to delete it after you have built all kits to be sent to translators.

The extraction process now takes place. Because you specified that you wish the phrases to be extracted and loaded in the project database in one step, you will see two status meters: an Extracting meter and a Loading meter. Because some processes in Translation Manager and Visual Translator may be lengthy, status meters will frequently inform you of how a step is progressing.

> **Note**
>
> Translation Manager requires that you are connected to all databases that need to be connected in order to build the kit. This is because the procedures must be capable of compiling. Translation Manager will remind you to connect before continuing. If you are not connected, you can back up and connect now using the Database Connect icon in the Translation Manager toolbar.

After the extraction is completed, you are presented with a Statistics window summarizing the results of the process. You see the total number of phrases extracted, and the number and percentage of them loaded into the database. This is a good indication of how much data the phrase filters left behind (see fig. 16.11). In this case, approximately 35 percent of the phrases were filtered away.

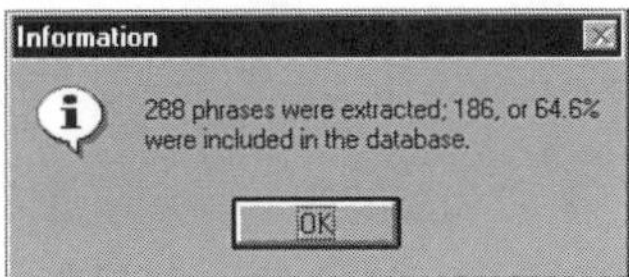

Fig. 16.11

Information Window: a summary of the extraction process.

This information points out a major benefit of Translation Manager. Because translators are typically paid by the word, the cleaner you can make the data through filtering out unnecessary text, the less costly doing the translations will be.

Now the Data tab window is filled with data (see fig. 16.12). Each translatable, nonfiltered source phrase has been added to the translation project database, along with information about the procedure from which it came, the number of occurrences of this phrase in that procedure, the line number of the occurrence, the length of the text phrase, and the statement type that generated or included that phrase.

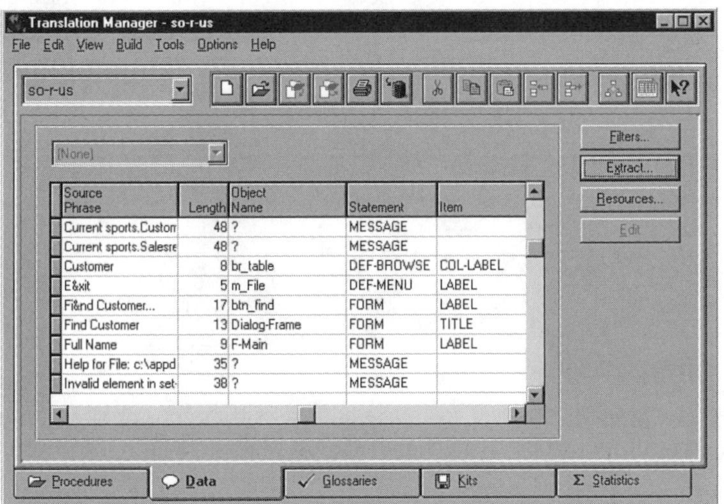

Fig. 16.12

A Data tab filled with phrases to be translated.

Not all fields of data are immediately visible in the browser. You can scroll across columns or down rows to see pertinent data. Or, you can change the display order of the fields in the browser.

Tip

Reviewing the phrases and the 4GL statements that generated them can be a good thing to do right now. You just extracted the text phrases by using the default filter settings. It might be useful to see exactly which phrases were extracted, and from which statement types they came. You might see that there are additional statement types that should be excluded (filtered out). This is very dependent on individual programming styles, and this is why such precise selectivity is given to you.

By reordering the columns to be Source Phrase, Statement, and Item, you can determine which filters to apply.

Choose the menu item View Order Columns, and specify a new column order in the Order Columns dialog. All possible columns are listed in a selection list, and you choose Source Phrase, followed by Statement, followed by Item.

For simplicity, assume that the phrases extracted and loaded are fine, and move on to the next step.

Creating Resource Procedures for the Kit

It is now time to create resource procedures for all those modules. Resource procedures are mock-ups of the real procedures that you wish to translate. They are used by the Visual Translator to imitate the original procedures, allowing the translator to visualize each screen, SmartObject, and so on. Resource procedures are like the original procedures except that they have had all logic and database access removed; what remains is the user interface portion.

To create resource procedures, click on the Resources button and you will be presented with the dialog shown in figure 16.13.

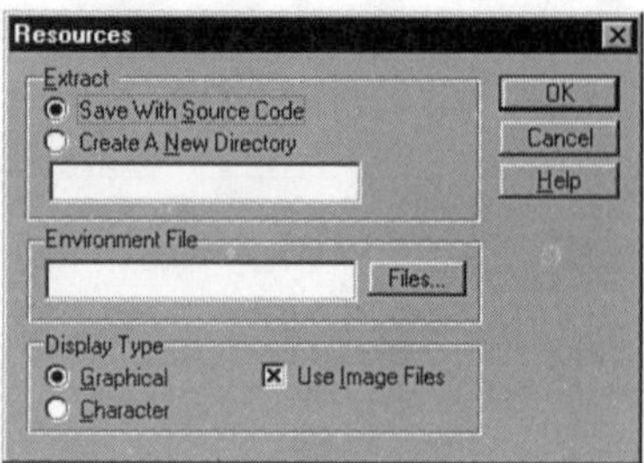

Fig. 16.13

Resources procedure dialog box.

You need to be sure that you are attached to all the databases that your program uses before the resource procedures can be created. Translation Manager will remind you of this.

There are certain selections you can make in this dialog:

- You can choose to save the resource procedures in the same directory with the source code, or you can place them in a separate directory. You should probably save them in a separate directory in order to keep files generated for translation purposes separate from files necessary for deploying your application. Here, however, you will save them with the source code to keep the example simple.
- If you use a different PROGRESS.INI file for your application (for font selections, colors, and so on), you should list it here in the Environment File fill-in, and it will be sent along with the project kit to the translator. This is needed if Visual Translator is to display an accurate facsimile of your application.
- If your application is a character-mode application, selecting Display Type Character will compile the resource procedures to render a character look. The default is Graphical.
- Finally, if your application uses image files (logos, icons, pictures, etc.), you should select the toggle Use Image Files. Again, you want the translator to see your application at translation time the way you see it when it is really running.

While Translation Manager is creating resource procedures, you will be given the status of the task. Translation Manager will display a status meter Creating Resource Files so that you know it is working.

When the process is complete, a final statistics screen will summarize the work accomplished. In figure 16.14, you see that eight resource procedures were created.

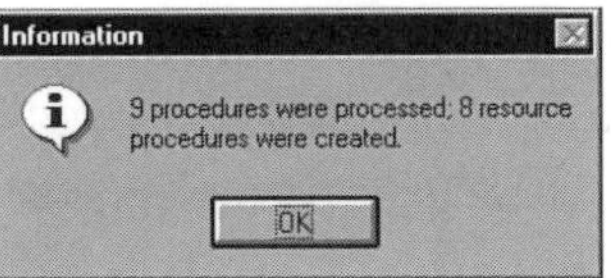

Fig. 16.14

Summary of the resource creation process.

Note that the Information window tells you that although nine procedures were processed, only eight have resource files created for them. Why would this be?

One way to find out is to go back to the Procedures tab and look at the file list browser. Doing so, you scroll through the columns until you get to the "Resources Generated?" column, and find that the procedure `q-sale_c.w` has no resource procedure.

This actually makes sense because `q-sale_w` is a query object and has no run-time visualized user interface to translate.

Having identified all procedures and text phrases to be translated, it is now time to build the glossary to be sent to the translator(s).

Building a Translation Glossary

Many companies have an established glossary of translations set up for frequently used terms. This glossary can come from hardcopy documentation previously translated, or from previously translated software. If such a glossary exists, the project manager will want to supply it to the translator, so that product translations are consistent with previous translations in other product components or revisions. In this step, you create a glossary to be sent to the translator.

> **Note**
>
> This is not absolutely necessary, and some companies have no glossary to provide to a translator. In this case, you could simply go on to the next step, although there is still a good reason to continue here. Translation Manager comes with built-in glossaries of software terms for certain languages, and it can't hurt to provide the translator with a head start.

First, select the Glossary tab. It comes up empty.

Say that you wish to add items to a glossary. This can be done term by term, but that is an arduous task. For simplicity, you will create a glossary using basic terms already supplied with Translation Manager. You click on the Add. button to bring up the Add Glossary dialog.

You fill in some fields requested in the Add Glossary dialog. This includes the name, source language, and target language for translations. In this case, you will create a glossary named English-to-French, which will hold terms that allow translation from English to French. Finally, you choose the toggle box to Include Microsoft Glossaries to add any terms which might be automatically supplied by Translation Manager.

When you click on the selection box for Include Microsoft Glossaries, another dialog automatically appears, as seen in figure 16.15.

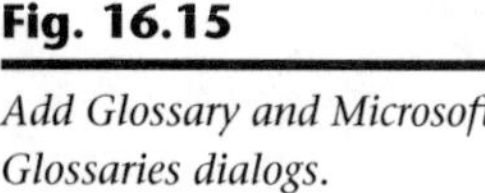

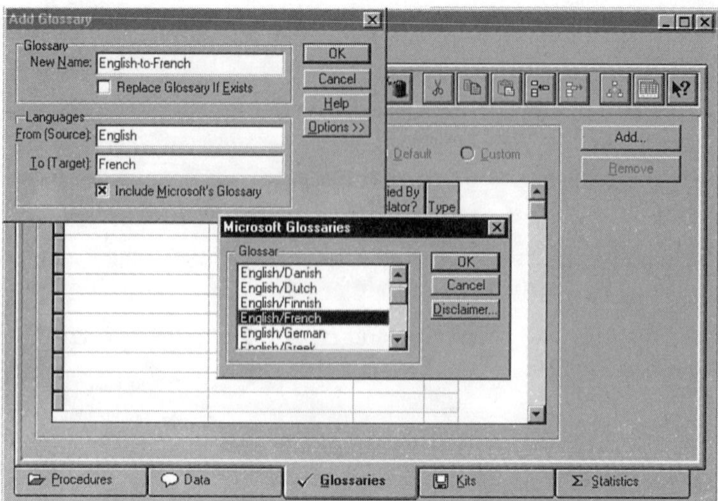

Fig. 16.15

Add Glossary and Microsoft Glossaries dialogs.

Translation Manager incorporates more than a dozen Microsoft glossaries. These glossaries vary in content from 400 items (for example Czech and Russian) to more than 5,000 items (for example Portuguese).

The glossaries are the same glossaries used by Microsoft for translating Microsoft applications such as Word and Excel. If you used similar terms in your translation, you will benefit from these glossaries.

Note

Progress has obtained the right to reproduce and incorporate these glossaries in the Translation Manager product, and they are provided at no additional cost.

See Appendix D for a complete list of the glossaries provided as of this printing, along with the number of phrases included in each. As more glossaries are made available from Microsoft, Progress intends to incorporate those as well.

Tip

Microsoft makes these glossaries available via FTP and in *The GUI Guide* (see Appendix D). Legal terminology accompanying those glossaries states that you may not publish them without the express permission of Microsoft. They are available for your own use, however. Occasionally checking Microsoft's address on CompuServe may turn up a new glossary before Progress re-releases it in Translation Manager. You would use the EXPORT function to incorporate it. It may take some massaging, however, depending on the format made available from Microsoft.

Select the Microsoft English/French glossary, and the terms from the built-in glossary will begin to load.

Again, this can take a minute or two, so Translation Manager provides a meter displaying the percentage completed and the terms being loaded.

After the loading has finished, Translation Manager gives you the summary statistics. Now you have a glossary full of terms. The browser in the Glossary tab is populated with translation data. This will be sent to the translator in the kit, and may be used to speed the translation as well as ensure that translations are consistent across the application.

Knowing that you will also send kits out to Swedish and German translators, you now click on the Add button to create two more glossaries for English-to-Swedish and English-to-German, and again use the Microsoft glossaries.

Now you have three language glossaries loaded. Using the browser, you can scroll through and see the Source and Target Phrases in the glossary. Figure 16.16 displays the English-to-French Glossary.

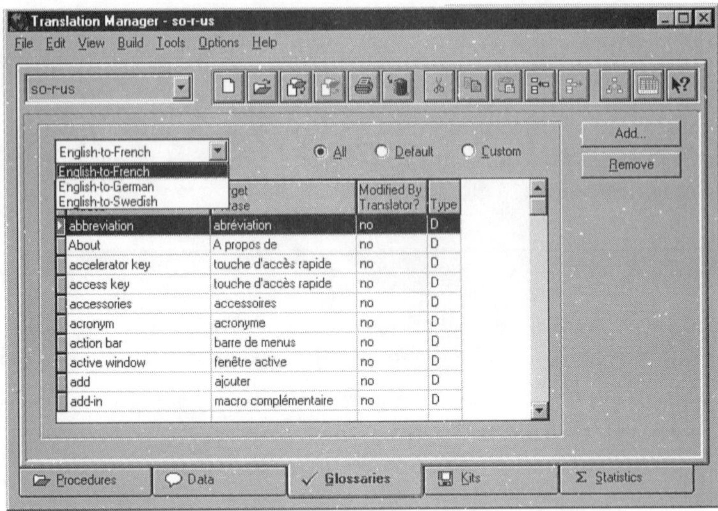

Fig. 16.16

French Glossary to be used for translations.

You are now ready to prepare the kits for the translators. But before you do this, it might be beneficial to take a look at how much data you have gathered together in the project.

Viewing the Statistical Details for This Project

This is not a mandatory step, but it is informative. Selecting the Tab folder Statistics, you can see information about the project. As seen in Figure 16.17, you see the number of procedures and, more importantly, the number of words and phrases to be translated.

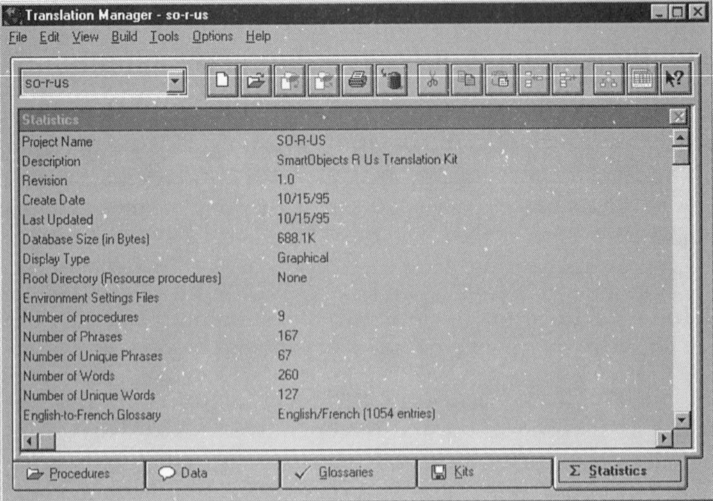

Fig. 16.17

Statistics for this translation kit.

The count of words and phrases is extremely useful. At this point, you know the magnitude of the translation project and can use this data to bid and schedule work with translators, as well as budget the expense internally.

Tip

Now is when you contact the potential translation services with estimates of the number of words and phrases to be translated. Take note that two numbers are reported: the total number of words and phrases and the number of *unique* words and phrases. Using Visual Translator, it should be necessary to translate a word or phrase only once, though the translator may visually inspect the translation in a number of places. Keep this in mind when negotiating.

You have performed a number of steps so far, and you are just about done preparing your application for translation. You have identified all the procedures to be translated. You have extracted the phrases to be translated, using a powerful filtering mechanism. You have built resource programs to help the translator visualize your application, and you have built a glossary of translations for the translator to use. You're now ready to bundle all these materials into a kit for the translator. You will send that kit, along with Visual Translator, to the translator for him or her to do the job.

Bundling Everything Together into a Kit

You now go to the Kits tab. This is where all kit management takes place. Using this tab, you will generate kits to be sent out to translators, and later you will also use it to consolidate those kits after they've been sent back to you from the translators.

Again, the tab comes up with an empty template, so you click on the Add button to create a kit, and name it FrenchKt. Because the name of the kit will be used to create a database, the kit name must be eight characters or fewer. Using the selection list for the Glossary Name, you choose the English-to-French glossary from the three glossaries you created earlier. The Add Kit dialog is pictured in figure 16.18.

Fig. 16.18

Adding a kit.

The kit gets added to the list of kit lists. You will repeat this step for the German and Swedish kits to be sent to the other translators. You follow the same steps although you will incorporate a different glossary. The new kits created will be GermanKt and SwedshKt.

Note

In the list of kits, all the kits have a status of NO under the ZIP column. It is possible to create a compressed version of the kit. This accomplishes two tasks: first, it makes a much smaller, self-contained file. Second, it maintains the necessary directory structure for Visual Translator to find everything.

The kits have now been completed. In your working directory, there are databases called FRENCHKT.DB, GERMANKT.DB, and SWEDSHKT.DB, containing information that should be sent to the translators along with Visual Translator.

The resource procedures that were created, and the PROGRESS.INI necessary for the application (if different), will also need to be sent. If the kit was zipped, this will happen automatically. If not, then these files will need to be copied by hand.

Tip

Translation Manager creates a file, called zipkit.lis, which lists all the files necessary to be sent to the translator. It is placed in the working directory.

You can take one last look at the Statistics tab, and scroll down to see the kit information. You see the three glossaries and their volume, as well as the three kits created. This will help in tracking what you've sent out. The Statistics Tab is seen in figure 16.19.

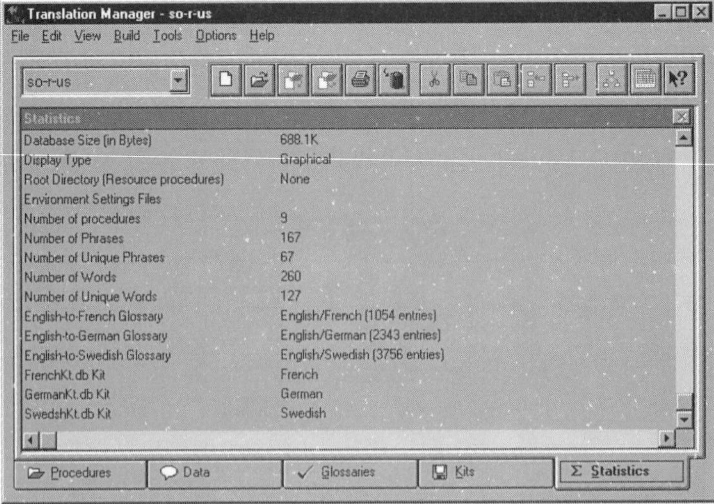

Fig. 16.19

List of kits and glossaries.

From here, you could start the Visual Translator, open the kit you have just created, and begin translation. You would do this when you do translation in-house and on the same system.

Typically, this is not the case, and translation will take place in another company. The translator will receive, load, and open your kit in order to begin translation. That process will be documented in the next chapter.

Advanced Topics—Tailoring Filters

You followed the simplest path through Translation Manager to create a translation kit.

At Step 3, Extracting the text to be translated, you chose the default filters as specified by the Filter Wizard. This generated a list of phrases to be sent to the translator.

As noted previously, you can look through the text extracted and look for text that does not need to be translated. If there are one or two text phrases, they can be directly deleted out of the list by selecting that row and deleting it. The row will then not be included in any kit.

If, however, many text phrases could be removed, it is a good investment of your time to determine their source. If you simply remove them by hand, then the next time that you kit this project for translation, or when you build kits for the next application project, they will reappear.

By sorting the Data Tab browser by Source Phrase, then Statement Type, then Item, you can see which 4GL statements were generating that text. Because every application developer or company has a different programming style, different keywords will generate unwanted strings for different people.

If you spot a particular statement that is generating unwanted strings, you can reenter the Filter Wizard by clicking on the Filters button in the Data Tab. Stepping through the screens, you can find the offending keyword, remove it from the list, and then apply the new keyword filters in the final screen.

Tip

If you plan to iteratively tailor your filter settings, it is important to note the steps built into the extract process. First, the procedures are compiled and *all* the text is extracted and placed in the string xref file. After this, the filters are applied to the string xref file, and the project database is loaded.

In the Extract dialog, you only need to Extract the phrases once (to create the string xref file). If you change the filter settings, when you reenter the Extract Dialog, choose the Skip Extract radio button, and you will avoid a lengthy and unnecessary process. You must load the database each time to see which phrases have been filtered.

Obviously, you should not choose the toggle Delete XREF When Load Complete if you plan to modify filters and reload the translation database.

From Here...

In this chapter, you have learned the translation process, and you have completed phase one of a three phase process. You have prepared your application for translation, and you have built kits to be sent to translators to translate your application.

Next, you will follow the translation process through the second and third phases: translating the application, and merging the translations back into the application, respectively. Both of these phases are covered in Chapter 17, "Translating Your Application."

For more details on topics covered in the first phase, Preparing for Translation:

- For more information on filters, see Appendix D, "Internationalization." The list of all user-selectable phrase filters available during the Extract process in Translation Manager may be found here.
- For more information on reserved keywords, see Appendix D, "Internationalization." *Reserved Keywords* are specific words or phrases which are used by the PROGRESS programming language, which should probably not be translated, and which are filtered out by Translation Manager by default.
- For more information on the Microsoft glossaries included with Translation Manager, see Appendix D, "Internationalization." Each glossary is listed, along with the number of entries contained in the glossary.

CHAPTER 17

Translating Your Application

Translating an application takes place in three stages with the PROGRESS Translation Management System. The first phase, preparing the application for translation, involves gathering the application components together, identifying the text phrases to be translated, and bundling the materials into a "kit" to be sent out to translators. This was covered in Chapter 16, "Preparing for Translation." In that chapter, you prepared the "Smart Objects R Us" application for translation and created a kit for a French translator.

The second and third phases—translating the application and consolidating translations—will be covered in this chapter. Following the steps for the second and third phases in this chapter, you will create a multilingual application.

In this chapter, you will learn:

- How to translate application modules visually
- How to translate text phrases in a global edit mode
- How to return the translation kit to the project manager
- How to consolidate the translations into the original application
- How to run and deploy the newly created multilingual application

Voice of Experience Movies

See Table G.3 in Appendix G, "Contents of CD," for a list of the Voice-of-Experience files for this chapter.

In Chapter 16 (phase one), you played the role of the project manager to generate the translation kit. In this chapter, you will play two roles. In phase two, you will be the translator translating the application. In phase three, you will again be the project manager consolidating the translator's work and building the application for two languages.

Translating with Visual Translator

Now you are in Paris, and you are the translator hired to put the application into French. You have been sent the tool, PROGRESS Visual Translator, along with a "kit" file called Frenchkt from the project manager. According to the project manager, the kit contains the text phrases to be translated, a preloaded glossary for you to use, and some support files to help you see how the application appears.

You load Visual Translator onto your PC, and you restore the French kit to your system.

> **Note**
>
> For now, this chapter will ignore the mechanics of loading the software and the kit, since the more important point is how to translate the application. Information on transferring kits between project manager and translator will be covered in the Advanced Topics section.

You are now ready to begin the translation. The major tasks you perform to translate an application can be summed up as follows:

1. Open the translation kit sent to you.
2. Add to the translation glossary.
3. Translate all the resource procedures, using either a visual mode or an edit mode.
4. View the statistics.
5. Bundle and return the kit to the project manager.

The following sections cover each of these tasks in detail. To start the translation process, you will start Visual Translator (see fig. 17.1). Starting Visual Translator can be done by clicking on it in the PROGRESS Desktop, clicking on the Visual Translator icon outside of the Desktop, or by pulling it down from the Tools Menu.

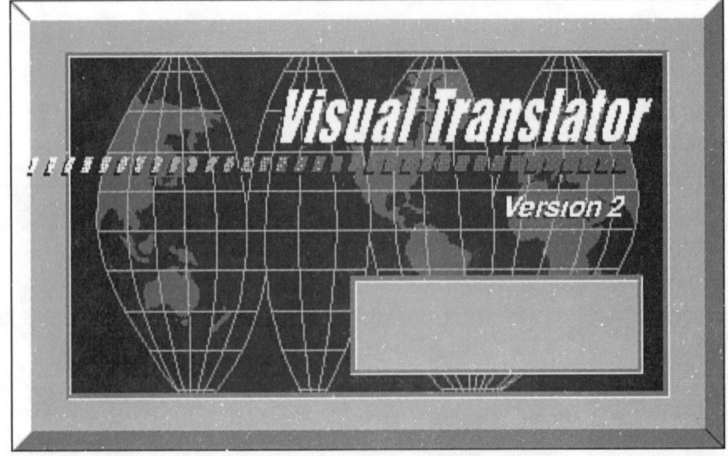
Visual Translator
Version 2

Fig. 17.1

Welcome to Visual Translator 2.0.

The opening screen of Visual Translator, shown in fig. 17.2, is empty, and you begin in the Procedures Tab. Visual Translator has the same look and feel as Translation Manager, and is made up of four tabs: Procedures, Translations, Glossaries, and Statistics. These tabs are for the following tasks:.

Procedures
This tab lists the modules to be translated, and reports the status of the translation effort so far on a module-by-module basis. It will also be used to invoke the visual mode for performing translations.

Translations
This tab contains the text phrases to be translated, along with translations which have been applied to those text phrases. It is used to translate the phrases in edit mode.

Glossaries
This tab contains the glossary used for performing translations. Source phrase—Translated phrase pairs are displayed here. This glossary continues to grow as translations are performed.

Statistics
This tab contains information about the translation effort. The translator will use it to confirm the size of the translation effort, and to track the progress.

These tab folders are similar to those found in the Translation Manager tool (see Chapter 16, "Preparing for Translation.").

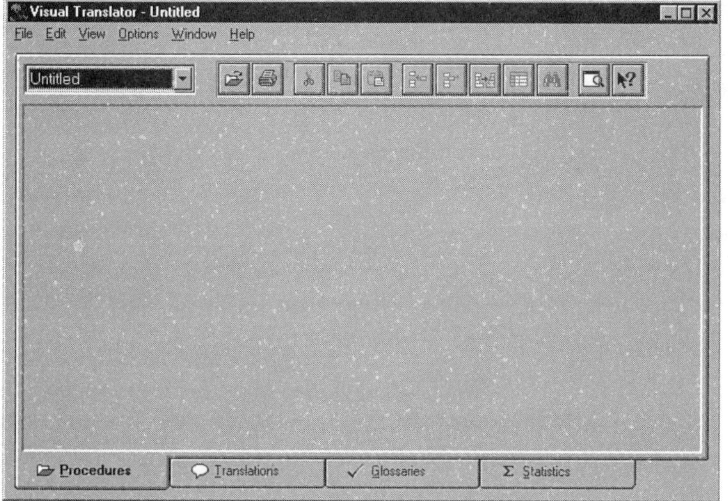

Fig. 17.2
Visual Translator Main Interface

Opening the Kit

To begin, you will open the kit named Frenchkt. This kit was built by the project manager in the previous chapter, and has now been sent to you. Opening the kit is done by pulling down the File menu and choosing Open (similar to Open dialog boxes found in most Windows applications).

After it is loaded, you are in the Procedures tab and see a list of procedures that you are to translate (see fig. 17.3).

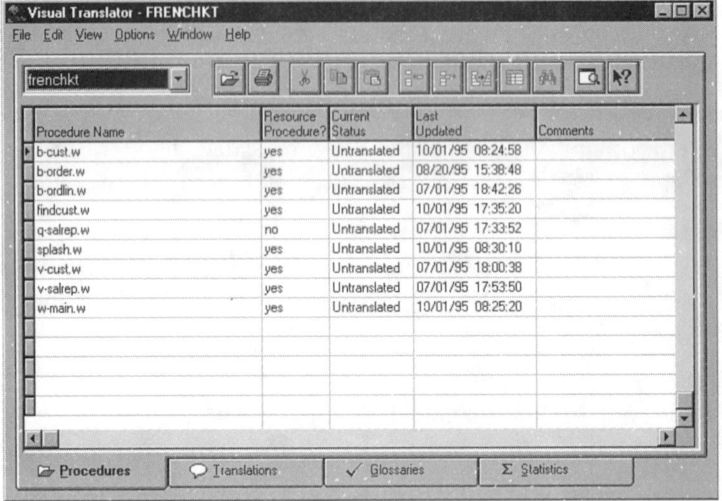

Fig. 17.3

The Procedures tab shows the list of procedures to translate.

Adding to the Translation Glossary

As an experienced translator, you know that the more automatic you can make the translation, the less time it will take you. That is to say, you can save time by not having to construct translations from scratch. If you have a collection of standard translations, you would like the program to use them. You go to the Glossaries tab (see fig 17.4), and examine the translations already sent to you for use.

Although there appear to be a few hundred supplied translations here, you have your own glossary, which you feel will be even more useful, and so you would like to incorporate your glossary with this one.

You choose Import from the File menu, and fill in the Import dialog box box shown in figure 17.5. The name of the file containing your own glossary is c:\appdir\eng-fre.glo, and you specify this in the File Name field.

It is important to specify to the import mechanism the codepage in which your data is stored. *Codepages* are specific encodings for data, and vary from language to language and from operating system to operating system. Visual Translator must be told the codepage of the data you wish to import so that it will be read in correctly. Most translators are aware of the codepage used by their language and system. In this case, you will accept the default of ISO8859-1, the codepage for Western European editions of UNIX, and a virtual match to the codepage also used by Microsoft Windows.

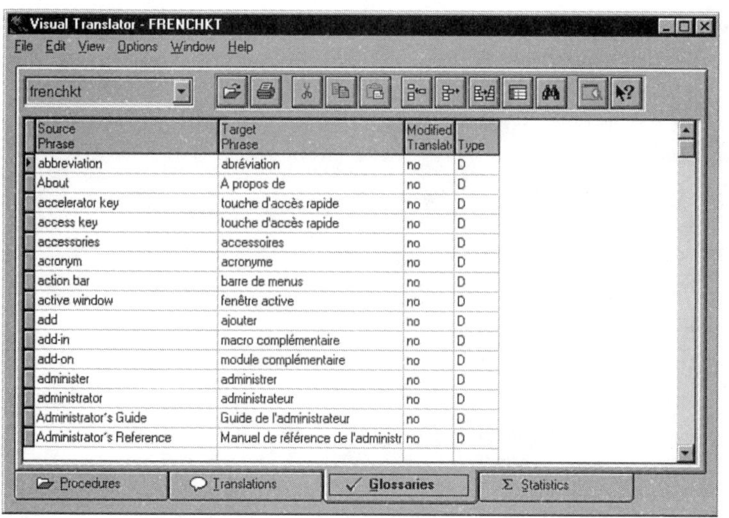

Fig. 17.4

The Glossaries tab shows the glossaries already set up.

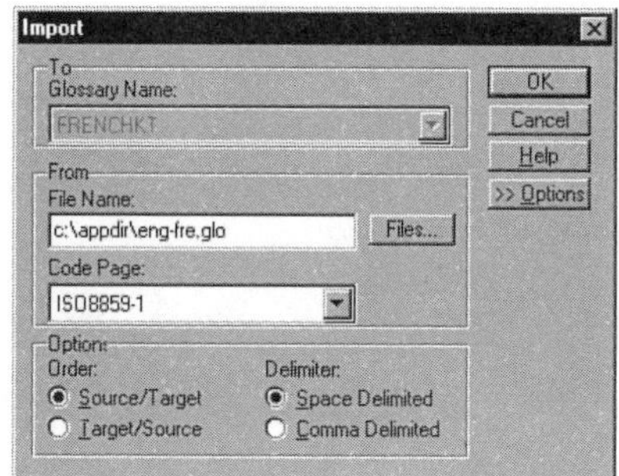

Fig. 17.5

The Import dialog box.

Note

Codepages were discussed briefly in Chapter 14, "Designing Your Global Application," and are discussed in great detail in Chapter 18, "Deploying Your Application Globally."

The import mechanism is capable of handling external text files organized in standard ways. Typically, source and translation strings are separated by either a space ("space-delimited quoted strings") or by commas ("comma-delimited files"). Your file is space-delimited, and the order of the phrases is Source (English) phrase, followed by Native (French) phrase. You designate this by selecting the appropriate radio buttons in the Import dialog box.

The import program opens this file, parses the text (while displaying a status meter since this can be a lengthy process), and returns a final summary status for the import process.

You will see that your terms have been added to the glossary. If you look at the Glossary column Type, the letter types will tell you what comes by default from the project manager, and what comes from your glossary. "D" stands for the Default glossary shipped to you; "C" stands for your Custom glossary. Any term imported into the project and any translation you interactively create will be marked "C." Now you are ready to perform the translations.

Translating the Resource Procedures

There are two modes for translating: visual mode and edit mode. Each mode has benefits for the translator.

In visual mode, you use the resource files (mock-ups) of the original procedures to translate the text phrases in situ. That is to say, you see the objects to be translated (buttons, labels, fields, etc.) exactly as they appear in the real application, and when you translate the text, you see it immediately appear on that object. This lets you see how your translations will appear on the screen when they are merged with the original application. You can see how the text phrases relate to other text phrases on the screen, and you can see if a translation will fit (on a button, for example).

In edit mode, you work directly with the text phrases and translate them field by field (or globally) without seeing how they appear in a mock-up screen. Edit mode is done using the new Version 8 browser, thus providing a "spreadsheet-like" interface. It is useful when the same phrase is used many times throughout the application and you only need to translate it once.

It is very easy to swap between the two modes, as you will do later.

You'll start with a simple program to translate: the splash screen for the application. Go to the Procedures tab shown in figure 17.6, and pick the splash.w procedure by clicking on the browser row handle, and then double-clicking on that row. You can alternatively choose View Procedure from the View menu.

You now see a mock-up of the splash.w routine you wish to translate. You will first translate the "Continue" button at the bottom. To do this, you double-click on the button object, and a Properties Window appears, as shown in figure 17.7.

> **Note**
>
> The Visualized procedure window and the Properties window may be moved around the screen for ease of reading.

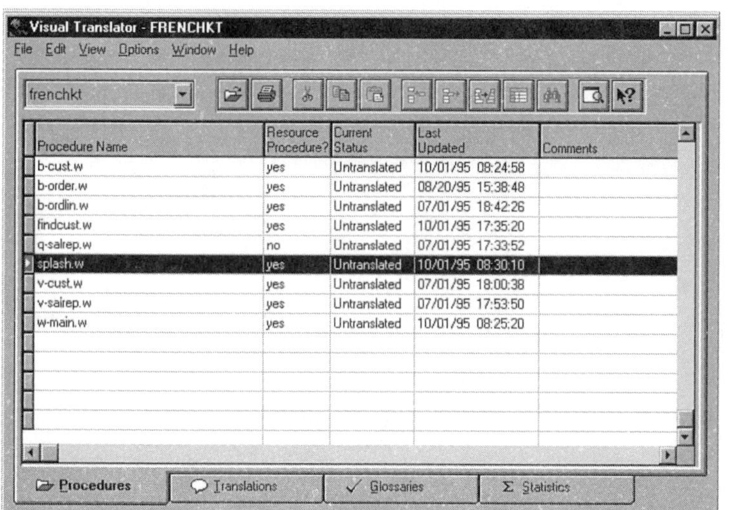

Fig. 17.6

Selecting a procedure to visualize and translate.

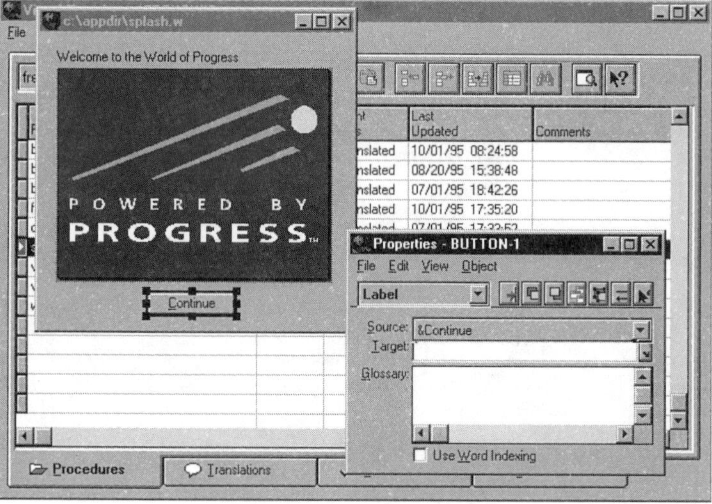

Fig. 17.7

A visualized procedure, with properties window, ready to translate

There are no translations offered by the glossary for the word "Continue," so you enter the translation by hand. You enter the French "Continuer" into the Properties window, and it is immediately reflected in the mocked-up resource procedure, as seen in figure 17.8. In this way, you can see the button in context, and can see that the translation you chose fits in the button object. If it hadn't, you would have either had to select a shorter translation, or you would have had to ask the project manager to make the button bigger.

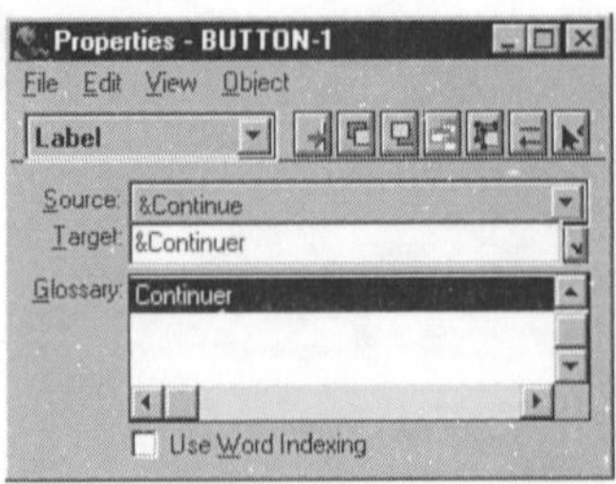

Fig. 17.8

The translation is immediately visualized.

You now can move to another phrase to be translated by selecting the Next Object/ Previous Object interface found in the Object menu. Or you could simply click on another object. In this case, the next object is "Welcome to the World of Progress," which you translate to "Bienvenue dans le Monde Progress," as seen in figure 17.9.

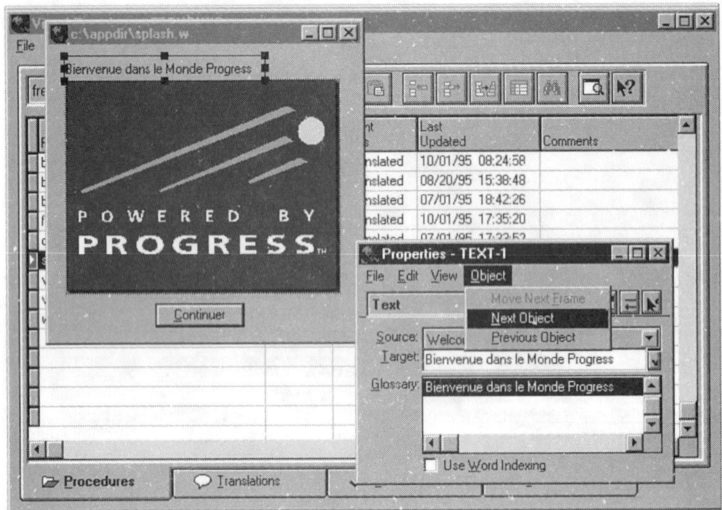

Fig. 17.9

Translating the next phrase in the splash screen.

The translation is again immediately reflected in the interface. Moving forward through the objects on the screen using the Object, Next and Object, Previous menu, you see that all the text phrases in the procedure are now translated.

Now you are ready to translate another procedure. You close the Properties window (although you can leave it open), and you close the splash.w visualization window. Now you are back at the Procedure tab and you choose the findcust.w procedure for translation. You double-click on it and its facsimile appears.

This time, however, you are pleasantly surprised: half of the objects are already translated! Translations for Name (Nom), OK (OK), Search (Rechercher), Cancel (Annuler), and help (aide), are automatically proposed. You simply have to accept them. This is that automatic translation from which you hoped to benefit.

These translations have been proposed to you because Visual Translator found entries for these phrases in the glossary while it was bringing up the visualization for findcust.w. You simply have to accept the translations by clicking on the check box next to the Target field in the Properties window. If you do not accept a translation, it will not be applied and will not appear in the list of translations in the Translations tab.

Not all the objects have been translated, however, so you could continue on by translating by choosing another object (for example, &Country).

Visual translation is one mode for doing translations. The second mode, edit mode, uses the PROGRESS Version 8 editable browser. This is much more helpful when doing global translations, where you would like to translate multiple instances of the same source phrase.

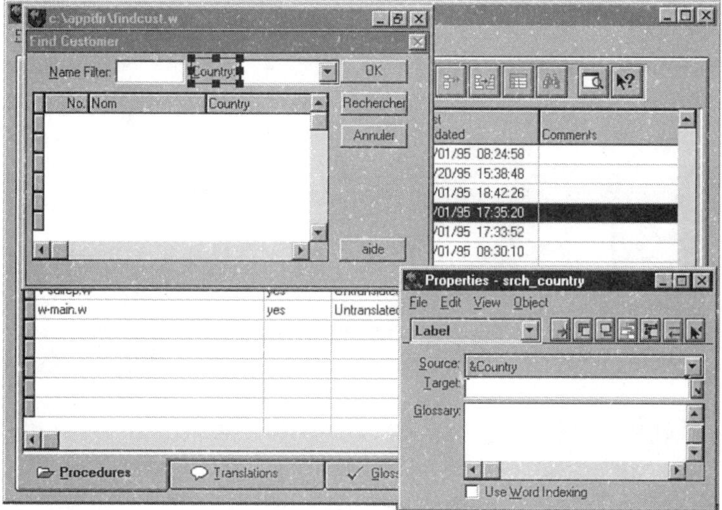

Fig. 17.10

The findcust.w procedure visualized.

You would like to try this method, so you close down the visualized findcust.w procedure, and also close down the Properties window. You go to the Translations tab shown in figure 17.11, and you are now looking at the translation browser, listing source and target phrases. Note that &Continue, &Country, and &Search now show up as translated.

> **Note**
>
> Visual Translator is "hot key" aware. Notice that some phrases begin with &. In PROGRESS, & in a word indicates that the character following it is to be used as a hot key, and will display with an underline. The glossary mechanism of Visual Translator will match translations in the
>
> (continues)

(continued)

glossary, whether or not they have an &. You can then place the hot key where you want in the translation phrase (or choose not to apply a hot key, as in the example for &Search/Rechercher).

Note also that it is possible to change the hot key value during the Visual Translation process. This would be expected by users of the translation. In France, you would want the hot key to reflect the translated word you are using, not the original source word.

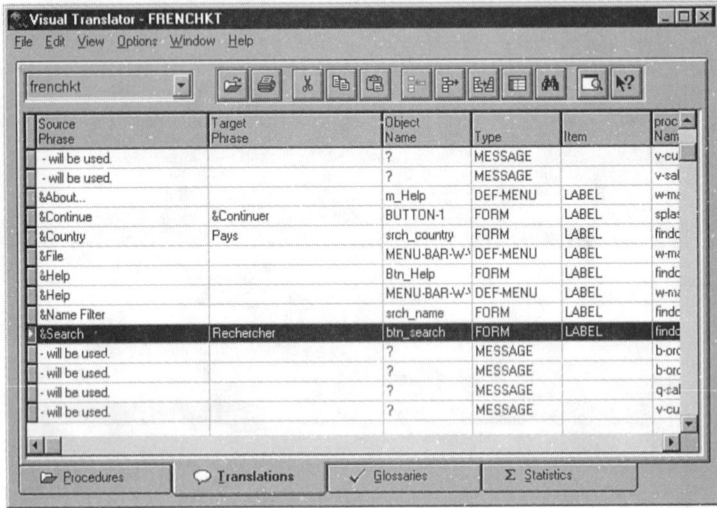

Fig. 17.11

The edit mode translation interface in the Translations tab.

To translate in edit mode, you simply choose the cell in the target column next to the source phrase you wish to translate, and then you type in the translation.

If you wanted to do global translations at this stage, you could use the Find, Replace or Goto commands in the Edit menu. These are similar functions to those found in most word-processing programs.

Suppose you would like to edit all the text phrases within one specific procedure. The organization of the browser, by default, is to present Source Phrase, followed by Target Phrase, followed by Object Name, Type, Item, Procedure Name, etc. For your purposes, you would like to change the order of the columns. Again, using standard Windows-like functions, you can do this.

You select Order Columns from the View menu and fill in the Order Columns dialog box (see fig. 17.12) by selecting fields from available choices. You choose to order the columns as Procedure Name, Source Phrase, and Target Phrase, followed by the rest.

This puts the columns in that order, but the data is still not ordered as you would like since you wish to see all the objects in the findcust.w procedure. You therefore sort the rows using the Procedure name as the primary sort key, Source Phrase as a secondary sort key, and Target Phrase as a tertiary sort key. This is done using the Sort function on the View menu (see fig. 17.13).

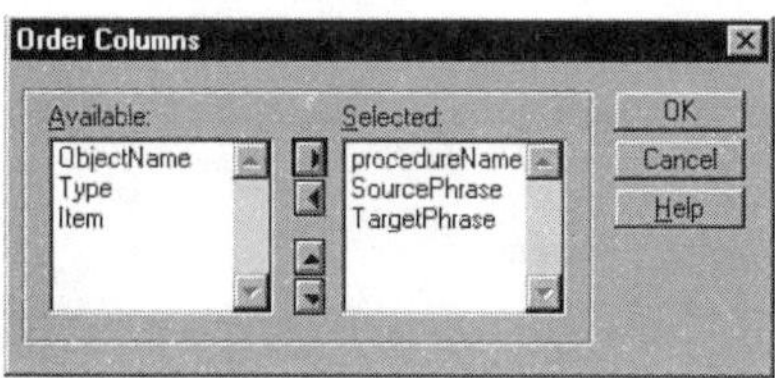

Fig. 17.12

Reordering the columns in edit mode.

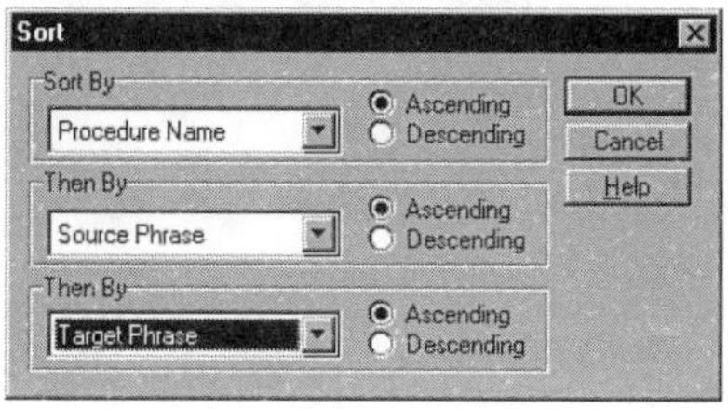

Fig. 17.13

Sorting the data in edit mode.

Now you can see all the objects that are found in the findcust.w procedure, and you can translate them. In Edit mode, this is easily done by filling in the cells under the Target Phrase by hand. You can also double-click on a Target Phrase cell, and bring up the glossary interface (properties window). If there are translations for this Source Phrase in the glossary, they will be recommended.

You fill in all the Target Phrase cells associate with the findcust.w procedure, and you can visualize it if you wish. This is done by double-clicking on it (see fig. 17.14).

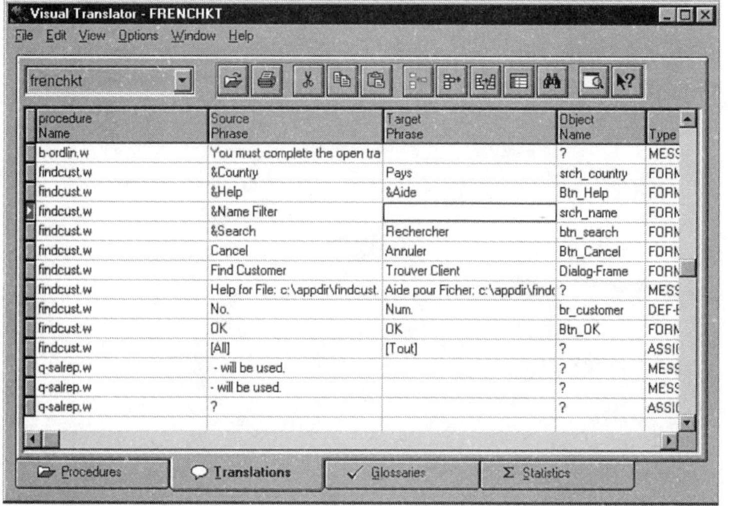

Fig. 17.14

Translating a procedure phrase-by-phrase in edit mode.

Having translated all the cells, if you return to the Procedures tab, you will see that the status of two of the procedures, splash.w and findcust.w. In figure 17.15, you see that all of the phrases in splash have been translated, and 9 of 10 in findcust.w are complete.

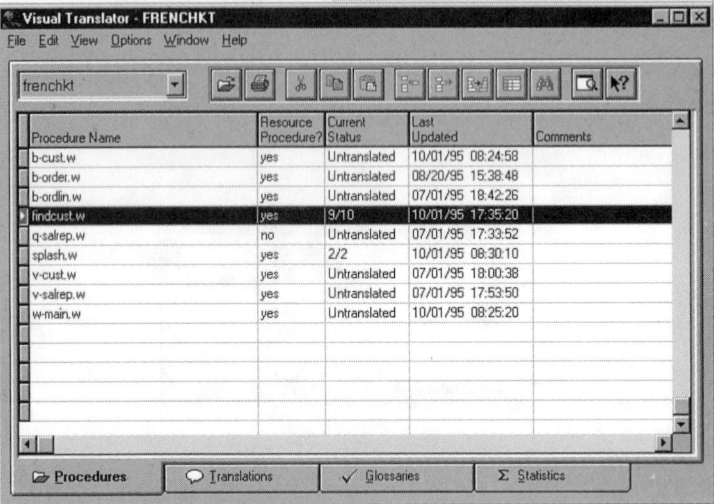

Fig. 17.15

Status of the translations in the Procedures tab.

Viewing Your Translation Statistics

You can now analyze the volume of work you have done so far. You probably looked at the Statistics tab shown in figure 17.16 once before, to verify that the job sent to you was the same size (number of words, number of procedures) as when you quoted your price when bidding the project.

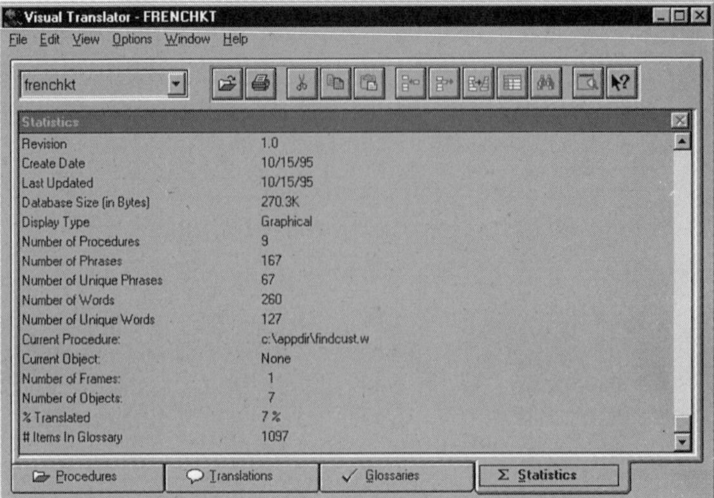

Fig. 17.16

Statistics for the translation effort.

Having done some translation work, now you check it to see how much of the project is complete. In this case, you see that you are 7% done (you have translated 7% of the phrases to be translated), and that the glossary has grown (from 1054 to 1097 entries).

You could continue on translating the entire kit, but you and the project manager agreed that you would send back the kit after a couple of procedures were translated. This is to verify that the process works, and that your translations are acceptable.

Now you will repackage the kit and return it to the project manager.

Returning the Kit to Project Manager

To send your current work-in-progress back to the project manager for approval, you simply close the kit, and return the kit to the project manager in the same way it was sent to you (diskette, e-mail, ftp, etc.). To close the kit, you choose Close from the File menu. More detail on how the kit can be bundled will be explained later, in the Advanced Topics section.

You have now completed the basic steps for phase two: translating the application. In this phase, you loaded a kit sent to you from the project manager, you loaded your own glossary of terms, and then you performed some translations. You did this in both visual mode (walking from button to button in a mock-up of a procedure) and edit mode (entering translations in a browser). You then bundled it all together and sent it back to the project manager.

It is time to enter phase three: consolidating the translations into the original application, and building a multilingual application. That is the purpose of the next section.

Project Manager: Consolidating the Translations

Now you are the project manager again. The translator has shipped the kit back to you with a couple of procedures that have been translated so that you can evaluate their work and do a trial run of the translation process. If they have been translated well, then they will be ready to be bundled into the original application. You will now take the final steps to integrate the translations, and ultimately, to deploy the translated application. Basically, you will do the following:

- Consolidate the translations with their original phrases in the application. This is done back in Translation Manager.
- Build the application with the original and newly-translated text phrases
- Run the application in the original and new language

Updating the Returned Kit

In phase one, you created the translation kit from within the overall SO-R-US project. The project contained all the information necessary to manage the original source of the application, the original text phrases, the original glossaries, and all the support files necessary to generate a kit. You will now re-integrate the translations contained in the returned translation: a process called *consolidation*.

You load the kit on to your system using the same format and process that you used to send it out (floppy disk, internet, FTP, etc.). You load the kit database into the directory from which it came. Then you invoke Translation Manager from either the PROGRESS Desktop or the Tools menu, as you did in the first phase (see Chapter 16), and open the project from which this kit was created. In this exercise, that project was named SO-R-US.

Consolidating the Translations

In the context of Translation Manager, "consolidation" refers to the process of taking the translations from the kit and matching them up to the original text phrases in the source code identified in the translation project. It also refers to the same process for the translations in the glossary returned with the kit.

You consolidate the kit following these steps. In the Kits tab, you select the Consolidate button and the Consolidate dialog box box appears (see fig. 17.17). You specify the kit which has just been returned from the translator, and which is to be consolidated (Frenchkt.db, in this case).

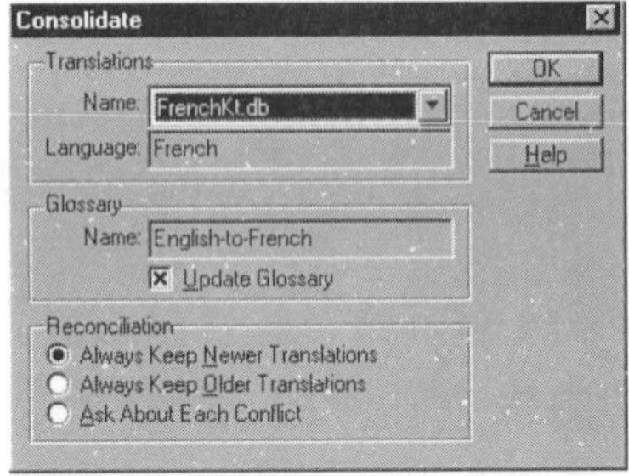

Fig. 17.17

Consolidating the translator's work.

You also make some decisions about how the translations are to be reconciled in case this is an update of a previously submitted kit. When consolidating in the translations from the kit, you can either accept all new translations, reject the newer ones in favor of the older ones, or be prompted each time there is a difference. In this case, you will simply accept the newer translations since this is the first time you have consolidated the translator's work.

Consolidation takes place in two steps:

1. First, the procedures' translations are consolidated into the translation project database. A Consolidating Translations status meter appears. In this case, 11 translations are consolidated.
2. Second, the glossary translations are consolidated the glossary. A Consolidating Glossary meter appears. In this case, 43 entries have been added.

The Kits browser list now reflects the newly consolidated kit (see fig. 17.18). The FrenchKt kit is marked as consolidated, and 11 phrases are now integrated into the project database.

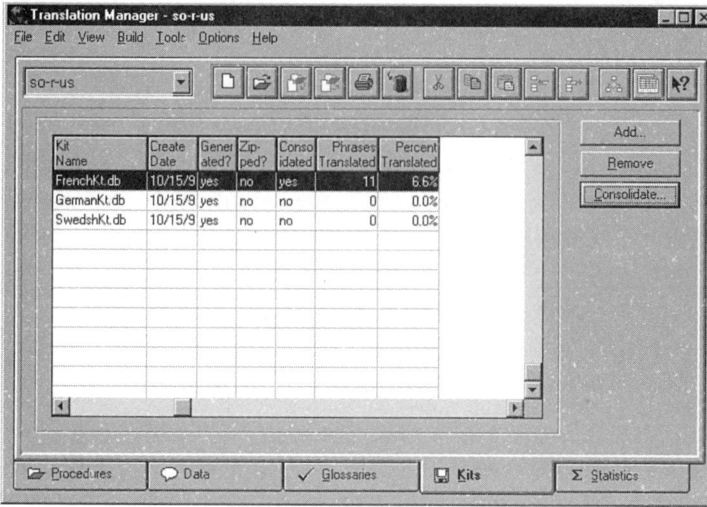

Fig. 17.18

The Kits tab keeps track of kit consolidation status.

Now it is time to try out the new translations by building them into the program executables. This is done in two steps: compiling and running.

Compiling the Program with Translations

Compiling and running the newly translated application is best done from the Procedures Tab. You enter the Procedures tab by clicking on it. Once there, you choose Compile from the Build menu. This brings up a Compile dialog box which allows you to control how you will perform the compile. This dialog box is pictured in figure 17.19.

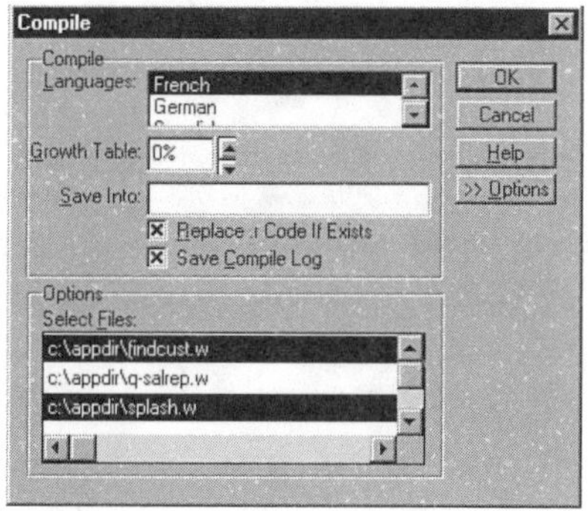

Fig. 17.19

The Compile dialog box, which makes the application multilingual.

In the Compile dialog box, you first choose the languages to compile into the executable. In this case, you choose French, and the compiler will compile the program for French and the original language (in this case, English). Next, you can specify a text growth factor. The default for this is 0% and, for simplicity, we will accept this for now.

The Save Into field allows you to specify a different directory in which to place the compiled code. In this case, you will choose the default (the same directory as the source code).

Finally, you click on the Options button, which brings up a file selection list. Since only two procedures were sent back translated, you select only the two files which were returned: findcust.w and splash.w.

Note

Text expansion is used for allowing text strings to grow beyond their original (untranslated) length. The need for text to grow during translation was discussed in Chapter 14, "Designing Your Global Application." Text expansion merits a longer discussion, and will be covered in the Advanced Topics section later in this chapter.

Finally, you click on the OK button, and the two procedures now compile.

You are now ready to see the result of all your work! The final step is to run the program, now multilingually. To do this, you choose Run from the Build menu, and bring up the Run dialog box. In this dialog box, you select the procedure and the language in which it should be run. To start, you run splash.r in the original (<unnamed>) language, and see splash.r run, as shown in figure 17.20.

Fig. 17.20

Running a procedure in the original language.

Now you wish to run it in French, so you again select Run from the Build menu. This time, however, you choose French from the selection list of languages. The result is pictured in figure 17.21.

Now you see the procedure running in French. Note that this is using the same executable, and that we never had to change a line of source code!

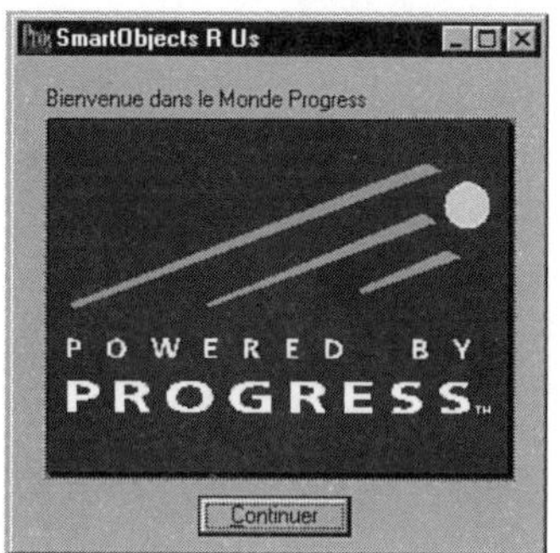

Fig. 17.21

A multilingual procedure has been created and runs in French.

Deploying Your Application

As has been seen, it is possible to create one set of executables (objects, .r code) which can store more than one language. How would you select which language to run in the field? Said another way, how would you deploy this multilingual application so that users have control over the language they see?

The parameter `CURRENT-LANGUAGE` determines which language should be used when running a PROGRESS-based program built with multiple languages. This can be set at run-time, as will be seen later. `CURRENT-LANGUAGE` can also be set by a parameter on the PROGRESS command line, or in the startup.pf file. That parameter `is -lng`, and would be set as follows.

Append to the PROGRESS command line (in the command for the Properties of a Windows Program Item, for example):

```
_prowin.exe -p _desk.p -lng French
```

In STARTUP.PF (add the following line):

```
-lng French
```

Figure 17.22 shows how you would run splash.r from the PROGRESS Procedure Editor in the original language.

Figure 17.23 shows how you would run splash.r from the PROGRESS Procedure Editor in a translated language (French).

You have now gone through the entire process of translating an application, and you have successfully created a multilingual application.

During this process, you skipped over two important topics:

- Transferring kit files between the project manager and translator
- Text growth at compile time.

The next section will now expand on these two subjects.

Fig. 17.22

Running a .r file in original language from procedure editor.

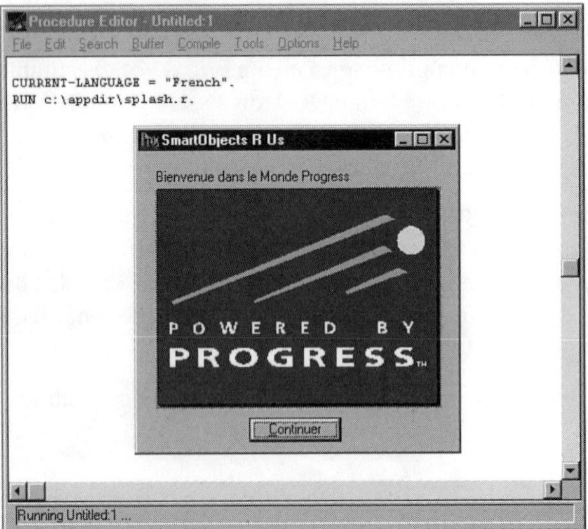

Fig. 17.23

Running an .r File in an alternative language.

Advanced Topics

Transferring Kit Files Between Project Manager and Translator

There are a number of files and components that Visual Translator requires to function properly. The various components are:

- The kit database. This is a PROGRESS database containing a number of tables for holding the names of the procedures to be translated, the text phrases to be translated, and one or more glossaries.
- The resource procedures (procedure facsimiles) used to visualize the original procedures. Resource procedures resemble the originals, except that all database access and business logic has been removed, leaving only user interface elements.

- Images files (optional). These are used to make the resource procedures resemble the original code as much as possible. If icons or images were used by the original code, they can be included in the kit for the translator.
- PROGRESS.INI file (if a tailored PROGRESS.INI file is used for running the application). This is necessary if default PROGRESS text fonts or colors have been changed by the application.

There are two ways to transfer these components between project manager and translator. Either the files can be left as is when creating a kit, or they can be compressed together and sent in one bundle (a "zipped kit"). Your specific translation process will determine which one to use.

Zipped Kits

If the project manager and the translator work for two different companies, then zipped kits will typically be used. The kits are built and transferred in this way:

- When the project manager Adds a kit in the Kits tab of Translation Manager, he or she chooses to Generate a Zip File in the Add Kit dialog box. This will take all necessary files and compress them together using a compression mechanism internal to Translation Manager. This mechanism is pkzip/pkunzip compatible, for those who are familiar with these programs.
- The zipped file is then transferred to the translator, either by floppy diskette, an e-mail attachment, ftp, or some other means.
- When the translator receives the compressed kit, he or she Loads the kit in the File menu of Visual Translator. This will decompress the file and place the required files in the appropriate directories for Visual Translator to locate.
- Throughout the rest of the translation process, the translator will Open and Close the kit from the File menu, rather than Loading and Saving it.
- When the translator is finished with the translation effort, he or she Saves the kit in the File Menu of Visual Translator. Saving the kit will re-compress it, readying it to be sent back in the same mechanism in which it was sent.
- The project manager then consolidate the kit, automatically decompressing it.

Non-Zipped Kits

If the project manager and translator will work on the same system, then zipping is not necessary. This would happen if the project manager and the translator are the same person (rare), or if the project manager plans to send the entire PC to the translator—already configured. In this case, zipping is not necessary, since the physical files are not being moved.

The process is quite simple for non-zipped kits:

- The project manager generates a kit, but chooses not to zip it.
- The translator can invoke Visual Translator and simply open the kit by name. All the other support files are in the same directories where the project manager left them, and Visual Translator will find them.

- The translator will simply Open and Close the kit during the translation process, and will never Load or Save it.
- When the translator is done translating the kit and has closed it for the last time, the project manager simply invokes Translation Manager and will immediately Consolidate the kit, since it is already in the directory where Translation Manager expects it.

Growing Text Strings at Compile Time

The need to allow text to grow in translations was discussed in Chapter 14, "Designing Your Global Application." There are two aspects to this: leaving enough space on the screen for the translations to fit, and allowing the text strings to physically grow and be integrated in a multilingual application. Text segment growth addresses the latter.

By default, Translation Manager (and the PROGRESS Compiler which it invokes) will build object code where translated phrases will be no longer than the original phrase. There are cases and languages, however, where this behavior will be too strict. A text growth mechanism has been included in Translation Manager to address this.

In the Compile dialog box during the Build process (one of the last steps you followed to build a multilingual application), the project manager can assign a growth factor to the translated strings.

The translator was allowed to translate text phrases to any length, whether shorter or longer than the source phrase. Although the translation could look too long (not fitting in buttons, etc.), the translation would be accepted. Hopefully, the translator would send back a comment to the project manager that a translation appeared to be too long, and that something in the original program needs to be changed (the button needs to be bigger, etc.).

Presumably you, the project manager, designed your screens so that text could expand proportionally to the length of the source phrase. The expansion varies, depending on the original length of the text. This, too, was covered in Chapter 14, "Designing Your Global Application."

Screen layout and design aside, when the translated phrases are returned to be compiled into the .r code, the project manager has control over how much the phrases should grow when compiled into another language.

Translation Manager (and the underlying PROGRESS Compiler) supports text string growth. Specifying a growth factor causes the length of every *translated* string to be increased as if it had been explicitly defined with a string attribute (":L10" for example).

The growth is variant, based on the following table used by Translation Manager. Table 17.1 has been published by many vendors, including IBM and Sun Microsystems (see Appendix D, "Internationalization," for those references).

Table 17.1 String Growth Table

Length of Source String	Additional Space
1-10 characters	200%
11-20 characters	100%
21-30 characters	80%
31-50 characters	60%
51-70 characters	40%
Greater than 70 characters	30%

Rules used by Translation Manager when applying text growth:

1. When the growth table factor is 0, as specified in the Compile dialog box in Translation Manager, then no growth is applied, and the translated string may be truncated to be no longer than the original source string.
2. When a growth table factor greater than 0 is applied, then that value is applied as a percentage of the value that would have been used from the table. For example, if you supply a growth table factor of 10, then 10% of the values in the table are applied. For a string 20 character long, the growth factor will be 2 characters (10% factor of 100% growth in the table for strings 20 characters long = 10% expansion x 20 characters = 2 characters). The maximum length for the translation in the object code will be 22 characters.
3. Only text strings which have been translated will have a growth factor applied.
4. Text strings which have had explicit length attributes applied to them will retain that explicit length (they will not have a growth factor applied). Explicit lengths are applied to text in 4GL code with the :Lxx attribute.
5. When a text string has had a growth factor applied, that growth factor will be applied to all the translations of that string (for multiple translations being compiled into one .r), and that length will be exactly the same for all languages.

> **Note**
>
> In fact, during the previous compilation of splash.w, a growth factor of 10 was applied. Otherwise, the French translation of "Continue" would not have displayed as "Continuer" (one character longer).

From Here...

You have now completed the process of translating an application. The important point is that you translated it by extracting the text phrases and user interface objects from the source code, translating the objects independently of the application, and then applied the translations and created a multilingual application without changing a line of source code.For more information related to topics in this chapter, refer to the following:

- Chapter 14, "Designing Your Global Application," covers issues of designing an application for translatability.
- Chapter 16, "Preparing for Translation," covers the steps which were take in preparation for this chapter.

Moving forward, it is now time to discuss the issues involved with deploying an application internationally. There are issues involved with installing and running your application in another country and in another language. This is covered in:

- Chapter 18, "Deploying Your Application Globally," which covers how to get your application to run in all global environments.

CHAPTER 18

Deploying Your Application Globally

Now that you have developed an application which is completely internationalized and localized, you are ready to deploy it. That is to say, you are ready to install it in various countries. A few challenges remain, but PROGRESS has utilities which will facilitate deployment.

In Chapter 14, "Designing Your Global Application," you learned about codepages and collations, and the need to remove any assumptions from code about specific character sets or sorting orders. Now that you are about to deploy your application, you will see why this is so important.

As stated earlier, different languages may require different characters sets. Furthermore, for a given character set, different hardware platforms, operating systems, and user interfaces may require different codepages. When all computer systems were host-based (a powerful computer with only dumb terminals talking to it), all points in the configuration used the same codepage, and this was not an issue.

However, with the advent of client-server computing, and more specifically, with heterogeneous client-server computing, it has become necessary to pay extra attention to codepages. Fortunately, PROGRESS has done most of the thinking to make this easy for you.

Take a simple example: the configuration most typical in the United States, Latin America, and Western Europe. Assuming Microsoft Windows Clients (using the DOS operating system) connected to a UNIX Server, the codepage configuration is shown in Figure 18.1. DOS uses codepage IBM850 (or IBM437, a very close precursor to IBM850), Microsoft Windows uses codepage 1252 (identical to codepage ISO8859-1 for all practical purposes), and UNIX Uses codepage ISO8859-1.

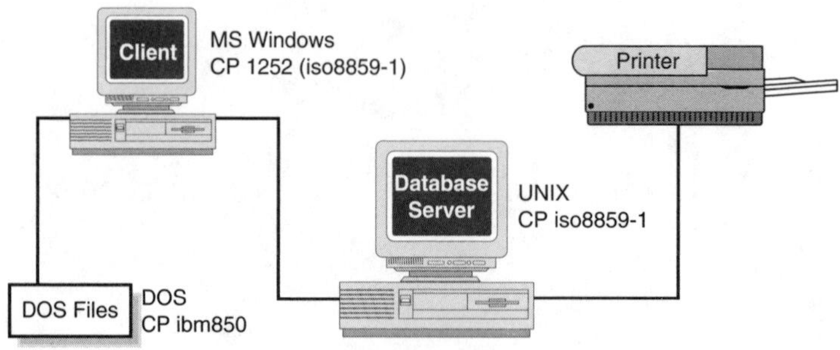

Fig. 18.1

Typical North American, Latin American, or Western European client/server configuration

If you want to read a DOS file in and process it on the client, do some processing (e.g., create a new record), and then store the data in a database on a UNIX server, someone must manage and map the different codepage values. With PROGRESS Version 6 and earlier, and with most other products, this was a difficult task which *you* had to manage. But starting with PROGRESS Version 7, and evolving with Version 8, PROGRESS does this codepage work transparently to your application. PROGRESS allows you to specify the codepage for the DOS file (using the startup `parameter` *-cpstream*), the Windows Client (the startup `parameter` *-cpinternal*), the database (the codepage is set in the actual database), and on the server (which can also have an explicit codepage set (using the startup parameter *-cpinternal* on the server startup command).

Character Sets and Codepages

Most English-speaking people would not know that these different codepages are operating behind the scenes. This is because the alphabetic characters used 99% of the time in English, "ABC...XYZ" and "abc...xyz," are stored in the lower half, or first 128 characters, of the codepage (characters 0-127) This is also called the "basic ASCII" range. Most codepages have the same first 128 characters, so to an English user, the various codepages appear identical.

Non-English Roman-based languages (German, French, Spanish, etc.) are very much affected by codepage differences. This is because many of the alphabetic characters they use (umlauted characters, accented characters, etc.) are stored in the upper 128 characters, also known as the "extended ASCII" range, or the "8-bit" range. It is in this upper set of characters that codepages differ from one another. For examples of different codepages, such as Hebrew, Arabic, Russian, Chinese, Japanese, and Korean, see Chapter 14, "Designing Your Global Application." Looking at Figure 18.2, you see the alphabetic characters as they are arranged in the Microsoft Windows Codepage for the Americas and Western Europe, also known as the "Latin-1" codepage.

> **Note**
>
> The first 32 characters in the codepage are not displayed in this utility, since they are almost always non-printing control characters.

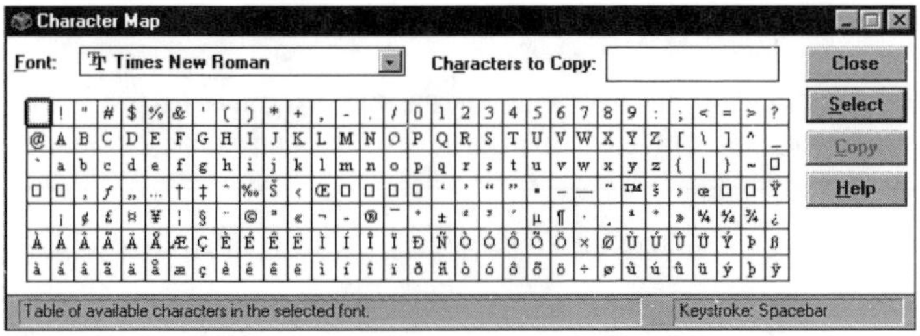

Fig. 18.2

Microsoft Windows Latin-1 codepage 1252 (virtually identical to ISO8859-1 for UNIX).

The English alphabet takes up the character range 65-91 (ABC...XYZ) and range 97 - 123 (abc...xyz), both in the lower range of 128 characters. Other alphabet characters used by other Western languages, e.g., ÄÅÆÇÈÉÖØ, etc., may be found in the upper 128 range. This range would be quite different if you were using a different codepage.

For example, by referring to Table D.4 in Appendix D, you can see the values of characters in the Western DOS codepage, IBM850, and the Western Microsoft Windows/UNIX codepage, ISO8859-1.

As you will see in Table D.4, the two codepages are identical for all printing and alphabetic characters for the first 128 characters (the lower half of the codepage). In some cases, the non-printing characters are not exactly the same, but it rarely matters. If you limited your communications to just the characters in the lower half of the codepage range, you would never notice a difference between the two codepages.

Now take a look at the extended range (second half) of the codepages, the characters above 127. You'll notice from the table that many character values differ between the IBM850 codepage and the ISO8859-1 codepage. For example, the German character Sharp-S (ß) has the value 225 in codepage IBM850, but the value 223 in the ISO8859-1 codepage. Conversely, for a given value, the representation may be quite different in different code pages. Character 229 is an Õ in codepage 850 and an å in codepage ISO8859-1. This is why it is critical that your software use the correct codepage for reading and writing.

In order to transfer data properly from a system with one codepage to a system with a different codepage, and to ensure that the data is still displayed correctly, it is necessary to map the values of the characters.

In earlier versions of PROGRESS (pre-7.2A), and with most of Progress Software's competitors today, that mapping is the application developer's responsibility. This task is difficult, time-consuming, and error-prone. In DOS/Windows systems, there is a facility providing this mapping ("oemtoansi" and "ansitooem"), but Windows provides nothing for mapping to UNIX systems.

PROGRESS Version 8 has a table-driven mechanism which provides such mappings for dozens of codepages. This mechanism does this mapping transparently to the application, simplifying development, testing, and deployment.

Note

The file containing all of these mapping tables that is used by PROGRESS is convmap.cp, a binary file found in $dlc\bin. It is created from convmap.dat, a text file found in $dlc\prolang.

As of this writing, the following codepages and codepage mapping tables are provided automatically in Version 8.

Table 18.1 Codepages Built into PROGRESS Version 8.0

Country	UNIX cp	DOS cp	Windows cp	Other cp
Americas and Western Europe	ISO8859-1	IBM850	ISO8859-1	
USA	ISO8859-1	IBM437,850	ISO8859-1	
Iceland	ISO8859-1	IBM861	ISO8859-1	
Eastern Europe	ISO8859-2	IBM852	1250	
Poland	ISO8859-2	IBM852	1250	Mazovia
Russia/Cyrillic	ISO8859-5	IBM866	1251	KOI8-R
Turkish	1254	IBM857	1254	
Greek	1253	IBM851	1253	
Hebrew	1255	IBM862	1255	
Arabic	1256	710, etc.		Naphitha 711, 721 ASMO 449, 707 Sakher 714 Mosad 786
China (PRC)	GB2312	GB2312	GB2312	
Japan	Shift-JIS	Shift-JIS	Shift-JIS	
Korea	KSC5601	KSC5601	KSC5601	
Taiwan (ROC)	BIG-5	BIG-5	BIG-5	
Thailand	620-2533	620-2533	620-2533	

The following AS/400 codepages and codepage mappings are also included in Version 8:

Country	Windows cp	AS/400 Codepage
Latin America,	ISO8859-1	IBM037
North America,		IBM278
Western Europe		IBM500

These codepage mappings will support most of the languages spoken in major global software markets. But suppose that a codepage specific to your country or system is not provided in the list above. It is a simple exercise to add your codepage table to PROGRESS and have it perform the automatic mapping for your table as well. The following sections will guide you through adding the support for a new codepage in PROGRESS.

Creating a New Codepage Table

In order to demonstrate how codepage tables are set up, you will create a fictitious codepage for a fictitious country.

Let's say you work in the country of Queland. In Queland, you have your own codepage. Your language is a compendium of the Scandinavian, Icelandic, and Western European languages, and in fact, you use almost all of the characters found in those alphabets. Newer systems in Queland use ISO8859-1 and IBM850, but your codepage, Que-1, has been used in Queland for years, and you have a great number of text files and databases which have the Que-1 encoding. You need to get at that data from PROGRESS without having to manually put the data through a conversion first.

Your Que-1 codepage table is organized in the following way:

1. To begin with, the lower 128 characters are the standard ASCII characters, like most codepages.
2. In Queland, you use more characters than the basic ASCII characters, including Å, Ä, Ö, etc. The upper 128 characters of your codepage include these characters, among others, and are organized as follows:

Table 18.2 The Upper Half of the Fictitious Que-1 Codepage for the Country Queland

Code Values	Characters
128-143	Å Ä Â Ã À Á Æ Ë Ê È É Ö Ô Õ Ó Ò
144-159	Ø Œ Ü Û Ù Ú Ÿ Y « » ‹ › " " ' '
160-175	å ä â ã à á æ ' ê è é ö ô õ ó ò
176-191	ø œ ü û ù ú ÿ y ÷ x ± 1/4 1/2 3/4 © ®
192-207	™ ‡ • ¤ | ¨ Ç Ð Ñ ß Þ ç ð ñ þ
208-223	Ï Î Ì Í ï î í ì ¥ £ ƒ ¢
224-239	Š š § ‰ ‚ „ " … ˆ ˜ ´ ° ¶ µ
240-255	– ¯ – – ¬ • ª º ¹ ² ³ ¡ ¿

Blank spaces in the table above represent non-printing characters. Every codepage has them, and yours is no exception. The only blank space in the upper 128 characters that is actually a printing character is the <non breaking space> character, which is character 240 in your codepage (160 in the ISO8859-1 codepage).

You may wish to add your codepage to PROGRESS so that it can be recognized, and so that mappings between Que-1 and the standard codepages are built into PROGRESS and occur automatically.

The following steps are a brief summary of what you need to do to add support for a codepage in PROGRESS. These steps will be explained in full throughout the remainder of this chapter.

1. Create a local copy of convmap.dat for your work.
2. Create an IS-ALPHA table, defining which characters in your character set are alphabetic, and which are not (which are numbers, punctuation, and so on).
3. Create one or more uppercase tables for all the alphabetic characters of your codepage.
4. Create one or more lowercase mapping tables for all the alphabetic characters in your codepage.
5. Create a mapping table between your codepage and ISO8859-1 (once you can do that, creating mapping tables to the other codepages of the family will be easy).
6. Create one or more collation tables for your codepage, to support your local sorting requirements.

Creating a Local Copy of convmap.dat

The file, convmap.dat, is found in the $dlc\prolang directory. It contains every codepage definition and collation table that is built into PROGRESS. You will copy that file to your local working directory, which you have set up to be C:\quework. (You're doing this on Microsoft Windows, since that is the most popular client available in Queland).

Tip

The header of the file convmap.dat lists the various codepages in the table. As the header points out, there are many codepage tables defined in this file which you can discard. This is a good thing to do, since it will save you compiling time, and will generate a smaller table of contents list in memory of all the codepages available in this session. It's also easier to work with a convmap.dat file after you've removed the unnecessary clutter. Remember, however, that you may need some of those codepages when you deploy your application in various countries.

In your case, you'll delete the Russian codepage family, the Turkish codepage family, the Greek, Hebrew, Arabic, Double Byte (Chinese, Japanese, and Korean), and AS/400 codepages, leaving behind the ISO8859-1 and IBM850 codepage tables. The result is that you now have a convmap.dat file suitable for the codepages you might find in Queland.

Creating an ISALPHA Table Identifying Alphabetic Characters

The ISALPHA table is a table that identifies, character by character, whether it is an alphabetic or a non-alphabetic (digit, punctuation, symbol) character. This table is necessary for PROGRESS, since PROGRESS uses this table to qualify characters in the Format statement. For example, only the alphabetic characters as defined in this table can be entered into a variable as defined below:

```
DEFINE VAR FOO AS CHAR FORMAT "A(10)"
```

The easiest way to create your Que-1 ISALPHA table is to copy an ISALPHA table from some other codepage. You'll use the ISALPHA table for ISO8859-1 as a base. This table can be found in Appendix D.

This is a good table to start with, since the first 128 characters should already be set up for you.

The way the ISALPHA table works in PROGRESS is simple. The table is composed of 256 values, numbered from 0 to 255. The n'th value in the table corresponds to the character numbered n in the codepage. If the value is 001, then the character is alphabetic. If the value is 000, then the character is non-alphabetic (numeric, symbolic, or non-printing).

You can examine a few sample characters by looking at the ISALPHA table for ISO8859-1 in Appendix D and at the ISO8859-1/IBM850 table, also found in Appendix D. The first 64 values of the ISALPHA table are all zeros. Looking at the Microsoft Character Map Utility table, you can confirm that the first 64 characters are, in fact, non-alphabetic. Note that Character Map doesn't display the first 32 characters in the codepage because they are non-printing. Looking at the next 32, you see that there are no alphabetic characters in these either.

The first value set to 001, indicating an alphabetic character, is value 65. Character 65 in the ISO8859-1 table is "A," and it is alphabetic. In fact the next 25 values are also set to 001, which correspond to characters 66 through 91 ("B" through "Z"). The next 5 are 000, which is correct, since none of "[\]^_" are alphabetic.

The table continues in this fashion. Here are a few characters that require a little thought before deciding whether they are alphabetic or not:

The copyright symbol, ©, character number 169, is not an alphabetic character (it's a symbol), and in the PROGRESS ISO8859-1 ISALPHA table, the entry number 169 is 000.

The German alphabetic character Sharp-S, ß, is character 223, and is set to 001 in the PROGRESS ISALPHA table. Sharp-S and other character ligatures and diphthongs (such as Æ, æ, Œ, and œ) are considered to be alphabetic.

The superscript character, ª, is character 170, and is set to 000 in the PROGRESS ISALPHA table. This is correct because, although it looks like an alphabetic character, it is really a footnote symbol.

Following this technique, you will create an ISALPHA table for the Que-1 codepage. Working with your favorite text editor, you derive the following table by copying the ISO8859-1 ISALPHA table to a new Que-1 ISALPHA table in your working version of CONVMAP.DAT. You are doing this in your working directory, which you set to c:\quework. When you have finished, the resulting table will be as follows:

```
#-----------------------------------------------------------------------
# This table contains the attributes for code page Que-1
CODEPAGE
CODEPAGE-NAME "QUE-1"
TYPE "1"
ISALPHA
/*000-015*/  000 000 000 000 000 000 000 000 000 000 000 000 000 000 000 000
/*016-031*/  000 000 000 000 000 000 000 000 000 000 000 000 000 000 000 000
/*032-047*/  000 000 000 000 000 000 000 000 000 000 000 000 000 000 000 000
/*048-063*/  000 000 000 000 000 000 000 000 000 000 000 000 000 000 000 000
/*064-079*/  000 001 001 001 001 001 001 001 001 001 001 001 001 001 001 001
/*080-095*/  001 001 001 001 001 001 001 001 001 001 001 000 000 000 000 000
/*096-111*/  000 001 001 001 001 001 001 001 001 001 001 001 001 001 001 001
/*112-127*/  001 001 001 001 001 001 001 001 001 001 001 000 000 000 000 000
/*128-143*/  001 001 001 001 001 001 001 001 001 001 001 001 001 001 001 001
/*144-159*/  001 001 001 001 001 001 001 001 000 000 000 000 000 000 000 000
/*160-175*/  001 001 001 001 001 001 001 001 001 001 001 001 001 001 001 001
/*176-191*/  001 001 001 001 001 001 001 001 000 000 000 000 000 000 000 000
/*192-207*/  000 000 000 000 000 000 000 001 001 001 001 001 001 001 001 001
/*208-223*/  001 001 001 001 001 001 001 001 000 000 000 000 000 000 000 000
/*224-239*/  001 001 000 000 000 000 000 000 000 000 000 000 000 000 000 000
/*240-255*/  000 000 000 000 000 000 000 000 000 000 000 000 000 000 000 000
ENDTABLE
ENDCODEPAGE
#-----------------------------------------------------------------------
```

The keywords in the table are as follows.

`CODEPAGE`. There are two types of tables in convmap.dat: codepage definition tables and collation tables. The CODEPAGE keyword specifies that you are defining the former.

`CODEPAGE-NAME "Que-1"`. The keyword allows you to name the codepage. It is mandatory that you limit the characters in the Codepage-Name to characters in the lower 128 range of the codepage, since these characters remain the same in most codepages, and you will need the codepage names to be portable across systems with varying codepages.

`TYPE "1"`. There are two types of ISALPHA tables. Type "1" tables are for defining whether characters are alphabetic or non-alphabetic for single-byte codepages. Type "2" tables are for defining valid lead-byte and trail-byte ranges for double-byte character sets. The Que-1 codepage is a single-byte codepage.

`ISALPHA`. There are a few types of codepage definition tables. The ISALPHA Keyword indicates that this table will define alphabetic versus non-alphabetic characters.

ENDTABLE. This indicates that the table data has ended. In some codepage definition tables, there can be more than one sub-table (for example, the Lead-Byte and Trail-Byte tables for ISALPHA Type "2").

ENDCODEPAGE. This indicates that the ISALPHA table in a codepage definition block has ended.

Numbers. The numeric value for each codepage entry is made up of a three-digit number. 000 represents a non-alphabetic character; 001 is alphabetic.

Comment Lines. As with PROGRESS and the C programming language, comments are started by /* and ended by */.

Lines starting with "#" are also valid comment lines. No termination character is required.

Blank Lines. Blank lines are ignored, and are useful for readability.

In summary, you assigned the values to the ISALPHA codepage definition table as follows:

> The base 0-127 characters were left alone, since they are the same as in the ISO8859-1 table.
>
> You zeroed out all of the character values for character values 128-255.
>
> You went back and set to "001" the character values in the range 128-143 ("Å" through "Ò").
>
> You set to "001" the character values in the range 144-151 ("Ø" through "Y").
>
> You set to "001" the character values in the range 160-175 ("å" through "ò").
>
> You set to "001" the character values in the range 176-183 ("ø" through "y").
>
> You set to "001" the character values in the range 199-207 ("Ç" through "þ").
>
> You set to "001" the character values in the range 208-215 ("Ï" through "í").
>
> You set to "001" characters 224 ("Š") and 225 ("š").

All other characters in the top 128 characters are non-alphabetic, and are set to "000."

Now that you have identified each alphabetic and nonalphabetic character in the Que-1 codepage with the ISALPHA table, it is time to create a table that identifies the uppercase and lowercase values for each alphabetic character in the Que-1 codepage.

Creating an Uppercase Table for Alphabetic Characters

The UPPERCASE-MAP table in convmap.dat is used to determine the uppercase values for each alphabetic character in the codepage. This table contains the values to be returned by the CAPS 4GL function (a function that returns the uppercase value of a given character).

The UPPERCASE-MAP table is again a table of 256 values, one for each character in the codepage. This time, however, the value held in the position is a pointer to the character in the codepage that is the uppercase value for that character.

For example, in the ISO8859-1 codepage, the value for entry 97 ("a") is 65. Character number 65 in the ISO8859-1 codepage is "A." which is the uppercase of "a." Refer to the ISO8859-1/IBM850 table in Appendix D to confirm these values.

Again, the first 128 characters of the Que-1 codepage are the same characters as the first 128 of ISO8859-1. It is not necessary that the uppercase rules should be the same for every language, but you know that it is true in Queish as well.

> **Note**
>
> An example of how two UPPERCASE-MAP tables can differ for the same codepage are the UPPERCASE-MAP tables for French-Canadian and French ("Basic"). In Parisian French, the uppercase for é is E, but in Canadian French, the uppercase for é is É. Since E and É have two different codepage values, the corresponding UPPERCASE-MAP tables are different.

For your uppercase_map, you copy the CASE table containing both the UPPERCASE-MAP and the LOWERCASE-MAP from the ISO8859-1 table in your working version of the CONVMAP.DAT file, and assign the following values to the UPPERCASE-MAP (among other values):

> The value for entry 175 ("ò") is 143. Character 143 in the Que-1 codepage is "Ò," which is the uppercase of "ò."
>
> The value for entry 136 ("Ê") is 136. This is because "Ê" is already an uppercase character, so the uppercase value for it is itself.
>
> The value for entry 202 ("ß") is 202. This is because the German Sharp-S has no uppercase/lowercase mapping.

You can confirm these values by referring to the Que-1 codepage definition Table 18.2.

Now that you have defined the uppercase table, it is time to define the lowercase table.

Creating a Lowercase Table for Alphabetic Characters

The LOWERCASE-MAP table holds the lowercase value for each character in the 256-character table. This table is used by the `LC` 4GL function (a function which returns the lowercase value of a character). Reversing the logic from above, and editing the LOWERCASE-MAP:

> The value for entry 143 ("Ò") is 175. Character 175 in the Que-1 codepage is "ò." which is the lowercase of "Ò."
>
> The value for entry 205 (the entry for "ð," small d-slash) is 205. This is because "ð" is already a lowercase character, so the lowercase value for it is itself.
>
> the value for entry 202 (the entry for "ß") is 202. This is because the German Sharp-S may be used as lowercase as well.

Here is the UPPERCASE-MAP and the LOWERCASE-MAP which you have just created for your Que-1 codepage:

```
#----------------------------------------------------------------------
# Case tables for code page Que-1 and case table basic
CASE
CODEPAGE-NAME QUE-1
CASETABLE-NAME BASIC
TYPE 1
UPPERCASE-MAP
   /*000-015*/  000 001 002 003 004 005 006 007 008 009 010 011 012 013 014 015
   /*016-031*/  016 017 018 019 020 021 022 023 024 025 026 027 028 029 030 031
   /*032-047*/  032 033 034 035 036 037 038 039 040 041 042 043 044 045 046 047
   /*048-063*/  048 049 050 051 052 053 054 055 056 057 058 059 060 061 062 063
   /*064-079*/  064 065 066 067 068 069 070 071 072 073 074 075 076 077 078 079
   /*080-095*/  080 081 082 083 084 085 086 087 088 089 090 091 092 093 094 095
   /*096-111*/  096 065 066 067 068 069 070 071 072 073 074 075 076 077 078 079
   /*112-127*/  080 081 082 083 084 085 086 087 088 089 090 123 124 125 126 127
   /*128-143*/  128 129 130 131 132 133 134 135 136 137 138 139 140 141 142 143
   /*144-159*/  144 145 146 147 148 149 150 151 152 153 154 155 156 157 158 159
   /*160-175*/  128 129 130 131 132 133 134 135 136 137 138 139 140 141 142 143
   /*176-191*/  144 145 146 147 148 149 150 151 184 185 186 187 188 189 190 191
   /*192-207*/  192 193 194 195 196 197 198 199 200 201 202 203 199 200 201 203
   /*208-223*/  208 209 210 211 208 209 210 211 216 217 218 219 220 221 222 223
   /*224-239*/  224 224 226 227 228 229 230 231 232 233 234 235 236 237 238 239
   /*240-255*/  240 241 242 243 244 245 246 247 248 249 250 251 252 253 254 255
ENDTABLE
LOWERCASE-MAP
   /*000-015*/  000 001 002 003 004 005 006 007 008 009 010 011 012 013 014 015
   /*016-031*/  016 017 018 019 020 021 022 023 024 025 026 027 028 029 030 031
   /*032-047*/  032 033 034 035 036 037 038 039 040 041 042 043 044 045 046 047
   /*048-063*/  048 049 050 051 052 053 054 055 056 057 058 059 060 061 062 063
   /*064-079*/  064 097 098 099 100 101 102 103 104 105 106 107 108 109 110 111
   /*080-095*/  112 113 114 115 116 117 118 119 120 121 122 091 092 093 094 095
   /*096-111*/  096 097 098 099 100 101 102 103 104 105 106 107 108 109 110 111
   /*112-127*/  112 113 114 115 116 117 118 119 120 121 122 123 124 125 126 127
   /*128-143*/  160 161 162 163 164 165 166 167 168 169 170 171 172 173 174 175
   /*144-159*/  176 177 178 179 180 181 182 183 152 153 154 155 156 157 158 159
   /*160-175*/  160 161 162 163 164 165 166 167 168 169 170 171 172 173 174 175
   /*176-191*/  176 177 178 179 180 181 182 183 184 185 186 187 188 189 190 191
   /*192-207*/  192 193 194 195 196 197 198 204 205 206 202 207 204 205 206 207
   /*208-223*/  212 213 214 215 212 213 214 215 216 217 218 219 220 221 222 223
   /*224-239*/  225 225 226 227 228 229 230 231 232 233 234 235 236 237 238 239
   /*240-255*/  240 241 242 243 244 245 246 247 248 249 250 251 252 253 254 255
ENDTABLE
ENDCASE
#----------------------------------------------------------------------
```

There are some new keywords in this table, as follows.

`CASE`. This indicates that case tables are about to follow for the Codepage definition.

`CASETABLE-NAME BASIC`. As mentioned before, it is possible to have multiple case tables for a single codepage. This keyword allows us to uniquely name this case table. PROGRESS will, by default, look for a BASIC casetable name for a given codepage, unless instructed otherwise via the `-cpcase` parameter (this will be discussed later in the chapter).

`TYPE 1`. Indicates that this is a case table for a single-byte codepage.

`UPPERCASE-MAP`. The table about to follow will be the uppercase mapping table, to be used by the CAPS function.

`LOWERCASE-MAP`. The table about to follow will be the lowercase mapping table, to be used by the LC function.

`ENDCASE`. End of named case tables definition.

Now that you have defined the alphabetic and case tables, two sets of tables remain to be defined: how to map this codepage to another codepage such as ISO8859-1, and how to collate (sort, order) the alphabet in this codepage.

Creating a Codepage Mapping Table

For the sake of brevity, you will just create a mapping table between Que-1 and ISO8859-1. This will be sufficient for Windows-based client configurations reading and writing old Que-1-based files. Once you can do a mapping between Que-1 and a member of the ISO8859-1 family, creating mapping tables to the other codepages of the family is easy.

To create the mapping table, you start with a table called "null" in your working version of the convmap.dat file, and make a copy of it. This table does a mapping from ISO8859-1 to ISO8859-1 (no mapping, effectively). You use it for its formatting, and proper use and placement of codepage keywords.

You will actually create two mapping tables: one to map from Que-1 to ISO8859-1, and one to map from ISO8859-1 to Que-1.

> **Note**
>
> This must be a two-way non-loss mapping. That is to say, if you convert value x to value y in going from Que-1 to ISO8859-1, then you should end with value x when you then convert value y back using the ISO8859-1 to Que-1 mapping. Otherwise, you would lose (and possibly corrupt) data. This is also referred to as a *round trip* conversion.

Again, this table is a 256-value table, with one value for each character in the codepage table. This time, the value held is the value of the character in the codepage to which you are mapping. For example, the character "ÿ" is value 255 in ISO8859-1, and value 182 in Que-1. Therefore, entry number 255 in the ISO8859-1 to Que-1 mapping table would have the value 182. Entry number 182 in the Que-1 to ISO8859-1 table would have the value 255.

Following this logic, you assign the mappings for each character, and here is the mapping table for the ISO8859-1 codepage to the Que-1 codepage you create:

```
#----------------------------------------------------------------------
# This is a the conversion table for ISO8859-1 to Que-1
CONVERT
```

```
SOURCE-NAME "ISO8859-1"
TARGET-NAME "QUE-1"
TYPE "1"
 /*000-015*/ 000 001 002 003 004 005 006 007 008 009 010 011 012 013 014 015
 /*016-031*/ 016 017 018 019 020 021 022 023 024 025 026 027 028 029 030 031
 /*032-047*/ 032 033 034 035 036 037 038 039 040 041 042 043 044 045 046 047
 /*048-063*/ 048 049 050 051 052 053 054 055 056 057 058 059 060 061 062 063
 /*064-079*/ 064 065 066 067 068 069 070 071 072 073 074 075 076 077 078 079
 /*080-095*/ 080 081 082 083 084 085 086 087 088 089 090 091 092 093 094 095
 /*096-111*/ 096 097 098 099 100 101 102 103 104 105 106 107 108 109 110 111
 /*112-127*/ 112 113 114 115 116 117 118 119 120 121 122 123 124 125 126 127
 /*128-143*/ 228 229 231 222 232 233 193 194 234 227 224 154 145 216 217 218
 /*144-159*/ 219 158 159 156 157 195 245 246 235 192 225 250 177 241 242 150
 /*160-175*/ 240 254 223 222 196 220 197 226 198 190 249 152 247 243 191 244
 /*176-191*/ 237 186 252 253 236 239 238 248 230 251 237 153 187 188 189 255
 /*192-207*/ 132 133 130 131 129 128 134 199 137 138 136 135 210 211 209 208
 /*208-223*/ 200 201 143 142 140 141 139 185 144 148 149 147 146 151 203 202
 /*224-239*/ 164 165 162 163 161 160 166 204 169 170 168 167 214 215 213 212
 /*240-255*/ 205 206 175 174 172 173 171 184 176 180 181 179 178 183 207 182
ENDTABLE
ENDCONVERT
#---------------------------------------------------------------------
# This is a the conversion table for Que-1 to ISO8859-1
CONVERT
SOURCE-NAME "QUE-1"
TARGET-NAME "ISO8859-1"
TYPE "1"
 /*000-015*/ 000 001 002 003 004 005 006 007 008 009 010 011 012 013 014 015
 /*016-031*/ 016 017 018 019 020 021 022 023 024 025 026 027 028 029 030 031
 /*032-047*/ 032 033 034 035 036 037 038 039 040 041 042 043 044 045 046 047
 /*048-063*/ 048 049 050 051 052 053 054 055 056 057 058 059 060 061 062 063
 /*064-079*/ 064 065 066 067 068 069 070 071 072 073 074 075 076 077 078 079
 /*080-095*/ 080 081 082 083 084 085 086 087 088 089 090 091 092 093 094 095
 /*096-111*/ 096 097 098 099 100 101 102 103 104 105 106 107 108 109 110 111
 /*112-127*/ 112 113 114 115 116 117 118 119 120 121 122 123 124 125 126 127
 /*128-143*/ 197 196 194 195 192 193 198 203 202 200 201 214 212 213 211 210
 /*144-159*/ 216 140 220 219 217 218 159 221 171 187 139 124 147 148 145 146
 /*160-175*/ 229 228 226 227 224 225 230 235 234 232 233 246 244 245 243 232
 /*176-191*/ 248 156 252 251 249 250 255 253 247 215 177 188 189 190 169 174
 /*192-207*/ 153 134 135 149 164 166 168 199 208 209 223 222 231 240 241 254
 /*208-223*/ 207 206 204 205 239 238 236 237 141 142 143 144 165 163 131 162
 /*224-239*/ 138 154 167 137 128 129 184 130 132 133 136 152 180 176 182 181
 /*240-255*/ 160 157 158 175 173 150 151 172 183 170 186 185 178 179 161 191
ENDTABLE
ENDCONVERT
#---------------------------------------------------------------------
```

The following are definitions of the new keywords.

`CONVERT`. This indicates that conversion tables are about to follow to map one codepage to another.

`SOURCE-NAME "Que-1"`. You are defining a conversion table from the Que-1 codepage to something else. Each entry number refers to the character value within the Que-1 codepage. The value it holds is the character value of the codepage to which you are mapping.

`TARGET-NAME "ISO8859-1"`. The codepage to which you are mapping the Que-1 codepage is ISO8859-1.

`ENDCONVERT`. End of named conversion definition.

Note

In both tables, the first 128 characters (0 to 127) have the same values as their entry number, since the Que-1 and ISO8859-1 codepages are identical for the lower ASCII characters.

For mapping your Que-1 codepage to ISO8859-1, the printing (alphabetic, numeric, and symbolic) characters were easy to identify and map. There are some characters, however, which are non-printing in both codepages. Your correct approach is to map non-printing characters to equivalent non-printing characters in the ISO8859-1 codepage. The mapping is sufficient to maintain a 1-to-1 relationship between the two codepages.

For reference, the non-printing characters mapped are:

Que-1 Codepage	ISO8859-1 Codepage
216	141
217	142
218	143
219	144
228	128
229	129
241	157
242	158

There is one apparently empty character in the upper half of the table which is a printing character: the non-break space character. In Que-1, it is char 240; in ISO8859-1, it is character 160. This unity is reflected in the mapping.

Note

As with the Que-1 codepage, in many real-world cases there will be no direct one-to-one mapping between codepages. There may be one or more characters in one codepage which cannot be found in another. For codepages provided with PROGRESS that fall into this category, non-printing characters are mapped to non-printing characters, and printing characters to their closest equivalent. The mapping is a two-way, non-destructive conversion.

You are almost done adding all the support for your codepage into PROGRESS. The only remaining table to add is the table that instructs PROGRESS how to properly sort your alphabet.

Creating a Que-1 Collation Table

The Que-1 codepage is now completely defined. It is now time to define the collation, or sorting order used in Queland.

Every language sorts its alphabet uniquely. It is important when generating reports that they be generated in culturally expected alphabetical order. PROGRESS collation tables provide this capability.

There are a number of collation tables already built into PROGRESS.

Latin America, North America, Western Europe:

- Basic, Danish, Finnish, German-Library, Icelandic, Norwegian, Swedish
- 72-basic, v6-basic, v6-Danish, v6-Swedish (for backward compatibility to older collations provided in PROGRESS Version 7.2 and prior)

Eastern Europe/Western Asia:

- Czech, Greek, Hungarian, Polish, Romanian, Russian, Turkish

Middle East/Gulf States:

- Hebrew, Arabic

Asia:

- Chinese GB2312 Order, Chinese BIG-5 Order, Japanese, Korean, Thai

A collation for Queish is not included in the PROGRESS set, so you will have to create one.

In Queland, the alphabet is ordered like this:

AÃÂBCÇĐDEFGHIJKLMÑNOÕÔPQRSTÞUÛVWXYZÅÄËÊÖÜŸ

There are also some accented characters and diphthongs, but they sort equivalently to their unaccented counterparts (i.e., you don't care what order they appear in, as long as they appear with their unaccented counterparts or equivalents). They are:

À = Á = A   Æ = Ä

È = É = E   Ì = Í = I

Ò = Ó = O   Ø = Œ = Ö

Ù = Ú = U   Y = Y

In Queland, you don't do anything special with Sharp-S and you don't sort it in your alphabet, so you'll let it sort among the non-alphabetic characters.

V

Internationalization

The lowercase alphabetic characters behave similarly:

aãâbcç defghijklmñnoõôpqrst þuûvwxyzåäëêöüÿ

Lowercase accented characters behave in the same way as their uppercase counterparts.

When mixing uppercase and lowercase characters, there are two ways to sort them: case-sensitively, and case-insensitively.

When sorting case-insensitively, the upper- and lowercase characters are treated equally. "N" and "n" can appear before or after each other, depending on their order in the database.

When sorting case-sensitively, either the uppercase or the lowercase character always comes first (has more weight).

In Queland, when ordering the alphabet case-sensitively, characters appear in the order: uppercase first, lowercase second. So the comprehensive, case-sensitive sorting order is as follows (entries in parentheses are equivalently sorted):

When all of the text is uppercase:

(AÀÁ)ÃÂBCÇĐD(EÈÉ)FGH(IÌÍ)JKLMÑN(OÒÓ)ÕÔPQRSTÞ(UÙÚ)ÛVWX(YÝ)ZÅ(ÄÆ)ËÊ(ÖŒ)ÜŸ

When all of the text is lowercase:

(aàá)ãâbcçðd(eèé)fgh(iìí)jklmñn(oòó)õôpqrstþ(uùú)ûvwx(yý)zå(äæ)ëê(öœ)üÿ

When the text is mixed:

(AÀÁ)(aàá)ÃãÂâBbCcÇçĐðDd(EÈÉ)(eèé)FfGgHh(IÌÍ)(iìí)JjKkLlMmÑñN(OÒÓ)(oò-ó)ÕõÔôPpQqRrSsTtÞþ(UÙÚ)(uùú)ÛûVvWwXx(YÝ)(yý)ZzÅå(ÄÆ)(äæ)ËëÊê(ÖŒ)(öœ)ÜüŸÿ

> **Note**
>
> This might look complicated, but it is no more complicated than most languages. People just don't realize how intricate the collation rules are for their language.

As with the other tables, collation assignments are done in PROGRESS through the use of two 256-character collation tables. There is a table for case-insensitive sorting, and a table for case-sensitive sorting. The case-insensitive table is used by default by PROGRESS, and the case-sensitive table is used by PROGRESS when you specify that a field or variable is case-sensitive in the dictionary or in the 4GL.

Each entry contains a value called a *sort weight*, a number between 1 and 255. The basic mechanism is easy:

- The lower the number, the earlier the character comes in the alphabet. For example, if you gave "E" a sort weight of 103 and "Å" a sort weight of 147, then "E" would come before "Å" in your alphabetic sorting.

- If two entries have the same sort weight, then they are equivalent as far as sorting is concerned, and will appear in whatever order they appeared in the database. For example, if you gave "O" and "Ò" a sort weight of 92, then they would be identical, for all practical purposes, in the sorting of the alphabet.
- In the case-insensitive tables, the upper- and lowercase of the same character will usually have the same sort weight.
- In the case-sensitive tables, far fewer characters will have the same sort weight. Uppercase and lowercase characters will have different sort weights.
- The value 000 is a special case. An entry assigned the sort weight of 000 will be sorted as the German Sharp-S character, and will sort as "ss" (between "sr" and "st").

You can refer to the collation tables for codepage ISO8859-1 in Appendix D to see how these rules have been applied.

Note

For historical (backward-compatibility) reasons, the Basic collation for ISO8859-1 in PROGRESS sorts the alphabet this way when using case-sensitive collation:

ABCD...XYZ abcd...xyz

All of the new codepages defined since Version 7.3, except for the double-byte codepages, have the case-sensitive sorting order of AaBb... It is a trivial exercise to create a new collation for ISO8859-1 which would do the same.

Now, you could copy and edit the ISO8859-1 collation tables by hand with your favorite editor—as you did with the ISALPHA, CASE tables, and MAP tables—to create a Queish collation, but this would be very tedious and error-prone.

Instead, you can use a program (.p) shipped by PROGRESS which has been specially written for creating collation tables. The program, MAKECOLL.P, may be found in the $dlc\prolang directory, and should be run from inside PROGRESS.

Before you do so, though, there are a few points and requirements of MAKECOLL.P:

- The program will automatically create an alphabetic order which is case-alternating AaBbCc, etc., for the case-sensitive sort.
- The program will display characters in the codepage of the -cpinternal setting you have specified in starting up PROGRESS. It is possible to create a collation for another, completely different codepage, but the characters displayed will be those for your current codepage and font, not the working codepage and font.
- The program requires that the tables for ISALPHA, the UPPERCASE-MAP, and LOWERCASE-MAP have already been defined for this codepage. This is because the program will use them to create automatically the case-alternating collation.

In order to do this, you will now need to compile your own copy of convmap.dat (which you have in your c:\quework directory) to create a convmap.cp. This is done by running the PROGRESS utility proutil as follows:

```
proutil -C codepage-compiler \quework\convmap.dat \quework\convmap.cp
```

You will now create the Queish collation by running MAKECOLL.P. MAKECOLL.P will look for a file called convmap.dat in your local working directory, c:\quework. You created this earlier.

You run MAKECOLL.P by opening it into the Procedure Editor, and running it. You can enter the Procedure Editor from either the PROGRESS Desktop, or you can enter it from the PROGRESS Tools menu. You open the procedure by choosing Open in the File menu, and finding MAKECOLL.P in the $DLC\PROLANG directory.

Figure 18.3 shows the first screen that is used to gather the basic information:

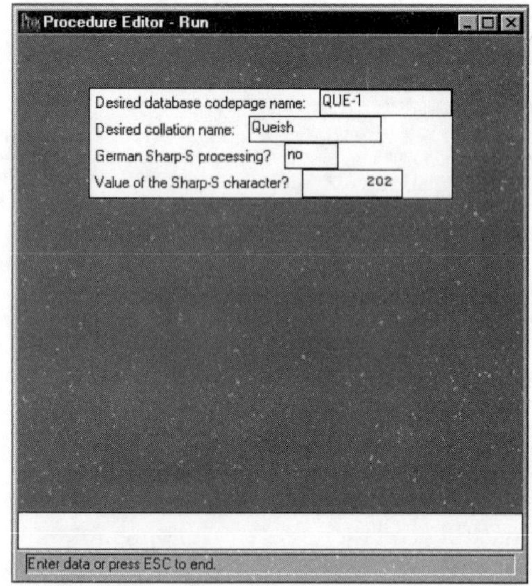

Fig. 18.3

Creating a collation table for Queish.

The desired database codepage name is Que-1 and the desired collation name will be Queish. As said before, you do not need German Sharp-S processing. The German Sharp-S character is 202, though you don't really need to fill in this value, since you don't care. This character will be sorted with the non-alphabetic characters.

Having filled in all the fields, type F2 to go to the next screen (see fig. 18.4), which is:

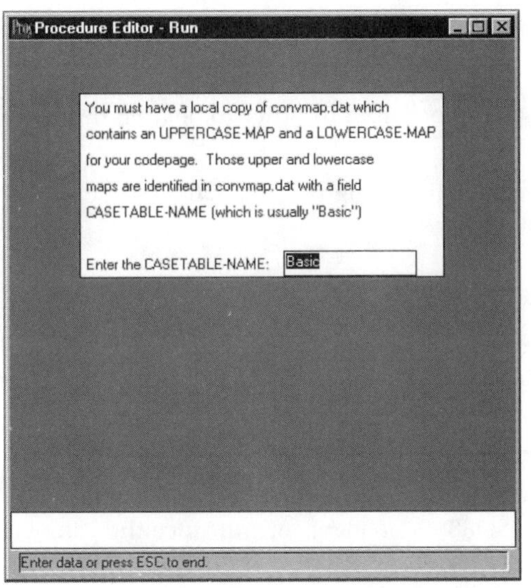

Fig. 18.4

Defining the casetable name.

The casetable name you have previously defined is Basic. This casetable will be used by MAKECOLL.P to do the automatic upper/lowercasing for case-sensitive and case-insensitive sorting. Some codepages have multiple case tables, which is why this must be specified (see fig. 18.5). Press F2 again to continue.

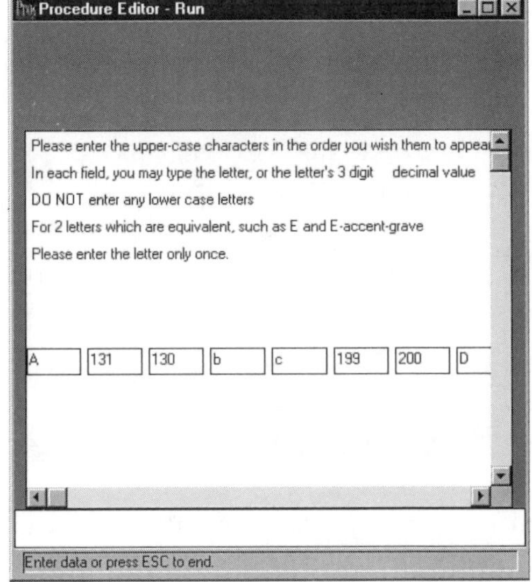

Fig. 18.5

Specifying the collation sequence.

In figure 18.5, you've started entering values in the table (it prompts you), supplying the alphabetic entries in the order you wish them to sort.

While inputting the entries, you have the option to input:

The uppercase character—gets interpreted as is;

The lowercase character—get uppercased in order to be used in the algorithm correctly;

The numeric value of the character, using the character's value in the target codepage.

> **Note**
>
> If you should accidentally input a character twice, the program will remove the redundant input (the first instance takes precedence).

You've entered the numeric equivalent for the extended Que-1 characters, since you are actually running this in the ISO8859-1 codepage, and since the values are different in the two codepages, different characters appear.

You fill in the entire collation list for Queish, and end up with the following (see fig. 18.6):

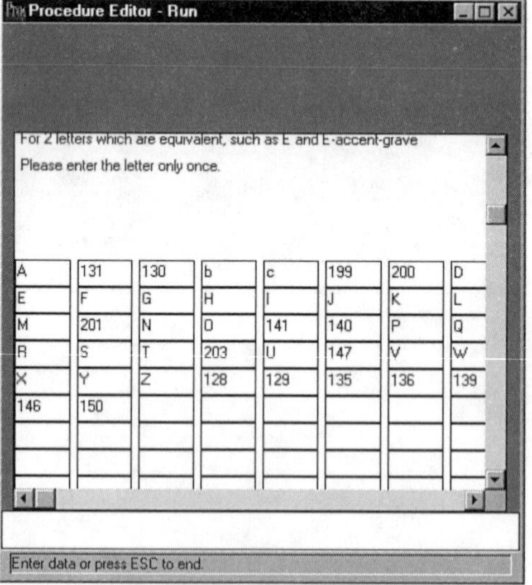

Fig. 18.6

Your Queish collation sequence.

These are all of the alphabetic characters that you want to sort. There are other alphabetic characters in your codepage, some of which you will equivalence to the characters above (the accented characters and diphthongs, for example), and some of which you'll ignore. The program will just put them at the end of the collating sequence—as good a place as any.

Press F2 to continue, and the program will automatically uppercase all the lowercase characters and remove redundancies (see fig. 18.7).

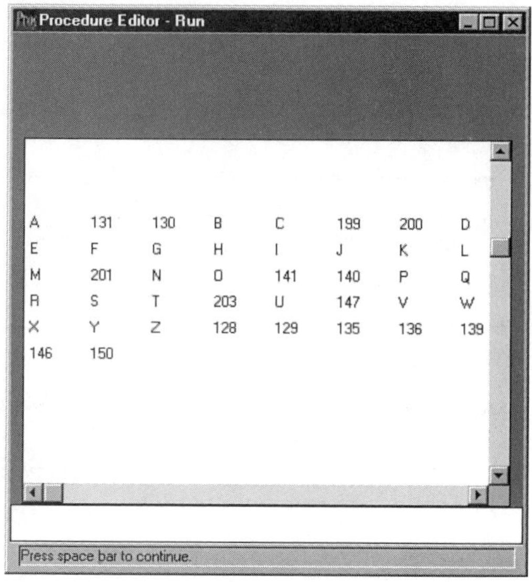

Fig. 18.7

Final, corrected alphabetic order.

The collation sequence has been adjusted to remove redundancies and to make all values uppercase. It now follows your desired alphabetic sequence as defined previously, so you can continue by again pressing F2.

In figure 18.8, you are being prompted to give assignments to those extended characters in the codepage to which you didn't explicitly give weights.

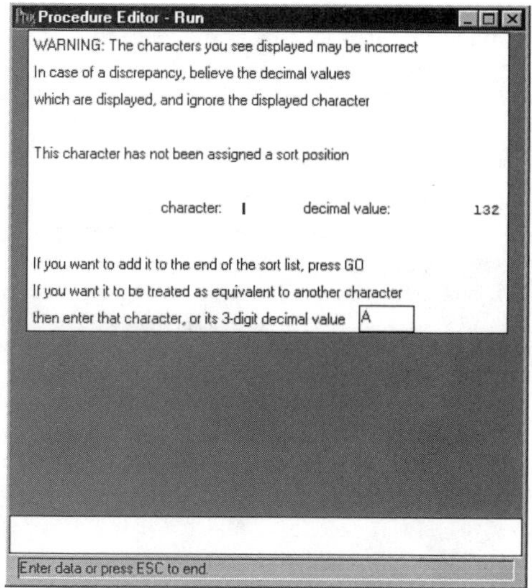

Fig. 18.8

Filling out the rest of the values.

Note

You will start with character 92. The program automatically weights the first 64 characters in the codepage with weights 1-64. The first character in your collation gets the value 65. You used all of the Roman alphabetic characters in the lower ASCII range, so the first unassigned character is 92, the first of 5 characters that separate uppercase Roman characters from the lowercase ones. You'll then step through the remainder of the codepage, being prompted for a value for every unassigned character.

When you don't care about a prompted character, you simply hit <carriage return>, and the program will assign it some value which gets it out of your collation sequence. When you *do* care about making an assignment, you input the character (or the codepage value) whose weight you would like it to equal.

Here, for example, you assign the character "À" (132) the same weight as "A." Note that since you are in a different codepage from the Que-1 codepage, the prompting character displayed is wrong (it is the ISO8859-1 character 132). For this reason, you should pay attention to the actual numeric value, not the character display of each character. Here, you entered "A," but you could have also entered a numeric value (for example, 65).

You continue inputting desired values for all the unweighted characters of the codepage. Finally, you reach the end, and the program is complete. You have now created a new collation table. MAKECOLL.P places a file named newcoll.dat in your working directory. Note: MAKECOLL.P always creates a file named NEWCOLL.DAT. If you wish to change the file name, you can edit MAKECOLL.P and change the name to any name you prefer.

Here is what the program generated:

```
#---------------------------------------------------------------------
# Collation tables for code page Que-1 and collation Queish
COLLATION
CODEPAGE-NAME QUE-1
COLLATION-NAME Queish
COLLATION-TRANSLATION-VERSION 1.0-16
CASE-INSENSITIVE-SORT
 /*000-015*/ 000 001 002 003 004 005 006 007 008 009 010 011 012 013 014 015
 /*016-031*/ 016 017 018 019 020 021 022 023 024 025 026 027 028 029 030 031
 /*032-047*/ 032 033 034 035 036 037 038 039 040 041 042 043 044 045 046 047
 /*048-063*/ 048 049 050 051 052 053 054 055 056 057 058 059 060 061 062 063
 /*064-079*/ 064 065 071 073 079 081 083 085 087 089 091 093 095 097 101 103
 /*080-095*/ 109 111 113 115 117 121 125 127 129 131 133 149 150 151 152 153
 /*096-111*/ 154 065 071 073 079 081 083 085 087 089 091 093 095 097 101 103
 /*112-127*/ 109 111 113 115 117 121 125 127 129 131 133 155 156 157 158 159
 /*128-143*/ 135 137 069 067 065 065 137 139 141 081 081 143 107 105 103 103
 /*144-159*/ 143 081 145 123 121 121 147 131 160 161 162 163 164 165 166 167
```

```
 /*160-175*/ 135 137 069 067 065 065 137 139 141 081 081 143 107 105 103 103
 /*176-191*/ 143 081 145 123 121 121 147 131 168 169 170 171 172 173 174 175
 /*192-207*/ 176 177 178 179 180 181 182 075 077 099 183 119 075 077 099 119
 /*208-223*/ 184 186 089 089 184 186 089 089 188 189 190 191 192 193 194 195
 /*224-239*/ 196 196 198 199 200 201 202 203 204 205 206 207 208 209 210 211
 /*240-255*/ 212 213 214 215 216 217 218 219 220 221 222 223 224 225 226 227
ENDTABLE
CASE-SENSITIVE-SORT
 /*000-015*/ 000 001 002 003 004 005 006 007 008 009 010 011 012 013 014 015
 /*016-031*/ 016 017 018 019 020 021 022 023 024 025 026 027 028 029 030 031
 /*032-047*/ 032 033 034 035 036 037 038 039 040 041 042 043 044 045 046 047
 /*048-063*/ 048 049 050 051 052 053 054 055 056 057 058 059 060 061 062 063
 /*064-079*/ 064 065 071 073 079 081 083 085 087 089 091 093 095 097 101 103
 /*080-095*/ 109 111 113 115 117 121 125 127 129 131 133 149 150 151 152 153
 /*096-111*/ 154 066 072 074 080 082 084 086 088 090 092 094 096 098 102 104
 /*112-127*/ 110 112 114 116 118 122 126 128 130 132 134 155 156 157 158 159
 /*128-143*/ 135 137 069 067 065 065 137 139 141 081 081 143 107 105 103 103
 /*144-159*/ 143 081 145 123 121 121 147 131 160 161 162 163 164 165 166 167
 /*160-175*/ 136 138 070 068 066 066 138 140 142 082 082 144 108 106 104 104
 /*176-191*/ 144 082 146 124 122 122 148 132 168 169 170 171 172 173 174 175
 /*192-207*/ 176 177 178 179 180 181 182 075 077 099 183 119 076 078 100 120
 /*208-223*/ 184 186 089 089 185 187 090 090 188 189 190 191 192 193 194 195
 /*224-239*/ 196 197 198 199 200 201 202 203 204 205 206 207 208 209 210 211
 /*240-255*/ 212 213 214 215 216 217 218 219 220 221 222 223 224 225 226 227
ENDTABLE
ENDCOLLATION
#-------------------------------------------------------------------------
```

Append the new collation table, stored in the file NEWCOLL.DAT, to your convmap.dat file in your local directory (c:\quework) by using your favorite editor. Before you can use this collation table, you must compile it. That is done using proutil. At the operating system level, you type:

```
proutil -C codepage-compiler \quework\convmap.dat \quework\convmap.cp
```

You can now replace the convmap.cp file in $dlc\bin with your own, or you can use the startup parameter `-convmap` to specify that you want PROGRESS to use a different convmap file. To do the latter, you would add to your startup parameters (or add to your startup.pf file):

```
-convmap \quework\convmap.cp
```

Now you have successfully integrated the new Que-1 codepage into the PROGRESS environment.

It will be necessary to remember to copy the new CONVMAP.CP file to the $DLC directory for PROGRESS to use it. Alternatively, you can use the `-convmap <filename>` startup option to tell PROGRESS to use your convmap.cp file.

Also, when you deploy your application, you will want to include this new CONVMAP.CP file so that the systems in the field will also have this new codepage support.

Using Deployment-Related Startup Parameters

As discussed above, different computers and operating systems may represent the same character set with different codepages. During the development phase, it is important to remember that codepages store alphabetic characters with different values.

It is also important to remember as you deploy an application that there may be different character set families and codepage mappings for different countries and languages.

The examples above were for the Western European, Latin American, and North American codepages IBM850 and ISO8859-1. Suppose you wish to deploy your application into Russia. Figure 18.9 shows what the Russian codepage environment looks like for heterogeneous client-server computing environments. Note that there are different codepages for DOS, Windows, and UNIX than in Western Europe. Also note that there are actually four different codepages being used in this configuration.

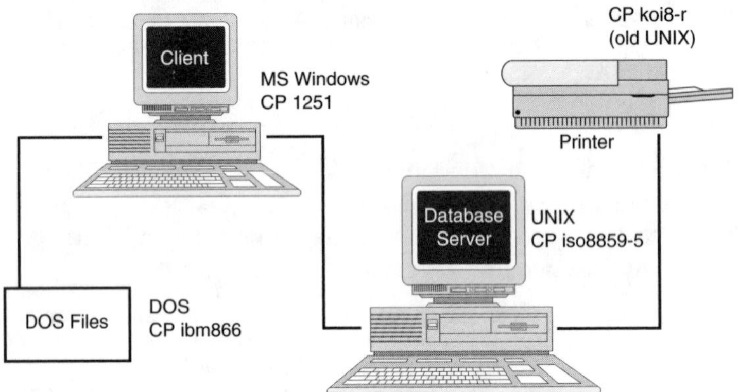

Fig. 18.9

Russian (Cyrillic) codepage in client/server.

How would you support these codepages in PROGRESS? Simply by setting the appropriate startup parameters and by creating an empty database with the correct codepage and collation loaded.

Here is the configuration, with the appropriate PROGRESS startup parameters used to designate codepage settings at all points in the configuration:

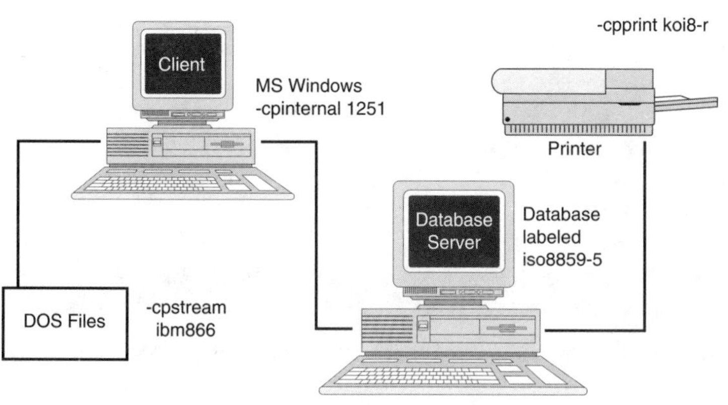

Fig. 18.10

Russian (Cyrillic) codepage in a PROGRESS configuration.

PROGRESS Startup Parameters

These startup parameters allow you to configure heterogeneous systems where codepages vary at different points in the configuration (as in the previous example for Russian Cyrillic codepages).

`-cpinternal`. This parameter allows you to set the codepage for PROGRESS to use for internal processing. For Microsoft Windows clients and UNIX clients, the default is ISO8859-1. For DOS clients, the default is IBM850.

`-cpstream`. This parameter allows you to set the codepage that PROGRESS uses when importing or exporting data and files. The default is IBM850.

`-cpterm`. This parameter allows you to set a codepage for the character-based client display different from the one you are using for internal client processing.

> **Note**
>
> In most GUI environments, the cpterm codepage is identical to the cpinternal codepage, and in fact, this is the default. There are cases where you might have a different terminal codepage from the processing codepages.
>
> Two examples: a UNIX 7-bit character terminal (does not support any 8-bit characters, and remaps characters such as {,},[,], to the extended characters of that character set (Ä, Ö, etc.). In this case you could use a codepage table to map from an extended character set to the display character set. PROGRESS, for example, includes Swedish-7bit, German-7bit, etc.
>
> A second example would be a Microsoft Windows screen doing UNIX character terminal emulation. The internal processing should probably be the ISO8859-x UNIX codepage, but the display codepage should be the Microsoft Windows codepage.

`-cpprint`. This parameter allows you to specify the codepage of a printer. The default is the value set by -cpstream, since the printer is a kind of stream.

V

Internationalization

`-cplog`. This parameter allows you to specify the codepage of the log file. The default is the value set by -cpstream.

`-codepage` argument to the `prolib` command. This parameter allows you to override the codepage setting in library files. Libraries are labeled with the codepage that is used to name all of the procedures. If they have been labeled incorrectly, or if you have a specific reason for overriding it, this may be used.

Tip

You probably want your library names to have the same codepage value as the rcode contained in those libraries.

Also, to aid portability of your application, you should probably also consider using only lower ASCII (lower 128) characters in the filenames for your code modules. As you have seen, in almost every codepage, the lower 128 characters are exactly the same, so you would not be remapping program names when moving from one codepage to another.

`-cpcoll`. This parameter allows you to specify a particular collation for the client to use. PROGRESS will use this value if specified (and if the collation can be found in convmap.cp). If you do not specify this value, PROGRESS will use the collation of the first database to which you connect. If you do not connect to a database, then PROGRESS will use the collation named Basic (found in convmap.cp) for the codepage set with `-cpinternal`.

Report Builder Command Line Parameters

Report Builder is a powerful tool for generating professional quality reports in PROGRESS Version 8. It brings together data from a variety of databases and other sources, and also functions in a heterogeneous client-server environment. Therefore, Report Builder must also accommodate different codepage configurations.

The following are Report Builder command line parameters that allow you to set the codepage for specific points in a Report Builder configuration. These values may be set on the Report Builder command line, in the startup.pf file, or in the rbstart.pf files.

`-rbcpreportin`. Specifies to Report Builder the codepage of the report definition files being read in. This is used to designate the codepage of the text fields, labels, report names, character string constants, etc. of .rdf's. When the reports are run, as with other applications, the default codepage for the execution is `-cpinternal`.

`-rbcpreportout`. The codepage to be used when creating and saving report definition files.

`-rbcpudfin`. Specifies to Report Builder the codepage of user-defined functions being imported.

`-rbcpudfout`. Specifies to Report Builder the codepage of user-defined functions being created and saved.

Additionally, PROGRESS Version 7 and Version 8 databases are labeled with the codepage of their contents. They also contain the specific collation used for building indexes and processing queries. Although you can retrieve this information via the DBCODEPAGE and DBCOLLATION functions, the information is stored and can be accessed by looking at the following fields of the _db record:

```
find first _db.
   display _db.db-xl-name.
   display _db.db-coll-name.
```

This can also be accomplished by:

```
display dbcodepage(1).
display dbcollation(1).
```

Determining Codepage-Related Environment Settings at Runtime

There are times when it would be useful to query at runtime what the settings in use are for the stream codepage, the internal processing codepage, and the current collation, among other information. This could be helpful when debugging behavior which is not understood, such as when the wrong character is displaying.

There are a number of ways to determine the settings of the codepage and collation environment parameters in use while your program is executing. You can access these like any other session handle, rcode info handle, or 4GL keyword.

Querying Session Parameters

PROGRESS session parameters allow you to see what the various settings are for codepages and collations around the configuration. This can help you understand problematic behavior when debugging a system being set up for the first time. These session parameters can also be read by 4GL programs, and certain PROGRESS 4GL statements and functions can operate with these values. See Chapter 15, "Developing Your Global Application," for PROGRESS 4GL statements and functions that are sensitive to codepage settings, and would use these session parameters.

SESSION:CHARSET. Contains the cpinternal codepage name. In PROGRESS Version 7.2, the startup parameters for codepages were -charset and -stream. These have been replaced with -cpinternal and -cpstream starting in Version 7.3. These are left for compatibility reasons.

SESSION:STREAM. Contains the cpstream codepage name. Again, in Version 7.2, the startup parameters for codepages were -charset and -stream. These have been replaced with -cpinternal and -cpstream starting in Version 7.3. These are left for compatibility reasons.

SESSION:CPINTERNAL. Contains the cpinternal codepage name. This is the codepage used for all PROGRESS internal processing on the client.

SESSION:CPSTREAM. Contains the cpstream codepage name. This is the codepage that all input and output streams are assumed to be working in, unless overwritten for printers and log files.

SESSION:CPTERM. Contains the codepage used for displaying to the terminal. In most GUI environments, the cpterm codepage is identical to the cpinternal codepage, and in fact, this is the default. There are cases, as detailed above, where you might have a different terminal codepage from the processing codepages.

SESSION:CPPRINT. Contains the printer codepage name. The default is the cpstream codepage.

SESSION:CPRCODEIN. This is the assumed codepage for text in rcode. The default is cpstream, but can be overridden with input parameter -cprcodein.

SESSION:CPRCODEOUT. This is the codepage to be used for writing out rcode text. The default is the cpinternal codepage.

SESSION:CPCASE. Contains the cpcase case conversion table name. This is the name of the casetable being used by the current session. In most cases, this will be Basic.

SESSION:CPCOLL. Contains the cpcoll value—the name of the currently active collation being used by this client session.

SESSION:CPLOG. Contains the cplog codepage name. This is the parameter for specifying the codepage to be used for writing the log file.

SESSION:DATE-FORMAT. Contains the string that is used to specify the order of days, months, years. This is set by the startup parameter -d.

SESSION:NUMERIC-FORMAT. Signifies which numeric format, American or European, is being used. The European date format is set by using the -e startup parameter.

CURRENT-LANGUAGE. Contains the current language being used in rcode files. When a program is compiled for multiple languages, that program supports multiple languages in its binary (executable) form. CURRENT-LANGUAGE is the language currently in use. See Chapter 17, "Translating Your Application," for more details.

Reading Rcode Information Handles

The following handles are useful to the system manager for understanding the contents of PROGRESS executable code on the system. If the system manager encountered strange behavior (the wrong characters are being displayed, the wrong translation language is being used, etc.), these RCODE-INFO (Rcode information) handles might be helpful to explain the events.

RCODE-INFO:LANGUAGES. As seen above, through the use of Translation Manager, rcode may be compiled in a number of languages. This handle will return the languages compiled into a program's rcode.

`RCODE-INFO:CODEPAGE`. Reports the codepage of the strings stored in a text segment of a program's `rcode`. By default, the strings stored in an `rcode`'s text segment are the `cpinternal` codepage of the session when it was compiled. It may have been overridden by the `cprcodeout` parameter.

> **Note**
>
> To be clear, when compiling code into `rcode`, PROGRESS reads in the procedure (.p, .w, etc.) using the `-cpstream` parameter, and writes `rcode` (.r) in the `-cpinternal` codepage (and labels it thus). When PROGRESS reads in `rcode`, it reads in the codepage set for that `rcode` file, and processes it and/or maps it to the current session's `cpinternal` codepage value. Of course, you can override this with the `cprcodein` and `cprcodeout` parameters.

Defining 4GL Functions

For the PROGRESS programmer, the following PROGRESS 4GL keywords and functions are useful to determine the specific codepage capabilities of the system at the site where the application is being run. All of these functions are callable from within the PROGRESS 4GL.

`DBCODEPAGE (`*`dbpointer`*`)`. This function returns the codepage of a database given as an input parameter.

In PROGRESS Command Reference terms, `dbpointer` may be an integer-expression, a logical-name, or an alias.

`DBCOLLATION (`*`dbpointer`*`)`. This function returns the collation name of a database given as an input parameter.

In PROGRESS Command Reference terms, `dbpointer` may be an integer-expression, a logical-name, or an alias.

`GET-CODEPAGES`. This function returns a comma-delimited list of all of the available codepages in memory for the current PROGRESS session.

`GET-COLLATIONS`. This function returns a comma-delimited list of all of the collations available in memory for a specified codepage.

> **Note**
>
> When PROGRESS is started, the convmap.cp file is read, and a table is set up in memory of all of the codepages found in the convmap.cp file. This is the list of codepages returned by the `Get-Codepages` function. All of those tables are not read into memory at this time (and, in fact, they probably never would be). The tables specified in the startup parameters certainly are read in at startup time, and when a database is connected, its codepage tables are read in if they are not there already. Likewise, if the codepage mapping parameters in some of the 4GL keywords invoke a codepage which has not already been read into memory, then those tables will be read in as well. Collation tables are handled in a similar fashion.

Miscellaneous Issues to be Resolved at Deployment Time

At this point, you are ready to deploy your application internationally. Before you deploy, however, there are a few remaining details to consider. The following sections cover some of the remaining issues to keep in mind as you get ready to deploy your application.

Installation Scripts

Installation scripts are programs run to install software. They will typically walk a user through the process of installing software to a system for the first time or update existing software with a later version. They are usually invoked from an obvious place, such as the root directory of a floppy disk.

There are a few international considerations for installation scripts:

- *Translation:* You should give serious consideration to translating the installation scripts. Some countries may not require the installation in their native language, but others will definitely require it.
- *Simplicity:* Installation scripts can be very complicated programs to run. Running them in a language which is not your own and following logic which may not be the way you think can make the installation process even more difficult. As much as possible, try to make the installation process straightforward.
- *Hardware Issues:* Be careful not to make any assumptions about the target hardware for the installation. If your installation script requires a 640 × 480 resolution screen, for example, you will have problems with the NEC PC 640 × 400 screen.

> **Note**
>
> An interesting point about the NEC PC: the floppy drive is C:, and the hard drives are lettered A: and B:! Be careful to allow your script to specify different source and target drives. Furthermore, media sizes are different. NEC used to ship with a floppy drive which supported only 1.2M floppies, not 1.44M. Depending on the media used in your target markets, you will have to provide your installation and program disks on diverse media.

Platform Availability

For the most part, you will rely on PROGRESS to protect you from hardware or operating system platform differences. However, if you require a certain operating system, be aware that its current version may not always be available in your target country.

For example, Microsoft Windows Version 3.1 shipped in North America and Western Europe (March 1992) fourteen months before it was available in Japan (May 1993).

The version for Korea followed two months later (July 1993), and the version for China (Windows 3.2) was available after that (January 1994)—20 months after the North American release. Additionally, there may be special editions of a platform for specific countries. There is a Solaris-J version of Solaris for Japan, for example.

Required Configurations

The basic system setup for a given platform may vary in other languages. For example, the input method editors for Double Byte Character Sets take up system memory. If the memory on your system was tight for supporting your program, you may not be able to fit your program in the available memory on a Chinese PC, for example. Also, certain hardware devices and services may not be as readily available in other countries. Fiber-optic lines for data communication are prohibitively expensive in some countries, and completely unavailable in others. CD-ROM and DAT drives may not be as prevalent in some countries as others, requiring you to provide floppy-based or cartridge software in some markets.

Product Components for International Use

There are four products available in PROGRESS Version 8 that cover or support all of the information above. They are as follows.

Translation Manager 2.0

This is the complete Translation Management program, including all software used by the Translation Project Manager and the Translator.

Visual Translator 2.0

This is the Translator's portion of the Translation Management system. It allows translators to perform translation through a procedure-oriented method (visually) or through a browser-oriented (edit mode).

International Supplement

Subdirectories of $dlc\prolang containing support files for many countries may be found in this product, along with convmap.dat, promsgs for over two dozen languages, .df files (dumpfiles) containing collation definitions for a variety of languages and codepages, as well as sample startup.pf files with codepages available for specific languages. This product is available at no charge, and can be included with any order.

Double Byte Supplement

This product contains the files necessary for running Double Byte Enabled PROGRESS. It contains a new `_prowin` executable, supporting double-byte character sets, as well as the probuildable objects to build your own double-byte client. Additionally, it contains the promsgs, .df files, and startup files for Japanese, Traditional Chinese, Simplified Chinese, and Korean. This product is available at no charge, and can be included with any order.

From Here...

In this chapter, you learned how to configure a system to handle varying character sets and codepages around the world. Although many codepages are already supported by PROGRESS, you have also learned how to add all of the tables necessary to integrate a new codepage into PROGRESS: ISALPHA tables, case tables, collation tables, and codepage mapping tables.

You have also learned about a number of queriable session and rcode parameters to help debug a system when codepage behavior is not as expected.

For more detailed information or references on internationalization, see the following:

- Chapter 14, "Designing Your Global Application," highlights the main issues involved in developing an application that is culturally acceptable (or culturally tailorable) for deployment in other countries.
- Chapter 15, "Developing Your Global Application," covers the *here's how to...*'s and *do*'s when developing an application in the PROGRESS environment.
- Chapter 16, "Preparing for Translation," covers the steps to prepare your application for translation, using the PROGRESS Translation Manager.
- Chapter 17, "Translating Your Application," covers the steps and hands-on information to convert your Progress application to another language using the PROGRESS Visual Translator.
- Appendix D, "Internationalization," provides a list of references on the subject of internationalization.

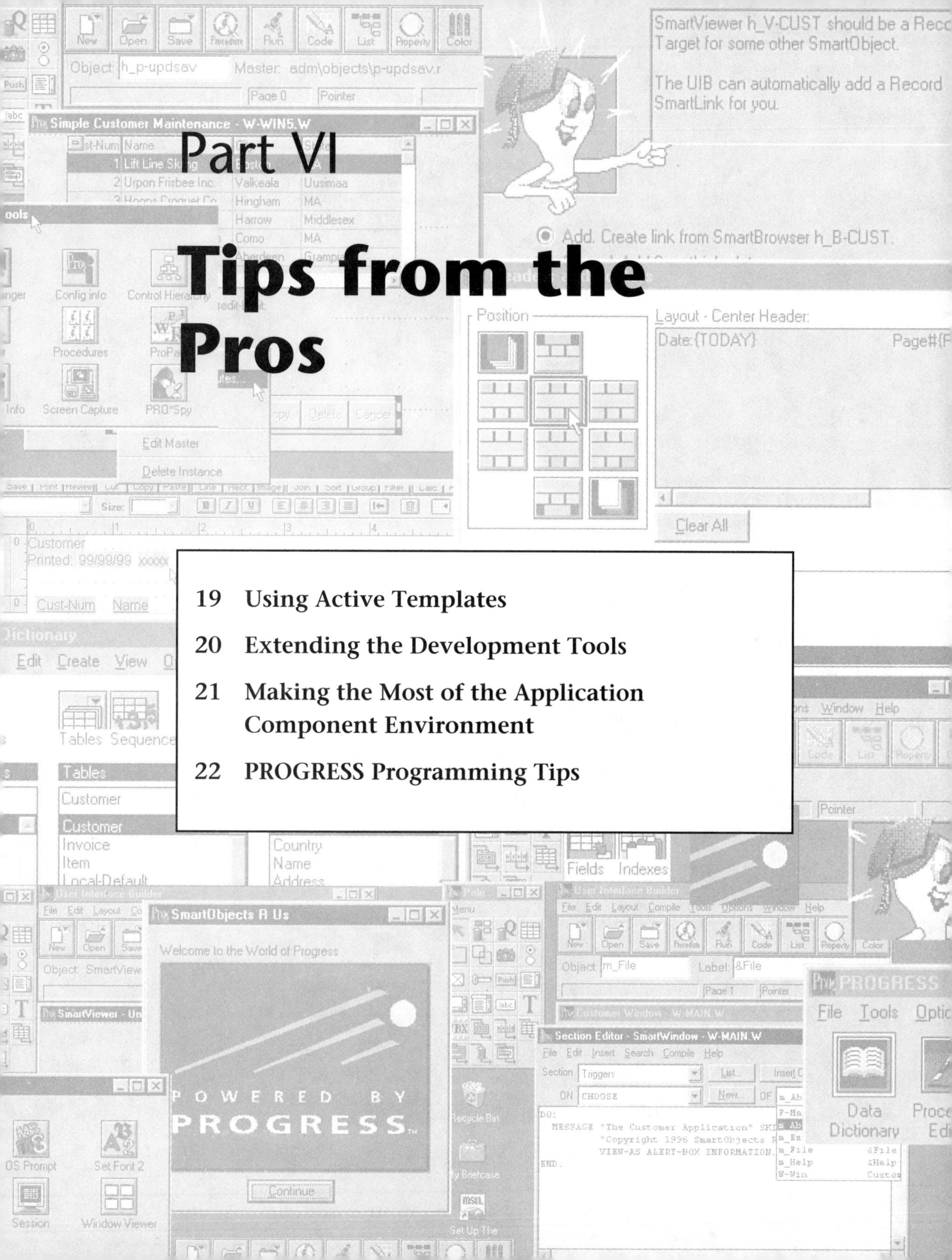

Part VI

Tips from the Pros

New
Open
Save
Procedure
Run
Code
List
Property
Color
Object: h_p-updsav
Master: adm\objects\p-updsav.r
Page 0
Pointer
SmartViewer h_V-CUST should be a Re
Target for some other SmartObject.
The UIB can automatically add a Reco
SmartLink for you.
Add. Create link from SmartBrowser h_B-CUST.
Simple Customer Maintenance - W-WIN5.W
st-Num
Name
City
State
1 Lift Line Skiing
Boston
MA
2 Urpon Frisbee Inc.
Valkeala
Uusimaa
Hingham
MA
Harrow
Middlesex
Como
MA
Aberdeen
Grampian
Changer
Config info
Control Hierarchy
Editor
Procedures
ProPath
Windows Info
Screen Capture
PRO*Spy
Edit Master
Delete Instance
Headers and Footers
Position
Layout - Center Header:
Date:{TODAY}
Clear All
Function List:
{TODAY} Today's date
{TIME} Time report started
{NOW} Current time
{COUNT} Records listed so far
{PAGE} Current page number
Customer
Printed: 99/99/99
Cust-Num
Name
City
State
Edit
Create
View
Options
Tools
Help
Tables
Sequences
Fields
Indexes
Customer
Invoice
Item
Local-Default
Cust-Num
Country
Name
Address
User Interface Builder
File
Edit
Layout
Compile
Tools
Options
Window
Help
Object:
Label:
Pointer
SmartObjects R Us
Welcome to the World of Progress
POWERED BY
PROGRESS
Continue
Object: m_File
Label: &File
Page 1
Section Editor - SmartWindow - W-MAIN.W
File
Edit
Insert
Search
Compile
Help
Section
Triggers
List...
ON
CHOOSE
New...
OF
DO:
MESSAGE "The Customer Application"
"Copyright 1996 SmartObjects
VIEW-AS ALERT-BOX INFORMATION.
END.
m_File
&File
m_Help
&Help
W-Win
Data
Dictionary
OS Prompt
Set Font 2
Session
Window Viewer
Recycle Bin
My Briefcase

Chapter 19

Using Active Templates

When assembling an application, one would like to do so quickly, with all the power and sophistication needed to do the job. Experienced developers know that many parts of a typical application are similar in appearance and function, so they tend to look for ways to reuse whatever they can. They draw upon code they have already written or use code from other sources. Without an organized repository of routines and code fragments, hunting down the right pieces of code is often a tedious and laborious task.

Voice-of-Experience Movies

See Table G.3 in Appendix G, "Contents of CD," for a list of the Voice-of-Experience files for this chapter.

How many times have you gone searching through your directories of source code to find that *right piece of code*? How many times have you spent so much time looking for code that you realize it's taking longer to find the code than it would have taken you to write it from scratch? Reusing code is supposed to save you time, isn't it? In this chapter, you will see how you can organize those common application pieces and use them in a flash!

Tips from the Pros

In this chapter, you will learn about:

- Using UIB Templates to standardize your code and to ensure a consistent look and feel.
- Creating active templates which interact with its users.
- UIB Extended Features (XFTRs) and how to use them effectively.

Using UIB Templates

The PROGRESS UIB gives you a way to construct a reusable unit called a *template*. A template is a PROGRESS 4GL source file which can be used to complete an application component.

Here are some typical uses for a UIB template:

- A window that is specifically tailored for your organization. It is the right size, color, and font. It has as all the default logic to handle different screen resolutions. It uses your preset window icon, and maybe even contains an image of your company logo.
- Building on the previous example, your window template could be more specific to certain database application tasks. For example, you could have a window that contains a preset menu bar containing various default menu items, and buttons that could save a record and close the window.
- A dialog box containing buttons, such as OK, Cancel and Help, which can be used through your application.
- SmartObjects.

When developing applications, a consistent look and feel is highly desirable. This is particularly true of GUI applications. It can be very frustrating and confusing to end-users when they cannot depend on consistent visual queues. You can ensure that everything is the right size, color, and font, as well as making sure that your common objects are all in the same location. Has your shop ever split up an application among several developers? When you put the pieces together, did you find that some developers put the OK and Cancel buttons in the upper right, and some across the bottom of their dialog? Having the entire team using the same templates can ensure a consistent look and feel.

While templates themselves solve many of the more mundane tasks of building applications, a developer using them still needs to adapt them to the task at hand. To put it another way, a developer using the standard window template still has to add database fields, browses, etc. More simply, from application to application, your standard templates may need to change for various reasons. You may wish that you could use the *same* set of templates in a variety of situations. In the next section, you'll see how this can be achieved.

Making Your Templates Active

It is possible to construct a template that performs specific user-defined actions when used in the PROGRESS UIB. Such a template is known as an *active template*.

Here are some common ways to use an active template:

- When a template is used, you can prompt the developer for information needed to tailor a window to a specific need. Here is where you may want to change the size, color, and font of a window, or prompt for the database fields and/or menu bar to be used. A developer may want to include a specific pre-processor section search routine in a dialog box.
- Offer online assistance to the developer using the template in the way of a cue card or a wizard. This makes your templates self-documenting and easy to use. ACE objects already do this, and we will discuss these later.
- Perform various functions during the UIB's processing of the new .w file.

A template is made active by user-defined sections in your template. These sections are known as an *extended feature* or *XFTR*.

If you've ever looked at a .w file, you've noticed that your 4GL code has been separated into various sections. This is so the UIB can read the file and reconstruct it. Here is an example of one typical section:

```
&ANALYZE-SUSPEND _UIB-CODE-BLOCK _CONTROL btn_hello C-Win
ON CHOOSE OF btn_hello IN FRAME DEFAULT-FRAME /* Hello */
DO:
  MESSAGE "Hello, world!" VIEW-AS ALERT-BOX.
END.
/* _UIB-CODE-BLOCK-END */
&ANALYZE-RESUME
```

Like the trigger code shown above, the XFTRs you construct also need to be processed by the UIB and, as such, have a similar appearance.

The Anatomy of an XFTR

An XFTR needs to be written in particular format so it can be processed properly. Let's look at the XFTR syntax:

```
&ANALYZE-SUSPEND _UIB-CODE-BLOCK _XFTR <name> <window> _INLINE
/* Actions: <realize> <edit> <destroy> <read> <write> */
<user-defined area>
/* _UIB-CODE-BLOCK-END */
&ANALYZE-RESUME
```

Table 19.1 Syntax Elements of an XFTR Command

Command Element	Function of the Command
<name>	The name of the XFTR
<window>	The name of the containing window
<realize>	The PROGRESS procedure you want to execute when the window is realized
<edit>	The PROGRESS procedure you want to execute when Edit is chosen from the Section Editor
<destroy>	The PROGRESS procedure you want to execute when the window is destroyed
<read>	The PROGRESS procedure you want to execute when the UIB reads the file in
<write>	The PROGRESS procedure you want to execute when the .W is written to disk
<user-defined area>	You can put anything you want here

When it's time to realize, edit, destroy, read, or write in the UIB, the UIB executes the procedure you've specified, if any, and passes the contents of the user-defined area to your procedure.

As you already know, several ACE objects contain XFTRs that implement cue cards, wizards, and auto-field generation. Let's start by looking at the cue card XFTR contained in the SmartViewer template that is located in the file (%DLC%\src\adm\template\vieweraf.w).

```
    &ANALYZE-SUSPEND _UIB-CODE-BLOCK _XFTR "SmartViewerCues" V-table-Win
    _INLINE
    /* Actions: adecomm/_so-cue.w ? adecomm/_so-cued.p ? adecomm/_so-cuew.p */
    /* SmartViewer,uib,49270

A SmartViewer is a procedure object which visualizes database fields.
A SmartViewer typically receives database records from a SmartQuery or
SmartBrowser.

CREATING A MASTER
Here's how you create a master:

    Step 1
    Draw database fields onto the SmartViewer design window.
    Step 2
    Save and close the SmartViewer.

Inserting An Instance
Here's how you insert an instance:

    Step 1
    Open or create a SmartContainer, such as a SmartWindow.
```

```
Step 2
Choose the SmartViewer master from the Object Palette.
Step 3
Draw the SmartViewer instance into the SmartContainer.
Step 4
Add all necessary SmartLinks between the SmartViewer and other
SmartObjects.
During assembly, the PROGRESS Advisor suggests links and creates them for you.
However, you can also add and remove SmartLinks with the SmartLinks dialog box.
To access this dialog box, choose the Procedure button from the UIB main window.
Then choose the SmartLinks button from the Procedure Settings dialog box.
*/
/* _UIB-CODE-BLOCK-END */
&ANALYZE-RESUME
```

Note that the name of this XFTR is SmartViewerCues. It is associated with the window named V-table-Win, and it has procedures defined for realize, destroy, and write. It also has some text in the user-defined area that is processed by these procedures.

Essentially, the cue card works as follows when the template is used:

- While processing the file, the UIB detects and stores each XFTR it finds.
- When the window is realized, the UIB executes adecomm/_so-cue.w and passes the user-defined area to the procedure.
- so-cue.w reads the first line of the user-defined area and breaks it into three pieces of data.

  The first is the type of cue card, which is also used in the title of the cue card's window. An example of a type of cue card is "SmartViewer."

  The second and third are used as the help file and help context, respectively, to use for its help button. In this case, the help file is the "uib" help file and the topic context for the SmartViewer cue card is 49270. When you press the Help button on the cue card, you will be brought directly to this topic in the UIB's help file.
- The rest of the user-defined area is used for the text to be displayed in the cue card.
- When the window is destroyed, the UIB runs adecomm/_so-cued.w, which destroys the cue card window.
- When the .W is written, the UIB runs adecomm/_so-cuew.w which effectively deletes the XFTR from the .W.

The source code for all the cue card routines are located in &DLC&\src\adecomm. Take a few minutes and look at the source files. You'll learn a great deal from them.

It is common, as XFTRs get more complex, to require information directly from the UIB or to get the UIB to do something that would otherwise be done manually. You will see in the next section how you can accomplish this.

UIB XFTR Advanced Programming Interface (API)

The Advanced Programming Interface (API) allows you to access information and methods within the UIB itself! This allows you customize the UIB to your needs and enhance its capabilities. You can use the API to construct your own UIB add-on tools, wizards and cue cards. There are several 4GL procedures that are designed to interface with the UIB in various ways. Here is a list of them and what they are designed to do:

adeuib/_uibinfo.p

This procedure is intended to allow you to peek into the UIB's internal data structures and ask for information about an object.

Syntax:

```
RUN adeuib/_uibinfo.p (INPUT  pi_context,
                       INPUT  p_name,
                       INPUT  p_request,
                       OUTPUT p_info).
```

where:

`pi_context` is an integer value that represents the "context" of the object to access. This value can be a:

> Context for an object, e.g., `RUN adeuib/_uibinfo.p (?,"Btn_OK","CONTEXT", OUTPUT i_context).`
>
> Context for the procedure, e.g., `RUN adeuib/_uibinfo.p (?, ?, "PROCEDURE", OUTPUT i_context).`
>
> Setting `pi_context` to `?` will imply the UIB's current procedure.

`p_name` is a character value that represents the name of the object to access. This value can be specified in the following forms:

```
Object [IN FRAME frame-name] [IN WINDOW window-name].
Object [IN FRAME frame-name] [IN PROCEDURE file-name].
```

If the frame or window phrase is omitted, then the current window and frame are assumed. If an object is unique in a window, then you may refer to it as `object IN WINDOW window-name`.

To refer to a window, frame, or procedure, preface the object with the type. For example: `FRAME f [IN WINDOW w]` to find frame `f`.

The following special cases also apply:

> `?` to get the current object (in the UIB's main window).
>
> `FRAME ?` to get the current frame.
>
> `WINDOW ?` to get the current window.
>
> `PROCEDURE ?` to get the current procedure.

p_request is a character value that defines what information is requested. The following is a list of values you can pass:

NAME: Return the name of the object.

PROCEDURE: The context for the procedure.

FILE-NAME: The name of the file where the object is stored.

TEMPLATE: Returns "TRUE" or "FALSE" depending on whether the current object is a UIB Template file.

TYPE: Returns the widget type of the object.

HANDLE: Returns the widget handle of the object.

PROCEDURE-HANDLE: Returns the procedure handle of the object (if it is a SmartObject)

CONTEXT: Returns the UIB context of the object. This value represents the recid of the object from where it is stored in the UIB's internal data structures.

CONTAINS *¦<comma-delimited list of widget types> [DISPLAY¦LIST-1¦etc. TRUE¦FALSE] [RETURN CONTEXT¦NAME]: Returns all or objects of a particular type. Optionally, you can specify an attribute that evaluates to a logical value, such as DISPLAY, LIST-1, ENABLE, etc. And you can elect to receive the contexts (default) or the names of the objects.

FRAMES: Returns all frames. This is shorthand for CONTAINS FRAME RETURN NAME.

FIELDS: Returns all database fields for a frame or browse widget.

EXTERNAL-TABLES: Returns the list of external tables for a procedure.

TABLES: Returns the tables used by a query, frame query, or browse.

4GL-QUERY: Returns the 4GL query for a query, frame query, or browse.

WBX-FILE-NAME: Name of the .wbx in which runtime attribute will be saved for the VBXs in a procedure.

COMPILE-INTO-DIR: The directory in which the .w will get compiled to.

p_info is a character value that contains the value returned.

adeuib/_accsect.p

This procedure allows you to read and write UIB sections.

Syntax:

```
RUN adeuib/_accsect.p (INPUT pcmode,
                       INPUT pi_context,
                       INPUT pc_section,
                       INPUT-OUTPUT pi_Srecid,
                       INPUT-OUTPUT pc_code).
```

where:

pcmode is a character value that defines the mode of operation. The following modes are valid:

GET: Returns the value of the section (or ?) specified.

SET: Changes the value of the section specified.

DELETE: Deletes the section specified.

pi_context is an integer value that represents the context of the object to access. If this value is ?, then the UIB will assume the current window or procedure.

pc_section is a character value that names the section to access. The following section names are valid:

DEFINITIONS: The Definitions section of the .w file.

MAIN-CODE-BLOCK: The Main Block section of the .w file.

TRIGGER:<event-name>: A user-interface trigger of the event specified.

PROCEDURE:<name>: An internal procedure of the name specified.

XFTR:<xftr-name>: An XFTR of the name and section specified.

pi_srecid is an integer value that represents the recid of the current section. If pc_section is ?, then this parameter is used to identify the section of interest.

pc_code is a character value that contains the contents (code) of the current section.

adeuib/_uib_crt.p

This procedure allows you to create objects in a design window.

Syntax:

```
RUN adeuib/_uib_crt.p (INPUT pi_parent,
                       INPUT pc_type,
                       INPUT pc_custom,
                       INPUT pd_row,
                       INPUT pd_column,
                       INPUT pd_height,
                       INPUT pd_width,
                       OUTPUT pi_context).
```

where:

pi_parent is an integer value that represents the context of the parent of the object to create. If this value is ?, then the current frame or window is assumed.

pc_type is a character value that is the name of the object to create. The name of any valid widget type, such as BUTTON, IMAGE, etc., can be specified.

pc_custom is a character value that specifies custom parameters for the object. Valid values are:

CUSTOM:<name>: The name of a custom entry from any loaded .cst file.

SmartObject:<object-file>: The name of a SmartObject to draw.

SPECIAL: <attribute-values>: An "on-the-fly" custom entry with a CHR(10) delimited list of attributes.

pd_row is a decimal value that is the row at which the object should be drawn.

pd_column is a decimal value that is the column at which the object should be drawn.

pd_height is a decimal value that is the height of the object being drawn.

pd_width is a decimal value that is the width of the object being drawn.

pi_context is an integer value that is the context of the object you have requested to draw. If the draw failed, the value of this parameter is ?.

adeuib/_uib_del.p

This procedure allows you to delete objects in a design window.

Syntax:

```
RUN adeuib/_uib_del.p (INPUT pi_context).
```

where:

pi_context is an integer value that represents the context of the object you want to delete.

adeuib/_uib_dlg.p

This procedure provides access to several of the UIB's dialog boxes, such as Query Builder, Column Editor and External Tables.

Syntax:

```
RUN adeuib/_uib_dlg.p (INPUT pi_context,
                       INPUT pc_dlgname,
                       INPUT-OUTPUT pc_args).
```

where:

pi_context is an integer value that represents the context of the object to pass to one of the dialogs.

pc_dlgname is a character value that is the name of the UIB dialog to call. Valid names are:

> QUERY BUILDER: Calls the UIB's Query Builder dialog. This dialog is used to create and/or modify any query for a frame, query, or browse object.
>
> COLUMN-EDITOR: Calls the UIB's Column Editor dialog. This dialog edits the database fields used in a browse object.
>
> EXTERNAL-TABLES: Calls the UIB's External Tables dialog. This dialog is used to add/delete database tables from the list of external tables of a procedure.

pc_args is a character value that represents the arguments passed to/from any of the dialogs. Valid values are:

> For Query-Builder

QUERY-ONLY: Allows only editing of the query. Does not allow you to add/modify the field list.

CHECK-FIELDS: The Query Builder should remind you to add database fields as well as give you access to them.

NO-FREEFORM-QUERY: Add this to either of the above, separated by a comma, to signify that the Freeform Query button should not appear on the Query Builder dialog. Use this option to disallow Freeform queries. (e.g. QUERY-ONLY, NO-FREEFORM-QUERY)

For External Tables

Specify the current list of external tables so that the dialog will put them into the list. You'll get back what the user said OK to.

For Column-Editor

None.

adeuib/_namespc.p

This procedure allows an XFTR to register names of variables or procedures so that they cannot be used by UIB users.

Syntax:

```
RUN adeuib/_namespc.p (INPUT pi_context,
                       INPUT pc_mode,
                       INPUT pc_list).
```

where:

p_Precid The context ID (usually the same as the recid) of the procedure object to access. If this is the context for a widget in the procedure, then the procedure is found anyway. If this is unknown then you will get the current procedure. (If a Procedure Object cannot be found then the procedure returns ERROR.)

pc_mode is a character value that is the name of the requested action. The syntax of this field is:

```
RESERVE|UNRESERVE [VARIABLE|PROCEDURE [NAME|NAMES]]
```

pc_list is a character value that is the list of names to add or remove.

Examples of How the UIB XFTR API Can Be Used

Let's look at where the cue card XFTR uses the UIB's API to get a better idea of how they can be used and why.

Cue cards are meant to appear only when a user, who is not the original author, uses a template to create a master file. They do so by selecting File,New as opposed to

File,Open. Therefore, the main cue card routine adecomm/_so-cue.w needs to know whether the file that activated it was opened as a "template" or used to create a master file.

A call to adeuib/_uibinfo.p, such as the one below, will determine this:

```
RUN adeuib/_uibinfo.p (trg-recid, ?, "TEMPLATE", OUTPUT cResult).
```

Another feature of the cue card is that it will destroy itself once a master file is saved. It does this by taking the XFTR's user-defined section and changing it to "Destroy on next read" when the master file is saved.

Each procedure to be called from an XFTR must have two mandatory parameters:

```
DEFINE INPUT        PARAMETER trg-recid AS INTEGER   NO-UNDO.
DEFINE INPUT-OUTPUT PARAMETER trg-code  AS CHARACTER NO-UNDO.
```

trg-recid identifies the context of the XFTR code-block in the UIB, and trg-code contains the contents of the XFTR's user-defined section. Notice that trg-code is an INPUT-OUTPUT parameter. This means that you can not only read the section, but also change its contents.

In the case of the cue card, when the master file containing it is saved, trg-code is changed to "Destroy on next read." This is saved into the .w in place of the original cue card text. When the cue card is opened in the UIB the next time, adecomm/_so-cue.w issues the following call to delete the XFTR code block if the value of its user-defined section is "Destroy on next read."

```
RUN adeuib/_accsect.p ("DELETE",?,?,INPUT-OUTPUT trg-recid,INPUT-OUTPUT
trg-code).
```

The next time this master is saved, the XFTR is no longer in the .w file.

Some other interesting calls to the UIB XFTR API are done by the wizards.

In adm/support/_wizqry.w, which is shared by both the SmartQuery and SmartBrowser wizards, the procedure needs to get the context of the .w's query, in the case of a SmartQuery, or the .w's browse, in the case of a SmartBrowser. Let's see what this procedure does in its Main Block:

```
    /* Get context id of procedure */
    RUN adeuib/_uibinfo.p (?, "PROCEDURE ?", "PROCEDURE", OUTPUT proc-recid).

    /* Get procedure type (SmartQuery or SmartBrowser) */
    RUN adeuib/_uibinfo.p (?, "PROCEDURE ?", "TYPE", OUTPUT objtype).

IF objtype = "SmartQuery" THEN
      RUN adeuib/_uibinfo.p (INT(proc-recid), "PROCEDURE ?",
         "CONTAINS QUERY RETURN CONTEXT", OUTPUT obj-recid).
    ELSE
      RUN adeuib/_uibinfo.p (INT(proc-recid), "PROCEDURE ?",
         "CONTAINS BROWSE RETURN CONTEXT", OUTPUT obj-recid).
```

The procedure gets the context of the current procedure. It uses the procedure context to determine the procedure's type. And depending on its type, it gets the context of the query or browse.

When the user hits the button to define or modify the query, a call is made to adeuib/_uib_dlg.p to run the Query Builder.

```
ASSIGN arg = "QUERY-ONLY,NO-FREEFORM-QUERY".

RUN adeuib/_uib_dlg.p (INT(obj-recid), "QUERY BUILDER", INPUT-OUTPUT arg).
```

Once the query is defined, a call is made to determine the 4GL of the query so it can be displayed.

```
RUN adeuib/_uibinfo.p(INT(obj-recid), ?, "4GL-QUERY", OUTPUT q-syntax).
```

We have seen how the built-in cue card and wizard XFTRs use the UIB XFTR API. In the next section, we'll get to write our own XFTR.

An Example of How to Write and Use an XFTR

Let's say that you write custom applications for a number of companies, and you want your SmartWindow templates to prompt you for a company's logo image whenever you create a new master file.

Our XFTR will need to do several things:

- Determine whether the object is a SmartWindow. If it is, we will prompt for an image.
- Determine whether the .w file is a "template." If so, we will not prompt for an image.
- Prompt for an image file on disk.
- Create the image on the frame inside the SmartWindow.
- Delete itself once the master file is saved.

You also need to think about which XFTR programs you'll need to write. For this example, you'll need one for the XFTR "realize" event, because you'll need to prompt for the image once the window is realized, and one for the XFTR "write" event, because you'll need to flag the XFTR for deletion when the master file is saved.

Use the following example to write your "Auto-Image" XFTR:

```
&ANALYZE-SUSPEND _UIB-CODE-BLOCK _XFTR "Auto-Image" W-Win _INLINE
/* Actions: primage.p ? ? ? wrimage.p */
/* _UIB-CODE-BLOCK-END */
&ANALYZE-RESUME
```

Copy src/adm/template/cntnrwin.w to c:/appdir/winimage.w. Open c:/appdir/winimage.w with the procedure editor and insert the "Auto-Image" XFTR just above the cue card XFTR.

The procedure primage.p would look something like the following:

```
/* Procedure Name: primage.p
 * Description: XFTR procedure to prompt for company image logo to
                * place in SmartWindow master.
 * Parameters:  INPUT trg-recid (int)
                * INPUT-OUTPUT trg-code (char)
 */

DEFINE INPUT        PARAMETER trg-recid AS INTEGER   NO-UNDO.
DEFINE INPUT-OUTPUT PARAMETER trg-code  AS CHARACTER NO-UNDO.

DEFINE VARIABLE cResult   AS CHARACTER NO-UNDO.
DEFINE VARIABLE logoname  AS CHARACTER NO-UNDO.
DEFINE VARIABLE objtype   AS CHARACTER NO-UNDO.
DEFINE VARIABLE fcontext  AS CHARACTER NO-UNDO.
DEFINE VARIABLE OKpressed AS LOGICAL   NO-UNDO INITIAL TRUE.
DEFINE VARIABLE icontext  AS INTEGER   NO-UNDO.

/* Is this .W a template? or not a SmartWindow?
   then do not prompt for image */
RUN adeuib/_uibinfo.p (trg-recid, ?, "TEMPLATE", OUTPUT cResult).
RUN adeuib/_uibinfo.p (?, "PROCEDURE ?", "TYPE", OUTPUT objtype).
IF cResult eq STRING(yes) OR objtype NE "SmartWindow" THEN RETURN.

/* Should we delete this XFTR ? */
IF TRIM(trg-code) = "/* Destroy on next read */" THEN DO:
  RUN adeuib/_accsect.p ("DELETE",?,?,INPUT-OUTPUT trg-recid,INPUT-OUTPUT
trg-code).
  RETURN.
END.

/* Prompt for the image file*/
SYSTEM-DIALOG GET-FILE logoname
  TITLE      "Choose Company Logo..."
  FILTERS    "Windows BMP files (*.bmp)" "*.bmp",
             "All Files (*.*)" "*.*"
  MUST-EXIST
  USE-FILENAME
  UPDATE OKpressed.
IF NOT OKpressed THEN RETURN. /* Abort on "Cancel" */

/* Create the image on the frame */
RUN adeuib/_uib_crt.p (?,
                       "IMAGE",
                       "SPECIAL:" + CHR(10) + "IMAGE-FILE " + logoname +
                       CHR(10) + "NAME logo",
                       1.0, 1.0, ?, ?,
                       OUTPUT icontext).
RETURN.
```

There are several important sections of the above code to point out.

Notice the section that begins with `/* Is this .W a template? or not a SmartWindow? then do not prompt for image */`. The program makes two calls to adeuib/_uibinfo.p, first to determine whether or not the .w is a template, and second to get the type of the .w.

Notice the section that begins with `/* Should we delete this XFTR ? */`. If the contents of the code block is `/* Destroy on next read /*` then the program makes a call to `adeuib/_accsect.p` and deletes the XFTR from the .w.

Notice the section that begins with `/* Create the image on the frame */`. The program makes a call to `adeuib/_uib_crt.p` to create an image widget in the .w with the filename chosen.

The procedure `wrimage.p` would look something like this:

```
/* Procedure Name: wrimage.p
                    * Description:  XFTR procedure to flag Auto-Image XFTR
 * to be deleted in a master file in SmartWindow master.
 * Parameters:     INPUT trg-recid (int)
                    * INPUT-OUTPUT    trg-code (char)
 */

DEFINE INPUT        PARAMETER trg-recid AS INTEGER   NO-UNDO.
DEFINE INPUT-OUTPUT PARAMETER trg-code  AS CHARACTER NO-UNDO.

DEFINE VARIABLE                cResult   AS CHARACTER NO-UNDO.

/* Is this .W a template, if so, do not flag XFTR for delete */
RUN adeuib/_uibinfo.p (trg-recid, ?, "TEMPLATE", OUTPUT cResult).
IF cResult eq STRING(yes) THEN RETURN.

/* Flag XFTR to be deleted */
ASSIGN trg-code = "/* Destroy on next read */".
RETURN.
```

Create these two programs and put them in your working directory. Also, make sure that you've added the XFTR to the template file.

To test your XFTR, click the New button on the UIB's main window. The New dialog box will be displayed. Click the Template button. The Template dialog box will appear, shown in figure 19.1. To locate `winimage.w`, click on Edit Path, add the path of the directory where you saved `winimage.w` and click on the path combo box. Select winimage.w.

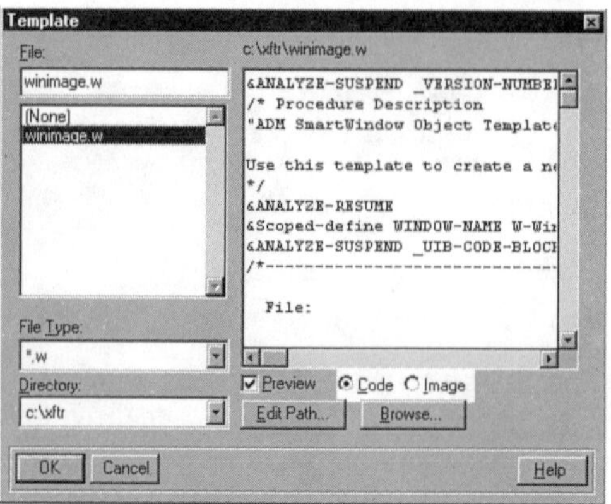

Fig. 19.1

Choose Template dialog box.

Click OK on the template dialog box to choose the template.

The template has been added to your available list of objects in the New dialog (see fig. 19.2). This allows you to create a master file from it.

Click OK on the New dialog to use the template.

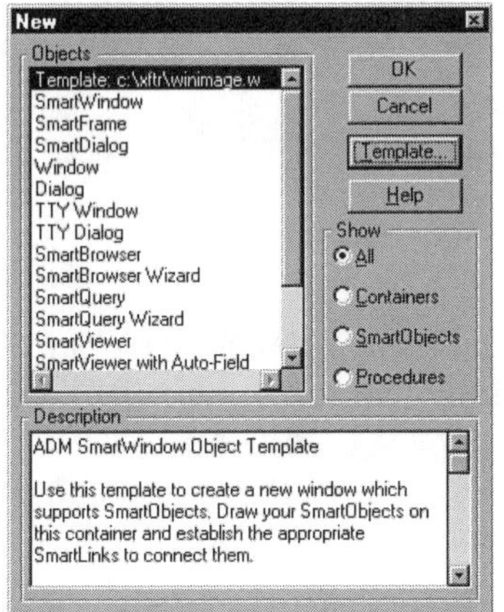

Fig. 19.2

New template chosen on New dialog.

The UIB will load this template file to create a new master file. Just after the window in the template is realized or made visible, the UIB will run `primage.p` and you will be prompted for an image file (see fig. 19.3). While the UIB loads a template, it registers any XFTRs which are encountered and processes them at the appropriate time.

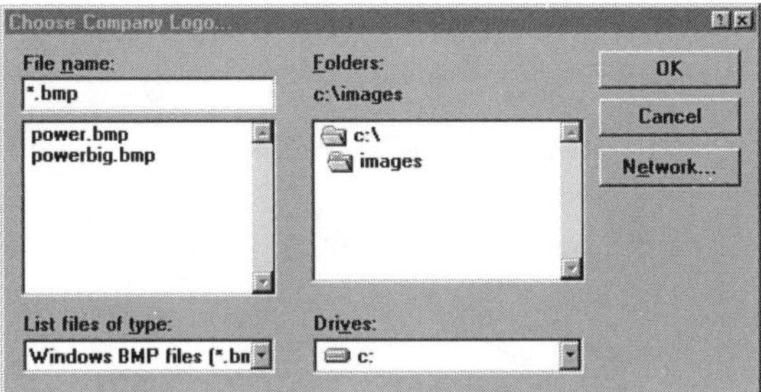

Fig. 19.3

XFTR prompts for an image file.

Select an image file such as dlc/gui/adeicon/powerbig.bmp and click OK. The UIB will now create an image widget on the SmartWindow's frame using the bitmap file you've chosen.

You learned a great deal about UIB templates and how to make them interact with the user. You took a look at the UIB's cue card feature. You took it apart and saw how it worked. You were introduced to XFTRs and you created an "active" template. Just imagine all the ways in which your templates can interact with their users.

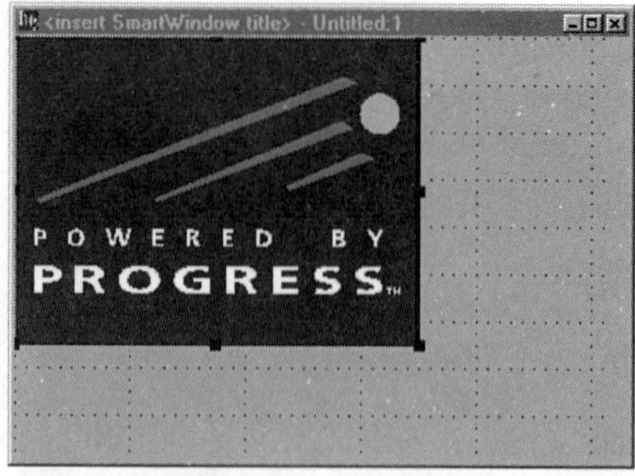

Fig. 19.4

SmartWindow with image created by XFTR.

From Here...

You can now create and implement your own XFTRs. By *activating* your templates you can customize your development environment and *leverage* the V8 tools. Active templates are an important function of making the most of the V8 ADM environment. The next chapters in Part VI, "Tips from the Pros," cover other advanced topics related to templates.

For more information on templates and other related subjects:

- Chapter 20, "Extending the Development Tools," will show more about customizing your development environment.
- Chapter 21, "Making the Most of the Application Component Environment," covers additional topics relating to UIB internals.

Chapter 20

Extending the Development Tools

Now that you have been using the PROGRESS tools, you may be wondering about how they work and, more importantly, how you can extend the environment to achieve your own goals. To fully explore this topic would take a whole book in itself. However, there are some particular issues that you will want to understand.

In this chapter, you will see where and how the PROGRESS tools can be customized and extended. You will also get an insider's look at how SmartObjects behave in the User Interface Builder (UIB).

Voice-of-Experience Movies

See Table G.3 in Appendix G, "Contents of CD," for a list of Voice-of-Experience files for this chapter.

Tips from the Pros

After reading this chapter, you should be able to:

- Customize the PROGRESS environment by editing the `progress.ini` file.
- Add pop-up menus and icons to the UIB's Object Palette to access your own SmartObjects and customized basic objects.
- Change the default characteristics of basic objects drawn in the UIB.
- Customize the PRO*Tools palette to add your own icons and tools.
- Understand where to intercept the standard file selection and file-saving mechanisms in the ADE tools.
- Create SmartObjects that take advantage of their intrinsic "UIB-mode."

Introduction to the PROGRESS.INI File

Applications written for Microsoft Windows typically need to store a lot of configuration and startup information. A convention established by Microsoft to store such pieces of information is known as an *initialization file* or *.INI* file. PROGRESS also uses an .INI file for this purpose; it is called progress.ini. This file is located in `DLC\bin` and stores information needed by the PROGRESS executable and ADE tools. PROGRESS Version 8 installs a default version of progress.ini that is manipulated by the PROGRESS environment at run-time.

A typical .INI file is divided into *sections* and *keys*. Sections are denoted as character strings enclosed in brackets (for example, `[Startup]`). Keys follow each section and are set equal to a particular value (e.g., `v6display=yes`). You can read and write to an .INI file using the 4GL statements `GET-KEY-VALUE` and `PUT-KEY-VALUE`.

In both Windows 95 and Windows NT, Microsoft is moving away from .INI files to a *registry* for user preferences and application information. The initial release of PROGRESS Version 8 supports only the traditional .INI file. Future releases will use the Windows registry.

PROGRESS will help you move from your .INI files to a registry. First, there will be a conversion tool in future PROGRESS releases that will take your .INI file and convert it into registry entries. Second, the `GET-KEY-VALUE/PUT-KEY-VALUE` syntax will be transparently upgraded to work with the Windows registry. As long as you use these PROGRESS commands, you will be insulated from the details of how settings are stored.

There are several noteworthy `progress.ini` parameters (see Table 20.1).

Table 20.1 Important Initialization Parameters

Parameter	Description
v6display	A logical value (yes/no) that indicates whether PROGRESS should startup in v6display mode. This mode provides compatibility for PROGRESS applications written for character-mode terminals.
ImmediateDisplay	A logical value that indicates whether PROGRESS should startup in immediate-display mode. When set to YES, PROGRESS will repaint the screen display after every I/O operation. When set to NO, PROGRESS waits until a 4GL statement blocks for input before updating the screen.
MultitaskingInterval	A numeric value that PROGRESS uses to adjust the way it handles cooperative multitasking. The higher the number, the longer PROGRESS retains control.
DefaultFont	The font used by PROGRESS to calculate the base character-unit size.
DefaultFixedFont	The font used by v6display.
Use-3D-Size	A logical value that determines whether the size of an object should include the space used by its 3D decoration.
DLC	The location of your DLC directory that is used to establish the root location of your PROGRESS installation.
PROPATH	Your PROGRESS PROPATH.
PROBUILD	Your path to PROBUILD.

You may decide to provide your own .INI file for your application that stores information relevant to it for a variety of purposes. A handy use for an .INI file is to store user preferences that are intended to restore a user's application to his liking.

For example, suppose you build an application where the user can state his preferences for what colors to use, what level of help should be provided, and what windows should be open. Naturally, you would not want the user to have to specify these preferences manually every time the application starts up. If your application saved these settings in the .INI file, then the application could read these settings at startup. You might create an .INI file as follows:

```
[Startup]
CueCards=On
LastWindowPosition=300,100
OpenWindowList=window1,window2,window3
ColorScheme=Rainbow
[ColorSchemes]
Rainbow=111,222,333
GrayScale=0,127,255
```

Depending on your environment, you may have created many `progress.ini` files for each of your projects. In evaluating problems with your environment, you need to be able to find out where the settings are coming from.

Tip

To find out the location of the progress.ini file that is currently in use, press the special key sequence Ctrl+Alt+Shift+F1. This key combination brings up the dialog box shown in figure 20.1.

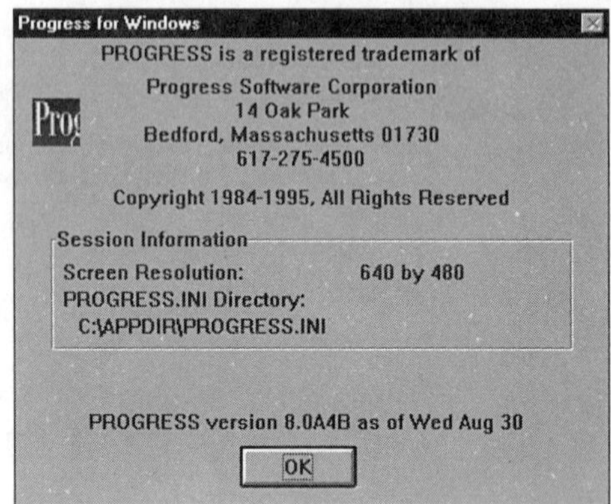

Fig. 20.1

Press Ctrl+Alt+Shift+F1 to see basic information about your PROGRESS session.

The UIB Object Palette

The UIB Object Palette can be extended in Version 8 of PROGRESS. The *Object Palette* is the palette window in the User Interface Builder in which you select the object you wish to draw in your current design window. This palette initially contains an icon for each of the basic objects, VBX's, and SmartObjects provided by PROGRESS. Each icon also has a pop-up menu listing various options related to each object.

You can extend the Object Palette, both by adding new icons and by adding additional pop-up menu items (by providing a *custom object,* or *.CST,* file). PROGRESS installs two such .CST files with Version 8 (which provide the default layout of the Object Palette). These files are located in `DLC\src\template` and are named `progress.cst` and `smart.cst`.

The custom object files have an additional function, which is to provide the entries that appear in the UIB's File, New dialog box and the pop-up menu on the New button, in the UIB's main window.

The purpose of a custom definition is three-fold:

- To configure a basic object to have customized characteristics, attributes, and trigger code.

  You may like to have multiple definitions for an object, each having different attribute settings. For example, you can define your button objects to have the same height and width. You can also inherit the characteristics from other custom definitions for the same object type.

- To add your own objects to the Object Palette.

  As you build your own SmartObjects, you might like to add them to the Object Palette so that they are readily available. You can also add palette items that represent any VBX objects you might use on a regular basis.

- To add your own object types to the File, New options.

  When you build your own templates for new classes of SmartObjects and other application components, you will want to add these to the list of new master files that you can create in the UIB.

You will write custom object definitions differently based on what you are tying to accomplish. Let's take a look at the different syntax:

- Customizing a basic object

```
*basic-object-type label
[DESCRIPTION [description-text-string]]
[attribute value]
[INHERIT name-of-entry]
[trigger-block]
```

- Defining a new object on the palette

```
#object-name &Default
[UP-IMAGE-FILE image-file [x,y]]
[DOWN-IMAGE-FILE image-file [x,y]]
[LABEL label-text-string]
[DB-CONNECT]
[NEW template-filespec]
[USE filename ¦
DIRECTORY-LIST directory-list
FILTER filespec
TITLE title-text-string-for-choose-dialog]
```

- Defining a custom definition for a new object

```
*object-name label
[USE filename ¦
 DIRECTORY-LIST directory-list
 FILTER filespec
 TITLE title-text-string-for-choose-dialog]
```

- Defining a Container, Procedure, or SmartObject type for the New dialog box

```
*NEW-CONTAINER label
[NEW-TEMPLATE template-name]

*NEW-PROCEDURE label
[NEW-TEMPLATE template-name]

*NEW-SMARTOBJECT label
[TYPE type-of-smartobject]
[NEW-TEMPLATE template-name]
```

> **Note**
>
> When you use a label of `&Default` next to an object-type, you will override the default for that object. For example, when you simply select that object and draw it on a design window, the `&Default` definition is what you will get.

Let's take a closer look at each of these files:

Understanding Custom Definitions in PROGRESS.CST

This file defines custom definitions for many of the basic objects, as well as several objects that appear in the New dialog box. When you define a custom object, it can appear in several locations on the Object Palette:

- In the pop-up menu associated with each palette item, accessed by a right-mouse click.
- In the menu bar next to each menu item corresponding to a given object.
- In the UIB's New dialog box.

Let's look at one of the definitions in this standard DLC\src\template\`progress.ini` file:

```
*BUTTON          &OK
DESCRIPTION      Standard Dialog OK Button
INHERIT          C&ustom Width/Color
AUTO-GO          YES
AUTO-END-KEY     NO
DEFAULT-BTN      YES
DEFAULT-STYLE    YES
LABEL            OK
NAME             Btn_OK
```

Suppose you were going to create an "OK" button from scratch. You would draw a basic button into a dialog box. This button would show as "Button 1" in the UIB. In order to turn it into an OK button for your application, you would have to go into the buttons property sheet and set many properties. You would:

- Change the label to **OK**.
- Set the attributes that cause the button to accept changes in a dialog box (AUTO-GO = YES, AUTO-END-KEY = NO, DEFAULT-BUTTON).
- Change the visualization of the button to be consistent with the width, color, and style of similar buttons in your application
- Give the object a more meaningful name: **Btn_OK**.

You would have to make these same changes every time you wanted to make a similar button in your application. Because OK buttons are standard user-interface elements, you would spend a lot of your time repeating the same steps.

Fortunately, you do not need to build standard buttons from scratch every time. The definitions in a custom object file store the attributes you would otherwise have to set in an object's property sheet. By choosing the custom object from the pop-up menu on the Object Palette, you are asking the UIB to create the button and make the changes automatically.

The standard `progress.cst` file contains many standard variations to the basic objects, such as the OK button definition above. As you identify additional standard objects in your own applications, you can create your own .CST files and add them to the UIB's Object Palette.

A complete list of the attributes for basic objects supported in custom object defintions is provided in Appendix E, "Custom Object Options."

The custom object definition shown above changes the characteristics of objects that you can select on the Object Palette. You may also like to change the characteristics of the files, windows, and dialog boxes that you can create with the UIB.

For example, you may find that you are always changing the size and shape of the new windows that you create with the UIB. Perhaps you are building windows that must fit on smaller, VGA, screens. You might like to define a variation of the Window template that is sized specifically for the VGA resolution. To accomplish this, you should make a copy of `DLC\src\template\window.w`, make your changes, and save it under another name, (for example, vgawin.w). Then you may write a custom definition like the following:

```
*NEW-CONTAINER &VGA Window
NEW-TEMPLATE src/template/vgawin.w
```

You can make these changes directly into the standard `progress.cst` file, or to your own .CST files.

> **Note**
>
> Changing a custom object file will not automatically cause the change to be reflected in the UIB. You must make sure the UIB uses those changes by restarting the UIB, or by choosing the Menu, Use Custom option on the UIB's Object Palette.
>
> Choosing Menu, Use Custom will bring up a dialog box showing all the custom object files in use. Pressing OK will instruct the UIB to reload the files, even if you do not change the list.

When a new custom object definition is loaded, you will see an entry in the New dialog box called *VGA Window*. If you choose this option, you will create a new master file based on the template file that you specified.

As you can see, this capability provides you with an enormous amount of customization ability. You can customize every aspect of the files you create and the objects you draw in the UIB (or, at least, every aspect supported by the UIB). There are many ways that you might take advantage of custom objects, including:

- Changing the default sizes of new windows and dialog boxes
- Changing the basic templates to have your own comments or header information in the files created
- Adding standard buttons to the Object Palette that execute standard functions in your application, such as sending or reading e-mail
- Adding fill-ins or combo-boxes initialized with specific values, or with customized validation code

Defining SmartObjects in SMART.CST

Just as `progress.cst` customizes to the basic objects in your PROGRESS session, `smart.cst` defines all the SmartObject extentions in PROGRESS Version 8.

This file, located in `DLC\src\template\smart.cst`, specifies which SmartObject templates are used in the File, New dialog box, as well as which SmartObject icons appear on the Object Palette. If you decide not to use `smart.cst`, the UIB would effectively be shut off from the SmartObject technology in Version 8.

Let's look at one of the definitions in this `smart.cst` file, which defines the entry for the SmartBrowser icon on the Object Palette:

```
#SmartBrowser   &Default
UP-IMAGE-FILE   adeicon/wp_up 28,196
DOWN-IMAGE-FILE adeicon/wp_down 28,196
LABEL           SmartBro&wser
DB-CONNECT
NEW-TEMPLATE    src/adm/template/browser.w
DIRECTORY-LIST  .,adm/samples
FILTER          b-*.*,b-*.w,b-*.r,*.*
TITLE           Choose SmartBrowser
```

This definition defines a new palette item for the SmartBrowser object. Since `&Default` was used in the definition, this becomes the default for a SmartBrowser object. A useful modification that you may wish to make is to the `DIRECTORY-LIST` and `FILTER` parameters.

If you decide to store some, or all, of your new SmartBrowsers in a particular directory, change `DIRECTORY-LIST`. (for example, `DIRECTORY-LIST src/sb`). Remember that you should list these directories relative to your `PROPATH` setting.

If you decide on a different file name prefix for your SmartBrowsers, you should change `FILTER` (for example, `FILTER sb*.r, sb*.w`).

Also note that the `DB-CONNECT` parameter indicates that the UIB will prompt you to connect a database if none are currently connected at the time you select this object.

You may also want to add your own objects to the palette, or even replace the standard ADM objects entirely. To delete a SmartObject from your environment, simply delete any definitions for it in the `smart.cst` file. If you want to add your own definition for your own objects, your new definition may look like the following:

```
#MyObject        &Default
UP-IMAGE-FILE    images/myobj-u
DOWN-IMAGE-FILE images/myobj-d
LABEL            &MyObject
DB-CONNECT
NEW-TEMPLATE     src/myobj/template/mobase.w
DIRECTORY-LIST   src/myobj
FILTER           mo*.w
TITLE            Choose MyObject
```

You can define variations to this new object by adding entries such as:

```
*MyObject        MyObject&A
USE              src/myobj/template/moa.w

*MyObject        MyObject&B
USE              src/myobj/template/mob.w
```

The entry needed to add this new object to the New dialog box's list is similar to the entry needed to add any template to the New dialog box. You can specify a `*NEW-CONTAINER`, `*NEW-SMARTOBJECT`, or `*NEW-PROCEDURE`. For each type, you specify the name of the template file to use (on the `NEW-TEMPLATE` line).

Earlier in this chapter, you saw how the VGA Window was added as a new type of container. The following code adds the new class of SmartObject.

```
*NEW-SMARTOBJECT This is &MyObject
TYPE             MyObject
NEW-TEMPLATE     src/myobj/template/mobase.w
```

Note

When you add a SmartObject type to both the New dialog box and the Object Palette, you can link the two by specifying the TYPE in the definition of the `*NEW-SMARTOBJECT`. However, if you do this, make sure that the "*" entries (defining the New dialog box entries) come after the corresponding "#" entry (defining the Object Palette item) in the .CST file.

Customizing Your PRO*Tools

If you're like most developers, you write handy little shortcut routines all the time that become hard to find when you need them. These routines might connect to particular databases, set up your PROPATH, or update tables in your database. Normally, to run these routines you would start a Procedure Window in the PROGRESS toolset and write a program to invoke your routine.

An easier way to keep these routines readily accessible is to add them to PRO*Tools. Adding a program to PRO*Tools is easy through PRO*Tools own customization dialog box (see fig. 20.2).

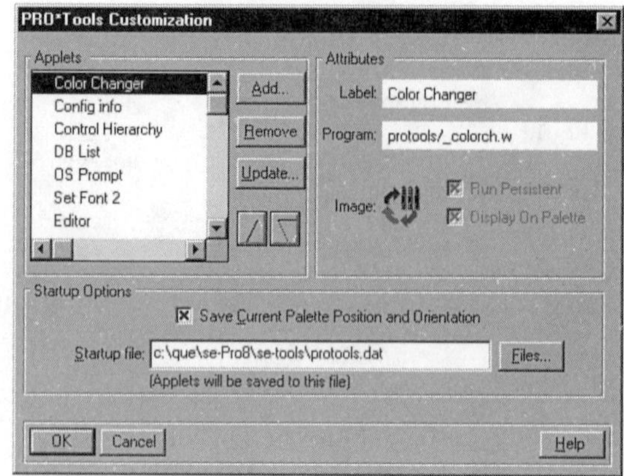

Fig. 20.2

*The PRO*Tools Customization dialog box.*

To invoke the PRO*Tools customization dialog box, follow these steps:

1. Click the right-mouse button in the PRO*Tools window. This pops up a menu that allows you to turn on PRO*Tools' menu bar.
2. Select the Menu Bar option. A menu bar will be added to the PRO*Tools window.
3. On that menu, choose the File, Customize option.

You are now ready to add your routine to the PRO*Tools palette:

1. Click the Add button. The Add PRO*Tools Applet dialog box appears (see fig. 20.3).

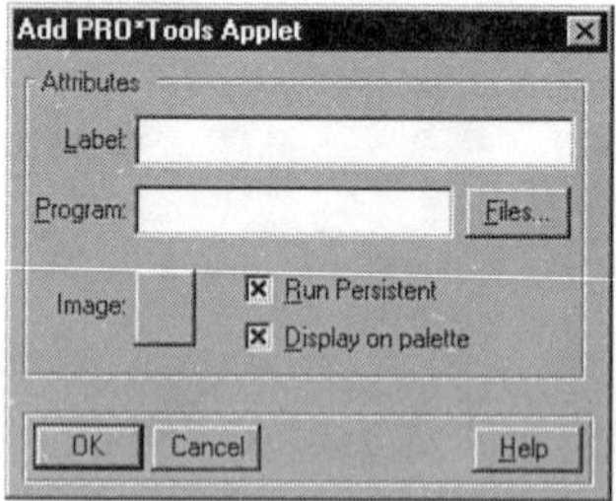

Fig. 20.3

*The Add PRO*Tools Applet dialog box.*

2. Type the name of your routine into the Program field. Optionally, you can use the Files button to browse for the file name of your program file.
3. If this routine is not meant to be run `PERSISTENT`, then do not check the Run Persistent check box.
4. You will also need to specify how your routine will look on the PRO*Tools palette. Do this by entering a name into the Label field, and clicking the Image button to specify a bitmap file.

5. Click OK to return to the PRO*Tools Customization dialog box.
6. Click OK again to save the new applet into the startup file.

Using the PRO*Tools Customization dialog box, you can do several things besides adding a program:

- You can Update the information for an existing entry.
- You can Remove existing programs.
- You can change the order in which the programs appear in the palette by clicking the up and down arrow buttons. This option is useful if you want to group related applets, or move the most common routines to the upper-left corner of the PRO*Tools palette.
- You can determine whether a program should be displayed in the palette window or not. This feature is useful if you want to minimize the size of your palette, but you don't want to throw out the definition of a palette entry. If you remove the entry entirely and then change your mind, you will have to remember all the attributes and re-type them into the Add PRO*Tools Applet dialog. It is much easier to simply choose not to display a defined item than it is to remove and then re-enter it.
- You can determine the name of the startup file in which the definitions of the programs are stored. It is possible to have many PRO*Tools startup files. You might create different files that have different options, perhaps depending on what project you are working on. Generally, however, most users stick with a single file.
- You can save the screen position and the visual orientation (for example, buttons only or buttons and labels) of the palette window. The name of the startup file and the palette position and orientation are saved to the user's `progress.ini`.

In a group development environment you may choose to have all developers share a PRO*Tools startup file. This way, the entire team can have access to the same tools, as well as having the ability to add new ones for everyone to use. An individual also has the ability to have his own startup file. To do this, the user should make private copies of `progress.ini` and `protools.dat`.

Writing Custom Handlers for Standard ADE Events

Most users of the UIB and the other PROGRESS tools will be happy with the standard behavior. However, there exists a class of power users who want to change the behavior of the tools at a very basic level. These are users who want to add some functionality to the UIB itself, perhaps by augmenting the Code Section Editor with a toolbar or adding new menu options to the UIB's main window.

Another class of power user will want to change the way the tools find and access files. Preeminent of these are people who want to add Source Code Control capabilities to the PROGRESS tools. These people want to intercept the tools when they open and save files, so that customized processing can occur.

The PROGRESS tools support these power users through a set of published ADE events and API procedures. This section describes the ADE events in PROGRESS Version 8, and describes the main procedures that effect file access.

This is an advanced topic. You do not need to understand any of this in the normal use of the PROGRESS tools. If you do want to intercept ADE events, then you will find yourself writing procedures to replace the standard handlers supplied by PROGRESS in `DLC/gui/adecomm`.

Tip

The source code for all the ADE event handlers can be found in the DLC\src\adecomm directory. Before you decide to write your own handlers, you should first check the source code.

Any information you find on these handlers, whether in this book or in PROGRESS' own documentation, may be outdated. Always go to the original source files. The information there is guaranteed to be the most accurate description of the ADE events.

The ADE events are a mechanism by which you can intercept certain events that occur inside ADE tools. These events are triggered by the UIB, Procedure Editor, and Procedure Window tools. Each time an event occurs, a procedure called `adecomm\_adeevnt.p` is called and is passed information, including the event which has occurred. To write an event handler for these events, you need to write your own version of `adecomm\_adeevnt.p` and perform the actions that are required.

A description of the parameters that are used to call `adecomm\_adeevnt.p` can be found in the original source file, `DLC\src\adecomm\_adeevnt.p`. They are summarized in table 20.2.

Input Parameters

Table 20.2 shows the parameters for adecomm_adeevnt.p.

Table 20.2 Parameters for adecomm_adeevnt.p

Parameter	Type	Description
p_product	Input	A character field in which the name of the ADE tool is passed. Valid values are "UIB" and "Editor."
p_event	Input	A character field in which the name of the event is passed.
p_context	Input	A character field that is a unique context string that can be used to compare the object, or context, of an event.

Parameter	Type	Description
p_other	Input	A character field that is used to pass additional information, such as the file name of the file being saved.
p_ok	Output	A logical field that can be used to allow or disallow an impending event. For example, returning FALSE to a BEFORE-SAVE event will cancel the SAVE event.

Output Parameters

The file `adecomm\_adeevnt.p` is called every time the UIB reads or writes a file. Each of these situations sends a different value of `p_event`. Table 20.3 shows events that are produced by the UIB during its processing of a source file.

Table 20.3 ADE File Events Issued by the UIB

Event Name	Description
New	Called after a new window/dialog box is created.
Before-Open	Called just before the .w is opened/created.
Open	Called after a window has been opened.
Before-Close	Called before a window is to be closed. Returning FALSE from `adecomm\_adeevnt.p` will cancel the close operation.
Close	Called after a window has been closed.
Before-Save	Called immediately before a window is saved, but after the name for the save has been decided on. Returning FALSE from `adecomm\_adeevnt.p` will cancel save operation.
Save	Called after a window has been saved.
Before-Run	Called before a file has been written to disk for a run. Returning FALSE from `adecomm\_adeevnt.p` will cancel the run operation.
Run	Called after a file has been executed.
Before-Debug	Same as Before-Run (except Debug has been chosen).
Debug	Same as Run (except Debug has been chosen).
Before-Check-Syntax	Called before a Check Syntax. Returning FALSE from `adecomm\_adeevnt.p` will cancel the Check Syntax operation.
Check-Syntax	Called after a Check Syntax.

In addition, the UIB also issues events when it starts up or shuts down. Table 20.4 shows events produced by the UIB during startup and shutdown of the UIB.

Table 20.4 ADE Tool Startup/Shutdown Events for the UIB

Event Name	Description
Startup	Called when the UIB has been loaded and initialized. This call occurs immediately before user input is allowed. In this case: `p_context = STRING` (procedure handle of the UIB main routine) `p_other = STRING` (widget-handle of the UIB main window).
Shutdown	Called when a user requests that the UIB shutdown. This event occurs before setting have been saved or objects destroyed. `p_context = STRING` (procedure handle of the UIB main routine) `p_other = STRING` (widget-handle of the UIB main window).

PROGRESS supplies a stubbed version of `adecomm\_adeevnt.p`. You can look at its comment header for additional information.

By using ADE Events, you are able to provide additional functionality and allow your tools to work in tandem with ADE tools.

An example of a tool that uses ADE Events heavily is RoundTable Source Code Control. It uses Open, Save, and Close events, among others, to facilitate the check-in and check-out of source files.

You can also manipulate the ADE tools directly. For example, upon startup of the UIB, you can use the handle of the UIB's main window to modify or add to the UIB's menubar. By this method, you can add access to your own tools, which will then be directly accessible by you and your developers.

The following custom version of `adecomm\_adeevnt.p` adds a menu item to the Tools menu of the UIB that, when chosen, runs the PROPATH Editor from PRO*Tools.

Listing 20.1 \examples\chap-20_adeevnt.p—Adding Menu Item to UIB Tools Menu

```
/* a custom version of adecomm\_adeevnt.p */

DEFINE INPUT        PARAMETER p_product  AS CHAR     NO-UNDO.
DEFINE INPUT        PARAMETER p_event    AS CHAR     NO-UNDO.
DEFINE INPUT        PARAMETER p_context  AS CHAR     NO-UNDO.
DEFINE INPUT        PARAMETER p_other    AS CHAR     NO-UNDO.
DEFINE       OUTPUT PARAMETER p_ok       AS LOGICAL  NO-UNDO INITIAL TRUE.

DEFINE VARIABLE h          AS WIDGET-HANDLE.
DEFINE VARIABLE MyMenuItem AS WIDGET-HANDLE.

/* NOTE: If you are creating dynamic widgets do not create
 * a widget-pool in this procedure. You want dynamic widgets
 * to use the UIB's widget pool
 */

/* If the UIB is starting up... */
IF p_product = "UIB" and p_event = "STARTUP" THEN
```

```
DO:
  ASSIGN h = WIDGET-HANDLE(p_other)
         h = h:MENUBAR
         h = h:FIRST-CHILD.
  DO WHILE VALID-HANDLE(h):
    /* Find the "Tools" menu-item */
    IF CAN-QUERY(h, "LABEL") THEN
      IF h:label = "&Tools" THEN
      DO:
        /* Create a new menu item under "Tools" */
        CREATE MENU-ITEM MyMenuItem
          ASSIGN PARENT = h
                 LABEL  = "&Edit PROPATH"
          TRIGGERS:
            ON CHOOSE PERSISTENT
                RUN protools/_propath.w.
          END TRIGGERS.
      END.
    ASSIGN h = h:NEXT-SIBLING. /* Find next menu-item */
  END.
END.

/* End of adecomm\_adeevnt.p */
```

This program would probably call one of your tools instead, however, it serves to illustrate how simple it is to customize your development environment.

There are two other procedures that can be used to override a tool's behavior: `adecomm\_getfile.p` and `adecomm\_chosobj.w`. These are the two procedures called by the UIB when it wants to ask the user to select a file. You would only consider changing these files if you want to change the way users look for files

adecomm_getfile.p

This procedure provides the native system-dialog used to select disk files. By modifying or replacing this procedure, you can customize the way in which disk files are chosen by the ADE tools.

You might consider modifying this file if you do not want UIB users to directly choose files from their disks. If you have a system where users need to check files in and out, you can consider modifying this `adecomm\_getfile.p`.

adecomm_chosobj.w

The other place that UIB users are asked to select files is on the UIB's Object Palette, when either SmartObject or VBX palette items are chosen. In both cases, the user is asked to directly choose a file from his hard disk. This file is then used to create the new instance of the object in the UIB.

If your organization wants to implement a system where SmartObjects are referenced indirectly, then you would want to consider changing this file. Once again, this would be considered a very advanced feature. If you decide to do this, you should check the comments in the actual source code before proceeding.

Enhancing SmartObjects in the UIB

SmartObjects behave differently when displayed in the UIB than when they are used in your application. In your application, SmartObjects are supposed to interact with the user. The user will be clicking buttons and entering data in fields. The user ultimately should not even be able to tell where one SmartObject ends and another begins.

Developers in the UIB, however, are not interested in the individual buttons or fields. They are concerned with each SmartObject as a single object. Developers want the SmartObjects to be selectable. They expect the SmartObject to move and resize at their command. Buttons and database fields inside each SmartObject should be visible, but disabled.

This behavior seems correct. You don't want SmartObjects to be changing data when you are in design-mode in the UIB, nor do you want your SmartObjects to move around your user interface in your deployed application.

How is this accomplished?

SmartObjects are just running PROGRESS procedures. The SmartObject that you see running in the UIB is exactly the same SmartObject that you run in your applications. How is it that the behavior of the object differs in the two environments?

The answer is that SmartObjects have a special mode of operation called `UIB-mode`.

> **Note**
>
> You should be aware that you really do not need to understand `UIB-mode` at all to use SmartObjects.
>
> However, if you do understand what `UIB-mode` is and how it is implemented in your SmartObject code, you can exploit `UIB-mode` to increase the capabilities of your SmartObjects.

In this section, you will see a series of examples designed to teach you about SmartObjects in the UIB. Each example is intended to produce an enhancement to the standard SmartObjects you receive from PROGRESS.

When you have finished this for next following sections, you should be able to:

- Change the basic behavior of SmartObjects in the UIB
- Modify the instance of a SmartObject as you drop it into a design window based on user preferences
- Create SmartObjects that are active in the UIB

Using the `UIB-Mode = Design` Attribute

There is really only one thing that the UIB does when it runs a SmartObject that is not normally done when the object is run as part of your application. The UIB sets the attribute:

UIB-Mode = Design

Setting `UIB-mode` tells the method, `adm-initialize`, to change its behavior. When `UIB-Mode` is set to `Design`, `adm-initialize` will dispatch the `UIB-mode` event. The `adm-UIB-mode` event procedure is the procedure that disables all the objects in a SmartObject and makes the SmartObject selectable and movable, as a single entity.

This gives you two places to change the behavior of a SmartObject in the UIB. You can localize or override `adm-initialize`, or you can localize or override `adm-UIB-mode`. Your local methods can:

- Change the characteristics of the SmartObject based on user preferences.
- Change the sensitivity or behavior of basic objects in the SmartObject so that the SmartObject becomes *active* in the UIB.

If you want to test if a given SmartObject is in design-mode in the UIB, you should use the `get-attribute` method and test the `RETURN-VALUE`. For example:

```
RUN get-attribute IN object-handle ("UIB-mode":U).
IF RETURN-VALUE eq "Design":U THEN DO:
  /* Insert custom code here ... */
END.
```

Using the `UIB-Mode = Preview` Attribute

In normal operation, the attribute `UIB-mode` will be unknown (?). There is another possible value of UIB-mode. When you are choosing SmartObjects from the Object Palette, there is an option to preview the object. In this situation, the SmartObject is run and `UIB-mode` is set to *Preview* (see fig. 20.4).

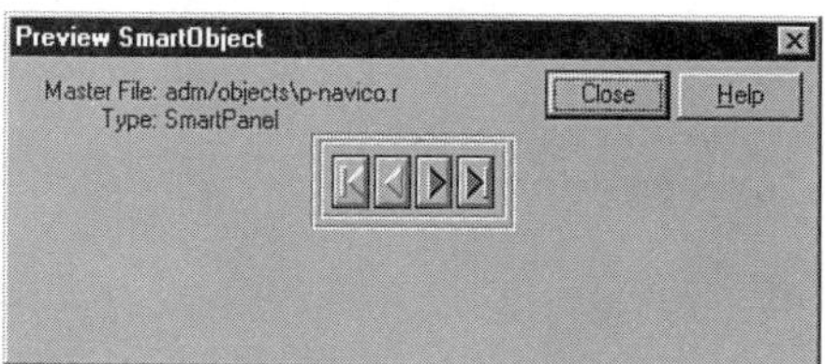

Fig. 20.4

Previewing a SmartObject from the UIB's Object Palette sets `UIB-mode = Preview`.

Using the `UIB-Mode = Design-Child` Attribute

There is one other `UIB-mode` case to consider. That is the case of SmartContainers used in the UIB. If you add a SmartFrame in a design window, the SmartFrame will be in *Design* `UIB-mode`. However, the SmartFrame will probably contain other SmartObjects. These are running within the SmartFrame and are not in Design mode themselves (that is, they should not be movable or resizable within the SmartFrame). If a SmartObject is a child of SmartContainer that is in Design mode, then `UIB-mode` is set to *Design-Child*.

Instance Wizards and Self-Initializing SmartObjects

You can take advantage of UIB-mode to create SmartObjects that interact with a developer as they are dropped into a SmartContainer from the UIB's Object Palette. This interaction goes by the general term of *Instance Wizard.*

Normally, the only automatic dialog box that occurs between developers and SmartObjects are the Template Wizards that are invoked when a new Master File is created from the UIB's File, New menu. These wizards take advantage of the XFTR technology and are fairly tedious to build.

Instance Wizards, on the other hand, can be quite simple to program. Also, their scope is quite limited. While template wizards modify the basic source code for a class of Master Files, instance wizards only change a single instance of a SmartObject by automatically setting the *instance attributes* of an object.

Creating a Simple "Wizard"

The simplest instance wizard is one that pops up the Instance Attribute dialog box as soon as a SmartObject is added to a SmartContainer. This is actually a useful function on a SmartObject where you expect the user to normally go into the Instance Settings dialog box at some point anyway. Automatically popping up the dialog will save the user some steps.

For example, suppose you want to create a version of the standard Update Panel that automatically lets the user change its instance attributes as soon as it is used. The following steps will produce a quick instance wizard.

1. Copy the standard update panel (usually in `c:\dlc\src\adm\objects\p-updsav.w`) into your working directory (for example, `c:\appdir`).
2. Rename the file to `p-updsvx.w` (where the "x" stands for the eXtended Update/Save SmartPanel).
3. Open the file in the UIB.
4. Add a method for local-UIB-mode as follows. At this point you are done and can save the file.

Listing 20.2 \examples\chap-20\p-updsvx.w—`local-UIB-mode` Procedure

```
/*------------------------------------------------------------
  local-UIB-mode

  Purpose: Override standard ADM method
  Notes:
    This procedure calls the normal instance attribute
    dialog box (adm-edit-attributes) when the object is
     first dropped into a design window. We know it is
     the "first" time because the attribute
     "Drawn-in-UIB" will not have been set .
------------------------------------------------------------*/
```

```
    /* Code placed here will execute PRIOR to standard
       behavior. */

    /* Is this the first time? Check if the object
       has been drawn in the UIB. */
    RUN get-attribute ('Drawn-in-UIB':U).
    IF RETURN-VALUE eq ? THEN DO:
      /* Run the normal Instance Attribute dialog. */
      RUN dispatch ('edit-attribute-list':U).
      /* Set Drawn-in-UIB this won't happen again. */
      RUN set-attribute-list ('Drawn-in-UIB = yes':U).
    END.

    /* Dispatch standard ADM method.                  */
    RUN dispatch IN THIS-PROCEDURE ('adm-UIB-mode':U ) .

    /* Code placed here will execute AFTER standard
       behavior.  */

  END PROCEDURE.
```

There are a few points to note about this method:

- You have only had to write only a few lines of code.
- You *did not* have to check for the attribute `UIB-mode` yourself because `adm-initialize` does this for you. The `UIB-mode` method is dispatched only if the SmartObject is indeed in design mode.
- You *did* have to add a new attribute, `Drawn-in-UIB`, to the SmartPanel. There is no built-in way for a SmartObject to tell if it is being created by the UIB for the first time. If you did not create and check the `Drawn-in-UIB` attribute, then the instance wizard would come up every time you opened a SmartContainer that contains this SmartPanel.

Setting SmartObject Defaults

You can also set up a SmartObject by reading default values from a file, such as the `progress.ini` file. The dialog box, or instance wizard, in the above example requires the developer to explicitly provide input for each instance. Using the `progress.ini` file allows the user to set attribute values once. The same settings will be used for every new instance of the object.

The statement `GET-KEY-VALUE` is a very useful way of storing SmartObject instance attributes. The syntax of this statement is as follows:

```
GET-KEY-VALUE SECTION section KEY name VALUE string.
```

Tip

You can store default values for SmartObject attributes in your `progress.ini` file.

A good convention to follow is to set:

```
SECTION    = SmartObject type
KEY        = Attribute Name
VALUE      = Attribute Value
```

You can read and set these attribute values in a local-initialize or local-UIB-mode method.

Suppose you want to change the default value of the border box in the SmartPanels. This attribute is called `Edge-Pixels`. Setting the value to 0 will turn off the border. Adding sections for SmartObject defaults to your environment would produce a `progress.ini` file of the form:

```
[SmartPanel]
EdgePixels = 0
```

You could read this value in the `local-UIB-mode` method.

```
/*-------------------------------------------------------
  local-UIB-mode

  Purpose: Override standard ADM method
  Notes:
    This procedure initializes the instance attributes
    for the SmartPanel by reading KEY-VALUES from the
    settings file.
---------------------------------------------------------*/
  DEF VAR c-value AS CHAR NO-UNDO.

  /* Code placed here will execute PRIOR to standard
     behavior. */

  /* Is this the first time? Check if the object
     has been drawn in the UIB. */
  RUN get-attribute ('Drawn-in-UIB':U).
  IF RETURN-VALUE eq ? THEN DO:
    /* Get the KEY-VALUE and set the attribute. */
    GET-KEY-VALUE SECTION 'SmartPanel':U
                  KEY     'Edge-Pixels':U
                    VALUE   c-value.
    IF c-value ne ? THEN
      RUN set-attribute-list
           ('Edge-Pixels =':U + c-value).

    /* Set Drawn-in-UIB this won't happen again. */
    RUN set-attribute-list ('Drawn-in-UIB = yes':U).
  END.
```

```
    /* Dispatch standard ADM method.                    */
    RUN dispatch IN THIS-PROCEDURE ('adm-UIB-mode':U ) .
    /* Code placed here will execute AFTER standard
       behavior.   */

  END PROCEDURE.
```

Tip

The easiest way to add values in the `progress.ini` is to use the `PUT-KEY-VALUE` statement. Editing the initialization file is always risky because you may make a spelling mistake or edit the wrong file.

Using `PUT-KEY-VALUE` in the Procedure Editor is generally safer. For example, run the following code instead of editing `progress.ini` directly:

```
PUT-KEY-VALUE SECTION 'SmartPanel'
              KEY 'Edge-Pixels'
              VALUE '0'.
```

A SmartFolder That Automatically Initializes Itself

Another example of localizing a SmartObject to take advantage of `UIB-mode` is a SmartFolder that initializes the number and label of the folder tabs based on the size of the object. In this example, the basic SmartFolder (`DLC\src\adm\objects\folder.w`) already has a `local-initialize` method that processes the instance attributes *before* the call to `UIB-mode`. In this case, you will need to modify `local-initialize` directly instead of adding a `local-UIB-mode` method.

1. Copy the standard SmartFolder (usually in `c:\dlc\src\adm\objects\folder.w`) into your working directory (e.g. `c:\appdir`).
2. Rename the file to `folderx.w` (the "x" is for. eXtended SmartFolder).
3. Open the file in the UIB.
4. Modify the method for `local-initialize` as follows. At this point, you are done and can save the file.

Listing 20.3 \examples\chap-20\folderx.w—`local-initialize` Procedure

```
/* ------------------------------------------------------
  local-initialize
    Purpose:
      Local version of the initialize method which
      starts up  the folder object. This runs
      initialize-folder with the folder attributes.
    Parameters:  <none>
    Notes:
  -------------------------------------------------------*/
```

(continues)

Listing 20.3 Continued

```
  DEF VAR c-labels AS CHARACTER NO-UNDO.
  DEF VAR tab-cnt  AS INTEGER   NO-UNDO.

  /* Is this instance in the UIB's design mode? */
  RUN get-attribute ('UIB-mode':U).
  IF RETURN-VALUE eq 'Design':U THEN DO:
    /* Is this the first time? Check if the object
       has been drawn in the UIB. */
    RUN get-attribute ('Drawn-in-UIB':U).
    IF RETURN-VALUE eq ? THEN DO:
      /* Create up to 5 tabs, where each tab is
         about 75 pixels wide. */
      ASSIGN
        tab-cnt = FRAME {&FRAME-NAME}:WIDTH-P / 75
        tab-cnt = MAX(1,MIN(tab-cnt,5))
        c-labels = SUBSTRING
             ('Page 1¦Page 2¦Page 3¦Page 4¦Page 5',
              1, (tab-cnt * 7) - 1).
      /* Setup the folder as desired. */
      RUN set-attribute-list
            ('FOLDER-TAB-TYPE = 2,
              FOLDER-LABELS = ':U + c-labels).
      /* Set Drawn-in-UIB this won't happen again.*/
      RUN set-attribute-list
            ('Drawn-in-UIB = yes':U).
    END.
  END.

  RUN initialize-folder.
  RUN dispatch IN THIS-PROCEDURE ('adm-initialize':U).

  RETURN.
END PROCEDURE.
```

Activating Your SmartObjects in the UIB

Buttons and controls in a SmartObject are *usually* disabled when the SmartObject is shown in the UIB as an element of some SmartContainer. This behavior, however, is actually under the control of the developer. You can change the SmartObject so that it can show data, have active fields, or have active buttons that help developers use the SmartObject in their applications.

The standard `adm-UIB-mode` is an event procedure that disables the contents of a SmartObject. After this standard behavior is run, you can program your SmartObject to enable some fields or objects.

Suppose you wanted a SmartViewer to show enabled fields while in the UIB. You would simply enable the fields in your `local-UIB-mode` procedure.

```
/*-------------------------------------------------------
  local-UIB-mode

  Purpose: Override standard ADM method
  Notes:   Enable fields at design time.
--------------------------------------------------------*/

  /* Code placed here will execute PRIOR to standard
     behavior. */

  /* Dispatch standard ADM method.                     */
  RUN dispatch IN THIS-PROCEDURE ('adm-UIB-mode':U ) .

  /* Code placed here will execute AFTER standard
     behavior.   */
  ENABLE {&ENABLED-FIELDS} WITH FRAME {&FRAME-NAME}.

END PROCEDURE.
```

You can see that there is only the single line that needs to be added to the `local-UIB-mode` procedure.

You should also remember that any field or object that you enable at design time will truly be active. All triggers and validation expressions will fire for these enabled objects.

Creating Your Own SmartObjects

SmartObjects are just PROGRESS procedures that are run persistently. If you are interested in producing your own stripped down SmartObjects, you should be aware of what the UIB expects, as a bare minimum, for a procedure to be recognized as a SmartObject.

The minimum requirements for a SmartObject to be compatible with the UIB are as follows:

- The Master File must exist.
- The Master File must be runnable as an independent object. This means *no parameters, no shared variables,* and *no compilation errors.* Also, any databases used in the SmartObject must be connected before the SmartObject will run.

  There is an exception here. You can, of course, use `NEW GLOBAL SHARED` variables in a SmartObject. Also, if you modify your PROGRESS environment to define some `SHARED` variables before the UIB starts up, these `SHARED` variables can be used in a SmartObject.
- The procedure must have contain methods for:

  ```
  dispatch
  set-attribute-list
  ```

  and ADM event procedures for:

  ```
  initialize
  destroy
  ```

- The UIB also tries to call the following methods

```
get-attribute
get-attribute-list
```

  and dispatch the following ADM events, if they are available:

```
hide
view
```

- If a SmartObject is supposed to be visualized in the UIB design window, it must return a value for:

```
RUN get-attribute ('ADM-OBJECT-HANDLE':U).
```

  If the RETURN-VALUE is not the handle of a FRAME, the UIB will not initialize the SmartObject. Instead, it will create a simple visualization based on the SmartObjects icon. (For example, a SmartWindow in the UIB has an ADM-OBJECT-HANDLE that is a window object. A SmartQuery has no ADM-OBJECT-HANDLE. Both of these objects have UIB created icons to show when they are being used.)

- If an SmartObject is visualized with a FRAME, the UIB checks for the following methods:

```
set-position
set-size
```

  SmartObjects that have a set-position method are MOVABLE in the UIB. SmartObjects with set-size are RESIZABLE in the UIB.

- A SmartObject that is visualized with a FRAME should also allow the UIB to set the parent of the FRAME as an attribute of the object, using:

```
RUN set-attribute ('ADM-PARENT=<handle>').
```

- The UIB also decides if a SmartObject can edit its own Instance Attributes by checking to see if the object supports the ADM event procedure:

```
edit-attribute-list
```

  If there is neither a local- or adm- version of this event, the UIB will disable the Edit Instance Attribute function on the SmartObject pop-up menu, and in the SmartObject's property sheet.

- In determining the capabilities of a SmartObject, the UIB checks the following attributes (using get-attribute):

```
SUPPORTED-LINKS
EXTERNAL-TABLES
INTERNAL-TABLES
```

  These attributes, which are displayed on the SmartInfo dialog box for each SmartObject, determine what links the UIB suggests should be added to this SmartObject when it is added to a SmartContainer.

- In particular, the UIB checks the SUPPORTED-LINKS attribute to see if the object is a PAGE-TARGET. If so, the UIB enables the Pages button on the Procedure Settings dialog box, and the Page number area in the status bar.

All this may sound pretty complicated. However, there is an easy way to achieve all the requirements for UIB support of a SmartObject.

Tip

The simplest way of creating a SmartObject is to ensure that `src\adm\method\smart.i` is included as one of the Method Libraries in the Procedure Settings dialog box.

The Method Library, `src\adm\method\smart.i`, defines all the basic methods and ADM events that the UIB expects a SmartObject to possess. It also defines the get- and set-attribute-list methods for all the standard attributes.

The one place you may have to write code is to assign the `adm-object-hdl` variable that is returned when a request is made to `get-attribute ('ADM-OBJECT-HANDLE':U)`. For any FRAME-based SmartObject (like a SmartPanel, SmartViewer, or SmartBrowser), this variable is set to the handle of the main frame. That is:

```
ASSIGN adm-object-hdl = FRAME {&FRAME-NAME}:HANDLE.
```

In general, `smart.i`, will correctly assign `adm-object-hdl` for you. However, in unusual cases, you may need to set this variable yourself. This would only happen in cases where your SmartObject was not based on a PROGRESS frame, or where you create all your objects dynamically.

Creating an Instance Attribute Editor

One of the events that the UIB expects to dispatch to a SmartObject is `edit-attribute-list`. The presence of this internal procedure (or the adm- or local-versions of it) tells the UIB that the SmartObject has instance attributes that can be set.

One of the ways that the UIB is open to custom extensions by developers is through this mechanism of editing instance attributes in SmartObjects. Instead of having the UIB handle the interface to SmartObject attributes, the UIB instead asks the SmartObject to edit its own attributes.

When you edit instance attributes for a SmartObject, you choose either the Instance Attributes function on the SmartObject pop-up menu, or the Edit button on the SmartObject's property sheet. In both cases, the UIB simply dispatches `edit-attribute-list` to the SmartObject.

`edit-attribute-list` is an ADM event and takes no parameters and returns no values. This event, however, handles all the setting of attributes in a SmartObject. Ultimately, the UIB needs to find out these attributes so that the .w file can be generated correctly. At this point, the UIB uses the `get-attribute-list` method in the SmartObject.

The biggest advantage of the `edit-attribute-list` event is that you, as a SmartObject fabricator, can build a user-friendly and appropriate dialog box for editing attributes. This dialog box can be optimized to the needs of a given SmartObject.

The disadvantage of this system is that you are required to build this dialog box for every SmartObject class that you create.

In this section, you will learn how to write a very simple Instance Attributes dialog box that lets you enter any and all attributes into a freeform editor. Figure 20.5 shows this simple dialog box, in use as a replacement for the standard Update SmartPanel.

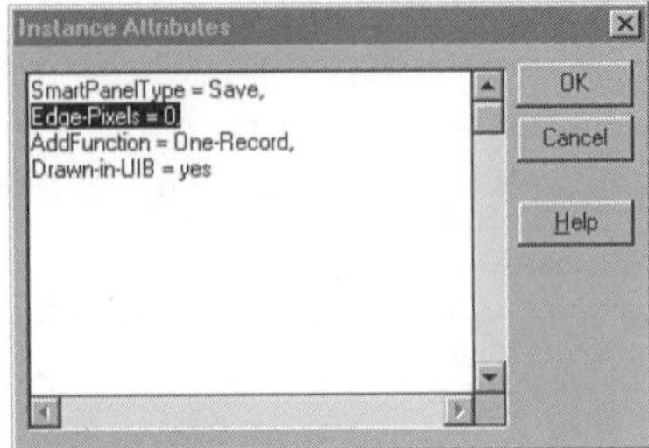

Fig. 20.5

You can write a simple Instance Attributes editor and use it when prototyping your own SmartObject classes.

To add your own Instance Attributes editor to a SmartObject, you can replace the standard `adm-edit-attribute-list` with your own `local-edit-attribute-list`, just as you would do to override any ADM event code. However, there is an easier way. If you look at the code for `adm-edit-attribute-list` (in `src\adm\method\smart.i`), you will see that the name of the dialog box being run is a preprocessor variable.

Tip

The easiest way to specify the file name of the Instance Attributes editor is to set the preprocessor variable, `adm-attribute-dlg`.

For example, to use a file, `\examples\chap-20\attr-edt.w`, you can add the following line to the Definition section of the SmartObject master file:

```
&Scoped-define adm-attribute-dlg \examples\chap-20\attr-edt.w
```

The file must have a single input parameter, which is the handle of the SmartObject.

The way these standard Instance Attribute dialog boxes work is that they take the handle of the SmartObject as their only input parameter. When the dialog box comes up, the SmartObject can then be queried for its current attributes (using get-attribute-list). These attributes can then be displayed in the dialog box. When the user presses OK, the new attributes can be assigned back to the SmartObject using attributes (using set-attribute-list).

To create the simple Attribute editor shown in figure 20.5, you should:

1. Create a new dialog box in the UIB using File, New. Choose the basic Dialog template (for example, *not* the SmartDialog).

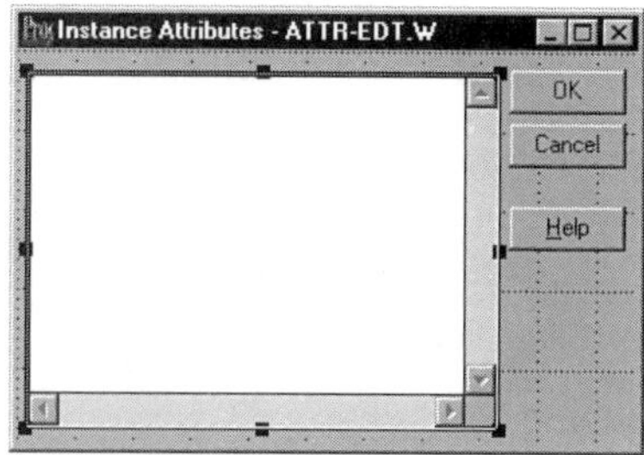

Fig. 20.6

Add an editor object to a basic dialog box.

2. Change the title of the dialog box to Instance Attributes.
3. Add an EDITOR object to the window. Name this object attr-list (see fig. 20.6).
4. Save this as, for example, `c:\appdir\attr-edt.w`.

At this point, you will need to edit the code for the dialog box. You will need to set the input parameters in the Definition section, and the logic in the Main Code Block.

1. Bring up the Code Section Editor in the UIB.
2. Edit the Definition section. Add a line to the parameters to define the handle of the SmartObject that is being edited:

```
DEFINE INPUT PARAMETER ph_SMO AS HANDLE NO-UNDO.
```

3. Change the Main Code Block as follows:

Listing 20.4 \examples\chap-20\attr-edt.w—Changing the Main Code Block

```
/* ******************  Main Block  ****************** */

/* Parent the dialog box to the ACTIVE-WINDOW.  */
IF VALID-HANDLE(ACTIVE-WINDOW) AND
   FRAME {&FRAME-NAME}:PARENT eq ?
THEN FRAME {&FRAME-NAME}:PARENT = ACTIVE-WINDOW.

/* Get the instance attributes from the object. */
RUN get-attribute-list IN ph_SMO (OUTPUT attr-list).

/* Now enable the interface and wait for the exit
   condition. */
MAIN-BLOCK:
DO ON ERROR   UNDO MAIN-BLOCK, LEAVE MAIN-BLOCK
   ON END-KEY UNDO MAIN-BLOCK, LEAVE MAIN-BLOCK:
  RUN enable_UI.
  /* Make sure there is no special cursor set. */
  RUN adecomm/_setcurs.p ('':U).
  WAIT-FOR GO OF FRAME {&FRAME-NAME}.

  /* Set the values in the object. NOTE: this will
     not, by default cause the object to rebuild
     itself. */
```

(continues)

Listing 20.4 Continued

```
    ASSIGN attr-list = TRIM(attr-list:SCREEN-VALUE).
    RUN set-attribute-list IN ph_SMO (attr-list).
    /* Reinitialize the object - this will rebuild it
       based on the new attribute values. */
    RUN dispatch IN ph_SMO ('initialize':U).
  END.
  RUN disable_UI.
```

Some points to note include:

- You only have to add five statements, plus comments, to the standard dialog box main block (shown in **bold** text).
- After you set the attributes back in the original SmartObject, you generally want to reinitialize it.

Resizing SmartObjects with `set-size`

Another method that the UIB looks for in a SmartObject is `set-size`. If `set-size` is found, the UIB will treat the object as RESIZABLE when `UIB-mode` is *Design*.

When a developer resizes a SmartObject in the UIB, either by directly manipulating the resize handles or by editing the geometry in the Group Properties window, the UIB calls the set-size method. The parameters for this method are the decimal values of Height and Width (in row and column units). For example:

```
RUN set-size IN object-handle
       (INPUT d-height,  /* Height, in rows   */
        INPUT d-width). /* Width, in columns */
```

Tip

Examples of `set-size` method can be found in the source code for the resizable PROGRESS-supplied objects: the SmartFolder and the SmartPanels.

Look at `src\adm\objects\folder.w` for the `set-size` method for the SmartFolder.

The SmartPanel methods are in a Method Library: `src\adm\methods\panelsiz.i`.

From Here...

In this chapter, you have learned how to:

- Customize the PROGRESS tools
- Extend both the UIB's Object Palette and the PRO*Tools application.

- Intercept ADE events for file opening and closing.
- Create SmartObjects that work with the UIB to extend their capabilities.

As you begin to write PROGRESS code to take advantage of these features, you are going to get more and more into the advanced areas of the PROGRESS 4GL. You can find additional information in the following chapters:

- Chapter 21, "Making the Most of the Application Component Environment." This chapter lists some of the best ways to use SmartObjects and the PROGRESS tools.
- Chapter 22, "PROGRESS Programming Tips." This chapter lists some of the issues and tricks of using the PROGRESS 4GL.
- Appendix F, "Structure of .w Files." This appendix examines the structure of files generated by the User Interface Builder. Because all SmartObjects are created in the UIB, the sections and arrangement of the underlying code is often of interest to the advanced developer.

Chapter 21

Making the Most of the Application Component Environment

This chapter is intended to aid you in making the most of the Application Component Environment (ACE). PROGRESS V8 provides you with a set of tools and a system for building applications using SmartObjects.

This chapter will help you use the ACE to its fullest potential. You will learn everything from simple tips and tricks of the tools, to ways of extending the environment to match your particular needs.

Voice-of-Experience Movies

See Table G.3 in Appendix G, "Contents of CD," for a list of the Voice-of-Experience files for this chapter.

The sections in this chapter will primarily teach through examples. While these examples will be helpful in themselves, they have been chosen for their generality. Taken as a whole, these examples will, we hope, teach you how to make best use of PROGRESS.

Tips from the Pros

After reading this chapter, you should be able to:

- Take advantage of preexisting code supplied by PROGRESS to write your own applications.
- Make better use of the User Interface Builder.
- Use the PRO*Tools applets to explore the inner workings of your applications.
- Understand how to write your own SmartObject classes.
- Add functionality to existing SmartObjects.

The Best of adecomm

PROGRESS provides many useful code fragments that you can use directly, or modify to meet your own needs. Many of these procedures were originally developed for PROGRESS' own internal needs. The PROGRESS Application Development Environment (ADE) is written in the PROGRESS 4GL. When you write your own 4GL code, you can use these same procedures.

The directory dlc\gui\adecomm contains many of the common utility procedures shared by the ADE tools. Because the dlc\gui directory is automatically placed in your PROPATH, this directory is usually referred to by its relative location, adecomm.

This section lists some of the most useful utilities in the adecomm directory. Each routine will be explained by example. Further documentation is available by directly examining the source code for each file.

Tip

Source code to all of adecomm, as well as other directories, is supplied in the dlc\src directory. ("dlc" refers here to the Progress installation root directory—usually C:\dlc. So adecomm source code will normally be installed in C:\dlc\src\adecomm.)

In addition to adecomm, the source code to many other tools is provided in the dlc\src directory. You can look in dlc\src for source code to tools such as:

PRO*Tools (in dlc\src\protools)

Procedure Editor (in dlc\src\adeedit)

Data Dictionary (in dlc\src\adedict)

ADM Support Code (in dlc\src\adm\support)

Tip

Add src (or c:\dlc\src) to the end of your PROPATH if you are working with any PROGRESS source code. This is because many of the source files use PROGRESS include files found in adecomm. Unless src is in your PROPATH, these source files will not compile.

Make sure that dlc\src follows dlc\gui in your PROPATH. If dlc\src is first, then the source files to the ADE common procedures (for example, in c:\dlc\src\adecomm) will be found before the compiled r-code (in c:\dlc\gui\adecomm). Everything will still work, but the whole PROGRESS tool set will slow down because none of the compiled versions of the common routines will be used.

The directory adecomm contains many of the common utility procedures shared by the ADE tools. The following sections list some of the most useful utilities in `adecomm`.

Common Dialogs: Font, Color, and Find File

Some of the most useful utilities are the standard color, font, and file dialogs used by the PROGRESS tools. These dialog boxes, which are written in the PROGRESS 4GL, reflect some of the idiosyncracies of PROGRESS, and are more appropriate to use than the standard Microsoft Windows common dialogs.

Tip

You do not want your users to change font or color by using the system dialogs for font or color. It is much safer to use the ADE procedures: `adecomm/_chsfont.p` and `adecomm/chscolr.p`.

This is because PROGRESS sets color and font for the entire PROGRESS session. If your user changes the values for a color or font number, then every use of this attribute will be affected. In particular, changing fonts can cause screens and objects to be unreadable, or worse, to give errors where objects won't fit in their parent.

The source code for the ADE standard dialogs is available for your use. Look at the source files for:

`adecomm/_chsfont.p`. Select a font based on the PROGRESS font number (0-255). This routine acts as a PROGRESS front end for the standard system font dialog (i.e., `SYSTEM-DIALOG FONT n.`).

`adecomm/_chscolr.p`. Select a color based on the PROGRESS color number (0-255). This routine acts as a PROGRESS front end for the standard system color dialog (i.e., `SYSTEM-DIALOG COLOR n.`).

`adecomm/_fndfile.p`. Select an *image, text,* or *template* file. The user can preview the file. (This is the file chooser used by the UIB to select templates or images, as in figure 21.1.) This procedure allows the user to browse for any other file using the standard system dialog (i.e., `SYSTEM-DIALOG GET-FILE...`). The other advantage of `_fndfile.p` over the common system dialog is that `fndfile.p` can return filenames relative to the PROGRESS `PROPATH`. Within PROGRESS you are much better off using relative pathnames than absolute names. (For example, `adecomm/_fndfile.p` is more portable than referring to `C:\dlc\gui\adecomm\_fndfile.p`.)

Fig. 21.1

You can use the UIB's file or image dialog in your own application by calling `adecomm/_fndfile.p` *directly.*

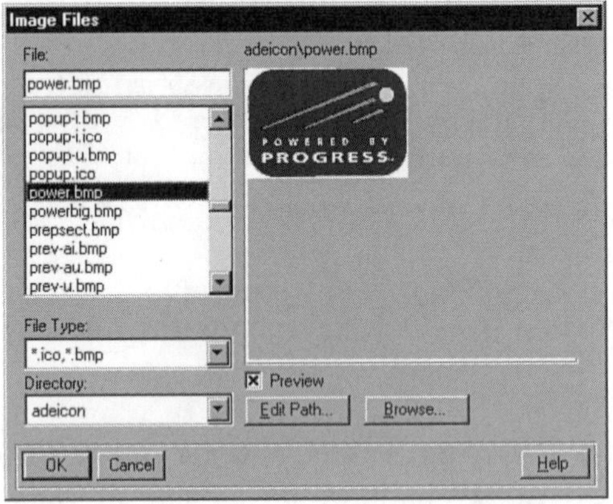

Parsing Filenames—`adecomm/_osfext.p` and `adecomm/_osprefx.p`

Programs written in the PROGRESS 4GL can be run on a variety of platforms, such as VMS, UNIX, as well as DOS. One aspect of this portability is the ability to support file names that are valid across operating systems. Among other things, this means:

- PROGRESS supports drive identifiers other than the traditional single letter DOS drives (for example, `C:\`).
- PROGRESS allows both slashes and backslashes as directory delimiters (for example, `/appdir/samples` is valid in PROGRESS, even though it is not directly supported by operating systems such as DOS).

One advantage to the PROGRESS 4GL is that it is easy for you to write code that is portable across operating systems. On the other hand, parsing a file name in your code can sometimes be tedious. Two routines in `adecomm` can help you here:

`adecomm/_osfext.p`—Return the file extension for any file on any PROGRESS platform (for example, ".p" out of `C:\test.dir\myfile.p`).

`adecomm/_osprefx.p`—Return the file path prefix for any file on any PROGRESS platform (for example, "C:\test.dir\" out of `C:\test.dir\myfile.p`).

Retrieving File Extensions—`adecomm/_osfext.p`

The following example shows how to retrieve the file extension using `adecomm/_osfext.p`. Running the following code from a Procedure Window will display the message `.p`.

You might use this routine in your own applications if you ask users to choose image files. Looking at the file extension, to see if it is .BMP, .PCX, or .GIF, can tell you what processing you might want to try on the file.

```
DEFINE VARIABLE c-fullname AS CHAR NO-UNDO.
DEFINE VARIABLE c-extension AS CHAR NO-UNDO.
```

```
c-fullname = "C:\test.dir\sample\myfile.p".
RUN adecomm/_osfext.p
      (INPUT  c-fullname,    /* OS File Name.    */
       OUTPUT c-extension). /* File Extension. */
MESSAGE "Extension is" c-extension VIEW-AS ALERT-BOX.
```

Note

`adecomm/_osfext.p` returns the name of the file extension including the "dot" seperator. If there is no file extension, then a null string ("") is returned.

Retrieving File Path Prefix—adecomm/_osprefx.p

It is often common for an application to want to rename a file, or copy it to another directory. Before you can do this, you will usually need to parse the full pathname into its directory and file name components.

The following example shows how to break a file into its base path and filename. Running the following code from a Procedure Window will divide the sample file `C:\test.dir\sample\myfile.p` into a prefix (`C:\test.dir\sample\`) and a filename (`myfile.p`).

```
DEFINE VARIABLE c-fullname AS CHAR NO-UNDO.
DEFINE VARIABLE c-prefix   AS CHAR NO-UNDO.
DEFINE VARIABLE c-filename AS CHAR NO-UNDO.

c-fullname = "C:\test.dir\sample\myfile.p".
RUN adecomm/_osprefx.p
      (INPUT  c-fullname,    /* OS File Name  */
       OUTPUT c-prefix,      /* File Prefix   */
       OUTPUT c-filename).   /* File name     */

MESSAGE c-fullname "is composed of" SKIP
        "Prefix:  " c-prefix SKIP
        "FileName:" c-filename
        VIEW-AS ALERT-BOX.
```

`adecomm/_osprefx.p` returns the directory prefix including the trailing slash "\."

The Procedure Window—adecomm/_pwmain.w

The Procedure Window is a simple ADE tool that creates an editor in a window, and allows a user to edit the contents of a file. There are many reasons why you might like to incorporate similar functionality in your own application (from editing text data files to previewing reports). You can call up a Procedure Window using the following call to `adecomm/_pwmain.w`.

```
/* Edit AUTOEXEC.BAT in a Procedure Window. */
RUN adecomm/_pwmain.w
    (INPUT "",                /* Parent ID string */
     INPUT "c:\autoexec.bat", /* File(s) to open  */
     INPUT "").               /* Startup commands */
```

```
/* NOTE: For testing purposes, there needs to be some
   event to end this procedure. */
DEFINE BUTTON btn-done LABEL "Done" AUTO-GO.
UPDATE btn-done.
```

Parameters to adecomm/_pwmain.p:

> *Parent ID string*—This is a character string that allows you to "parent" a Procedure Window to another ADE Tool. When the other tool exits, this Procedure Window will automatically close. This string is the name of the file that defines that ADE tool, such as _uib.p or _edit.p; however, you can leave this empty.
>
> *File(s) to open*—A comma-delimited list of files to open. A separate Procedure Window is opened for each filename in the list. If the list is empty ("") or unknown (?) then a new, empty buffer is created.
>
> *Startup string*—This parameter is a placeholder that is currently unused by adecomm/_pwmain.p. It may be used in future releases of PROGRESS. In Version 8, however, you should just leave this empty ("").

A classic use for the Procedure Window is to replace the UIB's code preview function. The UIB allows you to preview code in a dialog box. You can replace the UIB's code preview dialog box by calling the Procedure Window.

Listing 21.1 shows how you can replace the UIB's code preview function. You must save this code as adeuib/_prvw4gl.p. This file should be placed in your PROPATH ahead of the normal call to this file.

Listing 21.1 \examples\chap-21_prvw4gl.p—Replacing the UIB's Code Preview

```
/*-------------------------------------------------------------
File: _adeuib/_prvw4gl.p
Description:
    A replacement for the UIB's 4GL code previewer. This
    file copies the preview file into a temporary file:
            preview.p
    This file is then edited in a Procedure Window.

To use this file:
    Place this file in an ADEUIB sub-directory that will
    be found PRIOR to the basic DLC/GUI/ADEUIB directory
    in your PROPATH.

Input Parameters:
   pc_file  : File Name
   pc_msg   : Error to display at startup (this can be ?)
   pi_char  : Initial cursor-char offset
              (eg. COMPILER:ERROR-COLUMN)
   pi_line  : Initial cursor-line offset
              (eg. COMPILER:ERROR-ROW)
```

```
Output Parameters:
   <None>

NOTES:
  1) In this replacement procedure, we ignore pi_char and pi_line
---------------------------------------------------------*/
DEFINE INPUT PARAMETER pc_file   AS CHAR    NO-UNDO.
DEFINE INPUT PARAMETER pc_msg    AS CHAR    NO-UNDO.
DEFINE INPUT PARAMETER pi_char   AS INTEGER NO-UNDO.
DEFINE INPUT PARAMETER pi_line   AS INTEGER NO-UNDO.

/* Copy the input filename to a standard filename (because
   the UIB will delete the original file). */
OS-COPY VALUE(pc_file) preview.p.

/* Edit this file in a Procedure Window. NOTE that
   we parent it to the UIB so the window will be
   closed when the UIB exits. */
RUN adecomm/_pwmain.w
     (INPUT "_uib.p",       /* Parent ID string */
      INPUT "preview.p",    /* File(s) to open  */
      INPUT "").            /* Startup commands */

/* Show any messages */
IF pc_msg ne ? THEN
  MESSAGE pc_msg VIEW-AS ALERT-BOX ERROR BUTTONS OK.
```

The advantages of having Code Preview in a Procedure Window instead of a dialog box include the following:

- You can have the Procedure Window open while the Code Section Editor is open. This lets you cut and paste between files (which is difficult to do in the standard UIB's Code Preview dialog).
- You can save the file as a .p (without the UIB's special formatting).

The disadvantages of replacing Code Preview with a Procedure Window include:

- Changes to the file will not be reflected in the UIB.
- The preview file will not automatically be updated when you make changes in the UIB.
- Every time you click Compile, Code Preview, you will create a new copy of the Procedure Window, even if you are previewing the same file many times.

Telling the User to Wait—`adecomm/_setcurs.p`

You should always set the mouse pointer to its *wait* state when your application is performing some extended processing. PROGRESS provides two ways to change the mouse pointer.

- `SESSION:SET-WAIT-STATE`. Sets or cancels a wait-state that changes the mouse pointer for the PROGRESS session, and locks out user input.

- `<object handle>:LOAD-MOUSE-POINTER`. This method changes the mouse pointer when the mouse crosses over the object.

The former works best under Microsoft Windows, while the latter works best on OSF/ Motif. Neither should be used when you are batch processing.

The PROGRESS tools use the procedure `adecomm/_setcurs.p` to provide a single call that works across deployment platforms and operating systems.

The routine takes a single parameter, which can have the value of `"WAIT"` or `""` depending on whether you want to turn the wait cursor on or off.

The following example simply sets the cursor while it counts to 100.

```
DEFINE VARIABLE i AS INTEGER NO-UNDO.

/* Turn on the wait cursor. */
RUN adecomm/_setcurs.p ("WAIT":U).

/* Do a big task. */
DO i = 1 TO 100:
  DISPLAY i.
END.

/* Restore the cursor to the standard pointer */
RUN adecomm/_setcurs.p ("":U).
```

A Segmented Status-Bar—adecomm/_status.p and adecomm/_statdsp.p

Many of PROGRESS's tools, such as the UIB or Results, use a *status bar* that is composed of many distinct sections, with each section showing a different piece of information. (Note that this status bar is not truly an object. It is a PROGRESS frame with rectangles and text objects that simulate the look and behavior of a standard status bar.)

You can use this simulated status bar by calling the following `adecomm` procedures:

- `adecomm/_status.p` creates a status bar. The parameters for this procedure are shown in Table 21.1.

Table 21.1 Parameters for adecomm/_status.p

Parameter	Type	Description
hWindow	Input	The handle of the window to parent the status bar.
cLen	Input	A character list of the lengths of each box in the status bar. For example, "40,10,5" will create a status bar with three boxes approximately 40, 10, and 5 character units wide.

Parameter	Type	Description
TopLine	Input	A logical switch. If TRUE, a line will be drawn at the top of the status bar separating it from the rest of the window.
iFont	Input	Font number for status text (or ? if the system font is to be used).
OUTPUT Parameters		
hStatusFrame	Output	The handle of the status bar frame.
iFields	Output	The actual number of fields that have been created.

- adecomm/_statdsp.p displays text in a box in the status bar. The parameters for this procedure are shown in Table 21.2.

Table 21.2 Parameters for `adecomm/_statdsp.p`

Parameter	Type	Description
INPUT Parameters		
hStatusFrame	Input	The handle of the status bar frame created in adecomm/_status.p.
iPos	Input	The section of the status box to display the message in (for example, 2).
cMessage	Input	The character string for the message to display.

There are a few tricks involved in using this simulated status bar, as follows:

- `adecomm/_status.p` does not make the status bar frame visible. You have to do this yourself.
- The last box in the status bar sizes itself to fill the window (independent of the size you specified for it). Getting the box sizes correct will take some trial and error.
- Because `adecomm/_status.p` only simulates a status bar using a standard PROGRESS frame, it will not automatically move or resize when you change the size of the parent window. It is easiest to use when the window is not resizable (i.e., `window-handle:RESIZE = NO`).

The following example shows a sample use of the ADE status bar routines (see fig. 21.2).

Fig. 21.2

You can use standard adecomm *procedures to create a segmented status bar.*

The code needed to generate figure 21.2 is shown below.

Listing 21.2 \examples\chap-21\status.p—Using adecomm Procedures to Create a Segmented Status Bar

```
/* Define variables to store the handles of the status bar
   frame, and the window to parent it to. */
DEFINE VARIABLE hWindow AS WIDGET-HANDLE NO-UNDO.
DEFINE VARIABLE hStatus AS WIDGET-HANDLE NO-UNDO.
DEFINE VARIABLE iCount  AS INTEGER       NO-UNDO.

/* Create a window to hold the status bar. Don't use the
   default PROGRESS STATUS-AREA. */
CREATE WINDOW hWindow ASSIGN
  STATUS-AREA  = no
  MESSAGE-AREA = no
  RESIZE       = no
  WIDTH        = 72
  HEIGHT       =  5
  VISIBLE      = yes
  .

/* Create a status bar with three boxes. */
RUN adecomm/_status.p
     (INPUT  hWindow,      /* Parent Window   */
      INPUT  "30,15,10",   /* Size of Boxes   */
      INPUT  yes,          /* Show top bar    */
      INPUT  4,            /* Font            */
      OUTPUT hStatus,      /* Handle of Frame */
      OUTPUT iCount).      /* Boxes created   */

/* Make the status bar visible. */
hStatus:VISIBLE = yes.

/* Place some text in the various boxes. */
RUN adecomm/_statdsp.p (hStatus, 1, "Waiting...").
RUN adecomm/_statdsp.p (hStatus, 2, STRING(TODAY)).
RUN adecomm/_statdsp.p (hStatus, 3, "Page 1").

/* Wait for the user to close the window. */
WAIT-FOR WINDOW-CLOSE OF hWindow.
```

The PRIVATE-DATA for the status bar frame contains a list of the handles for each status text object. You can use these handles to add triggers that come up as shortcuts when your user double-clicks in the status area. Listing 21.3 would add a trigger to the second status box in the above example. (Add this right before the WAIT-FOR statement.)

Listing 21.3 \examples\chap-21\status2.p—Adding a Trigger to the Second Status Box

```
DEFINE VARIABLE h AS WIDGET-HANDLE NO-UNDO.

/* Get the handle of the second status box. */
h = WIDGET-HANDLE (ENTRY (2, hStatus:PRIVATE-DATA)).

/* Add a trigger (and make the text area sensitive to
   user action). */
ON MOUSE-SELECT-DBLCLICK OF h
DO:
  MESSAGE "Place shortcut action here." VIEW-AS ALERT-BOX.
END.

h:SENSITIVE = yes.
```

Keeping Windows on Top—adecomm/_topmost.p

You may occasionally want to make sure some component of your application is always available to the user. One way to do this is to force some window to always be on top. The UIB's Object Palette and the PRO*Tools palette both provide this as an option.

> **Tip**
>
> Always on Top works best when applied to small windows, such as tool palettes. This is because a window that is always on top covers other parts of the application. So use this feature sparingly.
>
> If you do use it, you should support a user preference to turn off this feature as a preference in your application.
>
> It is also important to allow the user to resize and move these windows so that they can get to the rest of your application.

The ability to keep a window on top is not directly supported by the PROGRESS 4GL. However, you can ask Microsoft Windows to keep a PROGRESS window on top by calling the appropriate DLL function (`SetWindowPos`, in user.exe). The ADE procedure `adecomm/_topmost.p` implements this for you (see Listing 21.4).

Listing 21.4 \examples\chap-21\topmost.p—Using ADE Procedure adecomm/_topmost.p

```
DEFINE VARIABLE result-code AS INTEGER NO-UNDO.

/* Make the CURRENT-WINDOW topmost. (Also, make it
   small so it won't cover everything.) */
VIEW CURRENT-WINDOW.
```

(continues)

Listing 21.4 Continued

```
ASSIGN CURRENT-WINDOW:HEIGHT = 2
       CURRENT-WINDOW:WIDTH  = 40.

RUN adecomm/_topmost.p
     (INPUT CURRENT-WINDOW:HWND, /* Pass the HWND */
      INPUT yes,                 /* YES - Topmost */
                                 /* NO - Normal   */
      OUTPUT result-code).       /* OK - non-zero */

/* Show the result code */
MESSAGE "Result Code =" result-code VIEW-AS ALERT-BOX.
```

Note

To use this procedure, you must pass in the `HWND attribute` associated with the PROGRESS window object. `HWND` is the underlying handle that Microsoft Windows uses to reference the PROGRESS window. This is different from PROGRESS' own handle attribute (`:handle`).

User Interface Builder Tips

The following tips and tricks give some ways to make the most of the PROGRESS User Interface Builder (UIB). These techniques will improve the performance of the UIB, as well as help you be more productive, and write better code.

Setting Up Your Progress Environment

When you are developing in the UIB, there are some default settings that you can use to optimize performance. The general rules are:

- Don't scrimp on the memory available to PROGRESS.
- Use a RAM disk for anything temporary or frequently used.
- Don't worry about database integrity or security during development.

For a moderately capable computer (with 16 megabytes of RAM or more), you may try the following parameters:

```
-mmax 5000
```

This is the size of the initial buffer, in kilobytes, that PROGRESS reserves for executing r-code. While this buffer does expand dynamically as needed, increasing this value will reduce the amount of swapping to the SRT file.

```
-Bt 200
```

-Bt is the size, in kilobytes, of the buffer that PROGRESS uses for temp-tables. Because both the UIB and SmartObjects make extensive use of temp-tables, this is a useful value to increase.

`-T E:\`. The `-T` parameter specifies the location of temporary files (for example, SRT swap file). If you can place this on a RAM disk you can improve swapping speed.

`-i`. In development mode, it is not necessarily important to use all of PROGRESS' crash protection. If you are using a "dummy" database for testing, there is no need to worry about data integrity. If there is a problem, just delete the database and make a new copy. The `-i` parameter specifies "no integrity" for the session.

To use these parameters, specify them on the command line that invokes PROGRESS. The following command line might be specified in Microsoft Windows—assuming you had an E:\ RAM drive and that you wanted to bring up the PROGRESS UIB directly (`-p _uib.p`).

```
PROWIN.EXE -p _uib.p -mmax 5000 -Bt 200 -i -T E:\
```

In addition to the startup parameters, you may want to move commonly called routines to a RAM drive and point to it in your `PROPATH`.

There are other ways of improving performance of PROGRESS applications, such as the use of procedure libraries or indexing your database. The suggestions in this section are not intended to tell you how to optimize every application you write. These parameter settings do, however, tell you how to improve the performance of the UIB while you are writing those applications.

Temp-Tables, Buffers, and Aliases

Dealing with temp-tables, buffers, and database aliases has always been difficult in the UIB. Version 8 provides some help in this area, but it is still not very easy.

First, here are some definitions of these terms:

- *Temp-Table*—A temp-table is a temporary database that exists only for a single user in a single session. The definition of the table does not come from a database file. Rather, temp-tables are defined in your code in the same way that a variable is defined (see the PROGRESS on-line help for `DEFINE TEMP-TABLE` for more information). Temp-tables act like PROGRESS *structures*.
- *Buffers*—You may want to refer to two different records from the same table in a procedure. (For example, an employee and the employee's manager both have records in the employee table.) PROGRESS provides one buffer for each table used in a procedure. You must define additional buffers yourself, using the `DEFINE BUFFER` statement (for example, `DEFINE BUFFER manager FOR employee`).
- *Aliases*—You may not want to use the name of a database directly. When you connect to a database, you can specify the *logical database name*. You can also create an *alias* for the database so that the same database can have multiple names, or many databases can have the same name (although never at the same time). (For more information, check out the help on the `CREATE ALIAS` statement.)

Temp-tables, buffers, and aliases raise an interesting problem for the UIB because the UIB does not have access to their definitions. There are two classes of variables that you can define in the UIB:

- Those that you create from the UIB's object palette.
- Those you define in the Code Section Editor.

The UIB knows everything about the first class and nothing about the second.

Buffers, aliases, and temp-tables cannot be selected from the UIB's object palette. They must be defined in code. This means that the UIB knows nothing about them. But what do you do if you want to create an object on the screen, or a column in a browse, that is connected to a field in a temp-table, buffer, or alias? There are a few ways to trick the UIB into dealing with these constructs.

Dealing with Temp-Tables, Buffers and Aliases in Browses and Queries

The easiest way to deal with your own temp-tables and buffers in a UIB-generated browse is to use the *freeform* option in the Query Builder. A freeform query allows you to write the code directly that defines the query and the columns in the browse. Because you write the code yourself, you are not limited to the variables and databases that the UIB knows about. You can reference any variable, temp-table, buffer, or alias that you want.

To use a *freeform query* you will need to:

1. Select the Browse object where you want to create a freeform query.
2. Double-click the Browse to bring up the Property Sheet for this object
3. In the Property Sheet, click the Query button. This will start the Query Builder.
4. Click the Freeform Query button. You will be asked to confirm this action. Choose the radio button that says you want to Allow Freeform Editing Of The Query and click OK.

   This will create two pseudo-events that you can edit in the Code Section Editor: `OPEN_QUERY` and `DISPLAY`. (These are not true PROGRESS events. Instead, they provide a location for you to write PROGRESS 4GL code that will be inserted into your source file at the points where the query is opened, and where the display list for the browse is defined.)
5. Accept your changes by clicking the OK button in all the dialog boxes until you return to the UIB.
6. Go to the Code Section Editor and edit the `OPEN_QUERY` and `DISPLAY` pseudo-events on the browse (see fig. 21.3).

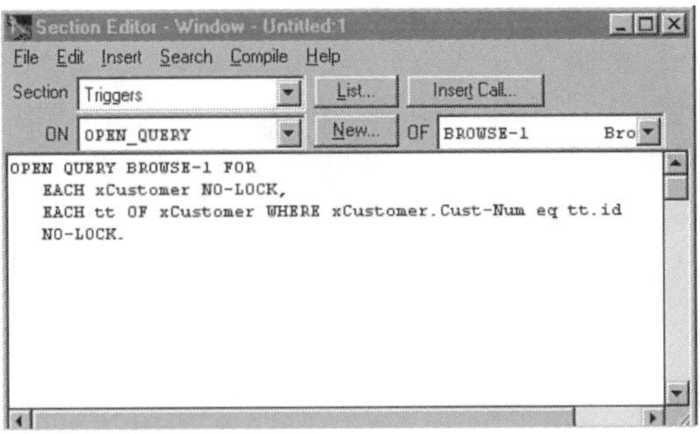

Fig. 21.3

Code Section Editor showing a freeform query entered as the `OPEN_QUERY` *pseudo-event.*

Tip

You can use an include file to define the query or browse columns in a freeform query. If you plan on reusing the same query or browse definition in multiple places in your application, just define these as an include file.

Use this include file in the `OPEN_QUERY` (or DISPLAY) pseudo-event in the UIB's Code Section Editor.

Using the Logical Database Name to Simulate a Runtime Alias

A simple way of getting the UIB to generate code using an alias is to connect to the database using a *logical database name*. The details behind aliases and logical database names are beyond the scope of this book. Suffice it to say that PROGRESS allows programmers to use names for databases in their code that differ from the physical names of the database files on the hard disk.

You can use this feature to have common code that works against many different physical databases. You might have a database for west coast sales (for example, `sls-west.db`), and one for east coast sales (for example, `sls-east.db`). Depending on which region you were interested in, you could create an `ALIAS` for the relevant database. For example, you might create an alias named `sls-curr`. Code that referenced the common alias could work against either database, while code that referenced each database directly could not work against the other one.

By default, the UIB does not actually insert the name of a database into the code it generates. This is generally the best default, unless you have multiple databases connected with common tables. In this case, you will want to turn on the database qualifiers in UIB-generated code. This is accomplished as follows:

1. Choose the Options, Preferences menu item from the UIB's menu bar. This brings up the Preferences dialog shown in figure 21.4.
2. In this dialog, check the toggle labelled Qualify Database Fields with Database Name.
3. Click OK to return to the UIB.

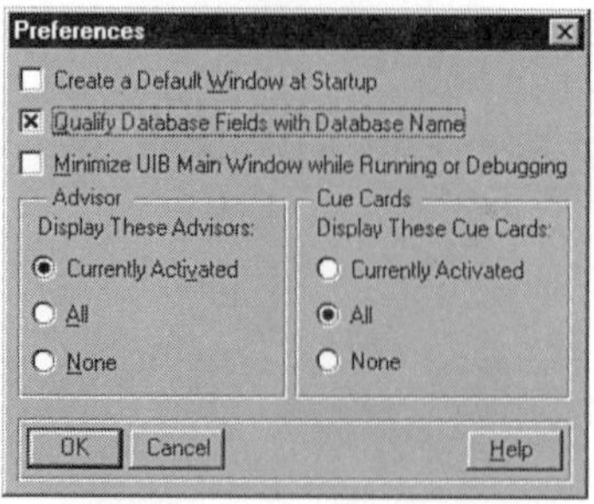

Fig. 21.4

Qualified Database Fields only should be used if you have multiple databases connected with common tables.

At this point, all code generated by the UIB will use the logical database name in referring to database fields. That is, field references will contain the trio of `database.table.field` (`SPORTS.Customer.Name` instead of simply `Customer.Name`).

Suppose, however, that you want to use an alias `current` for the sports database. Your code will have the line:

```
CREATE ALIAS current FOR DATABASE sports.
```

However, when you create browses or database fields in the UIB, the UIB will generate code that references "sports." The UIB won't know about the alternate alias name.

There are two ways around this. If you connect to the sports database giving it the logical database name of "current," then the UIB will generate code correctly using the name "current." (For example, the UIB will generate names as "current.customer.name" instead of "sports.customer.name.") Figure 21.5 shows the standard database connection dialog when the user specifies a logical database name.

Fig. 21.5

Connect to databases using a logical database name that matches the name of an alias your application will create at runtime.

> **Note**
>
> The trick of using a *logical database name* to simulate runtime *aliases* is simply a technique for getting the UIB to generate code with the correct database field naming.
>
> When you compile and deploy, your application, you will want to first make sure that databases are set up with the correct aliases. You do not want to keep changing the logical database name after your development is complete.

Using a Dummy Database to Support Temp-Tables and Buffers

If you create a database and connect it with the logical name "Temp-Tables," then the UIB will *never* write out the database name in the code it generates.

You can use this to have the UIB recognize the schema definition for buffers and Temp-Tables. Simply create a database that has tables that match the definition of your Temp-Tables or buffers. The UIB will read the schema for this database and allow you to choose fields and queries from this database. The generated code, however, will reference only the table and field name. This is just what you want for buffer and Temp-Table code.

The parts of the UIB that look at schema only look at connected database, not at temp-tables and buffers. However, when you connect your *dummy* Temp-Tables database, then all the tools will see the tables in that database. Figure 21.6 shows the standard Table Selector dialog in the UIB once you connect to a Temp-Tables database.

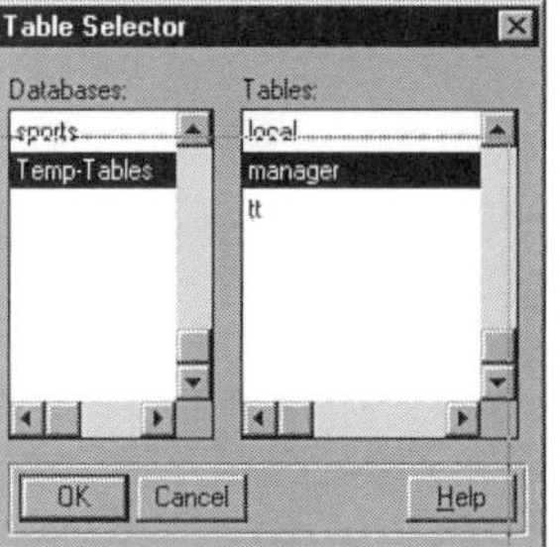

Fig. 21.6

Using a dummy database with logical name "Temp-Tables" will tell the UIB to generate code with just the table and field name.

When you actually go and compile your application, the PROGRESS compiler will look at the true Temp-Table and buffer definitions, and not at the Temp-Tables database.

Selecting the Window

Whenever you want to edit the properties of an object in the UIB, you simple select it and click the Property button, or just double-click on the object. This sounds nice and simple; however, you can almost never do it if the object of interest is a window.

Most windows are filled by a frame. Clicking in the middle of the window always selects the frame. You could make the window larger than the frame, but this means you will have space that is effectively unusable, so that is not really a solution.

Double-clicking in the window's title bar does not work because this is interpreted by Microsoft Windows as the shortcut to maximize the size of the window. While this will select the window object in the UIB, it will not bring up the property sheet.

Tip

The easiest way to select the window object itself is to simply deselect everything else. The easiest way to deselect everything is to box-select a region of a frame that contains nothing.

As shown in figure 21.7, if you click on a frame and drag out a region that contains no other objects, the UIB will select the window that contains the frame as the current object once you release the mouse button.

Once the window is chosen, simply choose the Property Sheet tool to view the window's property sheet (using the Property button on the toolbar, or menu-item Tools/Property Sheet).

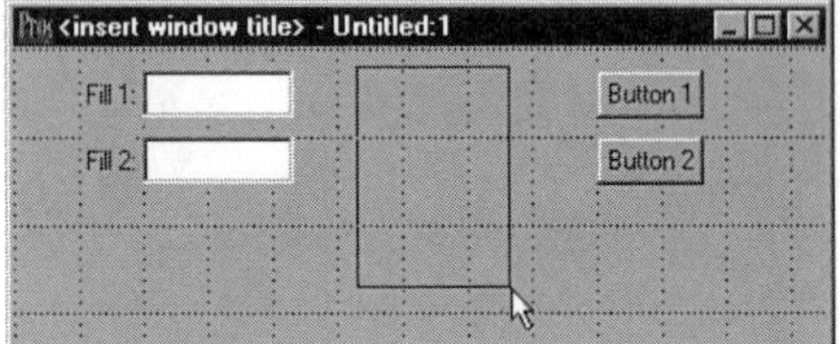

Fig. 21.7

Box-selecting an empty region in a frame is the quickest way of selecting the window object in the UIB.

Changing Object Types

The visualizations for fields specified in the Data Dictionary are not always the visualization you want to use in the UIB. While it is always possible to delete the object and re-create it as a different type you will lose any triggers or attributes that you have set in the original copy. The UIB provides a way of changing the visualization of an object that has been created.

The Group Properties window allows you to change the *type* of certain objects. You can change an object from an editor to selection-list, fill-in or combo-box, or you can change a fill-in to a slider or toggle box. (The specific valid combinations depend on the *datatype* of the object. For example, a LOGICAL variable can be a fill-in or toggle-box, but not an editor or slider.)

To use this feature, you must make sure that only one object is selected. Then bring up the Group Property sheet (choose the Window menu item, or click Ctrl+P). Select the Type row and select the new type from the list of valid-options, as shown in figure 21.8.

A related problem is what to do if you are happy with the *type* of an object, but want to change its data binding. If you want to connect an object to a database field or disconnect an object that is already connected, you can do this by clicking the Database Field button on the objects Property Sheet.

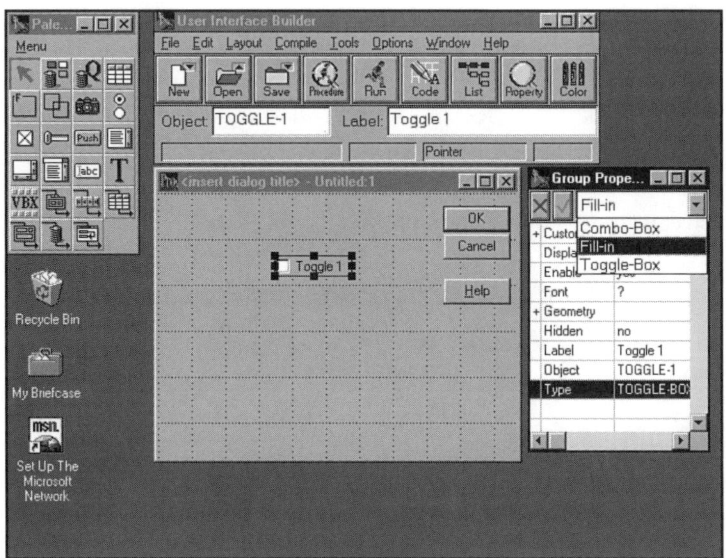

Fig. 21.8

Use the Group Property sheet on a single object to change the type of the visualization.

Tip

It is always better to change the type of an object than to delete and re-create it. Changing the type will not lose any attributes or trigger code associated with the object.

Use the Group Properties window if you want to change the type of visualization of an object in the UIB. If you want to change the database field associated with an object, then use the Database Fields button on the objects Property Sheet.

External Procedures in the UIB Code Section Editor

The UIB's Code Section Editor allows you to create an unlimited number of internal procedures in a .w file. However these can only be procedures coded in the PROGRESS 4GL. There is another kind of procedure supported by PROGRESS called "External Procedures."

External Procedures are routines that are defined in Dynamic Link Libraries (DLL) under Microsoft Windows. The syntax is similar to the definition for a regular internal procedure, except that you need to specify the name of the DLL file in the definition. To define an external procedure, you use the following code:

```
PROCEDURE proc-name EXTERNAL "dllname" :
```

Unfortunately, the UIB does not allow you to specify anything between the proc-name and the colon (:). So what can you do?

The answer is: "Cheat!" The UIB will store everything you type in the Code Section Editor even if it follows the `END PROCEDURE` statement.

If you want to define external procedures in the UIB, simply make a dummy internal procedure to hold all your DLL calls. Follow these steps:

1. Bring up the UIB's Code Section Editor.
2. Go to the Procedure section.
3. Create a new procedure, and name it **`DLL-routines`**.
4. Enter *all* your DLL calls in this one section (see fig. 21.9).

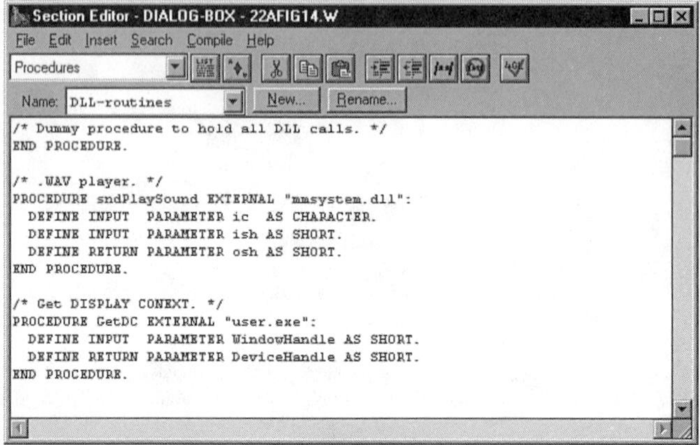

Fig. 21.9

Enter all your external procedure definitions into one UIB code section.

Tip

By placing all your DLL calls in one dummy procedure, you can import or export the entire set in a single .wx (UIB export) file.

Simply select the Edit, Copy to File option on the UIB Main Menu, and export the `DLL-routines` procedure (and no associated objects).

Aligning SmartObjects on Different Pages

When you open a SmartContainer that supports paging, the UIB shows all SmartObjects on the *base* page (page 0), plus the contents of one other design page. But suppose you have objects that are on pages 1 and 2 and you want to make sure they are in the same location. You could view page 1, check the coordinates of the objects there, then change to page 2 and check those objects, but this can be tedious, especially if there are lots of objects on many pages.

It would be very convenient to be able to box-select objects on multiple pages and move them together. This can be done by following these steps:

1. Bring up the Goto Page dialog by double-clicking on the page number in the UIB's status bar (or choose Edit, Goto Page).
2. Enter **?** in the Display Page Number field (see fig. 21.10). When you click OK in this dialog box, the UIB will display the contents of All Pages.

3. You can now select SmartObjects from multiple pages and move them directly, or by using the Group Property window.

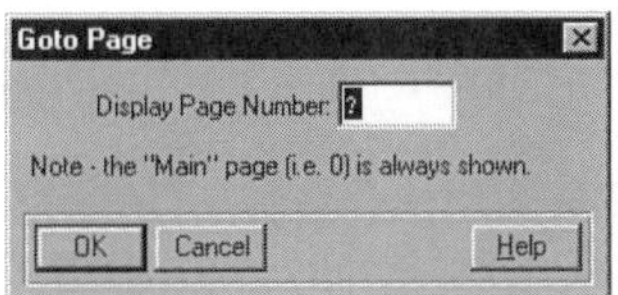

Fig. 21.10

The UIB will show all pages in a SmartWindow if you enter ? for the display page number.

Self-Initializing Custom Objects

The UIB allows you to create definitions for objects that can appear on the Object Palette. You define these objects in a custom object file and load it into the UIB using the Menu, Use Custom option on the Object Palette's menu. The standard files, PROGRESS.CST and SMART.CST, are examples of these custom object files.

◀◀ For more information on the mechanics of Custom Object files, see Chapter 20, "Extending the Development Tools."

In addition to specifying attributes for your custom objects, you can specify blocks of trigger code. The default definition for a Help button (in `DLC\src\template\progress.cst`) includes a `CHOOSE` trigger as well as `Name` and `Label` attributes.

```
*BUTTON          &Help
DESCRIPTION      Standard Help Button
DEFAULT-STYLE    YES
LABEL            &Help
NAME             Btn_Help
TRIGGER CHOOSE
DO: /* Call Help Function (or a simple message). */
  MESSAGE "Help for File: {&FILE-NAME}" VIEW-AS ALERT-BOX INFORMATION.
END.
END TRIGGER
```

It is also possible to use this feature to add code to an object that will initialize it. There are two facts about the UIB's Code Section Editor that you need to be aware of:

- Code you enter into the Code Section Editor gets copied directly to the .w file when you save. Code for triggers is placed after the object definitions and just before the Main Code Block.

▶▶ For more information on .w files, see Appendix F, "Structure of .w Files."

- The actual trigger code associated with an event is the code in the `DO:...END.` block. If you add statements after the `END` (and before the `END TRIGGER` in custom files), these statements are executed at the same level as the Main Code Block, and not as part of the trigger.

Figure 21.11 shows a CHOOSE trigger on a button in the Section Editor. The BELL statements are actually outside the trigger. Only the Message statement will be executed when the user clicks the button. The BELL will sound when the program is run.

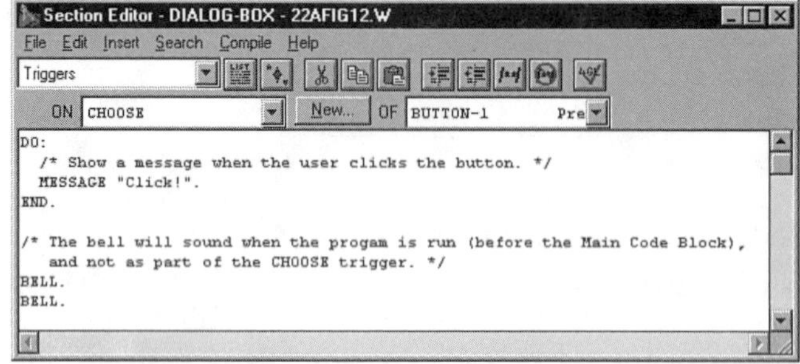

Fig. 21.11

Code can be entered outside of an actual trigger in the Section Editor. This code executes when the procedure file is first run, and not when the trigger fires.

The ability to add code outside the trigger in the Code Section Editor gives you the ability to add initialization code to an object. The advantages of adding initialization code here include:

- You can use the {&SELF-NAME} and {&FRAME-NAME} preprocessor variables in your initialization code.
- The initialization code is associated with the object. If you cut and paste the object, the initialization code is also copied. If you delete the object, the initialization code is also deleted.
- You can add initialization code as part of the definition of a Custom Object in your .CST file.

Tip

You can add initialization code to an object or custom object as part of a developer event. It is a good idea to establish a convention, such as always using U1 as the initialization event.

Add this initialization code after the normal DO:...END trigger block, and it will execute just before the Main Code Block.

In Chapter 22, "PROGRESS Programming Tips," you will see more examples of code that should be executed as part of the initialization of an object. For example, the "Labels on the Right" section defined the rlabel.p procedure, which could be executed as part of the Main Code Block. If you wanted to add this in the U1 trigger, the code (in the Section Editor) would be:

```
ON U1 OF FRAME f
DO:
  /* Do nothing as part of the trigger. The U1 trigger
     is only here to hold initialization code defined
```

```
        AFTER the trigger. */
    END.

    /* Do this initialization code. */
    RUN c:\appdir\rlabel.p (FRAME {&SELF-NAME}:HANDLE).
```

The same code would appear in a Custom Object file as:

```
*FRAME &Right Labels
TRIGGER U1
DO:
  /* Do nothing */
END.
/* Do this initialization before Main Code Block. */
RUN c:\appdir\rlabel.p (FRAME {&SELF-NAME}:HANDLE).
END TRIGGER
```

◀◀ For more information on using Custom Object files, see Chapter 20, "Extending the Development Tools."

SmartObject Tips

This section describes some techniques for enhancing the functionality and reusability of PROGRESS SmartObjects. You will see how to do the following:

- Add methods to SmartObjects.
- Create your own classes and templates.
- Reuse SmartContainers.

Modifying Search Filters in SmartQueries and SmartBrowsers

You may have noticed that the selection criteria in SmartQueries and SmartBrowsers are fixed when the object is created. For example, you can create a query `FOR EACH order WHERE order-date > 12/20/95` or `FOR EACH customer WHERE name BEGINS 'A'`. The query is compiled into the SmartObject by the PROGRESS compiler.

The advantage of compile-time binding in queries is that PROGRESS can optimize the database request based on database indices and capabilities of the data server. But does this mean that you have to build a different SmartObject every time you want to change the selection criteria on a query?

The answer is "No." It is actually rather simple to modify a SmartBrowser or SmartQuery to support a variable filter. Suppose you want to create a screen like the one shown in figure 21.12.

To create this screen, you first need to create a SmartBrowser with the following enhancements:

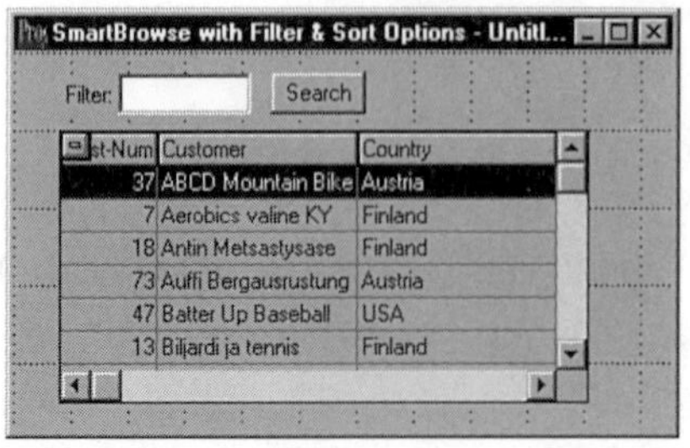

Fig. 21.12

This SmartBrowser has a variable filter that users can control by entering a filter in the fill-in field.

- The query in the SmartBrowser will use a variable to determine matching records. That is, the query will be

  ```
  FOR EACH customer WHERE customer.name MATCHES <filter variable>
  ```

- There need to be new methods that the container can call to set the *filter variable* and reopen the query.

To create this SmartBrowser, follow these steps:

1. Use File, New to bring up the New dialog. Select SmartBrowser with Wizard and click OK.
2. When the SmartBrowser Wizard comes up, skip over the External Tables screen.
3. Define the 4GL Query to be "`FOR EACH Customer WHERE Customer.Name MATCHES adm-filter`." Make sure adm-filter is not quoted in the final query. (Note: the variable *adm-filter* is not yet defined. This will happen later.)
4. Add fields to the SmartBrowser: Cust-Num, Name, and Country, for example.
5. Complete the SmartBrowser Wizard (by clicking the Next button, and then the Finish button).
6. Resize the SmartBrowser as necessary and then save the file as b-custf.w. (Note: the file will not compile. Don't bother looking at the errors.)

   Even though the file saved successfully, it did not compile. This is because the query you defined uses a variable that does not exist: adm-filter. In order to create this variable you need to:
7. Bring up the UIB Code Section Editor by clicking the Code button.
8. Go to the Definitions section and add the following local variable definition.

   ```
   /* Local Variable Definitions —          */
   DEFINE VARIABLE adm-filter AS CHAR INITIAL "*" NO-UNDO.
   ```

   You will have to add an initial condition to the filter so that the query will successfully open.
9. Save the file (as `b-custf.w`). It now saves and compiles.

> **Note**
>
> A completed version of this file is available on the accompanying CD-ROM as \examples\chap-21\b-custf.w.

The new SmartBrowser is now usable. In fact, you could use it in place of the SmartBrowser on Customer that you developed for the sample application in Part III of this book, "Creating a Sample Application." When the SmartBrowser runs, it will show customers whose names match "*" (i.e., all customers).

However, this is not exactly what is needed. You want to be able to control the filter variable from controls in other objects. You will have to add some methods to the SmartBrowser.

1. Return to the Code Section Editor for the SmartBrowser.
2. Go to the Procedures section and click on the New button.
3. Create a new procedure named `set-filter`, and set the code block as shown in Listing 21.5.

Listing 21.5 examples\chap-21\b-custf.w—`set-filter` Procedure

```
/*-------------------------------------------------------------
  Purpose:     Sets the filter variable and reopens the query
               (unless the AUTO-OPEN-QUERY attribute is turned off).
  Parameters:  pc_filter - the new filter variable
-------------------------------------------------------------*/
  DEFINE INPUT PARAMETER pc_filter AS CHAR    NO-UNDO.

  adm-filter = pc_filter.
  RUN get-attribute IN THIS-PROCEDURE ('AUTO-OPEN-QUERY':U).
  IF RETURN-VALUE ne 'no':U THEN RUN dispatch ('open-query':U).
END PROCEDURE.
```

This procedure allows another SmartObject to set the filter variable in the SmartBrowser, and then optionally reopen the query using that new variable. (Note: it would be fine, in this example, to always reopen the query. However, if you were setting a number of filter variables in a more complex query, you would want to have control of the query opening. That is why the `AUTO-OPEN-QUERY` attribute is checked.)

4. To complete the process, you should also add a method procedure that allows other SmartObjects to find out what filter variable is being used by the SmartBrowser. Create another new procedure in the SmartBrowser and name it `get-filter`. Set the code in the block as shown in Listing 21.6.

Listing 21.6 \examples\chap-21\b-custf.w—get-filter Procedure

```
/*------------------------------------------------------------------------
  Purpose:     Return the filter variable.
  Parameters:  pc_filter - the new filter variable.
-------------------------------------------------------------------------*/
  DEFINE OUTPUT PARAMETER pc_filter AS CHAR NO-UNDO.
  pc_filter = adm-filter.
END PROCEDURE.
```

5. You can now save your changes.

You can now use this object in your application. For example,

1. Use File, New to bring up the New dialog. Select SmartWindow and click OK.
2. Click the SmartBrowser icon from the Object Palette. Choose the master file you just created (i.e., b-custf.w).
3. Drop the object into your new SmartWindow. This will create an instance of the SmartBrowser. The name of this instance should be `h_b-custf`.
4. Click the Fill-In icon on the Object Palette and draw a fill-in on the SmartWindow near the SmartBrowser.
5. Select the fill-in and click the Code button to bring up the UIB's Code Section Editor.
6. You want to add a trigger that will fire when the user clicks the Return or Enter key in this field. Click the New button to create a new Trigger on the fill-in. Click the Keyboard Event button, and then press Enter.
7. After OK'ing the dialog boxes, you can now set the trigger code as follows:

```
ON RETURN OF Fill-in-1
DO:
  /* Use the value in the fill-in as the SmartBrowser Filter. */
  RUN set-filter IN h_b-custf (SELF:SCREEN-VALUE).
END.
```

8. You can now run the SmartWindow. Type any string into the fill-in and click the Enter key. The SmartBrowser will immediately reflect your changes. To test your code, try typing the following filter strings: *****, **B***, and ***ski***.

If you want to display the current value of the filter in the fill-in, a good place to do this is in a `local-initialize` procedure in the SmartWindow.

After the standard `adm-initialize` has executed, the SmartBrowser object will have been created, and its filter can be checked and displayed. The code to do this is as follows:

```
PROCEDURE local-initialize:
```

```
    /* Dispatch standard ADM method.                             */
    RUN dispatch IN THIS-PROCEDURE ( INPUT 'adm-initialize':U ) .

    /* Code placed here will execute AFTER standard behavior.    */
    RUN get-filter IN h_b-custf (OUTPUT Fill-in-1).
    DISPLAY Fill-in-1 WITH FRAME {&FRAME-NAME}.
  END PROCEDURE.
```

Changing Sort Order in SmartQueries and SmartBrowsers

Adding the functionality to change sort order in SmartBrowsers and SmartQueries is conceptually similar to adding filters. You will have to define access methods to get and set the sort order you want to use, and provide a way of using that sort order in the `OPEN QUERY` statement.

Suppose you wanted to add a `set-sort-by` method to the example above. There are three sort options we want to support: by Cust-Num, by Name, and by Country. Here are the steps to follow:

1. Open the file b-custf.w that you created in the last section.
2. Click the Code button to go to the Code Section Editor.
3. Go to the Definitions section and add a new local variable: `adm-sort-by`. (Note that we are assuming that the default sort order will be by `Cust-Num`.)

   ```
   /* Local Variable Definitions --                         */
   DEFINE VARIABLE adm-filter  AS CHAR INITIAL "*" NO-UNDO.
   DEFINE VARIABLE adm-sort-by AS CHAR INITIAL ?   NO-UNDO.
   ```

4. Go to the Procedures section and click the New button.
5. Create a new procedure named `set-sort-by` and set the code block as shown in Listing 21.7.

Listing 21.7 \examples\chap-21\b-custfs.w—`set-sort-by` Procedure

```
/*------------------------------------------------------------
  Purpose:     Sets the sort-by variable and reopens the query.
               (unless the AUTO-OPEN-QUERY attribute is turned off).
  Parameters:  pc_sort-by - the new sort-by variable
------------------------------------------------------------- */
  DEFINE INPUT PARAMETER pc_sort-by AS CHAR    NO-UNDO.

  adm-sort-by = pc_sort-by.
  RUN get-attribute IN THIS-PROCEDURE ('AUTO-OPEN-QUERY':U).
  IF RETURN-VALUE ne 'no':U THEN RUN dispatch ('open-query':U).
END PROCEDURE.
```

6. For completeness, add another new procedure and name it `get-sort-by`. Set the code in the block as shown in Listing 21.8.

Listing 21.8 \examples\chap-21\b-custfs.w—`get-sort-by` Procedure

```
/*------------------------------------------------------------------------
  Purpose:     Return the filter variable.
  Parameters:  pc_sort-by - the new filter variable.
------------------------------------------------------------------------*/
  DEFINE OUTPUT PARAMETER pc_sort-by AS CHAR NO-UNDO.
  pc_sort-by = adm-sort-by.
END PROCEDURE.
```

7. Save this file with a different name, b-custfs.w, using File, Save As on the UIB's menu bar.

You now are ready to change the query in the SmartBrowser so that it will change based on the value of adm-sort-by. In order to do this you will have to change the query on the browse to a Freeform query.

1. Double-click on the browse to bring up the Browse Property Sheet.
2. Choose the Query button to bring up the Query Builder.
3. Click on the Freeform Query button at the bottom of the dialog and verify that you do indeed want to use a Freeform query. Click OK on all the dialogs to return to the UIB design window.
4. Return to the Code Section Editor and change to the Trigger section. Select the `OPEN_QUERY` event for the Browse object. The code should be initialized to the existing query that you defined on the customer.
5. Type the Listing 21.9 code into the `ON OPEN_QUERY OF` code block for the browse object, `br_table` (note that the sorting by `cust-num` will be considered the default case).

Listing 21.9 \examples\chap-21\b-custfs.w—`ON OPEN_QUERY OF br_table` Trigger

```
CASE adm-sort-by:
  WHEN "name":U THEN
    OPEN QUERY br_table FOR EACH Customer
      WHERE Customer.Name MATCHES adm-filter NO-LOCK BY Customer.Name.
  WHEN "country":U THEN
    OPEN QUERY br_table FOR EACH Customer
      WHERE Customer.Name MATCHES adm-filter NO-LOCK BY
Customer.Country.
 OTHERWISE
    OPEN QUERY br_table FOR EACH Customer
      WHERE Customer.Name MATCHES adm-filter NO-LOCK BY Customer.Cust-
Num.
END CASE.
```

6. You can now save your file (as `b-custfs.w`).

If you wanted to use this sort-by function, you would simply call `set-sort-by` with the appropriate parameters. For example, you could add a combo-box or radio-set to set the sort-by option. The values of this object could then be used to set the sort-by attribute of the SmartObject. For example:

```
ON VALUE-CHANGED OF Radio-Set-1
DO:
  RUN set-sort-by IN h_b-custfs (SELF:SCREEN-VALUE).
END.
```

A completed test program that uses b-custfs.w and sets both the filter and sort-by options is available on the CD-ROM as \examples\chap-21\w-testfs.w.

> **Note**
>
> All the code you added to add filters and sort options to a SmartBrowser would work just as well on any SmartQuery.

Creating Your Own Method Library

If you want to add the same filter and sort-by capability to other SmartBrowsers and SmartQueries, you should create a Method Library. This new library could be added to individual master files, or to the standard SmartQuery and SmartBrowser templates.

In order to create a new Method Library, you need to do the following steps:

1. Use File, New to bring up the New dialog. Select Method Library and click OK. The UIB's Code Section Editor automatically comes into focus. You should also note that the Method Library is represented in the UIB as a blank window. No graphic objects can be added to this blank window.
2. Once in the Code Section Editor, go to the Definitions section. Add the definition of `adm-filter` and `adm-sort-by` from the above examples (see `b-custfs.w`).
3. Change to the Procedure section. Create new procedures for: `set-filter`, `get-filter`, `set-sort-by` and `get-sort-by`. These procedures should be the same as the ones you created for `b-custfs.w` in the previous section.
4. Save this as `filter.i`.

A completed copy of this method library is available on the CD-ROM as \examples\chap-21\filter.i.

If you ever need to add the filter or sort-by functions to a SmartBrowser or SmartQuery, all you need to do is add in this Method Library as follows:

1. Edit the Master File for the SmartObject (or just open it in the UIB).
2. Click the Procedure button on the UIB's Main Window to bring up the Procedure Settings dialog.
3. Click the Method Libraries button to bring up the Method Libraries dialog.

4. Click the Add button.
5. When the Add Method Library Reference dialog box comes up, type **filter.i** into the fill-in field and click OK.
6. You should be back in the Method Libraries dialog. Use the Move Up and Move Down buttons to make sure filter.i appears before any libraries that are going to use the variables defined in filter.i (see fig. 21.13).

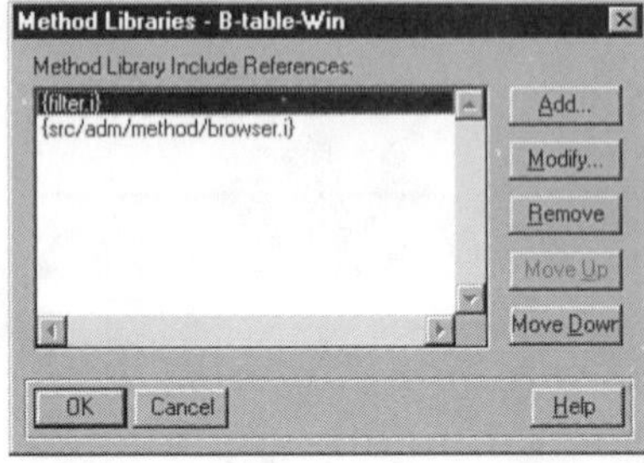

Fig. 21.13

Use the Method Libraries dialog box to add functionality to SmartObjects.

> **Tip**
>
> When you create your own Method Libraries, you will want to store them in a common directory such as src\adm\methods.
>
> You can store your own libraries with the standard PROGRESS libraries, or make your own directory structure and set your `PROPATH` accordingly.

Creating Your Own SmartObject Classes

At some point you will certainly want to create your own SmartObject classes. A SmartObject class is defined by its template file. The easiest way to build a SmartObject class is to start with an existing SmartObject template, copy it, and then modify it as necessary.

Suppose you wanted to create a generic SmartObject class that was "smart" enough to be dropped into any SmartContainer, but had no special links. You might want to use Master Files built from this class to build your own button bars or simple interface elements.

To create this "generic" class, follow these steps:

1. Copy the standard SmartViewer template, `DLC\src\adm\template\viewer.w`, to `simple.w`.
2. Open `simple.w` in a text editor. Remember that XFTRs cannot be edited in the UIB. The standard `viewer.w` contains the Cue Card instructions for SmartViewers. This code will need to be edited.

3. Find the Cue Card XFTR section and modify it as shown in Listing 21.10. Note that there is no help file defined for this new type. (Normally the help file would follow, `SimpleObject` on the third line of the XFTR section.)

Listing 21.10 \examples\chap-21\simple.w—XFTR Section

```
&ANALYZE-SUSPEND _UIB-CODE-BLOCK _XFTR "SimpleObjectCues" V-table-Win
➥_INLINE
/* Actions: adecomm/_so-cue.w ? adecomm/_so-cued.p ? adecomm/_so-cuew.p
/* SimpleObject
A SimpleObject is a basic SmartObject with no custom behavior.

* Creating a SimpleObject
1) Add basic objects, such as buttons and fields
2) Add code though the Code Section Editor.
3) Save and close the object.

*/
/* _UIB-CODE-BLOCK-END */
&ANALYZE-RESUME
```

4. Save the file and exit out the text editor.
5. Start up the UIB.
6. Open the file, `simple.w`. The type of the file will still say "SmartViewer." This is the next thing you will change.
7. Click the Procedure button on the UIB Main Window to bring up the Procedure Settings dialog.
8. Click the Advanced button to bring up the Advanced Procedure Settings dialog.
9. Change the Procedure Type by choosing New in the combo box. The New Procedure Type dialog appears. Enter the new type, **SimpleObject**, and click OK.
10. You are now back in the Advance Procedure Settings dialog. Select each of the Supported SmartLinks and click the Remove button. By default, this new SimpleObject will not support any special linking.
11. Uncheck the toggle box labelled Database fields. The SimpleObject will now only support basic objects.
12. Click OK to return to the Procedure Settings dialog.
13. Change the Description of the Procedure by typing:

    `ADM SimpleObject Template.`
    `Use this template to create a basic SmartObject that can contain basic objects.`

14. Click the Method Libraries button to bring up the list of Method Libraries used by this object.
15. Modify the list so that the only library is {src\adm\method\smart.i}.
16. Return to the Procedure Settings dialog, and click the Custom Lists button.
17. Make sure the custom lists are named LIST-1, LIST-2, ..., LIST-6.

18. Click OK in all the dialog boxes and return to the UIB Main Window.
19. Click the Code button to bring up the UIB's Code Section Editor.
20. Switch to the Definitions section. Change the references from "SmartViewer" to "SimpleObject."
21. Switch to the Main Block section. The Main Block needs to define two items: the root object that this SmartObject is based on, and what to do if it is run from the UIB. The basic object handle for the SimpleObject will be the default `FRAME`. The Main Block should be changed as shown in Listing 21.11.

Listing 21.11 \examples\chap-21\simple.w—Main Code Block

```
/* ***************************  Main Block  *************************** */

/* Define the root object of this type as the default FRAME. */
adm-object-hdl = FRAME {&FRAME-NAME}:HANDLE.

/* If testing in the UIB, initialize the SmartObject. */
&IF DEFINED(UIB_IS_RUNNING) <> 0 &THEN
  RUN dispatch IN THIS-PROCEDURE ('initialize':U).
&ENDIF
```

22. Click the List button in the Code Section Editor. This brings up the Sections dialog box. There are two procedures that can be removed from SimpleObject now that it does not support database fields: `adm-row-available` and `send-records`.
23. Select `adm-row-available` in the Sections dialog and click OK. The code for this procedure should now be shown.
24. Choose Edit, Delete Procedure from the menu bar. Confirm that you really want to delete the procedure.
25. Again click the List button. This time choose the `send-records` procedure.
26. Again choose Edit, Delete Procedure from the menu bar. Confirm that you really want to delete the procedure.
27. Again click the List button. This time select the procedure: `state-changed`. Remove the line that references the file: `{src/adm/template/vstates.i}`. This line includes the file listing the special states supported by SmartViewers. Because the SimpleObject has no special states, you can leave the `state-changed` procedure as shown in Listing 21.12.

Listing 21.12 \examples\chap-21\simple.w—`state-changed` Procedure

```
/* -----------------------------------------------------------
  Purpose:
  Parameters:  <none>
  Notes:
-------------------------------------------------------------*/
  DEFINE INPUT PARAMETER p-issuer-hdl AS HANDLE    NO-UNDO.
  DEFINE INPUT PARAMETER p-state      AS CHARACTER NO-UNDO.

  CASE p-state:
      /* Object instance CASEs can go here to replace standard behavior
         or add new cases. */

    END CASE.
END PROCEDURE.
```

28. Click the Save button on the UIB Main Window to store your changes to `simple.w`.

At this point you can create new SimpleObjects based on this template. You will have to choose the template file directly using the Template button on the File, New dialog box.

If you wish to add the SimpleObject class to the UIB's Object Palette and File, New list, you will have to create a custom object file that defines this. Chapter 20, "Extending the Development Tools," describes this process in more detail, but a quick summary of the steps would be:

1. Create two bitmaps (28 × 28 pixels): one for the up image and one for the down image that you wish to add to the Object Palette. (For example, create `myicon\simple-u.bmp` and `myicon\simple-d.bmp`.)
2. Create the following custom object file using a Procedure Window to define the SimpleObject class. Save this file as `simple.cst`.

Listing 21.13 \examples\chap-21\simple.cst—Custom Object File

```
/* simple.cst - local SmartObject file  */

#SimpleObject     &Default
UP-IMAGE-FILE    myicon/simple-u 0,0
DOWN-IMAGE-FILE myicon/simple-d 0,0
LABEL            &SimpleObject
DIRECTORY-LIST   .
FILTER           *.*
TITLE            Choose SimpleObject
NEW-TEMPLATE     simple.w

*NEW-SMARTOBJECT &SimpleObject
TYPE             SimpleObject
NEW-TEMPLATE     simple.w
```

3. Choose Menu, Use Custom to load this new custom object file into the UIB's Object Palette.

At this point, you will be able to create new SimpleObjects from the UIB's standard File, New dialog box. SimpleObject will appear in the list of SmartObjects that you can create in this dialog.

If you do in fact do this, and you try to save your new SimpleObject you will see that the UIB gives your new object a default file name of `v-table-.w`. This is the same default file name that would be used for a SmartViewer. There is no surprise here because the SimpleObject template was based on the SmartViewer template.

Tip

The UIB chooses the default file name for the new master file based on the *object name* of the window or dialog-box object in a file. For example, if the window object has a name WINDOW-1, then the default file name will be `window-1.w`.

If you want to change the default file name of files you create, you should change the name of the window object in the template used to create those files.

If you want all new SimpleObjects to have a name such as `s-object.w`, then all you have to do is change the name of the underlying window object. Unfortunately, this is harder than it should be because most SmartObject templates do not have a visible underlying window. The following steps will let you trick the UIB into changing the name of this hidden window.

1. Open the template file for SimpleObject, `simple.w`, in the UIB.
2. Click the Procedure button on the UIB's toolbar to enter the Procedure Settings dialog.
3. Click the Advanced button to start up the Advanced Procedure Settings dialog. Here is where we can trick the SmartObject into revealing its window object.
4. Check the Window toggle box in the group labelled Allow Addition of:. This will make the window object's property sheet available in the UIB.
5. Click OK in all the dialog boxes until you return to the UIB's main window. Ignore the warnings about setting Method Libraries correctly.
6. Click the List button on the UIB's toolbar and bring up the List Objects dialog. You should see a `WINDOW` object on that list with the name `v-table-win`.
7. Select the `WINDOW` object and click the Property button. The Property Sheet for object `v-table-win` should appear.
8. Change the name of the window to **s-object** by typing over the old name in the Object field.

9. Click OK on both the Property Sheet and List Objects dialog.
10. You are now ready to tell the UIB to hide the underlying window object again. This process will simply invert steps 1 to 5. First click the Procedure button; then click the Advanced button to return to the Advanced Procedure Settings dialog.
11. Turn off the Window toggle box.
12. Click OK until you return to the UIB. Once again ignore the Method Library warnings.
13. Save the file as `simple.w`.

Turning SmartContainers into Objects

As you build your applications, you will certainly find that many of your screens will share the same look and feel. You may have a standard layout for a maintenance screen based on a SmartWindow that contains Update and Navigation SmartPanels, one SmartQuery, and a SmartViewer. While you clearly need a new SmartQuery and SmartViewer to show different records tables, you may wonder why you need a separate SmartWindow for each table.

Surely it should be possible to have a single SmartWindow file, and just pass the file name of the SmartQuery and SmartBrowser to it.

Not only is this possible, it is the preferred approach. As much as possible, you should try to minimize the number of files in your application. If you can parameterize a whole screen down to a set of file names, this will improve the performance and maintainability of your application.

The steps you need to follow to change a SmartContainer into a reusable object are as follows:

1. Create a prototype that uses a particular set of SmartObjects.
2. For each SmartObject that you want to replace with a parameter or variable, go into that object's Property Sheet by double-clicking on the object.
3. Check the Parameterize as Variable toggle-box on the Property Sheet. This enables a fill-in field where you can type a name for the variable (see fig. 21.14). The UIB does not define this name for you. You will have to create this variable yourself in the Definition section. You can choose any name you want here, as long as it refers to a character variable defined somewhere in your procedure.
4. Define the variable name you used for each SmartObject in the Section Editor. You can define the variable as an internal variable or as an input parameter.
5. Save and compile the window file.

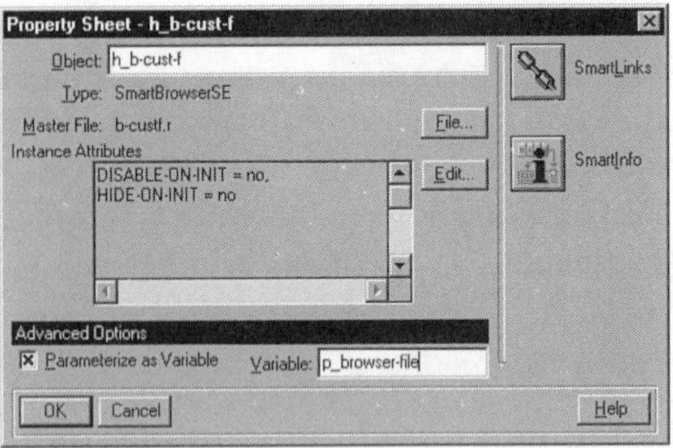

Fig. 21.14

Use the SmartObject Property Sheet to turn the specific Master File name into a variable.

You have just completed a container object that provides a framework to display or update many different tables. The difference between this object and other SmartContainers is that the new object is more general. The names of contained SmartObjects are not hard-coded into the file. Instead they must be passed as parameters or instance attributes to the SmartContainer.

You can also create SmartDialog objects. The CD-ROM contains an example of such an object in \examples\chap-21\d-v-updt.w. This SmartDialog takes two input parameters: the name of a SmartViewer, and the `ROWID` of a record to update with that SmartViewer. A logical value is returned depending on whether the user clicked OK in the dialog.

The advantage of this dialog is that it allows you to turn any SmartViewer into an update dialog box, without having to create new objects. The following code sample shows how you can call the SmartDialog for two separate tables.

```
DEFINE VARIABLE lOK AS LOGICAL NO-UNDO.

/* Update the first customer by passing a SmartViewer into the
   SmartDialog object. */
FIND FIRST Customer.
RUN \examples\chap-21\d-v-updt.w
        ('v-cust.w', ROWID(Customer), OUTPUT lOK).

/* Now update the salesrep using the same SmartDialog object. */
FIND Salesrep OF Customer.
RUN \examples\chap-21\d-v-updt.w
        ('v-salrep.w', ROWID(Salesrep), OUTPUT lOK).
```

Adding VBX Controls into a SmartViewer

You can add additional capabilities and pizazz to your SmartViewers by adding VBX controls. VBX controls can be *bound* to fields that are available from a data source. For example, you can represent a date using a calendar control.

Here are several things to consider if you want to use a VBX control in a SmartViewer:

- A VBX control should be appropriate for the SmartViewer. The control should be able to represent a single field or a series of fields for a single record.
- You will have to *bind* the VBX control to display and update the field by overriding several ADM events. Part of the binding may include converting the data. This will be different for each VBX control you use.
- Depending on the VBX control you may have to program how the control interacts with user.
- You may have to provide visual affordances to let the user know that the VBX control can be updated.

◄◄ For more information on VBX controls, refer to Chapter 5, "Further Exploration: Locking, Transactions, and VBXs."

Adding Calendar Controls

The following example will show you how to add calendar controls to a SmartViewer. The final result will look like figure 21.15.

- Use Crescent Software's calendar control to represent the promise and ship dates of the order table
- Learn which methods to override to bind the VBX controls into a SmartViewer
- Call a procedure that will automatically place the SmartViewer into a dialog box for update

As part of binding the calendars you will program them to display the current values of the fields, including the `NULL` value. You will create UI affordances to let the user know the calendars can be changed.

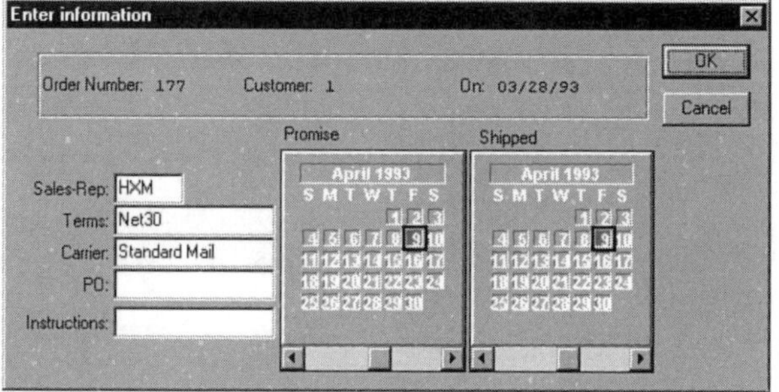

Fig. 21.15

The Proposed Update dialog box.

This example uses the CSCALDMO.VBX, and the rgb.i macro. These files can be found on the CD-ROM accompanying this book. Refer to Appendix G, "Contents of CD," for installation instructions.

Making the SmartViewer

You will start by creating the SmartViewer. Choose New followed by SmartViewer with AutoField.

1. Approximate the layout in figure 21.15 for the fill-in fields and rectangle only. From the order table add `Order-Num`, `Cust-Num`, `Order-Date`, `Sales-Rep`, `Terms`, `Carrier`, `PO`, and `Instructions`.
2. You don't want a user to be able to invalidate a record by typing over a primary index field. Make the `Order-Num`, `Cust-Num`, and `Order-Date` fill-ins be seen but not updatable. Change the `Enable` properties to **`No`** using the Group Properties Window.

> **Tip**
>
> You cannot create a SmartViewer that contains only VBX controls. There must be *at least one enabled* field in a SmartViewer.

3. Add the first calendar control. Choose `CSCALDMO` from the VBX picker. Change the name of the control to `prom-cal` and size of the control to 25 columns by 7 rows.

   Toggle the `Enable` property off. You do not want the user to be able to interact with calendar until in update mode.
4. Using the VB property Window change `DateType` to **`Crescent Serial Date`**, change `MarkColor1` to a nice shade of blue, change `FontName` to **`Arial`**, change `FontSize` to **`8`**, change `Scrollbar` to **`Horizontal`**, and change `ThreeD` to **`True`**.
5. You now need to make the second calendar. You can do this by copy and paste. Copy `prom-cal` and paste it. The calendar is completely copied, including the properties you set!

   Change the name of the new calendar to `ship-cal`. Position it next to `prom-cal`.
6. Add two texts. Change one to be **Promised:** and the other **Shipped:**.

Save your work as `v-ordx.w`.

Bind the VBX Controls

In general, to bind a VBX control into the SmartViewer you will need to make local versions of five ADM events and possibly add some definitions. The events are: `adm-initialize`, `adm-display-fields`, `adm-enable-fields`, `adm-disable-fields`, and `adm-assign-record`.

In our example, you will work with four ADM events and add code to the definition section. You will not need to write any special initialization for this example.

1. In the Definitions section add:

```
DEFINE VARIABLE s AS LOGICAL NO-UNDO.
```

This simply defines a logical variable to use as a return value when calling object methods. By defining it once at the top of the file, you won't have to define it in each procedure.

2. Add the code from the following tip. The "constant" will be needed later to display the dates into the calendars.

> **Tip**
>
> The Crescent Software calendar control stores the date as a signed integer in the property named `Date`. This number represents the number of days from December 31, 1979. You can only set the date by providing the date offset. Use PROGRESS date arithmetic to accomplish the conversion.
>
> Add the following code to your application:
>
> ```
> DEFINE VARIABLE crescent-start AS DATE NO-UNDO INITIAL "12/31/1979".
> ```
>
> In your code you use `crescent-start` as a constant by subtracting it from your date when setting the `Date` property.

3. To display the values of `promise-date` and `ship-date` you will make a local version of the `adm-display-fields` event. You must make the VBX controls display properly when there are values for the fields (including `NULL`) as well as when there is no record.

   Add the code in Listing 21.14 after the standard behavior comment:

Listing 21.14 \examples\chap-21\v-ordx.w—`local-display-fields` Procedure

```
/* Make sure any previous markings are removed */
ASSIGN s = ship-cal:SET-PROP("MarkType":U, 0, 0)
       s = prom-cal:SET-PROP("MarkType":U, 0, 0).
IF AVAILABLE ORDER THEN DO:
  /* Assign the dates, if there are any. Use the date constant. */
  IF order.ship-date <> ?
    THEN ASSIGN s = ship-cal:SET-PROP("Date":U, order.ship-date -
    ➥crescent-start)
                s = ship-cal:SET-PROP("MarkType":U, DAY(order.ship-
                ➥date), 1).

  IF order.promise-date <> ?
    THEN ASSIGN s = prom-cal:SET-PROP("Date":U, order.promise-date -
    ➥crescent-start)
                s = prom-cal:SET-PROP("MarkType":U, DAY(order.promise-
                ➥date), 1).
END.
ASSIGN s = ship-cal:REFRESH() /* Update the mark after display state is
➥resolved*/
       s = prom-cal:REFRESH().
```

4. Create a local version of `adm-enable-fields`. This event is called when a SmartViewer is going into `update`. You will make the calendars sensitive and *provide an affordance to let the user know the calendars can be changed.* In this example, make the text of the calendar white. Add the code in Listing 21.15.

Listing 21.15 \examples\chap-21\v-ordx.w—local-enable-fields Procedure

```
ASSIGN ship-cal:SENSITIVE = true
       prom-cal:SENSITIVE = true
       s = ship-cal:SET-PROP("ForeColor":U, {rgb.i 255 255 255}) /*
       ➥white */
       s = prom-cal:SET-PROP("ForeColor":U, {rgb.i 255 255 255}).
```

5. Create a local version `adm-disable-fields`. This event is called when a SmartViewer leaves `update`. Add the code in Listing 21.16.

Listing 21.16 \examples\chap-21\v-ordx.w—local-disable-fields Procedure

```
ASSIGN ship-cal:SENSITIVE = false
       prom-cal:SENSITIVE = false
       s = ship-cal:SET-PROP("ForeColor":U, {rgb.i 0 0 0}) /* black */
       s = prom-cal:SET-PROP("ForeColor":U, {rgb.i 0 0 0}).
```

6. Create a local version of `adm-assign-record`. This method is called only when the value of the field is to be changed, and is part of the transaction. Add the code in Listing 21.17.

Listing 21.17 \examples\chap-21\v-ordx.w—local-assign-record Procedure

```
ASSIGN Order.promise-date = DATE(INT(prom-cal:GET-CHAR-PROP("Month":U)),
                                 INT(prom-cal:GET-CHAR-PROP("Day":U)),
                                 INT(prom-cal:GET-CHAR-PROP("Year":U)))
       Order.ship-date = DATE(INT(ship-cal:GET-CHAR-PROP("Month":U)),
                              INT(ship-cal:GET-CHAR-PROP("Day":U)),
                              INT(ship-cal:GET-CHAR-PROP("Year":U))).
```

7. Save your work as `v-ordx.w`.

Tip

If a SmartViewer is only intended to be read-only then you only need to make a local version of `adm-display-fields`. If you are not sure what the future use of the SmartViewer is then it is better to program for update. The SmartViewer will be more robust.

Using the SmartViewer

The last step is to use this `v-ordx.w` in a file. We can use this SmartViewer as we would any SmartViewer that did not contain VBXs. For example, you can use it to update the record shown in a SmartBrowser. You can use it with the SmartDialog object that was shown in the previous section, `d-v-updt.w`. The following steps tie both the SmartViewer and the SmartDialog to a SmartBrowser on the Order table:

1. Create a SmartBrowser on all the Order records. Save this as `b-order.w`.
2. Create a new SmartWindow.
3. Drop the SmartBrowser, `b-order.w`, into the SmartWindow. The name of the SmartBrowser should be **`h_b-order`**.
4. Choose the Button tool from the UIB's Object palette and draw a button in the SmartWindow beside `h_b-order`.
5. Select the button. Change the name of the Object to **`Btn_update`** and the Label to **`Update`.**
6. Click the Code button to bring up the Section Editor. Add the following code for the `ON CHOOSE OF` trigger for `Btn_Update`.

```
DEFINE VARIABLE crowid AS CHARACTER NO-UNDO.
DEFINE VARIABLE ok     AS LOGICAL   NO-UNDO.
/* Provide the row from the browser to the dialog box */
RUN send-records IN h_b-order("order":U, OUTPUT cRowId).
RUN d-v-updt.w("v-ordx.w":U, TO-ROWID(cRowId), OUTPUT ok).
/* If the user chose OK then update the browser */
IF ok THEN RUN dispatch in h_b-order("Row-changed":U).
```

7. Click the Run button in the UIB. When the SmartWindow comes up, you will be able to scroll through the SmartBrowser. Every time you click the Update button, a SmartDialog will come up allowing you to change the Order fields using basic fill-ins, as well as the Calendar VBXs.

   You change the date simply by selecting a new date from the calendar. Try choosing OK and then Cancel.

PRO*Tools Tips

The PRO*Tools palette contains a series of small applications, or *applets*, that handle simple but common tasks. There is an applet to change the font used by the Procedure Editor, another to change PROPATH, and others to view all the objects and procedures in your PROGRESS session.

This section describes some of the more creative ways of using the applets in PRO*Tools. To start PRO*Tools, follow these steps:

1. Choose the Tools, PRO*Tools menu item from any of the PROGRESS tools (for example, the UIB or Procedure Editor). This will bring up the PRO*Tools palette.

2. If you want to see labels under the icons for the tools, use the right-mouse button anywhere in the PRO*Tools palette. This brings up a small pop-up menu. Select the Menu Bar option.
3. When the menu bar appears, choose the File, Labels option. The PRO*Tools palette will be redrawn with labels under the applet icons.
4. Click the button for any applet on the palette to bring up that tool.

Generally speaking, the PRO*Tools applets are quite obvious in their usage. All have on-line help describing their functionality (available by pressing the F1 key or clicking the Help button). You should explore these applets because while they don't do much, what they do can be very useful.

Control Hierarchy

The Control Hierarchy applet is particularly useful when debugging your applications. It provides an internal view into your PROGRESS session and allows you to see a list of the basic objects that are currently active. While developing, you may find problems such as unexpected behavior by windows and frames, or objects appearing in the wrong location or not appearing at all even though you know you've created them. Using the Control Hierarchy applet, you can query and verify the parenting of objects, as well as the existence of or location of objects.

For example:

1. Click the Control Hierarchy button on the PRO*Tools palette. This brings up the Control Hierarchy window.
2. Choose the menu item View, All Objects. You can now scroll through the list of not only your objects, but the objects used in all the PROGRESS tools.
3. Start up another PRO*Tool applet. You will note that the Control Hierarchy window does not automatically change to reflect the new objects used in this window.
4. Select View, Refresh to update the Control Hierarchy. You should be able to see the new tool in the list.

Procedure Object Viewer

The Procedure Object Viewer applet lists all the persistent procedures currently running in your PROGRESS session. When you select a procedure from the list, you can view all of the internal procedures contained within that procedure. You can also choose one from the list of internal procedures and Run it, or Dispatch it, if its name begins with `adm-` or `local-`.

This applet is also very useful when debugging your applications. It's common, when using persistent procedures, to create a "persistent procedure leak," that is, to have code that incorrectly runs a procedure multiple times, usually indicating a problem with correctly terminating your procedures. You may also have problems running internal procedures in a procedure that you think should be active or one that should contain the internal procedure you are attempting to run. This applet can quickly show you if you have more persistent procedures running than you should, or show you that you are not running the persistent procedures you think you are at any given moment. This applet also gives you a handy way to delete or close persistent procedures via the Apply "Close" and Delete buttons.

When using SmartObjects, you can use this applet to test your objects' methods. For example, you could select the persistent procedure representing a SmartViewer and directly dispatch `adm-hide` and `adm-view` to see if the object is responding properly to those internal procedures.

For example:

1. Click the Procedures button on the PRO*Tools palette. This brings up the Procedure Object Viewer window. This lists all the procedures that you have run `PERSISTENT` in your session.
2. Run a SmartObject application, such as `w-main.w`. This will create some new procedure objects (because all SmartObjects are PROGRESS procedures).
3. Select View, Refresh List of Procedure Objects to update the applet. You should now be able to see the new SmartObjects in the list.
4. Select one of the SmartObjects in the application (for example, `b-cust.w`). The list of Internal Entries will reflect the ADM events and methods in this object.
5. Choose the `adm-hide` event in the list of Internal Entries.
6. Click the Dispatch button. This will send the hide event to the object. If you look at your application, you will see that the SmartObject, `b-cust.w`, has disappeared.
7. Now select the `adm-view` event in the list of Internal Entries, and click the Dispatch button again. The SmartObjects should have come back.

Run Procedure Applet

The Run Procedure applet is handy to have running while you work, because it runs persistently and can be minimized on your desktop. It will always be available as a quick way to run PROGRESS procedures. You will no longer have to stop and load up a file in the Editor or UIB to run a PROGRESS procedure.

For example:

1. Click the Run button on the PRO*Tools palette. This brings up the Run Procedure window.
2. Type the name of some file to run into the fill-in. For example, you can type **protools_propath.w**. This is the name of the PRO*Tools `PROPATH` editor.
3. Click the Run button. The `PROPATH` editor will appear.

Session Attributes Applet

The Session Attributes applet shows you all of the attributes and values of the PROGRESS Session handle. It's handy for querying or validating many of these settings while writing or running your application. For example, differences in character-unit size may be the source of some strange object sizing when running your application on non-English versions of Windows. Using this applet to query the values of pixels-per-column and pixels-per-row will help you to determine the runtime adjustments you'll need to make in your application code to enable the application to run correctly in all supported environments. This applet is also handy to enable you to supply Progress Software Corporation's Technical Support with vital details about your operating environment.

For example:

1. Click the Session button on the PRO*Tools palette. This brings up the Session Attributes dialog.
2. Scroll this list to see the current values of all the attributes associated with the PROGRESS `SESSION` handle.

PROGRESS Window Viewer Applet

The PROGRESS Window Viewer applet shows you all the windows currently active in your PROGRESS session. You can determine the state of these windows and hide or view any of them. While developing your application, you can use this applet to locate windows that fail to appear. In this case, it will be useful to know whether the window really exists, or is simply hidden as a result of some faulty logic. Like the Object Hierarchy applet, the PROGRESS Window Viewer applet lists windows in a way that indicates how the windows are parented.

For example:

1. Make sure the UIB is started first.
2. Click the Window Viewer button on the PRO*Tools palette. This brings up the PROGRESS Window Viewer dialog. You should see that the User Interface Builder main window is on this list, with the UIB's Palette window listed below it.
3. Select the Palette window.
4. Click the Hide button. You will see that the UIB's Object Palette disappears, and the button label changes to "Show."
5. Click the Show button. The Palette comes back.

From Here...

In this chapter, you were exposed to some of the best ways of taking advantage of PROGRESS V8. You can find additional information in the following chapters:

- Chapter 22, "PROGRESS Programming Tips." This chapter lists some of the issues and tricks involved in using the PROGRESS 4GL.
- Chapter 6, "Utilizing Component-Based Development." This chapter lists the basics of SmartObjects and how they communicate.
- Chapter 19, "Using Active Templates." This chapter explains how to extend the capabilities of SmartObjects and templates through the use of Wizards and custom code.
- Chapter 20, "Extending the Development Tools." This chapter explains how to create and use Custom Object files.
- Appendix F, "Structure of .w Files." This appendix describes some interesting technical notes concerning how the UIB structures files.

Chapter 22

PROGRESS Programming Tips

This chapter is intended to help you write better PROGRESS code. The PROGRESS environment places very few restrictions on the developer. This power is one of the reasons that you do not need to drop down into 3GLs (like C, C++, or Pascal) to generate code necessary for mission-critical applications. However, this power also means that there are many ways to accomplish even the simplest tasks.

In the previous chapter, you saw how to take advantage of the SmartObjects and the PROGRESS tools to improve your productivity. This chapter focuses on tips for getting the most out of your PROGRESS 4GL code.

Voice-of-Experience Movies

See Table G.3 in Appendix G, "Contents of CD," for a list of the Voice-of-Experience files for this chapter.

After reading this chapter, you should be able to:

- Understand how to write code that is as reusable as possible;
- Write code to change your user interface dynamically;

Tips from the Pros

- Avoid the common mistakes made by many PROGRESS programmers;
- Improve the portability of your application across deployment platforms;
- Understand key issues of using fonts in PROGRESS.

Keyword Help

The on-line help facility (see fig. 22.1) in PROGRESS is very useful, especially when it comes to showing language elements and syntax.

Tip

The best way to get keyword help is from the Progress editors (Procedure Editor or UIB Section Editor). Simply select some text and press F1 (Help). The PROGRESS 4GL Help Viewer will come up, focused on the keyword that most closely matches the text you selected.

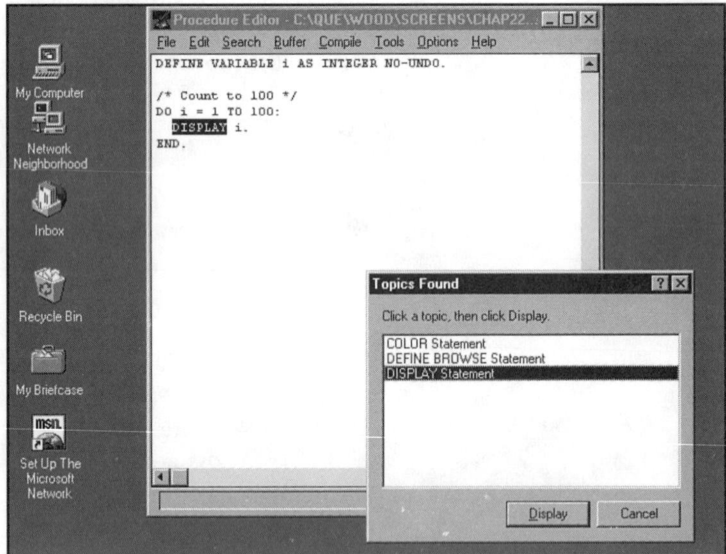

Fig. 22.1

Help for the entire PROGRESS language is available by highlighting text in the editor and pressing F1.

Writing Generic Code

Writing code is hard. Once you have developed a trigger or procedure that works, it would be nice to be able to reuse this code instead of rewriting it the next time you have to implement the same feature.

There are a variety of simple rules that you can follow to help you write generic code.

General Rules for Writing Generic Code

Generic code never refers to specific variables or objects. When you write generic code, always use indirection to refer to objects. PROGRESS supports indirection in many ways, including:

- System handles, such as `SELF`, `FOCUS`, or `CURRENT-WINDOW`
- Preprocessor variables, such as `SELF-NAME` or `FRAME-NAME`
- SmartLinks

The Underused `{&SELF-NAME}`

One of the more powerful, but least used, of the UIB-generated preprocessors is `SELF-NAME`. When you write a block of trigger code in the UIB's Section Editor, you can use the preprocessor `SELF-NAME`. `SELF-NAME` is defined as the name of the variable or object on which the trigger is defined.

> **Tip**
>
> For portable trigger code, always use `{&SELF-NAME}` to refer to the name of the underlying variable.

The best use of `SELF-NAME` is to allow you to assign variables that are not of character type.

For example, suppose you want to check the value of an integer fill-in for a variable `i-test`. You might normally write code of the form:

```
ON LEAVE OF i-test
DO:
  ASSIGN i-test.
  IF i-test > 10 THEN DO:
    MESSAGE "'i-test' must be less than 10."
             VIEW-AS ALERT-BOX.
    RETURN NO-APPLY.
  END.
END.
```

This code is fine, except for the fact that if you duplicate the fill-in as `i-test-2`, or rename it, the code will still refer to the original variable name, `i-test`. You will have to edit the code manually. The following *generic* version of the code performs the identical actions, but without directly referencing the variable name.

```
ON LEAVE OF {&SELF-NAME}
DO:
  ASSIGN {&SELF-NAME}.
  IF {&SELF-NAME} > 10 THEN DO:
    MESSAGE "'{&SELF-NAME}' must be less than 10."
            VIEW-AS ALERT-BOX.
    RETURN NO-APPLY.
  END.
END.
```

Use SmartLinks instead of Referring to SmartObjects Directly

In a SmartObject application, you should minimize the references to specific SmartObjects as much as possible. Where possible, use named SmartLinks instead.

> **Tip**
>
> It is always better to use references to SmartObjects by SmartLink type instead of referencing the handle of the SmartObject directly.

The entire purpose of the `notify` method is to allow the programmer to `dispatch` over a link instead of directly referencing a particular SmartObject. You should use a similar technique sending methods that have parameters.

For example, suppose you wanted to add a button to a SmartWindow that sets a filter in a SmartBrowser, named `h_b-cust`. You could write simple code to do this, as follows:

```
ON CHOOSE OF BUTTON-1
DO:
  RUN set-filter IN h_b-cust ('B*').
END.
```

It is much better, though, to establish a user-defined `FILTER` link to the SmartBrowser and reference this instead. You now have a button that can be used in any SmartObject context where a similar `FILTER` link has been defined.

```
ON CHOOSE OF BUTTON-1
DO:
  DEFINE VARIABLE c_filter-target AS CHARACTER NO-UNDO.
  /* See if there is a FILTER-TARGET. If so, set the filter
     in it. */
  RUN get-link-handle IN adm-broker-hdl
        (INPUT THIS-PROCEDURE,
         INPUT 'FILTER-TARGET':U,
         OUTPUT c_filter-target).
  IF NUM-ENTRIES(c_filter-target) eq 1
  THEN
    RUN set-filter IN WIDGET-HANDLE(c_filter-target) ('B*').
  ELSE
    MESSAGE 'FILTER-TARGET is undefined or not unique.'
            VIEW-AS ALERT-BOX ERROR.
END.
```

Of course, this code is more complex than the first example. However, it is also more reusable and more robust. Because the code will be used more often, you can spend the effort to write additional error-checking into the code.

Tricks for Enhancing Your User Interface

This section lists some simple (and not-so-simple) tips for sprucing up your user interface. There are a few common areas where developers want to go beyond the basic features supported by the PROGRESS language and tools.

In this section, you will see how to:

- Place labels on top or to the right of objects;
- Change the tab order on a screen dynamically.

Labels on the Right

PROGRESS places labels for data entry objects (e.g., fill-ins, editors) to the left of the object. However, some languages, such as Arabic, traditionally place labels in forms to the right of the data entry area.

In this section, you will learn how to right a small utility procedure that looks for all the labels in a frame and moves them to the right. Figure 22.2 lists the steps that your code must follow.

1. Find objects that have labels

   Last Name: [ ]

2. Move object to the column of the label

   [**Last Name:**]

3. Move the label to the right of the object

   [ ] **Last Name:**

4. Add a colon in front of the label

   [ ] **:Last Name:**

5. Hide the original colon

   [ ] **:Last Name**

Fig. 22.2

Steps to move standard side labels to the right side.

This procedure is an example of run-time manipulation of objects. Screens and labels will not be affected at design time (i.e., labels will still be on the left when you are creating them in the UIB). However, when the procedure is run, the labels will be flipped, one by one, as shown in figure 22.3.

The code to do this is quite simple. Enter the Listing 22.1 code into the Procedure Window, and save it as `rlabel.p` in your working directory. (Note: this procedure involves "walking the widget tree" and "moving widgets dynamically." These topics are covered in more detail later in this chapter.)

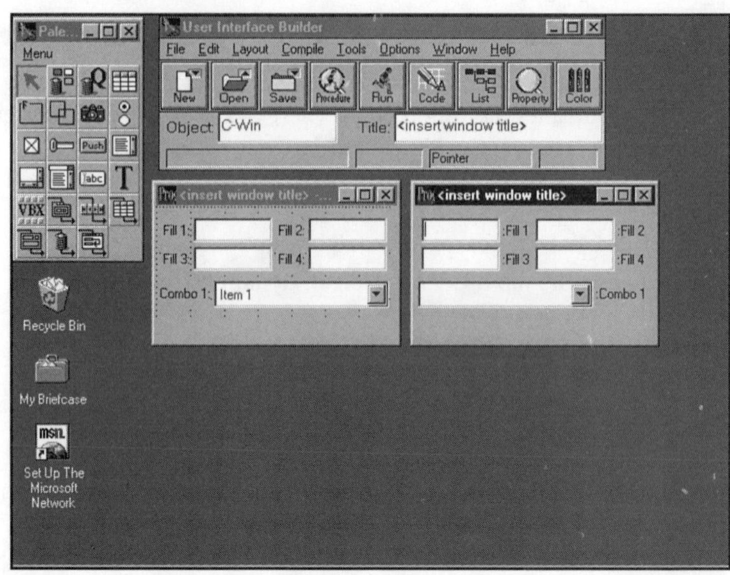

Fig. 22.3

Labels still appear on the left in the UIB, but will be moved dynamically, at run-time, to the right.

Listing 22.1 \examples\chap-22\rlabel.p—Flipping the Labels

```
/* ----------------------------------------------------
  File: rlabel.p

  Description: Look for all side-labels in the field-group
  of a frame and move the labels to the right.

  Input Parameters:
    ph_fldgrp - (HANDLE) Handle of the field-group
                of a PROGRESS Frame.
------------------------------------------------------ */
DEF INPUT PARAMETER ph_fldgrp AS HANDLE NO-UNDO.

DEF VAR h      AS HANDLE NO-UNDO.
DEF VAR hlbl   AS HANDLE NO-UNDO.
DEF VAR ifnt   AS INTEGER NO-UNDO.

/* Make sure we have a field group. If the user
   passed in a FRAME, then use the current iteration
   of that frame. Otherwise report an error. */
IF ph_fldgrp:TYPE eq "FRAME" THEN
  ph_fldgrp = ph_fldgrp:CURRENT-ITERATION.
ELSE IF ph_fldgrp:TYPE ne "FIELD-GROUP":U THEN DO:
  MESSAGE "rlabel.p expects a field-group."
          VIEW-AS ALERT-BOX ERROR.
  RETURN.
END.
```

```
/* Get the font of the frame (this is used for all
   labels). */
ASSIGN h    = ph_fldgrp:PARENT /* ie. the frame */
       ifnt = h:FONT.
/* Walk the widget tree of the field group and swap
   the positions of labels of the associated object. */
h = ph_fldgrp:FIRST-CHILD.
DO WHILE VALID-HANDLE (h):
  /* Does the object have a valid side-label? */
  IF CAN-SET (h, "SIDE-LABEL-HANDLE":U) THEN DO:
    hlbl = h:SIDE-LABEL-HANDLE NO-ERROR.
    IF VALID-HANDLE (hlbl) THEN DO:
      /* Put the field where the side-label is.
         Move the side label, add a leading colon.
         NOTE: we want to remove the trailing colon, but
         PROGRESS won't allow this on LABELS.  So we will
         shorten the viewed area of hlbl to hide the
         trailing colon. */
      ASSIGN
        h:X = hlbl:X
        hlbl:X = h:X + h:WIDTH-P + SESSION:PIXELS-PER-COL
        h:LABEL = ":" + h:LABEL
        hlbl:WIDTH-P = FONT-TABLE:GET-TEXT-WIDTH-P
                       (h:LABEL,ifnt)
             .
    END.
  END.

  /* Check the next widget. */
  h = h:NEXT-SIBLING.
END.
```

To use this utility, simply run it, passing in the handle of a field-group. For example, you could add the following lines at the top of the main code block of a file in the UIB's Code Section Editor.

```
/* *******************  Main Block  ******************* */

/* Move the labels in the current iteration of the frame
   to the right. */
RUN C:/appdir/rlabel.p
      (INPUT FRAME {&FRAME-NAME}:CURRENT-ITERATION).
```

In a SmartObject, you would usually add this code to the `local-initialize` event procedure.

```
PROCEDURE local-initialize :
/*------------------------------------------------------------------
  Purpose:     Override standard ADM method
  ------------------------------------------------------------------*/

  /* Code placed here will execute PRIOR to standard behavior. */
  RUN C:\appdir\rlabel.p (FRAME {&FRAME-NAME}:CURRENT-ITERATION).
```

```
    /* Dispatch standard ADM method.                               */
    RUN dispatch IN THIS-PROCEDURE ( INPUT 'initialize':U ) .

    /* Code placed here will execute AFTER standard behavior.     */

  END PROCEDURE.
```

For best results, you should make sure the frame is `HIDDEN` when you run `rlabel.p`. If the frame is visible, you will see the labels switch sides, which, though intriguing, will detract from the professionalism of your applications.

Tip

When you are writing your own SmartObjects, it is almost always better to place any special startup code in the `local-initialize` event procedure, rather than in the Main Code Block. (One of the most common errors of new SmartObject developers is to place too much code in the Main Code Block.)

The Main Code Block is executed when the object is created but before it has been positioned in its parent. Certain types of initialization code, such as setting the `LIST-ITEMS` of selection lists and combo-boxes, must be done after the object is in its parent. Doing these in the Main Code Block can, therefore, be a mistake.

Top/Printed Form Labels

A variation on "right" labels is "top" labels. In this example, you will learn:

- How to dynamically create a new object (in this case, a `TEXT` object that will act like a label);
- How to attach this `TEXT` widget as the `Side-Label-Handle` of an object. (By attaching it as a side label, you will be able to use the mnemonic Alt-key feature in Microsoft Windows to enable quick navigation of your application's interface.)

This procedure will work on a single object. We will pass both the handle of the object, and the text of the desired label.

Tip

In PROGRESS, you can specify the mnemonic "hot" key for a fill-in, menu item, or other user interface element by adding an ampersand (&) to the label in front of the letter you want to underline.

For example, you should set the label for standard File and Exit menu items as **&File** and **E&xit**, respectively. This will allow your users to go directly to the menu-items by pressing Alt+F and Alt+X.

If you want an ampersand to appear in a label, you indicate this by putting two ampersands in the label. The text **&Mileage && Tolls** would produce the label Mileage & Tolls.

Listing 22.2 adds a label above an object on the screen. The label is created as `TEXT`. It is positioned just above the object it is labeling. The `TEXT` is then connected to the object by setting the `Side-Label-Handle` attribute for the object. You can save this in your working directory as `c:\appdir\tlabel.p`.

Listing 22.2 \examples\chap-22\tlabel.p—Adding Label Above Object On-Screen

```
/* ---------------------------------------------------------------------
  File: tlabel.p

  Description: Add a text widget to the top of an object.
  The object must support a SIDE-LABEL-HANDLE.

  NOTE: if there is no room for the label to fit over the
  object, then the label may overlap the object.

  Input Parameters:
    ph_object - (HANDLE) Handle of object to be labelled
    pc_label  - (CHARACTER) Text of label
------------------------------------------------------------------- */
DEF INPUT PARAMETER ph_object AS HANDLE    NO-UNDO.
DEF INPUT PARAMETER pc_label  AS CHARACTER NO-UNDO.

DEF VAR hlbl   AS HANDLE NO-UNDO.

/* Make sure the object supports a label. */
IF NOT CAN-SET(ph_object, "SIDE-LABEL-HANDLE":U) THEN DO:
  MESSAGE "tlabel.p: Object cannot be labelled."
          VIEW-AS ALERT-BOX ERROR.
  RETURN.
END.

/* Create the label in the upper left corner of the object.
   We will move it up before we make it visible.*/
CREATE TEXT hlbl ASSIGN
  FORMAT = SUBSTITUTE ("X(&1)":U,MAX(1,LENGTH(pc_label)))
  SCREEN-VALUE = pc_label
  FRAME = ph_object:FRAME
  X     = ph_object:X
  Y     = ph_object:Y.

/* Connect the object with its label. */
ASSIGN ph_object:SIDE-LABEL-HANDLE = hlbl.

/* Now move the label up (add in a few pixels to allow
   for some whitespace between the label and the object).
   Then make it visible.  If the label won't fit on the
   screen, then it will just stay HIDDEN.  */
ASSIGN hlbl:Y = ph_object:Y - hlbl:HEIGHT-PIXELS - 2
       hlbl:HIDDEN = no
       NO-ERROR.  /* Suppress error messages. */
```

You use `tlabel.p` by calling it once for each object that you want to label on top. Suppose that you have an editor and a selection list, named `ed-desc` and `sl-region` respectively. You would add the following code to the top of the main code block, preferably before the window or dialog box is viewed.

```
/* ******************* Main Block ******************* */
/* Add top labels, where appropriate.*/
RUN C:/appdir/tlabel.p
      (INPUT ed-desc:HANDLE, INPUT "&Description:").
RUN C:/appdir/tlabel.p
      (INPUT sl-region:HANDLE, INPUT "Re&gion:").
```

Note that you must provide both the mnemonic ampersand (**&**) and the trailing colon (**:**) for your top labels. For side labels, you do not need to supply the colon—PROGRESS will add it for you.

Dynamic Changing of the Tab Order

You may also want to change the tab order in the user interface of the applications you write. By default, the UIB establishes a tab order that is left-to-right, and top-down. While this is satisfactory as a rough default, rarely will it be correct all the time.

There are many points to remember about tabbing in PROGRESS. These include:

1. Tabbing only works on the object in a frame. You cannot tab between frames that are parented to a window.
2. If multiple frames are parented to a common frame, then the child frames appear in the tab order of the parent frame. You will tab through the contents of one frame and then automatically move to the next frame.
3. You can navigate forward through the tab order by pressing the Tab key. Pressing Shift+Tab lets you navigate the tab-order backward.
4. Tab order is established in the order that variables are defined in the frame (e.g., how they first appear in `FORM`, `DEFINE FRAME`, or `DISPLAY` statements).
5. Objects that are created or parented dynamically are placed at the end of the tab order. (This is important because all VBX controls are created dynamically, and all SmartObjects are parented dynamically.)
6. If a frame has *not* been defined with `KEEP-TAB-ORDER`, then every time a variable is used in an `ENABLE` statement (or in a blocking statement that enables objects, such as `SET`, `PROMPT-FOR` or `UPDATE`), it moves to the end of the tab order.
7. You can move an object in the tab order by placing it before or after some other object. Use the methods `MOVE-BEFORE-TAB-ITEM` and `MOVE-AFTER-TAB-ITEM` to change tab order in this way.

Tip

The best way of dealing with tab order is to use the KEEP-TAB-ORDER attribute on frames. This will ensure that the tab order does not change in unexpected ways as a side effect of the Enable statement.

KEEP-TAB-ORDER is the default used by the PROGRESS UIB for newer frames and dialog boxes.

The methods MOVE-BEFORE-TAB-ITEM and MOVE-AFTER-TAB-ITEM are the preferred method of changing tab order. The Enable statement is often used to change tab order, but it has the additional side-effects of making objects both visible and sensitive. The following example shows how these methods are used.

```
/* Define a few fill-ins to use in the example. */
DEF VAR a AS CHARACTER NO-UNDO.
DEF VAR b AS CHARACTER NO-UNDO.
DEF VAR c AS CHARACTER NO-UNDO.
DEF VAR d AS CHARACTER NO-UNDO.
/* Define a return value for methods. */
DEF VAR lresult AS LOGICAL NO-UNDO.

/* Define the frame with KEEP-TAB-ORDER. */
DEFINE FRAME example
  a AT 10    b AT 10    c AT 10    d AT 10
  WITH SIDE-LABELS KEEP-TAB-ORDER.

/* Change the tab-order to d,c,b,a. */
ASSIGN lresult = c:MOVE-AFTER-TAB-ITEM (d:HANDLE)
       lresult = b:MOVE-AFTER-TAB-ITEM (c:HANDLE)
       lresult = a:MOVE-AFTER-TAB-ITEM (b:HANDLE)
       .
/* Test the tab-order. */
ENABLE ALL WITH FRAME example.
WAIT-FOR GO OF FRAME example.
```

Issues using the Attributes HIDDEN and VISIBLE

You are probably asking yourself why a concept like this is in a chapter titled "PROGRESS Programming Tips." Isn't the object attribute HIDDEN just the opposite of the VISIBLE attribute?

The answer is *No*. The basic rule to follow is simple.

Tip

Always use the attribute HIDDEN instead of VISIBLE when you set up objects in your user interface.

Setting the Visible attribute has side effects (described below). You should use the statement

```
<object handle>:HIDDEN = YES
```

instead of

```
<object handle>:VISIBLE = NO.
```

You will want to set the HIDDEN attribute to selectively show different aspects of your interface. In some cases, you may want to hide some fields from some users. In other cases you may want to hide a screen while you programmatically manipulate its contents.

The reason that Hidden should be used is that VISIBLE has side effects. VISIBLE was added to the PROGRESS 4GL in Version 7 to parallel the behavior of the keyword VIEW.

Both VIEW and VISIBLE, when applied to an object, implicitly make other objects visible. If you view a button, the frame that contains it and the window that contains the frame are also made visible. The following code sample shows this behavior when run from the Procedure Editor.

```
DEFINE BUTTON b LABEL "Hello, world".
DEFINE FRAME f
    b AT ROW 1 COLUMN 1
    WITH NO-LABELS.

ASSIGN b:VISIBLE = yes.
```

Running the above program will make the "Hello, world" button visible. But because the button won't actually be seen until the parent frame is made visible, PROGRESS will do that too. Compare this to the following program. It you run this program you should not be able to see either the frame or the button.

```
DEFINE BUTTON b LABEL "Hello, world".
DEFINE FRAME f
    b AT ROW 1 COLUMN 1
    WITH NO-LABELS.

ASSIGN b:HIDDEN = no.
```

Even though the button is not HIDDEN, the user never sees it because its container has not been explicitly viewed.

When you are setting up the contents of a frame, you want to control the timing of when that frame is made visible to your users. You do not want the frame to appear before it is ready to be seen. If you use the VISIBLE attribute on objects in the frame, there is a chance that the frame will appear before all your setup code has executed.

Because of these reasons, it is always safer to set the HIDDEN attribute.

Runtime Dynamics

At some point in the development of your application you will want to write code to dynamically modify the look of some screens. Perhaps you need to adjust the interface based on user preferences, or perhaps you need to change layout based on the screen size or font choices. Perhaps you want to make changes for different country markets. Perhaps you will want to make some of your windows resizable by your users.

Changing layout programmatically is quite easy once you master a few tricks of the PROGRESS 4GL. In this section, you will learn:

- How to move and resize objects, avoiding the most common errors;
- Why menus differ from other objects;
- Where objects are parented in the "widget tree."

If you have read previous chapters, you will have already seen examples of run-time manipulation of objects. In this chapter, the section "Labels on the Right" walked the widget tree to move all objects with labels. This section will list some of the tips you should follow when you write similar code.

Moving and Resizing Objects

Moving and resizing objects should be quite simple. What could be easier than just changing the attributes for `X`, `Y`, `WIDTH-PIXELS`, or `HEIGHT-PIXELS`? Well, things are never that simple. PROGRESS will not allow you to place a visible object in a position where it will not fit in its parent frame. This can complicate things if you are trying to change both the size and the position of an object.

The following code may or may not work.

```
ASSIGN btn:WIDTH-PIXELS = 100
       btn:X            = 50.
```

Suppose the button started out by being 50 pixels wide and up against the right edge of its parent. Because PROGRESS evaluates expressions line by line, setting the `WIDTH-PIXELS` to 100 will cause an error—the button won't fit in the frame. It doesn't matter to PROGRESS that you are about to set the `X` position to a valid value on the next line.

One way around this is to write complex assignment statements, where you would test to see whether the width was increasing; if is was, you would set `X` before setting `WIDTH-PIXELS`. However, there is a better way. PROGRESS only checks the geometry of visible objects. If you hide the object first, as shown below, then you will have solved the problem.

```
ASSIGN btn:HIDDEN       = yes
       btn:WIDTH-PIXELS = 100
       btn:X            = 50
       btn:HIDDEN       = no.
```

This leads to the first tip on run-time dynamics, which you should follow unless you are certain the object will never move outside its parent.

Tip

When manipulating the geometry of an object, first hide the object. Do not view the object again until you have finished all your assignments.

You may have noticed that all the run-time manipulation code in this book uses the attributes for pixel geometry (e.g., `X`, `Y`, `WIDTH-PIXELS`, `HEIGHT-PIXELS`) instead of the character-based versions (e.g., `ROW`, `COLUMN`, `WIDTH`, `HEIGHT`). There are three reasons for this:

1. Pixel attributes are integers. Character attributes are decimal. Integer mathematics is always a little more efficient and accurate.
2. You do not need to worry about rounding error. Ultimately, objects are placed on pixel borders when they are realized. Character units will be rounded to the nearest pixel. For example, a button 0.5 rows high positioned on row 1.5 will have a lower edge that drops below row 2.0 if there is an odd number of pixels per row. (Half of 23 is 12, in pixel math.)
3. Pixel coordinates are zero-based, whereas character coordinates are one-based. That is, the upper-left corner of a frame is `ROW = 1, COLUMN = 1` (which maps to `X = 0, Y = 0`). Experience shows that you are less likely to make mistakes in a zero-based system.

Of these reasons, the second is the most important.

Tip

Use the pixel geometry attributes (`X, Y, WIDTH-PIXELS, HEIGHT-PIXELS`, etc.) when dynamically setting geometry of objects.

Resizing Frames

In the same way that you cannot move an object unless you are sure it will fit in its frame, you cannot resize a frame unless you are sure that is bigger than all its contained objects.

The problem is compounded if you want to resize a frame and its children at the same time. If you want to make a frame bigger, simply resize the frame first, then resize the children. If, however, you want to shrink the frame, there is a problem. You cannot shrink the frame until the children have first been resized. But what if you are resizing the frame to be narrower in width, but taller in height? How do you handle this?

One solution to this problem would be simply to hide all the children first, then resize everything, and then go back and view the children again. However, this means that you will need to store a list of which children were originally hidden, so that you don't view them inappropriately.

A preferred solution takes advantage of the fact that frames (as well as dialog boxes and windows) can have a virtual size that differs from their viewport size. You can start the resizing operation by making sure that the virtual size is big enough to accommodate the worst-case situation. Then you can set the viewport size and the sizes of the children. Finally you can set the virtual size to its ultimate value. This is the next tip:

Tip

When resizing a frame and its contents, make sure the virtual size of the frame can accommodate the larger of the initial size or final size of all the children.

Set the virtual size to its correct value only after all the children have been moved.

You may want to hide the frame while you are working on it to avoid flashing.

An example of code to do this is given in the `set-size` method for SmartPanels. SmartPanels are resizable in the UIB. When the panel is resized, its child buttons are resized and rearranged to fit the frame. The source code for this ADM method can be found in the DLC\src\adm\method\panelsiz.i method library.

In the following example, however, we are going to size proportionally all the contents of a frame. There is some special code in here to handle the case of objects that cannot be resized. For example, PROGRESS Browse objects are not resizable. You also cannot set the height of a combo box.

Listing 22.3 \examples\chap-22\frm-size.p—Sizing all Contents of Frame

```
/*------------------------------------------------------
  File: frm-size.p
  Purpose: Changes the size and shape of the panel.  This
  routine spaces the buttons to fill the available space.

  Input Parameters:
    ph_frame    - the handle of the frame
    pd_height-p - the desired height (in pixels)
    pd_width-p  - the desired width  (in pixels)

  Notes:
    This procedure assumes that the target frame:

        - is not hidden
        - is not scrollable
        - has a single iteration without column labels
------------------------------------------------------*/
```

(continues)

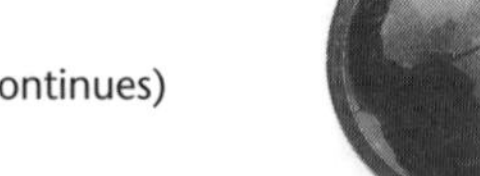

Listing 22.3 Continued

```
DEFINE INPUT PARAMETER ph_frame    AS HANDLE  NO-UNDO.
DEFINE INPUT PARAMETER pd_height-p AS INTEGER NO-UNDO.
DEFINE INPUT PARAMETER pd_width-p  AS INTEGER NO-UNDO.

DEFINE VAR x-border AS INTEGER NO-UNDO.
DEFINE VAR y-border AS INTEGER NO-UNDO.
DEFINE VAR x-mult AS DECIMAL NO-UNDO.
DEFINE VAR y-mult AS DECIMAL NO-UNDO.

DEFINE VAR h AS HANDLE  NO-UNDO.

/* Make the frame SCROLLABLE and reset the virtual size
   of the frame to accommodate any growing children.
   This may cause scrollbars to appear, so hide the frame
   during resizing. */
ASSIGN ph_frame:HIDDEN     = yes
       ph_frame:SCROLLABLE = yes.
IF pd_height-p > ph_frame:VIRTUAL-HEIGHT-PIXELS THEN
  ph_frame:VIRTUAL-HEIGHT-PIXELS = pd_height-p.
IF pd_width-p > ph_frame:VIRTUAL-WIDTH-PIXELS THEN
  ph_frame:VIRTUAL-WIDTH-PIXELS = pd_width-p.

/* How much should we scale the size of the children?
   Note that the frame border will not be resized.  If we
   have the size of the frame, the border will grow
   proportionally, and take more of the frame.  So we need
   to subtract the border size in deciding how much to
   scale the children. */
ASSIGN x-border = ph_frame:BORDER-LEFT-PIXELS +
                  ph_frame:BORDER-RIGHT-PIXELS
       y-border = ph_frame:BORDER-TOP-PIXELS +
                  ph_frame:BORDER-BOTTOM-PIXELS
       x-mult = (pd_width-p - x-border) /
                (ph_frame:WIDTH-PIXELS - x-border)
       y-mult = (pd_height-p - y-border) /
                (ph_frame:HEIGHT-PIXELS - y-border).

/* Walk the widget tree and scale all the children. */
ASSIGN h = ph_frame:CURRENT-ITERATION /* The field-group */
       h = h:FIRST-CHILD.             /* First true child */
DO WHILE VALID-HANDLE(h):
  /* We need to call this file recursively if one of the
     children is another frame. */
  IF h:TYPE eq "FRAME":U
  THEN RUN VALUE(THIS-PROCEDURE:FILE-NAME)
           (INPUT h,
            INPUT h:HEIGHT-PIXELS * y-mult,
            INPUT h:WIDTH-PIXELS * x-mult).
  ELSE DO:
    /* Unfortunately, there are some objects that cannot
       be resized dynamically - BROWSES and COMBO-BOX
```

```
       height.  Assign the new sizes NO-ERROR to deal with
       these cases.  If an error occurred, make sure the
       frame can still hold all its children. */
    ASSIGN h:X = h:X * x-mult
           h:Y = h:Y * y-mult
           h:WIDTH-PIXELS = h:WIDTH-PIXELS * x-mult
           h:HEIGHT-PIXELS = h:HEIGHT-PIXELS * y-mult
           NO-ERROR.
  END.
  /* Check the new frame size of the frame against the new
     size of the child. */
  ASSIGN
    pd_width-p  = MAX (pd_width-p,
                       h:X + h:WIDTH-PIXELS + x-border)
    pd_height-p = MAX (pd_height-p,
                       h:Y + h:HEIGHT-PIXELS + y-border).
  /* Get the next child. */
  h = h:NEXT-SIBLING.

END.
/* Now size the frame to its new size. */
ASSIGN ph_frame:SCROLLABLE    = no
       ph_frame:WIDTH-PIXELS  = pd_width-p
       ph_frame:HEIGHT-PIXELS = pd_height-p
       ph_frame:HIDDEN        = no.
```

Note that this routine calls itself recursively using the `THIS-PROCEDURE:FILE-NAME` attribute. The expression:

```
RUN VALUE (THIS-PROCEDURE:FILE-NAME) ...
```

always calls the file recursively because `THIS-PROCEDURE:FILE-NAME` evaluates to the name of the file as it was called.

Resizing Dialog Boxes

Resizing dialog boxes presents a special complication, because you must take into account the size of the dialog box border. Actually, this statement applies to all frames with borders (and dialog boxes are really a special class of frame). However, frames in windows generally do not have borders, whereas dialog boxes always do.

The issue with frame and dialog box borders is that, while the border is counted in the size of the frame, it is unusable space that children cannot occupy. The *usable* space in a dialog box is its size *minus* the size of the borders. This poses a particular problem when a dialog box is resized, because the borders are a fixed size, so the usable space changes as a fraction of the total geometry.

The example in the previous section, "Resizing Frames," shows how you can use the `FRAME-BORDER` attribute to account for border geometry. This brings us to our next tip:

Tip

When sizing any frame in general, and any dialog box in particular, don't forget to account for the size of the border, using the following attributes:

```
FRAME-BORDER-LEFT-PIXELS
FRAME-BORDER-RIGHT-PIXELS
FRAME-BORDER-TOP-PIXELS
FRAME-BORDER-BOTTOM-PIXELS
```

Warning: do not take the shortcut of assuming that the left border is equal to the right border. This is an invalid assumption on some window systems supported by PROGRESS.

Deleting Dynamic Objects with Pop-up Menus

This section highlights one of the subtleties in PROGRESS' handling of dynamic widgets. Normally, if you delete a container widget, then its children will also be deleted. This rule does not apply to pop-up menus or menu bars.

More and more interfaces support pop-up menus that provide quick access to the most important functions. This is especially true in Windows 95. If you decide to add pop-up menus to your PROGRESS applications, you should be aware that you will need to explicitly to delete the pop-up menu.

The following code fragment shows that a pop-up menu outlives its owner.

```
DEF VAR h     AS HANDLE NO-UNDO.
DEF VAR hmenu AS HANDLE NO-UNDO.

/* Create a popup menu and attach it to a button.*/
CREATE MENU hmenu ASSIGN
  POPUP-ONLY = yes.

CREATE BUTTON h ASSIGN
  POPUP-MENU = hmenu.

/* Delete the button. */
DELETE WIDGET h.
MESSAGE "Is the popup menu still valid?" SKIP
        "Answer: " VALID-HANDLE (hmenu)
        VIEW-AS ALERT-BOX.
```

If you use dynamic menus attached to dynamic widgets, you should be aware of the following. Before you delete an object that has a dynamic pop-up menu or menu bar, explicitly delete the menu. Otherwise you will slowly use up the memory in your system by storing "orphan" menus.

For example:

```
/* Delete the popup menu before deleting the owner. */
IF VALID-HANDLE(h:POPUP-MENU) THEN DELETE WIDGET h:POPUP-MENU.
/* Delete the owner. */
DELETE WIDGET h.
```

Orphan menus are particularly annoying because there is no way to find them again. Once the owner has been deleted, there is no way to "walk the widget tree" and find the menu.

Walking the Widget Tree

You have seen the mixed metaphor, "walking the widget tree," used a few times in this chapter. This is a mixed metaphor because you *walk a path*, or *climb a tree*—generally, you don't do your walking in a tree. The term refers to a technique of looping through all the basic widgets (for example, objects) that the PROGRESS session knows about. Because all widgets are arranged in a parent-child relationship, the structure is called a "widget tree." Walking the widget tree is the process of starting with a parent and iterating through all its children.

You should understand the structure of the widget tree, because it provides a very convenient way of applying a common action to every item in your user interface. If you couldn't traverse the tree, then you would have to store explicitly the handles or names for every object, and access them one by one.

You have already seen a few examples earlier in this chapter that walk the widget tree. The procedure `rlabel.p`, in the "Labels on the Right" section walked the widget tree to find labels that needed to be moved. The procedure `frm-size.p`, in "Resizing Frames," walked the widget tree to find and resize the children of a frame.

You may also have used the Control Hierarchy applet in PRO*Tools (see fig. 22.4) which displays the widget tree in an indented browse.

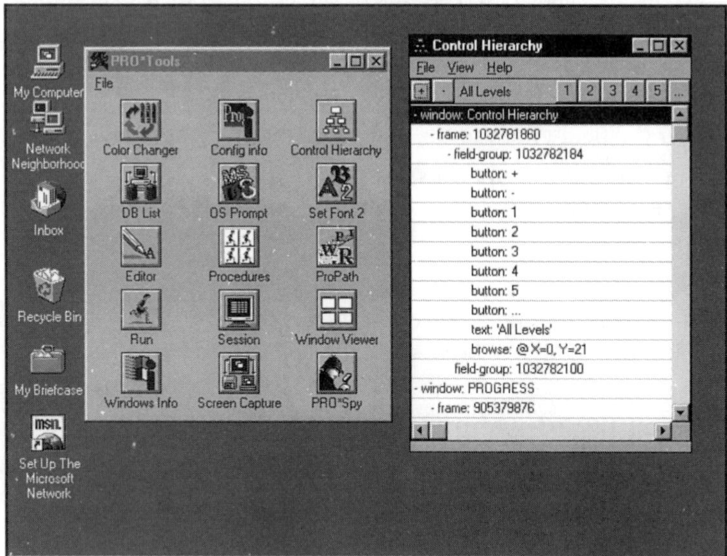

Fig. 22.4

*The Control Hierarchy PRO*Tool displays the widget tree.*

The basic code for walking the widget tree looks at the first child of an object. A loop iterates over the siblings of this object until no more children are found.

```
/* Look at all the children on h_parent. */
h = h_parent:FIRST-CHILD.
DO WHILE VALID-HANDLE(h):
  /* Act on this object. */
  ...

  /* Get the next child. */

  h = h:NEXT-SIBLING.
END.
```

There are a few issues that you may need to be aware of when you explore the widget tree.

- The root of the widget tree is the `SESSION` handle. When a window object is created, its default parent is the `SESSION` handle. To start your widget walk on the first window, get the `SESSION:FIRST-CHILD`.
- A window can have only frames, dialog boxes, or other windows as its children.
- Frames and dialog boxes do not contain any basic objects directly. All frames contain an invisible object called a `field-group`. Field-groups are automatically created with the frame. There is one field-group for each iteration of a frame (and one spare to allow PROGRESS to manipulate data without flashing the screen).
- You must go through the field-group to find the contents of a frame. The active field-group is stored as the `CURRENT-ITERATION` of the frame. Your widget walking code should contain statements similar to the following:

  ```
  ASSIGN h = h_frame:CURRENT-ITERATION
         h = h:FIRST-CHILD.
  ```

  This code walks over the field-group to the first basic object in the frame.
- All basic objects (such as fill-ins or buttons) are parented to the field-group. You can access the `FRAME` handle directly using the `FRAME` attribute.

  `h:PARENT` is the field-group
  `h:FRAME` is the frame
- Menus have parents and children that are other menus or menu items. To access a menu from a basic object, you need to look at the object's `POPUP-MENU` or `MENU-BAR` attribute.
- To find the basic object associated with a menu, chech the `OWNER` attribute of the menu.

Font Tips

PROGRESS handles fonts in a unique and often confusing manner. Instead of specifying a font by its name (e.g., Courier, 12-point, bold), you are required to specify a font number (from 0 to 255). These numbers map to the named fonts as specified in the `[fonts]` section of the `progress.ini` file.

◄◄ For more information on the progress.ini file, see Chapter 20, "Extending the Development Tools."

The next most important issue about PROGRESS is that all objects are sized relative to the `DefaultFont`. This is normally the system font used by your computer. In particular, the width of a column in this font is equal to the average width of characters in the system font. The height of a row is equal to the height of a fill-in field, including the border decoration, in this font. (This means that a standard PROGRESS character cell is about 7 by 26 pixels.)

When PROGRESS sizes objects, it uses this standard character cell. Generally speaking, this helps the portability of your application, because when you change to a new system font or a new computer, all the sizes of objects are scaled according to the system font in use. However, this holds true only if you are using the system font in those objects (or a font that is some fixed multiple of the system font).

Tip

The biggest portability problem you will face involves fonts. The problem is not the size of the fonts but rather the *ratio of sizes* between the fonts you use and the PROGRESS `DefaultFont`.

The fewer fonts you use, the easier it will be to deploy on different platforms.

There is one area where the absolute size of the fonts you use will matter. When you mix text data with graphic elements such as images or rectangles, you will have to deal with sizing issues when the font changes. While the character data will scale in response to the system font, the images and graphic elements of your interface will not. You should also note that any application contains graphic elements—the 3D borders, scrollbars, and button decoration are all created in pixels. Changing fonts will not change the sizes of these graphic elements.

Tip

It is generally easier for PROGRESS to handle *increases* in font sizes than *decreases*. If portability and deployment are important to you, you should design and compile your screens using the standard (or "small") font with a 640 by 400 pixel screen size.

When testing this screen, run the compiled code using the "large" font on an 800 by 600 pixel screen. This screen size is a fair approximation of the worst case your deployed application will face.

The previous tip made a point of telling you to compile your application with one font and screen resolution before testing with another font and screen resolution. This is very important advice. The PROGRESS compiler will change the details of a layout based on the fonts available at compile-time. If you compile on the fly, PROGRESS will do a better job with fonts and layout because the fonts used will be those currently available on your computer. However, compiling on the fly will slow down your application.

When you deploy an application, you will be deploying *compiled r-code*. The case you want to test is how this r-code, which was optimized by the compiler for one set of fonts, will run on a window system that uses some other font.

A final comment is that no application compiled in one environment will be totally portable to other environments. You should expect to have to tweak your layouts at run-time by moving objects or resizing them to fit screens and different fonts. What you want to aim for is to minimize this work. If you follow the tips listed above, then your run-time manipulation should not be too onerous.

There are some other issues that you should be aware of when working with fonts in PROGRESS.

1. Set the `FONT` attribute to **?** (the "unknown" value) to choose the default font.
2. The font of most objects can be inherited from their parent. If you set the font of a button to **?**, then it will use the font used by its parent frame. The exception to this rule is frames themselves.
3. Frames never inherit their font from their parent.
4. The default font is different for integer and decimal fill-ins than for all other datatypes. This is because numeric fill-ins expect a fixed-width font for the "input mask" to work correctly. (With a proportional font, the position of the comma and decimal places moves as you enter data into the field.)
5. You can set the default fonts only by changing the values in the `[Startup]` section of your `progress.ini` file. You must restart PROGRESS before these changes will take effect. The parameters you must change are:

   ```
   [Startup]
   DefaultFont = System
   DefaultFixedFont = FixedSys
   ```

6. By convention, font `0` is set to be the same font as the `DefaultFixedFont`. Font `1` is set to be the same as the `DefaultFont`. This convention allows you to set the font of character fill-ins to a fixed font, and the font of integer fill-ins to be proportional. If you change either `DefaultFont` or `DefaultFixedFont` in the `[Startup]` section of your `progress.ini`, you should change font `0` or font `1` in the `[fonts]` section.

Many PROGRESS developers, especially those working with Windows 95, would like their applications to use the small plain font that is standard in Windows 95. PROGRESS sets font `4` to be `MS San Serif, size = 8`. This is the font closest to the one in Windows 95.

While you could set the font for various windows and frames to font 4, you are going to have some problems when you deploy to different platforms. Your best portability will only come if the basic font in use is the PROGRESS `DefaultFont`.

However, if you change the `DefaultFont` to `MS Sans Serif, size = 8`, then you will find that the Progress tools themselves, including the UIB, will start to look different. The ADE tools are applications written in PROGRESS. They are subject to the same font problems as your application. If you change to a small `DefaultFont` then the screens and dialog boxes in the Progress tools may not display correctly: labels on toggle boxes might be truncated; images won't be centered on some buttons; and, occasionally, some dialogs will cease to display entirely.

A good compromise solution is to use a 8- or 10-point font as the `DefaultFont`. You will be able to use a good-looking font and still find that both your application and the ADE tools are portable in different environments. (The choice of 9 or 10 points depends on your environment. Generally speaking, use the 10-point font on Microsoft Windows 3.1 (or Windows NT), and the 8-point font in Windows 95.)

To set this up, change the `DefaultFont` and `DefaultFixedFont` (and font 0 and font 1) in your progress.ini file.

```
[Startup]
...
DefaultFont=MS Sans Serif, size=8
DefaultFixedFont=Courier New, size=8
...
[fonts]
...
font0=Courier New, size=8
font1=MS Sans Serif, size=8
```

> **Note**
>
> If you ask Progress Software Corporation directly, they will tell you never to change the `DefaultFont`. They will instead recommend that you use the same fonts on all platforms you intend to run on.
>
> However, most of the figures used in this book were done on Microsoft Windows 95 using an 8-point, MS Sans Serif font, as this works reasonably well on 640x480 screens.

Working with Persistent Procedures

Typically, a procedure is written in a "top-down" fashion. During execution, it starts at the top and runs down to the bottom and terminates, thus ending its scope. Running a procedure in "persistent" mode allows you to run a procedure in such a way that it remains active and in scope until you explicitly delete it or otherwise notify it that it should terminate itself. This mechanism alone yields unique and powerful ways to design your application.

The PROGRESS Application Component Environment uses this technology in areas such as PRO*Tools and SmartObjects. You too can use persistent procedures in your applications in ways that can make them more powerful and modular.

Since the internal procedures of a persistent procedure are available to be run from other procedures, you can design your persistent procedures to encapsulate all the behavior and data they need to become powerful stand-alone application components. Objects such as SmartObjects and the PRO*Tools palette are examples of persistent procedures that utilize this type of design. They are all designed to exhibit certain behavior which can be activated or altered at run-time by running various internal procedures within them.

When to Use Schema Triggers

Schema triggers, built into your database, ensure that all procedures will conform to the same standards, which in turn validate the integrity of the data. Building triggers into your database forces everyone's procedures to obey those rules. For example, if an order record should not exist without a customer record, then a schema trigger on the delete event of a customer should delete all that customer's orders.

You can also use schema triggers to provide security in a database. For example, you can disallow access to any record in the database by adding a schema trigger on the find event for that table. The schema trigger checks the user ID of the user requesting the record and disallows the find if the user does not have the necessary access privilege.

Since PROGRESS does not give you a direct way of getting the number of records in a table, you can use schema triggers to maintain a record count field in the table. For example, a `Create` trigger adds one to the count and `Delete` subtracts one from the count.

You can also use schema triggers to maintain log files that can be used to measure the load on a database. For example, a `Find` trigger may write out a message to a log file every time it's run. This data could be used to find out the intensity of user queries of the database. You may also use this method to track the utilization of a particular subset of users.

When schema triggers are defined, you have the ability to designate whether or not they can be overridden by a user's code. This gives a user the ability to define "session" schema triggers that can override ones defined in the database. Be careful not compromise data integrity with this feature.

If any batch jobs are to be run against your database, make sure that you do not include user-interface components, such as dialog boxes and alert boxes, into your schema triggers; they could prevent your batch jobs from completing successfully.

From Here...

You have just finished the last chapter in this book. Now is the time for you "leave the nest" and boldly explore the world of PROGRESS.

However, you are not entirely on your own. There are many places for you to go for additional help, including:

- Appendix C, "Important Information for PROGRESS Software Users." This appendix gives a complete list of contacts at Progress Software Corporation, including more information on the above sources.
- Appendix G, "Contents of CD." The CD-ROM is a very good source of further PROGRESS information. In particular, the CD-ROM contains a version of the PROGRESS Knowledge Base, a database of commonly asked technical support questions.
- PROGRESS Technical Support. PROGRESS is always available to answer technical support questions for any registered user. Check your documentation for a number to call.
- Progress Software Corporation Training. There are, of course, many areas of the PROGRESS environment that could not be covered in this book. PROGRESS training can help you learn about the rest of it.
- PROGRESS E-mail Group (PEG). This is an on-line PROGRESS Users Group where you can post questions or perhaps help users less knowledgeable than yourself. Check the CD-ROM accompanying this book for more information on the PEG.

For more information on the PEG, check out their Web page at http:\\www.happmis.com\peg.html

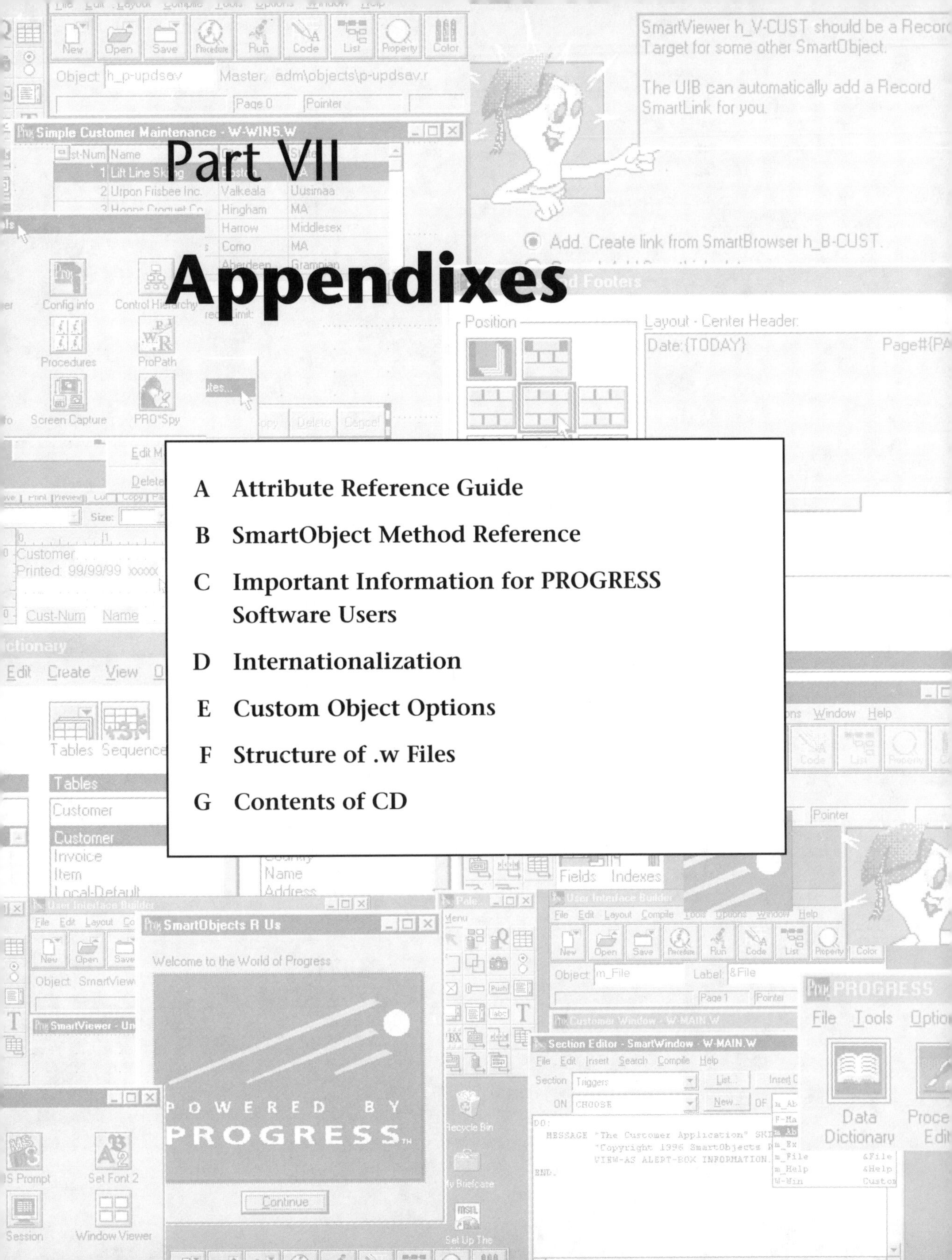

Part VII

Appendixes

New
Open
Save
Procedure
Run
Code
List
Property
Color
Object: h_p-updsav
Master: adm\objects\p-updsav.r
Page 0
Pointer
SmartViewer h_V-CUST should be a Target for some other SmartObject.
The UIB can automatically add a Re
SmartLink for you.
Simple Customer Maintenance - W-WIN5.W
Name
City
State
1 Lift Line Skiing
Boston
MA
2 Urpon Frisbee Inc.
Valkeala
Uusimaa
Hingham
MA
Harrow
Middlesex
Como
MA
Aberdeen
Grampian
PRO*Tools
Config info
Control Hierarchy
Editor
Procedures
ProPath
Screen Capture
PRO*Spy
Edit Master
Delete Instance
Add. Create link from SmartBrowser h_B-CUST.
Headers and Footers
Position
Layout - Center Header:
Date:{TODAY}
Clear All
Function List:
{TODAY} Today's date
{TIME} Time report started
{NOW} Current time
{COUNT} Records listed so far
{PAGE} Current page number
Customer
Printed: 99/99/99
Cust-Num
Name
City
State
Edit
Create
View
Options
Tools
Help
Tables
Sequences
Fields
Indexes
Customer
Cust-Num
Customer
Invoice
Item
Local-Default
Cust-Num
Country
Name
Address
User Interface Builder
File
Edit
Layout
Compile
Tools
Options
Window
Help
Object:
Label:
Pointer
Fields
Indexes
SmartObjects R Us
Welcome to the World of Progress
POWERED BY
PROGRESS
Continue
Object: m_File
Label: &File
Page 1
Pointer
Section Editor - SmartWindow - W-MAIN.W
File
Edit
Insert
Search
Compile
Help
Section
Triggers
ON
CHOOSE
DO:
MESSAGE "The Customer Application"
"Copyright 1996 SmartObjects
VIEW-AS ALERT-BOX INFORMATION.
END.
Recycle Bin
Set Up The
File
Tools
Data
Dictionary
OS Prompt
Set Font 2
Session
Window Viewer

APPENDIX A

Attribute Reference Guide

This appendix serves as a quick reference to all attributes and methods for Progress "widgets." A *widget* is another name for a Windows control.

Attributes for an object are data elements containing information about the object. Methods are functions relative to the object.

An analogy for the difference between attributes and methods uses a person as the object. The person has *attributes*: hair color, height, weight, IQ, etc. The person has *methods*: run, eat, sleep, laugh, etc.

This appendix is presented as a quick reference for all attributes and methods. Information about related objects, the attribute's return variable type and whether the attribute is Read Only or Read/Write is included to go beyond PROGRESS' on-line help system.

This alphabetical list will help you quickly locate the desired attribute or method.

Attribute Reference

An attribute is a *characteristic* of an object. If the object in question is a widget, the attribute may define a visible or functional characteristic. If the object is a system handle, the attribute may define a functional characteristic.

Think of the set of attributes associated with an object as the object's properties as one would see in a property sheet.

Attributes can be readable, writable, or both. Whether or not an attribute is readable or writable depends on a number of factors (for example, the widget type, system handle type, widget realization, etc.).

In this attribute reference, we list all attributes in alphabetical order along with attribute value type (integer, handle, etc.), which object types it pertains to and a short synopsis of the attribute.

The attribute value type is indicated following the attribute name with character=(char), integer=(int), decimal=(dec), logical=(log), handle=(handle). (R/W) indicates that the attribute is readable and writable while (Read) indicates readable only, and (Write) indicates write only.

A

ACCELERATOR (char) (R/W) Objects: MENU-ITEM

Specifies the key-label of the keyboard accelerator for the menu item.

APPL-ALERT-BOXES (logical) (R/W) Objects: SESSION handle

If TRUE, messages are viewed as alert boxes rather than in the default message area.

ATTR-SPACE (logical) (R/W) Objects: FILL-IN, TEXT

If ATTR-SPACE is TRUE, spaces for visual attributes are reserved on each side of the widget. The default value is FALSE.

AUTO-END-KEY (logical) (R/W) Objects: BUTTON

If AUTO-END-KEY is TRUE for a button, when the button is chosen the current frame will receive the ENDKEY event.

AUTO-GO (logical) (R/W) Objects: BUTTON

If AUTO-GO is TRUE for a button, when the button is chosen the current frame will receive the GO event.

AUTO-INDENT (logical) (R/W) Objects: EDITOR

If AUTO-INDENT is TRUE, each new line of text automatically indents to line up with the preceding line.

AUTO-RESIZE (logical) (R/W) Objects: (BUTTON, COMBO-BOX, EDITOR, FILL-IN, RADIO-SET, SELECTION-LIST,SLIDER,TEXT,TOGGLE-BOX)

If AUTO-RESIZE is TRUE, the widget automatically resizes when the contents of the widget changes. If AUTO-RESIZE is FALSE, the widget retains its original size.

AUTO-RETURN (logical) (R/W) Objects: FILL-IN

If AUTO-RETURN is TRUE, upon reaching the last character of entry in a fill-in the LEAVE event triggers and the focus is shifted to the next widget in the tab order. For the last widget of the tab order, a GO event will trigger.

AUTO-ZAP (logical) (R/W) Objects: FILL-IN

If AUTO-ZAP is TRUE, when the user begins typing in the field, the entire initial value is erased before the user's text appears. If AUTO-ZAP is FALSE, text entered by the user is inserted into existing text at the current cursor position in the field.

AVAILABLE-FORMATS (char) (Read) Objects: CLIPBOARD

Returns a comma-separated list of names that specify the formats available for the data currently stored in the clipboard.

B

BACKGROUND (Handle) (Read) Objects: DIALOG-BOX, FRAME

Returns a widget handle for the background iteration of the frame or dialog box.

BATCH-MODE (Logical) (Read) Objects: SESSION HANDLE

Reports whether the current PROGRESS session is running in batch or interactive mode.

BGCOLOR (Int) (R/W) Objects: BROWSE,BUTTON,COMBO-BOX,DIALOG-BOX,EDITOR,FILL-IN, FRAME, IMAGE, LITERAL, MENU, MENU-ITEM,RADIO-SET, RECTANGLE, SELECTION, LIST, SLIDER,SUB-MENU, TEXT,TOGGLE-BOX,WINDOW

Specifies the color number for the background color of the widget (graphical interfaces only).

BLANK (Logical) (R/W) Objects: FILL-IN, TEXT

Suppresses the display of sensitive data in a field. Used for password fields.

BLOCK-ITERATION-DISPLAY (Logical) (Read) Objects: FRAME

Specifies if the frame contains the NO-HIDE option or if the frame has multiple iterations.

BORDER-BOTTOM-CHARS (Dec) (Read) Objects: DIALOG-BOX, FRAME

Returns the thickness, in character units, of the border at the bottom of the frame or dialog box.

BORDER-BOTTOM-PIXELS (Int) (Read) Objects: DIALOG-BOX, FRAME

Returns the thickness, in pixel units, of the border at the bottom of the frame or dialog box.

BORDER-LEFT-CHARS (Dec) (Read) Objects: DIALOG-BOX, FRAME

Returns the thickness, in character units, of the border at the left side of the frame or dialog box.

BORDER-LEFT-PIXELS (Int) (Read) Objects: DIALOG-BOX, FRAME

Returns the thickness, in pixel units, of the border at the left side of the frame or dialog box.

BORDER-RIGHT-CHARS (Dec) (Read) Objects: DIALOG-BOX, FRAME

Returns the thickness, in character units, of the border at the right side of the frame or dialog box.

BORDER-RIGHT-PIXELS (Int) (Read) Objects: DIALOG-BOX, FRAME

Returns the thickness, in pixel units, of the border at the right side of the frame or dialog box.

BORDER-TOP-CHARS (Dec) (Read) Objects: DIALOG-BOX, FRAME

Returns the thickness, in character units, of the border at the top of the frame or dialog box.

BORDER-TOP-PIXELS (Int) (Read) Objects: DIALOG-BOX, FRAME

Returns the thickness, in pixel units, of the border at the top of the frame or dialog box.

BOX (Logical) (R/W) Objects: FRAME

Specifies that the frame has a graphical border around it.

BOX-SELECTABLE (Logical) (R/W) Objects: DIALOG-BOX, FRAME

Enables or disables box-selection direct manipulation events for the frame or dialog box (graphical interfaces only).

BUFFER-CHARS (Int) (R/W) Objects: EDITOR

Specifies the number of characters a user can enter on each line of the editor (character mode only).

BUFFER-LINES (Int) (R/W) Objects: EDITOR

Specifies the number of lines a user can enter into the editor (character mode only).

C

CANCEL-BUTTON (Handle) (Write) Objects: DIALOG-BOX, FRAME

Specifies a button widget in the frame or dialog box to receive the CHOOSE event when a user cancels the current frame or dialog box by pressing the ESC key.

CENTERED (Logical) (R/W) Objects: FRAME

Specifies whether PROGRESS automatically centers the frame in a window.

CHARSET (Char) (Read) Objects: SESSION-HANDLE

Returns the current setting for the Character Set (-charset) parameter.

CHECKED (Logical) (R/W) Objects: MENU ITEM (Toggle), TOGGLE-BOX

Specifies the display state for a toggle box or a toggle box menu item.

CODE (Int) (Read) Objects: LAST-EVENT Handle

Returns a numeric code associated with the last event.

COLUMN (Dec) (R/W) Objects: BROWSE BUTTON,COMBO-BOX, DIALOG-BOX,EDITOR,FIELD-GROUP,FILL-IN, FRAME, IMAGE, LITERAL,RADIO-SET,RECTANGLE,SELECTION-LIST, SLIDER,TEXT,TOGGLE-BOX,WINDOW,LAST-EVENT

Specifies the column position of the left edge of the widget or the column position of the mouse cursor for the last mouse event on the display. (Read-Only attribute for LAST-EVENT handle.)

CRC-VALUE (Int) (Read) Objects: RCODE-INFO handle

Returns the cyclic redundancy check (CRC) code for the r-code file specified by the RCODE-INFO:FILE-NAME attribute.

CURRENT-ITERATION (handle) (R/W) Objects: DIALOG-BOX, FRAME

Specifies a widget handle for the current iteration of the frame or dialog box.

CURRENT-WINDOW (handle) (R/W) Objects: Procedure HANDLES, THIS-PROCEDURE handle

Specifies a current window for the specified procedure.

CURSOR-CHAR (Int) (R/W) Objects: EDITOR

Specifies the current character position of the text cursor on the current text line in an editor widget.

CURSOR-LINE (Int) (R/W) Objects: EDITOR

Specifies the line within an editor widget where the text cursor is positioned.

CURSOR-OFFSET (Int) (R/W) Objects: EDITOR, FILL-IN

Specifies the character offset of the cursor within the widget.

D

DATA-ENTRY-RETURN (Logical) (R/W) Objects: SESSION handle

Specifies the behavior of the RETURN key for the fill-in widgets of a frame.

DATA-TYPE (Char) (R/W) Objects: COMBO-BOX, EDITOR, FILL-IN, RADIO-SET, RECTANGLE, SELECTION-LIST, SLIDER, TEXT, TOGGLE-BOX

Returns a character value that represents the data type of the field associated with the widget.

DATE-FORMAT (Char) (R/W) Objects: SESSION Handle

Specifies the format used to represent dates during the current PROGRESS session.

DBNAME (Char) (Read) Objects: COMBO-BOX, EDITOR, FILL-IN, RADIO-SET, RECTANGLE, SELECTION-LIST, SLIDER, TEXT, TOGGLE-BOX

Returns the logical name of the database from which the field is taken.

DCOLOR (Int) (R/W) Objects: BROWSE, BUTTON, COMBO-BOX, DIALOG-BOX, EDITOR, FILL-IN, FRAME, IMAGE, LITERAL, MENU, MENU-ITEM, RADIO-SET, RECTANGLE, SELECTION-LIST, SLIDER, SUB-MENU, TEXT, TOGGLE-BOX, WINDOW

Specifies the color number for the display color of the widget in character mode. Ignored in graphical environment.

DDE-ERROR (Int) (Read) Objects: FRAME

Returns the error condition returned by the most recent exchange in a DDE conversation associated with the frame (MS-Windows only).

DDE-ID (Int) (Read) Objects: FRAME

Returns the DDE channel number of the most recent conversation involved in an exchange.

DDE-ITEM (Char) (R/W) Objects: FRAME

Returns the name of the data item affected by the most recent conversational exchange.

DDE-NAME (Char) (Read) Objects: FRAME

The DDE-NAME attribute records the application name involved in the most recent conversational exchange.

DDE-TOPIC (Char) (Read) Objects: FRAME

Returns the topic name of the most recent DDE conversation.

DEBLANK (Logical) (R/W) Objects: FILL-IN

Determines the processing of leading blank spaces in fill-in widgets during user input.

DEFAULT (Logical) (R/W) Objects: BUTTON

Specifies the button as a default button.

DEFAULT-BUTTON (Handle) (Write) Objects: DIALOG-BOX, FRAME

Specifies a button as a default button for the frame or dialog box.

DELIMITER (Char) (R/W) Objects: COMBO-BOX, RADIO-SET, LIST

Specifies the character used to separate values input to or output from a combo box or selection list.

DISPLAY-TYPE (Char) (Read) Objects: SESSION handle

Indicates the type of display used in the session. Example: "TTY" for character display.

DOWN (Int) (R/W) Objects: BROWSER, FRAME

Specifies the number of iterations in a down frame that contain data or number of potential rows in a browse widget.

DRAG-ENABLED (Logical) (R/W) Objects: SELECTION-LIST

Specifies that the user can simultaneously hold down the mouse select button and drag the mouse cursor through the selection list.

DYNAMIC (Logical) (Read) Objects: BROWSE, BUTTON, COMBO-BOX, DIALOG-BOX, EDITOR, FIELD-GROUP, FILL-IN, FRAME, IMAGE, LITERAL, MENU, MENU-ITEM, RADIO-SET, RECTANGLE, SELECTION-LIST, SLIDER, SUB-MENU, TEXT, TOGGLE-BOX, WINDOW

Reports whether the widget is a dynamic or static widget.

E

EDGE-CHARS (Dec) (R/W) Objects: RECTANGLE

Specifies the width, in character units, of the rectangle's edge.

EDGE-PIXELS (Int) (R/W) Objects: RECTANGLE

Specifies the width, in pixel units, of the rectangle's edge.

EMPTY (Logical) (Read) Objects: EDITOR

Indicates whether or not the SCREEN-VALUE attribute for the editor contains text.

ERROR (Logical) (Read) Objects: COMPILER, ERROR-STATUS handle

Reports a compile-time or run-time error condition.

ERROR-COLUMN (Int) (Read) Objects: COMPILER handle

Returns the character position at which a compiler error occurred.

ERROR-ROW (Int) (Read) Objects: COMPILER handle

Returns the line number at which a Compiler error occurred.

EVENT-TYPE (Char) (Read) Objects: LAST-EVENT handle

The EVENT-TYPE attribute returns the type of the last event. Examples: KEYPRESS, MOUSE, PROGRESS.

EXPAND (Logical) (R/W) Objects: RADIO-SET

Controls size of the radio buttons in a radio set.

F

FGCOLOR (Int) (R/W) Objects: BROWSE, BUTTON, COMBO-BOX, DIALOG-BOX, EDITOR, FILL-IN, FRAME, IMAGE, LITERAL, MENU, MENU-ITEM, RADIO-SET, RECTANGLE, SELECTION-LIST, SLIDER, SUB-MENU, TEXT, TOGGLE-BOX, WINDOW

Specifies the color number for the foreground color of the widget.

FILE-NAME (Char) (R/W) Objects: (See handles list below)

Specifies the name of a file. Used in conjunction with the handles: COMPILER, FILE-INFO, RCODE-INFO, THIS-PROCEDURE

FILE-OFFSET (Int) (Read) Objects: COMPILER handle

Returns the character offset in the source file in which a Compiler error occurred.

FILE-TYPE (Char) (Read) Objects: FILE-INFO handle

Returns a string of characters that indicate the type of file that is currently specified for the FILE-INFO handle.

FILLED (Logical) (R/W) Objects: RECTANGLE

Controls the display of the background color of the rectangle.

FIRST-CHILD (handle) (Read) Objects: DIALOG-BOX, FIELD-GROUP, FRAME, MENU, SUB-MENU, WINDOW, SESSION-HANDLE

Returns the handle of the first widget created in the container widget or the current session.

FIRST-PROCEDURE (Handle) (Read) Objects: SESSION handle

Returns the first entry in the list of all current persistent procedures for the current session.

FIRST-TAB-ITEM (Handle) (R/W) Objects: FIELD-GROUP

Determines the first widget in the tab order of the field group.

FONT (Int) (R/W) Objects: BROWSE, BUTTON, COMBO-BOX, DIALOG-BOX, EDITOR, FILL-IN, FRAME, IMAGE, LITERAL, MENU, MENU-ITEM, RADIO-SET, RECT ANGLE, SELECTION-LIST, SLIDER, SUB-MENU, TEXT, TOGGLE-BOX, WINDOW

Specifies the font number for font of the widget (graphical interfaces only).

FOREGROUND (Logical) (Read) Objects: FIELD-GROUP

Reports whether the field group is a foreground or a background field group.

FORMAT (Char) (R/W) Objects: COMBO-BOX, FILL-IN, TEXT, TOGGLE-BOX

Specifies the text format for the widget.

FRAME (Handle) (R/W) Objects: BROWSE, BUTTON, COMBO-BOX, EDITOR, FILL-IN, IMAGE, LITERAL, RADIO-SET, RECTANGLE, SELECTION-LIST, SLIDER, TEXT, TOGGLE-BOX

Specifies the handle of the frame in which the widget appears.

FRAME-COL (Dec) (Read) Objects: BROWSE, BUTTON, COMBO-BOX, EDITOR, FILL-IN, IMAGE, LITERAL, RADIO-SET, RECTANGLE, SELECTION-LIST, SLIDER, TEXT, TOGGLE-BOX

Returns the location, in character units, of the left edge of the widget relative to the frame that contains the widget.

FRAME-NAME (Char) (Read) Objects BROWSE,BUTTON,COMBO-BOX, EDITOR,FILL-IN,IMAGE,LITERAL,RADIO-SET, RECTANGLE,SELECTION-LIST,SLIDER,TEXT,TOGGLE-BOX

Returns the name of the frame that contains the widget.

FRAME-SPACING (Int) (R/W) Objects: SESSION handle

Specifies the number of display units between frames in a window.

FRAME-ROW (Dec) (Read) Objects: BROWSE,BUTTON,COMBO-BOX, EDITOR,FILL-IN,IMAGE,LITERAL,RADIO-SET, RECTANGLE,SELECTION-LIST,SLIDER,TEXT,TOGGLE-BOX

Returns the location, in character units, of the top edge of the widget relative to the frame that contains the widget.

FRAME-X (Int) (Read) Objects: BROWSE,BUTTON,COMBO-BOX, EDITOR, FILL-IN,IMAGE,LITERAL,RADIO-SET, RECTANGLE,SELECTION-LIST,SLIDER,TEXT,TOGGLE-BOX

Returns the location, in pixels, of the left edge of the widget relative to the frame that contains the widget.

FRAME-Y (Int) (Read) Objects: BROWSE,BUTTON,COMBO-BOX, EDITOR, FILL-IN,IMAGE,LITERAL,RADIO-SET, RECTANGLE, SELECTION-LIST,SLIDER,TEXT,TOGGLE-BOX

Returns the location, in pixels, of the top edge of the widget relative to the frame that contains the widget.

FULL-HEIGHT-CHARS (Dec) (Read) Objects: WINDOW

Returns the maximum internal height of the window, in character units.

FULL-HEIGHT-PIXELS (Int) (Read) Objects: WINDOW

Returns the maximum internal height of the window, in pixel units.

FULL-PATHNAME (Char) (Read) Objects: FILE-INFO Handle

Returns the absolute pathname of the file specified in the FILE-NAME attribute.

FULL-WIDTH-CHARS (Dec) (Read) Objects: WINDOW

Returns the maximum internal width of the window, in character units.

FULL-WIDTH-PIXELS (Int) (Read) Objects: WINDOW

Returns the maximum internal width of the window, in pixel units.

FUNCTION (Char) (Read) Objects: LAST-EVENT handle

Returns the names of high-level events based on the EVENT-TYPE attribute value.

G

GRAPHIC-EDGE (Logical) (R/W) Objects: RECTANGLE

Specifies a graphical edge for the rectangle (character mode only).

GRID-FACTOR-HORIZONTAL (Int) (R/W) Objects: FRAME

Determines spacing, in horizontal grid units, between the horizontal grid lines of the frame (graphical interfaces only).

GRID-FACTOR-VERTICAL (Int) (R/W) Objects: FRAME

Determines spacing, in vertical grid units, between the vertical grid lines of the frame (graphical interfaces only).

GRID-SNAP (Logical) (R/W) Objects: FRAME

Turns the grid alignment behavior on or off for the frame (graphical interfaces only).

GRID-UNIT-HEIGHT-CHARS (Dec) (R/W) Objects: FRAME

Determines the height, in character units, of a vertical grid unit on the frame (graphical interfaces only).

GRID-UNIT-HEIGHT-PIXELS (Int) (R/W) Objects: FRAME

Determines the height, in pixel units, of a vertical grid unit on the frame (graphical interfaces only).

GRID-UNIT-WIDTH-CHARS (Dec) (R/W) Objects: FRAME

Determines the width, in character units, of a vertical grid unit on the frame (graphical interfaces only).

GRID-UNIT-WIDTH-PIXELS (Int) (R/W) Objects: FRAME

Determines the width, in pixel units, of a vertical grid unit on the frame (graphical interfaces only).

GRID-VISIBLE (Logical) (R/W) Objects: FRAME

Controls the display of the grid associated with the frame (graphical interfaces only).

H

HANDLE (Handle) (Read) Objects: BROWSE,BUTTON,COMBO-BOX, DIALOG-BOX,EDITOR,FIELD-GROUP,FILL-IN, FRAME, IMAGE,LITERAL,MENU,MENU-ITEM,RADIO-SET, RECTANGLE, SELECTION-LIST,SLIDER,SUB-MENU, TEXT,TOGGLE-BOX,WINDOW

Returns a handle to the widget.

HEIGHT-CHARS (Dec) (R/W) Objects: BROWSE,BUTTON,COMBO-BOX,DIALOG-BOX,EDITOR,FIELD-GROUP,FILL-IN, FRAME, IMAGE,LITERAL,RADIO-SET, RECTANGLE, SELECTION-LIST,SLIDER,TEXT,TOGGLE-BOX, WINDOW, SESSION Handle

Specifies the height, in character units, of the widget. For SESSION Handle, returns height of display and is Read-Only attribute.

HEIGHT-PIXELS (Int) (R/W) Objects: BROWSE,BUTTON,COMBO-BOX,DIALOG-BOX,EDITOR,FIELD-GROUP,FILL-IN, FRAME, IMAGE,LITERAL,RADIO-SET, RECTANGLE, SELECTION-LIST,SLIDER,TEXT,TOGGLE-BOX, WINDOW, SESSION Handle

Specifies the height, in pixel units, of the widget. For SESSION Handle, returns height of display and is Read-Only attribute.

HELP (Char) (R/W) Objects: BROWSE,BUTTON,COMBO-BOX, EDITOR, FILL-IN, IMAGE,LITERAL,RADIO-SET, RECTANGLE, SELECTION-LIST,SLIDER,TEXT,TOGGLE-BOX

Specifies the help text for the field.

HIDDEN (Logical) (R/W) Objects: BROWSE,BUTTON,COMBO-BOX,DIALOG-BOX,EDITOR,FILL-IN, FRAME, IMAGE, LITERAL,RADIO-SET,RECTANGLE,SELECTION-LIST, SLIDER,TEXT,TOGGLE-BOX,WINDOW

Controls the implicit display behavior of the widget.

HORIZONTAL (Logical) (R/W) Objects: RADIO-SET, SLIDER

Specifies the orientation of the slider or the radio buttons in the radio set.

HWND (Int) (Read) Objects: BROWSE,BUTTON,COMBO-BOX,DIALOG-BOX,EDITOR,FIELD-GROUP,FILL-IN, FRAME, IMAGE, LITERAL, MENU,MENU-ITEM,RADIO-SET, RECTANGLE, SELECTION-LIST,SLIDER,SUB-MENU,TEXT,TOGGLE-BOX,WINDOW

Returns an integer value for an MS-Windows handle to the window that contains the widget.

I

IMMEDIATE-DISPLAY (Logical) (R/W) Objects: SESSION handle

Determines the frequency of screen updates for the current session.

INDEX (Int) (Read) Objects: FILL-IN, TEXT

Returns the subscript value of the array element referenced by the current widget.

INNER-CHARS (Int) (R/W) Objects: EDITOR, SELECTION-LIST

Specifies the number of data columns within a selection list or editor widget.

INNER-LINES (Int) (R/W) Objects: COMBO-BOX, EDITOR, SELECTION-LIST

Specifies the number of data lines within a combo box drop down list, editor widget, or selection list.

INTERNAL-ENTRIES (Char) (Read) Objects: PROCEDURE Handles and THIS-PROCEDURE handle

Returns a comma-separated list containing the names of all internal procedures declared in the specified external procedure.

ITEMS-PER-ROW (Int) (R/W) Objects: CLIPBOARD

Determines how multiple items are formatted when written to the system clipboard using the CLIPBOARD handle.

L

LABEL (Char) (R/W) Objects: BUTTON,COMBO-BOX,EDITOR,FILL-IN,MENU-ITEM,RADIO-SET,SELECTION-LIST,SLIDER,SUB-MENU,TEXT,TOGGLE-BOX,LAST-EVENT Handle

Specifies the label of a widget or the name of a low-level event. Also used with LAST-EVENT handle as Read-Only attribute.

LABELS (Logical) (Read) Objects: EDITOR, FILL-IN, FRAME, TEXT

Returns the label display state of the widget.

LANGUAGES (Char) (Read) Objects: RCODE-INFO handle

Returns a comma-separated list of all languages compiled into the r-code file specified by RCODE-INFO:FILE-NAME attribute.

LARGE (Logical) (R/W) Objects: EDITOR

Determines the text capacity of the editor (MS-Windows only). A large editor can handle up to 64K of text.

LAST-CHILD (Handle) (Read) Objects: DIALOG-BOX, FIELD-GROUP, FRAME, MENUSUB-MENU, WINDOW, SESSION Handle

Returns the handle of the last widget created in the container widget or the current session.

LAST-PROCEDURE (Handle) (Read) Objects: SESSION handle

Returns the last entry in the list of all current persistent procedures in the current session.

LAST-TAB-ITEM (Handle) (R/W) Objects: FIELD-GROUP

Determines the last widget in the tab order of the field group.

LENGTH (Int) (Read) Objects: EDITOR

Returns the length (number of characters) of the current content of the editor widget.

LINE (Int) (Read) Objects: FRAME

Returns the current logical line number (iteration number) of the frame.

LIST-ITEMS (Char) (R/W) Objects: COMBO-BOX, SELECTION-LIST

Specifies a delimiter-separated list of items associated with the combo box or selection list.

M

MANUAL-HIGHLIGHT (Logical) (R/W) Objects: BUTTON, COMBO-BOX, EDITOR, FILL-IN, FRAME, IMAGE, LITERAL, RADIO-SET, RECT ANGLE, SELECTION-LIST, SLIDER, TEXT, TOGGLE-BOX

Controls the use of a customized highlight design for the selection of the widget.

MARGIN-HEIGHT-CHARS (Dec) (Read) Objects: BUTTON

Returns the height difference, in character units, of the margin applied to the top and bottom of a button when it is a default button in OSF/Motif.

MARGIN-HEIGHT-PIXELS (Int) (Read) Objects: BUTTON

Returns the height difference, in pixel units, of the margin applied to the top and bottom of a button when it is a default button in OSF/Motif.

MARGIN-WIDTH-CHARS (Dec) (Read) Objects: BUTTON

Returns the width difference, in character units, of the margin applied to the left and right of a button when it is a default button in OSF/Motif.

MARGIN-WIDTH-PIXELS (Int) (Read) Objects: BUTTON

Returns the width difference, in pixel units, of the margin applied to the left and right of a button when it is a default button in OSF/Motif.

MAX-CHARS (Int) (R/W) Objects: EDITOR

Specifies the maximum number of characters that the editor widget can hold.

MAX-DATA-GUESS (Int) (R/W) Objects: BROWSE

Specifies the number of records in a browse query.

MAX-HEIGHT-CHARS (Dec) (R/W) Objects: WINDOW

Specifies the maximum height of the window, in character units.

MAX-HEIGHT-PIXELS (Int) (R/W) Objects: WINDOW

Specifies the maximum pixel of the window, in character units.

MAX-VALUE (Int) (R/W) Objects: SLIDER

Specifies the maximum value for the slider.

MAX-WIDTH-CHARS (Dec) (R/W) Objects: WINDOW

Specifies the maximum width of the window, in character units.

MAX-WIDTH-PIXELS (Int) (R/W) Objects: WINDOW

Specifies the maximum width of the window, in pixel units.

MENU-BAR (Handle) (R/W) Objects: WINDOW

Specifies the widget handle of a menu bar associated with the window.

MENU-KEY (Char) (R/W) Objects: BROWSE, BUTTON, COMBO-BOX, DIALOG-BOX, EDITOR, FILL-IN, FRAME, RADIO-SET, SELECTION-LIST, SLIDER, TOGGLE-BOX, WINDOW

Specifies the accelerator key sequence that activates the pop-up menu for the widget.

MENU-MOUSE (Int) (R/W) Objects: BROWSE, BUTTON, COMBO-BOX, DIALOG-BOX, EDITOR, FILL-IN, FRAME, RADIO-SET, SELECTION-LIST, SLIDER, TOGGLE-BOX, WINDOW

Specifies the mouse button on a three-button mouse that activates the pop-up menu for the widget.

MESSAGE-AREA (Log) (R/W) Objects: WINDOW

Controls the appearance of the message area in the window.

MESSAGE-AREA-FONT (Int) (R/W) Objects: WINDOW

Specifies the font number of the font used in the window's message area.

MIN-HEIGHT-CHARS (Dec) (R/W) Objects: WINDOW

Specifies the minimum height of the window, in character units.

MIN-HEIGHT-PIXELS (Int) (R/W) Objects: WINDOW

Specifies the minimum height of the window, in pixel units.

MIN-VALUE (Int) (R/W) Objects: SLIDER

Specifies the minimum value of the slider.

MIN-WIDTH-CHARS (Dec) (R/W) Objects: WINDOW

Specifies the minimum width of the window, in character units.

MIN-WIDTH-PIXELS (Int) (R/W) Objects: WINDOW

Specifies the minimum width of the window, in pixel units.

MODIFIED (Logical) (R/W) Objects: COMBO-BOX, EDITOR, FILL-IN, RADIO-SET, SELECTION-LIST, SLIDER, TEXT, TOGGLE-BOX

Indicates whether or not the contents SCREEN-VALUE attribute for the widget has changed.

MOVABLE (Logical) (R/W) Objects: BUTTON, COMBO-BOX, EDITOR, FILL-IN, FRAME, IMAGE, LITERAL, RADIO-SET, RECTANGLE, SELECTION-LIST, SLIDER, TEXT. TOGGLE-BOX

Enables the widget to receive direct manipulation events (graphical interfaces only).

MULTIPLE (Logical) (R/W) Objects: BROWSE, SELECTION-LIST, CLIPBOARD

Specifies the behavior controlling the selection of items from a browse widget or selection list widget.

MULTITASKING-INTERVAL (Int) (R/W) Objects: SESSION handle

Indicates how the PROGRESS session interacts with MS-Window's cooperative multitasking environment (MS-Windows only).

N

NAME (Char) (R/W) Objects: BROWSE,BUTTON, COMBO-BOX, DIALOG-BOX, EDITOR, FIELD-GROUP, FILL-IN, FRAME, IMAGE, LITERAL, MENU, MENU-ITEM, RADIO-SET, RECTANGLE, SELECTION-LIST, SLIDER, SUB-MENU, TEXT, TOGGLE-BOX, WINDOW

Returns a string identifier for the widget.

NEXT-SIBLING (Handle) (Read) Objects: BROWSE,BUTTON,COMBO-BOX, DIALOG-BOX,EDITOR,FIELD-GROUP,FILL-IN, FRAME, IMAGE,LITERAL,MENU-ITEM,RADIO-SET, RECTANGLE,SELECTION-LIST,SLIDER,SUB-MENU, TEXT, TOGGLE-BOX,WINDOW,SESSION Handle,THIS-PROCEDURE Handle,All procedure handles

Returns the handle associated with the next entry in the list of all current persistent procedures in the current session relative to the specified procedure.

NEXT-TAB-ITEM (Handle) (Read) Objects: BROWSE,BUTTON,COMBO-BOX,EDITOR,FILL-IN,RADIO-SET,SELECTION-LIST, SLIDER,TOGGLE-BOX

Returns the widget handle of the next widget in the tab order of a field group relative to the specified widget.

NUM-BUTTONS (Int) (Read) Objects: RADIO-SET

Returns the number of items in the radio set.

NUM-COLUMNS (Int) (Read) Objects: BROWSE

Returns the number of columns in the browse.

NUM-ENTRIES (Int) (R/W) Objects: COLOR-TABLE, FONT-TABLE handles

Specifies the number of entries in the table (graphical interfaces only).

NUM-FORMATS (Int) (Read) Objects: CLIPBOARD

Returns the number of formats available for reading the data currently stored in the clipboard.

NUM-ITEMS (Int) (Read) Objects: COMBO-BOX, SELECTION-LIST

Returns the number of entries in a combo box or selection list.

NUM-ITERATIONS (Int) (Read) Objects: BROWSER, FRAME

Returns the number of currently visible foreground iterations for a frame or the number of rows currently visible in a browse widget.

NUM-LINES (Int) (Read) Objects: EDITOR

Returns the number of lines in the editor widget.

NUM-LOCKED-COLUMNS (Int) (R/W) Objects: BROWSER

Specifies the number of leading columns locked in the browse widget.

NUM-MESSAGES (Int) (Read) Objects: ERROR-STATUS handle

Returns the number of error messages currently available through the ERROR-STATUS handle.

NUM-SELECTED-ROWS (Int) (Read) Objects: BROWSER

Specifies the number of rows currently selected in the browse widget.

NUM-SELECTED-WIDGETS (Int) (Read) Objects: DIALOG-BOX, FRAME, WINDOW

Returns the number of widgets in a frame or window that the user has selected for direct manipulation.

NUM-TABS (Int) (Read) Objects: FIELD-GROUP

Returns the number of widgets with tab positions in the field group.

NUM-TO-RETAIN (Int) (Read) Objects: FRAME

Returns the number of frame iterations to retain when a down frame scrolls to a new set of iterations.

NUMERIC-FORMAT (Char) (R/W) Objects: SESSION handle

Specifies the meanings of commas and periods within numeric values.

O

ON-FRAME-BORDER (Logical) (Read) Objects: LAST-EVENT handle

Returns TRUE if the last event was a mouse event that occurred on a frame border.

OVERLAY (Logical) (R/W) Objects: FRAME

Specifies whether or not the frame can overlay other frames on the display.

OWNER (Handle) (Read) Objects: MENU

Returns the handle of the widget associated with the menu widget.

P

PAGE-BOTTOM (Logical) (R/W) Objects: FRAME

Specifies the frame as a footer frame in paged output.

PAGE-TOP (Logical) (R/W) Objects: FRAME

Specifies the frame as a header frame in paged output.

PARAMETER (Char) (Read) Objects: SESSION handle

Access the value of the Parameter (-param) parameter specified upon initiation of the current session.

PARENT (Handle) (R/W) Objects: BROWSE,BUTTON,COMBO-BOX, DIALOG-BOX,EDITOR,FIELD-GROUP,FILL-IN, FRAME, IMAGE,LITERAL,MENU-ITEM,RADIO-SET, RECTANGLE, SELECTION-LIST,SLIDER,SUB-MENU,TEXT,TOGGLE-BOX

Specifies the handle for the parent widget of the widget.

PATHNAME (Char) (Read) Objects: FILE-INFO handle

Returns the absolute or relative pathname of the file specified by the FILE-NAME attribute of the FILE-INFO handle.

PERSISTENT (Logical) (Read) Objects: Procedure handles and THIS-PROCEDURE handle

Reports whether the procedure is persistent or not.

PFCOLOR (Int) (R/W) Objects: BROWSE,BUTTON,COMBO-BOX,DIALOG-BOX,EDITOR,FILL-IN,FRAME,MENU,MENU-ITEM,RADIO-SET, RECTANGLE,SELECTION-LIST,SLIDER,SUB-MENU, TOGGLE-BOX,WINDOW

Specifies the color number for the color of the widget when the widget has input focus (character mode only).

PIXELS-PER-COLUMN (Int) (Read) Objects: SESSION handle

Returns the number of pixels in each column of the display.

PIXELS-PER-ROW (Int) (Read) Objects: SESSION handle

Returns the number of pixels in each row of the display.

POPUP-MENU (Handle) (R/W) Objects: BROWSE,BUTTON,COMBO-BOX, DIALOG-BOX,EDITOR,FILL-IN,FRAME,RADIO-SET, SELECTION-LIST,SLIDER,TOGGLE-BOX.WINDOW

Specifies the pop-up menu associated with the widget.

POPUP-ONLY (Logical) (R/W) Objects: MENU

Specifies the menu as a pop-up menu or a menu bar.

PREV-SIBLING (Handle) (Read) Objects: BROWSE, BUTTON, COMBO-BOX, DIALOG-BOX, EDITOR, FIELD-GROUP, FILL-IN, FRAME, IMAGE, LITERAL, MENU-ITEM, RADIO-SET, RECTANGLE, SELECTION-LIST, SLIDER, SUB-MENU, TEXT, TOGGLE-BOX, WINDOW, SESSION Handle, THIS-PROCEDURE Handle, All procedure handles

Returns the handle associated with the previous entry in the list of all current persistent procedures in the current session relative to the specified procedure.

PREV-TAB-ITEM (Handle) (Read) Objects: BROWSE,BUTTON,COMBO-BOX,EDITOR,FILL-IN,RADIO-SET,SELECTION-LIST, SLIDER,TOGGLE-BOX

Returns the widget handle of the previous widget in the tab order of a field group relative to the specified widget.

PRINTER-CONTROL-HANDLE (Int) (R/W) Objects: SESSION handle

Returns the current context for a print job in MS-Windows.

PRIVATE-DATA (Char) (R/W) Objects: BROWSE, BUTTON, COMBO-BOX, DIALOG-BOX, EDITOR, FIELD-GROUP, FILL-IN, FRAME, IMAGE, LITERAL, MENU-ITEM, RADIO-SET, RECTANGLE, SELECTION-LIST, SLIDER, SUB-MENU, TEXT, TOGGLE-BOX, WIN DOW, SESSION Handle, THIS-PROCEDURE Handle, All procedure handles

Stores an arbitrary string value associated with the widget.

PROGRESS-SOURCE (Logical) (R/W) Objects: EDITOR

Controls how the editor widget wraps lines of 4GL source code that are longer than the display width of the editor widget (character mode only).

R

RADIO-BUTTONS (Char) (R/W) Objects: RADIO-SET

Specifies the label and value associated with each radio button in the radio set.

READ-ONLY (Logical) (R/W) Objects: BROWSE, EDITOR, MENU-ITEM

Specifies whether or not the widget is for display purposes only.

RESIZABLE (Logical) (R/W) Objects: BUTTON,COMBO-BOX, EDITOR, FILLIN, FRAME, IMAGE, LITERAL,RADIO-SET, RECTANGLE, SELECTION-LIST, SLIDER,TEXT,TOGGLE-BOX

Specifies that the user can resize the widget at run time (graphical interfaces only).

RESIZE (Logical) (R/W) Objects: WINDOW

Specifies that the user can resize the window at run time (graphical interfaces only).

RETURN-INSERTED (Logical) (R/W) Objects: EDITOR

Defines the behavior of a RETURN event for the editor (MS-Windows only).

ROW (Dec) (R/W) Objects: BROWSE,BUTTON,COMBO-BOX,DIALOG-BOX,EDITOR,FIELD-GROUP,FILL-IN, FRAME, IMAGE, LITERAL,RADIO-SET,RECTANGLE,SELECTION-LIST, SLIDER,TEXT,TOGGLE-BOX,WINDOW,LAST-EVENT Handle

Specifies the row position of the top edge of the widget relative to the top edge of a parent widget or the display.

RULE-ROW (Dec) (R/W) Objects: DIALOG-BOX, FRAME

Specifies the location, in character units, to place the horizontal bar that separates the default button from the rest of the frame or dialog box (OSF/Motif only).

RULE-Y (Int) (R/W) Objects: DIALOG-BOX, FRAME

Specifies the location, in pixels, to place the horizontal bar that separates the default button from the rest of the frame or dialog box (OSF/Motif only).

S

SCREEN-LINES (Dec) (Read) Objects: WINDOW

Returns the number of display lines available in the window, in character units.

SCREEN-VALUE (Char) (R/W) Objects: COMBO-BOX, EDITOR, FILL-IN, LITERAL, RADIO-SET, SELECTION-LIST, SLIDER, TEXT, TOGGLE-BOX

Specifies the data value in the screen buffer associated with the widget.

SCROLL-BARS (Logical) (R/W) Objects: WINDOW

Controls the availability of scroll bars for the window.

SCROLLABLE (Logical) (R/W) Objects: DIALQG-BOX, FRAME

Controls the scrolling capabilities of the frame or dialog box.

SCROLLBAR-HORIZONTAL (Log) (R/W) Objects: EDITOR, SELECTION-LIST

Controls the display of a horizontal scroll bar for the editor or selection list.

SCROLLBAR-VERTICAL (Log) (R/W) Objects: EDITOR, SELECTION-LIST

Controls the display of a vertical scroll bar for the editor or selection list.

SELECTABLE (Logical) (R/W) Objects: BUTTON, COMBO-BOX, EDITOR, FILL-IN, FRAME, IMAGE, LITERAL, RADIO-SET, RECTANGLE, SELECTION-LIST, SLIDER, TEXT, TOGGLE-BOX

Specifies that the widget is selectable for direct manipulation at run time (graphical interfaces only).

SELECTED (Logical) (R/W) Objects: BUTTON, COMBO-BOX, EDITOR, FILL-IN, FRAME, IMAGE, LITERAL, RADIO-SET, RECTANGLE, SELECTION-LIST, SLIDER, TEXT, TOGGLE-BOX

Indicates whether the widget is selected (highlighted).

SELECTION-END (Int) (Read) Objects: EDITOR

Returns the offset of the first character after the end of the currently selected text in the editor.

SELECTION-START (Int) (Read) Objects: EDITOR

Returns the offset of the first character of the currently selected text in the editor.

SELECTION-TEXT (Char) (Read) Objects: EDITOR

Returns the currently selected text in the editor.

SENSITIVE (Logical) (R/W) Objects: BROWSE, BUTTON, COMBO-BOX, DIALOG-BOX, EDITOR, FIELD-GROUP, FILL-IN, FRAME, IMAGE, LITERAL, MENU, MENU-ITEM, RADIO-SET, RECTANGLE, SELECTION-LIST, SLIDER, SUB-MENU, TEXT, TOGGLE-BOX, WINDOW

Controls the ability of the widget to receive input focus and events.

SEPARATORS (Logical) (R/W) Objects: BROWSE

Controls the display of row and column separators in the browse widget.

SIDE-LABEL-HANDLE (Handle) (R/W) Objects: COMBO-BOX, EDITOR, FILL-IN, RADIO-SET, SELECTION-LIST, SLIDER, TEXT

Specifies a widget handle to the side label for the widget.

SIDE-LABELS (Logical) (R/W) Objects: FRAME

Controls the display location of labels relative to widgets in the frame.

SORT (Logical) (R/W) Objects: COMBO-BOX, SELECTION-LIST

Determines whether or not to sort new additions to the item list of the widget (MS-Windows and character interfaces only).

STATUS-AREA (Logical) (R/W) Objects: WINDOW

Controls the display of the status area of the window.

`STATUS-AREA-FONT` (Int) (R/W) Objects: `WINDOW`

Specifies the font number for font used in the status area of the window (graphical interfaces only).

`STOPPED` (Logical) (Read) Objects: `COMPILER` handle

Indicates whether or not the last compilation stopped prior to completion.

`STREAM` (Char) (Read) Objects: `SESSION` handle

Returns a value that specifies the character set used for operating system file I/O—"ibm850" or "iso8859-1."

`SUB-MENU-HELP` (Logical) (R/W) Objects: `SUB-MENU`

Designates a submenu as the "Help" menu on the menu bar (OSF/Motif only).

`SUBTYPE` (Char) (R/W) Objects: `COMBO-BOX, FILL-IN, MENU-ITEM`

Specifies the subtype of the widget.

`SUPPRESS-WARNINGS` (Logical) (R/W) Objects: `SESSION` handles

Controls the display of warning messages during a PROGRESS session.

`SYSTEM-ALERT-BOXES` (Logical) (R/W) Objects: `SESSION` handle

Directs the display of system messages to either the default message area or to alert boxes.

T

`TAB-POSITION` (Int) (Read) Objects: `BROWSE, BUTTON, COMBO-BOX, EDITOR, FILL-IN, RADIO-SET, SELECTION-LIST, SLIDER, TOGGLE-BOX`

Indicates the tab order of the widget within its field group.

`TABLE` (Char) (Read) Objects: `COMBO-BOX, EDITOR, FILL-IN, RADIO-SET, RECTANGLE, SELECTION-LIST, SLIDER, TEXT, TOGGLE-BOX`

Returns the name of the database table containing the field associated with the widget.

`TEMP-DIRECTORY` (Char) (Read) Objects: `SESSION` handle

Returns the directory where PROGRESS stores temporary files during the session.

`TEXT-SELECTED` (Logical) (Read) Objects: `EDITOR`

Indicates whether or not text is currently selected in the editor.

`THREE-D` (Logical) (R/W) Objects: `DIALOG-BOX, FRAME, WINDOW, SESSION` handle

Determines if the widget displays using a three-dimensional format (MS-Windows only).

`TITLE` (Char) (R/W) Objects: `BROWSE, DIALOG-BOX, FRAME, MENU (pop-up only), WINDOW`

Specifies the title string displayed for the widget.

TITLE-BGCOLOR (Int) (R/W) Objects: BROWSE, DIALOG-BOX, FRAME, MENU (pop-up only)

Specifies the color number for the background color of the widget title.

TITLE-DCOLOR (Int) (R/W) Objects: DIALOG-BOX, FRAME, MENU

Specifies the color number for the character-mode display color of the widget title (character mode only).

TITLE-FGCOLOR (Int) (R/W) Objects: BROWSE, DIALOG-BOX, FRAME, MENU (pop-up only)

Specifies the color number for the foreground color of the widget title.

TITLE-FONT (Int) (R/W) Objects: BROWSE, DIALOG-BOX, FRAME, MENU (pop-up only)

Specifies the font number for the font of the widget title.

TOGGLE-BOX (Logical) (R/W) Objects: MENU-ITEM

Determines if the menu item is a toggle menu item.

TOP-ONLY (Logical) (R/W) Objects: FRAME

Determines if another frame can overlay the frame.

TYPE (Char) (Read) Objects: (All widgets)

Returns the type of the widget or handle.

V

V6DISPLAY (Char) (R/W) Objects: SESSION handle

Controls whether PROGRESS uses Version 7 or Version 6 rules to govern the layout and display behavior of widgets in MS-Windows.

VALUE (Char) (R/W) Objects: CLIPBOARD

Specifies the data value(s) in the system clipboard.

VIRTUAL-HEIGHT-CHARS (Dec) (R/W) Objects: DIALOG-BOX, FRAME, WINDOW

Specifies the maximum height of the widget, in character units.

VIRTUAL-HEIGHT-PIXELS (Int) (R/W) Objects: DIALOG-BOX, FRAME, WINDOW

Specifies the maximum height of the widget, in pixels.

VIRTUAL-WIDTH-CHARS (Dec) (R/W) Objects: DIALOG-BOX, FRAME, WINDOW

Specifies the maximum width of the widget, in character units.

VIRTUAL-WIDTH-PIXELS (Int) (R/W) Objects: DIALOG-BOX, FRAME, WINDOW

Specifies the maximum width of the widget, in pixels.

VISIBLE (logical) (R/W) Objects: BROWSE, BUTTON, COMBO-BOX, DIALOG-BOX, EDITOR, FIELD-GROUP, FILL-IN, FRAME, IMAGE, LITERAL, MENU, MENU-ITEM, RADIO-SET, RECTANGLE, SELECTION-LIST, SLIDER, SUB-MENU, TEXT, TOGGLE-BOX, WINDOW

Specifies whether a widget is currently visible on the screen.

W

WARNING (Logical) (R/W) Objects: COMPILER handle

Indicates whether or not the last compilation produced warning messages.

WIDTH-CHARS (Dec) (R/W) Objects: BROWSE, BUTTON, COMBO-BOX, DIALOG-BOX, EDITOR, FIELD-GROUP, FILL-IN, FRAME, IMAGE, LITERAL, RADIO-SET, RECTANGLE, SELECTION-LIST, SLIDER, TEXT, TOGGLE-BOX, WINDOW, SESSION Handle

Specifies the width of the widget or the display used in the current session, in character units.

WIDTH-PIXELS (Int) (R/W) Objects: BROWSE, BUTTON, COMBO-BOX, DIALOG-BOX, EDITOR, FIELD-GROUP, FILL-IN, FRAME, IMAGE, LITERAL, RADIO-SET, RECTANGLE, SELECTION-LIST, SLIDER, TEXT, TOGGLE-BOX, WINDOW, SESSION Handle

Specifies the width of the widget or the display used in the current session, in pixel units.

WIDGET-ENTER (Handle) (Read) Objects: LAST-EVENT

Provides a handle, in a trigger associated with the ENTRY event or LEAVE event, to the next widget to receive input focus.

WIDGET-LEAVE (Handle) (Read) Objects: LAST-EVENT

Provides a handle, in a trigger associated with the ENTRY event or LEAVE event, to the widget that had input focus prior to the event.

WINDOW (Handle) (Read) Objects: MENU, MENU-ITEM, SUB-MENU

Returns the window that owns the menu or contains the owner of the menu, submenu, or menu item.

WINDOW-STATE (Int) (R/W) Objects: WINDOW

Indicates the current visual state of the window in the window system.

WINDOW-SYSTEM (Char) (Read) Objects: SESSION handle

Returns the name of the windowing system being used—OSF/Motif, MS-Windows, or character mode (TTY).

WORD-WRAP (Logical) (R/W) Objects: EDITOR

Determines whether word wrapping is enabled for the editor widget.

Method Reference

A method is a *function* of an object. While attributes are properties and data elements associated with an object, a method performs a specific function for the object.

Most methods return a logical value unless otherwise specified.

A

ADD-FIRST Objects: COMBO-BOX, SELECTION-LIST

Adds one or more items to the beginning of the combo box list or selection list.

ADD-LAST Objects: COMBO-BOX, RADIO-SET, SELECTION-LIST

Adds one or more items to the end of the combo box list, radio-set list or selection list.

C

CANCEL-BREAK Objects: DEBUGGER handle

Removes a specified breakpoint from a debugging session.

CLEAR Objects: DEBUGGER handle

Removes all breakpoints from the debugging session, cancels logging, purges all commands in the DEBUGGER command queue, and clears all panels in the Debugger window except the button panel.

CLEAR-SELECTION Objects: EDITOR

Removes the highlight from the currently selected text.

CONVERT-TO-OFFSET Objects: EDITOR

Converts a row and column value to a character offset in an editor widget. Returns the offset as an integer.

D

DEBUG Objects: DEBUGGER handle

Starts the DEBUGGER in stand-alone mode. It initializes the DEBUGGER and immediately transfers control to the DEBUGGER while blocking the invoking procedure.

DELETE Objects: COMBO-BOX, RADIO-SET, SELECTION-LIST

Deletes an item from a combo box, radio set, or selection list.

DELETE-CHAR Objects: EDITOR

Deletes the character at the current text cursor position.

DELETE-CURRENT-ROW Objects: BROWSE

Deletes the most recently selected row from a browse.

DELETE-LINE Objects: EDITOR

Deletes the line that currently contains the text cursor.

DELETE-SELECTED-ROW Objects: BROWSE

Deletes the nth selected row from a browse.

DESELECT-ROWS Objects: BROWSE

Deselects all currently selected rows in the browse and clears the associated database buffer.

DESELECT-SELECTED-ROW Objects: BROWSE

Deselects the nth selected row in a browse.

DISABLE Objects: RADIO-SET

Disables the radio set button.

DISPLAY-MESSAGE Objects: DEBUGGER handle

Displays the specified character string in the data panel of the Debugger window.

E

ENABLE Objects: RADIO-SET

Enables the specified radio button within the radio set.

ENTRY Objects: COMBO-BOX, SELECTION-LIST

Returns the character-string value of the specified list entry.

F

FETCH-SELECTED-ROW Objects: BROWSE

Returns the character-string value of the specified list entry.

G

GET-BLUE-VALUE Objects: COLOR-TABLE handle

Returns the blue component (integer) of an entry in the color table.

GET-DYNAMIC Objects: COLOR-TABLE handle

Returns TRUE if the entry in the color table is a dynamic color.

GET-GREEN-VALUE Objects: COLOR-TABLE handle

Returns the green component of an entry in the color table.

GET-ITERATION Objects: FRAME

Returns the widget handle for the field group that represents the nth visible iteration of the frame.

GET-MESSAGE Objects: ERROR-STATUS handle

Returns the error message associated with the nth error that occurred during the execution of a statement run with the NO-ERROR option.

GET-NUMBER Objects: ERROR-STATUS handle

Returns the error number associated with the nth error that occurred during the execution of a statement run with the NO-ERROR option.

GET-RED-VALUE Objects: COLOR-TABLE handle

Returns the error number associated with the nth error that occurred during the execution of a statement run with the NO-ERROR option.

GET-SELECTED-WIDGET Objects: DIALOG-BOX, FRAME, WINDOW

Returns the handle of the selected widget in a dialog box, frame, or window.

GET-TAB-ITEM Objects: FIELD-GROUP

Returns the handle of a widget at a specified tab position in a field group.

GET-TEXT-HEIGHT-CHARS Objects: FONT-TABLE handle

Returns the height, in character units, of the specified font. If no font is specified, the method returns the height of the default font.

GET-TEXT-HEIGHT-PIXELS Objects: FONT-TABLE handle

Returns the height, in pixels, of the specified font. If no font is specified, the method returns the height of the default font.

GET-TEXT-WIDTH-CHARS Objects: FONT-TABLE handle

Returns the width, in character units, of the string using the specified font. If no font is specified, the method calculates the width of the string using the default font.

GET-TEXT-WIDTH-PIXELS Objects: FONT-TABLE handle

Returns the width, in pixels, of the string using the specified font. If no font is specified, the method calculates the width of the string using the default font.

I

INITIATE Objects: DEBUGGER handle

Initializes the DEBUGGER, but does not pass control to the DEBUGGER immediately. To start the DEBUGGER from the procedure in application mode, you must set a breakpoint using the SET-BREAK method that the procedure encounters. When the procedure encounters the breakpoint, the DEBUGGER takes control of the procedure at that point.

INSERT Objects: COMBO-BOX, SELECTION-LIST

Inserts a new item before a specified item in a combo box or selection list.

INSERT-BACKTAB Objects: EDITOR

Inserts a new item before a specified item in a combo box or selection list.

INSERT-FILE Objects: EDITOR

Inserts the text of filename into the editor widget at the current location of the text cursor.

INSERT-STRING Objects: EDITOR

Inserts a string into the editor widget at the current location of the text cursor.

`INSERT-TAB` Objects: `EDITOR`

This method works differently depending on the insert mode status. If insert mode is on, it inserts one to four spaces from the current cursor position to the next four-space tab stop. If insert mode is off, it moves the cursor to the next four-space tab stop without inserting any characters.

`IS-ROW-SELECTED` Objects: `BROWSE`

Returns `TRUE` if a specified row in the browse is currently selected.

`IS-SELECTED` Objects: `SELECTION-LIST`

Returns `TRUE` if a specified list item is a currently selected item in the selection list.

L

`LOAD-ICON` Objects: `WINDOW`

Specifies the file that contains the icon to be used when the window is minimized.

`LOAD-IMAGE` Objects: `BUTTON, IMAGE`

Reads the image contained in a specified file. When applied to a button widget, the image is used for the button in its up state, and also for its down state if a separate down state image is not specified. For buttons, this is equivalent to the `LOAD-IMAGE-UP` method.

`LOAD-IMAGE-DOWN` Objects: `BUTTON`

Reads the image contained in a specified file. The image is used for the button in its down state only.

`LOAD-IMAGE-INSENSITIVE` Objects: `BUTTON`

Reads the image contained in a specified file. The image is used for the button in its insensitive state.

`LOAD-IMAGE-UP` Objects: `BUTTON`

Reads the image contained in a specified file. The image is used for the button in its up state. The image is also used for the down state if a separate down image is not specified. This method is equivalent to the `LOAD-IMAGE` method.

`LOAD-MOUSE-POINTER` Objects: `BROWSE, BUTTON, COMBO-BOX, DIALOG-BOX, EDITOR, FIELD-GROUP,FILL-IN, FRAME, IMAGE, MENU, MENU-ITEM, RADIO-SET, RECTANGLE, SELECTION-LIST, SLIDER, SUB-MENU, TOGGLE-BOX, WINDOW`

Specifies the mouse pointer to display when the pointer is moved over the widget. If you apply this method to a frame, field group, or window, the same mouse pointer is displayed when it is moved across all child widgets within the frame, field group, or window. However, if you load a different mouse pointer for a child widget, the child widget mouse pointer is displayed when it is moved over that child.

`LOOKUP` Objects: `COMBO-BOX, SELECTION-LIST`

Returns the index of the specified item in a combo box list or selection list.

M

`MOVE-AFTER-TAB-ITEM` Objects: `BROWSE,BUTTON,COMBO-BOX, EDITOR,FILL-IN,RADIO-SET,SELECTION-LIST, SLIDER,TOGGLE-BOX`

Assigns the applied widget to the tab position after a specified widget. Both the applied widget and the specified widget must be in the same field group.

`MOVE-BEFORE-TAB-ITEM` Objects: (same as `MOVE-AFTER-TAB-ITEM`)

Assigns the applied widget to the tab position before a specified widget. Both the applied widget and the specified widget must be in the same field group.

`MOVE-COLUMN` Objects: `BROWSE`

Repositions a column in a browse widget.

`MOVE-TO-BOTTOM` Objects: `BROWSE,BUTTON,COMBO-BOX,EDITOR,FILLIN, FRAME, IMAGE, LITERAL,RADIO-SET, RECTANGLE, SELECTION-LIST,SLIDER,TEXT,TOGGLE-BOX,WINDOW`

Moves the widget to the bottom (or back) of other widgets of the same class on the screen.

`MOVE-TO-EOF` Objects: `EDITOR`

Moves the cursor position in an editor to the end of the current text.

`MOVE-TO-TOP` Objects: `BROWSE,BUTTON,COMBO-BOX,EDITOR,FILL-IN, FRAME, IMAGE, LITERAL,RADIO-SET, RECTANGLE, SELECTION-LIST,SLIDER,TEXT,TOGGLE-BOX, WINDOW`

Moves the widget to the top (or front) of other widgets of the same class on the screen.

R

`READ-FILE` Objects: `EDITOR`

Clears an editor widget, reads the contents of a specified text file into the widget, and sets the widget's `MODIFIED` attribute to `FALSE`.

`REFRESH` Objects: `BROWSE`

Forces PROGRESS to refresh the display of the current rows in the browse.

`REPLACE` Objects: `COMBO-BOX, RADIO-SET, SELECTION-LIST, EDITOR`

Replaces an item in a combo box, radio set, or selection list. Replaces an existing text string in an editor with a new text string.

`REPLACE-SELECTION-TEXT` Objects: `EDITOR`

Replaces the currently selected text in an editor widget with the new text.

S

SAVE-FILE Objects: EDITOR

Saves the current contents of the editor widget to a specified text file and sets the widget's MODIFIED attribute to FALSE.

SCROLL-TO-CURRENT-ROW Objects: BROWSE

Scrolls a browse (if necessary) to bring the currently selected row into view. If the browse supports multiple selections, then SCROLL-TO-CURRENT-ROW brings the most recently selected row into view.

SCROLL-TO-ITEM Objects: SELECTION-LIST

Scrolls a selection list so that a specified, existing list item appears at the top of the list.

SCROLL-TO-SELECTED-ROW Objects: BROWSE

Scrolls a browse (if necessary) to bring a specified selected row into view.

SEARCH Objects: EDITOR

Searches for a specified string in an editor widget starting from the current text cursor position.

SELECT-FOCUSED-ROW Objects: EDITOR

Selects the row that currently has focus in a browse widget.

SELECT-NEXT-ROW Objects: BROWSE

Deselects a currently selected row in a browse and selects the row after the deselected row.

SELECT-PREV-ROW Objects: BROWSE

Deselects a currently selected row in a browse and selects the row before the deselected row.

SELECT-ROW Objects: BROWSE

Deselects any selected rows in a browse and then selects the specified row.

SET-BLUE-VALUE Objects: COLOR-TABLE handle

Specifies the blue component of an entry in the color table.

SET-BREAK Objects: DEBUGGER handle

Sets a specified breakpoint for a debugging session.

SET-DYNAMIC Objects: COLOR-TABLE handle

Sets a color entry to a dynamic or static color

SET-GREEN-VALUE Objects: COLOR-TABLE handle

Specifies the green component of an entry in the color table.

SET-RED-VALUE Objects: COLOR-TABLE handle

Specifies the red component of an entry in the color table.

SET-SELECTION Objects: EDITOR

Selects the text in an editor widget between two specified character offsets.

SET-WAIT-STATE Objects: SESSION handle

Sets or cancels a PROGRESS wait state that blocks user input.

V

VALIDATE Objects: COMBO-BOX, DIALOG-BOX, EDITOR, FILL-IN, FRAME, RADIO-SET, SELECTION-LIST, SLIDER, TOGGLE-BOX

Executes any validation tests established in a database or by the VALIDATE option of the Format phrase.

APPENDIX B

SmartObject Method Reference

The following tables list the methods that make up the Application Development Environment (ADE). All of the following methods can be found under the /src/adm/method/ directory in the subdirectories listed below.

Table B.1 provides the descriptions for methods located in src/adm/method/smart.i.

Table B.1 Methods Located in src/adm/method/smart.i

Method	Description
ADM-Destroy	Destroys a SmartObject and any SmartObjects contained within it.
ADM-Disable	Disables all enabled objects.
ADM-Edit-Attribute-List	Runs a SmartObjects attribute dialog procedure to get runtime parameter settings.
ADM-Enable	Enable an object—all components except db fields, which are enabled using ENABLE-FIELDS.
ADM-Exit	Passes an exit request to a SmartObjects container.
ADM-Hide	Hides an object and deactivates any SmartLinks that depend on it.
ADM-Initialize	Enables and views an object unless its attributes indicate this should not be done. Cascades 'initialize' to descendents.
ADM-Show-Errors	Displays system error messages.
ADM-UIB-Mode	Sets an object's attributes to indicate that it's being run in "design-mode" inside the UIB.
ADM-View	Views an object and activates/reactivates links
Dispatch	Determines whether to run the LOCAL or STANDARD (adm-) or no-prefix version of a method in the current procedure.
Get-Attribute	Returns the value of a std variable or attribute-table entry.
Get-Attribute-List	Returns a list of settable attributes in an object.
New-State	Notifies other objects of a state change.
Notify	Sends an event to all objects of a particular linktype.

(continues)

Table B.1 Continued

Method	Description
Set-Attribute-List	Sets attributes of an object from a comma-separated List.
Set-Position	Moves an object to a specified position.

Table B.2 provides the descriptions for methods located in src/adm/method/containr.i.

Table B.2 Methods Located in src/adm/method/containr.i

Method	Description
ADM-Change-Page	Views objects on a newly selected page, initializing them if the page has not yet been seen.
Delete-Page	Destroys all objects on the current page.
Init-Object	Runs an object procedure PERSISTENT and initializes default links.
Init-Pages	Initializes one or more pages in a paging control without actually viewing them. This can be used either for initializing pages at startup without waiting for them to be selected, or for creating additional or replacement pages after startup.
Select-Page	Makes a new set of objects associated with a page number current, by hiding the previous page, if any, creating the objects in the new page if the page hasn't been initialized, and viewing the new page.
View-Page	Makes a new set of objects associated with a page number current, without hiding the previous page, if any, creating the objects in the new page if the page hasn't been initialized, and viewing the new page.

Table B.3 provides the descriptions for methods located in src/adm/method/tableio.i.

Table B.3 Methods Located in src/adm/method/tableio.i

Method	Description
ADM-Add-Record	Initiates a record add. Displays initial values but does not create the record. That is done by adm-assign-record.
ADM-Apply-Entry	Applies ENTRY to the first enabled object in the current object.
ADM-Assign-Record	Assigns changes to a single record. Creates record if 'add' or 'copy'.
ADM-Assign-Statement	Assigns field values from within assign-record.
ADM-Cancel-Record	Cancels an add,update or copy.
ADM-Copy-Record	Creates new record with values from thecurrent record buffer instead of the template record.
ADM-Current-Changed	Error message and action if a user has changed the record being updated while the current user had it NO-LOCK.

Method	Description
ADM-Delete-Record	Deletes the current record.
ADM-Disable-Fields	Disables all enabled fields.
ADM-Enable-Fields	Enable all db fields in the {&ENABLED–FIELDS} list for the default frame. Refind the current record SHARE-LOCKED, and redisplay it in case it has changed.
ADM-End-Update	Does final update processing, including reopening the query on an add so that the new record becomes part of the query, and notifying others that a record has changed and that the update is complete.
ADM-End-Update	Does final update processing, including reopening the query on an add so that the new record becomes part of the query, and notifying others that a record has changed and that the update is complete.
ADM-Reset-Record	Redisplays values from the record buffer for the current record.
ADM-Update-Record	Defines a transaction within which assign-record commits changes to the current record.
Check-Modified	Either checks or clears the Modified attribute of all the enabled widgets in this object. Done as part protecting users from losing updates in the record changes or the application exits.
Get-ROWID	Furnishes the rowid of the current record or "previously current" record (in the event of a cancelled Add or Copy, for example) to a requesting procedure (typically reposition-query). Note that the rowid is saved only for certain update operations, in order to allow repositioning after the update is complete or has been cancelled. Get-rowid should not be used as a general way to get the ROWID of the current record. send-records should be used instead.
Set-Editors	Set the attributes of editor widgets properly. They must be SENSITIVE AND READ-ONLY if disabled, ELSE SENSITIVE AND not READ-ONLY. Otherwise they will be unscrollable and possibly the text will be invisible when they are disabled.

Table B.4 provides the descriptions for methods located in src/adm/method/query.i.

Table B.4 Methods Located in src/adm/method/query.i

Method	Description
ADM-Get-First	Gets the first record in the defaultquery.
ADM-Get-Last	Gets the last record in the default query.
ADM-Get-Next	Gets the next record in the default query.
ADM-Get-Prev	Gets the previous record in the default query.

Table B.5 provides the descriptions for methods located in src/adm/method/panelsiz.i.

Table B.5 Methods Located in src/adm/method/panelsiz.i

Method	Description
Count-Buttons	Counts the number of buttons in a frame.
Set-Size	Sets the size and shape of a SmartPanel.

Table B.6 provides the descriptions for methods located in src/adm/method/record.i.

Table B.6 Methods Located in src/adm/method/record.i

Method	Description
ADM-Display-Fields	Displays the fields in the current record.
ADM-Open-Query	Opens the default or browse query.
ADM-Row-Changed	Executed when a new record or set of records is retrieved locally (as opposed to passed on from another procedure). Handles default display or browse open code and then signals to RECORD-TARGETs that a fresh record or set of joined records is available.
Reposition-Query	Gets the current rowid from the calling procedure, and repositions the current query to that record.

Additional methods that are used to control the A.C.E.'s behavior at run-time are contained within the A.C.E.'s broker process.

Table B.7 lists the methods contained within the broker procedure.

Table B.7 Methods Contained in src/adm/objects/broker.p

Method	Description
Add-Link	Adds a procedure handle to the link-table for a particular link type, in both directions.
Broker-New-State	Allows a procedure to send a state change message to another.
Broker-Notify	Sends an event in the form of a method invocation to all objects of a particular link type.
cleanup-links	Checks for any leftover links that point to invalid objects and get rid of them. This can happen if an application is stopped without explicitly destroying each object.
Get-Link-Handle	Returns the current procedure handle(s) for the specified link.
Modify-Deactivate-Links	Adds or removes link types from the list of those to be disabled when an object is hidden.
Remove-All-Links	Removes all links as part of destroying a procedure.
Remove-Link	Removes a procedure handle from the link-tables for a particular link type.

Method	Description
Request	Sends a request to another procedure.
Request-Attribute	Requests an attribute from an object with the specified link type and returns the attribute value
Set-Active-Links	Turns links on or off when the current object is viewed or hidden; touches only the links that are marked as ok to deactivate (adm-deactivate-links).
Set-Broker-Owner	This procedure allows the procedure which initialized the broker (or potentially some other procedure) to declare itself to be the "owner" of the broker process. When this procedure runs Remove-All-Links to indicate that it is terminating, the broker will look for another owner or terminate itself.
Set-One-Active-Link	Sets an individual link's active flag on or off.
Set-Watchdog	Turns the watchdog (PRO*Spy) flag on for a proc and its contained descendants.
Split-Link	Splits a link name such as RECORD-SOURCE into its base link type (RECORD) and link direction (SOURCE).
State-Changed	User uses this to control the behavior for State linktypes.

Appendix C

Important Information for PROGRESS Software Users

This appendix lists Progress' offices, conferences and seminars, international subsidiaries, and worldwide user groups. Your entry into the Progress community will be greatly enhanced by getting in touch with the listed contacts.

Progress Software's 1996 Conferences

Progress Software will host three regional conferences in 1996.

- The 1996 Americas User Conference & Expo will be held June 3-6 in Boston, Massachusetts.
- The 1996 Asia/Pacific Users Conference & Expo will be held August 11-13 in Queensland, Australia.
- The 1996 European Users Conference & Expo will be held September 23-25 in Brussels, Belgium.

Progress Software's conferences offer a variety of sessions that address the business and technical issues of designing, developing, deploying, and marketing PROGRESS applications. Attendees have the opportunity to network closely with fellow members of the PROGRESS community and have questions answered directly by Progress Software staff. The product expositions give attendees a chance to view PROGRESS-based applications and PROGRESS-compatible solutions offered by Progress Software Application Partners, Hardware Vendors, and System Integrators.

For more information on the conferences, please call 1-617-280-4000.

The Smart Move for Smart Business Seminar Series

Consider attending Progress Software's newest seminar series, The Smart Move for Smart Business.

Harnessing the Power of Component Assembly for Application Development, the series examines the advantages of component-assembly techniques and how they relate to enterprise client/server development. Attendees will learn several effective strategies for leveraging the power of component assembly, how to define a clear path to a component assembly environment, and how to evaluate application development environments for true component-assembly techniques. An introduction to the PROGRESS Version 8 Application Component Environment (ACE) and PROGRESS SMARTOBJECTS is also provided.

For more information on The Smart Move for Smart Business seminar series, please call 1-800-989-3773 (U.S. and Canada only).

SmartObject Market Program

With the emergence and acceptance of PROGRESS Version 8 and the Application Development Model, the opportunity to develop and distribute plug and play components for business applications is excellent. You've probably been saying to yourself, "There is a real opportunity here to provide third-party SmartObjects and sell them to the Progress community."

Well, we agree. Imagine having the ability to develop components as small as a particular graphical control or as large as entire line of business applications and have the vast PROGRESS user base in which to market them.

If you're interested in finding out more about this exciting new business opportunity, send an e-mail to smartobject-market@progress.com.

PROGRESS User Groups

The following is a list of PROGRESS user groups sorted by the country or continent.

United States User Groups

Arizona
Tim Thellman
Arizona Corporation Commission
(602) 542-0671

Bay Area
John Campbell
White Star Software
(415) 857-0686

Carolinas, PROGRESS Users Network of
Frank Samuelson
6641 Belfield Court
Clemmons, NC 27012
(910) 766-6693

Chicago Area
Paul Guggenheim
Paul Guggenheim & Associates, Inc.
(708) 498-2299

Cleveland Area
Chris Howard
MDSS, Inc.
(216) 861-8100

Colorado Area
Bob Mann
J.D. Edwards & Company
(303) 488-4920

Colorado Users Group
Lola Carter
LogicData
3650 South Yosemite Suite 202
Denver, Colorado 80237
(303) 694-4400

Delaware Valley
Jonathan A. Shevelew
Protech Systems
1-800-268-1144
jashevelew@aol.com.

Florida
Sam Wingate
Automation Resources
(813) 287-2747

Florida—South (South Florida Progress Users Group)
Paul Duggan
Professional Computer Consulting, Inc.
(305) 424-9569

Harrisburg
Theresa Cermanski
Commonwealth of Pennsylvania, Bureau of Management Information Systems
(717) 787-4076

Indiana
Marty Rhodes
Single Source Systems
(317) 253-0665
Delbert Crocker
Greg White
IN PROGRESS
(317) 635-7020 ext. 741
(317) 595-8437

Iowa
Mark Franke
Strouss & Associates
515-472-2602 ext 11

Kansas
Rob Gonzalez
Benchmark Computer Systems
(800) 279-9192

Kentucky
Tyler McCain
Zion Group
(615) 665-9220

Louisiana
Peter Langworthy
Syscon Corporation
(504) 887-0258

Maine
Arthur Fink
Arthur Fink Consulting
(207) 774-3465

Mid-Atlantic—PROGRESS Users, Middle Atlantic (P.U.M.A.)
David Kosek
Travel Technologies Group
(703) 739-9080

Mid-South (Tennessee)
Jim Carlson
Sedgwick James
(901) 684-3810

Midwest—Upper
Phil Hane
Dynamic Data Systems
(612) 484-6355

Minnesota
Ayrlahn Johnson
UMPUG
(708) 850-5251

Missouri
Russ Bryant
Trinity Technology Consulting, Inc.
(314) 230-7337

New York
John Gowran
Automated Technologies Management LTD.
(212) 249-1665
jgowran@interport.com

Ohio
Charles Griesemer
Griesemer & Associates
(513) 335-7399

Oregon
Richard Uchytil, President
283 NE Kinsale Ct.
Hillsboro, OR 97124
(503) 520-7614
rich@cray.com

Pennsylvania—Consortium of PROGRESS Users (CPU), Liberty Bell Chapter
Bruce McIntyre
McIntyre Designs, Inc.
(215) 322-1895

PROGRESS E-Mail Group (PEG)
Gregory Higgins
Happ Management Systems
(708) 593-6130

Southeastern
Chris Longo
United Systems, Inc.
(404) 457-0340

Southern California
Richard Smith
Lab FUSION, Inc.
(909) 592-8134

Tennessee
Tyler McCain
Zion Group
(615) 665-9220

Texas—Dallas Area
Rick McFarland
Outside Force
(817) 633-8133

Texas—Houston Area
Paul Castanias
AIC
(713) 869-3420
Doug Williams
Hurst, Paul & Associates
(713) 460-9386

Utah
Kent Koffard
Call Business Systems
455 East 400 South
Salt Lake City, Utah 84111
(801) 364-7007

Utah—InterMountain
Steve Rydalch
National Filter Media
(801) 363-6736

Virginia
c/o Allegro Consultants, Ltd.
PO Box 4581 Richmond, VA 23220
Doug Lucy
(804) 355-3085
allegro@well.sf.ca.us

Washington State
Don Pickering
Delta Management
(206) 391-2000 x559

Wisconsin
Ron Alexander
Industrial Electric
(414) 782-2255

Canadian User Groups

Also see the following section, "PROGRESS North America Offices," for more information about Canadian locations.

British Columbia
Peter Beblo
Law Society of British Columbia
(604) 669-2533

Canadian PROGRESS User Group (CPUG)—Manitoba Chapter
Dan Keizer
Federated Insurance
(204) 786-6431

Canadian PROGRESS User Group (CPUG)—Montreal Chapter
David McCabe
Rampart Partitions, Inc.
(514) 676-6644

Canadian PROGRESS User Group (CPUG)—Ottawa Chapter
Ralph Koschade
Hagenbart Systems
(613) 224-6192

Canadian PROGRESS User Group (CPUG)—Quebec Chapter

Vincent Pouliot
(514) 688-7964

European, Middle Eastern, and African User Groups

Austria

Hans-Werner Lhotzky
Progress Software GesmbH
43 222 696603

Finland

Mikko Fagerstrom
Kaukomarkkinat Oy
358 0 521 5704

France

Denis Luglia
DCL
33 67219443

Germany—Northern

Dr. Michael Krause
HGT—B&K GmbH
49 2505 602

Germany—Southern

Robert Fey
Büro für neue Systeme GmbH
49 761 408648

Netherlands

Marcel Vlendre
Walvis Software BV
31 15 619911

Norway

Dan Siggerud
DAN-NOR-MANAGEMENT A/S
47 2 41 68 15

Russia—PROGRESS Russian Users Society (PROGRUS)

Andrei Orehov
Banking Information Systems, Ltd.
+7 095 369 9724

South Africa—Gauteng Progress Linking Users and Solutions (PLUS)

Leon Coetsee
27 11 315 6980
leonc@realtime.co.za

South Africa—Western Cape

Progress Linking Users and Solutions (PLUS)
Mark Lawrence
27 21 244350
markl@realtime.co.za

Sweden

Lars Britts
Forsta Bassangvagen 7
46 8 665 09 45

Switzerland

Stephan Strub
Stasoft AG
41 61 736707

United Kingdom

Julie Clift-Thompson
44-181-651-1112

Australian User Groups

New South Wales

Peter Solomon
Genesys Computer Corporation
+61/2 969 1477

New Zealand

C/- Chris Easton
PO Box 99243
Newmarket
Auckland, New Zealand
ph: 64,9,5201853
fx: 64,9,5223339
Email: mark@cogita.co.nz

Queensland

Graham Hobson
Sterling Systems
+61/7 3832 2500

South Australia

Peter Schelvis
Orlando Wyndham Group
+61/8 208 2444

North America Offices

The following is information for contacting Progress offices in North America.

California—Northern

Progress Software Corporation
900 Larkspur Landing Circle, Suite 205
Larkspur, CA 94939
Phone: (415) 461-8068
Fax: (415) 461-9543

California—Southern

Progress Software Corporation
4590 MacArthur Boulevard, Suite 550
Newport Beach, CA 92660
Phone: (714) 251-1148
Fax: (714) 251-1772

Colorado—Denver

Progress Software Corporation
Denver Corporate Center Tower III
7900 East Union Avenue, Suite 1100
Denver, Colorado 80237
Phone: (303) 220-4700
Fax: (303) 220-4701

Florida

Progress Software Corporation
1200 N. Federal Highway, Suite 200
Boca Raton, FL 33432-2845
Phone: (407) 392-7470
Fax: (407) 392-9576

Georgia

Progress Software Corporation
3091 Governors Lake Drive, Suite 200
Norcross, GA 30071
Phone: (404) 416-1166
Fax: (404) 416-1020

Illinois

Progress Software Corporation
2215 York Road, Suite 310
Oak Brook, IL 60521
Phone: (708) 990-1450
Fax: (708) 990-9590

Michigan

Progress Software Corporation
100 West Big Beaver Road, Suite 200
Troy, MI 48084
Phone: (810) 680-6700
Fax: (810) 680-6709

Minnesota

Progress Software Corporation
8400 Normandale Lake Blvd., Suite 920
Minneapolis, MN 55437
Phone: (612) 921-8440
Fax: (612) 921-2371

Missouri

Progress Software Corporation
111 West Port Plaza, Suite 600
St. Louis, MO 63146
Phone: (314) 542-3171
Fax: (314) 542-3167

New Jersey

Progress Software Corporation
33 Wood Avenue South, Suite 600
Iselin, NJ 08830
Phone: (908) 603-3898
Fax: (908) 603-3897

New York

Progress Software Corporation
528 Plum Street, Suite 200
Syracuse, NY 13204-1434
Phone: (315) 466-8911
Fax: (315) 466-9891

New York—New York City

Progress Software Corporation
100 Park Avenue, 16th Floor
New York, NY 10017
Phone: (212) 880-6471
Fax: (212) 880-6499

North Carolina—Chapel Hill

Progress Software Corporation
Building 600
1829 East Franklin Street
Chapel Hill, NC 27514
Phone: (919) 933-0920
Fax: (919) 933-8525

North Carolina—Charlotte

Progress Software Corporation
6201 Fairview Road, Suite 200
Charlotte, NC 28210
Phone: (704) 643-8111
Fax: (704) 552-6332

Ontario—Ottawa

Progress Software Corporation
440 Laurier Avenue West
Ottawa, Ontario K1R 7X6
Phone: (613) 782-2222
Fax: (613) 782-2269

Ontario—Toronto

Progress Software Corporation
2085 Hurontario Street, Suite 300
Mississauga, Ontario L5A 4G1
Phone: (905) 949-1600
Fax: (905) 949-1445

Quebec

Progress Software Corporation
Centre de la Cite' Pointe-Claire
1, rue Holiday, Tour Est, Niveau 5
Pointe-Claire, Quebec H9R 5N3
Phone: (514) 694-6287
Fax: (514) 694-5023

Texas

Progress Software Corporation
545 John Carpenter Freeway, Suite 500
Irving, TX 75062
Phone: (214) 444-0146
Fax: (214) 444-0274

Washington

Progress Software Corporation
777 108th Avenue, N.E. Suite 600
Bellevue, WA 98004
Phone: (206) 646-4858
Fax: (206) 646-3007

Washington, D.C.

Progress Software Corporation
8150 Leesburg Pike, Suite 700
Vienna, VA 22182
Phone: (703) 827-6551
Fax: (703) 448-8836

World Headquarters

Progress Software Corporation
14 Oak Park
Bedford, MA 01730
Phone: (617) 280-4000
Fax: (617) 280-4075

Progress International Offices

The following is a listing of Progress international offices.

Europe

European Headquarters

Progress Software Europe BV
Alan Facey, EMEA
Shipping Address:
Rivium Boulevard 84
2909 LK Capelle a/d IJssel
The Netherlands

Correspondence:
P.O. Box 172
2900 AD Capelle a/d IJssel
Telephone: 31 10 202 1799
Fax: 31 10 202 2314

Technical Services Centre, EMEA
Peter C.A. de Jong, Director
67 Schorpioenstraat
3067 GG Rotterdam
The Netherlands
Telephone: 31 10 286 5222
Fax: 31 10 286 5225
Cust. Hotline: 31 10 286 5220

Austria

Progress Software GesmbH
Alfred Stumfoll, Managing Director
SCS Buerocenter B2
A-2334 Voesendorf, Austria
Telephone: 43 1 696 603
Fax: 43 1 696 603 99

Belgium

Progress Software NV
Guy Puttemans, Managing Director
Excelsiorlaan 79, 81, b8
B-1930 Zaventem, Belgium
Telephone: 32 2716 0420
Fax: 32 2725 3409

Czech Republic

Progress Software, SPOL. S.R.O.
Jiri Gregor, Managing Director
Pobocna 1
140 00 Prague 4, Czech Republic
Telephone: 42 2 6121 7884
Fax: 42 2 6121 7885

Denmark

Progress Software A/S
Peder Welch Nelson, Managing Director
Tornerosevej 127
2730 Herlev, Denmark
Telephone: 45 42 84 88 66
Fax: 45 42 84 47 32

Finland

Progress Software Oy
Jyrki Maukonen, Managing Director
Sinikalliontie 18B
SF-02630 Espoo, Finland
Telephone: 358 0 502 4420
Technical Support: 358 0 502 4425
Fax: 358 0 5024 4211

France—Lyon

Progress Software S.A.
15 Boulevard Viviers
Merle
69003 Lyon, France
Telephone: 33 72 36 08 33
Fax: 33 72 35 00 49

France—Paris

Progress Software S.A.
Mihai Sturdza, Managing Director
3 Place de Saverne
BP 98
92901 Paris la Defense
Telephone: 33 1 41 16 16 00
Fax: 33 1 41 16 16 01

Germany—Cologne

Progress Software GmbH
Herbert Steinbach, Managing Director
Konrad-Adenauer-Str. 13
50996 Cologne 50, Germany
Telephone: 49 221 93 57 90
Fax: 49 221 93 57 978

Germany—Frankfurt

Progress Software GmbH
Guenther Derstroff, Field Sales
Westendstr. 19
60325 Frankfurt, Germany
Telephone: 49 69 975 46246
Fax: 49 69 975 46110

Germany—Munich

Progress Software GmbH
Furstenrieder Strabe 279
81377 Munich, Germany
Telephone: 49 89 74 13 05 0
Fax: 49 89 74 13 05 48

Germany—Hamburg

Progress Softrware GmbH
Peter Rump, Sales
Geschaeftsstelle Hamburg
Glockengiesserwall 26
20095 Hamburg 1, Germany
Telephone: 49 40 3010 4200
Fax: 49 40 3010 4299

Germany—Stuttgart

Progress Software GmbH
Dieter Ott, Sales
Geschaftsstelle Stuttgart
Konigstr. 56
71073 Stuttgart, Germany
Telephone: 49 711 18293 0
Fax: 49 711 2237218

The Netherlands

Progress Software BV
Mike Gallagher, Mng. Director
Rivium Boulevard 82
2909 LK Capelle a/d IJssel
The Netherlands
Telephone: 31 10 202 2799
Fax: 31 10 202 2201

Norway

Progress Software A/S
Tor Lau, Director, Nordic Operations
Fekjan 13
N1361 Billingstadsletta, Norway
Telephone: 47 66 84 88 55
Fax: 47 66 98 14 73
Bjornar Andersen, Managing Director
Telephone: 47 66 98 14 50
Fax: 47 66 98 14 53

Spain

Progress Software Int. Corp. (Suc.) Espana
Francisco Fernandez, Managing Director
Centro Empresarial El Plantio
Ochandiano, 12 1st Floor Izqda
28023 Madrid, Spain
Telephone: 34 1 307 7714
Fax: 34 1 372 9936

Sweden

Progress Software Svenska AB
Klas Berlin, Managing Director
Box 1124
S-164 22 KISTA, Sweden
Telephone: 46 8 632 6700
Technical Support: 46 8 632 6740
Fax: 46 8 632 6701

Switzerland

Progress Software AG
Rolf Zemp, Managing Director
Bernstr. 390
CH-8953 Dietikon, Switzerland
Telephone: 41 1 742 15 50
Fax: 41 1 742 15 51

United Kingdom—Basingstoke

Progress Software Limited
Jim Bush, Managing Director
The Square, Basing View
Basingstoke, Hampshire
England RG21 2EQ
Telephone: 44 1 256 816 668
Fax: 44 1 256 463 226

United Kingdom—Stockport

Progress Software Limited
Regent House
Stockport
Cheshire
England SK4 1BS
Telephone: 44 1 61 476 6505
Fax: 44 1 61 476 6527

United Kingdom—Glasgow

Progress Software Limited
Craigie Hall
6 Rowan Road
Glasgow
G416BS
Scotland
Telephone: 44 1 41 427 6884
Fax: 44 1 41 427 4947

Asia/Pacific

Australia—Melbourne

Progress Software Pty. Ltd.
Stephen Brady, Director, Asia/Pacific
1911 Malvern Road
Malvern East, 3145
Australia
Telephone: 613 9 885 0544
Fax: 613 9 885 9473

Australia—Sydney

Progress Software Pty. Ltd.
Greg Harrison, National Sales Manager
Level 2
25 Ryde Road
Pymble, NSW
2073
Australia
Telephone: 612 498 7555
Fax: 612 498 7498

Australia—Brisbane

Progress Software Pty. Ltd.
Ric Sibley, Sales
Level 8
303 Coronation Drive
Miltion QLD 4064
Telephone: 617 367 3911
Fax: 617 367 3767

Australia—Canberra

Progress Software Pty. Ltd.
Rowland Chambers
10 Thesiger Court, Deakin
Canberra
Australia
Telephone: 616 202 8862
Fax: 616 202 8855

Australia—Perth

Progress Software Pty. Ltd.
Parkwater
1 Havelock Street
West Perth WA 6005
Australia
Telephone: 619 429 8868
Fax: 619 429 8871

Hong Kong

Progress Software Ltd.
Dennis Ng
Managing Director
Room 1903
Goldmark Building
502 Hennessy Road
Causeway Bay
Hong Kong
Telephone: 852 882 5303
Fax: 852 882 1332

Japan

Progress Software K.K.
Alaska Nakagawa Bldg.
3-11-3 Akasaka
Minato-ku
Tokyo 107
Japan
Telephone: 81 3 3584 5211
Fax: 81 3 3584 5225

Malaysia

Progress Software Corp. (S) Pte. Ltd.
Paul Kwa, Managing Director
79 Robinson Road
#13-08 CPF Building
Singapore 068897
Telephone: 65 222 2526
Fax: 65 227 2192

Singapore

Progress Software Corp. (S) Pte. Ltd.
Paul Kwa, Managing Director
79 Robinson Road
#13-08 CPF Building
Singapore 068897
Telephone: 65 222 2526
Fax: 65 227 2192

Latin America

Mexico—Mexico City

Progress Software, S.A. de C.V.
Hector Vela, Managing Director
Insurgentes Sur 667 - 6 piso
Col. Napoles
Mexico, D.F. 03810
Telephone: 525 687 5206
Fax: 525 687 7163

Mexico—Monterrey

Progress Software, S.A. de C.V.
Francisco Ramirez, Branch Manager
Edificio Losoles
Av. Lazaro Cardenas #2400
Desp. C-31-7
Garza Garcia, Nuevo Leon
C.P. 66220
Mexico
Telephone: 528 363 29 50
Fax: 528 363 22 82

Progress International Distributors

The following is a list of Progress international distributors.

Brazil

PGS Software LTDA
Luiz Soldatelli
Luis Turon (technical rep.)
Rl. a Geraldo Flausino
Gomes 78-15 Andar
04575-060
Sao Paulo SP
Brazil
Telephone: (55) 11 505 0011
Fax: (55) 11 505 1775
E-Mail:
soldatelli.%pgs_software_ltda@mcimail.com

PGS Software LTDA
Miguel Abuhab
Rua Presidente de Moraes, 80
82218-000-Joinville-SC
Brazil
Telephone: (55) 474 41 7000
Fax: (55) 474 417034

Central America—Florida Office

Sigma Industries
Mauricio Hidalgo
Chien Nguyen
10570 N.W. 27th Street
Suite 103
Miami, Florida 33172
Telephone: (305) 592 0282
Fax: (305) 592 1005
E-Mail: 75554.1224@compuserve.com

Chile

Sistemas Multipro, S.A.
Mario Herane
Felipe Montenegro (technical rep.)
Nueva De Lyon 96
Oficina 402
Santiago,
Chile
Telephone: 562 252 0336 562-232-4748
Fax: 562 252 0337
E-Mail: sistemas@mailnet.rdc.cl

Colombia

Argos World Ltd.
Juan Garcia
Jorge Carrera
CRO 20 #89-08
Bogota
Colombia
Telephone: 571 616 6099
Fax: 571 218 9239
E-Mail: jorge.cabrera@sprintcol.sprint.com

Croatia

Infodesign
Mr. Marijan Pucko
Ms. Masa Smokvina
Mr. Damir Hulgev (technical rep.)
Andrijeviceva 12
10000 Zagreb
Croatia
Telephone: 385 1 177096
Fax: 385 1 177097
E-Mail: masa@open.hr

Ecuador

Nomac, S.A.
Gustavo Cajiao
Av. Colombia 1573
Casilla 17 07 9178
Quito, Ecuador
Telephone: (593 2) 222 073/75
Fax: (593 2) 568 226
E-Mail: gcajiao@unisys.com.ec
monicag@unisys.com.cc

Greece

Singular S.A.
Nikos Hatzimichail
Thanasis Daglis (technical rep.)
45, Koniari Str.
11471 Athens
Greece
Telephone: (30) 1 646 3956
Fax: (30) 1 644 2429
E-Mail: nicholas@singular.ath.forthnet.gr

Honduras

COMPUTO Y DESARROLLO S.A.
Rafael Rivera
Col. Parmira 2123
Av. Republic De Panama
Tequeigalpa, Honduras
Telephone: (504) 313 201
Fax: (504) 325 838

Hungary

Rolitron Informatika Kft.
Andras Olah
Laszlo Stankovics (technical rep.)
H-1138 Budapest
Vaci ut 168/A
Hungary
Telephone: (36) 1 270 5120
Fax: (36) 1 270 5132
E-Mail: olah@rolitron.hu

Iceland

Taeknival
Hjortur Gretarsson
Bjarni Bergsson
Skeifan 17
P.O. Box 8294
128 Reykjavik, Iceland
Telephone: (354) 568 1665
Fax: (354) 568 0664
E-Mail: hjortur@ismennt.is

India

JD Technosoft
N. Shiva Kumar
Puneet Mohan (technical rep.)
A-2 Shopping Complex
Masjid moth, greater Kailash-II
New Delhi 110048
India
Telephone: (91) 11 642 8936
(91) 11 646 9050
Fax: (91) 11 642 6533
E-Mail: delhi.jkt@axcess.net.in

Indonesia

Programa Reka Piranti
Edhi Purnomo
Kartono Taslim (technical rep.)
JL Boulevard Barat
Blok LC 7/51
Kelapa Gading
Jakarta 14240
Indonesia
Telephone: (62) 21 452 2465
(62) 21 452 5110
Fax: (62) 21 452 4311

Israel

Moding Ltd
Mr. Yoram Zehavi
Barry Shultz (technical rep.)
1 Ha'ormanut Street
Poleg Industrial Park
P.O. Box 8026
Netanya 42160
Israel
Telephone: 972 9 85 1110
Fax: 972 9 85 1114
E-Mail: moding@shani.co.il

Italy

Technologica S.P.A.
Pino Vaccarella
Alberto Caronna (technical rep.)
Via del Serfico, 75
1-00142 Rome
Italy
Telephone: 39 6 5190 207
Fax: 39 6 5190 131

ICOS S.R.I.
Riccardo Maiarelli
Roberto Giuntoli (technical rep.)
Via Bersaglieri del Po. 23
44100 Ferrara (FE)
Italy
Telephone: (39) 532 210047
Fax: (39) 532 247946

Korea

Pro's Korea Co., Ltd.
Mr. Lee, President
Kee Chul Lee
Mr. Choi, Technical Rep.
Dong-il B/D 4F
107 Yangjae-Dong
Seocho-ku
Seoul, Korea 137-130
Telephone: (82) 2 577 6818
Fax: (82) 2 579 4115
E-Mail: progress@soback.kornet.nm.kr

Lebanon

Gulf Stars For Technology
Billing:
Sami Araji
P.O. Box Shouran 136547
Snoubra
Lebanon
Shipping:
Sheri Lynn Bldg., 2nd Floor
Madame Curie Street
Snoubra
Beirut
Lebanon
Telephone: 961 1 810978
Fax: 961 1 811306

Macedonia

ALEKS d.o.o.
Andre Bozovic
Ms. Cona Paskoska
IVO Ribar Lola 74/111
Skopje, 91000
Macedonia
Telephone: 389 91 255 792
Fax: 389 91 118 406
389 91 114 583

ABV Information Technologies
55 Wynford Heights Cr.
Don Mills, ON M3C1L4
Telephone: 416 446 6055
Fax: 416 446 6432
E-Mail: programa@indo.net.id

Malaysia

PSM Technology SDN BHD
Law Siew Ngoh
36 Jalan SS22/21, Damansara Jaya
47400 Petaling Jaya, Selangor
Malaysia
Telephone: 603 717 3022
Fax: 603 717 1317

New Zealand

QED Software
Jon Perry
Johannes Suwantika (technical rep.)
135 Dominion Road
PO Box 3673
Auckland 1, New Zealand
Telephone: (64) 9 630 1066
Fax: (64) 9 630 9324
E-Mail: jim@qed.co.nz

Peru

C.D.R.
Hans Peter
507 Calle Hernan Velarde
179 Lima, Peru
Telephone: (511) 433 4249
Fax: (511) 433 3507 (511) 433 3218
(Territory includes Uruguay, Paraguay, and Bolivia)

Poland

CSBI S.A.
Slawomir Chlon
Jacek Stochlok (technical rep.)
Spotka z o.o.
02-119 Warzawa
ul. Pruszkowska 17
Poland
Telephone: (48) 39 12 02 39
Fax: (48) 39 12 04 48
E-Mail: progresse.csbi.waw.pl

Portugal

ENS
Jorge Dias
Rua Simao Bolivar, 239-8
4470 Maia
Portugal
Telephone: (35) 129 418 902
Fax: (35) 129 441 192
E-Mail: ens.por@telepac.pt

Philippines

Information Managers
Anthony Abrera
Carlo Doran
Ground Floor, MJL Building
1175 Pasong Tamo Street
Makati Metro, Manila, Philippines
Telephone: (632) 890 7348
Fax: (632) 890 7327

Russia

CSBI E.E.
Boris Melenevski
Dmitry Stepanov (technical rep.)
Vladimir Serbin
2 Pobedy Square
196143
St. Petersburg
Russia
Telephone: 7812 293 0521
Fax: 7812 293 3513
E-Mail: b.melenevski@csbi.spb.su

Saudi Arabia

Saudi Co. Electronics System
Soufyan Al-Kabbani
P. O. Box 107
Riyadh 11411
Saudi Arabia
Telephone: 966 1 476 6876
Fax: 966 1 478 4164

Singapore

Progress Software Corp. (S) Pte. Ltd.
Wong Jak
Sales Manager
79 Robinson Road
#13-08 CPF Building
Singapore 0106
Telephone: (65) 222 2526
Fax: (65) 227 2192
E-Mail:
wjk@shogun.singapore.progress.com

South Africa—Cape Town

Realtime Computer
Neil Hinrichsen
35 Wale Street, 4th Floor
Cape Town 8001
South Africa
Telephone: (27) 21 24 4350
Fax: (27) 21 22 1507
E-Mail:
neilh@realtime.co.za
admin@realtime.co.za
mkting@realtime.co.za
techsupport@realtime.co.za

South Africa—Johannesburg

Realtime Computer
Leon Coetsee
2nd Floor
37 Bath Avenue
Rosebank
Johannesburg 2196
South Africa
Telephone: (27) 11 880 9057
Fax: (27) 11 880 7718
E-Mail: leonc@realtime.co.za

Taiwan

Top Business Machines
Geoffrey Wu
Brian Tsai
11 F, 149, Sec. 2
Ming Sheng E. Road
Taipai, Taiwan R.O.C.
Telephone: 886 2 503 3006
Fax: 886 2 505 2603
E-Mail: oscar@oitop.fstop.com.tw
alice@olitop.fstop.com.tw

Thailand

PSP (Thailand) Co., Ltd.
Mr. Pramote Ukkeedech
Vichai Kraisingkorn (technical rep.)
29 VANISSA Bldg.
3rd Floor soi Chidlom
Ploechit Road,
Bangkok 10330, Thailand
Telephone: (66) 22 51 5330
Fax: (66) 22 54 6397
E-Mail: vichai@morakot.nectec.or.th

Turkey

Servodata
Haydar Bektas
Cem Konuralp (technical rep.)
Bilgisayar ve Yazilim San. Ve Tic. Ltd. Sti.
Buyukdere Cad. Rasit Riza Sk 1/2
80650 Mecidiyekoy
Istanbul
Turkey
Telephone: (90) 212 212 10 45
Fax: (90) 212 212 10 60

United Arab Emirates—Dubai

Fourth Dimension Systems
Hussam Alnouri
Zabeel Business Center
P.O. Box 8070
Dubai, United Arab Emirates
Telephone: 971 436 7782
Fax: 971 436 8128

Venezuela

Sistemas Prosiga SP, S.A.
Tito Gallegos
Manuel Casado
Edsel Garcia (technical rep.)
Callie 3-A, Centro Profesional
La Urbina, Piso 11 of 11E-La Urbina
Caracas, Venezuela
Telephone: (58) 22 41 4641
(58) 22 41 6529
Fax: (58) 22 41 5270
E-Mail: prosiga@spail.lat.net

Progress International Application Partners

Argentina

Overall
Mr. Jorge Garavelli
Mendoza 575 2 Piso of "A"
Rosario 2000
Argentina
Telephone: 54 41 210 327
Fax: 54 41 263 376
E-Mail: jorge.garavelli@sur.turbo.net

El Dante S.A.I.C.
Mr. Vincente Speranza
Lisandro de la Torre 1760 (5006)
Cordoba, Argentina
Telephone: 54 51 55 6950
Fax: 54 51 55 3684

El Date Florida
Jorge Hoberman
Telephone: 305-374-2334
Fax: 305-374-7713

Vergani Y Asociados S.R.L.
Miguel D'Uva—Rodolfo Yaryura
Pichincha 364 Piso 3 Of. "A" "B"
Buenos Aires, Argentina
Telephone: 541 951 6285
Fax: 541 951 4544

Close Up S.A.
Roberto Goti
Thamas 2486
1 Piso
Buenos Aires, Argentina
Telephone: 541 771 3088/3089
Fax: 541 774 2167

Computel S.A.
Carlos R. Rodrigues
Aranguren 443, 6th Piso
1405 Capital Federal
Republica, Argentina
Telephone: 541 983 7821
Fax: 541 903 1972

Perino & Boente
Reconqvista 737
Piso 3F
1003 Buenos Aires, Argentina
Telephone: 54 1 311 0806 Fax: 54 1 313 1813

Baltic States

BMS Ltd.
Chuck Park
Paldiski Mnt. 77A-24
Tallinn EE0006
Estonia
Telephone: 3725 230 300
Fax: 3726 395 021

AS Microsystems
Mr. Piret Spiirt
Andres Kukke (technical rep.)
Ravala PST, 8C
Tallinn EE0001
Estonia
Telephone: 372 6 312 099

IC Systems
Ulo Puskarf
Sakala 19
Tallinn, Estonia
Telephone: 372 630 8900
Fax: 372 630 8901

Bermuda

Business Systems Ltd.
Ken Lamb
12 Par-la-ville Road
Richmond House
Hamilton, Bermuda
Telephone: (809) 295-8777
Fax: (809) 295-1149

Softpro System Services
Sinclair Packwood
Suite No. 385
48 Par-la-ville Road
Hamilton HM 11, Bermuda
Telephone: 809-292-5048
Fax: 809-292-5047

Cameroon

CGICOM
Mr. FomeKong Josue'
BP12588
Yaounde
Cameroon, Africa
Telephone: 237 23 4991
Fax: 237 22 6567

China

Vanda Software
Peter Sham
Xue Yuan Nan Lu 70
Hai Dian, China
Telephone: 861 831 5522
Fax: 861 834 1633

Cypress

4th GL Prodata
Mr. Kleanthis Hadjisoteriou
P.O. Box 1301
54-58 Evagoras Ave.
Nicosia, Cyprus
Telephone: 3572 463 046
Fax: 3572 464 568

Greece

C.S.D. Ltd.
Ms. M. Liuaniov
Mesogion Ave. & 2 Papada Street
Athens, Greece 115 25
Telephone: 30 1 692 751
Fax: 30 1 692 6860

Ivory Coast

Informatique Development
Zone 3—15, Rue DES Carrossiers
01 BP 3907 Abidjan 01
Cote D'Ivoire, Africa
Telephone: 225 2525 14
Fax: 225 35 13 85

Sodeci S.A.
Mr. Sem
D.O.I.M. Sem
Avenue Cristiani
OIBP 1843 Abidjan 01
Cote D'Ivoire, Africa
Telephone: 225 23 3022
Fax: 225 24 2033

Kenya

Memory Information Systems Ltd.
Mr. Peter Wahinya
P.O. Box 26430
Kenya, Africa
Telephone: 254 2 216767
Fax: 254 2 219634

Lithuania

Baltic Amadeus
Audrius Beniusis
Akademijos 4
2600 Vilnius, Lithuania
Telephone: 370 2 611 677
Fax: 370 2 623 970
E-Mail: abenas@amadeus.aiva.lt

Nigeria

Inlaks Computers
Mr. J.C. Chaney
180 Awolowo Road
Ikoyi
Lagos Island, Lagos
Nigeria
Telephone: 234 12 69 1874
Fax: 234 12 69 0605

Portugal

Timesharing, S.A.
Dr. Rui Pedroso
Av dos Combatentes, n43/43A-6
Edificio "Green Park"
1600 Lisboa, Portugal
Telephone: 351 1 720 8000
Fax: 351 1 727 3956

Puerto Rico

Computer Distributors, Inc.
Mr. Jose Acevedo
P.O. Box 11954
Caparra Heights Station
San Juan, Puerto Rico
Telephone: 809-793-3434
Fax: 809-793-6354

JKG Systems
Ambar #2 Villa Blanca
Caguas, 00725
Puerto Rico
Telephone/Fax: 809-746-3774

Romania

Crescendo
Aurel Carstoiu
Razvan Nedelcu (technical rep.)
13 Fecioarei Street
Bucharest—2, Romania
Telephone: 401 211 18 60 401 211 18 58
Fax: 401 210 76 40

Genesys Software Romania SRL
Sorin Baltag
Slatineanu 23—27, ap. 3
Bucharest—1, Romania
Telephone: 401 638 49 44
Fax: 401 638 49 44 401 311 08 97
E-Mail: office@genesys.evnet.ro

Russia

BIS, Ltd.
Stanislav Zelentsov
Andrei Orehov (technical rep.)
Scherbakovskaya 3, office 401
Moscow 105318
Russia
Telephone: 7 095 369 1793
Fax: 7 095 369 6310
E-Mail: nd@bis.msk.su

"2 Plus" Ltd.
Mr. Emil Zlatev
Ms. Nin Ditcheva
10, Ivac Voivoda Str.
1124 Sofia, Bulgaria
Telephone: 359 2 466173
Fax: 359 2 445409

Sri Lanka

Computer Information Systems (PTE) Ltd.
Nazrul Sheriff
Rohan Sirisena (technical rep.)
No. 17
Duplication Road
Colombo 5, Sri Lanka
Telephone: 94 1 50 1103 94 1 593 262
Fax: 94 1 58 0190

APPENDIX D

Internationalization

This appendix contains supporting information for Part V, "Internationalization." This information is organized in sections, corresponding to the individual chapters. At the end of this appendix is a list of references where you will find more information on the subject of internationalization.

Supporting Information for Translation Manager and Visual Translator

This section contains detailed information on some of the internal mechanisms used by Translation Manager and Visual Translator. For more information about Translation Manager, see Chapter 16, "Preparing for Translation." For more information on Visual Translator, see Chapter 17, "Translating Your Application."

Filters

In Translation Manager, the project manager applies filters to the text phrases being extracted from the application. The filters help the project manager determine exactly which text phrases should be translated. Using those filters, a subset of phrases is placed in a kit to be sent out for translation.

The filters available in Translation Manager are grouped into 12 categories, listed in Table D.1. Using the Filter Wizard in Translation Manager, the specific 4GL statements filtered in or out may be tailored. 19 4GL statements are, by default, filtered IN. These are identified in ***bold italics***.

Table D.1 4GL Statements Filters by Category

Category	Keyword
Labels	***Button*** ***Display*** Enable

(continues)

Table D.1 Continued

Category	Keyword
	Form/Frame ***Menu*** Prompt-For Set Update
Column-Labels	***Browse*** Enable ***Form/Frame*** Set Update
Messages	***Regular Expression*** ***Expressions in Titles*** ***Pause*** ***Status Default*** ***Status Input***
List Items/ Radio-Buttons	Radio Buttons Combo-Box List-Items Selection-List List-Items
Titles	***Browse*** ***Display*** Enable For ***Form/Frame*** Insert ***Menus*** Prompt-For Repeat Set Update
Assignments	Current-Language ***Expression*** Non-Alpha Promsgs Propath Termcap
Formats	Character Date Logical Non-Alpha Numeric
Run Statements	Input-Parameter Non-Alpha
Comparisons	If Statement When (Case) Where (For) While (Do)

Category	Keyword
Other	Create Export Image-File (Button) Image-File (Image) ***Put*** ***Put Screen*** ***Text in Frames***
PSC Keywords	(see list below)
Custom Filters	(User-definable)

Keywords

There are 84 keywords used internally in PROGRESS to control program logic. By accidentally translating one of these keywords, a translator could introduce bugs in program logic. For this reason, those keywords can be selectively filterout out. By default, 79 are filtered out, and five are included in the translation database (identified in ***bold italics*** below) because they can occur in normal text phrases as well. The keywords are shown in Table D.2.

Table D.2 Keywords Filtered by Translation Manager

ABORT

ANY-KEY

ANY-PRINTABLE

BACK-TAB

BACKSPACE

BELL

CHOOSE

CLEAR

CURSOR-DOWN

CURSOR-LEFT

CURSOR-RIGHT

CURSOR-UP

DEFAULT-ACTION

DELETE-CHARACTER

DESELECTION

EMPTY-SELECTION

END

END-BOX-SELECTION

(continues)

Table D.2 Continued

END-ERROR
END-MOVE
END-RESIZE
ENDKEY
ENTER-MENUBAR
ENTRY
ERROR
GO
GUI
HELP
HOME
INSERT-MODE
ITERATION-CHANGED
LEAVE
LEFT-END
LEFT-MOUSE-CLICK
LEFT-MOUSE-DBLCLICK
LEFT-MOUSE-DOWN
LEFT-MOUSE-UP
MENU-DROP
MIDDLE-MOUSE-CLICK
MIDDLE-MOUSE-DBLCLICK
MIDDLE-MOUSE-DOWN
MIDDLE-MOUSE-UP
MOUSE-EXTEND-CLICK
MOUSE-EXTEND-DBLCLICK
MOUSE-EXTEND-DOWN
MOUSE-EXTEND-UP
MOUSE-MENU-CLICK
MOUSE-MENU-DBLCLICK
MOUSE-MENU-DOWN
MOUSE-MENU-UP
MOUSE-MOVE-CLICK

MOUSE-MOVE-DBLCLICK

MOUSE-MOVE-DOWN

MOUSE-MOVE-UP

MOUSE-SELECT-CLICK

MOUSE-SELECT-DBLCLICK

MOUSE-SELECT-DOWN

MOUSE-SELECT-UP

NEXT-FRAME

OFF-END

OFF-HOME

PREV-FRAME

RECALL

RETURN

RIGHT-END

RIGHT-MOUSE-CLICK

RIGHT-MOUSE-DBLCLICK

RIGHT-MOUSE-DOWN

RIGHT-MOUSE-UP

ROLLBACK

SCROLL-MODE

SELECTION

START-BOX-SELECTION

START-MOVE

START-RESIZE

STOP

TAB

TTY

VALUE-CHANGED

WINDOW-CLOSE

WINDOW-MAXIMIZED

WINDOW-MINIMIZED

WINDOW-RESIZED

WINDOW-RESTORED

Microsoft Language Glossaries

As of this writing, 14 Microsoft Language Glossaries are included with Translation Manager 2.0. These language glossaries provide a translation mapping from English to the target language. Progress Software leaves these glossaries in their original state, as provided from Microsoft. During the project definition phase of Translation Manager, the glossaries are loaded in, and duplicates are removed. Table D.3 summarizes, by language, the total entries, the duplicates removed, and the final result of loading.

Table D.3 Microsoft Glossaries Statistics

Target Language	Records	Duplicates	Total Loaded
Czech	454	3	451
Danish	1468	105	1363
Dutch	767	70	697
Finnish	1329	23	1306
French	1083	29	1054
German	1315	26	1289
Greek	5652	827	4825
Hungarian	1009	77	932
Italian	518	3	515
Norwegian	1718	199	1519
Portuguese	5554	59	5495
Russian	423	18	405
Spanish	1070	28	1042
Swedish	1463	50	1413

IBM850 and ISO8859-1 Codepages

As discussed briefly in Chapter 14, "Designing Your Global Application," and in detail in Chapter 18, "Deploying Your Application Globally," codepages vary from computer platform to computer platform, operating system to operating system, and language to language.

PROGRESS includes a powerful mechanism for defining and mapping data between codepages. This section includes sample tables used for managing character sets and codepages.

The two codepages detailed below, IBM850 and ISO8859-1, are the codepages used in Western Europe, North America, and Latin America for character set support. Codepage IBM850 is the codepage used for DOS, and ISO8859-1 is the codepage used for most UNIX systems. ISO8859-1 is almost identical to the Microsoft Windows codepage for the same region: 1252.

Table D.4 compares the values between the IBM850 codepage and the ISO8859-1 codepage. This is used to demonstrate that two codepages used for representing the same character set can be very different.

Note

Val = Numeric value of the character

850 = IBM850

ISO = ISO8859-1

n/p = non-printing character

SP = Space character

As seen in Table D.4, the first half of the two codepages is identical. In fact, this is true of most codepages: characters numbered 0 to 127 are usually kept the same, providing some level of portability between systems and languages.

Table D.4 Lower Range of IBM850 and ISO8859-1 Codepages

Val	850	ISO	Val	850	ISO	Val	850	ISO	Val	850	ISO
0	n/p	n/p	32	SP	SP	64	@	@	96	`	`
1	n/p	n/p	33	!	!	65	A	A	97	a	a
2	n/p	n/p	34	"	"	66	B	B	98	b	b
3	n/p	n/p	35	#	#	67	C	C	99	c	c
4	n/p	n/p	36	$	$	68	D	D	100	d	d
5	n/p	n/p	37	%	%	69	E	E	101	e	e
6	n/p	n/p	38	&	&	70	F	F	102	f	f
7	n/p	n/p	39	'	'	71	G	G	103	g	g
8	n/p	n/p	40	(	(	72	H	H	104	h	h
9	n/p	n/p	41	)	)	73	I	I	105	I	i
10	n/p	n/p	42	*	*	74	J	J	106	j	j
11	n/p	n/p	43	+	+	75	K	K	107	k	k
12	n/p	n/p	44	,	,	76	L	L	108	l	l
13	n/p	n/p	45	-	-	77	M	M	109	m	m
14	n/p	n/p	46	.	.	78	N	N	110	n	n
15	n/p	n/p	47	/	/	79	O	O	111	o	o

(continues)

Table D.4 Continued

Val	850	ISO	Val	850	ISO	Val	850	ISO	Val	850	ISO
16	n/p	n/p	48	0	0	80	P	P	112	p	p
17	n/p	n/p	49	1	1	81	Q	Q	113	q	q
18	n/p	n/p	50	2	2	82	R	R	114	r	r
19	n/p	n/p	51	3	3	83	S	S	115	s	s
20	n/p	n/p	52	4	4	84	T	T	116	t	t
21	n/p	n/p	53	5	5	85	U	U	117	u	u
22	n/p	n/p	54	6	6	86	V	V	118	v	v
23	n/p	n/p	55	7	7	87	W	W	119	w	w
24	n/p	n/p	56	8	8	88	X	X	120	x	x
25	n/p	n/p	57	9	9	89	Y	Y	121	y	y
26	n/p	n/p	58	:	:	90	Z	Z	122	z	z
27	n/p	n/p	59	;	;	91	[	[	123	{	{
28	n/p	n/p	60	<	<	92	\	\	124	|	|
29	n/p	n/p	61	=	=	93	]	]	125	}	}
30	n/p	n/p	62	>	>	94	^	^	126	~	~
31	n/p	n/p	63	?	?	95	_	_	127	n/p	n/ p

Table D.5 shows the extended range of IBM850 and ISO8859-1 codepages. Note that the characters stored in the upper half of these two codepages are very different. Although they are the same characters for the most part, their numeric value is different, thus requiring mapping when moving data from a system with one codepage to a system with another codepage.

Table D.5 Extended Range of IBM850 and ISO8859-1 Codepages

Val	850	ISO	Val	850	ISO	Val	850	ISO	Val	850	ISO
128	Ç	n/p	160	á	NBS	192	n/p	À	224	Ó	à
129	ü	n/p	161	í	¡	193	n/p	Á	225	ß	á
130	é	‚	162	ó	¢	194	n/p	Â	226	Ô	â
131	â	ƒ	163	ú	£	195	n/p	Ã	227	Ò	ã
132	ä	„	164	ñ	¤	196	n/p	Ä	228	õ	ä
133	à	…	165	Ñ	¥	197	n/p	Å	229	Õ	å
134	å		166	ª	¦	198	ã	Æ	230	µ	æ
135	ç	‡	167	º	§	199	Ã	Ç	231	Þ	ç
136	ê	ˆ	168	¿	¨	200	n/p	È	232	þ	è

Val	850	ISO	Val	850	ISO	Val	850	ISO	Val	850	ISO
137	'	‰	169	®	©	201	n/p	É	233	Ú	é
138	è	Ṡ	170	¬	ª	202	n/p	Ê	234	Û	ê
139	•	‹	171	1/2	«	203	n/p	Ë	235	Ù	ë
140	"	Œ	172	1/8	¬	204	n/p	Ì	236	y	il
141	"	n/p	173	¡	–	205	n/p	Í	237	Y	í
142	Ä	n/p	174	«	®	206	n/p	Î	238	¯	î
143	Å	n/p	175	»	¯	207	¤	Ï	239	´	ï
144	É	n/p	176	n/p	°	208	δ	Đ	240	–	ð
145	æ	'	177	n/p	±	209	Đ	Ñ	241	±	ñ
146	Æ	'	178	n/p	2	210	Ê	Ò	242	=	ò
147	ô	"	179	n/p	3	211	Ë	Ó	243	1/8	ó
148	ö	"	180	n/p	´	212	È	Ô	244	¶	ô
149	ò	•	181	Á	µ	213	1	Õ	245	§	õ
150	û	–	182	Â	¶	214	Í	Ö	246	÷	ö
151	ù	—	183	À	·	215	Î	x	247	,	÷
152	ÿ	˜	184	©	,	216	Ï	Ø	248	°	ø
153	Ö	™	185	n/p	1	217	n/p	Ù	249	¨	ù
154	Ü	š	186	n/p	º	218	n/p	Ú	250	·	ú
155	ø	›	187	n/p	»	219	n/p	Û	251	1	û
156	£	œ	188	n/p	1/8	220	n/p	Ü	252	3	ü
157	Ø	n/p	189	¢	1/2	221	|	Y	253	2	y
158	X	n/p	190	¥	1/4	222	i	þ	254	□	Þ
159	*f*	Ÿ	191	n/p	¿	223	n/p	ß	255	NBS	ÿ

ISO8859-1 Codepage Tables

This section includes the tables important to define and work with codepage ISO8859-1, the codepage used in Western Europe, North America, and Latin America for UNIX systems. It is also very similar to the Microsoft Windows codepage for the same region: 1252.

The following table is used by PROGRESS to determine, for each value in the ISO8859-1 codepage, whether it is a valid alphabetic character or whether it is non-alphabetic (numeric, punctuation, symbollic, etc.). If an entry has a value of 001, it is alphabetic. If an entry has a value of 000, it is non-alphabetic.

```
CODEPAGE
CODEPAGE-NAME "ISO8859-1"
TYPE "1"
ISALPHA
/*000-015*/  000 000 000 000 000 000 000 000 000 000 000 000 000 000 000 000
/*016-031*/  000 000 000 000 000 000 000 000 000 000 000 000 000 000 000 000
/*032-047*/  000 000 000 000 000 000 000 000 000 000 000 000 000 000 000 000
/*048-063*/  000 000 000 000 000 000 000 000 000 000 000 000 000 000 000 000
/*064-079*/  000 001 001 001 001 001 001 001 001 001 001 001 001 001 001 001
/*080-095*/  001 001 001 001 001 001 001 001 001 001 001 000 000 000 000 000
/*096-111*/  000 001 001 001 001 001 001 001 001 001 001 001 001 001 001 001
/*112-127*/  001 001 001 001 001 001 001 001 001 001 001 000 000 000 000 000
/*128-143*/  000 000 000 000 000 000 000 000 000 000 000 000 000 000 000 000
/*144-159*/  000 000 000 000 000 000 000 000 000 000 000 000 000 000 000 000
/*160-175*/  000 000 000 000 000 000 000 000 000 000 000 000 000 000 000 000
/*176-191*/  000 000 000 000 000 000 000 000 000 000 000 000 000 000 000 000
/*192-207*/  001 001 001 001 001 001 001 001 001 001 001 001 001 001 001 001
/*208-223*/  001 001 001 001 001 001 001 000 001 001 001 001 001 001 001 001
/*224-239*/  001 001 001 001 001 001 001 001 001 001 001 001 001 001 001 001
/*240-255*/  001 001 001 001 001 001 001 000 001 001 001 001 001 001 001 001
ENDTABLE
ENDCODEPAGE
```

The following table is used by PROGRESS to determine the upper and lower case values for all characters in the ISO8859-1 codepage. The ISO8859-1 codepage is the codepage used in Western Europe, North America, and Latin America for UNIX systems. It is also virtually identical to the Microsoft Windows codepage 1252 for the same regions.

There are two tables: the UPPERCASE-MAP is used to determine the uppercase values for all entries in the codepage, the LOWERCASE-MAP is used to determine the lowercase values for all entries in the codepage.

The value stored at each location in the table is the value of the uppercase (or lowercase) value for that character. For example, in the UPPERCASE-MAP table, the value in entry number 97 is 65, meaning that the uppercase for character 97 (a) is 65 (A).

```
# Case tables for code page iso8859-1 and case table basic
CASE
CODEPAGE-NAME ISO8859-1
CASETABLE-NAME BASIC
TYPE 1
UPPERCASE-MAP
   /*000-015*/  000 001 002 003 004 005 006 007 008 009 010 011 012 013 014 015
   /*016-031*/  016 017 018 019 020 021 022 023 024 025 026 027 028 029 030 031
   /*032-047*/  032 033 034 035 036 037 038 039 040 041 042 043 044 045 046 047
   /*048-063*/  048 049 050 051 052 053 054 055 056 057 058 059 060 061 062 063
   /*064-079*/  064 065 066 067 068 069 070 071 072 073 074 075 076 077 078 079
   /*080-095*/  080 081 082 083 084 085 086 087 088 089 090 091 092 093 094 095
   /*096-111*/  096 065 066 067 068 069 070 071 072 073 074 075 076 077 078 079
   /*112-127*/  080 081 082 083 084 085 086 087 088 089 090 123 124 125 126 127
   /*128-143*/  128 129 130 131 132 133 134 135 136 137 138 139 140 141 142 143
   /*144-159*/  144 145 146 147 148 149 150 151 152 153 154 155 156 157 158 159
   /*160-175*/  160 161 162 163 164 165 166 167 168 169 170 171 172 173 174 175
   /*176-191*/  176 177 178 179 180 181 182 183 184 185 186 187 188 189 190 191
   /*192-207*/  192 193 194 195 196 197 198 199 200 201 202 203 204 205 206 207
```

```
   /*208-223*/  208 209 210 211 212 213 214 215 216 217 218 219 220 221 222 223
   /*224-239*/  192 193 194 195 196 197 198 199 200 201 202 203 204 205 206 207
   /*240-255*/  208 209 210 211 212 213 214 247 216 217 218 219 220 221 222 089
ENDTABLE

LOWERCASE-MAP
   /*000-015*/  000 001 002 003 004 005 006 007 008 009 010 011 012 013 014 015
   /*016-031*/  016 017 018 019 020 021 022 023 024 025 026 027 028 029 030 031
   /*032-047*/  032 033 034 035 036 037 038 039 040 041 042 043 044 045 046 047
   /*048-063*/  048 049 050 051 052 053 054 055 056 057 058 059 060 061 062 063
   /*064-079*/  064 097 098 099 100 101 102 103 104 105 106 107 108 109 110 111
   /*080-095*/  112 113 114 115 116 117 118 119 120 121 122 091 092 093 094 095
   /*096-111*/  096 097 098 099 100 101 102 103 104 105 106 107 108 109 110 111
   /*112-127*/  112 113 114 115 116 117 118 119 120 121 122 123 124 125 126 127
   /*128-143*/  128 129 130 131 132 133 134 135 136 137 138 139 140 141 142 143
   /*144-159*/  144 145 146 147 148 149 150 151 152 153 154 155 156 157 158 159
   /*160-175*/  160 161 162 163 164 165 166 167 168 169 170 171 172 173 174 175
   /*176-191*/  176 177 178 179 180 181 182 183 184 185 186 187 188 189 190 191
   /*192-207*/  224 225 226 227 228 229 230 231 232 233 234 235 236 237 238 239
   /*208-223*/  240 241 242 243 244 245 246 215 248 249 250 251 252 253 254 223
   /*224-239*/  224 225 226 227 228 229 230 231 232 233 234 235 236 237 238 239
   /*240-255*/  240 241 242 243 244 245 246 247 248 249 250 251 252 253 254 255
ENDTABLE
ENDCASE
```

The following tables are the collation tables used for sorting characters in the ISO8859-1 codepage. ISO8859-1 is the codepage used in Western Europe, North America, and Latin America. It is also virtually identical to Microsoft Windows codepage 1252 for the same region.

There are two tables: a `CASE-SENSITIVE-SORT` table, which makes a distinction between upper and lower case chararacters when comparing them, and a `CASE-SENSITIVE-SORT` table, which makes no distinction between upper and lower case characters when comparing them.

The value stored at each entry is the character's *sort weight*. The lower the weight number, the earlier that entry comes in the alphabet. For example, in the `CASE-SENSITIVE-SORT` table, the weight for entry 65 (A) is 65 and the weight for entry 66 (B) is 66, meaning that B sorts after A, since it has a higher weight value.

```
# Collation tables for code page iso8859-1 and collation
# Basic
COLLATION
CODEPAGE-NAME ISO8859-1
COLLATION-NAME BASIC
COLLATION-TRANSLATION-VERSION 1.0-16
CASE-INSENSITIVE-SORT
   /*000-015*/  000 001 002 003 004 005 006 007 008 009 010 011 012 013 014 015
   /*016-031*/  016 017 018 019 020 021 022 023 024 025 026 027 028 029 030 031
   /*032-047*/  032 033 034 035 036 037 038 039 040 041 042 043 044 045 046 047
   /*048-063*/  048 049 050 051 052 053 054 055 056 057 058 059 060 061 062 063
   /*064-079*/  064 065 066 067 068 069 070 071 072 073 074 075 076 077 078 079
   /*080-095*/  080 081 082 083 084 085 086 087 088 089 090 091 092 093 094 095
   /*096-111*/  096 065 066 067 068 069 070 071 072 073 074 075 076 077 078 079
   /*112-127*/  080 081 082 083 084 085 086 087 088 089 090 123 124 125 126 127
```

```
  /*128-143*/  176 177 178 179 180 185 186 187 188 191 192 193 194 195 196 197
  /*144-159*/  200 201 202 203 204 205 206 213 217 218 219 220 223 242 254 158
  /*160-175*/  255 173 189 156 207 190 221 245 249 184 229 174 199 240 199 238
  /*176-191*/  248 241 253 252 239 230 244 250 247 251 229 175 172 171 243 168
  /*192-207*/  065 065 065 065 065 143 146 067 069 069 069 069 073 073 073 073
  /*208-223*/  068 078 079 079 079 079 079 158 157 085 085 085 085 089 222 000
  /*224-239*/  065 065 065 065 065 143 146 067 069 069 069 069 073 073 073 073
  /*240-255*/  068 078 079 079 079 079 079 246 157 085 085 085 085 089 222 089
ENDTABLE

CASE-SENSITIVE-SORT
  /*000-015*/  000 001 002 003 004 005 006 007 008 009 010 011 012 013 014 015
  /*016-031*/  016 017 018 019 020 021 022 023 024 025 026 027 028 029 030 031
  /*032-047*/  032 033 034 035 036 037 038 039 040 041 042 043 044 045 046 047
  /*048-063*/  048 049 050 051 052 053 054 055 056 057 058 059 060 061 062 063
  /*064-079*/  064 065 066 067 068 069 070 071 072 073 074 075 076 077 078 079
  /*080-095*/  080 081 082 083 084 085 086 087 088 089 090 091 092 093 094 095
  /*096-111*/  096 097 098 099 100 101 102 103 104 105 106 107 108 109 110 111
  /*112-127*/  112 113 114 115 116 117 118 119 120 121 122 123 124 125 126 127
  /*128-143*/  176 177 178 179 180 185 186 187 188 191 192 193 194 195 196 197
  /*144-159*/  200 201 202 203 204 205 206 213 217 218 219 220 223 242 254 158
  /*160-175*/  255 173 189 156 207 190 221 245 249 184 229 174 199 240 198 238
  /*176-191*/  248 241 253 252 239 230 244 250 247 251 229 175 172 171 243 168
  /*192-207*/  065 065 065 065 065 143 146 067 069 069 069 069 073 073 073 073
  /*208-223*/  209 078 079 079 079 079 079 158 157 085 085 085 085 089 232 000
  /*224-239*/  097 097 097 097 097 134 145 099 101 101 101 101 105 105 105 105
  /*240-255*/  208 110 111 111 111 111 111 246 155 117 117 117 117 121 231 121
ENDTABLE
ENDCOLLATION
```

The following table is used by PROGRESS to map characters between the UNIX codepage ISO8859-1 for Western Europe, North America, and Latin America, and the DOS codepage IBM850 for the same region.

The value for each entry in the table is the codepage entry for the target codepage. For example, in the ISO8859-1 to IBM850 table, the value for entry 255 (ÿ) is 152, the value for ÿ in codepage IBM850. You can refer to Table D.5 above to verify this.

```
# This contains the data needed to convert from iso8859-1 to IBM codepage
850

CONVERT
SOURCE-NAME "ISO8859-1"
TARGET-NAME "IBM850"
TYPE "1"
  /*000-015*/  000 001 002 003 004 005 006 007 008 009 010 011 012 013 014 015
  /*016-031*/  016 017 018 019 020 021 022 023 024 025 026 027 028 029 030 031
  /*032-047*/  032 033 034 035 036 037 038 039 040 041 042 043 044 045 046 047
  /*048-063*/  048 049 050 051 052 053 054 055 056 057 058 059 060 061 062 063
  /*064-079*/  064 065 066 067 068 069 070 071 072 073 074 075 076 077 078 079
  /*080-095*/  080 081 082 083 084 085 086 087 088 089 090 091 092 093 094 095
  /*096-111*/  096 097 098 099 100 101 102 103 104 105 106 107 108 109 110 111
  /*112-127*/  112 113 114 115 116 117 118 119 120 121 122 123 124 125 126 127
  /*128-143*/  176 177 178 179 180 185 186 187 188 191 192 193 194 195 196 197
  /*144-159*/  200 201 202 203 204 205 206 213 217 218 219 220 223 242 254 159
  /*160-175*/  255 173 189 156 207 190 221 245 249 184 166 174 170 240 169 238
  /*176-191*/  248 241 253 252 239 230 244 250 247 251 167 175 172 171 243 168
```

```
  /*192-207*/  183 181 182 199 142 143 146 128 212 144 210 211 222 214 215 216
  /*208-223*/  209 165 227 224 226 229 153 158 157 235 233 234 154 237 232 225
  /*224-239*/  133 160 131 198 132 134 145 135 138 130 136 137 141 161 140 139
  /*240-255*/  208 164 149 162 147 228 148 246 155 151 163 150 129 236 231 152
ENDTABLE
ENDCONVERT
```

The following table is used by PROGRESS to map characters between the DOS codepage IBM850 for Western Europe, North America, and Latin America, and the UNIX codepage ISO8859-1 for the same region.

The values in this table work in the same way as the previous table, only for the reverse direction.

```
# This contains the data needed to convert from IBM codepage 850 to iso8859-1
CONVERT
SOURCE-NAME "IBM850"
TARGET-NAME "ISO8859-1"
TYPE "1"
  /*000-015*/  000 001 002 003 004 005 006 007 008 009 010 011 012 013 014 015
  /*016-031*/  016 017 018 019 020 021 022 023 024 025 026 027 028 029 030 031
  /*032-047*/  032 033 034 035 036 037 038 039 040 041 042 043 044 045 046 047
  /*048-063*/  048 049 050 051 052 053 054 055 056 057 058 059 060 061 062 063
  /*064-079*/  064 065 066 067 068 069 070 071 072 073 074 075 076 077 078 079
  /*080-095*/  080 081 082 083 084 085 086 087 088 089 090 091 092 093 094 095
  /*096-111*/  096 097 098 099 100 101 102 103 104 105 106 107 108 109 110 111
  /*112-127*/  112 113 114 115 116 117 118 119 120 121 122 123 124 125 126 127
  /*128-143*/  199 252 233 226 228 224 229 231 234 235 232 239 238 236 196 197
  /*144-159*/  201 230 198 244 246 242 251 249 255 214 220 248 163 216 215 159
  /*160-175*/  225 237 243 250 241 209 170 186 191 174 172 189 188 161 171 187
  /*176-191*/  128 129 130 131 132 193 194 192 169 133 134 135 136 162 165 137
  /*192-207*/  138 139 140 141 142 143 227 195 144 145 146 147 148 149 150 164
  /*208-223*/  240 208 202 203 200 151 205 206 207 152 153 154 155 166 204 156
  /*224-239*/  211 223 212 210 245 213 181 254 222 218 219 217 253 221 175 180
  /*240-255*/  173 177 157 190 182 167 247 184 176 168 183 185 179 178 158 160
ENDTABLE
ENDCONVERT
```

For more information on codepages and characters sets, see Chapter 18, "Deploying Your Application Globally."

Other Sources of Internationalization and Localization Information

The following is a partial listing of other references on internationalization and localization information. There are hundreds of references on internationalization, and the sources listed below are a good introduction. Many of them contain very comprehensive reference listings of their own.

The references are grouped into multiple sections: references available from Progress Software, and references available from the industry in general, organized by subject.

References Available from Progress Software

The following manuals are available from Progress Software. They are typically included with a new purchase of PROGRESS, but may also be ordered separately.

- "PROGRESS System Administration Guide," Appendix A (Version 8.0). This contains information on codepages and character sets.
- "PROGRESS Translation Manager Guide." This manual is the reference guide for using Translation Manager, and covers the process from the project manager's viewpoint.
- "PROGRESS Visual Translator Guide." This manual is the reference guide for using Visual Translator, and covers the process to be usedby translators.
- "Double Byte Enabled PROGRESS Guide." This manual gives an overall explanation of the double byte enabled versions of PROGRESS.

Bibliographic Reference

This bibliography contains a list of hundreds of references on a variety of areas of internationalization.

- Lasovick, Susan. *GLOBALIZATION, An Annotated Bibliograph*y. Polyglot publishing, 1995.

Cultural References

The following references cover cultural differences and conventions around the world. These are not programming references, and make for light, but interesting reading.

- Axtell, Roger. *The DO'S and TABOOS of International Trad*e. John Wiley & Sons, 1989. ISBN 0-471-61637-0.
- Axtell, Roger. *DO's and TABOOS around the Wor*ld. John Wiley & Sons, 1990. ISBN 0-471-59528-4.
- Axtell, Roger. *The DO's and TABOOS of Body Language Around the Wor*ld. John Wiley & Sons, 1991.
- Fast, Julius. *Body Languag*e. MJF Books, 1970. ISBN 1-56731-004-4.

Technical References

The following references are written for application designers and programmers. They are of a technical nature, but also provide good overviews of the subject.

- Lunde, Ken. *Understanding Japanese Information Processing*. O'Reilly & Associates, Inc, 1993. ISBN 1-56592-043-0.
- Uren, Howard, and Perinotti. *Software Internationalization and Localization, an Introductio*n. Van Nostrand Reinhold, 1993. ISBN 0-442-01498-8.
- Unicode Consortium. *The UNICODE Standard: Worldwide Character Encoding, Version 1.0, Volumes 1 and* 2. Addison-Wesley, 1992. ISBN 0-201-60845-6.
- Taylor, David. *Global Software*. Springer-Verlag, 1992. ISBN 0-387-97706-6.

Vendor Literature

Some of the best sources on internationalization are materials written by operating system and computer vendors. While they can be very system-specific, and may have certain prejudices built in, in sum they contain good information.

- Kano, Nadine. *Developing International Software for Windows 95 and Windows NT.* Microsoft Press, 1995. ISBN 1-55615-840-8.
- *The GUI Guide.* Microsoft Press, 1993. ISBN 1-55615-538-7. This contains earlier versions of the 14 glossaries currently incorporated into Translation Manager.
- American Electronics Association. *Soft Landing in Japan.* AEA Publications, 1992.
- Gray, Pamela. *Catalyst: A Guide to Doing Business in Europe.* Sun Microsystems, 1992.
- National Language Design Guide Series, IBM publications, numbers 8001-8004 (Series SE09).
- Garneau, Dennis. *Keys to Sort and Search for Culturally Expected Results.* IBM publication number GG24-3516.

APPENDIX E

Custom Object Options

This appendix lists the legal attributes for custom object definitions in User Interface Builder (UIB) custom object files (*.cst). Entries in these files allow you to add customized object definitions to the UIB's Object Palette.

The attributes and values that are legal in custom object definitions are essentially the same attributes that are supported by your PROGRESS code. However, the purpose of custom object definitions is to initialize the characteristics of objects created in the UIB. Some attributes, such as `TITLE-BAR`, are not PROGRESS runtime attributes and are valid only in the UIB. There are also some runtime attributes, such as `SENSITIVE` and `SELECTED`, that are not supported in custom object definitions.

Table E.1 shows the list of custom object attributes. Attribute names can be abbreviated, as long as the abbreviation is not ambiguous with another attribure.

Table E.1 Custom Object Attributes

Attribute	Type	Valid on Objects
AUTO-END-KEY	L	Butt
AUTO-GO	L	Butt
AUTO-INDENT	L	Edit
AUTO-RESIZE	L	Butt Edit Fill Sele Slid Togg
AUTO-RETURN	L	Fill
BGCOLOR	I	Fram Brow Butt Comb Edit Fill Imag Radi Rect Sele Slid Togg Text
BLANK	L	Fill
BOX-SELECTABLE	L	Fram
CANCEL-BTN	L	Butt
COLUMN-SCROLLING	L	Brow
DATA-TYPE	C	Comb Fill Radi
DEBLANK	L	Fill

(continues)

Table E.1 Continued

Attribute	Type	Valid on Objects
DEFAULT-BTN	L	Butt
DEFAULT-STYLE	L	Butt
DISPLAY	L	Comb Edit Fill Radi Sele Slid Togg
DOWN	L	Fram
DRAG-ENABLED	L	Sele
EDGE-PIXELS	I	Rect
ENABLE	L	Brow Butt Comb Edit Fill Imag Radi Rect Sele Slid Togg
EXPAND	L	Radi
FGCOLOR	I	Fram Brow Butt Comb Edit Fill Imag Radi Rect Sele Slid Togg Text
FILLED	L	Rect
FONT	I	Fram Brow Butt Comb Edit Fill Radi Sele Slid Togg Text
FORMAT	C	Comb Fill
GRAPHIC-EDGE	L	Rect
HEIGHT	D	Fram Brow Butt Comb Edit Fill Imag Radi Rect Sele Slid Togg Text
HEIGHT-P	I	Fram Brow Butt Comb Edit Fill Imag Radi Rect Sele Slid Togg Text
HELP	C	Brow Butt Comb Edit Fill Radi Sele Slid Togg
HIDDEN	L	Fram Brow Butt Comb Edit Fill Imag Radi Rect Sele Slid Togg
HORIZONTAL	L	Radi Slid
IMAGE-DOWN	C	Butt
IMAGE-FILE	C	Butt Imag
IMAGE-INSENSITIVE	C	Butt
INHERIT	C	Fram Brow Butt Comb Edit Fill Imag Radi Rect Sele Slid Text Togg
INITIAL-VALUE	C	Comb Edit Fill Radi Sele Slid Togg
INNER-LINES	I	Comb
KEEP-TAB-ORDER	L	Fram
LABEL	C	Fram Brow Butt Comb Fill Togg
LARGE	L	Edit
LAYOUT-UNIT	L	Fram Brow Butt Comb Edit Fill Imag Radi Rect Sele Slid Togg Text
LIST-ITEMS	C	Comb Radi Sele

Attribute	Type	Valid on Objects
LOCK-COLUMNS	I	Brow
MANUAL-HIGHLIGHT	L	Fram Butt Comb Edit Fill Imag Radi Rect Sele Slid Togg
MAX-CHARS	I	Edit
MAX-DATA-GUESS	I	Brow
MAX-VALUE	I	Slid
MIN-VALUE	I	Slid
MOVABLE	L	Fram Butt Comb Edit Fill Imag Radi Rect Sele Slid Togg
MULTIPLE	L	Brow Sele
NAME	C	Fram Brow Butt Comb Edit Fill Imag Radi Rect Sele Slid Togg
NATIVE	L	Fill
NO-ASSIGN	L	Brow
NO-BOX	L	Fram Brow
NO-HELP	L	Fram
NO-HIDE	L	Fram
NO-LABEL	L	Comb Fill
NO-LABELS	L	Fram Brow
NO-ROW-MARKERS	L	Brow
NO-UNDERLINE	L	Fram
NO-UNDO	L	Comb Edit Fill Radi Sele Slid Togg
NO-VALIDATE	L	Fram
OPEN-QUERY	L	Fram Brow
OVERLAY	L	Fram
PAGE-BOTTOM	L	Fram
PAGE-TOP	L	Fram
PRIVATE-DATA	C	Fram Brow Butt Comb Edit Fill Imag Radi Rect Sele Slid Togg
READ-ONLY	L	Edit
RESIZABLE	L	Fram Butt Comb Edit Fill Imag Radi Rect Sele Slid Togg
RETAIN	I	Fram
RETURN-INSERTED	L	Edit
SCROLLABLE	L	Fram
SCROLLBAR-HORIZONTAL	L	Edit Sele

(continues)

Table E.1 Continued

Attribute	Type	Valid on Objects
SCROLLBAR-VERTICAL	L	Edit Sele
SELECTABLE	L	Fram Butt Comb Edit Fill Imag Radi Rect Sele Slid Togg
SENSITIVE	L	Fram
SEPARATORS	L	Brow
SIDE-LABELS	L	Fram
SIZE-TO-FIT	L	Fram
SORT	L	Comb Sele
TITLE	C	Fram Brow
TITLE-BAR	L	Fram Brow
TITLE-BGCOLOR	I	Fram
TITLE-FGCOLOR	I	Fram
TOP-ONLY	L	Fram
USE-DICT-EXPS	L	Fram
VIEW	L	Fram
VIEW-AS-TEXT	L	Fill
VIRTUAL-HEIGHT	D	Fram
VIRTUAL-HEIGHT-P	I	Fram
VIRTUAL-WIDTH	D	Fram
VIRTUAL-WIDTH-P	I	Fram
WIDTH	D	Fram Brow Butt Comb Edit Fill Imag Radi Rect Sele Slid Togg Text
WIDTH-P	I	Fram Brow Butt Comb Edit Fill Imag Radi Rect Sele Slid Togg Text
WORD-WRAP	L	Edit

Table E.2 lists the object type abbreviations used in Table E.1.

Table E.2 Object Name Abbreviations Used in Table E.1

Abbreviation	Full Object Name
Brow	Browse
Butt	Button
Comb	Combo-Box
Edit	Editor
Fill	Fill-in
Fram	Frame
Imag	Image
Radi	Radio-Set
Rect	Rectangle
Sele	Selection-List
Slid	Slider
Text	Text
Togg	Toggle-box

Table E.3 lists the datatype abbreviations used in Table E.1.

Table E.3 Datatype Abbreviations Used in Table E.1

Abbreviation	Datatype
C	Character String
D	Decimal
I	Integer
L	Logical (Yes/No or True/False)

APPENDIX F

Structure of .w Files

Files generated by the User Interface Builder (UIB) have a very specific structure that allows them to be read back into the UIB. Unlike many graphic development environments, PROGRESS stores all screen layouts in simple text files. There is no "resource file" or "screen description language" that is distinct from standard PROGRESS source code.

When you specify a screen layout in the UIB, the UIB creates a file of PROGRESS source code that will recreate that layout when you run your program. This can sometimes be rather complex. PROGRESS supports the following two distinct models to describe objects and their attributes:

- *Compiled Frame Definitions*. Before version 7, PROGRESS did almost all layout at compile time. Layout was based on a FORM statement which defined all the elements of a FRAME. Compile-time layout has two advantages. First, the layout can be computed once, when the file is compiled, rather than every time the file is run. Second, PROGRESS can bind database fields to screen objects and allow for efficient transfer of data to and from the screen.
- *Run-time Attribute Setting*. Starting in version 7, PROGRESS allowed objects to be created and manipulated using executable statements. When you assign a value to an `object:attribute`, you are changing attributes dynamically. Run-time layout can adjust itself to the needs of a user, or to screen resolution.

  One attribute that you cannot set at run-time is the database binding. That means that you cannot automatically connect a field in our database to an object that is created dynamically. Nor can you change the data binding of an existing object. This is a significant limitation in a database application.

  Another problem with run-time attribute settings is speed. PROGRESS evaluates each line of your run-time code individually. If you do a significant amount of run-time manipulation, you may find your application will become sluggish.

When the UIB generates a file, it tries to find a balance between these two techniques. Generally speaking, a UIB .w file does as much as possible using compiler layout. This basic interface is then modified using run-time attribute settings to set attributes that cannot be set at compile time.

Understanding &ANALYZE-SUSPEND

When the UIB opens a file, it needs to parse this file the same way the compiler would. To do this, the UIB uses a special version of the compiler to analyze the layout of frames. This ANALYZER processes the original file and literally throws out all the source code that does not affect compile-time frame layout.

Essentially, the ANALYZER only looks at those statements that define the layout of frames (for example, DEFINE FRAME, DISPLAY, UPDATE and FORM statements). Every other statement is passed over. This includes statements that define variables not used in a frame, statements that create objects dynamically, and statements that set size and position of objects (outside of a frame definition).

If you go into a .w file with the Procedure Editor and edit it, you may find that your changes are lost when you open the file in the UIB. That is because the ANALYZER is discarding your changes before they ever get to the UIB.

However, if the ANALYZER is throwing out everything not directly related to compile-time frames, then why is any run-time code retained at all? Why does the ANALYZER ignore the run-time settings that the UIB generates, as well as the code, comments and triggers that you write in your code.

The answer is &ANALYZE-SUSPEND. If you look at a .w file in an editor you will see that blocks of code are surrounded by statements that begin:

```
&ANALYZE-SUSPEND _UIB-CODE-BLOCK _CUSTOM _DEFINITIONS f
...
&ANALYZE-RESUME
```

The code between an &ANALYZE-SUSPEND and &ANALYZE-RESUME is totally ignored by the ANALYZER. It is as if these lines did not exist. Consider the following simplified .w file. This file is similar to any file that you might create with the Progress UIB.

```
&ANALYZE-SUSPEND _VERSION-NUMBER UIB_v8r1 GUI
&ANALYZE-RESUME
&Scoped-define WINDOW-NAME CURRENT-WINDOW
&Scoped-define FRAME-NAME F
&ANALYZE-SUSPEND _UIB-CODE-BLOCK _CUSTOM _DEFINITIONS f
/*-----------------------------------------------
  File: edit-atr.w
  -----------------------------------------------*/
DEFINE INPUT PARAMETER ph_SMO AS HANDLE NO-UNDO.

/* _UIB-CODE-BLOCK-END */
&ANALYZE-RESUME


&ANALYZE-SUSPEND _UIB-PREPROCESSOR-BLOCK

/* *********  Preprocessor Definitions  ************* */

&Scoped-define PROCEDURE-TYPE DIALOG-BOX
```

```
/* Name of first Frame and/or Browse and/or first Query */
&Scoped-define FRAME-NAME F

/* Standard List Definitions                            */
&Scoped-Define ENABLED-OBJECTS attr-list Btn_Cancel Btn_Help Btn_OK
&Scoped-Define DISPLAYED-OBJECTS attr-list

/* Custom List Definitions                        */
/* List-1,List-2,List-3,List-4,List-5,List-6      */

/* _UIB-PREPROCESSOR-BLOCK-END */
&ANALYZE-RESUME

/* **************  Control Definitions  ************* */

/* Define a dialog box                                  */
DEFINE BUTTON Btn_Cancel AUTO-END-KEY
     LABEL "Cancel"
     SIZE 12 BY 1.08
     BGCOLOR 8 .

DEFINE BUTTON Btn_OK AUTO-GO
     LABEL "OK"
     SIZE 12 BY 1.08
     BGCOLOR 8 .

DEFINE VARIABLE attr-list AS CHARACTER
     VIEW-AS EDITOR NO-WORD-WRAP
     SCROLLBAR-HORIZONTAL SCROLLBAR-VERTICAL
     SIZE 49 BY 8.5 NO-UNDO.

/* ****************  Frame Definitions  *************** */

DEFINE FRAME f
     Btn_OK AT ROW 1.38 COL 52
     attr-list AT ROW 1.5 COL 2 NO-LABEL
     Btn_Cancel AT ROW 2.69 COL 52
     SPACE(1.13) SKIP(4.72)
    WITH VIEW-AS DIALOG-BOX KEEP-TAB-ORDER
         SIDE-LABELS NO-UNDERLINE THREE-D  SCROLLABLE
         TITLE "Instance Attributes"
         CANCEL-BUTTON Btn_Cancel.



/* *************** Procedure Settings **************** */

&ANALYZE-SUSPEND _PROCEDURE-SETTINGS
/* Settings for THIS-PROCEDURE
   Type: DIALOG-BOX
   Allow: Basic,Browse,DB-Fields,Query
 */
&ANALYZE-RESUME _END-PROCEDURE-SETTINGS


/* ******  Runtime Attributes and UIB Settings  ****** */
```

```
&ANALYZE-SUSPEND _RUN-TIME-ATTRIBUTES
ASSIGN
       FRAME F:SCROLLABLE = FALSE.

/* _RUN-TIME-ATTRIBUTES-END */
&ANALYZE-RESUME

/* ****************  Control Triggers  **************** */

&Scoped-define SELF-NAME f
&ANALYZE-SUSPEND _UIB-CODE-BLOCK _CONTROL f f
ON WINDOW-CLOSE OF FRAME F /* Instance Attributes */
DO:
  APPLY "END-ERROR":U TO SELF.
END.

/* _UIB-CODE-BLOCK-END */
&ANALYZE-RESUME

&UNDEFINE SELF-NAME

&ANALYZE-SUSPEND _UIB-CODE-BLOCK _CUSTOM _MAIN-BLOCK f

/* *****************  Main Block  ******************* */

/* Parent the dialog-box to the ACTIVE-WINDOW.  */
IF VALID-HANDLE(ACTIVE-WINDOW) AND
   FRAME {&FRAME-NAME}:PARENT eq ?
THEN FRAME {&FRAME-NAME}:PARENT = ACTIVE-WINDOW.

/* Get the instance attributes from the object. */
RUN get-attribute-list IN ph_SMO (OUTPUT attr-list).

/* Now enable the interface and wait for the exit condition. */
MAIN-BLOCK:
DO ON ERROR   UNDO MAIN-BLOCK, LEAVE MAIN-BLOCK
   ON END-KEY UNDO MAIN-BLOCK, LEAVE MAIN-BLOCK:
  RUN set-up.
  RUN adecomm/_setcurs.p ('':U).
  WAIT-FOR GO OF FRAME {&FRAME-NAME}.

  /* Set the values in the object. NOTE: this will not,
     by default, cause the object to rebuild itself. */
  ASSIGN attr-list.
  RUN set-attribute-list IN ph_SMO (INPUT attr-list).
  /* Reinitialize the object - this will rebuild it based
     on the new attribute values. */
  RUN dispatch IN ph_SMO ('initialize':U).
END.

/* _UIB-CODE-BLOCK-END */
&ANALYZE-RESUME

/* **************  Internal Procedures  ************** */

&ANALYZE-SUSPEND _UIB-CODE-BLOCK _PROCEDURE set-up f
```

```
PROCEDURE set-up :
/*----------------------------------------------------
  Purpose:     setup the User Interface
  Parameters:  <none>
  Notes:       Here we display/view/enable the widgets in
               the user-interface.
-----------------------------------------------------*/
  DISPLAY attr-list WITH FRAME f.
  ENABLE Btn_OK attr-list Btn_Cancel Btn_Help
      WITH FRAME f.
END PROCEDURE.

/* _UIB-CODE-BLOCK-END */
&ANALYZE-RESUME
```

When this file is opened by the UIB, it is divided into two separate streams. The first stream is the code that the ANALYZER should look at. It is a collection of all the lines that are not in an &ANALYZE-SUSPEND block. The mechanical stripping out of the &ANALYZE-SUSPEND blocks leaves a very unusual looking file, containing lots of blank lines and comments that seem out of place. However, this file is only used by the ANALYZER itself. The important lines are those that define the frames in the file. These lines are present in this first stream.

```
&Scoped-define WINDOW-NAME CURRENT-WINDOW
&Scoped-define FRAME-NAME F




/* **************  Control Definitions  ************* */

/* Define a dialog box                                */
DEFINE BUTTON Btn_Cancel AUTO-END-KEY
     LABEL "Cancel"
     SIZE 12 BY 1.08
     BGCOLOR 8 .

DEFINE BUTTON Btn_OK AUTO-GO
     LABEL "OK"
     SIZE 12 BY 1.08
     BGCOLOR 8 .

DEFINE VARIABLE attr-list AS CHARACTER
     VIEW-AS EDITOR NO-WORD-WRAP
     SCROLLBAR-HORIZONTAL SCROLLBAR-VERTICAL
     SIZE 49 BY 8.5 NO-UNDO.


/* ****************  Frame Definitions  *************** */

DEFINE FRAME f
     Btn_OK AT ROW 1.38 COL 52
     attr-list AT ROW 1.5 COL 2 NO-LABEL
     Btn_Cancel AT ROW 2.69 COL 52
     SPACE(1.13) SKIP(4.72)
```

```
    WITH VIEW-AS DIALOG-BOX KEEP-TAB-ORDER
         SIDE-LABELS NO-UNDERLINE THREE-D  SCROLLABLE
         TITLE "Instance Attributes"
         CANCEL-BUTTON Btn_Cancel.


/* *************** Procedure Settings **************** */


/* ******  Runtime Attributes and UIB Settings  ****** */


/* ****************  Control Triggers  **************** */

&Scoped-define SELF-NAME f

&UNDEFINE SELF-NAME


/* **************  Internal Procedures  ************** */
```

You will note that this subset of the file effectively contains only the DEFINE VARIABLE and the DEFINE FRAME statements (as well as miscellaneous comments and preprocessor lines). This is the part that is compiled into the static frame layout.

This frame layout information must be a valid PROGRESS file all by itself. It must compile without any errors. The ANALYZER is a subset of the COMPILER. If it contained a compiler error, the ANALYZER would not be able to parse it, and the file could not be loaded into the UIB.

A general issue here is that the ANALYZER really has no knowledge of any of the code blocks that you write in the UIB's Code Section Editor. This is why you cannot use variables (or temp-tables or buffers) that you define in the Definitions Section as objects in the frame layouts. The ANALYZER would not be able to compile the references to variables in the DEFINE FRAME statement and the file will not load into the UIB.

Remember that the ANALYZER created two streams. The first stream stripped out the &ANALYZE-SUSPEND/&ANALYZE-RESUME blocks. The second stream contains only these blocks.There are two broad classes of these &ANALYZE-SUSPEND blocks.

- There are blocks that you enter through the Code Section Editor that contain your own application code. These are identified by the second token on the &ANALYZE-SUSPEND statement. These are the _UIB-CODE-BLOCK sections. They are read into the UIB verbatim when a .w file is opened.
- All other blocks are created by the UIB. They hold either run-time code, preprocessor definitions, or comments that the UIB needs to read in order to recreate the file when it is opened. These sections will be parsed by the UIB. They should never be changed by a developer outside the UIB.

There is also a class of XFTR (Extended Feature) sections that the UIB supports. XFTRs allow you to add your own code generation capability to a .w file. XFTRs are covered in Chapter 19, "Using Active Templates."

Tip

If you have to edit a UIB-generated file in a simple text editor, limit your changes to sections that you could have edited in the Code Section Editor.

Almost any section starting with &ANALYZE-SUSPEND _UIB-CODE-BLOCK ...
and ending with

```
/* _UIB-CODE-BLOCK-END */
&ANALYZE-RESUME
```

is safe to edit in any editor. This includes the Definition section, the Main Code Block, and all triggers and user-defined procedures.

(The exception to this are the UIB-maintained internal procedures, such as *enable_UI,* or *adm-create-objects*. Changes made to these sections will be lost when the UIB reads in the file.)

Occasionally you may want to edit other sections of a .w file in a text editor. Perhaps you want to generalize the file with preprocessor variables that add or remove sections of the layout, or which define standards. However, if you make edits outside the _UIB-CODE-BLOCK sections, your changes will be lost if you ever bring the file back into the UIB.

Tip

If you do make changes in non-standard sections of the file you should remove the first line of the file as well:

```
&ANALYZE-SUSPEND VERSION-NUMBER UIB_v8r1 GUI
```

Removing this line will tell the UIB not to try to read this file. If you try to open the file in the UIB, the UIB will offer to open it in a Procedure Window instead.

Types of &ANALYZE-SUSPEND Sections

As you look through a .w file, you will see that there are many types of &ANALYZE-SUSPEND sections. Each type of section is identified by the second token on the &ANALYZE-SUSPEND line. For example:

```
&ANALYZE-SUSPEND _RUN-TIME-ATTRIBUTES
```

or

```
&ANALYZE-SUSPEND _UIB-CODE-BLOCK _CONTROL btn-ok f-dialog
```

or

```
&ANALYZE-SUSPEND _PROCEDURE-SETTINGS
```

Each of these sections is read and parsed individually by the UIB when a file is opened. The major sections are:

`&ANALYZE-SUSPEND _VERSION-NUMBER`
This section denotes the version of the UIB that last generated and saved the .w file. The version number is also used internally to provide compatibility, when possible, and when not possible, used to trigger any appropriate warning messages. It is suggested that you not edit this version number manually.

`&ANALYZE-SUSPEND _UIB-PREPROCESSOR-BLOCK`
The preprocessor section is the place in which the UIB writes out all of the preprocessors it generates. This section cannot be edited by hand since it is regenerated each time the file is saved. A list of preprocessors generated by the UIB can be seen clicking Preprocessor Name in the Section Editor's pop-up menu. This section is mostly generated from data stored elsewhere in the .w file, however, it is read for the ADM Supported SmartLinks, and the names of the Custom Lists.

`&ANALYZE-SUSPEND _CREATE-DYNAMIC`
Creates the containers needed for VBX controls.

`&ANALYZE-SUSPEND _CREATE-WINDOW`
Defined the attributes for the `WINDOW` object. This section does not appear if the UIB defines a dialog-box.

`&ANALYZE-SUSPEND _PROCEDURE-SETTINGS`
This section is pure comment. It stores the information displayed in the Procedure Settings dialog box within the UIB.

`&ANALYZE-SUSPEND _RUN-TIME-ATTRIBUTES`
One of the most important sections is the `RUN-TIME-ATTRIBUTES` section. This block stores attributes that have been set for each individual object in its property sheet. The comments in this section are just as important as the run-time assignment statements. Both are needed for the UIB to be able to reconstruct a .w file.

`&ANALYZE-SUSPEND _QUERY-BLOCK`
A `QUERY-BLOCK` is created to store all the data needed by the Query Builder. There is generally one query block for each `QUERY`, `BROWSE`, and `FRAME` in your application.

`&ANALYZE-SUSPEND _UIB-CODE-BLOCK`
All code entered through the Section Editor is stored as UIB Code Blocks. This includes the Definition Section, Main Code Block, Triggers and Procedures. These sections are read in line-by-line and stored in the UIB. These are the only sections that it is safe to change outside the UIB.

Types of _UIB-CODE-BLOCK Sections

There are four distinct types of _UIB-CODE-BLOCK sections:

- *Definitions Section.* The definitions section is accessed through the Section Editor. This is a area in which you should place any header information or standard comments and definitions for all of your globally accessed variables (explicitly written or via include files), parameters (INPUT, OUTPUT, INPUT-OUTPUT) and temp-tables. You may also insert code here which needs to be performed this early in the program.
- *Control Definitions Section.* The control definitions section is where the definitions of all the user-interface objects drawn in the UIB are written. This section cannot be edited by hand.
- *Main Block Section.* The main block section is the section of code which typically gets executed before the WAIT-FOR statement. Some defaults are generated by the UIB for the purposes of initializing and terminating the procedure. This code can be edited directly in the Section Editor.
- *Internal Procedures Section.* The internal procedures section is the section of the .w file which the UIB writes out all of the internal procedure defined in the procedure. Three in particular are generated automatically by the UIB. They are as follows:

```
enable_UI
```

This is the default enabling procedure used by the UIB's default code in the Main Block section. This internal procedure does the following:

1. Displays objects that are defined to be displayed in the object's property sheet.
2. Enables objects that are defined to be enabled in the object's property sheet.
3. Opens any queries that are defined to be automatically opened.

```
disable_UI
```

This is the default disabling procedure used by the UIB's default code in the Main Block section. This internal procedure does the following:

1. Deletes the window created in the procedure.
2. Deletes the procedure if the procedure was RUN PERSISTENT.

```
Control_Load
```

This internal procedure is generated by the UIB when you add one or more VBX's to your procedure. The purpose of this procedure is to handle the instantiation of the VBX's as well as to load in their attribute settings from the .wbx file associated with the .w file.

Settings for Template .w Files

The procedure settings section is where the settings of a procedure are stored. These settings generally are those chosen in the procedures Advanced Procedure Settings dialog box.

The Advanced Procedure Settings dialog box is only available to a procedure if it is a template. For a .w file to be a template, the word `Template` must be specified on the line marked `Type:` as shown below.

```
/* ********************* Procedure Settings ********************** */

   &ANALYZE-SUSPEND _PROCEDURE-SETTINGS
   /* Settings for THIS-PROCEDURE
      Type: SmartWindow Template
      Allow: Basic,Browse,DB-Fields,Query,Smart,Window
    */
   &ANALYZE-RESUME _END-PROCEDURE-SETTINGS
```

Tip

The UIB does not support changing a .w file into a template. However, if you want to do this, you can edit the source file by hand and type the word **template** next to the procedure type in the Procedure Settings section.

There are really very few differences between how the UIB deals with a Template .w file, as compared to a normal .w file.

- Templates allow you to access the Advanced Procedure Settings dialog box.
- Templates never display their Cue Cards or Wizards when opened in the UIB.
- Templates are never compiled when they are saved.

APPENDIX G

Contents of CD

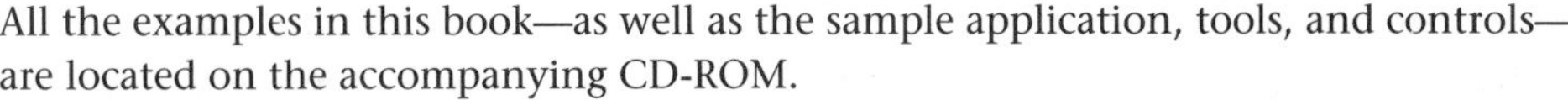

All the examples in this book—as well as the sample application, tools, and controls—are located on the accompanying CD-ROM.

You will also find a few surprises located in different directories on the CD-ROM.

Table G.1 Directories within CD-ROM

Directory	Description
\	Root directory of Special Edition CD-ROM
examples\	Source directory for all examples code introduced in each chapter
chap-nn	"nn" represents the chapter number
movies	All the Voice-Of-Experience movies
partners	Root level for all Partner documents and software
samples\	Miscellaneous code samples
ed4win	Ed For Windows text editor demo
forehelp	ForeHelp Windows help authoring tools demo
image	Various image files
kbase	The PROGRESS Knowledge Base
sound	Various sound files
source	Various PROGRESS code samples
se-pro8	Root directory of Special Edition Tools
utils\	Root level for various utilities
vfw	Video for Windows Drivers
vbx\	Root level for Visual Basic Controls
crescent	Crescent Software controls
graph	Matrix Link control
msgfilte	Maximized Software control

CD-ROM Installation

There are no special instructions for installing any of the example software from the CD-ROM. Since the CD is organized by chapter, you might want to just copy the appropriate files for each chapter over to your working directory as you read through the text.

Add-On Directory (\SE-PRO8)

Many of the programs and routines discussed in this book augment the standard PROGRESS Version 8 tools.

These files are stored in the directory \se-pro8 on the CD-ROM.

If you copy this directory onto your local drive and place it in your PROPATH (ahead of the standard C:\DLC, and C:\DLC\GUI), then you'll be able to take advantage of the various enhancements to the PROGRESS tool set.

The directory structure is shown in Table G.2.

Table G.2 Directories in SE*Tools

Directory	Description
se-pro8\	Root directory of Special Edition Tools
adeuib	Replacements and enhancements to UIB
adecomm	Replacements and enhancements to ADE Common
image	Special bitmaps and images
se-adm\	Special Edition add-ons to the standard ADM directory
se-adm\objects	Support files for the ADM extensions
se-adm\support	Support files for the ADM extensions
se-tools	Additional Special Edition Tools (SE*Tools) that add to the PRO*Tools palette
src\	Source directory for all the files. This directory contains all the source files for the SE-Pro8 directory.

Most files are included in directories as source sode and compiled r-code.

There is one routine in this directory that lets you set up all the PRO*Tool add-ons. This file is se-setup.w.

After you have copied the se-pro8 directory to your local hard disk, you will need to run se-setup.w and then restart PROGRESS before all the changes will take effect.

Installation Process

To install the *Special Edition PROGRESS V8* tools, follow these steps:

1. Create an SE-PRO8 directory on your hard drive.

   ```
   mkdir c:\SE-PRO8
   ```

2. Change into that directory.

   ```
   cd c:\SE-PRO8
   ```

3. Copy the SE-PRO8 from the CD-ROM onto your hard drive.

   ```
   xcopy d:\se-pro8\*.* c: /s
   ```

4. Start the PROGRESS Desktop. From there, start PRO*Tools.
5. Add the SE-PRO8 directory to your PROPATH in front of %DLC%/GUI. Save the PROPATH setting or you will lose access to SE*Tools when you next start up PROGRESS.
6. Use the RUN applet in PRO*Tools to run se-setup.w. This file should be in your PROPATH, thanks to the previous step.
7. Set the desired defaults, as shown in figure G.1.
8. Click OK.

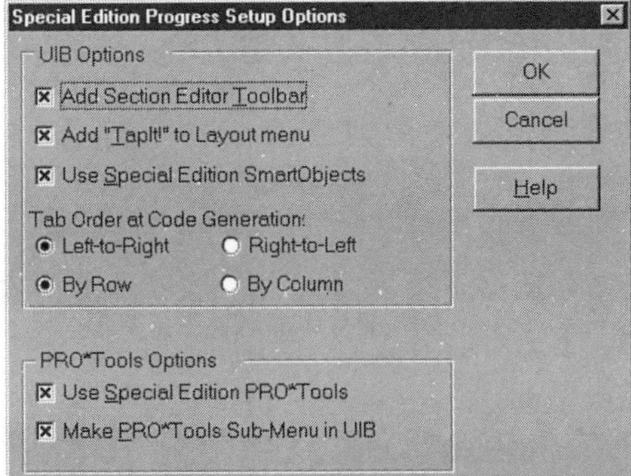

Fig. G.1

*Suggested settings for SE*Tools are set by running the setup file se-setup.w.*

When you restart PROGRESS, you will have all the Special Edition Tools available in the User Interface Builder. If you ever want to change the installed SE*Tools, simply run se-setup.w again.

Contents of SE-Pro8 Root Directory

SE-PRO8 is the root directory. It must be included in your PROPATH *ahead* of the PROGRESS DLC and DLC/GUI directories.

SE-Pro8/SE-SETUP.W

This file brings up a property sheet that shows all the options for SE*Tools. You should run this file to setup the SE*Tools options you wish to use (see fig. G.1).

Contents of SE-Pro8/ADEUIB Directory

This directory replaces some of the standard UIB routines, and adds new routines as well.

SE-Pro8/ADEUIB/_PRVW4GL.P

This is the replacement for the UIB's Code Preview property sheet. Instead of a property sheet, this replacement copies the preview code into a preview file, preview.p. This is then displayed in a Procedure Window.

There are two major advantages to this replacement routine:

- Because it is not a property sheet, you can keep the preview code visible while you cut and paste into the Section Editor.
- You can use all standard editor functions in the window, including Search and Save As.

The disadvantages include the following:

- You can change the file in the UIB and the preview window *won't* change.
- You can edit the preview file and the UIB won't be able to read those changes.

Contents of SE-Pro8/ADECOMM Directory

This directory replaces some of the standard ADE common routines. In particular, it watches the startup of the UIB and Code Section Editor and modifies these tools.

SE-Pro8/ADECOMM/_ADEEVNT.P

This file augments the standard ADE event handler, `_adeevnt.p`. The first time this file is called, it searches for the standard `adecomm/_adeevnt.p` in the rest of the PROPATH. This is stored in the NEW GLOBAL variable, `q_old_adevent`. All calls to the replacement `_adeevnt.p` are handled by the new routine, and then passed onto the old one.

There are two events handled by the replacement `_adeevnt.p`:

- *Section Editor Startup*. This calls SE-tools/_sestrt.p which adds a Toolbar to the Section Editor.
- *UIB Startup*. This calls SE-tools/_uibstrt.p, which adds the TapIt! tool to the UIB.

Contents of SE-Pro8/SE-ADM Directory

This directory contains the code for various enhancements to ADM objects.

SE-Pro8/SE-ADM/OBJECTS

This directory contains the extended versions of the standard PROGRESS SmartPanel and SmartFolder.

The SmartFolder, folderx.w, is self-adjusting when drawn in the UIB. The number of pages in the folder is initialized based on the size of the folder drawn in the UIB.

The SmartPanels are designed to check the PROGRESS.INI file for standard attributes. The attributes checked are all in a `[SmartPanel]` section, as follows:

```
[SmartPanel]
Edge-Pixels = 0
AddFunction = One-Record
Right-to-Left = First-on-Left
```

Contents of SE-Pro8/SE-Tools Directory

This directory contains the code for various new features that can be added to the PROGRESS environment.

SE-Pro8/SE-Tools/_TAPIT.W

This file brings up a window that lets you nudge selected objects in the UIB. All selected UIB widgets can be moved up, down, left, or right (in pixel increments).

This procedure is called from the Layout, Tapit! menu on the UIB's Main window. This menu item is added by se-tools/_uibstrt.p depending on the `UIBAddTapitMenu` `KEY-VALUE` in your PROGRESS.INI file.

```
[SE*Tools]
UIBAddTapItMenu = YES
```

SE-Pro8/SE-Tools/_PER-RUN.P

This file is needed to run PRO*Tools applets persistently from menu items created in setools/_pt-subm.p.

SE-Pro8/SE-Tools/PROTOOLS.DAT

A replacement file for the default PROTOOLS.DAT. This file lists all the default tools plus some extra applets supplied in SE-Tools.

SE-Pro8/SE-Tools/_PT-SUBM.P

This file reads the PRO*Tools data file and creates a submenu under the UIB's Tools menu where each PRO*Tool applet is an individual menu item.

This routine allows you to have direct access to all PRO*Tools from the UIB Main menu.

This submenu is only created if the PROGRESS.INI file contains:

```
[QUE*Tools]
UIBAddPROToolsMenu = YES
```

SE-Pro8/SE-Tools/_PLAYVOE.P

This program plays the Voice-Of-Experience movies from PRO*Tools.

SE-Pro8/SE-Tools/SE-V8.CST

This file adds some new items to the UIB's Object Palette and the File/New property sheet in the UIB.

SE-Pro8/SE-Tools/_SESTRT.P

This file rearranges some of the existing objects in the UIB's Code Section Editor and creates many new buttons that give you shortcut access to the Section Editor's functions.

The toolbar is only created if there is a startup KEY-VALUE in your PROGRESS.INI file.

```
[SE*Tools]
UIBSectionEditorToolbar = YES
```

SE-Pro8/SE-Tools/_UIBSTRT.P

This file adds some menu items to the UIB's menu bar, including:

- Layout, Tapit! Window
- Tools, PRO*Tools becomes a Sub-menu listing all PRO*Tools.

Voice-of-Experience Movies (\MOVIES)

There is a subdirectory on the CD devoted to the Voice-Of-Experience movies that accompany the text of the book. These movies denoted by the icon to the left are guides to many of the examples presented in the text.

To fully appreciate the movies, you should have a sound card installed in your computer. The movies not only show, in easy-to-follow steps, how to complete a particular task, they also *talk* you through each task.

The voices on the movies are those of the authors, so you will be able to easily follow along as if each author is sitting next to you and your computer.

If you don't have sound capabilities on your computer. You will still be able to see how easy it is to create applications using PROGRESS V8.

All of the Voice-Of-Experience movies are located in the \MOVIES subdirectory. They are Windows video files (.AVI) that can be played from PRO*Tools using the VOE Player. You can also run them directly using the Windows Media Player.

> **Note**
>
> If you are running under Windows 3.x you will need to install the Video For Windows Runtime drivers. See "Installing Video for Windows" at the end of this appendix.

To save hard drive space, you can play each movie directly from the CD-ROM.

The list of Voice-Of-Experience movies is shown in Table G.3.

Table G.3 Voice-Of-Experience Movies

V-O-E Movie	Description/Speaker
	Chapter 2: Getting Started with ADE Tools **Speaker: Steven Feinstein**
CH02-001.avi	Tour of ADE development tools
	Chapter 3: *Using ADE End-User Tools* **Speaker: Steven Feinstein**
CH03-001.avi	Tour of ADE end-user tools
	Chapter 4: *Introducing PROGRESS Language* **Speaker: George Kassabgi**
CH04-001.avi	4GL language examples
	Chapter 5: Further Exploration: *Locking, Transactions,* and VBXs **Speaker: *David Lee***
CH05-001.avi	VBX integration examples
	Chapter 6: *Utilizing Component-Based Development* **Speaker: *Gerry Seidl***
CH06-001.avi	Creating a SmartViewer
CH06-002.avi	Creating a SmartBrowser
CH06-003.avi	Creating a SmartQuery
CH06-004.avi	Assembling a working SmartWindow
CH06-005.avi	Defining External Tables for a SmartObject
	Chapter 7: *SmartObject Links and Messages* **Speaker: *George Kassabgi***
CH07-001.avi	PROGRESS SmartObjects linking and messaging
	Chapter 8: *SmartObject Internals* **Speaker: *George Kassabgi***
CH08-001.avi	PROGRESS SmartObjects anatomy tour

(continues)

Table G.3 Continued	
V-O-E Movie	**Description/Speaker**
	Chapter 9: *A Sample GUI Application* **Speaker: *George Kassabgi***
CH09-001.avi	Sample application PROGRESS SmartObjects
	Chapter 10: *Connecting the Components* **Speaker: *George Kassabgi***
CH10-001.avi	Connecting sample application PROGRESS SmartObjects
	Chapter 11: *Adding Menu Bar and Report Components* **Speaker: *Bill Wood***
Ch11-001.avi	Adding a Menu Bar to the Sample Application
Ch11-002.avi	Creating the Welcome "Splash" Screen in the Sample Application
Ch11-003.avi	Adding a TIMER VBX to the Welcome Screen
Ch11-004.avi	Creating a Search Dialog in the Sample Application
Ch11-005.avi	Report Builder: Creating the *Customer Address* Report
Ch11-006.avi	Report Builder: Adding a Calculated Field to the Customer Address Report
Ch11-007.avi	Report Builder: Creating the Orders by Customer Report
	Chapter 16: *Preparing for Translation* **Speaker: *Michael Jannery***
CH16-001.avi	Opening a new project, adding procedures, extracting phrases and doing the filters
CH16-002.avi	Adding a glossary, building a kit
	Chapter 17: *Translating Your Application* **Speaker: *Michael Jannery***
CH17-001.avi	Opening a kit, adding a custom glossary, visual translation
CH17-002.avi	Re-ordering, re-sorting browser, edit mode translations, statistics and closing kit
CH17-003.avi	Consolidating kit, build-compile, build-run in two languages translating in edit mode

V-O-E Movie	Description/Speaker
	Chapter 19: *Using Active Templates* **Speaker: *Gerry Seidl***
CH19-001.avi	Turning Cue Cards Off/On in the UIB
CH19-002.avi	How to write and use an XFTR
	Chapter 20: *Extending the Development Tools* **Speakers: *Bill Wood* (1-4) and *Gerry Seidl* (5-10)**
Ch20-001.avi	Enhancing SmartObjects: A Simple Instance Wizard
Ch20-002.avi	Enhancing SmartObjects: Reading Default Attributes from progress.ini
Ch20-003.avi	Enhancing SmartObjects: A Self-initializing SmartFolder
Ch20-004.avi	Creating a Simple Instance Attribute
CH20-005.avi	Adding a custom entry to the Object Palette
CH20-006.avi	Adding a new icon to the Object Palette
CH20-007.avi	Adding a template to the NEW dialog/pop-up menu
CH20-008.avi	Adding a program to PRO*Tools
CH20-009.avi	A tour of the Object Palette
CH20-010.avi	Using the PRO*Tools Presistent Object Viewer to test SmartObject behavior
	Chapter 21: *Making the Most of the Application Component Environment* **Speakers: *Bill Wood* (1-8) and *David Lee* (9)**
Ch21-001.avi	Replacing the UIB's Code Preview Dialog (using `adecomm/pwmain.p`)
Ch21-002.avi	Creating a Segmented Status Bar (using `adecomm/_status.p`)
Ch21-003.avi	Adding Trigger Code Outside the `DO:...END`. Block
Ch21-004.avi	Enhancing SmartBrowsers: Adding Search Filters
Ch21-005.avi	Enhancing SmartBrowsers: Adding Sort-By Options
Ch21-006.avi	Creating Your Own Method Library (filter.i)
Ch21-007.avi	Creating A New SmartObject Class: `SimpleObject`
Ch21-008.avi	Changing the Default File Name for a SmartObjectTemplate
Ch21-009.avi	Adding VBX Controls in a SmartViewer

(continues)

Table G.3 Continued

V-O-E Movie	Description/Speaker
	Chapter 22: *PROGRESS Programming Tips* **Speaker: *Bill Wood***
Ch22-001.avi	Adding Right-Labels to a SmartViewer (`rlabel.p`)
Ch22-002.avi	Adding Top Labels in a SmartViewer (`tlablel.p`)
Ch22-003.avi	Resizing a Frame and its Children (`frm-size.p`)
Ch22-004.avi	Changing `progress.ini` Fonts for Windows 95

> **Note**
>
> Once the movie is running, you can control the playback of each Voice-Of-Experience movie by using the VCR-type buttons on the media player.

PROGRESS Knowledge Base (\SAMPLES\KBASE)

The PROGRESS Knowledge Base (PKB) is an up-to-date technical reference database providing customers with immediate access to information on known solutions to problems, error message explanation, and other related facts. The PKB is derived from experiences of Progress Software Corporation's worldwide technical support engineers, developers, and application partners. The PKB offers full featured query, search, and data retrieval functionality.

We are offering an initial version of the PROGRESS Knowledge Base on the CD-ROM. Contact Progress Software Corporation for the fully supported and updated version of the PROGRESS Knowledge Base. In the \SAMPLES\KBASE subdirectory you will find a README.TXT file with complete installation instructions.

Included VBXs (\VBX)

PROGRESS V8 supports the integration of Visual Basic custom controls. We are including four controls on the CD-ROM:

- CSCALDMO.VBX
- CSMTRDMO.VBX
- GRAPHX.VBX
- MSGFILTE.VBX

CSCALDMO.VBX (\VBX\CRESCENT)

This is a pop-up calendar that can be used to graphically select and/or display dates. You can move through the dates using either the built-in scroll bar or the keyboard. Set the `GetArrows` property to `True` to navigate using the keyboard.

CSMTRDMO.VBX (\VBX\CRESCENT)

This is a range bar that can be used to graphically show percentages or numerical values in a horizontal or vertical bar. You can easily change the direction of the bar using the `FillType` property.

These files (CSCALDMO.VBX & CSMTRDMO.VBX), along with their associated license file (QP4SPEC1.LIC), are located in the \VBX\CRESCENT subdirectory on the CD-ROM. To use the VBXs, you will need to copy all of the files to your \WINDOWS\SYSTEM directory. These VBXs are fully functional, but are not fully licensed. They have special splash-screens that appear during design mode.

To order Crescent products, or for more information, please contact the Crescent Division of Progress Software Corporation:

Telephone: 800-35BASIC (22742) between 8 a.m. and 8 p.m. (EST)

International callers: 617-280-3000

Fax: 617-280-4025 (to the attention of "Crescent Sales")

CompuServe: 70662,2605

Internet address: crescent@progress.com

Home Page: http://www.progress.com/crescent/

Bulletin Board System: 617-280-4221

CompuServe Windows Components Forum A: simply type **GO COMPA**

Mailing Address: Crescent Division of Progress Software, 14 Oak Park, Bedford, MA 01730 USA

GRAPHX.VBX (\VBX\GRAPH)

This is a graphing control that can be used to integrate many popular graphs, including pie and bar, into your PROGRESS applications.

The \VBX\GRAPH subdirectory has sample code and a README.WRI file that includes full installation instructions.

For further information, contact:

Matrix Link Limited
Unit 7, Fellgate Court, Newcastle, Staffs, ST5 2UA, UK
Telephone: +44-1782-715716
Fax: +44-1782-715717
E-Mail: Sales@matrixlk.demon.co.uk

MSGFILTE.VBX (\VBX\MSGFILTE)

This is a control that allows you to trap WINDOWS messages that are being sent to a PROGRESS application window. As an example, you can use such a control to implement a drag-and-drop of files from the file manager into a PROGRESS window or even use it to watch for incoming email.

The \VBX\MSGFILTE subdirectory has a drag-and-drop example and a README.TXT file that includes control properties and installation instructions.

For further information, contact:

Maximized Software, Inc.
18195 McDurmott, Suite A
Irvine, CA 92714
Telephone: 714.955.5800
Fax: 714.955.5801
info@maximized.com
http://maximized.com/

Progress Software's Application Partner Forum

In 1994, more than $1 Billion USD of Progress-based applications were sold worldwide. Most of that success is attributed to Progress Software's Application Partners.

In the subdirectory \PARTNERS you will find dedicated subdirectories for a sampling of the Progress Software's Application Partner community. Inside each subdirectory you will find a document file (for example, README.TXT or README.DOC) that will provide more information about the Partner and files in each subdirectory.

Banking Information Systems, Ltd. (\PARTNER\BIS)

Banking Information Systems, Ltd.
Moscow 105318
PO Box 89, Sherbakovskaya 3, Suite 401
Telephone: +7 095 369 9724
Fax: +7 095 369 6310
info@bis.msk.su
http://www.demos.su/firms/bis/bis.html

Bradley Ward Systems, Inc. (\PARTNER\BWI)

Bradley Ward Systems, Inc.
750 Hammond Drive
Building 10, Suite 200
Atlanta, GA 30328
Telephone: 404.256.4855
Fax: 404.256.1871

Center for Human Drug Research (\PARTNER\CHDR)

Centre for Human Drug Research
Zernikedreef 10
2333 CL Leiden, The Netherlands
Telephone: +31.71.246416
Fax: +31.71.246499
promasys@chdr.leidenuniv.nl

Computer Applications Ltd, (\PARTNER\CAL)

Computer Applications Ltd,
Rivington House, Drumhead Road,
Chorley, PR6 7BX, UK.
Telephone: +44 1257 231011
Fax: +44 1257 230927
mike@calnet.demon.co.uk

Ethitec (\PARTNER\ETHITEC)

Ethitec
37 MILLSTONE LANE, LEICESTER, LE1 5JN, ENGLAND
Telephone: (0044) 116 247 0806
Fax: (0044) 116 254 4172
simonw@ethitec.demon.co.uk

House of Speed, Ltd. (\PARTNER\SPEED)

House of Speed, Ltd.
Hawes Hill Court
Drift Road
Winkfield Windsor
Berkshire SL4 4QQ, UK

Lyons Computer PTY, Ltd. (\PARTNER\LYONS)

Lyons Computer PTY, Ltd.
Unit 8, 31 Black Street
Milton QLD 4064
Telephone: (07) 367 1533
Fax: (07) 367 1538
nerida@lyons.oz.au

MDA Computing (\PARTNER\MDA)

MDA Computing
Amy Johnson House
15 Cherry Orchard Road
Croydon, CR9 6BB,UK.
Telephone: 0181 680 1677,
Fax: 0181 760 0023,
100302.3640@compuserve.com

Minerva Industrial Systems plc (\PARTNER\MINERVA)

Minerva Industrial Systems plc,
Bovis House, Lansdown Road UK
Cheltenham, GL50 2JA.
Telephone: +44 (0) 1242 242566
Fax: +44 (0) 1242 236107

Mycor, Inc. (\PARTNER\MYCOR)

Mycor, Inc.
23 Vreeland Road
Florham Park, NJ 07932
Telephone: 201.301.0600 or 1.800.MYCOR-GL

North Coast Systems, Inc. (\PARTNER\NCS)

North Coast Systems, Inc.
P. O. Box 299
The Sea Ranch, CA 95497
Telephone: (707)785-3948 or (408)374-3404
Fax: (800)230-8574
wpm@mcn.org

Office Automation Consultants, Inc. (\PARTNER\OAC)

Office Automation Consultants, Inc.
1101 Veterans Blvd., Suite 4
Kenner, LA 70062-5221
Telephone: 504.467.8000
Fax: 504.469.3690

POSability Systems, Inc. (\PARTNER\POS)

POSability Systems, Inc.
4020 N. MacArthur
Suite 122-232
Irving, TX 75038
Telephone: 214.444.9777
Fax: 214.401.0675
72633.3664@compuserve.com

Professional Computer Consulting, Inc. (\PARTNER\PROGTOOL)

Professional Computer Consulting, Inc.
13600 Roanoke St.
Davie, FL 33325
Telephone: 800.738.4426 or 954.424.9569
Fax: 800.424.9395 or 954.424.9395
ProgTools@aol.com
http://emory.com/~emory/progress/progress.html

Progressive Consultants, Inc. (\PARTNER\PCI)

Progressive Consultants, Inc.
8027 Leesburg Pike
Suite 403
Vienna, VA 22182-2710
Telephone: 703.790.9316
Fax: 703.790.9248
pci-net@ix.netcom.com

RJW Services, Ltd. (\PARTNER\RJW)

RJW Services, Ltd.
9, Castle Street
ForFar, Angus DD8 3AE
Telephone: 0307-461000
Fax: 0307-461100

Source One Unlimited (\PARTNER\SOURCE1)

Source One Unlimited
Computer Consultants
4421 Othello Drive
Fremont, CA 94555
Telephone: 510.797.0821
Fax: 510.797.4186
gsingh@infolane.com

Systemcare, Ltd (\PARTNER\MFOUR)

Systemcare Limited
10 Belasis Court
Belasis Hall Technology Park
Billingham Cleveland TS23 4AZ
Telephone: +44 (0)1642-370326
Fax: +44 (0)1642-370412

Total Systems plc (\PARTNER\TOTALSYS)

Total Systems plc
394 City Road
London EC1V 2QA UK
Telephone: 0171 837 2844
Fax: 0171 837 0452
totalsys@dircon.co.uk

Walker Martyn Software, Ltd. (\PARTNER\WALKER)

Walker Martyn Software, Ltd.
1 Park Circus Place
Glasgow
G3 6AU
Telephone: +44 141 332 7999
Fax: +44 141 331 2820
sales@walkermartyn.co.uk

ForeHelp (\SAMPLES\FOREHELP)

ForeHelp provides advanced help authoring tools for windows. The CD-ROM includes a demo version of the system.

The demo software is fully functional, so you can try out all the ForeHelp features. Excluded are the spelling dictionary and thesaurus. You are limited to 10 topics when creating projects.

Help files are also included for more information on ForeHelp and its add-on products (FOREINFO.HLP) and international distributors (DISTRIBS.HLP). You can run the help files directly from your CD-ROM drive, or copy the .hlp files—along with the .DLL files—to a local directory to run.

For more information contact:,

ForeFront, Inc.
4710 Table Mesa Drive Suite B
Boulder, CO 80303
Telephone: 303-499-9181
Fax: 303-494-5446

Ed For Windows (\SAMPLES\ED4WIN)

Ed For Windows is an intelligent, language-sensitive editing tool. You will find that Ed For Windows had been customized to understand the PROGRESS environment. One nice feature in particular is the color-coded highlighting of PROGRESS keywords.

To install the demo version of ED For Windows run the INSTALL.EXE procedure that is located in \SAMPLES\ED4WIN.

For more information contact:,

Soft As It Gets P/L
12 Fairview Grove
Glen Iris, 3146
Victoria, Australia
Telephone: +61 3 885 4445
Fax: +61 3 885 4444
E-mail: saig@ozemail.com.au

Installing Video for Windows (\UTILS\VFW)

To play Voice-of-Experience movies on your Windows 3.x system, you must install the VfW runtime library. The installation will require a few changes to your Windows .INI files, and will install an updated version of the Windows Media Player.

To install the VfW run-time library, follow these steps:

1. Open the Program Manager and choose File, Run.
2. Use the Browse dialog box to locate SETUP.EXE in the subdirectory \UTILS\VFW.
3. Click OK.

The runtime libraries will be installed in your \WINDOWS\SYSTEM directory. To activate the VfW drivers, you must restart Windows.

Index

Symbols

A

D

E

F

J

K

L

M

N

O

Q

R

S

T

U

V

X

Y

Z

PLUG YOURSELF INTO...

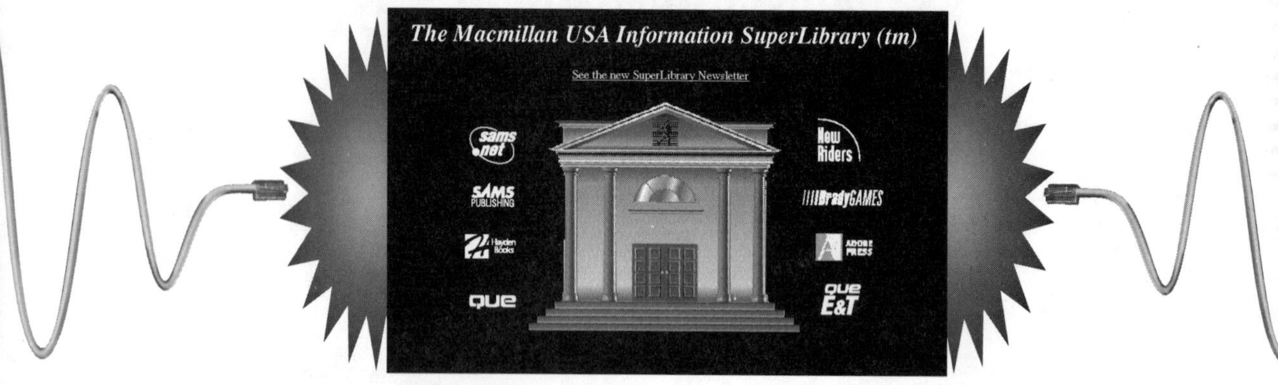

THE MACMILLAN INFORMATION SUPERLIBRARY™

Free information and vast computer resources from the world's leading computer book publisher—online!

FIND THE BOOKS THAT ARE RIGHT FOR YOU!

A complete online catalog, plus sample chapters and tables of contents!

- STAY INFORMED with the latest computer industry news through our online newsletter, press releases, and customized Information SuperLibrary Reports.
- GET FAST ANSWERS to your questions about QUE books.
- VISIT our online bookstore for the latest information and editions!
- COMMUNICATE with our expert authors through e-mail and conferences.
- DOWNLOAD SOFTWARE from the immense Macmillan Computer Publishing library:
  - Source code, shareware, freeware, and demos
- DISCOVER HOT SPOTS on other parts of the Internet.
- WIN BOOKS in ongoing contests and giveaways!

TO PLUG INTO QUE:

WORLD WIDE WEB: **http://www.mcp.com/que**

FTP: ftp.mcp.com

Complete and Return this Card for a *FREE* Computer Book Catalog

Thank you for purchasing this book! You have purchased a superior computer book written expressly for your needs. To continue to provide the kind of up-to-date, pertinent coverage you've come to expect from us, we need to hear from you. Please take a minute to complete and return this self-addressed, postage-paid form. In return, we'll send you a free catalog of all our computer books on topics ranging from word processing to programming and the internet.

r. ☐ Mrs. ☐ Ms. ☐ Dr. ☐

ame (first) ☐☐☐☐☐☐☐☐☐☐☐ (M.I.) ☐ (last) ☐☐☐☐☐☐☐☐☐☐☐☐☐☐☐

ddress ☐☐☐☐☐☐☐☐☐☐☐☐☐☐☐☐☐☐☐☐☐☐☐☐☐☐☐☐☐☐☐☐☐☐☐

☐☐☐☐☐☐☐☐☐☐☐☐☐☐☐☐☐☐☐☐☐☐☐☐☐☐☐☐☐☐☐☐☐☐☐

ty ☐☐☐☐☐☐☐☐☐☐☐☐☐☐☐ State ☐☐ Zip ☐☐☐☐☐ ☐☐☐☐

one ☐☐☐ ☐☐☐ ☐☐☐☐ Fax ☐☐☐ ☐☐☐ ☐☐☐☐

ompany Name ☐☐☐☐☐☐☐☐☐☐☐☐☐☐☐☐☐☐☐☐☐☐☐☐☐☐☐☐☐☐☐☐☐

mail address ☐☐☐☐☐☐☐☐☐☐☐☐☐☐☐☐☐☐☐☐☐☐☐☐☐☐☐☐☐☐☐☐☐

Please check at least (3) influencing factors for purchasing this book.

- ont or back cover information on book ☐
- ecial approach to the content ☐
- ompleteness of content ☐
- uthor's reputation ☐
- blisher's reputation ☐
- ook cover design or layout ☐
- dex or table of contents of book ☐
- ice of book ☐
- ecial effects, graphics, illustrations ☐
- her (Please specify): ______________ ☐

How did you first learn about this book?

- w in Macmillan Computer Publishing catalog ☐
- ecommended by store personnel ☐
- w the book on bookshelf at store ☐
- ecommended by a friend ☐
- eceived advertisement in the mail ☐
- w an advertisement in: ______________ ☐
- ad book review in: ______________ ☐
- her (Please specify): ______________ ☐

How many computer books have you purchased in the last six months?

- is book only ☐
- 3 to 5 books ☐
- ooks ☐
- More than 5 ☐

4. Where did you purchase this book?

- Bookstore ☐
- Computer Store ☐
- Consumer Electronics Store ☐
- Department Store ☐
- Office Club ☐
- Warehouse Club ☐
- Mail Order ☐
- Direct from Publisher ☐
- Internet site ☐
- Other (Please specify): ______________ ☐

5. How long have you been using a computer?

- ☐ Less than 6 months
- ☐ 6 months to a year
- ☐ 1 to 3 years
- ☐ More than 3 years

6. What is your level of experience with personal computers and with the subject of this book?

	With PCs	With subject of book
New	☐	☐
Casual	☐	☐
Accomplished	☐	☐
Expert	☐	☐

Source Code ISBN: 0-7897-0493-5

7. Which of the following best describes your job title?

- Administrative Assistant
- Coordinator
- Manager/Supervisor
- Director
- Vice President
- President/CEO/COO
- Lawyer/Doctor/Medical Professional
- Teacher/Educator/Trainer
- Engineer/Technician
- Consultant
- Not employed/Student/Retired
- Other (Please specify): ____________________

8. Which of the following best describes the area of the company your job title falls under?

- Accounting
- Engineering
- Manufacturing
- Operations
- Marketing
- Sales
- Other (Please specify): ____________________

9. What is your age?

- Under 20
- 21-29
- 30-39
- 40-49
- 50-59
- 60-over

10. Are you:

- Male
- Female

11. Which computer publications do you read regularly? (Please list)

____

Comments: ____________________

Fold here and scotch-tape to ma

NO POSTAGE NECESSARY IF MAILED IN THE UNITED STATES

BUSINESS REPLY MAIL

FIRST-CLASS MAIL PERMIT NO. 9918 INDIANAPOLIS IN

POSTAGE WILL BE PAID BY THE ADDRESSEE

ATTN MARKETING
MACMILLAN COMPUTER PUBLISHING
MACMILLAN PUBLISHING USA
201 W 103RD ST
INDIANAPOLIS IN 46290-9042

Licensing Agreement